# ECONOMIC ANALYSIS AND OPERATIONS RESEARCH:
# OPTIMIZATION TECHNIQUES IN QUANTITATIVE ECONOMIC MODELS

# STUDIES
# IN MATHEMATICAL AND
# MANAGERIAL ECONOMICS

*Editor*

## HENRI THEIL

VOLUME 10

1969

NORTH-HOLLAND PUBLISHING COMPANY – AMSTERDAM · LONDON

*Economic Analysis and Operations Research:*

# OPTIMIZATION TECHNIQUES IN QUANTITATIVE ECONOMIC MODELS

*by*

## JATI K. SENGUPTA

*Professor of Economics and Statistics*
*Iowa State University (Ames)*

and

## KARL A. FOX

*Distinguished Professor and Head*
*Department of Economics*
*Iowa State University*
*(Ames)*

1969

NORTH-HOLLAND PUBLISHING COMPANY – AMSTERDAM · LONDON

Library of Congress Catalog Card Number 70–89939
Standard Book Number 7204 3310 x

PRINTED IN THE NETHERLANDS

# INTRODUCTION TO THE SERIES

This is a series of books concerned with the quantitative approach to problems in the behavioral science field. The studies are in particular in the overlapping areas of mathematical economics, econometrics, operational research, and management science. Also, the mathematical and statistical techniques which belong to the apparatus of modern behavioral science have their place in this series. A well-balanced mixture of pure theory and practical applications is envisaged, which ought to be useful for universities and for research workers in business and government.

The Editor hopes that the volumes of this series, all of which relate to such a young and vigorous field of research activity, will contribute to the exchange of scientific information at a truly international level.

THE EDITOR

# PREFACE

This book presents in a comprehensive manner the salient results of linear and nonlinear programming, dynamic and variational programming, control methods, and probabilistic optimization techniques which are applicable to microeconomic models. Its primary objective is to acquaint economists with the economically-relevant techniques of operations research.

From an economist's point of view, the book also illustrates that the theory of quantitative economic policy can be extended and interpreted to include the various optimization techniques presented here. The difference is that the techniques are here applied to decision-making situations involving individual firms (and individual nonmarket institutions) rather than national economies.

The book is not a textbook in the conventional sense, as it includes numerous results and concepts arising from the authors' own research. The areas in which original results are reported include (a) probabilistic programming, (b) models of resource allocation and planning in educational institutions, (c) the use of central place theory to clarify (1) the nature of competition and complementarity among retail firms and (2) the bases for regionalizing national economic policies, and (d) suggestions for the symmetrical analysis of market and nonmarket institutions as components of a general social system.

The unifying theme throughout the book is the need for integrating the two approaches of operations research and economics. This integration is stressed in ch. 1, where the theory of quantitative economic policy is used as a bridge between economic theory and operations research; in chs 6 and 7, where applications to specific microeconomic models are drawn both from operations research and economics; and in ch. 8, where the operations research techniques of decomposition or decentralization are extended to the regionalization of national economic policy and to the analysis of external economies among retail firms in shopping plazas or centers.

Most of the materials in chs 2, 3, 4 and 5 were developed in connection with a graduate course in operations research taught by one of the authors.

VII

This course has had an unusually large enrollment and has drawn students from economics, statistics, industrial engineering and other engineering fields.

The primary reason for integrating these chapters with chs 1, 6, 7, 8 and 9 has already been noted. For several years the authors, together with Erik Thorbecke and Hylke van de Wetering, have conducted a graduate workshop in the theory of economic policy based on the pioneering work of Jan Tinbergen with extensions by Theil and others, including ourselves. One result of this collaboration was a book by Fox, Sengupta and Thorbecke entitled *The theory of quantitative economic policy: with applications to economic growth and stabilization* (Amsterdam: North-Holland Publishing Company and Chicago: Rand McNally, 1966, 514 pp.). In that book we showed that optimizing models could be applied fruitfully in several fields of economics, including economic growth and development planning, economic stabilization policy, urban and regional economics, and agricultural economics. Between us, we have taught and written in all of these areas.

During 1967 and 1968 the present authors have also collaborated in applying optimizing techniques to models of university departments and groups of departments. Universities are of great interest in themselves and also as examples of nonmarket institutions in general. Our experience with university administration in a fairly complex setting and with the use of objective functions of policy-makers in the theory of economic policy has encouraged us to go further with optimizing models (as distinct from simulation models) of university departments and groups of departments than other researchers who have thus far come to our attention. Our experience with government agencies, along with the current emphasis on planning, programming and budgeting systems (PPBS) in the United States, leads us to believe that optimizing models of public agencies and their components at national, regional, state and sub-state levels will be developing rapidly in the years just ahead.

Finally, contact with scholars in several fields has led one of us to believe that the time is ripe for experimentation with optimizing models that include both economic and noneconomic components of social systems. The suggestions along these lines in ch. 9 are necessarily somewhat speculative. However, given the many and urgent problems requiring public officials to make quantitative decisions *as if* they had optimizing models of the relevant social systems, we make no apology for juxtaposing the mathematical techniques of operations research with suggestions for their extension to models of social systems involving more than economic dimensions. The recent (1968) publication of the *International Encyclopedia of the Social Sciences*, the first of its kind since the 1930's, should greatly facilitate communication among social scientists in connection with these and other multidisciplinary endeavors – and operations research is *par excellence* a multidisciplinary field!

We believe this book offers considerable flexibility for use as a text in operations research for graduate students in economics, industrial engineering, statistics and other fields who are interested in economic applications of optimizing techniques within firms and/or nonmarket institutions. Beginning students who want a broad overview of deterministic programming methods should emphasize chs 1, 2, 3 and 6. Advanced students and research workers should find much new ground covered in chs 4, 5, 6, 7, 8 and 9 as well as some insights (in ch. 1) into the similarities among economic theory, operations research, and the theory of quantitative economic policy.

The authors owe a special note of thanks to Dr. T. Krishna Kumar, who has done an excellent job of proofreading the typescript in all its mathematical detail and of correcting some slips in our original mathematical statements.

We appreciate the excellent and expeditious typing of Helen Brown and Carolyn Hartzler and their careful attention to the mathematical sections. Special thanks are due to Helen Brown and Wesley H. Ebert for their organizational assistance in getting the typescript completed on time in spite of the extreme mobility of authors and typists during the summer months of 1968.

October 9, 1968

JATI K. SENGUPTA
KARL A. FOX

# TABLE OF CONTENTS

Chapter 3. NONLINEAR AND DYNAMIC PROGRAMMING

Chapter 4. SENSITIVITY ANALYSIS IN PROGRAMMING

# Chapter 1

# ECONOMIC POLICY AND OPERATIONS RESEARCH

By traditional standards operations research is clearly an interdisciplinary field. During the past decade or two, some engineers have become increasingly involved in economic problems and some economists have become increasingly involved in problems once regarded as the sole provinces of engineers.

The problems of a firm are always partly economic and partly technological. On a pragmatic basis, every large industrial concern has accomplished some sort of integration of principles of engineering with principles of economics. However, the explicit integration of engineering and economic approaches on the scientific level, involving extensive journal publication across both fields, has been an exponential development of the 1950's and 1960's.

It is hard to imagine the development of operations research in the absence of large-scale computers. The quantitative and operational problems encountered in many different fields of science and engineering can all be translated into computer language. Thus, homologous systems and mathematical isomorphisms which used to pass unnoticed by specialists in different applied fields are becoming more widely recognized. Optimizing models with mathematical programming structures are appearing in a multitude of increasingly transparent disguises. It seems at times that almost every problem of applied science and engineering (which, after all, are goal-directed human activities) can be given an optimizing formulation, and that anything worth doing is worth doing not merely well but optimally!

Economic theory may be viewed as a theory of optimal decisions concerning the allocation of limited resources. The theory of consumption and the theory of the firm both center formally on the optimization of objective functions subject to certain restrictions.

The theory of quantitative economic policy, as pioneered by Tinbergen [1–3] and extended by Theil [4] and others provides a bridge between economic theory and operations research. Economic theory as such is mathematical and abstract; it can be communicated most efficiently in this form. The theory of economic policy had to be quantitative and operational, requiring careful measurement of variables and the specification and estimation of

1

econometric models. Many extensions and applications of the theory of quantitative economic policy have been presented by Fox, Sengupta and Thorbecke [5]. The operational characteristics of the theory of economic policy applied to problems of economic growth and stabilization gave the initial impetus to our concern with operations research techniques as such (see e.g., Sengupta [6–11]). The optimizing techniques are of particular interest to us and will be so, we believe, to most economists.

### 1.1. *Economic models and the methods of operations research*

It will be worthwhile to describe more specifically some of the similarities and points of contact between the theoretical models used by economists and the methods of operations research.

### 1.1.1. *Optimizing models in static economic theory*

Microeconomic theory is essentially a theory of optimal decisions. The optimizing model involved in the theory of consumer behavior may be expressed as follows:

$$\max U = f(q_1, q_2, ..., q_n)$$

subject to

$$\sum_{i=1}^{n} p_i q_i = Y,$$

where the $q_i$ are quantities of $n$ consumer goods and services, the $p_i$ are the corresponding market prices, and $Y$ is the consumer's income, assumed fixed; the consumer's utility function, $U$, depends directly only on the quantities consumed, $q_i$ ($i = 1, 2, ..., n$).

Utility is usually treated as an ordinal (rather than a cardinal) magnitude. Confronted with two sets of quantities of the same commodities, the consumer is viewed as being able to state that he prefers set $A$ to set $B$, or that he prefers set $B$ to set $A$, or that he is indifferent as between the two. An *indifference curve* involving (say) commodity 1 and commodity 2 would be the locus of all combinations of quantities of the two commodities that would be equally acceptable to the consumer in question. In the normal case, sets of the two commodities which included larger quantities of commodity 1 than before and the same quantities of commodity 2 would lie on higher indifference curves, and so would sets which included the same quantities of commodity 1 as before but larger quantities of commodity 2. A higher indifference curve implies a higher value of $U$, but (in the ordinal approach) "how much higher" is indeterminate; $U$ is defined only up to a monotonic transformation. This mild assumption is enough to permit a unique optimal solution to the maximization problem (i.e., we do not need cardinal values of $U$ for this purpose). We also assume that the consumer's indifference surface (in the $n$ dimensional quantity-space) is convex toward the origin.

The constrained maximization of $U$ leads to the following $n$ expressions

$$\frac{\partial U}{\partial q_i} + \lambda p_i = 0, \qquad i = 1, 2, ..., n$$

where $\lambda$ is a Lagrangean multiplier. The last unit of $q_i$ depletes the fixed income resource $Y$ by $p_i$ dollars and the last unit of $q_j$ depletes it by $p_j$ dollars; if this allocation of his income is optimal, the marginal utilities of $q_i$ and $q_j$ to the consumer must be proportional to their prices: $(\partial U/\partial q_i)/(\partial U/\partial q_j)$ $= \lambda p_i/\lambda p_j = p_i/p_j$. The value of $\lambda$ is never determined; in theory it is an "exchange rate" which converts marginal dollars into marginal utilities. In programming terminology, $\lambda$ corresponds to the shadow price of the income restriction; if the income resource were increased by one dollar, the consumer's utility, $U$, would be increased by $\lambda$ units of his own internal and unspecified currency.

In operations research applications, optimizing models almost always employ cardinal objective functions. However, the weights assigned to units of output in some applications may be rather arbitrary, in which case the value of the objective function, $W = \sum_{i=1}^{n} c_i q_i$, may be essentially a quantity index number with the $c_i$ $(i = 1, 2, ..., n)$ as index number weights. For example, Cartter [12] constructed an index of publications by university departments of economics in which a theoretical or research book was regarded as equivalent to six journal articles. If our aim were to maximize the objective function

$$W = x_1 + 6x_2$$

subject to

$$\begin{bmatrix} a_{11} & a_{12} \\ a_{21} & a_{22} \end{bmatrix} \begin{bmatrix} x_1 \\ x_2 \end{bmatrix} \leqq \begin{bmatrix} b_1 \\ b_2 \end{bmatrix}$$

where $x_1$ is the number of articles, $x_2$ is the number of books, $b_1$ is faculty time available for research, $b_2$ is research time available from graduate assistants and the $a_{ij}$'s are input-output coefficients, we would obtain the same optimal solution values for $x_1$ and $x_2$ if we maximized

$$W_0 = \lambda(x_1 + 6x_2),$$

where $\lambda$ is any scalar number whatsoever.

The objective function $W_0$ is still cardinal, as it implies that the value of two books is twice as great as the value of one book; an ordinal objective function would simply imply that two books were worth more than one and three books were worth more than two. However, strictly ordinal utility functions might be compatible with the present stage of thinking of some university administrators and of decision-makers in other nonmarket institutions, particularly if the outputs are as heterogeneous as (say) numbers of B.A. majors in music and numbers of research publications in molecular biology. An indifference map based on judgments of a university administrator that specified combinations of outputs are preferable to others would help to clarify questions involving *relative* marginal utilities (to him) of different activities. Given a "technology matrix" describing the input levels required to support different combinations of outputs and a set of resource limitations, ordinal utility would be sufficient to yield the optimal set of activity levels implied by his indifference map and to explore the implications (for optimal activity levels) of changes in the resource constraints. However, the university administrator is under some pressure (both self-imposed and external) to justify his allocation of resources in terms of contributions to the larger society and this leads on toward a cardinal objective function in which efforts are made to assign market-like prices to some university outputs and "reasonable" relative weights to others.

Economists have perhaps overemphasized the ordinality of utility. Its principal attraction is that all the theorems of industry-wide and economy-wide equilibrium can be derived without requiring economists to attempt quantitative comparisons of microevents taking place within the psyches of different individuals. Consumption theory proves only that interpersonal comparisons of utility are *unnecessary* in a particular context; it does not prove that interpersonal comparisons of welfare are impossible, undesirable or unnecessary in broader social contexts. The derivation of ordinal utility functions for two university presidents would mean that each could make optimal choices according to his own value system in his own domain without generating a cardinal number to support invidious comparisons with the other. It would not mean that cardinal comparisons of the total *social value products* of two universities are impossible or undesirable when the business of measurement and conceptualization is farther advanced.

Mathematical programming has been applied so widely in recent years to problems of firm (including farm) behavior that it seems easiest to state the linear programming formulation first (in vector and matrix notation):

$$\max W = v'x \qquad v, x: n.1$$

subject to

$$Ax \leqslant b \qquad b : m.1$$
$$x \geqslant 0 \qquad A : m.n$$

where $x$ is a vector of the levels of $n$ outputs (activities), $v'$ is a row vector of net revenue (i.e., selling price minus the cost of variable inputs) per unit of each output, $W$ is total net revenue, $A$ is an $m$ by $n$ matrix of technical coefficients $a_{ij}$ ($i = 1, 2, ..., n$ and $j = 1, 2, ..., m$) which specify the amount of the $j$th restriction required to support one unit of the $i$th activity, and $b$ is a vector of $m$ constraints, including resources (plant capacity, land area, labor force, etc.) which are regarded as fixed within the time period to which the optimization applies; the level of each activity must be either positive or zero.

Suppose that in the optimal solution activity 1 is most limited by resource 1. Each unit of $x_1$ requires $a_{11}$ units of $b_1$; if $b_1$ is increased by one unit $x_1$ can be increased by $1/a_{11}$ units and $W$ can be increased by $v_1/a_{11}$ units. In this situation the shadow price or marginal value product of resource 1 when $W$ is optimized is $v_1/a_{11}$.

The $b$ vector is analogous to the fixed factors or fixed costs in economic theory. The definition of $v$ as net revenue (or, $v = p - c$, where $p$ is selling price and $c$ is the cost of all variable inputs per unit of output) and the specification that $v$ is independent of $x$ imply a horizontal demand curve and a horizontal variable cost curve. Thus, marginal revenue equals average revenue and marginal cost equals average variable cost for each output; the marginal revenue and marginal cost curves for each output are parallel horizontal lines. Under these conditions the classical theory of the firm will not give us an equilibrium solution; the still-profitable expansion of each activity is stopped short by one or another of the $m$ constraints. (We could perhaps argue that at this point the marginal cost curve shoots up vertically and intersects the marginal revenue curve from below, thus satisfying the equilibrium condition of economic theory.)

The linearity assumptions of this particular model seem unduly restrictive as compared with the continuous nonlinear functions which have been used in stating the economic theory of the firm. Nonlinear forms of programming are also available and are presented in ch. 3. However, we shall content ourselves at this point with a brief statement of the optimizing model of economic theory in the case of a single-product firm (adapted from Samuelson [13, pp. 57–89]):

$$\max \pi = R(x) - A - V(x, w_1, w_2, ..., w_m)$$

subject to

$$x = f(y_1, y_2, ..., y_n)$$

where $\pi$ is net revenue, $x$ is the level of output, $R(x)$ is gross revenue, $A$ is total fixed cost, the $w_i$ $(i = 1, 2, ..., m)$ are (constant) prices of the $m$ variable inputs, $V(x, w_1, w_2, ..., y_n)$ is the production function expressing $x$ in terms of all inputs, fixed as well as variable (hence $n \geqslant m$).

Looking first at the revenue and cost relationships we note that maximization of net revenue requires

$$\frac{\partial \pi}{\partial x} = \frac{\partial R}{\partial x} - \frac{\partial V}{\partial x} = 0,$$

or

$$\frac{\partial R}{\partial x} = \frac{\partial V}{\partial x},$$

i.e., marginal revenue must equal marginal cost; also

$$\frac{\partial^2 \pi}{\partial x^2} = \frac{\partial^2 R}{\partial x^2} - \frac{\partial^2 V}{\partial x^2} < 0,$$

i.e., the marginal revenue curve must intersect the marginal cost curve from above.

If we assume the firm is small enough relative to the total market so that its selling price $p$ is independent of $x$, we may write gross revenue as $R(x) = px$; also, $V = \sum_{i=1}^{m} w_i y_i$. To determine the amounts of the inputs $y_i$ required under the optimal solution, we write $\pi = px - A - \sum_{i=1}^{m} w_i y_i$, and, substituting $f(y_1, y_2, ..., y_m)$ for $x$, we obtain $m$ expressions as follows:

$$\frac{\partial \pi}{\partial y_i} = p \frac{\partial x}{\partial y_i} - w_i = 0,$$

or

$$p \frac{\partial x}{\partial y_i} = w_i, \qquad i = 1, 2, ..., m.$$

Here $w_i$ is the marginal cost of a unit of $y_i$, $\partial x / \partial y_i$ is the marginal *physical* product of $y_i$ in terms of $x$, and $p \, \partial x / \partial y_i$ is the marginal *value* product of $y_i$; at the optimal solution the marginal value product of each variable input is equal to its marginal cost. Also,

$$\frac{\partial^2 \pi}{\partial y_i^2} = p \frac{\partial^2 x}{\partial y_i^2} < 0, \qquad i = 1, 2, ..., m$$

$$\frac{\partial^2 \pi}{\partial y_i \partial y_j} = p \frac{\partial^2 x}{\partial y_i \partial y_j} < 0, \qquad i, j = 1, 2, ..., m; i = j$$

if $\pi$ is a well-behaved maximum.

Diminishing returns (diminishing marginal physical productivity) is usually stressed as the normal case in expositions of the economic theory of the firm; however, optimal solutions are possible even under increasing returns if the marginal revenue curve is downward sloping and sufficiently steep to intersect the (downward sloping) marginal cost curve from above. A downward sloping marginal revenue curve would imply a nonlinear objective function in programming terms; if selling price were a linear (downward sloping) function of output, the equivalent programming objective function would be quadratic.

In elementary expositions of the theory of the firm, little attention is given to the fixed costs; over the time period relevant to the optimization, fixed costs are fixed and that is that. However, the fixed factors do give rise to rents or quasi-rents, and it turns out that these are equivalent to the shadow prices of the binding restrictions in a programming model. Suppose $y_k$ is a fixed factor in the short run, for example, the floor area of a factory; $y_k$ is not available for use as a policy instrument to increase net revenue in the short run. Nevertheless, it pays to ask the conditional question, by how much *could* we increase net revenue if we did have additional floor space? The answer is given by $\partial \pi / \partial y_k = p(\partial x / \partial y_k)$, where $\partial x / \partial y_k$ is the marginal physical productivity of $y_k$ in terms of $x$ and $p$ (assuming a horizontal demand curve) is the marginal revenue per unit of $x$. Suppose $\partial \pi / \partial y_k = \$10$ per year per net square foot of factory floor space; the firm is then faced with a decision (based on longer-run considerations) as to whether it should invest in additional floor space. If this decision is made in an optimizing framework, the period over which expected net revenue should be optimized would typically be at least five years and possibly more than ten.

The above exposition has assumed a single-product firm. If the firm can produce two products, we can define a production-possibilities frontier which is the locus of all possible combinations of quantities of the two commodities which can be produced within the limits of the firm's resource constraints. If additional resources are provided, the firm can produce more of one or both commodities. For any fixed set of resources, and for specified actual or relative prices for the two outputs, the firm can maximize its revenue by producing at the point of tangency between the production-possibilities frontier or *isoquant* and what might be called the *isoprice line*. These principles can be extended to any number of products.

In the theory of the firm, then, we have a price-guided allocation of resources and a cardinal objective function, net revenue, which depends on the market prices of the firm's outputs and inputs and the slopes (if any) of the market demand curves for its outputs and the market supply curves for its inputs.

We will mention only briefly some of the subproblems within the theory of the firm. If a firm is one of many producing a standardized product, for example wheat or cotton, the proprietor must sell whatever he produces at the market price; he cannot use his selling price as a policy instrument to influence his net revenue. His strategy must be one of cost minimization, or, more precisely, one of producing at a level at which his marginal cost is equal to the market price. This is atomistic competition; the firm faces a horizontal demand curve for its output. This means a constant price and a linear gross revenue function.

*Monopolistic competition* is, in fact, widely pervasive [14, 15]. Firms produce somewhat differentiated products, so that commodity $A_i$ is perceived by a significant number of consumers as somewhat different from commodity $A_j$, where $i, j \, (i \neq j)$ run over the $n$ firms which produce the generic commodity $A$. Under these circumstances, sales of firm $i$ depend on its own price and also on the prices charged by its $n-1$ competitors. Mathematically, the situation may be characterized as follows:

$$q_i = f\,(p_1, p_2, p_3, \ldots, p_n); \qquad i = 1, 2, \ldots, n$$

$$\frac{\partial q_i}{\partial p_i} < 0, \quad \frac{\partial q_i}{\partial p_j} > 0 \quad \text{for all} \quad i, j \, (i \neq j).$$

The "leverage" of selling price as a policy instrument for firm $i$ in increasing its net revenue will depend upon the slope of the demand curve which confronts it; that is, the demand curve for commodity $A_i$. It appears that the slope of this demand curve can be influenced by advertising (or, more generally, selling costs) designed to increase the perceived differences in the minds of consumers as between commodity $A_i$ and the other $n-1$ basically similar products.

Holdren [16] has pointed out that, under conditions of monopolistic competition, the policy variables open to a firm include both price and nonprice offer variations. Formally, we may write

$$q_i = f\,(p_1, p_2, p_3, \ldots, p_n; \qquad a_1, a_2, a_3, \ldots, a_n),$$

where $(\partial q_i/\partial p_i) < 0$ and $(\partial q_i/\partial p_j) > 0$ as before and, in addition,

$$\frac{\partial q_i}{\partial a_i} > 0 \quad \text{and} \quad \frac{\partial q_i}{\partial a_j} < 0 \quad \text{for all} \quad i, j \, (i \neq j);$$

$a_i$ is a nonprice offer variation (such as air conditioning the store, providing free parking for customers, etc.) or index of nonprice offer variations open to the $i$th firm. We define $a_i$ in such a way that a larger value tends to increase sales of the $i$th firm and to reduce sales of its competitors.

We will not bother here to discuss other variants of market structure such as oligopoly and monopoly, or their counterparts on the buying side, oligopsony and monopsony (or the counterpart of monopolistic competition which is monopsonistic competition [17]).

A few general comments are in order about the nature of optimizing models in static economic theory. First, they have been developed and presented in terms of classical mathematics involving continuous functions. Second, the case of atomistic competition has been given a great deal of emphasis in most expositions of economic principles. Along with this has gone a considerable emphasis on the resource allocation aspects of decision-making; consumers and firms accept market prices as given and adjust their purchases or their production patterns accordingly. Third, empirical research on the decision-making processes of firms engaged in monopolistic competition is inherently difficult, as product differentiation takes many forms; a great many such firms are in fact multiproduct firms, which raises aggregation and index number problems; and, since price and nonprice offer variations are strategic policy instruments, the considerations leading to the selection of particular strategies may be regarded as trade secrets.

### 1.1.2. *Methods of operations research*

Ackoff [18] lists the essential features of operations research as "its systems (or executive) orientation, its use of interdisciplinary teams, and its methodology... The systems approach to problems is based on the observation that in organized systems the behavior of any part ultimately has some effect on the performance of every other part". The problems relevant to major decisions in a large firm may cut across several scientific fields. Careful quantification of the more important relationships and successive expansions and reformulations of the initial model are characteristic of the systems approach. Also, when objective functions are difficult to formulate, the mathematical model of a system may be used to *simulate* a number of alternative time paths (over a prescribed planning horizon) reflecting alternative assumptions about developments in the environment external to the firm and/or alternative policy decisions which might be made by the firm. We will make few references to simulation models in this book.

Apart from the systems approach and simulation, the primary methods of operations research can be broadly subsumed under mathematical programming in all its ramifications. These include linear, nonlinear and dynamic programming and their variants; control theory and variational techniques; and the many aspects of probabilistic programming.

In the context of operations research applications in industry, Ackoff states that "most problems fall into one, or a combination, of a small number of basic types". He enumerates these as the inventory problem, the allocation problem, the queuing problem, the sequencing problem, the routing problem, the replacement problem, the competition problem, and the search problem [18; pp. 293–294].

Most of these problems lead, in fact or in principle, to models which involve optimizing an objective function subject to specified constraints. Analogies with the models of economic theory are close and pervasive, particularly in the area of firm behavior. The economic theory of the firm deals with price-guided resource allocation and price-weighted objective functions. The majority of operations research models within a firm have, in the background at least, the price-weighted objective function of the firm. The immediate objectives of some models may be stated in terms of physical performance characteristics, but the choice of performance characteristics embodies economic considerations and/or has economic repercussions.

When operations research methods are applied to nonmarket institutions such as universities, the absence of recognized market prices for many outputs presents initial difficulties [19–22]. We will make some comments about these in chs 7 and 9. Some outputs of a university can be translated into market-like magnitudes, such as the expected increases in career incomes of students who complete four-year college programs rather than ending their formal educations with high school diplomas. The allocation of university resources between (1) outputs with market-like "prices" and (2) other outputs can be shown to imply subjective "prices" for the latter which can be translated into market-like equivalents.

## 1.2. *The theory of quantitative economic policy and operations research*

Macroeconomic theory underwent a profound revolution in the 1930's. This was preceded and accompanied by systematic efforts in the United States and other countries to develop time series estimates of what we now call the national income and product accounts. Superficially, these accounts represented nothing more than an application of double-entry bookkeeping to national aggregates of all firms, all households and all units of government. Basically, however, they provided (together with related series on employment, production, prices and monetary phenomena) an integrated set of performance measures for a national economy. J. M. Keynes provided a general theory as to how the principal aggregative variables were related functionally, why it was possible for an economy to stagnate at considerably less than full employment, and how a national government could intervene to bring about economic recovery and subsequently to maintain high and relatively stable employment.

With knowledge and power comes responsibility. The Employment Act of 1946 stated that it is the policy of the United States government to promote maximum employment, production and income consistent with certain qualitative considerations. To steer a complicated system one needs to know the effects of the control variables upon the state variables and to have criteria for adjusting the controls. Other governments assumed similar responsibilities following World War II.

### 1.2.1. *Econometric models of national economies and their policy implications*

Jan Tinbergen [23; 1939] was the first person to construct an econometric model of a national economy. Later, Tinbergen's series of books on the theory of economic policy [1–3; 1952, 1954, 1956] supplied a bold new interpretation of the relationship of econometric models to the practical formulation of economic policies.

Tinbergen's theory of economic policy can be summarized in terms of fig. 1.[1]

The three basic ingredients of his quantitative economic policy model are as follows; a welfare function $W$ of the policy maker, which is a function of $I$ target variables $y_i$ and $J$ instrument variables $z_j$; a quantitative model $M$, which sets up statistical or empirical relationships essentially between the $I$ target variables and the $J$ instrument variables; and a set of boundary conditions or constraints on the target, the irrelevant and the instrument variables. The policy model may be a fixed target or a flexible target model; in the former, $W$ contains fixed target values, but in the latter, such target values are chosen as will optimize the welfare function $W$.

The model $M$ specifies the set of quantitative relations among the variables. Such relations in their original form, as distinct from the "reduced form", are called structural relations, and their coefficients are called structural coefficients. These structural relations may be divided into three groups:

---

[1] Fig. 1.1 and most of the following six pages are excerpted from Fox, Sengupta and Thorbecke [5].

Fig. 1.1. The theory of economic policy[1]

| Exogenous Variables | System of structural relation-ships connecting all variables: The "model" | Endogenous Variables | Utility, welfare or "objective function" |

Policy Instruments                    Goals or "target variables"

$$z_1 \\ z_2 \\ \vdots \\ z_j$$          $$y_1 \\ y_2 \\ \vdots \\ y_i$$          $$W$$

"Data" or noncontrollable factors[2]          Side-effects or "irrelevant variables"

$$u_1 \\ u_2 \\ \vdots \\ u_k$$          $$x_1 \\ x_2 \\ \vdots \\ x_s$$

[1] Classification of variables based on J. Tinbergen.
[2] Not subject to control by the policy-maker or level of government that sets the goals and uses the policy instruments in question.

behavioral, technical and definitional. The most important equations are the behavioral ones, which contain essentially quantitative theories and hypotheses about empirical economic behavior, for example, demand or supply relations or the reactions of economic groups to risk and uncertainty.

The variables of the model $M$ may be classified into four different types, the "target" variables $(y_i)$, which are to be purposefully (though indirectly) influenced by the policy maker; the "instrument" variables $(z_j)$, which are the means available to the policy maker; the "data" $(u_k)$, which are not subject to control by the policy maker, and the "irrelevant" variables $(x_s)$, which are side effects in which the policy maker is not interested.

If for *ad hoc* reasons we regard some economic variables $(x_s)$ as irrelevant for a given policy decision, we can in most cases eliminate them from a complete model by algebraic means, leaving a set of equations containing only policy instruments and targets (plus the effects of strictly noncontrollable variables). Fig. 1.1 may help to clarify the classification of variables in the Tinbergen-type policy model. The random components of the policy model are not explicit in the diagram. Furthermore, the light arrow running from the instrument vector to the welfare function $W$ probably understates the importance of this connection because a cost imputation on the basis of either shadow prices or direct monetary expenditure can in most cases be made for the instrument variables used by a policy maker. In any case, the welfare function $W$ can incorporate as elements instrument variables in addition to the target variables as such.

There are two useful ways of looking at these different variables of economic policy. From the standpoint of econometric theory, the "endogenous" variables comprise the targets and the irrelevant variables, while the "exogenous" variables comprise the instrument variables and the "data". Thus the unknowns are the endogenous variables, whose values are to be estimated from known values of the exogenous variables. In the theory of economic policy, however, the unknowns of the problem are the instrument variables and the irrelevant variables, whereas the knowns are the targets and the data.

One consequence of this difference in standpoint is best understood in terms of the concept of consistency in the policy sense as distinct from an equational sense. Suppose the policy model consists of $N$ independent structural equations which contain $I$ target variables, $J$ instruments, $K$ data (or noncontrollable) variables and $S$ irrelevant variables. *Equational* consistency requires that the total number of endogenous variables (i.e., dependent or unknown variables) should equal the number of independent structural equations, i.e., $N=I+S$. Consistency in the policy sense, for a *fixed target* policy model, requires that the number of instrument variables should equal that of the targets, i.e., $J=I$. By combining these we get $J+S=N$, which gives us the necessary condition to solve for all the unknowns of our policy problem.

We must note that for a *flexible target* policy model it is not necessary to satisfy the consistency condition $J=I$.

Assuming linearity and eliminating the vector $(x)$ of irrelevant variables, an economic policy model may be very simply specified in terms of three systems of equations:

$$\text{Optimize } W = a'y + b'z \quad \text{(preference function)} \quad (1.1)$$

under the conditions

$$Ay = Bz + Cu \quad \text{(the model } M\text{), and} \quad (1.2)$$

$$\begin{aligned} y_{\min} \leqslant y \leqslant y_{\max} \\ z_{\min} \leqslant z \leqslant z_{\max} \end{aligned} \quad \text{(boundary conditions)}, \quad (1.3)$$

where $A$, $B$ and $C$ are matrices of coefficients of appropriate orders $y$, $z$ and $u$

are appropriate column vectors of targets, instruments and data. If the matrix $A$ is square and nonsingular, the "reduced form" of the model $M$ in (1.2) can be obtained by multiplying both sides of equation (1.2) by the inverse of $A$:

$$y = (A^{-1}B)z + (A^{-1}C)u. \tag{1.2.1}$$

For purposes of statistical estimation of the structural coefficients, the reduced-form equations (1.2.1) play a fundamental role, because in some cases least-squares theory can be very easily applied to the reduced form but not to the original system (1.2).

Since for the policy problem our unknown is the vector $z$ of instruments, we solve for $z$ from equation (1.2):

$$Bz = Ay - Cu. \tag{1.2.2}$$

If the matrix $B$ has constant elements and is square and nonsingular, the inverse of $B$ exists and hence the vector of instruments $z$ can be uniquely solved from equation (1.2.2) by premultiplying both sides by $B^{-1}$, i.e.,

$$z = (B^{-1}A)y - (B^{-1}C)u = Gy + Hu. \tag{1.2.3}$$

The nature of the dependence of $z$ upon $y$ is associated with different types of structures of the matrices $B$ and $A$:

(i) If $B$ and $A$ are strictly *diagonal* matrices, then to each target there corresponds one and only one instrument and vice versa. There is no simultaneity in the relationship between the instruments and the targets. The practical implication would be that the policy maker could pursue each target with a single highly specific instrument. Or, he could afford to assign responsibility for each target and its unique instrument to a different cabinet officer or agency head without providing any mechanism for coordination or even communication among these officials!

(ii) If the matrices $B$ and $A$ are strictly *triangular* and of similar dimensionality, the policy model given by equation (1.2.2) is called recursive (or correspondingly consecutive). In this case we have a "pure causal chain" model, to use a concept developed by Wold in his theory of estimation. The two-way simultaneity of relations between the vectors $z$ and $y$ (i.e., $z$ affecting $y$ and $y$ affecting $z$) can be reduced to a unilateral dependence.

We must emphasize that $z$ and $y$ are *vectors*:

$$z = \begin{bmatrix} z_1 \\ z_2 \\ \vdots \\ z_J \end{bmatrix}, \qquad y = \begin{bmatrix} y_1 \\ y_2 \\ \vdots \\ y_I \end{bmatrix}.$$

Even if most of the $z_j$'s were unilaterally dependent on certain of the $y_i$'s, the *vectors z* and *y* would be interdependent (or show two-way simultaneity) if any one (or more) of the $y_i$'s depended on one or more of the $z_j$'s.

If the matrices $A$ and $B$ are strictly triangular, the first element $z_1$ of the vector $z$ will depend only on the single element $y_1$ of vector $y$ and other data ($u$). The second element $z_2$ will depend on $z_1, y_1, y_2$ and other data, but since $z_1$ has already been solved in terms of $y_1$, we have $z_2$ depending only on $y_1$, $y_2, y_3$, and not on any $y_i$ higher than $i = 3$. Apart from the advantages of this pattern for statistical estimation, such a strictly recursive model allows a very simple policy interpretation. Specifically, if each equation were assigned to a different policy maker, the system of equations would specify a hierarchy such that a policy maker in a given position need not look at the instruments selected by those who are *below* his position in the hierarchy of equations in order to determine his own optimal policy.

(iii) If many of the elements of the matrices $B$ and $A$ are zero (which some-times occurs in practice in input-output models and in investment planning), it may happen that such matrices are *quasi-diagonal* or *block-diagonal* rather than strictly diagonal. This means that each matrix contains square submatrices which, after appropriate arrangement of rows and columns, form blocks on the principal diagonal, the off-diagonal elements being zero.

In this case of a block-diagonal policy model, the overall model could be split (or decomposed) into two or more independent parts depending on the number of blocks in the block-diagonal form. A centralized plan (model) could thus be decentralized into "relatively independent" subplans (sub-models) which would permit efficient decentralized decision-making.

(iv) Again, if the matrices $B$ and $A$ are *quasi-triangular* or *block-triangular*, i.e., triangular in blocks of submatrices, the set of instruments corresponding to any given block can be solved for without any knowledge of other instru-ments belonging to blocks which are *lower* in the hierarchy. In this case the overall central plan (or model) could be split into separate "unilaterally dependent" plans (or models).

So far we have assumed implicitly, if not explicitly, that we are discussing a fixed-target policy model; we may presume that some welfare function $W$ lies behind the selection of target values, but $W$ itself is not specified. In fact, however, a Tinbergen-type policy model may be fixed, flexible, random or mixed. In the *flexible* case we select the instruments to optimize the welfare function $W$ subject to the conditions of the model. In the *random* case we optimize the expected value (or some appropriate deterministic equivalent such as the variance or the probability that $W$ takes a particular value or falls within a particular confidence interval) of the preference function. The randomness in the model may enter either through errors of statistical estimation of the model $M$ from past observational data or because the targets set may have random components (or intervals within which random variation will be tolerated). A model is *mixed* when some targets are fixed, some are flexible and still others are random. Various other combinations are possible, e.g., some targets may be allowed to take only integral values, some may be continuous except at some "jump points", etc.

The concept of "efficiency" used in the theory of economic policy is also important. This concept is applicable to a flexible target policy model and also to the random and mixed cases. Suppose for simplicity we write the welfare function $W$ as a scalar function of the target variables, the instruments and random terms $(v)$; that is, $W = W(y_1, y_2, ..., y_I; z_1, z_2, ..., z_J, v)$ after appropriate substitutions through the model. Then, assuming differentiability and other regularity conditions, we may state that the optimum set of instruments would be given by solving the following set of $J$ partial differential equations which are the necessary conditions for an extremum (optimum):

$$\frac{dW}{dz_j} = \sum_{i=1}^{I} \frac{\partial W}{\partial y_i} \frac{\partial y_i}{\partial z_j} + \frac{\partial W}{\partial z_j} = 0, \qquad j = 1, 2, ..., J \qquad (1.4)$$

provided the random term $v$ is identically zero and the second-order condition for a maximum or minimum is fulfilled. The term $(\partial y_i / \partial z_j)$ expresses the effectiveness of the instrument $z_j$ in inducing a change in the value of the target $y_i$ when all other instruments are kept constant. Hence the term $\sum_{i=1}^{I} (\partial W / \partial y_i)(\partial y_i / \partial z_j)$ expresses the sum of all marginal (partial) effects upon $W$ of a unit change in $z_j$ acting indirectly through the target variables $y_i$. The direct effect of the instrument $z_j$ upon $W$ is specified by the term $\partial W / \partial z_j$.

These efficiency indicators, which are partial measures of impact of the use of instruments, may be used to construct numerical tables to indicate the rates of substitution between different instruments. It should be noted that these indicators are not in terms of elasticities, hence comparisons of the effectiveness of different instruments are not free from the units in which these instruments are measured.

*An illustrative example.* As a simple example let us consider a linear macroeconomic model [2] with two fixed targets: a given value of balance of payments

---

[2] This has been adapted from Theil [24].

$(B=B^*)$ and a given volume of employment $(N=N^*)$ and two instruments: government expenditure for consumption $(G_c)$ and for investment $(G_i)$. The model is

Domestic output: $\qquad Y=C+I+X+G_c+G_i$ (definition),

Imports: $\qquad M=a_1C+a_2I+a_3X+a_4G_c+a_5G_i$ (behavior equation),

Consumption: $\qquad C=bY$ (behavior equation),

Employment: $\qquad N=eY$ (technical relation),

Balance of payments: $\qquad B=p_xX-p_mM$ (definition).

The boundary conditions on each of the variables are that they must belong to the real nonnegative interval $(0, \infty)$, which is closed at the left end but open at the right end. Here we have

Endogenous variables: $\qquad$ 5: $Y, M, C, B, N$,

Exogenous variables: $\qquad$ 4: $I, X, G_c, G_i$,

Target variables: $\qquad$ 2: $B=B^*, N=N^*$,

Instrument variables: $\qquad$ 2: $G_i, G_c$,

Data variables: $\qquad$ 2: $I, X$,

Irrelevant variables: $\qquad$ 3: $Y, M, C$.

After rearrangement of terms and appropriate substitution, we get

$$\begin{aligned}
N = N^* &= b_1(I+X) + b_1G_c + b_1G_i, \\
B = B^* &= p_xX - g_2I - g_3X - g_4G_c - g_5G_i,
\end{aligned} \qquad (1.5)$$

where the constant coefficients are $b_1=e/(1-b)$ and $g_i=p_ma_i+p_ma_1b/(1-b)$ for $i=2, 3, 4, 5$.

Since the data variables $I, X$ are not controlled by the policy-maker, they must be either forecast from past data (projected) or replaced by judgment estimates. We denote these values by $I_0$ and $X_0$. Substituting these known values in system (1.5), we can check the system for mathematical consistency in the sense of the existence of solutions. Since the number of targets equals the number of instruments in this case we can solve for "unique" values of the instruments $G_i, G_c$, if their coefficient matrix is nonsingular, i.e.,

$$\begin{bmatrix} G_i \\ G_c \end{bmatrix} = \begin{bmatrix} b_1 & b_1 \\ -g_4 & -g_5 \end{bmatrix}^{-1} \begin{bmatrix} N^* - b_1(I_0+X_0) \\ B^* - (p_x-g_3)X_0 - g_2I_0 \end{bmatrix}. \qquad (1.6)$$

Suppose we reduce our two instruments to only one, i.e., $G=G_i+G_c$, by defining $a_4=a_5$ and hence $g_4=g_5$. We cannot now achieve the two arbitrarily-fixed targets in general, because the system (1.5) now defines two equations in one unknown $(G)$. However, if we reduce the two equations to one by defining $W=w_1N+w_2B$ where $W=W^*$ is the value of the fixed target, we again have consistency in the policy sense and under the usual regularity conditions the policy model can be solved. We note that the nonnegative weights $w_1$, $w_2$ specify the barter terms of trade between the two objectives $N$ and $B$, which together specify the preference function of the policy-maker. Further, it should be noted that a special case of the flexible policy model can be incorporated in the solution (1.6) of our policy model if we impose the condition that $B^*$ must take the minimum possible value, zero.

### 1.2.2. *Connections between consumption theory and the theory of economic policy*

Theil [4] drew a very specific analogy between the theory of economic policy and the theory of consumption. He pointed out that ordinal utility was sufficient in principle to lead the policy-maker to select the optimal set of values of the instrument variables (according to his own preference ordering, of course). Theil's model is essentially

$$\max W = f(x, y) \qquad x : m \cdot 1$$
$$y : n \cdot 1$$

subject to

$$Qy = Rx + s \qquad Q : n \cdot n$$
$$R : n \cdot m$$
$$s : n \cdot 1$$

where $x$ is a vector of $m$ instruments, $y$ is a vector of $n$ targets, $Q$ is a matrix with scalar numbers on the diagonal and zeros elsewhere, $R$ is a matrix of coefficients specifying the effects of the instruments on values of the (normalized) targets $q_i y_i$, and $s$ is a vector of constants (each $s_i$ is a linear combination of the "data" variables, whose values are regarded as predetermined constants during the optimization period, and any constant term in the equation expressing $y_i$ as a function of the instruments and "data"). The $y_i$ may be expressed in different units, such as per capita disposable income (in dollars), total employment (millions of workers), the consumer price index (1957–59 = 100), and so on; the diagonal elements in $Q$, $q_i$ ($i = 1, 2, ..., n$) may be thought of as analogous to prices per unit of $y_i$, in that each unit of $y_i$ uses up $q_i$ units of the restriction imposed (or resource provided) by the $i$th equation.

The income constraint of consumption theory is here replaced by the set of $n$ reduced-form equations derived from the econometric model (i.e., those equations which express the target variables as functions of the instruments and "data" after the vector of irrelevant variables has been eliminated from the original structural system). To impose the present constraint set we write

$$\max W - \lambda'(Qy - Rx - s),$$

where $\lambda$ is a column vector of $n$ Lagrangean multipliers. Maximization leads to

$$\frac{\partial W}{\partial x} + R'\lambda = 0$$

$$\frac{\partial W}{\partial y} - Q'\lambda = 0$$

where $\partial W/\partial x$ and $\partial W/\partial y$ are column vectors of the marginal welfare contributions or "utilities" of the instruments and the target variables respectively.

For clarity, we may write typical individual rows of the vectors of first derivatives as

$$\frac{\partial W}{\partial x_j} + (\lambda_1 r_{1j} + \lambda_2 r_{2j} + \cdots + \lambda_n r_{nj}) = 0, \qquad j = 1, 2, \ldots, m$$

and

$$\frac{\partial W}{\partial y_i} - \lambda_i q_i = 0, \qquad\qquad i = 1, 2, \ldots, n.$$

If $W$ has been given a cardinal specification, each $\partial W/\partial x_j$ will be a cardinal number and each $\lambda_i$ will be the shadow price of the $i$th equation, in units of $W$, at the optimal solution. If $W$ has been given an ordinal specification, the *ratio* of the marginal "utilities" of any two instruments $x_j$ and $x_k$ can be expressed as

$$\frac{\partial W/\partial x_j}{\partial W/\partial x_k} = \frac{(\lambda_1 r_{1j} + \lambda_2 r_{2j} + \cdots + \lambda_n r_{nj})}{(\lambda_1 r_{1k} + \lambda_2 r_{2k} + \cdots + \lambda_n r_{nk})}.$$

This ratio will not be affected if we multiply both numerator and denominator by the same scalar $k$ (say), where $k$ is any real number whatsoever.

### 1.2.3. *The theory of economic policy as a bridge between economic theory and operations research*

The theory of quantitative economic policy provides a bridge between economic theory and operations research. It grew out of a problem which was of intense practical concern, the Great Depression of the 1930's, and the need to provide an operational method for steering national economies in such a way that major depressions would never happen again. It required careful quantitative specification of the structural relationships among major economic variables; a classification of these variables into (especially) targets and instruments closely analogous to the *state* variables and *control* variables of optimal control theory (see Kumar [25]); and the formulation of performance criteria in the forms of (1) fixed target values for some of the state variables or (2) sets of values of some state variables and some control variables to be selected optimally according to an objective function (either cardinal or ordinal) of a policy-maker.

The specification of objective functions in the theory of economic policy involves essentially the same problem that confronts us in specifying objective functions for universities and other nonmarket institutions, i.e., the absence of generally recognized prices for all or many of the outputs. Van Eijk and Sandee [26], analyzing the context of economic policy in the Netherlands as of 1956, decided that against a 100 million guilder balance of payments surplus $(E-M)$ could be set 400 million guilders of government expenditure $(x_G)$, or 500 million guilders of investment $(i)$, or a 2 percent increase in real wages $(w_R)$, or a 1.33 percent decrease in consumer prices $(p_c)$, or an 0.5 percent increase in employment $(a)$, or a 200 million guilder surplus $(S_G)$ of government receipts over government expenditures. These were marginal rates of substitution or "barter terms of trade" among the six variables listed; from these a linear objective function could be written as

$$W = 1.0(E - M) + 0.25x_G + 0.20i + 5.0w_R - 7.5p_c + 0.20a + 0.50S_G + \text{constant}$$

subject to specified upper and lower limits within which the targets (and implicitly the instruments) could be varied. Theil [27] specified quadratic objective functions representing (1) the trade unionist position, (2) the employer position, and (3) a neutral position and worked out the implications of each for optimal time paths of the same set of target and instrument variables in the Netherlands over a three-year horizon, using the same 40-equation model of the Dutch economy to link target and instrument variables in all cases. On one level, the "barter terms of trade" could be discussed as matters of taste or intuition, with different policy-makers bringing to bear their own judgements and experiences as tempered by recent political platforms and by the public and private statements of persons wielding political or intellectual influence. On another level, they suggest the need for further clarification as to who is hurt (or helped), how, and how much by a unit change in each national aggregative variable.

The Tinbergen and Theil models were developed primarily in the context of economic stabilization policy. Independently, a literature has grown up in the context of economic development planning, and many models of national economies have now been formulated in mathematical programming terms; (see, e.g., Adelman and Thorbecke [28]). The simplest (one-period) programming model for a national economy would be

$$\max W = \text{GNP} = v'x \qquad v, x: n.1$$

subject to

$$Ax \leqslant b, \qquad A: m.n$$
$$x \geqslant 0 \qquad b: m.1$$

where $v$ is a vector of values added in each of $n$ sectors of the economy, $x$ is a vector of output levels in the $n$ sectors, $A$ is a "technology matrix" specifying the amounts of each limited resource needed to support a unit of output in each sector, and $b$ is a vector of resource or capacity constraints.

The objective function here is stated in dollars, and the GNP (gross national product) is then taken as the sole criterion of the performance of the economy. We could, however, use alternative objective functions (employment, price stability, balance of payments equilibrium, a balanced government budget, etc.) either separately or in combination; in the latter case we again have the problem of selecting appropriate weights or "prices" for some nonmarket (or at least nondollar) variables. Alternatively, we could, say, maximize GNP subject to a specified minimum level of employment; in this case the shadow price of the employment constraint would represent its marginal cost in terms of dollars of GNP foregone in order to achieve the last unit of required employment. If we maximized employment subject to a minimum level of GNP, the shadow price of the GNP constraint would be the marginal cost in terms of manyears of employment foregone in order to achieve the last unit of required GNP. In either case we have implicitly established terms of trade between dollar and nondollar magnitudes.

Extensive discussions of programming, control theory, and probabilistic aspects of the theory of economic policy may be found in Fox, Sengupta and Thorbecke [5; pp. 171–282]; the probabilistic aspects are very thoroughly treated by Theil [4].

### 1.3. The plan of the book

Ch. 1 has briefly reviewed the use of optimizing concepts in economic theory and in the more recently developed theory of quantitative economic policy. In ch. 2 we will plunge immediately into the methods of operations research.

Operations research has sometimes been characterized by economists as "the econometrics of the firm". Most of the models of operations research involve objective functions to be optimized; sets of input-output type relationships or, more generally, structural relationships among variables; and resource and other constraints upon the levels of outputs that can be achieved. In many practical and realistic cases, they also involve dynamic and probabilistic aspects.

Chs 2, 3, 4 and 5 present the salient methods of linear, nonlinear and dynamic programming, control theory and variational techniques, and probabilistic programming which are applicable to microeconomic models, mostly within individual firms. Ch. 6 presents a considerable range of operations research models which have been applied to problems of decision-making in firms and, in a few cases, to investment planning and project selection by firms and/or government agencies.

Ch. 7 presents some very recent applications of optimizing techniques to models of university departments and groups of departments and provides an introduction to the rapidly-growing literature on operations research approaches to the planning of educational systems at the national level and at the level of particular universities.

Ch. 8 presents additional results on decentralization or decomposition techniques and develops some implications of central place theory for the optimal regionalization of national economic policies and for defining the environments in which competing and complementary retail firms actually operate. Ch. 9 discusses some problems of measuring the noneconomic outputs of a society, problems which must be provisionally solved if optimizing techniques are to be applied symmetrically to market and nonmarket institutions and to the economic and noneconomic components of general social systems.

### REFERENCES

[1] Tinbergen, J., *On the theory of economic policy*. Amsterdam: North-Holland Publishing Co., 1952. Second revised edition, 1955.

[2] Tinbergen, J., *Centralization and decentralization in economic policy*. Amsterdam: North-Holland Publishing Co., 1954.

[3] Tinbergen, J., *Economic policy: principles and design*. Amsterdam: North-Holland Publishing Co., 1956.

[4] Theil, H., *Economic forecasts and policy*. Amsterdam: North-Holland Publishing Company, 1958. Second revised edition, 1961, 424-444.
Theil, H., *Optimal decision rules for government and industry*. Amsterdam: North-Holland Publishing Company and Chicago: Rand McNally, 1964.

[5] Fox, K. A., J. K. Sengupta and E. Thorbecke, *The theory of quantitative economic policy: with applications to economic growth and stabilization*. Amsterdam: North-Holland Publishing Company and Chicago: Rand McNally; 1966.

[6] Sengupta, J. K., "The stability of truncated solutions of stochastic linear programming", *Econometrica*, Vol. 34, 1966, 77-104.

[7] Sengupta, J. K., "Stochastic linear programming with chance constraints", accepted for publication in *International Economic Review*, 1968.

[8] Sengupta, J. K., G. Tintner and C. Millham, "On some theorems of stochastic linear programming with applications", *Management Science*, Vol. 10, October 1963.

[9] Sengupta, J. K., "Distribution problems in stochastic and chance-constrained programming", K. A. Fox, G. V. L. Narasimham and J. K. Sengupta, ch. 17 in: *Economic models, estimation and risk programming: Essays in honor of Gerhard Tintner*. Berlin: Springer-Verlag, 1969.

[10] Sengupta, J. K. and J. H. Portillo-Campbell, "A fractile approach to linear programming under risk", (sent for publication, 1968).

[11] Sengupta, J. K. and B. C. Sanyal, "Sensitivity analysis methods for a crop-mix problem in linear programming". To appear in *Unternehmensforschung*.

[12] Cartter, A. M., *An assessment of quality in graduate education*. Washington, D.C.: American Council on Education, 1785 Massachusetts Avenue, N.W., 1966.

[13] Samuelson, P. A., *Foundations of economic analysis*. Cambridge: Harvard University Press, 1947. Also available in paperback edition, New York: Atheneum, 1965.

[14] Chamberlin, E. H., *The theory of monopolistic competition*. Cambridge: Harvard University Press, 1933.

[15] Kuenne, R. E. (ed.), *Monopolistic competition theory: studies in impact. Essays in honor of Edward H. Chamberlin*. New York: John Wiley and Sons, 1967.

[16] Holdren, B. R., *The structure of a retail market and the market behavior of retail units: a theory of the multiproduct firm*. Englewood Cliffs, N.J.: Prentice-Hall, 1960.

[17] Nicholls, W. H., *Imperfect competition within agricultural industries*. Ames: Iowa State University Press, 1941.

[18] Ackoff, R. L., "Operations research", *International Encyclopedia of the Social Sciences*. Macmillan and Free Press, 1968, Vol. 11, 290-294.

[19] Fox, K. A. and J. K. Sengupta, "The specification of econometric models for ptanning educational systems: An appraisal of alternative approaches", *Kyklos*, Vol. 21, No. 4, 1968.

[20] Fox, K. A., F. P. McCamley and Y. Plessner, *Formulation of management science models for selected problems of college administration*. Final report (cyclostyled) submitted to U.S. Department of Health, Education and Welfare, November 10, 1967, Department of Economics, Iowa State University, Ames, Iowa, 117 pp.

[21] Plessner, Y., K. A. Fox and B. C. Sanyal, "On the allocation of resources in a university department", accepted for publication in *Metroeconomica*, 1968.

[22] McCamley, F. P., *Activity analysis models of educational institutions*. Unpublished Ph.D. dissertation, 1967. Ames: Iowa State University Library, 235 pp.

[23] Tinbergen, J., *Statistical testing of business cycle theories, Vol. II: Business cycles in the United States of America, 1919-1932*, Geneva: League of Nations, 1939.

[24] Theil, H., "On the theory of economic policy", *American Economic Review*, Vol. XLVI, May 1956, 360-366.

[25] Kumar, T. K., *On the existence of an optimal economic policy*. Unpublished Ph.D. dissertation, 1965. Ames: Iowa State University Library.

[26] Van Eijk, C. J. and J. Sandee, "Quantitative determination of an optimum economic policy", *Econometrica*, Vol. 27, 1959, 1-13.

[27] Theil, H., "Linear decision rules for macrodynamic policy problems". In: B. Hickman (ed.), *Quantitative planning of economic policy*. Washington: Brookings Institution, 1965, 18-42.

[28] Adelman, I. and E. Thorbecke (eds.), *The theory and design of economic development*. Baltimore: Johns Hopkins Press, 1966.

# Chapter 2

# METHODS OF LINEAR PROGRAMMING: EXTENSION AND APPLICATIONS

Linear programming is perhaps the single technique which has found the most widespread application in economic and operations research models. Since nonlinear functions could under certain conditions be approximated by linear functions, methods of linear programming have been applied even to basically nonlinear problems with suitable modifications.

Two aspects of linear programming have received special attention in recent years, e.g. (i) the activity analysis formulation and the associated price-guided rules for resource allocation (usually termed decomposition techniques) and (ii) special situations such as integer linear programming and linear fractional functional programming in which the problems, though not strictly linear, could be solved by modified simplex-type algorithms. The following methods of linear programming and related techniques are presented here: standard algorithms of linear programming, linear fractional functional programming, integer linear programming, techniques of decomposition, and recursive linear programming.

## 2.1. Methodology of linear programming

Two aspects of the methodology of linear programming (LP) will be briefly discussed here, since the broad framework of LP is presumed to be known: (a) computational aspects of simplex or simplex-like procedures and (b) duality and its uses.

### 2.1.1. Computational aspects of LP

In a standard LP problem we have to find a vector $x=(x_1,...,x_n)$ which maximizes the objective function

$$z = c'x \qquad\qquad A: m.n$$

*Primal*: under the restrictions $c, x: n.1$

$$Ax \leqslant b; \quad x \geqslant 0 \qquad b: m.1.$$

24

By introducing $m$ slack variables $(x_{n+1}, ..., x_{n+m})$ and appropriate changes of dimensionality of $c$, $x$ and $A$ the problem can also be written as

$$\max z = c'x \tag{2.1}$$

under the restrictions

$$Ax = b \qquad A: m.(m + n) \tag{2.2}$$

$$x \geqslant 0 \qquad c, x: (n + m).1. \tag{2.3}$$

Assuming without loss of generality that the problem is feasible and that every basic feasible solution is nondegenerate, define a partition of vector $x$ into two subvectors, one in the basis $(x_B)$, the other not in the basis $(x_N)$. Let the appropriate conformable partition of matrix $A$ in (2.2) be denoted by $B$ and $N$.

Then

$$\underset{(m+n.1)}{x} = \begin{bmatrix} \underset{(m.1)}{x_B} & \underset{(n.1)}{x_N} \end{bmatrix} \qquad \underset{(m.m+n)}{A} = \begin{bmatrix} \underset{(m.m)}{B} & \underset{(m.n)}{N} \end{bmatrix}$$

$$\underset{(m+n.1)}{c} = \begin{bmatrix} \underset{(m.1)}{c_B} & \underset{(n.1)}{c_N} \end{bmatrix}.$$

The restriction (2.2) now becomes

$$Bx_B + Nx_N = b$$

i.e.

$$x_B = -B^{-1}Nx_N + B^{-1}b; \tag{2.4}$$

since $B$ is nonsingular by assumption. Also the objective function reduces to

$$z = c'_B x_B + c'_N x_N = (c'_N - c'_B B^{-1}N) x_N + c'_B B^{-1}b. \tag{2.5}$$

Now the particular basis we have taken in $x_B$ is the optimal basis only if

$$c'_N - c'_B B^{-1}N \leqslant 0 \qquad \text{(for all activities not in the basis)}. \tag{2.6}$$

For, if this condition (2.6) is not satisfied, it may be possible to increase (or maintain) profit $z$ in (2.5) by bringing in an activity from the set of activities $x_N$ which is more (or equally) profitable at the margin than some other activity in the set $x_B$. Denoting $c'_B B^{-1}N$ by $z'_N$ and $c'_N - z'_N$ by $\Delta'_N$ the optimality condition (2.6) can be expressed as

$$\Delta'_N = c'_N - z'_N \leqslant 0 \quad \text{(for all activities not in the basis)}. \tag{2.7}$$

The same thing can be expressed in terms of individual activity variables $x_j$. Let the optimal (maximum) basic feasible solution be $(x_1, ..., x_m, 0, ..., 0)$

and the associated basis (column) vectors be $P_1, P_2, ..., P_m$. Since these basis vectors are linearly independent, we may write

$$P_j = \sum_{i=1}^{m} x_{ij}P_i; \qquad (j = 1, 2, ..., m + n) \tag{2.8}$$

and use the coefficients $x_{ij}$ to define the quantities

$$z_j = \sum_{i=1}^{m} x_{ij}c_i; \qquad j = 1, ..., m + n \tag{2.9}$$

$$\Delta_j = c_j - z_j; \qquad j = 1, 2, ..., m + n. \tag{2.10}$$

For the optimal basis $\Delta_j = 0$ ($j = 1, 2, ..., m$ in the basis) and for all other activities not in the basis $\Delta_j \leqslant 0$ ($j = m+1, ..., m+n$).

If we have a feasible basis which is not optimal, then for that basis one can write (2.4) as

$$x_B = B^{-1}b \qquad (\text{setting } x_N = 0) \tag{2.11}$$

and utilize the following lemma to move from one basic feasible solution to another till the maximal profit level is reached.

*Lemma 2.1*

For any activity $k$ not in the current basis the change in profit resulting from the introduction of a unit of output $x_k$ into the basis is given by

$$\Delta_k = c_k - \sum_{i=1}^{m} c_i \, \Delta x_{Bi} \qquad (\text{index } i \text{ denotes basis})$$

$$= c_k - y_B' a_k$$

where $a_k$ is the $k$th column vector of basis $B$ with $m$ elements and $y_B'$ is the $m$-component row vector $y_B' = c_B' B^{-1}$ measuring implicit (or shadow) prices or 'dual' variables.

*Proof*: Starting from (2.11) let us introduce one unit of commodity $k$ not in the basis (i.e., $x_k$ is a nonbasic variable) into the basis (2.11); as a result at least some outputs in the basis $x_i$ (also denoted as $x_{Bi}$) have to change from $x_i$ to $x_i - \Delta x_{Bi}$ where $\Delta x_{Bi}$ denotes a small change in the level of basic activity $x_i$ which of course may be zero for some or all activities $i$. Hence

$$\sum_{j=1}^{m} a_{ij}(x_j - \Delta x_{Bj}) + a_{ik} = b_i$$

i.e.

$$B(x_B - \Delta x_B) + a_k = b$$

i.e.

$$\Delta x_B = B^{-1} a_k.$$

Then

$\Delta_k =$ opportunity cost of not producing the commodity $k$

$$= c_k - \sum_{i=1}^{m} c_i \, \Delta x_{Bi}$$

where the $i$th component of $\Delta x_B$ denoted by $\Delta x_{Bi}$ is given by the $i$th element of the column vector $(B^{-1} a_k)$. Defining $y'_B = c'_B B^{-1}$ as the vector of (provisional) dual prices, $\Delta_k$ can also be written as $(c_k - y'_B a_k)$. From the definition of $y_B$ it is also apparent that for any activity $j$ in the current basis

$$y'_B a_j = c_j \qquad (a_j \text{ is the } j\text{th column of basis } B)$$

since

$$y'_B B = c'_B B^{-1} B = c'_B.$$

The following lemma can also be easily proved.

*Lemma 2.2*

Let $u_i = x_{n+i}$ $(i = 1, \ldots, m)$ be the slack variables of the primal problem and $x_j$ $(j = 1, \ldots, n)$ be the other variables and let $y_i$ be the dual variables $(i = 1, \ldots, m)$ defined in lemma 2.1 as the vector $y_B$, then

$$x_j \, \Delta_j = 0, \text{ for all } j \text{ in the basis or not } (j = 1, 2, \ldots, n),$$
$$y_i u_i = 0, \text{ for all } i \text{ in the basis or not } (i = 1, 2, \ldots, m).$$

The simplex procedure begins with a basic feasible solution and then proceeds by changing one vector in the basis at each iteration by following the two criteria, one for the incoming activity and the other for the outgoing activity;

(i) incoming activity is $x_k$ and the column vector $a_k$ or $P_k$ enters the basis if,

$$c_k - z_k = \max_j (c_j - z_j), \; c_j - z_j > 0 \tag{2.12}$$

(ii) outgoing activity is $x_r$ and the outgoing vector is column $r$ of basis $B$ if,

$$x_{Br}/x_{rk} = \min_{i \in B} (x_{Bi}/x_{ik}); \; x_{ik} > 0. \tag{2.13}$$

Now this condition arises in the following way. Since the incoming vector is $P_k$, the unknown nonnegative amount $\theta$ at which it is to be used is to be chosen as large as the resource vector $b = P_0$ and the feasibility condition allow.

$$\text{Now } P_0 = \sum_{i \in B} x_i P_i - \theta P_k + \theta P_k$$

but by (2.8) with $j = k$,

$$P_k = \sum_{i \in B} x_{ik} P_i$$

$$\therefore P_0 = \sum_{i \in B} (x_i - \theta x_{ik}) P_i + \theta P_k.$$

Now if $\theta$ is chosen such that $(x_i - \theta x_{ik}) \geqslant 0$, $\theta \geqslant 0$ then the feasibility condition is satisfied. (If every $x_{ik} \leqslant 0$ then $\theta$ can be made arbitrarily large and positive without violating feasibility and thereby resulting in an infinite optimum (i.e. unbounded solution).) If, as is usual, some $x_{ik} > 0$ then the choice of $\theta$ is fixed by the feasibility conditions to $x_i/x_{ik} \geqslant \theta \geqslant 0$. The largest value that $\theta$ can take is then given by the *minimum* of the ratios

$$\theta = \min_{i \in B} (x_i/x_{ik}) = x_r/x_{rk}; \ x_{ik} > 0.$$

Note that in the text tableau the new coefficients $\bar{x}_{ij}$ analogous to the $x_{ij}$ in (2.8) are determined by

$$\bar{x}_{ij} = x_{ij} - x_{rj} \cdot (x_{ik}/x_{rk}); \qquad i = 1, 2, \ldots, m \quad \text{and} \quad i \neq r$$

$$\bar{x}_{rj} = x_{rj}/x_{rk}; \qquad (j = 1, 2, \ldots, n; \qquad x_k \text{ basic}, x_r \text{ nonbasic}).$$

Sometimes degeneracy can occur in applying the criteria for incoming and outgoing activities. For instance the criterion (2.12) $\max_j (c_j - z_j)$ when $c_j - z_j > 0$ may be satisfied by more than one incoming activity. This tie can be broken by selecting the vector with the largest index $j$. Similarly for the outgoing vector if there is a tie, choose the vector for which $x_{ik}$ is the greatest; if this does not break the tie one should choose from among the remaining vectors the one with the smallest index $i$. This should terminate cycling. Also the method of perturbation [1] may be applied.

*Revised simplex method*

One disadvantage of the standard simplex method, particularly for computers, is that at each iteration of computation we have to calculate those elements of a tableau which are not directly used in finding the values of basic feasible variables. Since it is not known in advance which particular values will be in the basis, calculation of all the elements is necessary, even though at each iteration we really need to know only the elements of the entering column, the new basic variables and their values.

The revised simplex method provides a means of reducing the load of extra computation at each iteration of the simplex tableau. Further, those LP problems in which artificial variables are required over and above the slack variables are treated in the revised simplex technique by what is known as the two-phase method [2, 3] rather than by the $-M$ pricing technique.

For standard LP problems with no artificial variables the revised simplex algorithm may be briefly summarized. Writing the objective function $z = c'_B x_B$ as $z - c'_B x_B = 0$ and adjoining it to a basic feasible solution we get

$$\begin{bmatrix} 1 & -c'_B \\ 0 & B \end{bmatrix} \begin{bmatrix} z \\ x_B \end{bmatrix} = \begin{bmatrix} 0 \\ b \end{bmatrix} \quad \text{or,} \quad x_B^{(1)} = \begin{bmatrix} z \\ x_B \end{bmatrix} = \begin{bmatrix} 1 & c'_B B^{-1} \\ 0 & B^{-1} \end{bmatrix} \begin{bmatrix} 0 \\ b \end{bmatrix}.$$

Further

$$\Delta_j = c_j - z_j = c_j - c'_B B^{-1} a_j \qquad \text{($a_j$ is the $j$th column vector of}$$
$$P_j = \sum_{i \in B} x_{ij} P_i = B^{-1} a_j \qquad \text{matrix $A$, also denoted $P_j$).}$$

Treating $x_B^{(1)}$ as the initial basic feasible solution, we proceed as in the standard simplex method. If all $\Delta_j \leqslant 0$ the optimal solution is reached; otherwise we select the vector $a_k$ (that is, $P_k$) to enter the basis and the vector $a_r$ (that is, $P_r$) to leave the basis just as in the simplex procedure.

*Dual simplex method*

In this method our main concern is to obtain a maximum (but not necessarily feasible) solution in the sense that a basis $B$ is determined such that $Bx = b$ and $c_j - z_j \leqslant 0$ for all $j$ *and* the basis vector $x$ is unrestricted in sign. The computational procedure is to transform the components of the unrestricted-in-sign vector $x$ by changing a single basic variable at a time in such a manner that the components of vector $x$ become nonnegative while always maintaining the optimality criterion $c_j - z_j \leqslant 0$. The variable to leave the basis is the most negative $x_{Bi}$ i.e., $x_{Br}$ say, and the acitivity entering the basis is $x_k$ if,

$$\frac{c_k - z_k}{x_{rk}} = \min_j \left( \frac{c_j - z_j}{x_{rj}} \right), \ x_{rj} < 0.$$

If there exists no $x_{rj} < 0$, then there is feasible solution. This method is useful for problems where finding the initial feasible basis is difficult and therefore this method is applied in integer linear programming e.g. Gomory's algorithm discussed in section 2.3 later.

*Other methods*

Methods alternative to the simplex algorithm have been proposed by various authors e.g. the multiplex method (Frisch [4]), gradient methods (Arrow, Hurwicz, Uzawa and others [5]), method of feasible directions (Zoutendijk [6]) and the various combinatorial methods (Kantorovic [7] and others [8]). However, for linear programming problems the ease and flexibility of the simplex method appear to be overwhelming factors in its favor.

*2.1.2. Duality and its uses*

To every primal LP problem: $\max z = c'x$, $Ax \leqslant b$, $x \geqslant 0$ there corresponds a dual LP problem: $\min w = b'y$, $A'y \geqslant c$, $y \geqslant 0$ with the basic property that, if either problem has an optimal (feasible) solution, then so does the other and further the optimal objective function values of the two problems are equal. Several other results on duality are worth mentioning:

(a) if the primal has an unbounded solution, the dual has no solution;

(b) if the vectors $x$ and $y$ are feasible for the primal and the dual LP problems respectively, then $c'x \leqslant b'y$;

(c) any optimal feasible solution pair $(x^*, y^*)$ satisfies the saddle point property (allowing a game-theoretic interpretation)

$$\phi(x, y^*) \leqslant \phi(x^*, y^*) \leqslant \phi(x^*, y)$$

where     $\phi(x, y) = c'x + y'(b - Ax)$     (pay-off function)

$(x, y) =$ feasible strategies of players in a two-person zero-sum game;

(d) if the primal LP has a *unique* feasible vector $x^*$ giving the maximum value of $z$, the dual LP need not necessarily have a *unique* (only one) optimal (feasible) vector $y^*$; and

(e) any dual variable at the optimal point $y^*$ can be interpreted as the marginal net profitability of the corresponding resource; that is, $y_i^* = \partial z^*/\partial b_i$ where $z^*$ is the maximum value of the objective function in the primal maximization problem. For any basic feasible solution in the primal, the marginal values $\partial z_B/\partial b = \partial(c_B'x_B)/\partial b = \partial(c_B'B^{-1}b)/\partial b$ can be defined (they are usually known as the provisional dual prices); however they are not necessarily nonnegative.

*Theorem 2.1* (Charnes, Cooper and Thompson [9])

If the primal feasible set $X = (x|Ax \leqslant b; x \geqslant 0)$ is nonempty and bounded, then the dual feasible set $Y=(y|y'A \geqslant c', y \geqslant 0)$ is nonempty but unbounded (i.e. has no upper bound).

*Proof*: Consider the primal $(\max g'x, Ax \leqslant b, x \geqslant 0)$ and the dual $(\min b'y, y'A \geqslant g', y \geqslant 0)$ problems, where $g$ is an $n$-element column vector with all elements equal to unity. Then since $X$ is nonempty and bounded, there exist, by the duality theorem, optimal feasible solutions $x^*$ to the primal and $y^*$ to the dual such that $y^{*'}A \geqslant g'$ and $y^* \geqslant 0$. Define a scalar (positive) number $h_0$ by $h_0 = \max(1, c_1, ..., c_n)$ for any bounded collection (i.e. row vector $c' = (c_1, ..., c_n)$ such that $y = hy^*$ where $h \geqslant h_0$. Then $y'A = hy^{*'}A \geqslant \geqslant hg' \geqslant h_0 g' \geqslant c'$; also $y \geqslant 0$. Hence the set $Y$ contains the infinite ray $(y|y = = hy^*, h \geqslant h_0)$ and therefore has no upper bound.

### Theorem 2.2

Let the primal feasible set $X$ defined above be nonempty, bounded, and containing at least two basic feasible solutions and let $y^*$ be the dual variable corresponding to the optimal primal vector $x^*$; further let $x$ be any basic feasible solution, distinct from $x^*$, leading to a value of the primal objective function $z$ next to the maximum value $z^*$ $(z < z^*)$; similarly let $y$, distinct from $y^*$, be any basic feasible solution in the dual problem leading to a value of the dual objective function $w$, next to the minimum value $w^*$ $(w > w^*)$. Under such conditions not both of the following can occur:

$$w = \text{dual to } z \text{ and } w > w^*.$$

A proof of this result may be easily worked out by applying the method of contradiction [10].

There is one very important implication of the above theorems: i.e., the duality aspect is specifically restricted only to the optimal solution.

The concept of duality or the related concept of shadow prices of resources has played an important role in several kinds of practical situations to which LP has been applied. Three specific uses are worth mentioning:
(a) the dual variables $y_i^*$ as shadow prices provide relative efficiency indicators for the different resources, thereby providing helpful guides in resource allocation if the original budgets are increased:
(b) since the following relations hold (Saaty, Webb [11])

$$\partial z^*/\partial a_{ij} = -x_j^* y_i^* \qquad (a_{ij} \text{ belonging to optimal basis})$$

at the optimal, these partial derivatives can be used, after proper normalization, as indicators of the sensitivity of the program to changes in input coefficients; and

(c) the dual variables, especially those called provisional dual prices, play a fundamental role in methods of decomposition of a large LP problem, especially one with a block-triangular or nearly block-triangular coefficient matrix.

The concept of duality can be easily extended to time-continuous [12] LP problems which frequently arise in many industrial applications. Define the following two sets $X_F$ and $Y_F$ of bounded measurable functions

$$X_F = \left\{ x: [0, T] \text{ such that } Ax(t) \leqslant b(t) + \int_0^t Dx(s)\, ds \right.$$

$$\left. \text{and } x(t) \geqslant 0, \text{ for } 0 \leqslant t \leqslant T; x: n.1 \right\}$$

$$Y_F = \left\{ y: [0, T] \text{ such that } y'(t) A \geqslant c'(t) + \int_t^T y'(s) D\, ds \right.$$

$$\left. \text{and } y(t) \geqslant 0 \text{ for } 0 \leqslant t \leqslant T; y: m.1 \right\}.$$

Here $A, D: m.n$ and $x(t)$ is an $n$-vector, $y(t)$ is an $m$-vector. If the two sets $X_F$ and $Y_F$ are nonempty, then they define feasible vectors for the primal and the dual continuous LP problems:

### Primal problem

Find $\bar{x}(t) \in X$ such that

$$\int_0^T c'(t)\, \bar{x}(t)\, dt = \max_x \left\{ \int_0^T c'(t)\, x(t)\, dt; x \in X_F \right\}.$$

### Dual problem

Find $\bar{y}(t) \in Y_F$ such that

$$\int_0^T b'(t)\, \bar{y}(t)\, dt = \min_y \left\{ \int_0^T b'(t)\, y(t)\, dt; y \in Y_F \right\}.$$

If such functions $\bar{x}(t), \bar{y}(t)$ exist they are called optimal solutions. (Note that if $D$ is a zero matrix and $b(t), c(t)$ are constants independent of time we get the standard static LP primal and dual problems.)

*Theorem 2.3* (Tyndall and others [12])

If there exist functions $\bar{z}$ in $X_F$ and $\bar{y}$ in $Y_F$ such that

$$\int_0^T c'(t)\,\bar{x}(t)\,\mathrm{d}t = \int_0^T b'(t)\,\bar{y}(t)\,\mathrm{d}t$$

then $\bar{x}(t)$ and $\bar{y}(t)$ are the optimal solutions of their respective problems.

*Proof*: Since it holds that for all $x(t)$ in $X_F$

$$\int_0^T c'(t)\,x(t)\,\mathrm{d}t \leqslant \int_0^T b'(t)\,\bar{y}(t)\,\mathrm{d}t = \int_0^T c'(x)\,\bar{x}(t)\,\mathrm{d}t$$

and for all $y(t)$ in $Y_F$

$$\int_0^T b'(t)\,y(t)\,\mathrm{d}t \geqslant \int_0^T c'(t)\,\bar{x}(t)\,\mathrm{d}t = \int_0^T b'(t)\,\bar{y}(t)\,\mathrm{d}t$$

therefore the result.

This theorem has applicability in (a) the linear dynamic continuous version of the Leontief input-output model and (b) in production scheduling models in which a pay-off function over time is optimized.

An important aspect of duality in linear programming is that it allows a game theoretic interpretation (i.e. a saddle value problem).

*Theorem 2.4* (Kuhn and Tucker [13])

In order that the nonnegative vectors $(x_0, y_0)$ provide a solution of the saddle value problem i.e.

$$\phi(x, y_0) \leqq \phi(x_0, y_0) \leqq \phi(x_0, y) \quad \text{for all} \quad x \geqslant 0, y \geqslant 0$$

where $\phi(x, y) = c'x + y'(b - Ax)$ is the Lagrangian function of a linear program, the necessary conditions are

$$\phi_{x_0} = (\partial\phi/\partial x)_{x=x_0} \leqq 0; \ \phi'_{x_0}x_0 = 0; \ x_0 \geqslant 0 \tag{2.14}$$

$$\phi_{y_0} = (\partial\phi/\partial y)_{y=y_0} \geqq 0; \ \phi'_{y_0}y_0 = 0; \ y_0 \geqslant 0. \tag{2.15}$$

The sufficient conditions are that $\phi(x, y_0)$ be concave in $x$ and $\phi(x_0, y)$ be convex in $y$ around the points $(x_0, y_0)$.

Now consider a maximization-type LP model with the primal constraint set $X$ and the contraint set of the dual problem (which is a minimization problem) as $Y$. Let the vector $x$ in $X$ be the strategy set of player I (in the primal maximization problem) and the vector $y$ in $Y$ that of player II (in the dual minimization problem) and the scalar pay-off function is $\phi(x, y)$ as defined above. This pay-off function has the interpretation that it specifies the amount of gain to player I for a given $y$, which is also the amount of loss to player II for a given $x$. Now if player I fixes his strategy $x_0$ and announces this beforehand, the best that player II can do is to select $y_0$ such that $\phi(x_0, y_0)$ gives the minimum of $\phi(x_0, y)$ over all $y \in Y$, i.e.

$$\phi(x_0, y_0) = \min_y \phi(x_0, y) = \min_y \max_x \phi(x, y). \tag{2.16}$$

Similarly, if player II announces his optimal strategy as $y_0$, then the best that player I can do is to maximize $\phi(x, y_0)$ over $x \in X$, i.e., to select a strategy $x_0$ such that

$$\phi(x_0, y_0) = \max_x \phi(x, y_0) = \max_x \min_y \phi(x, y). \tag{2.17}$$

These two conditions (2.17) and (2.18) may be easily identified with saddle point property at $(x_0, y_0)$:

$$\phi(x_0, y) \geqslant \phi(x_0, y_0) \quad \text{and} \quad \phi(x, y_0) \leqslant \phi(x_0, y_0)$$

which implies optimality in LP models.

Now for a given LP model, let there exist vectors $x, y$ satisfying the Kuhn-Tucker necessary conditions of theorem 3.4; then the following relations hold:

$$Ax - b \leqslant 0; \quad -A'y + c \leqslant 0; \quad c'x - b'y \leqslant 0. \tag{2.18}$$

Now define a positive scalar constant $v$ such that the set $(\bar{x}, \bar{y}, \bar{v})$ provides all feasible strategies where $\bar{x} = x/v$, $\bar{y} = y/v$, $\bar{v} = 1/v$ and the sum of all components of the strategy set is unity, i.e.

$$\sum_j \bar{x}_j + \sum_i \bar{y}_i + \bar{v} = v^{-1} \left( \sum x_j + \sum y_i + 1 \right) = 1$$

i.e.

$$v = \sum x_j + \sum y_i + 1.$$

With the strategy set $(\bar{x}, \bar{y}, \bar{v})$ the relations (2.18) become

$$\begin{bmatrix} 0 & -A' & c \\ A & 0 & -b \\ c' & -b' & 0 \end{bmatrix} \begin{bmatrix} \bar{x} \\ \bar{y} \\ \bar{v} \end{bmatrix} \leqq 0. \tag{2.19}$$

Now since each component of the strategy vector $s=(\bar{x}, \bar{y}, \bar{v})$ is nonnegative and the sum of all its elements add up to unity, this defines an equivalent game problem. Since the coefficient matrix of (2.19) is skew-symmetric, the value of this equivalent two-person game is zero i.e. the saddle value problem for the matrix game (2.19) has a zero saddle-point solution. Note that if one element of the vector $s$, say $s_k=1$, while all other components of $s$ are zero, we have a pure strategy for player I, otherwise the strategies are said to be mixed.

Two remarks about the saddle-value interpretation of LP models may be added. First, we note that the above results help us to characterize the neighborhood of the optimal solution specified by the nonnegative vectors $(x_0, y_0)$ where $x_0$ is the maximizing solution of the primal LP and $y_0$ is the minimizing solution of the dual LP. For instance, let $\bar{x}$ be the maximizing solution vector of the primal LP model with parameters $(\bar{A}, \bar{b}, \bar{c})$ and the maximand $\bar{z}=\bar{c}'\bar{x}$; then it can be shown [14] that $\bar{z}$ is convex in $\bar{c}$ and concave in $\bar{b}$. Thus, let $c$ be any vector in the neighborhood of $\bar{c}$, such that the maximizing vector $x$ in this case is feasible and different from $\bar{x}$. Then by the saddle value theorem

$$\phi(\bar{x}, \bar{y}) = \phi(\bar{x}) = \bar{z} = \bar{c}'\bar{x} = \phi(\bar{c}) \text{ say, and } \phi(x, y) = \phi(x) = c'x = \phi(c),$$

say.

Now the equation of the tangent plane at $\bar{c}$ i.e.

$$\phi(\bar{c}, \bar{x}) + (c - \bar{c})' (\partial\phi/\partial c)_{c=\bar{c}, x=\bar{x}} = c'\bar{x}$$

lies below the curve $\phi(c, x)=c'x$, since with given $c$, the vector $x$ is optimal i.e. $c'x \geqslant c'\bar{x}$, both $x$, $\bar{x}$ feasible. Hence $\phi(\bar{c})=\phi(\bar{x}, \bar{y})=\bar{z}$ is convex in $\bar{c}$. Similarly, it can be shown that $\bar{z}$ is concave in vector $\bar{b}$, by using the duals to the two primal problems. These results are useful in parametric problems and decomposition techniques. Also, if the variations in the elements of the price vector $c$ are random in a probabilistic sense we can apply Jensen's inequality, i.e.

$$E\phi(c) \geqslant \phi(Ec) \tag{2.20}$$

where $E$ is the expectation operator and $\phi(c)=\phi(c, x)$ is the optimal maximand. If the statistical distribution of the quantity $m=Ec$ is non-degenerate, then the above inequality (2.20) is strict and this implies that replacing the random vector $c$ in a probabilistic linear program by its expected value and solving the resulting deterministic LP model would generally underestimate the expected level of optimal profits.

Second, since the Kuhn-Tucker theorem is more general in its application, it could be invoked for situations which are bilinear rather than linear. As an example consider the simple Von Neumann model of an expanding economy [15], where we intend to determine the optimal non-negative pair $(\bar{x}, \bar{\delta})$ for the following problem:

$$\text{maximize } \delta, \text{ subject to } \delta A x \leqq x, \, x \geqslant 0 \qquad (2.21)$$

where $\delta$ is a scalar, $A$ is a nonnegative $n$-rowed square matrix satisfying the condition of productivity i.e., $x \geqslant Ax$ for an $n$-element activity vector $x$. Writing the saddle-value function as

$$\phi(\delta, x, y) = \delta + y'(x - \delta Ax)$$

and applying theorem 2.4, it can be easily shown that if there exists a non-negative triple $(\bar{\delta}, \bar{x}, \bar{y})$ satisfying

$$\phi(\delta, x, \bar{y}) \leqslant \phi(\bar{\delta}, \bar{x}, \bar{y}) \leqslant \phi(\bar{\delta}, \bar{x}, y)$$

for all nonnegative elements $(\delta, x, y)$ in the appropriate feasible sets, then at the optimal we must have

$$\bar{x} = \bar{\delta} A \bar{x}, \, \bar{x} \geqslant 0.$$

More generalized versions of such models are available and in those cases [16] the computational procedures have to use game theory methods of constructing equivalent games and solving them by techniques known; e.g., fictitious play or sequential search.

### 2.2. *Linear fractional functional programming*

The structure of a linear fractional functional (LFF) program is as follows:

$$\text{maximize } z = \frac{\sum_{j=1}^{n} c_j x_j + c_0}{\sum_{j=1}^{n} d_j x_j + d_0} \qquad (2.22)$$

under the restrictions

$$\sum_{j=1}^{n} a_{ij} x_j \leqslant b_i \quad \text{and} \quad x_j \geqslant 0 \quad (i = 1, \dots, m). \qquad (2.23)$$

Since the graph of (2.22) is hyperbolic on the $(x, z)$ coordinate system, the LFF program is also called a hyperbolic program. Various computational methods, each requiring slight modifications of the finite simplex routine, have been proposed (Isbell and Marlow, Martos, Charnes and

Cooper, Gilmore and Gomory, Swarup [17] and others) in the literature. However, each algorithm is basically dependent on the two following properties of the objective function $z$, i.e.

(a) although the functional $z$ is neither convex nor concave, its local maximum is also a global maximum, and

(b) the maximum of $z$ if it occurs at a finite point also occurs at a primal feasible solution of the constraint set defined by (2.23).

### 2.2.1. Computational methods

If the convex set of restrictions (2.23) defines a convex polyhedral $P$ such that the denominator of $z$ in (2.22) is strictly positive for all feasible values of $x$ in $P$, then the following result holds.

### Theorem 2.5 (Martos)

The linear fractional function $z$ in (2.22) has a finite maximum on the convex polyhedral set $P$ which is attained on at least one vertex of the polyhedron. *Proof*: Let $P_1, ..., P_s$ be the vertices of the convex polyhedral $P$. Then any feasible point (i.e. a vector point) $q$ of $P$ can be expressed as a convex linear combination of these vectors i.e.,

$$q = g_1 P_1 + \cdots + g_s P_s = \sum_{i=1}^{s} g_i x_{ji} \qquad (2.24)$$

where $g_1, ..., g_s$ are constants such that $g_i \geqslant 0$ and $\sum_i g_i = 1$ $(i = 1, ..., s)$ and $x_{ji}$ denotes the $j$th activity in $P_i$. Now denote the numerator of $z$ by $N$ and the denominator by $D$ assume that among the vertices the objective function value $z$ is maximum at $P_h$, that is

$$z(P_h) \geqslant z(P_i); i = 1, ..., s$$

i.e.

$$N(P_h) D(P_i) \geqslant D(P_h) N(P_i). \qquad (2.25)$$

Multiplying both sides of (2.25) by $g_i$ and adding from $i = 1$ to $i = s$

$$N(P_h) \sum_i g_i D(P_i) \geqslant D(P_h) \sum_i g_i N_i(P_i) \qquad (2.26)$$

but

$$\sum_i g_i D(P_i) = \sum_{i=1}^{s} g_i \left( \sum_{j=1}^{n} d_j x_{ji} - d_0 \right)$$

$$= \sum_j d_j \left( \sum_i g_i x_{ji} \right) - d_0 \sum_i g_i$$

$$= \sum_j d_j q - d_0 \sum_i g_i = D(q), \text{ say.}$$

Similarly

$$\sum_i g_i N(P_i) = N(q), \text{ say.}$$

Using (2.26)

$$N(P_h)/D(P_h) \geqslant \frac{N(q)}{D(q)} \quad \text{i.e.} \quad z(P_h) \geqslant z(q).$$

This theorem shows the applicability of the simplex routine.

Now for computation the restriction (2.23) is converted into equalities by slack variables $x_{n+i} \geqslant 0$ $(i = 1, ..., m)$

$$\sum_{j=1}^{n} a_{ij} x_j + x_{n+i} = b_i.$$

We start with a basic feasible solution in which $m$ basic variables are positive and the others (nonbasic variables) are zero. Then the basic variables $x_s$ can be expressed in terms of nonbasic ones $\bar{x}_q = x_{m+q}$ i.e.

$$x_s = p_{s0} + \sum_{q=1}^{n} p_{sq} \bar{x}_q; \quad (s = 1, 2, ..., m: \text{basic}). \tag{2.27}$$

Then since nonbasic variables $\bar{x}_q$ could be put to zero

$$x_s = p_{s0} > 0 \quad (s = 1, ..., m: \text{basic})$$
$$\bar{x}_q = 0 \quad (q = 1, ..., n: \text{nonbasic}).$$

*Step 1*: Express the objective function $z$ of (2.22) in terms of nonbasic variables by using (2.27); then take the first partial derivative $(\partial z/\partial \bar{x}_j) = z_j$ say, i.e., if

$$z = \left( \alpha_0 + \sum_{j=1}^{n} \alpha_j \bar{x}_j \right) \Big/ \left( \beta_0 + \sum_{j=1}^{n} \beta_j \bar{x}_j \right)$$

then

$$\partial z/\partial \bar{x}_j = z_j = \left( \Delta_j + \sum_{\substack{k=1 \\ j \neq j}}^{n} \delta_{kj} \bar{x}_k \right) \Big/ \left( \beta_0 + \sum_{j=1}^{n} \beta_j \bar{x}_j \right)^2 \tag{2.28a}$$

where

$$\Delta_j = \beta_0 \alpha_j - \alpha_0 \beta_j$$
$$\delta_{kj} = \beta_k \alpha_j - \beta_j \alpha_k.$$

Since the nonbasic variables in (2.28a) can be put to zero, therefore (2.28a) can be written as

$$z_j = z_j^B = \Delta_j / \beta_0^2 \quad \text{where} \quad z_j^B = z_j \tag{2.28b}$$

of (2.28a) with all nonbasic $\bar{x}_q = 0$.

Note from (2.28a) that the numerator of $z_j$ does not involve $\bar{x}_j$ and since the denominator of $z_j$ is always positive, therefore any amount of increase in $\bar{x}_j$ cannot affect the sign of $z_j$ except through the coefficients, i.e. through $\varDelta_j$. Hence either $z_j^B > 0$ for some $j$ or $z_j^B \leqslant 0$ for all $j = 1, ..., n$. The latter case (i.e. $\varDelta_j \leqslant 0$ for all $j$) defines an optimal basis.

*Step 2*: In case $z_j^B > 0$ for some $j$, one changes the basis by the following criteria:

(i) activity $x_k$ enters the basic feasible set (i.e. then $\bar{x}_k = x_k$ in the new basis), if after calculating $z_j^B$ for all nonbasic activities $j = 1, ..., n$, $\bar{x}_k$ is chosen such that $z_k^B$ is the largest positive (finite) number; and

(ii) activity $x_r$ leaves the basic feasible set (i.e then $x_r = \bar{x}_r$ in the new basis), to be replaced by $\bar{x}_k$ above and $x_r$ is selected by choosing for $r$ that value of $s$ in the basis for which the ratio $(p_{so}/|p_{sk}|)$ with $p_{sk} < 0$ is minimum over $s = 1, ..., m$.

*Step 3*: With the outgoing activity $x_r$ and incoming activity $x_k$ we get a new basis at which the objective function $(\bar{z})$ is usually higher than (though in case of degeneracy it can be equal to) the old value (i.e. $\bar{z} \geqslant z$). Since the number of basic feasible solutions of the constraint set is finite, this iterative procedure terminates. (In cases of cycling the same methods used in the simplex routine are applicable.) Note however that in step 3 we can again express the basic variables in terms of the nonbasic ones as follows: ($x_r$ nonbasic, $x_k = \bar{x}_k$ basic)

$$x_s = \bar{p}_{s0} + \bar{p}_{sr} x_r + \sum_{\substack{q=1 \\ q \neq k}}^{n} \bar{p}_{sq} \bar{x}_q \qquad (s \neq r, \quad s = 1, 2, ..., m : \text{basic})$$

where

$$\bar{p}_{s0} = p_{s0} - p_{r0}\left(p_{sk}/p_{rk}\right)$$
$$\bar{p}_{sq} = p_{sq} - p_{rq}\left(p_{sk}/p_{rk}\right)$$
$$\bar{p}_{sr} = p_{sk}/p_{rk} .$$

Charnes and Cooper [18] have deloped a LP model equivalent to the LFF problem specified by (2.22) and (2.23) under the same assumption as in theorem 1. Let $t$ be a nonnegative scalar such that $y = tx$. Then the equivalent LP problem is

$$\text{maximize } L(y, t) = c'y + c_0 t \qquad (2.29a)$$

under the restrictions

$$Ay - bt = 0 \qquad (2.29b)$$
$$d'y + d_0 t = 1 \qquad (2.29c)$$
$$y \geqslant 0, t \geqslant 0. \qquad (2.29d)$$

The first restriction here corresponds to $Ax=b$ where we assume without loss of generality $x'_B=(x_1,...,x_m)$ as basic variables and $x'_N=(x_{m+1},...,x_n)$ as nonbasic. Let the conforming partitions be

$$x = \begin{bmatrix} x_B \\ x_N \end{bmatrix}; \quad c = \begin{bmatrix} c_B \\ c_N \end{bmatrix}; \quad d = \begin{bmatrix} d_B \\ d_N \end{bmatrix}; \quad \text{and } A = [B \ N]$$

then

$$x_B = B^{-1}b - B^{-1}Nx_N.$$

Define further $z_j^{(1)}=c'_B B^{-1}a_j$ and $z_j^{(2)}=d'_B B^{-1}a_j$ where $a_j$ is the $j$th column of matrix $A$ corresponding to $x_j$. Then the objective function $z$ of the LFF program and its first derivative evaluated at the basis can be written after a little algebraic manipulation as:

$$z = \left[ N^{(1)} + \sum_{j=m+1}^{n} (c_j - z_j^{(1)})\, x_j \right] \Big/ \left[ D^{(1)} + \sum_{j=m+1}^{n} (d_j - z_j^{(2)})\, x_j \right] \quad (2.30)$$

$$\frac{\partial z}{\partial x_j} = z_j^B \quad \text{(i.e. with } x_N = 0\text{)}$$
$$= [D^{(1)}(c_j - z_j^{(1)}) - N^{(1)}(d_j - z_j^{(2)})]/(D^{(1)})^2 \quad (2.31)$$

where $N^{(1)}=c'_B B^{-1}b+c_0$ and $D^{(1)}=d'_B B^{-1}b+d_0$.

Now for the equivalent LP problem, since from (2.29b)

$$y_B = B^{-1}bt - B^{-1}Ny_N$$

therefore (2.29c) can be written as

$$(d'_B B^{-1}b + d_0)t = D^{(1)}t$$

i.e.

$$t - \left[ 1 - \sum_{j=m+1}^{n} (d_j - z_j^{(2)})y_j \right] \Big/ D^{(1)} = 0 \quad \text{(using (2.29c))}.$$

Finally the objective function $L$ of equivalent LP may be written as

$$L = \frac{N^{(1)}}{D^{(1)}} + \left[ \sum_{j=m+1}^{n} \{D^{(1)}(c_j - z_j^{(1)}) - N^{(1)}(d_j - z_j^{(2)})\}\, y_j \right] \Big/ D^{(1)} \quad (2.32)$$

$$\vdots$$
$$\partial L/\partial y_j = [D^{(1)}(c_j - z_j^{(1)}) - N^{(1)}(d_j - z_j^{(2)})]/D^{(1)}$$
$$j = m + 1, ..., n.$$

Note that when the nonbasic variables are equated to zero (i.e. all $x_j \in x_N$ and all $y_j \in y_N$ are zero), $z$ of (2.30) equals $L$ of (2.32). Further, the sign of $z_j^B$ depends on

$$\Delta_j = D^{(1)}(c_j - z_j^{(1)}) - N^{(1)}(d_j - z_j^{(2)}) \quad (2.33)$$

whereas the sign of $(\partial L/dy_j)$ depends on

$$\bar{\Delta}_j = [D^{(1)}(c_j - z_j^{(1)}) - N^{(1)}(d_j - z_j^{(2)})]/D^{(1)}. \qquad (2.34)$$

Hence the optimality conditions are

$$\Delta_j \leqslant 0\,(j = m + 1, ..., n: \text{nonbasic}) \text{ for LFF program}$$
$$\bar{\Delta}_j \leqslant 0\,(j = m + 1, ..., n: \text{nonbasic}) \text{ for equivalent LP}.$$

Similarly the simplex criteria for moving from one feasible basis to another are analogous, e.g. the incoming activity $x_k$ is chosen by

$$\Delta_k = \max_j \Delta_j; \qquad (\Delta_j > 0) \text{ in LFF program}$$
$$\bar{\Delta}_k = \max_j \bar{\Delta}_j; \qquad (\bar{\Delta}_j > 0) \text{ in equivalent LP}.$$

Two remarks about LFF programs may be added. First, we have so far assumed that the feasible set of constraints (2.23) contains "good points" in the sense that either the denominator $D(x)$ of $z$ is positive for all feasible $x$ or if $D(x)=0$ for some feasible $x$, then the numerator $N(x)$ of $z$ is negative.

Martos [18] has distinguished three sets of points in a LFF program, e.g.,

(a) the set of "good points" defined by those feasible points $x$ at which either the denominator $D(x)$ of $z$ is positive or, if $D(x)=0^+$ (i.e., tends to zero from above) for some feasible $x$, then the numerator $N(x)$ of $z$ is negative. (Note however that in the latter case the feasible point $x$ cannot be optimal, since the objective function $z$ becomes infinite this way through negative values and therefore $z$ does not reach a maximum value).

(b) the set of "bad points" (or inadmissible points) defined by those feasible points $x$ at which either $D(x)<0$ or $D(x)=0^-$ (i.e. tends to zero from below) with $N(x)>0$. (Note that by observing the sign of the partials $\partial z/\partial x_j$ it is intuitively clear that if the feasible set $X$ contains only bad points defined above, then the function $z$ is not bounded from above and hence the LFF problem has no finite solution); and

(c) the set of singular points defined by those feasible points $x$ for which $D(x)=N(x)=0$. In this case the fractional function $z$ is not ordinarily defined. Nevertheless, from a practical viewpoint, if there is such a singular point $x_0$ among the nonsingular points of the constraint set $X$ at which although $z$ is not defined its limit superior

$$\lim_{x \to x_0} \sup (N(x)/D(x))$$

exists, the problem should be considered solvable.

Now consider a nonlinear extension [19] of the fractional problem, where the convex constraint set $X$ is as before, i.e. $X=\{x|Ax\leqslant b, x\geqslant 0\}$ is assumed closed, bounded and connected but the numerator $N(x)$ is assumed to be any concave, continuous, nonlinear (real-valued) scalar function of vector $x$ in $X$ and the denominator $D(x)$ of $z=N(x)/D(x)$ is assumed to be any convex, continuous, nonlinear (real-valued) scalar function of vector $x$ in $X$. Further, $D(x)$ is assumed positive for all $x\in X$. Under these assumptions the following theorem holds:

*Theorem 2.6*

Under the above assumptions, the vector $x_0$ is an optimal solution of the nonlinear fractional problem

$$\max\{N(x)/D(x); \quad x\in X\} = N(x_0)/D(x_0) = z_0$$

if and only if

$$\max\{N(x)-z_0D(x); \quad x\in X\} = F(z_0) = 0.$$

*Proof*: Now since $x_0$ is the optimal solution, therefore

$$z_0 = N(x_0)/D(x_0) \geqslant N(x)/D(x) \quad \text{for all} \quad x, x_0 \in X$$

which implies

$$N(x) - z_0D(x) \leqslant 0 \quad \text{for all} \quad x\in X$$

and in particular if $x=x_0$, then $N(x_0)-z_0D(x_0)=0$. To prove the converse, let $x_0$ solve the problem $F(z_0)=0$, then by hypothesis

$$N(x) - z_0D(x) \leqslant N(x_0) - z_0D(x_0) = 0 \quad \text{for all} \quad x, x_0 \in X.$$

This implies

$$N(x) - z_0D(x) \leqslant 0 \quad \text{for all} \quad x\in X$$

and in particular for $x=x_0$, $N(x_0)-z_0D(x_0)=0$. Hence the result. Note, however, that the solution vector $x_0$ may not be unique.

This theorem is useful in developing a computatonal algorithm for nonlinear fractional programming problems satisfying the conditions of theorem 2.6. For instance, define

$$F(z) = \max_x (N(x) - zD(x); \quad x\in X, \quad z \text{ scalar})$$

and let the scalar numbers $z_1, z_2$ be such that $z_2>z_1$, that with $z_1$ fixed, $x_1$

is the optimal vector maximizing $F(z_1)$ and that with $z_2$ fixed, $x_2$ is the optimal vector maximizing $F(z_2)$. Then for $x_1, x_2$, and $x$ in the constraint set $X$, we have

$$F(z_2) = \max_x (N(x) - z_2 D(x)) = N(x_2) - z_2 D(x_2) < N(x_2) - z_1 D(x_2)$$
$$\text{since} - z_2 < - z_1$$
$$\leqslant \max_x (N(x) - z_1 D(x)) = F(z_1).$$

This implies in other words that $F(z)$ is strictly monotone decreasing in the scalar number $z$ and in particular $F(z)=0$ has a unique solution. This suggests the following iterative method of computation:

*Step 1*: Assume $z=z_1=0$ and solve $F(z_1)=F(0)=\max N(x)$, $x \in X$; denote the optimal solution vector $x_1$ and compute the scalar quantity $z_2 = N(x_1)/D(x_1)$. This step is admissible if $z_2 \geqslant 0$.

*Step 2*: Treating $z_2$ as a fixed nonnegative constant, solve the LP model $F(z_2)=\max(N(x)-z_2 D(x))$, $x \in X$ and let $x_2$ be the optimal solution vector; use $x_2$ to define $z_3 = N(x_2)/D(x_2)$ and the iterations continue.

*Step 3*: We stop at the $k$th iteration if $F(z_k)$ is either zero or less than a very small preassigned positive quantity $\delta$. In the latter case the $\delta$-termination rule defines an approximately optimal solution in the $\delta$-approximate sense.[1]

### 2.2.2. Applications of LFF

One of the most useful applications of LFF programming is to be found in linear macrodynamic models of national planning based on input-output analysis. Let $Y(t)$ denote the real net national product (income) which is the sum total of sectoral net products $\sum_i Y_i(t)$ where

$$\Delta Y_i(t) = Y_i(t+1) - Y_i(t) = b_i I_i(t) + b_{i0}$$
$$Y_i(t) = C_i(t) + I_i(t).$$

Here $I_i, C_i$ are sectoral investment and consumption respectively. One conventional type of planning model sets up maximization of growth of real national income as the objective function. Then the following type of model results:

$$\text{maximize } \Delta Y/Y = \frac{\sum_i (b_i I_i(t) + b_{i0})}{\sum_i C_i(t) + \sum_i I_i(t)}$$

---

[1] See, for example, [19].

subject to the restrictions

$$C_i(t) \geqslant C_i(0) > 0$$
$$I_i(t) \geqslant I_i(0) > 0$$
$$C_i(t) \geqslant C_i(\min); \qquad I_i(t) \leqslant I_i(\max).$$

Here $C_i(\min)$ denotes the minimum consumption level preassigned for some sector and $I_i(\max)$ denotes the maximum preassigned level of investment for some sector.

For computational illustration consider the following:

$$\text{maximize } z = (3x_1 + 6x_2)/(x_1 + 4x_2 + 7)$$

under the restrictions

$$3x_1 + 4x_2 + x_3 = 2$$
$$x_1 + 4x_2 + x_4 = 1; \quad x \geqslant 0 \quad (x_3, x_4 \text{ are slack}).$$

Consider the initial basis made up of $x_3$, $x_4$. Expressing all basic variables in terms of nonbasic variables we get $x_3 = 2$, $x_4 = 1$, $x = 0$. Evaluate $\partial z/\partial x_1 = \frac{3}{7}$ and $\partial z/\partial x_2 = \frac{6}{7}$ which implies that $x_2$ should be the new incoming acticity. Now if $x_2 = \frac{1}{2}$ then $x_3 = 0$ or, if $x_2 = \frac{1}{4}$, $x_4 = 0$; therefore $x_4$ should be the outgoing activity. At the second iteration, the new basis is $(x_2, x_3)$. At the third iteration we get the optimal basis $x_1 = \frac{1}{2}$, $x_2 = \frac{1}{8}$ with $z = \frac{9}{32}$.

A special type of problem arises in the safety first principle of risk programming, where the vector $c$ of the objective function $z = c'x$ of an LP problem has random components and we have to apply a Tchebycheff-type inequality [20] to specify relatively distribution-free inequality

$$\text{Prob}(z \leqslant r) \leqslant \frac{\text{Var } z}{(\text{mean } z - r)^2} = \frac{x'Vx}{(\bar{c}'x - r)^2}$$

where $V$ is the variance-covariance matrix, $\bar{c}$ is the mean vector and $r$ is the preassigned disaster level the chance of which is intended to be minimized. In default of minimizing $\text{Prob}(z \leqslant r)$ (since the distribution characteristics may not be known), the safety first principle [21] operates through minimizing $(x'Vx)/(\bar{c}'x - r)^2$ subject to the usual (nonstochastic) restrictions of a LP model $Ax \leqslant b$, $x \geqslant 0$. This problem has the structure of a nonlinear fractional functional programming model.[2]

---

[2] Various aspects of risk programming are discussed in ch. 5.

## 2.3. Integer linear programming

An integer LP problem is a linear programming problem in which some or all of the activities $x_j$ are required to be integers. An all integer LP problem may be stated as:

$$\text{maximize } z = c'x \tag{2.35a}$$

$$\text{subject to } Ax = b \quad A: m.n; \\ x: n.1; \tag{2.35b}$$

$$x \geqslant 0 \tag{2.35c}$$

$$\text{all } x_j \text{ are integers } 0, 1, 2, \ldots \tag{2.35d}$$

Since the variables or activities here are not allowed to take any (continuous) values between the integers $(0, 1, \ldots)$, two of the basic properties of the simplex algorithm fail to operate. First, the integer feasible solutions of an integer LP do not form a convex set. Second, the existing computational methods of integer LP based on the theory of cuts (Gomory, Dantzig, Fulkerson and others) generally require restricting the feasible area of LP to a minimal convex set which includes all integer solutions; this tends not only to increase the dimensionality of the problem but to involve difficulties of degeneracy and round off difficulties for a digital computer.

### 2.3.1. Computational aspects

We will mention in this section two different methods of computation e.g. (i) the methods of successive cuts and (ii) the branch and bound technique. Consider the first method and suppose we have solved the LP problem defined by (2.35a) through (2.35c) with $B$ as the optimal basis and let $N$ be the index-set of $j$ corresponding to the nonbasic variables. Further define the vector $q_j = B^{-1}a_j$, $(j = 1, \ldots, n)$ where $a_j$ is the $j$th column of matrix $A$ and let $q_0 = B^{-1}b$. Now for an ordinary LP problem any feasible solution satisfies

$$x_B = q_0 - \sum_{j \in N} q_j x_j \quad \text{(note that } x_B = q_0 - B^{-1}Nx_N), \tag{2.36a}$$

where the basic feasible solution is $x_B = q_0$, $x_N = 0$.

Consider the $i$th equation of (2.36a)

$$x_{Bi} = q_{i0} - \sum_{j \in N} q_{ij} x_j \quad (i = 1, \ldots, m). \tag{2.36b}$$

Now three cases are possible:

(i) if $q_{i0}$ is an integer for all $i$ ($i=1,...,m$) then the solution $x_j=0$ for $j \in N$ specifies an integer solution;

(ii) if $q_{i0}$ is not an integer but $q_{ij}$ is an integer, then the problem is not feasible (i.e., there cannot exist an all integer feasible solution). If we suppose the contrary and assume that there exists an all integer solution (including $x$'s) under these conditions, then $x_j$ must be a positive integer or zero for all $j$. Also by assumption $q_{ij}$ is an integer; hence $\sum_{j \in N} q_{ij}x_j$ must be an integer, but from (2.36b), $x_{Bi}$ cannot be an integer if $q_{i0}$ is not an integer; and

(iii) both $q_{i0}$ and $q_{ij}$ are not integers in some or all components. Let $q_{i0} = = k_{i0}+f_{i0}$ where $k_{i0}$ is the integral part (i.e. the largest integer less than or equal to $q_{i0}$) and $f_{i0}$ is the fractional part. Similarly define $q_{ij}=k_{ij}+f_{ij}$ where $k_{ij}$ is the integral part and $f_{ij}$ is the fractional part. Then by assumption

$$1 > f_{i0} > 0 \text{ since } q_{i0} \text{ is not integral, and} \tag{2.36c}$$

$$f_{ij} \geqslant 0, j \in N \text{ by construction (note that } -3.5 = -4+0.5). \tag{2.36d}$$

Then (2.36b) becomes

$$x_{Bi} = k_{i0} - \sum_{j \in N} k_{ij}x_j + f_{i0} - \sum_{j \in N} f_{ij}x_j. \tag{2.36e}$$

Now if any all integral solution exists to the LP problem, then $x_{Bi}$ is an integer; but $(k_{i0}-\sum_{j \in N} k_{ij}x_j)$ is an integer by construction, hence $(f_{i0} - -\sum_{j \in N} f_{ij}x_j)$ must be an integer.

By (2.36d), $\sum_{j \in N} f_{ij}x_j$ cannot be negative; then from (2.36c) it follows that

$$f_{i0} - \sum_{j \in N} f_{ij}x_j \leqslant 0. \tag{2.37}$$

This is a necessary condition for the existence of an all-integer solution. Define

$$s_i = -f_{i0} + \sum_{j \in N} f_{ij}x_j \qquad \text{(i.e. } s_i \geqslant 0). \tag{2.38}$$

The variable $s_i$ is usually called Gomory's slack variable, since this method has been developed by Gomory [22]. We adjoin the restricting equation (2.38) for this variable to the original LP problem defined in equation (2.35). Note the effects of constraint (2.37) on the original LP problem. First, it cuts off chunks of feasible space of the continuous LP model containing both integer and noninteger solutions. Second, the optimal solution of the continuous LP model (i.e. equations (2.35a) through (2.35c)) does not satisfy the necessary condition (2.37) (i.e. the old optimum is eliminated). Third, the process of adjoining restriction (2.38) to the original basis means we add another column to the basis. Since for the new basis the initial solution $s_i = -f_{i0}$ is negative. this is not feasible. This indicates that we have to solve the new LP problem either by introducing artificial variables or by the dual simplex method considered before in section 2.1.1. If the solution to the new LP problem does not have the integrality properties, one has to repeat the entire procedure by introducing more Gomorian cuts. This cutting plane method is continued till an optimal feasible all integer solution is reached. Gomory has proved the convergence of such a procedure (see Hadley [23]).

Consider the following example [24]:

$$\max z = -10x_1 + 111x_2 + 0x_3 + 0x_4$$

under the restrictions

$$-x_1 + 10x_2 + x_3 = 40; \qquad x_1 + x_2 + x_4 = 20;$$
$$x_j = \text{nonnegative integers } (j = 1, \dots, 4).$$

Disregarding integral requirements, the optimal simplex tableau for this problem is

| | | $N$ | | |
|---|---|---|---|---|
| $c_B$ | $B$ | $x_3$ | $x_4$ | $k_{i0}+f_{i0}$ |
| $-10$ | $x_1$ | $-\frac{1}{11}$ | $\frac{10}{11}$ | $14+\frac{6}{11}$ |
| $111$ | $x_2$ | $\frac{1}{11}$ | $\frac{1}{11}$ | $5+\frac{5}{11}$ |
| | $z_j$ | $11$ | $1$ | $460 = $ optimal $z$. |

Consider the largest positive of the ratios ($f_{i0}/f_{ij}$; $i \in B, j \in N$ i.e. $5, \frac{6}{10}, -6$) and determine $x_2$ as the activity on which the Gomory constraint is imposed by denoting $s_2 = x_5$ where

$$s_i - \sum_{j \in N} f_{ij}x_j = -f_{i0} \qquad (i = 2)$$

i.e., $x_5 - \left(\frac{1}{11}\right)x_3 - \left(\frac{1}{11}\right)x_4 = -\frac{5}{11}$.

Adjoin this as a new row to the original tableau and apply either the artificial variable technique or the dual method; the final optimal integer solution is $x_1 = 10$, $x_2 = 5$, $x_4 = 5$ and $x_3 = 0$. Note that in this case the optimal integral solution is much different from the old optimal solution (i.e. $x_1 = 14 + \frac{6}{11}$, $x_2 = 5 + \frac{5}{11}$, $x_3 = 0 = x_4$).

In some cases of transportation-type models where it is relatively easy to find a feasible solution with all integers, one could apply a second algorithm by Gomory [25], which proceeds from one all-integer solution of the constraints to another till the optimal has been found. There is another interesting method due to Land and Doig [26] which is most suitable for linear integer problems in which only a few selected variables have to be integral. This method, much like the technique of Gomory-type cuts, starts from the optimal tableau of a simplex solution disregarding integral requirements, then systematically reduces the value of the objective function till the activity (or activities) satisfy integral requirements. (The systematic reduction here is done through a sequence of linear programs.) Thus if the activity $x_1$ is to be made an integer, we reduce the maximum value $z$ of the continuous LP model to a value for which either the minimum of $x_1$ is the nearest lower nonnegative integer or the maximum of $x_1$ is the nearest higher nonnegative integer. Then keeping $x_1$ fixed at either its maximum or minimum integral values, we branch out to make activity $x_2$ integral and so on. Note that for any activity $x_i$ in the current basis, whether integral or not, the set $(x_i, z(x_i))$ defines a convex region (where $z(x_i)$ is the value of the objective function for the basis containing $x_i$), since given any two values $x_i^{(1)}$, $x_i^{(2)}$ in a small neighborhood of $x_i$ and the corresponding values of the objective function $z(x_i^{(1)})$, $z(x_i^{(2)})$ it is possible to find an intermediate value of $z$ between these two limits by taking suitable linear combination of $(x_i^{(1)}, x_i^{(2)})$.

Now consider a standard maximization-type LP model denoted by $P(k)$ where $r$ variables $x_k$ $(k=1,...,r)$ are required to be integers $(0, 1,...)$ where $r \leqslant n$, $n$ being the total number of activities. For instance, if $k=0$ then none of the activities $x_k$ are required to be integers, e.g. we have no integral requirement. Denote by $S_k$ the set of all feasible solutions and the corresponding objective function values of LP problems $P(k)$ and by $\bar{S}_k$ the set of all nonfeasible solutions to problems $P(k)$. Note that $\max_x z = z(x)$, $x \in S_r \leqslant \max z = z(x)$, $x \in S_{r-1} \leqslant \cdots \leqslant \max z = z(x)$, $x \in S_0$. Denoting $\max z = z(x)$, $x \in S_k$ $(k=0, 1,...,r)$ by $z^{(k)}$ this implies that the maximand $z^{(r)}$ is bounded above by $z^{(r-1)}$, which is bounded above by $z^{(r-2)}$ and so on till the maximum upper bound $z^{(0)}$ is reached, which however does not satisfy any integral requirement. This suggests the following sequence of computation starting from $z^{(0)}$ with the associated solution vector $x^{(0)}$.

*Step 1.* Starting from $z^{(0)} \in S_0$ and assuming that it does not satisfy integral requirements, select an activity $x_j^{(0)}$ in the basis $x^{(0)}$ to be made integral (e.g. by using a criterion of farthest distance from a near integer value of all basic activities in $x^{(0)}$) and then set up the following pair of LP problems:

(i) max $z = c'x$, subject to $P(0)$ and $x_j = x_j^{(0)} = [x_j^{(0)}]$ where $[x_j^{(0)}]$ is the greatest integer less than or equal to $x_j$;

(ii) max $z$, subject to $P(0)$ and $x_j = x_j^{(0)} = [x_j^{(0)}] + 1$. Let the maximands of these two problems be denoted by $z_{jm}^{(0)}$ and $z_{jM}^{(0)}$ $(z_{jm}^{(0)} \leqslant z_{jM}^{(0)})$ and if they exist they are necessarily elements of the set $S_1$. Two cases are now possible: either one (or both) of the two LP problems are feasible or none of them are. In the latter case it would be usually true that $x_j$ cannot be made integral and hence the whole problem is infeasible; however, because of degeneracy it is sometimes advisable to try constraints of the type $x_j = [x_j^{(0)}] - 1$. In the former case, we denote $z^{(1)} = \max(z_{jm}, z_{jM})$ by considering only those maximands which are feasible. Note the value of $x_j$ at $z^{(1)}$, e.g. $x_j = v$, say; then each resource amount $b_i$ is reduced by $a_{ij}v$ to set up a new LP problem with dimensions reduced by one.

*Step 2*: The iterations continue to determine the sequence of maximands $z^{(0)}, z^{(1)}, ..., z^{(N-1)}$, till the highest unlabeled maximand not in the set $\bar{S}_j$ for any $j$ is given the labor $z^{(N)}$.

*Step 3*: After the sequence $z^{(0)}, z^{(1)}, ..., z^{(N-1)}$ has been generated up to $(N-1)$ such that we have only one variable left to be made integral, we can apply either Gomory's all integer algorithm or all the earlier steps, but now restricted to the set $S_{r-1}$. In the latter case appropriate constraints are applied to any activity which has not yet been constrained at an integral value and the maximand of set $S_r$ is labeled $z^{(N)}$. (Note that although in steps 1 and 2 the integral requirement is introduced for one activity at a time, as in the usual simplex routine, step 3 involves going through different integral feasible solutions till the optimal is found.)

A few comments are perhaps in order. First, note that in cases when more than one Gomory-cuts like (2.38) are to be selected (since more than one component of $q_{i0}$ may be nonintegral), as yet there is no single criterion that will work in all cases, although criteria based on largest $f_{i0}$, largest of the ratios $f_{i0}/f_{ij}$, etc. have been proposed on the analogy of the simplex routine. Second, Hadley has observed that the computational experience with Gomory's method has not been very encouraging, as the number of iterations required for convergence is generally found to be very large. Also the problems of degeneracy have not all been solved. The relative powers of the two algorithms presented above are also unknown.

It would seem both possible and desirable to devise a good continuous nonlinear approximation (good defined with a preassigned degree of tolerance, of course) for solving integer LP problems. One useful result of integer LP models, however, remains that at the optimal solution, the duality interpretation holds.

### 2.3.2. *Model applications*

(a) One of the earliest models of integer linear programming is a plant allocation model due to Koopmans and Beckmann [27]. Given *n indivisible* plants, *n* possible locations and the expected profitability $c_{ki}$ of plant *k* in location *i*, the problem is to find an assignment of plants $x_{ki}$ (i.e. plant *k* at location *i*) for all *k*, $i = 1, ..., n$ such that the sum total of profits is the highest possible (of course without violating the constraints). Mathematically the problem is to determine the decision variables $x_{ki}$ which

$$\text{maximize} \sum_k \sum_i c_{ki} x_{ki} \qquad (2.39a)$$

under the restrictions

$$\sum_i x_{ki} = 1 \text{ (i.e. one plant of each kind only is available),} \qquad (2.39b)$$

$$\sum_k x_{ki} = 1 \text{ (i.e. one location of each kind only is available),} \qquad (2.39c)$$

$[x_{ki}] = X$ where $X$ defines a permutation matrix of which each
row and each column contain a single element unity,     (2.39d)
all other elements being zero.

This model assumes no interaction between plant locations, i.e. one location has no neighborhood effects on the other locations through transportation costs or otherwise. (Otherwise the problem would be at the least a quadratic integer programming problem.) The following feature of duality is worth mentioning. Let the plants (*k*) and locations (i) be renumbered in such a way that in the *optimal assignment* each plant is matched with the location bearing the same number. Then there must exist a system of shadow prices ($q_k$ for *k*th plant i.e. (2.39b) and $r_k$ for *k*th location i.e. (2.39c) such that
(i) $c_{kk} = q_k + r_k$
(ii) $c_{ki} \leqslant q_k + r_i$, $k, i = 1, ..., n$
and conversely, if such a system of shadow prices can be determined for any feasible assignment, then that assignment is an optimal one (e.g. condition (ii) implies that the shadow price or rental imputed to a plank *k* is the highest amount that could be earned by this plant in any location).

(b) Situations of capital budgeting and project selection (Weingartner [28], Alan Manne and others [29]) offer another interesting field of application. Perhaps the simplest problem in this category is as follows: given *n independent* projects with all project outlays and returns discounted appropriately, the decision problem is to choose the optimal project-mix under a specific budget constraint for each time period e.g.

$$\text{maximize} \sum_{j=1}^{n} c_j x_j \qquad (2.40a)$$

under the restrictions

$$\sum_j a_{tj}x_j \leqslant b_t (t = 1, \ldots, T) \tag{2.40b}$$

$$0 \leqslant x_j \leqslant 1, x_j \text{ an integer } (j = 1, \ldots, n). \tag{2.40c}$$

Here $c_j$ = net present value of returns from project $j$; $x_j = 0$ if the $j$th project is not selected and 1 if it is selected; $a_{tj}$ = present value of outlays on project $j$ in time period $t$; $b_t$ = present value of total budget restrictions at period $t$. If $x_j$ could take any value between 0 and 1 (i.e., if a fraction of a project $j$ could be selected), then a dual problem to (2.40) could be easily written down:

$$\text{minimize } \sum_{t=1}^{T} b_t y_t \tag{2.41a}$$

under the restrictions                    (dual problem)

$$\sum_{t=1}^{T} a_{tj}y_t + u_j \geqslant c_j \tag{2.41b}$$

$$y_t \geqslant 0, u_j \geqslant 0; \quad j = 1, \ldots, n. \tag{2.41c}$$

Denote the optimal solutions of the primal $(x_j^*)$ and the dual LP problems $(y_t^*, u_j^*)$ by asterisks; now since the optimal solution must satisfy the dual restrictions (2.41b), hence

$$u_j^* \geqslant c_j - \sum_{t=1}^{T} a_{tj}y_t^*; \quad (j = 1, \ldots, n) \tag{2.41d}$$

and in particular, if project $j$ is selected (i.e. $x_j^* > 0$) then (2.41d) holds with strict equality. In the simplex routine, the optimality is checked by the criteria $(c_j - z_j) \leqslant 0$ for all $j = 1, \ldots, n$ and in particular for the activities in the optimal basis $c_j - z_j = 0$. In this problem it is easy to check that $z_j$ at optimal $= \sum_t a_{tj}y_j^*$. Hence

$$\text{for optimal projects only: } \sum_{t=1}^{T} a_{tj}y_t^* = c_j \tag{2.42a}$$
$$\scriptstyle (0 < x_j^* \leqslant 1)$$

($j$ extends over accepted projects only),

$$\text{for all other projects: } c_j - \sum_t a_{tj}y_t^* \leqslant 0 \tag{2.42b}$$
$$\scriptstyle (x_j^* = 0)$$

($j$ extends over projects not in the optimal basis).

The relation (2.42a) implies that for each optimal project selected (even at fractional levels) the present value $(c_j)$ must equal the present value of all future outlays $(\sum_t a_{tj}y_t^*$, where $y_t^*$ represents the shadow prices of the capital budget restrictions). (Incidentally it may be noted that this simple type of capital budgeting model has been extended in various ways to include interdependent projects, contingent projects, etc.)

(c) Other applications of the integer LP model are in (i) production sequencing problems where certain operations or activities must run in a definite sequence, (ii) PERT (program evaluation and review techniques) and CPM (critical path methods) techniques of analysis for complex construction projects, (iii) personnel assignment to jobs, and (iv) transportation problems with indivisible commodities.

Two comments may be added about the general approach of integer LP techniques. First, there is as yet no satisfactory (computational) method available for combining integer LP problems with the situations in which any of the parameters $(A, b, c)$ or the restrictions have probabilistic components for one reason or another. Although discrete probability distributions offer an important possibility here, this has not been attempted so far. Second, integer LP techniques are appropriate for only a very small portion of the many economic situations characterized by indivisibility (or lumpiness) of inputs or other variables. As a matter of fact, the two most important effects of indivisibility, e.g. external (or neighborhood) effects and interdependence effects, are practically precluded from consideration by the linearity assumption of integer linear programming.

### 2.4. Techniques of decomposition

Decomposition techniques are those methods of subdividing one (or a sequence of) programming problem(s) into subproblems (each being a programming problem) such that the subproblems are linked in some fashion to allow the sequence of subproblem optima to converge to the overall optimum of the original program. Decomposition techniques are not restricted exclusively to LP problems. In the context of LP problems it is useful to classify five types of decomposition methods, e.g.,

(a) decomposition algorithms for LP problems with special coefficient structures (e.g. block-triangular) developed by Dantzing and Wolfe [30];

(b) methods of two-level planning developed by Kornai and Liptak [31], in which the resource allocation vector is reshuffled to attain conformability (or feasibility) and optimality of sector programs with the overall program;

(c) the active approach developed by Tintner and Sengupta [32] in connection with stochastic linear programming, in which the resource vector is partitioned into a linear combination of allocation vectors such that the solutions other than the overall optimal solution can be analyzed both deterministically and stochastically;

(d) methods of decentralization developed by Arrow, Hurwicz [33] and others (Koopmans); and

(e) delegation models of an activity-analysis type based, for example, on methods of analyzing a LP model with a vector objective function into a sequence of properly constructed LP models (Koopmans and others [34]).

Although these five types of decomposition methods have many basic similarities, the contexts in which the methods originate, the ways the computational algorithms are developed and the manners in which the economic implications are analyzed are generally different. Some of the most common similarities are: (i) the use of shadow-price guided allocation at one stage or another, (ii) economy in use of information through decomposition in one form or another, and (iii) flexibility in decision-making through decentralization.

### 2.4.1. *Method of Dantzig and Wolfe*

Consider a large LP problem in which the coefficient matrix is partitioned into nonzero blocks $A_j$ and $B_j$ with a corresponding partition of the resource vector such that some resources are specific to the $j$th subproblem, whereas others are like overheads required by all activities. The overall program may be formulated as follows: determine an $n_j$ element column vector $x_j$ $(j=1, ..., n)$ which will

$$\text{maximize } \sum_{j=1}^{n} c_j' x_j$$

under the restrictions $\qquad c_j : n_j . 1 \qquad (2.43a)$

$$\sum_{j=1}^{n} A_j x_j = b \qquad A_j : m . n_j \qquad (2.43b)$$

$$b : m . 1$$

$$B_j x_j = b_j \quad (\text{all } j = 1, ..., n) \qquad B_j : m_j . n_j \qquad (2.43c)$$

$$x_j \geqslant 0 \quad (\text{all } j) \qquad b_j : m_j . 1 . \qquad (2.43d)$$

This is a LP problem in $\sum_{j=1}^{n} n_j$ variables subject to $m + \sum_j m_j$ constraints. Note that the constraints (2.43c) are subprogram constraints specific to $x_j$ only, whereas (2.43b) denotes joint constraints, so to say.

Now assume for simplicity that the subprogram constraints (2.43c) define a convex set

$$S_j = \{x_j \mid x_j \geqslant 0, B_j x_j = b_j\} \qquad (2.44)$$

which is bounded for each $j = 1, ..., n$. For a given $j$, let the set of extreme points of the convex polyhedron $S_j$ be $W_j = \{x_{j1}, x_{j2}, ..., x_{jr_j}\}$; then define

$$P_{jk} = A_j x_{jk} \quad \text{and} \quad c_{jk} = c_j x_{jk} \quad \text{for} \quad k = 1, 2, ..., r_j. \quad (2.45)$$

Now the extremal problem equivalent to the original LP problem is to determine the decision variables $s_{jk}$ $(j = 1, ..., n; \ k = 1, ..., r_j)$ which are in fact nonnegative weights which

$$\text{maximize} \sum_j \sum_k c_{jk} s_{jk} \quad (2.46a)$$

under the restrictions

$$\sum_j \sum_k P_{jk} s_{jk} = b \quad (m \text{ constraints}) \quad (2.46b)$$

$$\sum_k s_{jk} = 1 \quad (n \text{ constraints}) \quad (2.46c)$$

$$s_{jk} \geqslant 0 \quad \text{all} \quad j = 1, 2, ..., n \quad \text{and} \quad k = 1, 2, ..., r_j. \quad (2.46d)$$

To prove the equivalence, note that any point $x_j$ of the set $S_j$ may be written as a convex combination of its extreme points i.e. $\sum_k x_{jk} s_{jk}$ where $s_{jk} = \{s_{j1}, s_{j2}, ..., s_{jr_j}\}$ would satisfy the weight conditions (2.46c) and (2.46d). Then (2.46b) is equivalent to (2.43b) and (2.46a) is equivalent to (2.43c) in view of (2.45).

Note that the equivalent extremal problem has $(m+n)$ columns in the basis. Since there are $(m+n)$ constraints (i.e. the $m$ joint constraints (2.43b) and each of the $m_j$ constraints of the $j$th subproblem (2.43c)), the reduction in computation is considerable if the $m_j$ are large. Now if we apply the revised simplex method to the extremal problem (2.46), we will have "provisional dual prices" $y$: $(m.1)$ and $\bar{y}$: $(n.1)$ in every feasible basis (note the standard LP analogy: $y_B' = c_B' B^{-1}$ i.e . $y' A_j = c_j$) satisfying

$$y' P_{jk} + \bar{y}_j = c_{jk} \quad (2.47a)$$

for basic columns drawn from the $j$th partition, i.e.

$$y' A_j x_{jk} + \bar{y}_j = c_{jk}. \quad (2.47b)$$

Multiplying both sides by $s_{jk}$ and summing over $k$, we get

$$y' A_j x_j + \bar{y}_j = c_j x_j.$$

To describe the iterative steps, consider the provisional dual prices $y$, $\bar{y}$ to set up the following subproblem with a modified objective function:

$$\text{maximize } (c_j - y'A_j)\, x_j \qquad\qquad (2.48a)$$

$$\text{under the restrictions (2.43c), (2.43d)}. \qquad\qquad (2.48b)$$

Assume that an extreme point $\bar{x}_j$ of the set $S_j$ defined in (2.44) solves the maximization problem (2.48) for any $j=1,\dots,n$. Now define $\bar{x}_{j0}$ by the following criterion

$$\varDelta_0 = (c_{j0} - y'A_{j0})\bar{x}_{j0} - \bar{y}_{j0} = \max_{j}\left[(c_j - y'A_j)\bar{x}_j - \bar{y}_j\right]$$
$$(j = 1, 2, \dots, n) \qquad (2.49a)$$

i.e.

$$\varDelta_0 = \bar{c}_{j0} - z_{j0} \text{ where } z_{j0} = y'A_{j0}\bar{x}_{j0} + \bar{y}_{j0},\ \bar{c}_{j0} = c_{j0}\bar{x}_{j0}. \qquad (2.49b)$$

If $\varDelta_0 \leqslant 0$, then the basis is optimal and the nonnegative weights $(s_{jk})$ solve the equivalent problem and the original problem. If $\varDelta_0 > 0$ for some $j$, then the original problem is not solved and by (2.49a) we construct a new column and its associated profit coefficient for the equivalent extremal problem and form a new feasible basis with the new column replacing another by the usual simplex routine. The process is repeated till $\varDelta_0 \leqslant 0$ for all $j$, i.e. till optimality of the original problem is reached.

### Theorem 2.7

The decomposition algorithm (i.e., the iterative calculations applied to sub-problems (2.48) by using (2.49a)) terminates in a finite number of steps yielding a solution to the equivalent extremal problem (2.46) and hence to the original problem (2.43).

*Proof*: Since the simplex algorithm for LP problems is known to terminate in a finite number of steps, it is sufficient to show that the criterion (2.49a) applied to subproblem (2.48) yields a solution to the equivalent extremal problem. It is easy to note from (2.47b) and (2.49b) that the optimality case $\varDelta_0 \leqslant 0$ for *all* $j$ corresponds to

$$c_{jk} - y'A_j x_{jk} - \bar{y}_j \leqslant 0 \qquad (\text{all } j \text{ including } j=j_0)$$

and if $\varDelta_0 > 0$ for some $j$ and $j=j_0$ is chosen by the criterion (2.49a), then this must provide a new column and its associated profit coefficient for the equivalent extremal problem as

$$(A_{j0}x_{j0}, 0, \dots, 1, 0, \dots, 0) \quad \text{and} \quad c_{j0}x_{j0} \qquad (2.50)$$

satisfying

$$c_{j0k} - y'A_{j0}x_{j0k} - \bar{y}_{j0} > 0;$$

hence the result.

Note that even if the subproblems (2.48) have unbounded solutions in the sense that there exists a nonnegative vector $\hat{x}_j$ such that $B_j\hat{x}_j=0$ and $(c_j-y'A_j)\hat{x}_j>0$ (i.e. $\lambda\hat{x}_j$ with $\lambda>0$ is also a solution), then since the simplex solutions of the subproblem (2.48) generate a finite number of possible rays, the only change required in adding the new column is to rewrite the new basis in (2.50) as

$$(A_j\hat{x}_j, 0, \ldots, \quad 0, \ldots, 0) \qquad (2.51)$$

since we cannot apply the $\max_j$ criterion of (2.49a). The difference of (2.51) from (2.50) is that 1 has been omitted in (2.51) in the new column to be added so that the variable $s_{jk}$ associated with this new column need not satisfy the constraint $\sum_k s_{jk}=1$.

The most important field of application of the decomposition principle is in economic planning where there are two levels of operation, the central and the subdivisional. At the microeconomic level of a large corporate organization, the *central program* is specified by the equivalent extremal problem (2.46) (which has only the common resources, vector $b$, whereas the specific resources, vector $b_j$ are absent) and each of $j$ subdivisions of the central organization has a *subdivisional program*: max $c_j x_j$ under the restrictions (2.43c), (2.43d). Now the iterations can be described as a set of two-way exchange of information, e.g.

*Step 1*: Each subdivision (there are $j$ of them) submits a feasible *subdivisional program* based on central profit coefficients $c_j$.

*Step 2*: The center preassigns a revised set of profit coefficients which equals the old coefficient ($c_j$) plus a bonus or penalty, depending on whether this subdivisional program creates external economies or diseconomies for the overall central program. With revised profit coefficients the subdivisional program appears as problem (2.48).

*Step 3*: Each subdivision otherwise acts independently except for the revision of profit coefficients by the center at each iteration.

*Step 4*: At each iteration, the center considers the optimal solution of the $j$th subdivisional program (2.48), applies the criterion (2.49a) and if $\Delta_0>0$ for some $j$, then it introduces a new column to the basis of the equivalent extremal problem (2.46) and computes a new set of dual prices $y$ and $\bar{y}$ which determine the bonus or penalty element of the next revised profit coefficients for each subdivisional program. The iterations continue till the overall central problem (2.43) or (2.46) is solved.

### 2.4.2. Method of Kornai and Liptak

In this method the overall central program (termed the OCI problem i.e., overall central information) is decomposed into subprograms (termed sector programs) that can be solved by mutually independent 'sectors' coordinated by the center (i.e. central agency). Let the primal and dual versions of the OCI problem (in vector-matrix notations) be

$$\textit{Primal:} \quad \max c'x, \, Ax \leqslant b; \qquad x \geqslant 0 \tag{2.52a}$$

$$\textit{Dual:} \quad \min y'b, \, y'A \geqslant c', \, y \geqslant 0. \tag{2.52b}$$

Let $A = [A_1, ..., A_n]$, $x' = (x'_1, ..., x'_n)$, $c' = (c'_1, ..., c'_n)$ be the mutually corresponding partitions; then the OCI problem becomes

$$\max \sum_{i=1}^{n} c'_i x_i \quad \text{with} \quad \sum_{i=1}^{n} A_i x_i \leqslant b; \qquad x_i \geqslant 0 \quad (i = 1, ..., n) \tag{2.53a}$$

$$\min y'b \quad \text{with} \quad y'A_i \geqslant c'_i; \qquad y \geqslant 0 \quad (i = 1, ..., n). \tag{2.53b}$$

Partition the resource vector $b$ as the sum of vectors $u_i$

$$u_1 + \cdots + u_n = b \tag{2.54a}$$

where each vector $u_i$ representing allocation of resources is of the same dimension as the column vector $b$. Now define a quantity $u$

$$u = \begin{bmatrix} u_1 \\ \vdots \\ u_n \end{bmatrix}; \qquad (u_i \text{ is a vector}) \tag{2.54b}$$

composed of the allocation vectors $u_i$; then a specification of $u$ defines the central problem (2.52) whereas its component vector $u_i$ specifies the $i$th sector component of the central problem. Once $u_i$ is determined by the center, the $i$th sector programming problem can be formulated as

$$\textit{Primal:} \quad \max c'_i x_i, \, A_i x_i \leqslant u_i; \qquad x_i \geqslant 0 \tag{2.55a}$$

$$\textit{Dual:} \quad \min y'b, \, y'_i A_i \geqslant c'_i; \qquad y_i \geqslant 0, \, y \geqslant 0 \tag{2.55b}$$

where $y_i$ is the $i$th component of the conforming partition of $y$. Two levels of programs are thus defined; the OCI or central program in (2.52) and the sector programs in (2.55), and the allocation vectors $u_i$ link the two-level programs.

Now denote the feasible sets of $x$ and $y$ in the OCI program (2.52) by $X$ and $Y$ respectively and the feasible set of sector allocations $u_i$ by $U$.

Further, let $X^*$, $Y^*$ and $U^*$ be the respective sets corresponding to optimal solutions in $X$, $Y$ and $U$. Now it can be shown that for any feasible allocation program $u$ (i.e. feasible in its components $u_i$ for the sector programs), each sector optimum

$$f_i(u_i) = \max c_i' x_i = \min y_i' u_i \qquad (i = 1, \ldots, n \quad \text{and} \quad x_i \in X, \, y \in Y)$$

is a continuous and piecewise-linear concave function of $u_i$ and hence their sum, the overall optimum, i.e.

$$f(u) = f_1(u_1) + f_2(u_2) + \cdots + f_n(u_n)$$

is well defined under all $u_i$ in the feasible set $U$. Hence the central level OCI problem may be formulated as a program for decomposing the set $U$ into sector allocations $u_i$ which maximize the linear concave programming problem $f(u) = \sum_{i=1}^{n} f_i(u_i)$ and thereby determine the set $U^*$ consisting of the optimal programs.

*Theorem 2.8*

Any two-level problem derived from a solvable OCI problem is itself also solvable and its solution is equivalent to the OCI problem:

$$U^* \text{ nonempty and } X^* = \underset{u^* \in U^*}{\text{union of sets }} X^*(u^*). \qquad (2.56a)$$

Further, the maximum of the overall optimum is equal to the optimum of the OCI problem:

$$\max_{u \in U} f(u) = f(u^*) = \max_{x \in X} c'x = \phi; \qquad (u^* \in U^*). \qquad (2.56b)$$

*Proof*: The first part is easily proved by contradiction (for, if there is a central program $u$ with a component $u_i$ which does not solve the $i$th sector program, then $u$ with $u_i$ is not feasible and hence the two-level problem is not defined for that $u_i$). For the second part, note that

$$\max_{x \in X} c'x = \max_{\substack{x \in X(u) \\ u \in U}} c'x = \max_{u \in U} \left( \max_{x \in X(u)} c'x \right)$$

$$= \max_{u \in U} \left( \sum_{i=1}^{n} \max c_i' x_i, \, x_i \in X_i(u_i) \right),$$

since by definition $X = X(u) = $ union of sets $X_i(u_i)$

$$= \max_{u \in U} \left( \sum_{i=1}^{n} f_i(u_i) \right) = \max_{u \in U} f(u) = f(u^*) = \phi.$$

The computational solution of this two-level planning problem is achieved by setting up a polyhedral game between two groups of players, the center (maximizing player) and the team of sectors (minimizing player). The strategies of the center are feasible allocation patterns (i.e. elements $u$, $u_i$ in $U$), those of the team of sectors are the feasible shadow price systems in the duals of the sector programs, and the pay-off function is the sum of the dual sector objective functions. For instance, if $V$ be the union of dual *feasible* sets in the sector problems (i.e. union of $Y_i$ where $y_i \in Y_i$) the one can write (2.56b) as

$$f(u^*) = \max_{u \in U} \min_{v \in V} (v'u) = \phi^*. \qquad (2.56c)$$

Here $U$ is the feasible set of strategies of the maximizing and $V$ of the minimizing player and the homogeneous bilinear function $(v'u)$ may be identified as the pay-off function of the game.

Kornai and Liptak have suggested using the fictitious play method of Brown and Robinson [35] to solve this polyhedral game. In this method, against each central strategy $(u \in U)$, it is feasible to state an optimal counter strategy $v^* = v^*(u)$, while against sector strategy $v \in V$, it is feasible to state an optimal counter strategy $u^* = u^*(v)$, i.e.

$$v^*(u)'u = \min_{v \in V}(v'u); \qquad v'u^*(v) = \max_{u \in U}(v'u).$$

The regular fictitious play of the regular polyhedral game $(U, V)$ then simply means following a convergent rule of the strategy series $(u^*(1), \ldots, u^*(N))$ and $(v^*(1), \ldots, v^*(N))$ such that

$$\lim_{N \to \infty} \phi^*(N) = \phi$$

where $\phi$, and $\phi^*$ are given in (2.56c) and (2.56b).

For a termination at a finite stage $N_\delta < \infty$, the $\delta$-termination rule may be used, where the $\delta$-termination ($\delta$ is an arbitrary small positive number which may be preassigned) of the regular fictitious play of the game is defined as follows: let $N_\delta$ be the least positive integer for which

$$\phi^*(N_\delta + 1) - \phi^*(N_\delta) \leqslant \delta$$

holds. Then the iterations are terminated in phase $N_\delta$.

Kornai and Liptak have applied the decomposition methods of two-level planning to problems of optimal resource allocations in development planning in a multi-sector framework. A similar scope of application exists in multi-regional planning problems.

### 2.4.3. *Active approach of Tintner and Sengupta*

Consider the usual LP problem

$$\max c'x \qquad (2.57a)$$

under the restrictions      $c, x: n.1$

$$A: m.n$$

$$Ax \leqslant b; \qquad x \geqslant 0 \qquad b: m.1. \qquad (2.57b)$$

Define a new set of decision variables $u_{ij}$ which represent relative allocation proportions

$$b_i = \sum_{j=1}^{n} b_i u_{ij}; \qquad u_{ij} \geqslant 0, \; \sum_{j=1}^{n} u_{ij} \leqslant 1. \qquad (2.58)$$

By using these decision variables the active approach specifies a separable problem for each $x_j$ as

$$\max c_j x_j \qquad (2.59a)$$

under the restrictions

$$a_{ij} x_j \leqslant b_i u_{ij}; \qquad \text{all } i = 1, 2, ..., m \qquad (2.59b)$$

$$u_{ij} \geqslant 0, \sum_j u_{ij} \leqslant 1, \quad x_j \geqslant 0; \qquad j = 1, 2, ..., n. \qquad (2.59c)$$

This can also be written more generally as

$$\text{maximize } z = c'x = z(U) \qquad (2.60a)$$

under the restrictions

$$AX \leqslant BU; \qquad x \geqslant 0 \qquad (2.60b)$$

$$X = \text{diag. matrix}: (x_1, ..., x_n) \qquad (2.60c)$$

$$B = \text{diag. matrix}: (b_1, ..., b_m) \qquad (2.60d)$$

$$U = u_{ij} \quad \text{with} \quad 0 \leqslant u_{ij} \leqslant 1. \qquad (2.60e)$$

### *Lemma 2.3*

If there exists a finite optimal solution $x^*$ to the LP problem (2.57), then there also exists an optimal allocation matrix $U^*$ satisfying problem (2.60) and attaining the same value of the objective function $z^*$. (This can be proved by the method of contradiction.)

### *Lemma 2.4*

If for an arbitrary allocation matrix $U$ defined in (2.60e) the objective function value under the active approach (2.60) be denoted as $z_A$ and if for that $U$ there exists a feasible $x$ satisfying (2.57) with its objective function denoted by $z_P$ then

$$z_A \leqslant z_P .$$

(Proof is omitted here; see Tintner and Sengupta [32].)

Now consider the $j$th separable program (2.59). For a given $j = 1, ..., n$ let $W_j = (x_{j1}, x_{j2}, ..., x_{jr_j})$ be the set of all extreme points of the set defined by the feasibility constraints (2.59b) and (2.59c), where each feasible $x_j$ (and hence the elements $x_{jr_j}$ of set $W_j$) is a function of $u_{ij}$. We assume for simplicity that ther are $r_j$ extreme points for each $j$th subprogram (2.59). Further define

$$P_{jr} = a_j x_{jr} \quad \text{and} \quad c_{jr} = c_j x_{jr} . \tag{2.61}$$

For $r = 1, ..., r_j$ and $j = 1, ..., n$ and $a_j = j$th column of $A$, where each $x_{jr}$ may also be denoted by $x_{jr}(u_{ij})$ as a function of the allocation ratios $u_{ij}$. Now we construct an equivalent LP problem

$$\text{maximize} \sum_j \sum_r c_{jr} s_{jr} \tag{2.62a}$$

under the restrictions

$$\sum_j \sum_r P_{jr} s_{jr} \leqslant b \quad . \quad b : m . 1 \tag{2.62b}$$

$$\sum_r s_{jr} = 1 \tag{2.62c}$$

$$s_{jr} \geqslant 0 \quad \text{for all } j = 1, ..., n \quad \text{and} \quad r = 1, ..., r_j . \tag{2.62d}$$

Note that the variables $s_{jr}$ are simply nonnegative weights defining the coefficients of linear combinations of the feasible solutions of different subproblems. Now since any point $x_j = x_j(u_{ij})$ of the feasible set defined by (2.59b) and (2.59c) can be expressed as a convex combination of its extreme points, therefore

$$x_j = \sum_r x_{jr} s_{jr} \quad \text{satisfying (2.59b), (2.59c), (2.62c), (2.62d).} \tag{2.63}$$

By using (2.63) it is easy to prove the following lemma:

*Lemma 2.5*

If there exist numbers $(s_{jr})$ solving the problem (2.62), then the same numbers also solve the original LP problem (2.57).

Now let us define provisional dual prices $y$: $(m.1)$ and $\bar{y}$: $(n.1)$ as in

(2.47) before, corresponding to the problem (2.62) and satisfying

$$y'P_{jr} + \bar{y}_j = c_{jr} \tag{2.64a}$$

i.e.

$$y'a_jx_{jr}(u_{ij}) + \bar{y}_j = c_{jr}; \qquad (a_j = j\text{th column of } A). \tag{2.64b}$$

Using these quantities the $j$th subproblem (2.59) with a modified objective function may be written as

$$\text{maximize } (c_j - y'a_j) x_j \tag{2.65a}$$

under the restrictions

$$(2.59b) \quad \text{and} \quad (2.59c) \quad \text{and} \quad x_j = x_j(u_{ij}) \tag{2.65b}$$

In this form it is easy to apply the decomposition algorithm of Dantzig and Wolfe.

Two remarks about the active approach should be added. First, it uses the method of reshuffling the resource vector through allocation ratios, just like the method of Kornai and Liptak, but nonetheless sets up the subprograms (2.65) with revised profit coefficients much like the decomposition algorithm developed by Dantzig and Wolfe. Second, the active approach is developed essentially to show that the statistical distribution of the optimal objective function (when the program parameters $(A, b, c)$ have random components) conditional on the choice of allocation matrix $U[u_{ij}]$ has interesting features which could be utilized in minimizing the probability of a specified level of risk. In particular the allocation ratios $(u_{ij})$ could in some cases be so determined that the optimal risk-minimizing decision rule would be sequentially improved according as the different moments of the distribution of the optimal objective function could be specified with precision with more samples or more information. (Some of these aspects are discussed in some detail in ch. 5.)

### 2.4.4. *Decentralization methods of Arrow and Hurwicz*

Assume there are $k = 1, 2, \dots, K$ independent firms, for each of which the superscript $k$ is used and the feasible set is denoted by $X^{(k)} = \{x^{(k)} | A^{(k)}x^{(k)} \leqslant \leqslant b^{(k)}; x^{(k)} \geqslant 0\}$ for $k = 1, \dots, K$ and further let $X = \sum_{k=1}^{K} x^{(k)}$ denote the aggregate of (feasible) activity vectors i.e. $X = \{x \mid x = \sum_k x^{(k)}; x^{(k)} \in X^{(k)}\}$. The objective function for any feasible $x^{(k)}$ is denoted by $z(x^{(k)})$. Now the aggregate collection of optimal feasible vectors $(\bar{x})$ defined by

$$\bar{x} = \sum_k \bar{x}^{(k)} \tag{2.66a}$$

such that

$$\bar{x} \in X \tag{2.66b}$$

$$z(\bar{x}^{(k)}) = \max_{x^{(k)} \in X^{(k)}} (z(x^{(k)})); \qquad (k = 1, 2, ..., K) \tag{2.66c}$$

is said to satisfy the decentralization property, since it can be shown that

$$\max_{x \in X} z(x) = z(\bar{x}). \tag{2.66d}$$

Conversely, if (2.66d) holds and there exists $\bar{x}^{(k)}$ satisfying    (2.66e)
(2.66a), then (2.66c) must hold.

Operationally, however, great problems remain in identifying and computing a method of aggregating optimal activity vectors $\bar{x}$ according to (2.66a) satisfying the decentralization property. These problems are mainly (a) those of aggregation over input-output coefficient matrices of firms which may not be homogeneous (in fact the very concept of homogeneity may have to be redefined) and (b) those of constructing a sequence of LP problems through appropriately defined dual prices linked by some form of aggregation rule (e.g. compare Theil's concept of a linear and perfect aggregation rule). However, very strong implications may sometimes be derived if, for an aggregate of firms called a sector, an aggregate optimal feasible set $\bar{x}$ (defined in (2.66a)) having the decentralization property can be determined.

One implication is that such a system satisfies conditions of an *efficient* system (Pareto optimality) in the sense that if $\bar{x}^{(k)}$ maximizes profits for the $k$th firm, then $\sum_k \bar{x}^{(k)}$ maximizes profits for the whole sector (i.e. individual profit maximization leads to the maximization of profits for the whole sector – an ideal of perfect competition) and also conversely (i.e. decomposition and superposition are both defined). Further, the dual prices derived from an efficient system defined as above could be compared with market prices and the implicit costs of deviation of the two sets of prices could be considered as a broad measure of the deviation from the perfectly competitive framework.

It is possible to show that the property of decentralization has great scope for application in problems of national resource allocation and planning. Following the Arrow-Hurwicz analysis, let us assume there are $s$ commodities of which $n$ are final goods, the rest being primary commodities; there are $m$ processes of production, $x_j$ denotes the level of activity of the $j$th process and $g_{ij}(x_j)$ denotes the amount of commodity $i$ produced by the $j$th process at the level $x_j$; (a negative value for $g_{ij}(x_j)$ refers to the primary commodities used as inputs). Let $y_i$ be the final goods $(i = 1, 2, ..., n)$, and the central

planning authority (or the whole economy) is assumed to have a scalar
objective function

$$f(y_1, ..., y_n) \tag{2.67a}$$

which is maximized under the production constraints

$$y_i \leqslant \sum_{j=1}^{m} g_{ij}(x_j) + q_i, \qquad (i = 1, ..., n) \tag{2.67b}$$

$$\sum_{j=1}^{m} g_{ij}(x_j) + q_i \geqslant 0, \qquad (i = n+1, ..., s) \tag{2.67c}$$

where $q_i$ is the initial availability.

If the objective function (2.67a) and input functions $g_{ij}(x_j)$ are concave,
then the Kuhn-Tucker conditions apply to this problem (2.67). If the optimal
(feasible) solution to this problem exists, then there must exist a nonnegative
vector $\bar{u}$ of (optimal) dual prices such that the Lagrangian function $L(y, x, \bar{u})$
can be written as

$$
\begin{aligned}
L(y, x, \bar{u}) = f(y_1, ..., y_n) &+ \sum_{i=1}^{n} \bar{u}_i \cdot \left( \sum_{j=1}^{m} g_{ij}(x_j) - y_i + q_i \right) \\
&+ \sum_{i=n+1}^{s} \left[ \bar{u}_i \cdot \left( \sum_{j=1}^{m} g_{ij}(x_j) + q_i \right) \right] \\
&= \left[ f(y_1, ..., y_n) - \sum_{i=1}^{n} \bar{u}_i y_i \right] \\
&+ \left[ \sum_{j=1}^{m} \left( \sum_{i=1}^{s} \bar{u}_i g_{ij}(x_j) \right) \right] + \left[ \sum_{i=1}^{s} \bar{u}_i q_i \right] \\
&= [Q_1] + [Q_2] + [Q_3] \text{ say}.
\end{aligned}
\tag{2.67d}
$$

If the optimal vectors of $x$ and $y$ are $\bar{x}, \bar{y}$ then the Kuhn-Tucker optimality
conditions applied to the Lagrangian (2.67d) imply that

> the function $Q_1 = f - \sum_{i=1}^{n} \bar{u}_i y_i$ reaches its maximum
> with respect to $y$ at $\bar{y} = (\bar{y}_1, ..., \bar{y}_n)'$; and $\qquad$ (2.67e)

> the function $\sum_{i=1}^{s} \bar{u}_i g_{ij}(x_j)$ which depends only on $x_j$
> reaches its maximum for each $j$ at $\bar{x}_j$. $\qquad$ (2.67f)

In other words, if $\bar{u}_i$ is conceived of as the shadow price of commodity $i$,
then the function $\sum_{i=1}^{s} \bar{u}_i g_{ij}(x_j)$ can be identified with the profit function
$\bar{p}_j(x_j)$, say, where profit

$$\bar{p}_j(x_j) = \sum_{i=1}^{s} \bar{u}_i g_{ij}(x_j) \tag{2.67g}$$

is evaluated at the optimal (or equilibrium) prices $\bar{u}_i$.

The set of shadow prices $u_i$ converging to the optimal shadow prices may now act as the guiding principle of decentralized planning. For instance, assume that a "manager" (or regional authority) is appointed for each process and that a "helmsman" (or central planning authority) is entrusted with the task of choosing final goods (vector $y$). Then suppose at the first stage (or first iteration) the vector of prices set is $u^{(1)} = (u_1^{(1)}, u_2^{(1)}, ..., u_n^{(1)})$, where the superscript indicates the stage of iteration. The managers are asked to take these prices as given and to maximize their own profit

$$p_j^{(1)}(x, u^{(1)}) = \sum_{i=1}^{n} u_i^{(1)} g_{ij}(x_j) \qquad (2.67h)$$

at these prices by choosing the levels of activity of processes $x_j$ only. With the same set of prices $u^{(1)}$, the helmsman maximizes the difference between utility and costs, i.e., $Q_1^{(1)} = f(y_1, ..., y_n) - \sum_{i=1}^{n} u_i^{(1)} y_i$ by choosing only the final goods $(y_1, ..., y_n)$. If the price set $u_i^{(1)}$ is not optimal and hence not equal to $\bar{u}_i$ (which satisfies the Kuhn-Tucker conditions) but the overall problem is feasible, then the vector $u^{(1)}$ is revised successively to $u^{(2)}, u^{(3)}, ...,$ $u^{(N)}$, say, till the optimal set of dual prices $\bar{u}$ is reached. The rule of revision follows the "gradient method", according to which oversupplied (excess of supply over demand) goods are imputed lower prices (including zero prices) and undersupplied goods are successively imputed higher prices. (Gradient methods are discussed in ch. 3.)

(Note that if (2.67a) is a linear function of $y_i$ and $g_{ij}(x_j) = a_{ij} x_j$ where $a_{ij}$ is constant, the above principles apply to linear programming problems. However, in this case, the *gradient method* of iterations would generate oscillations if not constrained further.)

### 2.4.5. Delegation models of Koopmans

Here, as in the Arrow-Hurwicz framework of decentralized decision-making guided by a shadow price system, the essential strategy is to develop the concept of a proper set of prices through which the functions of delegated management may be performed. Following Koopmans (1951), let the vector of commodities $y$ be partitioned into three subvectors as

$$y' = (y'_F, y'_I, y'_P) \qquad (2.68a)$$

where $y_F$ = final commodity components (subvector), $y_I$ = intermediate commodity components (subvector) and $y_P$ = primary commodity components (subvector). These subvectors satisfy the conditions

$$y_F \geqslant 0, \quad y_I = 0, \quad -y_P \leqslant -N_P \qquad (2.68b)$$

where $-N_P \geqslant 0$ is a vector of primary stipulations. Let $A(m.n)$ be the input-output matrix relating activities and commodities, with partitions $A_F$, $A_I$, $A_P$ conforming to those of $y$ in (2.68a) such that

$$Ax = y; \quad x \geqslant 0 \qquad (2.68c)$$

where $y$ satisfies conditions (2.68a) and (2.68b). Now assuming the existence of a solution vector $y$ satisfying (2.68a) through (2.68c), a vector point $\bar{y}$ is said to be *efficient in the sense of Koopmans*, if and only if there does not exist any other point $y$ with the property

$$y_F \geqslant \bar{y}_F \quad \text{and} \quad y_F \neq \bar{y}_F \qquad (\bar{y} \text{ efficient}). \qquad (2.69)$$

Note that the vector inequalities (2.69) assume only partial ordering (i.e. the concept of efficiency in the sense of Koopmans is based on the optimization of a vector objective function).

If an efficient vector point in the sense of Koopmans exists, then an appropriate set of (dual) shadow prices can be devised, which could be used as a functional basis for delegated management. Let

$$p' = (p'_F, p'_I, p'_P) \qquad (2.70a)$$

be a vector of prices associated with final, intermediate and primary commodities respectively. Then Koopmans has shown that a necessary and sufficient condition for the efficiency of vector $y$ is that there exists a vector $p$ associated with $y$ satisfying the following conditions

$$p'y = 0 \quad \text{(i.e. } p'_F y_F + p'_P y_P = 0 \text{ since } y_I = 0\text{)} \qquad (2.70b)$$

$$p'A \leqslant 0 \qquad (2.70c)$$

$$p_F > 0, \quad p_{P=} \geqslant 0, \quad p_{P>} = 0 \qquad (2.70d)$$

where $p_{P=}$ is the subvector of prices associated with those primary commodities which are used to capacity (i.e. $(y_P)_k = (N_P)_k$ for any commodity $k$ in this group) and $p_{P>}$ is the subvector of prices associated with those primary commodities which are not used to capacity.

Relation (2.70b) with (2.70d) implies that if $p'_F y_F > 0$ for the outputs, then some of the components of $p_{P=}$ must be positive to obtain an offsetting amount, $p'_P y_P < 0$ for the inputs, since the condition $p'y = 0$ could not hold otherwise. Further, this relation may be viewed as a scheme of imputation of shadow prices in terms of which all the output value produced by the system is imputed to the inputs of primary commodities in some *optimal* fashion.

Denoting by $a_k$ $(k=1,...,n)$ the $k$th column of input-output matrix $A$ which is associated with $x_k$, the relation (2.70c) can be rewritten as

$$p'a_k = p'_F a_k(\text{F}) + p'_I a_k(\text{I}) + p'_P a_k(\text{P}) \leqslant 0 \qquad (2.70\text{e})$$

where $a_k(\text{F})$, $a_k(\text{I})$ and $a_k(\text{P})$ are respectively associated with $p_F$, $p_I$ and $p_P$. An optimality interpretation of this condition (2.70e) is possible, if it is assumed that each column of matrix $A$ is controlled by a manager. Then, whenever $p'a_k > 0$ the manager in charge of the $k$th activity should expand, since in opportunity cost terms this expansion of the $k$th activity will lead to a $y_F$ which is better in the sense of Koopmans-type efficiency. Again whenever $p'a_k < 0$ this means that the cost of activating this column ($k$th column) exceeds the benefits it can produce and in this case the condition $x_k^* \leqslant 0$ is imposed at the corresponding optimum. Hence $p'a_k \leqslant 0$ must hold for all $k$ at the optimum level.

For price-guided administration of the decomposed framework, Koopmans has proposed the following set of rules which in effect specify the different stages of iterations:

Assume a custodian for each commodity, a manager for each activity and a helmsman at the center (e.g. central planning board); then the rules are:

*Step 1*: (For the helmsman): Choose a vector $p_F$ of positive prices on all final commodities and inform each custodian of such a commodity of its price.

*Step 2*: (For all custodians): Buy and sell your commodity *up to the limit*, from and to managers at one price only announced before all managers.

*Step 3*: (For all custodians of final commodities): Announce to managers the price set on your commodity by the helmsman.

*Step 4*: (For all custodians of intermediate commodities): Announce a tentative price on your commodity. If demand by managers falls short of supply by managers, lower your price. If demand exceeds supply, raise it.

*Step 5*: (For all custodians of primary commodities): Regard the available supply from nature (i.e. relevant component of $-N_P$) as part of the supply of your commodity. Then follow the rule on custodians of intermediate commodities with two exceptions: do not announce a price lower than zero, but accept a demand below supply at zero price if necessary.

*Step 6*: (For all managers): Maintain activities of zero profitability at a constant level. Expand activities of positive profitability by increasing orders for the necessary inputs with and offers of the outputs in question to, the custodians of those commodities.

A very useful and convenient way of proving Koopmans' theorem on efficiency pricing has been formalized by Charnes and Cooper [36] in terms of the concept of "antecedents of efficient points". These antecedent points can be interpreted as activity vectors $x$ which can further be identified with the optimal solution of a pair of dual LP problems associated with the vector optimization problem of Koopmans. Now the sets of all antecedents of efficient points are defined as unions of convex polyhedral sets. Such unions are not, in general convex. However the linear image of a convex set is convex; by this property the transform $Ax = y$ carries the antecedent points $x$ into $y$ which are unions of polyhedral convex sets and the same holds for efficiency prices defined in the sense of Koopmans.

Now following Charnes and Cooper, define the following pair of primal and dual problems in vector-matrix form:

*Primal*:

$$\text{maximize } v^{0'} A_F x \tag{2.71a}$$

subject to

$$- A_P x \leqslant - N_P \tag{2.71b}$$

$$- A_I x = 0 \tag{2.71c}$$

$$x \geqslant 0, \, v^0 > 0; \tag{2.71d}$$

*Dual*:

$$\text{minimize } - w_P' N_P \tag{2.72a}$$

subject to

$$- w_P' A_P - w_I' A_I \geqslant v^{0'} A_F \tag{2.72b}$$

$$w_P \geqslant 0 \quad \text{but } w_I \text{ unrestricted in sign.} \tag{2.72c}$$

Here $v^0$ is a column vector of parameters which are systematically varied in advance according to prescribed rules in order to locate all the efficient points (and efficient prices); i.e. a set of efficient points is located by the process of optimizing the LP problem (2.71) with each given set of parameters in $v^0$.

In terms of the primal and dual models (2.71) and (2.72), the first part of Koopmans' result on efficiency pricing may be stated as a theorem:

*Theorem 2.9*

If the set $(y_F', y_I', y_P') = (x^{*'} A_F', x^{*'} A', x^{*'} A_P')$ and $x^*$ defines an optimal solution to the primal LP (2.71), then $y' = (y_F', y_I', y_P')$ is necessarily an efficient point and $p' = (p_F', p_I', p_P') = (v^{0'}, w_I^{*'}, w_P^{*'})$ are the corresponding efficiency prices, where $w_I^*$, $w_P^*$ are parts of an optimal solution to the dual LP problem (2.72).

*Proof*: Note that condition (2.70c) is identical with (2.72b). Further, in respect of (2.70b),

$$p'y = v^{0'}A_Fx^* + w_P^{*'}A_Px^* \qquad (2.73a)$$

since by (2.71c) $w_I^{*'}A_Ix^* = 0$. Again from LP problems (2.71) and (2.72), if for any activity $r$, $-(A_Px^*)_r < (-N_P)_r$ then its dual, $(w_P^*)_r = 0$. Hence $(A_Px^*)_k = (N_P)_k$, $k \neq r$ so that

$$w_P^{*'}A_Px^* = w_P^{*'}N_P. \qquad (2.73b)$$

Further, by the duality theorem applied to (2.71) and (2.72),

$$v^{0'}A_Fx^* = w_P^{*'}(-N_P) = -w_P^{*'}N_P. \qquad (2.73c)$$

By using (2.73c) and (2.73b), (2.73a) can be rewritten as

$$p'y = 0. \qquad (2.73d)$$

This is the same condition as (2.70b). Thus the first two sets of conditions of efficiency pricing in the sense of Koopmans are shown to hold at the optimum. Condition (2.70d) can also be shown to hold, since $p_F > 0$ is identical with $v^0 > 0$, and the remaining two parts of condition (2.70d) are already used in (2.73b) and (2.73c) to derive (2.73d).

Hence the proof is complete. Any commodity vector $y$ which has $x^*$ (an activity vector) as its antecedent is efficient and $p' = (v^{0'}, w_I^{*'}, w_P^{*'})$ is the corresponding vector of efficiency prices. (Note however that Koopmans' concept of efficiency is meaningful only when solutions with $y_F \geq 0$ exist and are bounded from above.)

Now theorem 2.9 only characterizes the efficiency pricing conditions; computation problems still remain as to how to compute a feasible $v_F > 0$ corresponding to any given efficient point. Let $\bar{y}_F$ be any given efficient point; then following Charnes and Cooper this point may be associated with the following primal-dual LP problems:

*Primal*:

$$\text{minimize} - e_F' z_F \qquad (2.74a)$$

subject to

$$A_Fx - y_F = 0 \qquad (2.74b)$$

$$A_Ix = 0 \qquad (2.74c)$$

$$A_Px - y_P = 0 \qquad (\bar{y}_F: \text{an efficient point}) \qquad (2.74d)$$

$$y_P \geqslant N_P \tag{2.74e}$$

$$y_F - z_F = \bar{y}_F \tag{2.74f}$$

$$x \geqslant 0, z_F \geqslant 0; \tag{2.74g}$$

*Dual*:

maximize $w'_P N_P + t'_F \bar{y}_F$ (2.75a)

subject to

$$u'_F A_F + u'_I A_I + u'_P A_P \leqslant 0 \tag{2.75b}$$

$$- u'_F + t'_F = 0 \tag{2.75c}$$

$$- u'_P + w'_P = 0 \tag{2.75d}$$

$$- t'_F \leqslant - e'_F \tag{2.75e}$$

$$w_P \geqslant 0. \tag{2.75f}$$

Here $e_F$ is a vector with all unit elements having the same number of components as $y_F$.

*Theorem 2.10*

The vector point $\bar{y}_F$ is efficient, if and only if $(\min e'_F z_F) = e^{*'}_F z^*_F = 0$, where $z^*_F$ is an optimal solution of (2.74).

*Proof*: If the point $\bar{y}_F$ is not efficient, but the problem has efficient solutions, then it is possible to find a vector point $y_F \geqslant \bar{y}_F$ and $y_F \neq \bar{y}_F$. Thus $z_F = = y_F - \bar{y}_F \geqslant 0$ and $z_F \neq 0$, so that $- e'_F z_F < 0$ when $\bar{y}_F$ is not efficient. Thus $y_F$ is efficient implies $e'_F z^*_F = 0$. On the other hand, if

$$0 = e'_F z^*_F = \max e'_F z_F = \max e'_F (y_F - \bar{y}_F), \quad \text{when} \quad z_F = y_F - \bar{y}_F \geqslant 0$$

then

$$0 = \max e'_F (y_F - \bar{y}_F) \geqslant e'_F (y_F - \bar{y}_F) \geqslant 0$$

hence $y_F - \bar{y}_F = 0$ for all $y_F \geqslant \bar{y}_F$. Thus $\bar{y}_F$ is efficient. This completes the proof and shows how to obtain a vector $v^*_F$ for $\bar{y}_F$.

Now if by hypothesis $\bar{y}_F$ is efficient, then $z^*_F = 0$ and $y^*_F = \bar{y}_F$ and therefore $y^*_F$ is efficient. Assuming finite solutions, the duality theorem implies that

$$t^{*'}_F \bar{y}_F + w^{*'}_F N_P = 0 \quad \text{i.e.} \quad t^{*'}_F \bar{y}_F = w^{*'}_P (- N_P), \quad \text{where} \quad N_P \leqslant 0. \tag{2.76a}$$

Further, the inequality (2.75e) $t'_F \geqslant e'_F$ implies $t^{*}_F > 0$. It can be shown that the vector $t^*_F$ will eventually turn out to be the desired vector $v^0_F$.

### 2.4.6. General remarks

Several general remarks may be made about the three basic facets of decomposition techniques, e.g. (i) the computational algorithms, (ii) the economic implications of the two-level procedures of resource planning which closely resemble the Walrasian concept of tâtonnement [37], and (iii) the relation of decomposition to the rules of aggregation in economic models [38].

First, the question of the relative power and efficiency of different methods of decomposition applied to linear models is not fully resolved. The ease of applicability of simplex-type algorithms in LP models is an overwhelming factor in favor of the method of Dantzig and Wolfe and several improvements of the standard simplex routine [39] have been suggested; these improvements include (a) successive revision of not only $c_j$ coefficients but also of central resources (i.e. their sectoral allocations) for the sector problems through using a dual version of the equivalent extremal problem, and (b) adjoining some interior movements along with movements on the boundaries of the simplex.

Second, the fact that decomposition techniques essentially incorporate a process of pricing and exchange which is basically similar to a competitive market model has interesting economic implications not all of which have been completely explored. For example, a spatial model of price equilibrium [40] based on distances between regions and competitive demand-supply interactions shows certain features of truncation and indivisibility in the competitive pricing process, for which no analogy in the decomposition process has been conceptualized. However, Malinvaud [41] has emphasized that the two-level processes of decomposition may encounter infeasibility and sometimes quasi-concavity [42].

Third, the relation of decomposition to techniques of aggregation in LP models is not sufficiently explored, although some preliminary work in this line is available [43]. As a simple illustration [43] consider the LP model for aggregating a number of farms in a homogeneous agricultural region. Let the LP model for the $k$th farm $(k=1,...,n)$ be:

$$\max c_k' x_k \quad \text{with} \quad A_k x_k \leqslant b_k; \qquad x_k \geqslant 0 \qquad (2.77)$$

where, $c_k, x_k: r.1; A_k: h.r; b_k: h.1; h \leqslant r$ under the following restrictions

$$A_k = A_0 \quad \text{for all} \quad k = 1, ..., n \quad \text{where} \quad A_0: h.r, \qquad (2.77a)$$

i.e. all farms have identical input-output coefficient matrices;

$$c_k = u_k c_0, (k = 1, ..., n) \quad \text{where} \quad u_k > 0 \text{ is a scalar,} \qquad (2.77b)$$

i.e. all farms have only proportional variations in their
net returns vectors;
the indices of optimal activities in the optimal basis must be
the same for all farms, i.e. the optimal output vectors of different
farms must be qualitatively homogeneous. $\qquad$ (2.77c)

Now construct an aggregated LP model with parameters

$$c^* = \sum_{k=1}^{n} c_k, \quad b^* = \sum_{k=1}^{n} b_k; \qquad A^* = A_0 \text{ defined in } (2.77a) \qquad (2.78)$$

and let $x_0^*$ be its optimal solution $(x_0^* \geqslant 0)$; let $\bar{x}_k$ be the optimal (feasible) solution of the LP model (2.77) for the $k$th firm. Now if it turns out that $x_0^* = \sum_{k=1}^{n} \bar{x}_k$, then the aggregation is defined to be exact and perfect. It can be easily proved [43] that the sufficient conditions for exact and perfect aggregation are given by (2.77a) and (2.77c). In case there are small errors in the elements of $A_k$ such that conditions (2.77a) and (2.77c) are satisfied in a probabilistic sense, i.e. the optimal solution vector $\bar{x}_k$ associated with $(A_k, b_k, c_k)$ is such that $\sum_{k=1}^{n} \bar{x}_k$ tends stochastically with probability unity to $x_0^*$ associated with $(A^*, b^*, c^*)$, then the aggregation is perfect but probabilistic. It is still an open question how to define a process of valid aggregation (e.g. without aggregation bias) when condition (2.77a) is not satisfied.

A last general remark about the concept of optimality in decomposition techniques is in order. If decomposition is viewed as a problem of aggregation (e.g. how to aggregate a number of LP models which have some resource and other links), then in the aggregative LP model the optimizing objective may sometimes have to be replaced by a satisfying objective (the latter concept is due to Simon [44]). In terms of the latter concept, an LP problem with a vector-valued objective function necessitates a distinction between 'optimality' and what is called a '*non-inferiority*' by Zadeh [45] in the context of control theory.

Let the set of solutions of an LP problem with a vector optimization function be denoted by $S$, and by a partial ordering let us associate with each system of solutions $X$ in $S$ the following three disjoint subclasses of $S$ with respect to a specific subset $X_0$ of $X$:

(i) the subclass denoted by $S_1$ of all systems of solutions which are better than (superior to) those in $X_0$;

(ii) the subclass denoted by $S_2$ of all systems of solutions which are inferior to or equal to those in $X_0$; and

(iii) the subclass denoted by $S_3$ of all systems of solutions which are not comparable.

Since every system in $S$ falls into one of these three categories, the union of $S_1$, $S_2$ and $S_3$ is $S$. Now let $C$ denote a subclass of $S$ satisfying the constraints. Then the following definitions are meaningful:

*Definition 1*: A system of solutions $X_0$ in $C$ is *noninferior* in $C$ if the intersection of $C$ and $S_1$ with respect to $X_0$ (i.e., $S_1(X_0)$) is empty.

*Definition 2*: A system of solutions $X_0$ in $C$ is optimal in $C$, if $C$ is contained in $S_2 = S_2(X_0)$. This means that every system of solutions in $C$ is inferior to or equal to $X_0$.

From these definitions it follows at once that if $X_0$ is optimal then it is necessarily noninferior, but not conversely.

### 2.5. *Recursive linear programming*

Recursive programming refers to methods of programming which incorporate a recursive relation at one stage or another. Here recursiveness implies a relation of precedence; e.g. a sequence of LP problems may be defined in which the objective function, the constraints and the resource vector parameters may depend upon the primal and/or dual solution variables of the preceding LP problems (the precedence being over time). Richard Day [46] has made interesting applications of one type of recursive linear programming method in predicting annual production and supply levels in the cotton producing region (Delta area) of Mississippi under four technical stages, three soil classes and four fertilizer levels over the period 1940–59.

#### 2.5.1. *A simple model of RLP (R. Day's model)*

To illustrate a simple model of recursive linear programming (RLP), consider the land utilization problem for two crops:

$$\text{maximize } c_1(t) \, x_1(t) + c_2(t) \, x_2(t) \tag{2.79a}$$

under the restrictions

$$x_1(t) + x_2(t) \leqslant \bar{x} \quad \text{(available land, fixed)} \tag{2.79b}$$

$$x_i(t) \leqslant (1 + \bar{b}_i) \, x_i(t-1); \quad (i = 1, 2) \tag{2.79c}$$

$$x_i(t) \geqslant (1 - b_i) \, x_i(t-1); \quad (i = 1, 2) \tag{2.79d}$$

$$x_i(t) \geqslant 0; \quad i = 1, 2. \tag{2.79e}$$

Here $x_i(t)$ = acreage of the $i$th crop at period $t$, $c_i(t)$ is its net return per acre, $\bar{b}_i$ and $b_i$ are upper and lower flexibility coefficients, assumed constant. The upper flexibility constraints (2.79c) are capacity constraints on the farmer's production which may be imposed due to internal or external credit rationing. The lower flexibility constraints (2.79b) reflect the reluctance of farmers to withdraw too rapidly from the production of any given crop. Generally it is assumed that $\bar{b}_i$ and $b_i$ lie within [0, 1], since these are reaction parameters. Now in this example, because of lower bounds in (2.79d), there should be at least two variables positive, if there is a feasible basis. For a given $t$ (i.e., given $c_i(t)$) the optimal feasible basis is selected each time by the optimizing principle (2.79a), and the sequence of periods for which a given optimal basis with specific optimal activities holds is defined as a phase. Thus the observed variation of acreages over time for different crops (which lies behind the usual supply function concept of economists) may be explained in terms of multiple phases – i.e., a change-over from one phase to another depending on the restrictions and the optimizing principle. For example, assume for problem (2.79) the initial condition $x_i(0)$ ($i = 1, 2$) and $c_1(t) > c_2(t)$ for the first two phases and $c_1(t) < c_2(t)$ for the third phase, then the following phases are conceivable:

Phase 1
$$\begin{cases} x_i(t) = (1 + \bar{b}_i)^t\, x_i(0); & i = 1, 2; \qquad t = 1, 2, ..., t_1 \quad (2.80a) \\ \text{(both crops in optimal basis)} \end{cases}$$

Phase 2
$$\begin{cases} x_1(t) = (1 + \bar{b}_1)^t\, x_1(t_1) \\ x_2(t) = \bar{x} - x_1(t) \quad t = t_1 + 1, t_1 + 2, ..., t_2 \qquad (2.80b) \\ \text{(first crop in optimal basis)} \end{cases}$$

Phase 3
$$\begin{cases} x_1(t) = \bar{x} - x_2(t) \\ x_2(t) = (1 - b_2)^t\, x_2(t_2); \qquad t = t_2 + 1, t_2 + 2, ..., t_3 \qquad (280c) \\ \text{(second crop in optimal basis)}. \end{cases}$$

However, economically the most interesting source of change from one phase of equated constraints to another is provided by the changes in $c_i(t)$ through prior changes in market prices (through aggregate net demand functions) and price expectations. In vector notation, the vector $c(t)$ which is based on expected prices (i.e. the vector $p(t-1)$ of past prices as in the well-known "cobweb" model of lagged supply response) assuming the yield per acre to be fixed, provides the optimizing choice of phases and determines the optimal acreage vector $x(t)$ for the two crops. The total supply of these two crops helps again to determine the market price $p(t)$, depending on which phase holds in the system. Thus the recursive relation has the following sequence: $p(t-1) \rightarrow c(t) \rightarrow$ optimal $x(t)$ at the optimal phase $\rightarrow$ aggregate supply interacting with aggregate market demand $\rightarrow$ new market price $p(t) \rightarrow$ the system starts again.

Several economic features of the recursive process have been pointed out by Day. First, this sort of model predicts supply relations (or acreage changes) over time through recursive interactions between market price and expected price (expectation based on lagged prices) and between aggregate supply and demand determining a market price. Generally, it is presumed that prices change first, then net returns and then the outputs undergo multiple phases, although this results in a system of stable multivariable cobweb cycles. (Sometimes before a phase change, two price adjustment curves may intersect; this could perhaps explain some of the cases of apparently downward-sloping supply curves estimated from time-series data.) Second, it indicates the role of parameters $\bar{b}_i$, $b_i$ behind the usual concept of supply elasticity used by economists in regional models, and that in some phases not all of these parameters may be statistically identifiable. For instance, in phase 1 above, the time series estimates of aggregate acreages can be used to estimate $\bar{b}_1, \bar{b}_2$ but for this period ($t=1, 2, ..., t_1$) aggregate acreage data *cannot* statistically identify $b_1, b_2$. Similarly in phase 3, only $b_2$ is identifiable and estimable and none of the other parameters are. This raises a new type of statistical estimation problem which has also been called the problem of estimating parameters with data obeying two or more separate regimes. Also this has some relations with estimation problems in censored and truncated statistical models. The regime problem is discussed in the next sections. Third, it should be mentioned that recursive relations could be introduced in many other alternative ways; for instance, through reinvested profits the budget for the resource vector could be changed recursively over time.

### 2.5.2. *A model of technical change*

The simple recursive model presented in the earlier section could be generalized to incorporate technical change and its diffusion effects. R. Day considers the following situation where the first crop can be produced by using either of two technical methods, the old and the new. Let the superscripts 1 and 2 denote the two techniques and $x_1^{(1)}(t-1)$, $x_1^{(2)}(t-1)$ be the actual capacities (in number of acres for the first crop) utilized during the year $(t-1)$. Further denote the maximal potential investment by $I_i^*(t)$ and assume that it can be related to the immediate past levels of capacity utilization, i.e.

$$I_1^*(t) = x_1^{(i)}(t) - x_1^{(i)}(t-1) = \Delta x_1^{(i)} \leqslant \beta_1 x_1^{(i)}(t-1) \qquad (2.81a)$$

i.e.,

$$x_1^{(i)}(t) \leqslant (1 + \beta_i)\, x_1^{(i)}(t-1); \qquad i = 1, 2. \qquad (2.81b)$$

Then a dynamic model could be set up as follws:

$$\text{maximize} \left[ c_1^{(1)}(t-1)\, x_1^{(1)}(t) + c_1^{(2)}(t-1)\, x_1^{(2)}(t) + c_2(t-1)\, x_2(t) \right] \quad (2.82a)$$

under the restrictions

$$x_1^{(1)}(t) + x_1^{(2)}(t) + x_2(t) \leqslant \bar{x} \qquad \text{(available land: fixed)} \qquad (2.82b)$$

$$x_1^{(1)}(t) \leqslant (1 + \beta_1)\, x_1^{(1)}(t-1) \qquad (2.82c)$$

$$x_1^{(2)}(t) \leqslant (1 + \beta_2)\, x_1^{(2)}(t-1) \qquad (2.82d)$$

$$x_1^{(1)}(t) + x_1^{(2)}(t) \geqslant (1 - b_1)\left[ x_1^{(1)}(t-1) + x_1^{(2)}(t-1) \right] \qquad (2.82e)$$

$$x_2^{(t)} \leqslant (1 + \bar{b}_2)\, x_2(t-1) \qquad (2.82f)$$

$$x_2^{(t)} \geqslant (1 - b_2)\, x_2(t-1) \qquad (2.82g)$$

all $x_1^{(1)}(t)$, $x_1^{(2)}(t)$, $x_2(t)$ nonnegative for all $t$.

Given the initial values $x_1^{(1)}(0)$, $x_1^{(2)}(0)$, $x_2(0)$ the model could be analyzed into phases. Note that the coefficients of the objective function are lagged by one year, since it is assumed that the expected price at $t$ is equal to the past experienced price (a more general formulation is also possible). Now if in model (2.82) we have $c_1^{(2)}(t) > c_1^{(1)}(t) > c_2(t)$, then although $x_1^{(1)}(t)$ will eventually fall and $x_1^{(2)}(t)$ will eventually rise, yet the growth of the total $(x_1^{(1)}(t) + x_1^{(2)}(t))$ may be slow, since it is likely that while the capacity of the new technique of production is small, investment and expansion may still continue for the old technique. This shows that new methods of agricultural production (e.g. introduction of hybrid corn) represent the features of what is called a diffusion process in the theory of stochastic processes. (R. Howard's Markov process model in a dynamic programming context provides a good analogy to a stochastic RLP model; this is discussed in ch. 5.)

It is apparent that models like (2.82) can be generalized and applied in the context of dynamic input-output models (Leontief, Solow and others [47]) of the whole economy, where the objective function coefficients (i.e., the vector $c(t-1)$ could be so defined as to reflect the discounted net relative contributions of the various activities. (Alternatively, a cumulative discounted sum (over time) of linear objective functionals could be selected as the objective function.)

### 2.5.3. *Statistical estimation with the RLP model*

In connection with the estimation of parameters $\bar{b}_i$, $b_i$ belonging to different phases or regimes, we referred to the problem of estimating parameters obeying two or more regimes which is presented by a RLP model. From a statistical viewpoint there are at least three types of analytical problems:
(a) the problem of regimes or phases and how to estimate parameters in such a case;
(b) the problem of stability of the optimal solution belonging to any given phase or regime, when stability is measured either deterministically or stochastically; and
(c) the problem of designing appropriate control variales to ensure stability up to a prescribed level, when a changeover is made from one phase to another.
Partial solutions to these problems are available, although they are not entirely satisfactory.

(a) Consider the first case and assume that we have to solve the following modified problem (due to Quandt [48]): Given a series of observations we have to estimate the simple regression model

$$y = a_1 x + u_1; \qquad u_1 \sim N(0, \sigma_1) \quad (t \text{ observations}) \qquad (2.83a)$$

$$y = a_2 x + u_2; \qquad u_2 \sim N(0, \sigma_2) \quad (T - t \text{ observations}) \qquad (2.83b)$$

with two scalar parameters $a_1$, $a_2$ which belong to two different regimes which are fixed by a specific value of any outside variable, in this case time (i.e., $t_1 =$ the first $t$ observations and $t_2 = T - t$ where $T$ is the total number of sample observations). Assuming normality and independence of the errors $u_1$, $u_2$, the likelihoods of samples of $t$ observations from (2.83a) and $(T - t)$ observations from (2.83b) are easily computed as $L_1$, $L_2$) i.e.

$$L_1 = (\sigma_1 \sqrt{2\pi})^{-t} \exp\left[ -(2\sigma_1^2)^{-1} \sum_{i=1}^{t} (y_i - a_1 x_i)^2 \right]$$

$$L_2 = (\sigma_2 \sqrt{2\pi})^{-t} \exp\left[ -(2\sigma_2^2)^{-1} \sum_{j=t+1}^{T} (y_j - a_2 x_j)^2 \right]$$

and the likelihood of the entire sample is

$$L = L_1 \cdot L_2 .$$

Define $L_0 = \log L = \log L_1 + \log L_2$ and then, taking $\partial L_0 / \partial a_i = 0$ and $\partial L_0 / \partial \sigma_i = 0$ $(i = 1, 2)$, we obtain ML estimates, $\hat{a}_i$, $\hat{\sigma}_i$ say. Putting these values in

$L_0 = L_0(t)$ we get

$$L_0(t) = - T \log \sqrt{2\pi} - t \log \hat{\sigma}_1 - (T - t) \log \hat{\sigma}_2 - \tfrac{1}{2}T. \qquad (2.84)$$

Then we find by numerical and programming methods that value of $t = t^*$ for which

$$L_0(t^*) \geqslant L_0(t^* - 1) \quad \text{and} \quad L_0(t^*) \geqslant L_0(t^* + 1).$$

An approximate but operational procedure would be to calculate the value of the likelihood function $L_0(t)$ in (2.84) for *all possible values* of $t$ in $[1, T]$ and select as the maximum likelihood estimate that value of $t$ which corresponds to the maximum maximorum. Define the likelihood ratio $\lambda = = L(\hat{w})/L(\Omega) = \hat{\sigma}_1^t \hat{\sigma}_2^{T-t}/\hat{\sigma}^T$ where $\hat{\sigma} =$ standard error of estimate taking all observations; then for all practical purposes it can be taken that $(-2 \log \lambda)$ for large $T$ has the approximate distribution of a chi-square variate, although the exact conditions for this approximation are not applicable here. Approximate small tests are also available. Some economic applications have also been reported [49].

(b) Before analyzing the second case note that the RLP model (2.79) can be written in vector-matrix notation as

$$\max c'(t) x(t) \qquad (2.85a)$$

under the restrictions

$$e'x(t) \leqslant \bar{x} \qquad (2.85b)$$

$$Ax(t) \leqslant TAx(t - 1) \qquad (2.85c)$$

$$x(t) \geqslant 0, \text{ all } t = 1, 2, \ldots \qquad (2.85d)$$

where

$$T = \text{diag.} \left[ 1 + \bar{b}_1, 1 + \bar{b}_2, - (1 - b_1), - (1 - b_2) \right],$$

$$A = \begin{bmatrix} 1 & 0 \\ 0 & 1 \\ -1 & 0 \\ 0 & -1 \end{bmatrix}; \quad e = \begin{bmatrix} 1 \\ 1 \end{bmatrix}; \quad c(t) = \begin{bmatrix} c_1(t) \\ c_2(t) \end{bmatrix}; \quad x(t) = \begin{bmatrix} x_1(t) \\ x_2(t) \end{bmatrix}.$$

It is easy to note that for $n$ activities $x_i(t)$ $(i = 1, \ldots, n)$ this formulation will still hold, except that we have to add the dimensions of the relevant vectors and matrices. Further, if the matrix $T$ is not diagonal, then there is simultaneity in the equated constraints which are in fact systems of linear simultaneous difference equations for which different types of stability (e.g.

Lagrange, Liapunov or Poincaré [50]) can be discussed in any one phase. Further, if residual additive errors are present for each set of simultaneous linear difference equations, then there is the problem of stability of the optimal solution vector in any given phase, stability being measured in terms of variance.

(c) In the third case, additional decision variables like the allocation ratios $u_{ij}$ in Tintner's active approach are introduced and a desired level of stability is approached through an appropriate use of the decision variables (this will be discussed in the context of probabilistic programming in ch. 5).

## REFERENCES

[1] Charnes, A., "Optimality and degeneracy in linear programming", *Econometrica*, Vol. 20, No. 2, 1952, 160–170.
[2] Hadley, G., *Nonlinear and dynamic programming*. London: Addison-Wesley, 1964.
[3] Vajda, S., *Mathematical programming*. London: Addison-Wesley, 1961.
    Gass, S. I., *Linear programming: methods and applications*. New York: McGraw-Hill, 1958.
[4] Frisch, R., "The multiplex method for linear programming", *Sankhya*, Vol. 18, 1957, 329–362.
[5] Arrow, K. J., L. Hurwicz and H. Uzawa (eds.), *Studies in linear and nonlinear programming*. Stanford: Stanford University Press, 1958.
[6] Zoutendijk, G., *Methods of feasible directions*. Amsterdam: Elsevier Publishing, 1960.
[7] Kantorovich, L. V., *Economic calculation of optimal utilization of resources*. Moscow: USSR Academy of Sciences, 1959.
[8] Beale, E. M. L., "An alternative method for linear programming", *Proceedings of Cambridge Philosophical Society*, Vol. 50, 1954, 513–523.
[9] Charnes, A., W. W. Cooper and G. L. Thompson, "Some properties of redundant constraints and extraneous variables in direct and dual linear programming problems", *Operations Research*, Vol. 10, No. 5, 1962.
[10] Sengupta, J. K., "On the stability of truncated solutions under stochastic linear programming", *Econometrica*, Vol. 34, 1966, 77–104.
[11] Webb, K. W., "Some aspects of the Saaty linear programming sensitivity equation", *Operations Research*, Vol. 10, 1962, 266–267.
[12] Tyndall, W. F., "A duality theorem for a class of continuous linear programming problems", *SIAM Journal*, Vol. 13, No. 3, 1965.
[13] Kuhn, H. W. and A. W. Tucker, "Nonlinear programming". In: *Proceedings of Second Berkeley Symposium on Mathematical Statistics and Probability*, Berkeley, 1951.
[14] Charnes, A. and W. W. Cooper, "Systems evaluation and repricing theorems", *Management Science*, October 1962.
[15] Gale, D., *Theory of linear economic models*. New York: McGraw-Hill, 1960.
[16] Kemeny, J. G., O. Morgenstern and G. L. Thompson, "A generalization of the Von Neumann model of an expanding economy", *Econometrica*, Vol. 24, 1956, 115–135.
[17] Swarup, K., "Linear fractional functional programming", *Operations Research*, Vol. 13, No. 6, 1029–1036.
[18] Charnes, A. and W. W. Cooper, "Programming with linear fractional functionals" *Naval Research Logistics Quarterly*, Sept.-Dec. 1962.

Martos, B., "Hyperbolic programming", *Naval Logistics Quarterly*, June-Sept. 1964, 135–155.

[19] Dinkelbach, W., "On nonlinear fractional programming", *Management Science*, Vol. 13, No. 7, 1967, 492–497.

[20] Sengupta, J. K., "Safety first rules under chance-constrained linear programming", (To be published in *Operations Research*).

[21] Roy, A. D., "Safety first and the holding of assets", *Econometrica*, Vol. 20, 1952.

[22] Gomory, R. E., "Outline of an algorithm for integer solutions to linear programs", *Bulletin of American Mathematical Society*, Vol. 64, 1958, 275–278.

Dantzig, G. B., "Discrete variable extremum problems", *Operations Research*, Vol. 5, 1957, 266–277.

[23] Hadley, G., *Nonlinear and dynamic programming, op. cit.*

[24] Vajda, S., *Mathematical programming, op. cit.*

[25] Gomory, R. E., "All-integer programming algorithm", *IBM Research Center, Research Report* RC 189, 1960.

[26] Land, A. H. and A. Doig, "An automatic method of solving discrete programming problems", *Econometrica*, Vol. 28, 1960, 497–520.

[27] Koopmans, T. C. and M. Beckmann, "Assignment problems and the location of economic activities", *Econometrica*, Vol. 25, 1957, 53–76.

[28] Weingartner, H. M., *Mathematical programming and the analysis of capital budgeting problems*. Englewood Cliffs, N. J.: Prentice Hall, 1963.

[29] Manne, A. S. and H. M. Markowitz, *Studies in process analysis*. New York: John Wiley, 1963; Cowles Foundation Series, Vol. 18.

[30] Dantzig, G. B. and P. Wolfe, "The decomposition principle for linear programs", *Operations Research*, Vol. 8, 1960, 101–111.

[31] Kornai, J. and Th. Liptak, "Two-level planning", *Econometrica*, Vol. 33, 1965, 141–169.

[32] Sengupta, J. K. and G. Tintner, "The approach of stochastic linear programming: a critical appraisal", (authors; sent for publication).

Sengupta, J. K., G. Tintner and C. Millham, "On some theorems of stochastic linear programming with applications", *Management Science*, Vol. 10, 1963.

[33] Arrow, K. J. and L. Hurwicz, "Decentralization and computation in resource allocation". In: R. W. Pfouts (ed.), *Essays in Economics and Econometrics*. Chapel Hill: University of North Carolina, 1960.

[34] Charnes, A. and W. W. Cooper, "On the theory and computation of delegation models: K-efficiency, functional efficiency and goals", *Proceedings of Sixth International Meeting of the Institute of Management Science*, Part I. Paris, 1960, 56–91.

[35] Robinson, J., "An iterative method of solving a game", *Annals of Mathematics*, Vol. 54, 1951, 296–301.

[36] Charnes, A. and W. W. Cooper, *Management models and industrial applications of linear programming*. New York: Wiley, 1961.

[37] Morishima, M., *Equilibrium, stability and growth*, Oxford: Clarendon, 1964.

[38] Sengupta, J. K., "Methods of dynamic decomposition", (author; unpublished manuscript, December 1967).

[39] Abadie, J. M. and A. C. Williams, "Dual and parametric methods in decomposition". In: R. L. Graves and P. Wolfe (eds.), *Recent Advances in Mathematical Programming*. New York: McGraw-Hill; 1963.

[40] Samuelson, P. A., "Spatial price equilibrium and linear programming", *American Economic Review*, Vol. 42, No. 3, 1952, 284–303.

[41] Fox, K. A., "Spatial price equilibrium and process analysis in the food and agricultural sector". In: A. S. Manne and H. M. Markowitz, *Studies in Process Analysis, op. cit.*

Malinvaud, E., "Decentralized procedures for planning". In: E. Malinvaud, and M. O. Bacharach (eds.), *Activity analysis in the theory of growth and planning, op. cit.*

[42] Hurwicz, L., "Programming involving many variables and constraints". In: E. Malinvaud and M. O. Bacharach (eds.), *Activity analysis in the theory of growth and planning, op. cit.*

[43] Day, R. H., "On aggregating linear programming models of production", *Journal of Farm Economics*, Vol. 45, 1963, 797–813.

[44] Simon, H. A., *Models of man*. New York: Wiley, 1957.

[45] Zadeh, L. A., "Optimality and nonscalar valued performance criteria", *IEEE Transactions on Automatic Control*, Vol. AC-8, No. 1, 1963, 59–60.

[46] Day, R., *Recursive programming and production response*. Amsterdam: North-Holland, 1963.

[47] Fox, K. A., J. K. Sengupta and E. Thorbecke, *Theory of quantitative economic policy*. Amsterdam: North-Holland, 1966.

[48] Quandt, R. E., "Tests of the hypothesis that a linear regression system obeys two separate regimes", *Journal of the American Statistical Association*, Vol. 55, 1960, 324–330.

[49] Sengupta, J. K. and G. Tintner, "An approach to a stochastic theory of economic development with applications". In: *Problems of economic dynamics and planning: Essays in honor of M. Kalecki*. Warsaw: PWN Polish Scientific Publishers, 1964.

[50] Struble, R. A., *Nonlinear differential equations*. New York: McGraw-Hill, 1962.

# Chapter 3

# NONLINEAR AND DYNAMIC PROGRAMMING

Nonlinear programming (NLP) refers to those programming methods which generalize the LP formulation in several respects, e.g. the linearity, duality, and the sensitivity of optimal solutions. In its general form the NLP problem is to find an $n$-dimensional vector $x$ within the feasible set $C = \{x|g_i(x) \geqslant 0,$ $x \geqslant 0,\ i = 1, ..., m\}$ which maximizes (or minimizes) a scalar function $f(x)$ of vector $x$, given that $g_i(x)$ for each $i$ is a scalar function of vector $x$. If each $g_i(x)$ is concave in $x$, then the constraint set $C$ can be shown to be convex and further, if the objective function $f(x)$ is concave in every $x \in C$ and a feasible solution exists, then it can be shown that an optimal feasible solution $x^0$ also exists in the sense that $f(x^0) \geqslant f(x)$, for $x, x^0 \in C$. This defines a concave programming problem as follows:

$$\text{maximize } f(x) = f(x_1, ..., x_n)$$

under the restrictions
$$
\begin{aligned}
& x : n . 1 \qquad (3.1) \\
& g_i : m . 1
\end{aligned}
$$

$$g(x) = (g_i(x)) \geqslant 0,\ x \geqslant 0$$
$$i = 1, ..., m.$$

Quadratic programming problems of the usual type are special cases of concave programming. Now if the restriction functions $g_i(x)$ are differentiable and satisfy the so-called "constraint qualification" (which specifies that there are no singularities on the boundary of the contraint set $C$) and the objective function $f(x)$ is also concave and differentiable then we have the basic theorem of Kuhn and Tucker [1] which proves that the necessary conditions for the vector $x^0$ to solve the concave program (3.1) are that there exists an $m$-dimensional nonnegative vector $y^0$ such that

$$\phi_x^0 \leqslant 0; \qquad x^{0'}\phi_x^0 = 0 \qquad (3.2a)$$

$$\phi_y^0 \geqslant 0; \qquad y^{0'}\phi_y^0 = 0 \qquad (3.2b)$$

where $\phi = \phi(x, y) = f(x) + y'g(x)$ and $\phi_x^0$ is the notation for the vector of partial derivatives of $\phi(x, y)$ evaluated at the point $x = x^0$ and prime denotes transposition. The sufficient conditions for a maximum (which in effect specify the concavity of the functions $f(x)$ and $g_i(x)$ and hence that of $\phi(x, y)$ for a fixed feasible $y$) are:

$$\phi(x, y^0) \leqslant \phi(x^0, y^0) + (x - x^0)' \phi_x^0 \tag{3.3a}$$

$$\phi(x^0, y) \geqslant \phi(x^0, y^0) + (y - y^0)' \phi_y^0. \tag{3.3b}$$

Since $f(x)$ and $g(x)$ are concave functions, it is not difficult to show that for fixed $y^0$, $\phi(x, y^0)$ is concave in $x$ and for fixed $x^0$, $\phi(x^0, y)$ is convex in $y$ and this feature together with the assumption of differentiability of $f(x)$ and $g(x)$ imply the sufficient conditions (3.3a) and (3.3b). For instance, condition (3.3a) defines in its right-hand side a tangent plane to the surface of a point $(x^0, y^0)$ lying everywhere above $\phi(x, y^0)$ as $x$ is varied, holding $y$ fixed at $y^0$.

A scalar function $f(x)$ of vector $x$ is defined to be concave (strictly concave), if the chord joining any two points $(x^{(1)}, x^{(2)})$ in the domain of $x$ lies everywhere on or below the function, i.e.

$$f\left(\alpha x^{(1)} + (1 - \alpha) x^{(2)}\right) \geqslant \alpha f\left(x^{(1)}\right) + (1 - \alpha) f\left(x^{(2)}\right) \tag{3.4a}$$

where $\alpha$ is a scalar constant $0 \leqslant \alpha \leqslant 1$ and the sign ($>$) holds for strictly concave functions. If $f(x)$ is differentiable in $x$, then the concavity around a vector point $x_0$ can be alternatively expressed by the following tangency condition

$$f(x_0) + (x - x_0)' (\partial f / \partial x)_{x=x_0} \geqslant f(x) \tag{3.4b}$$

where again the strict inequality sign ($\geqslant$) holds for strict concavity. For twice differentiable functions $f(x)$ which are quadratic in $x$ at $x_0$ (or functions which allow quadratic Taylor-series expansion around $x_0$ very closely in a given domain), concavity may also be specified by the condition that the matrix of second partial derivatives

$$H = \left[\frac{\partial^2 f(x)}{\partial x_i \partial x_j}\right]_{x=x_0} \qquad i, j = 1, ..., n \tag{3.4c}$$

be negative semi-definite (negative definiteness for strict concavity). A square matrix, $H$, is negative semi-definite if for all vectors $x$, $x'Hx \leqslant 0$. That is, considering the principal minors of the matrix $H$ of orders $1, 2, ...$ up to $n$, if the first-order principal minor has a nonpositive determinant, the second-order minor has a nonnegative determinant and the signs of successive-order minor determinants continue to alternate, then the matrix $H$ is negative semi-definite. (Analogous definitions of convexity of a function can be formulated by noting that if $f(x)$ is concave, then $-f(x)$ is convex.)

The notion of concavity of a function has been generalized by Arrow, Enthoven and Hurwicz [2] to what has been termed quasi-concavity. A concave function $f(x)$ satisfies the second order conditions of a maximum, i.e.

$$d^2 f = \sum_{i=1}^{n} \sum_{j=1}^{n} f_{x_i x_j} \, dx_i \, dx_j \leqslant 0$$

but this need not hold for a quasi-concave function in the entire domain of $x$. If the function $f(x)$ is quasi-concave and differentiable, then it has a diminishing marginal rate of substitution if $f_x = (\partial f / \partial x_j; j = 1, \ldots, n)$ is positive, or an increasing marginal rate of transformation if $f_x < 0$ between any pair of variables $x_i, x_j$ or any distinct composite variables. For instance, the function $f(x) = x_1 x_2$ of two scalar variables $x_1, x_2$ is quasi-concave for nonnegative $x_1, x_2$. Again, the production function $y = x_1^{m_1} x_2^{m_2}$ $(m_i > 0, i = 1, 2; x_1 = \text{labor input}, x_2 = \text{capital input}, y = \text{output})$ is quasi-concave but not concave whenever $m_1 + m_2 > 1$. Any concave function is quasi-concave but the converse does not necessarily hold.

Arrow and Enthoven have shown that the Kuhn-Tucker *necessary* conditions (3.2a), (3.2b) are not *sufficient* for a constrained maximum, if the functions $f(x)$, $g(x)$ are differentiable, satisfy the constraint qualifications of Kuhn and Tucker, but are quasi-concave rather than concave. A scalar function $f(x)$ of an $n$-dimensional column vector $x$ is defined to be quasi-concave, if for any pair of points $(x, x^0)$ in the domain of $x$

$$f(x) \geqslant f(x^0) \qquad \text{implies} \qquad f(\alpha x + (1 - \alpha) x^0) \geqslant f(x^0) \qquad (3.5a)$$

where $\alpha$ is a scalar constant, $0 \leqslant \alpha \leqslant 1$. For differentiable functions this definition can also be expressed as:

$$f(x) \geqslant f(x^0) \qquad \text{implies} \qquad f_x^{0'}(x - x^0) \geqslant 0 \qquad (3.5b)$$

where $f_x^0$ is the column vector of first partials with a typical element $(\partial f / \partial x_j)_{x=x^0}$ evaluated at $x = x^0$ (also called the gradient vector). Alternatively, if $f(x)$ is twice differentiable and quasi-concave in a certain domain of $x$, then $((-1)^r D_r) \geqslant 0$ for $r = 1, 2, \ldots, n$ for all $x$ in its domain, where $D_r$ is the following bordered determinant composed of the partial derivatives:

$$D_r = \begin{vmatrix} 0 & f_{x_1} & \cdots & f_{x_r} \\ f_{x_1} & f_{x_1 x_1} & \cdots & f_{x_1 x_r} \\ \vdots & \vdots & & \\ f_{x_r} & f_{x_r x_1} & \cdots & f_{x_r x_r} \end{vmatrix}.$$

A sufficient condition for $f(x)$ to be quasi-concave for $x \geqslant 0$ is that $D_r$ has the sign of $(-1)^r$ for all $x$ and all $r = 1, ..., n$. Note that if $f(x)$ is strictly concave and we define the matrix $H$ of second partials as in (3.4c), then the determinant $H_r$ must have the sign of $(-1)^r$ with $(-1)^r H_r > 0$ for all $r = 1, 2, ..., n$ where

$$H_r = \begin{vmatrix} f_{x_1 x_1} \cdots f_{x_1 x_r} \\ \vdots \\ f_{x_r x_1} \cdots f_{x_r x_r} \end{vmatrix}.$$

Another way of defining a quasi-concave function $f(x)$ without assuming differentiability is that the scalar function $f(x)$ is quasi-concave at $\bar{x} = c$, where $c$ is a constant vector if the set $S : \{x \mid f(x) \geqslant c\}$ is convex (this definition is identical with that of (3.5a)).

### 3.1. Methods of nonlinear programming

Before we discuss the extension of the Kuhn-Tucker necessary conditions to include quasi-concave functions, consider a simple example with one scalar variable $x$, i.e.

$$\text{maximize } f(x) = (x - 1)^3 \quad \text{with} \quad g(x) = 2 - x \geqslant 0, \, x \geqslant 0;$$

here $f(x)$ is quasi-concave and differentiable. By applying Kuhn-Tucker necessary conditions at $(x^0, y^0)$ we get

$$3(x^0 - 1)^2 - y^0 \leqslant 0; \qquad 3x^0(x^0 - 1)^2 - x^0 y^0 = 0; \qquad y^0(2 - x^0) = 0$$

which are satisfied by $x^0 = 1$, $y^0 = 0$ but the maximum of the objective function occurs at $x^0 = 2$, $y^0 = 3$ and not at $x^0 = 1$, $y^0 = 0$. To include such quasi-concave functions the Kuhn-Tucker necessary conditions have been generalized by Arrow-Enthoven-Hurwicz. In order to satisfy the constraint qualification, they define $x_{i_0}$ as "relevant variable", if there is some point [1] in the constraint set (i.e. $g(x) \geqslant 0$), say $x^*$ at which $x_{i_0}^* > 0$. The following theorem is then proved:

---

[1] The role of the "relevant variable" clause is to restate the so-called 'constraint qualification' of the Kuhn-Tucker theorem. With the constraint qualification, the Kuhn-Tucker theorem may be restated as:
*Theorem:* Let the functions $f(x)$, $g(x)$ mentioned in (3.1) be differentiable and concave for $x \geqslant 0$ such that there exists some $\hat{x} \geqslant 0$ for which $g(\hat{x}) = g_i(x) > 0$ $(i = 1, 2, ..., m)$; then $x^0$ is an optimal solution, if there is some vector $y^0 \geqslant 0$ such that $(x^0, y^0)$ is a saddle point of $\phi(x, y)$. (The constraint qualification is discussed in some detail in the next section, section 3.1.1.)

*Theorem 3.1* (Arrow-Enthoven)

Let $f(x)$ be a differentiable quasi-concave function of the $n$-dimensional vector $x$ and let $g(x)$ be an $m$-dimensional differentiable quasi-concave vector function, both defined for $x \geqslant 0$. Let $(x^0, y^0)$ satisfy the Kuhn-Tucker necessary conditions and let one of the following conditions be satisfied:

(a) $f_{x_{i_0}}^0 < 0$ for at least one variable $x_{i_0}$

(b) $f_{x_{i_1}}^0 > 0$ for some relevant variable $x_{i_1}$

(c) $f_x^0 \neq 0$ and $f(x)$ is twice differentiable in the neighborhood of $x_0$

(d) $f(x)$ is concave.

Then $x^0$ maximizes $f(x)$ subject to the constraints $g(x) \geqslant 0$, $x \geqslant 0$.

*Proof:* An outline of the proof for some cases can be specified. For instance, consider part (a). Let the three nonnegative vector points $x^0$, $x^1$, $x^2$ belong to the constraint set $C = \{x \mid g(x) \geqslant 0, x \geqslant 0\}$ such that $x^2 = x^0 + h$, $h$ being the unit vector in the $i_0$th direction and $x^0$ satisfies the Kuhn-Tucker (KT) necessary conditions and $f(x)$, $g(x)$ are quasi-concave differentiable functions. By using the identity $f_x^{0'}(x^1 - x^0) = (x^1 - x^0)'(f_x^0 + y^{0'}g_x^0) - (y^{0'}g_x^0)'(x^1 - x^0)$ and the KT necessary conditions on the saddle point function $\phi(x, y) = f(x) + y'g(x)$ at $x^0$ and the quasi-concavity, it is easy to show that $f_x^{0'}(x^1 - x^0) \leqslant 0$. Now by the hypothesis of (a), $f_x^{0'}(x^1(t) - x^0) < 0$ for a scalar constant $t$ $(0 \leqslant t \leqslant 1)$ where $x^1(t) \equiv (1 - t)x^1 + tx^2$, also by quasi-concavity $f(x) \geqslant f(x^0)$ implies $f_x^{0'}(x - x^0) \geqslant 0$. Combining these two results $f(x^1(t)) < < f(x^0)$ but as $t \to 0$, $x^1(t) \to x^1$, hence $f(x^1) \leqslant f(x^0)$.

For part (b), using the result $f_x^{0'}(x^1 - x^0) \geqslant 0$ for $x^1$, $x^0 \in C$ and the hypothesis that for some nonnegative $x^*$ in $C$ and for some $i_0$, $f_{x_{i_0}}^0 > 0$ and $x_{i_0}^* > 0$ we have $f_x^{0'}x^* > 0$. Letting $x^1 = x^*$, $f_x^{0'}x^0 > 0$, these imply $f_x^{0'}(x^* - x^0) < 0$. Noting that $x^*$ may be equated to $x^2 = 0$ of the proof in part (a), the same outline of proof applies. Note that if $x^{0'}f_x^0 > 0$, then the hypothesis (b) is necessarily satisfied.

For part (c) an intuitive and heuristic outline of proof is to note that since $f_x^0$ is not zero around $x^0$, there is a neighborhood around $x^0$ for which either part (a) or part (b) must hold, since the so-called constraint qualification is assumed to be satisfied. Similarly for part (d), we combine the two relations,

$$f_x^{0'}(x - x^0) + f(x^0) \geqslant f(x) \qquad \text{(by concavity)}$$

and,

$$f_x^{0'}(x - x^0) \leqslant 0 \text{ since } x^0 \text{ satisfies the KT necessary conditions}$$

which imply $f(x^0) \geqslant f(x)$ for all $x \in C$ around the point $x^0$.

### 3.1.1. *Constraint qualifications* [3–5]

A few remarks may now be made the so-called 'constraint qualifications' which must be satisfied before any concave programming algorithms based on the KT necessary conditions are developed. Very broadly speaking, these constraint qualifications are intended to exclude singularities on the boundary of the constraint set and the possibility of nonattainability of the optimal point (or points) because of corners and isolated points.

Consider a vector point $\bar{x}$ in the constraint set $C$ and let the set of indices $(i=1, ..., m)$ of the restrictions $g_i(\bar{x}) \geqslant 0$ be divided into two subsets $E$ and $F$ as:

$$E: \{k: g^k(\bar{x}) = 0, \bar{x} \in C\}$$
$$F: \{k: g^k(\bar{x}) > 0, \bar{x} \in C\}$$

where the notation $g^k(\bar{x})$ is used to denote the $k$th element of the vector function $g(x)$ evaluated at $\bar{x}$ in the feasible constraint set $C$. Now define the following three terms: a contained path with origin at $\bar{x}$, an attainable direction at $\bar{x}$ and a locally constrained direction.

A *contained path* with origin at $\bar{x}$ and direction $s = (s_1, ..., s_n)$ is a vector function $p(t)$ of the real (scalar) variable $t(t \geqslant 0)$ in an interval beginning at $t = 0$ satisfying the following three conditions:

(i) $p(t)$ is defined for all $0 \leqslant t \leqslant \hat{t}$ for some $\hat{t} > 0$,

(ii) $p(t=0) = p(0) = \bar{x}$ with $p(t) \in C$ for all $0 \leqslant t \leqslant \hat{t}$ and
$C = \{x \mid g(x) \geqslant 0, x \geqslant 0\}$,

(iii) $p(t)$ has a right-hand derivative at $t = 0$ such that $(dp(t)/dt)_{t=0} = s$.

A vector $s = (s_1, ..., s_n)$ is defined to be *an attainable direction* at the point $\bar{x}$, if there is a contained path beginning at $\bar{x}$ and with direction $s$ with components $(s_1, ..., s_n)$. Further the $n$-component vector $s$ is defined to be *a locally constrained direction*, if it holds that

$$g^{k'}_{x=\bar{x}} s \geqslant 0 \quad \text{for all} \quad k \in E, \quad \text{i.e.} \quad g^{E'}_{x=\bar{x}} s \geqslant 0$$

where the index set $E$ is defined as before and $g_{x=\bar{x}}$ denotes the partial derivative of $g(x)$ with respect to $x$ evaluated at $\bar{x}$. New denote the set of all attainable directions at any given $\bar{x} \in C$ by $\bar{A}$ and the set of all locally constrained directions at $\bar{x} \in C$ by $\bar{L}$. The KT constraint qualification may now be characterized in several ways in terms of the above concepts:

(a) *KT constraint qualification*: Every locally constrained direction is attainable, i.e. $\bar{L}$ is a proper subset of $\bar{A}$. This qualification requires that for any point $\bar{x}$ in the constraint set $C$, there is a contained path with $p(t=0)=p(0)=\bar{x}$ in any direction $s$ satisfying

    (i) if $g^k(\bar{x})=0$,   then   $\bar{g}_{x=\bar{x}}^{k'}s>0$;     (note: $k\in E$)

    (ii) if $\bar{x}_j=0$,   then   $s_j\geqslant 0$;     $j=1,...,n$.

In other words, the tangent hyperplane at $\bar{x}$ for a given specific constraint $g^k(x)$ where $k\in E$ defined by $\bar{g}_{x=\bar{x}}^{k'}(x-\bar{x})=0$ divides the space into two half spaces if the partial derivative $\bar{g}_{x=\bar{x}}^k$ is not zero; of these two half spaces one contains the constraint set. The KT constraint qualification then requires that the direction $s$ satisfying condition (i) points into or along the boundary of that half space containing the constraint set.

    (b) *Nondegeneracy condition*: The rank of the matrix $\bar{g}_{x=\bar{x}}^E=(\partial g^k/\partial x_j)_{x=\bar{x}}$ where $k\in E$ equals the number of effective constraints, i.e. the constraints for which $g^k(\bar{x})=0$, $\bar{x}>0$. To indicate why this nondegeneracy condition implies the KT constraint qualifications, consider an arbitrary column vector $u$ with positive elements; then by the hypothesis of the rank condition, there must exist a vector $s^*$ such that $\bar{g}_{x=\bar{x}}^{E'}s^*=u>0$, since $\bar{g}_{x=\bar{x}}^E$ is of full rank. Then either by theorem 3.1 (part (b)), it can be shown that an optimal solution exists and is attainable, or one can construct a contained path such that $s+\alpha s^*$ is attainable. Taking the latter case, define $p(t)=\bar{x}+(s+\alpha s^*)t$ for $t\geqslant 0$, $s\in L$, $\alpha=$ a positive real (scalar) number, and consider any index $k\in E$ at $t=0$ for which

$$\frac{\mathrm{d}g^k(p(t))}{\mathrm{d}t}=\bar{g}_{x=\bar{x}}^{k'}(s+\alpha s^*)=\bar{g}_{x=\bar{x}}^{k'}s+\alpha\bar{g}_{x=\bar{x}}^{k'}s^*\geqslant\alpha\bar{g}_{x=\bar{x}}^{k'}s^*$$

since $\bar{g}_{x=\bar{x}}^{k'}s\geqslant 0$ by definition of the set $\bar{L}$. But by the hypothesis of the nondegeneracy condition, $\bar{g}_{x=\bar{x}}^{k'}s^*=u>0$. Hence $\mathrm{d}g^k(p(t))/\mathrm{d}t\geqslant 0$ at $t=0$. If the constraint set $C$ is convex this implies that for $t$ sufficiently small, $g^k(p(t))$ has a local right-hand minimum at $t=0$, i.e.

$$g^E(p(t))\geqslant g^E(p(0))=g^E(\bar{x})=0\qquad\text{for }t\text{ sufficiently small}.$$

But for sufficiently small $t$, $g^F(p(0))>0$, $g^F(p(t))\geqslant 0$ where the subset $F$ is set of indices $k$ for which $g^k(\bar{x})>0$. Hence the function $p(t)$ is a contained path in $C$ with attainable directions $(s+\alpha s^*)$. Since $u$ and $t$ are arbitrary, therefore $\bar{L}$ is contained in $\bar{A}$.

    (c) *Slater condition*: Each restriction $g_i(x)$ is concave in $x$ so that the constraint set $C$ is convex and for some nonnegative vector point $x^*$, it holds that $g(x^*)>0$. To prove the result that this implies KT qualification, note that by hypothesis the constraint set $C$ is convex, hence $C$ has an interior; this implies that the set $\bar{L}$ must have an interior. Hence for each

$k \in E$, there must exist a vector $s \in L$ such that $\bar{g}^{k'}_{x=\bar{x}} s \geqslant 0$ (otherwise, if $\bar{g}^{k}_{x=\bar{x}} s = 0$ for *all* $s \in \bar{L}$, then this implies $\bar{g}^{k}_{x=\bar{x}} = 0$ which is contrary to the hypothesis). But $\bar{g}^{k}_{x=\bar{x}} s \geqslant 0$ implies that for components $s_k$ and $s_j$ of $s$

$$\bar{g}^{k'}_{x=\bar{x}} s_k > 0 \quad \text{and} \quad \bar{g}^{k'}_{x=\bar{x}} s_j \geqslant 0 \quad \text{for} \quad j, k \in E.$$

Now define $s^* = \sum_{k \in E} s_k$; then this means $\bar{g}^{E'}_{x=\bar{x}} s^* > 0$. This implies the KT constraint qualifications.

(d) *Karlin condition*: The constraint vector $g(x)$ is concave and for every (dual) vector $y \geqslant 0$, there exists a (primal) vector $x$ such that $y'g(x) > 0$. It is easy to show that this condition is implied by the Slater condition, for the vector $s^*$ in the Slater condition can be replaced by the vector $y$. Hence the Karlin condition also implies the KT constraint qualifications.

(e) *Hurwicz condition*: Any direction $s = (s_1, \ldots, s_n)$ at $\bar{x}$ is attainable for all $\bar{x} \in C$ and all $s$ satisfying $\bar{g}'_{x=\bar{x}} s + g(\bar{x}) \geqslant 0$. In finite dimensional spaces the Hurwicz condition implies the KT constraint qualification, since in the former we may consider only those components $k$ for which $g^k(\bar{x}) = 0$. (However, in infinite dimensional spaces (e g the infinite horizon models) the Hurwicz condition may be more general.)

From an operational viewpoint the above results on constraint qualifications may be conveniently put in a theorem [3] using only conditions that are easily applicable.

*Theorem 3.2*

Let $g(x) = (g_i(x); i = 1, \ldots, m)$ be an $m$-dimensional, differentiable, quasi-concave vector function of vector $x$. Let $g(x^*) > 0$ for some $x^* \geqslant 0$ and for each index $k$, either let $g^k(x)$ be concave or for each $\bar{x}$ in the constraint set let $\bar{g}^k_{x=\bar{x}} \neq 0$ where $\bar{g}^k_{x=\bar{x}} = $ the $k$th component of $(\partial g/\partial x)_{x=\bar{x}}$. Then $g(x)$ satisfies the constraint qualifications.

Several applications of quasi-concave programming have been discussed by Arrow and Enthoven, particularly in the theory of consumer choice and the production model of a firm. Since the log-linear production function $y = x_1^{m_1} x_2^{m_2}$ with $m_1 + m_2 > 1$ and $m_1 > 0$, $m_2 > 0$ where $y = $ output, $x_1 = $ capital input, and $x_2 = $ labor input is quasi-concave, the following optimization problem for a single firm enterprise is a quasi-concave programming problem:

$$\text{minimize total input costs} = p_1 x_1 + p_2 x_2$$
$$\text{under the restrictions: } x_1 \geqslant 0, x_2 \geqslant 0$$
$$y \geqslant \bar{y}, y = x_1^{m_1} x_2^{m_2}, m_1 + m_2 > 1,$$

$\bar{y} = $ preassigned output limit, $p_i = $ unit costs assumed fixed. Another important application is in the field of decomposition techniques applied to nonlinear programs [6] which have already been discussed in ch. 2.4. The point that gradient methods are applicable to quasi-concave programs satisfying the constraint qualifications is of great importance in an economic sense, since the successive steps of computation implied by the gradient method can be interpreted in fact as pricing rules for a competitive market model.

### 3.1.2. Duality in NLP models

A special case of concave (or quasi-concave) programming, other than quadratic programming, that has been analyzed and applied very widely is the case in which the constraint set $g(x) = b - Ax$ is linear but the objective function $f(x)$ is only a concave function, not necessarily quadratic. This sort of concave programming has found wide applications in several applied fields such as inventory control, production scheduling and the micro theory of the firm and to problems of national economic planning. Theoretically speaking there are at least two important lines of research work in this field. One is the development of the duality theorems and the second is the development of special computational techniques which are simplex-like procedures.

If $f(x)$ is a weakly concave differentiable function and $\nabla f(x_0)$ is the gradient vector evaluated at $x_0$ such that it exists with the condition that the matrix

$$(\partial/\partial \nabla f(x_0))(\partial x_0/\partial \nabla f(x_0))$$

of second partial derivatives of $x_0$ with respect to $\nabla f(x_0)$ also exists, then the following duality relation has been derived by Dorn and others [7].

| *Primal* | *Dual* |
|---|---|
| maximize $z = f(x)$ | minimize $Q = f(x_0) - x_0'\nabla f(x_0) + y'b$ |
| under the conditions | under the conditions |
| (1)  $Ax \leqslant b$ | (1)  $A'y - \nabla f(x_0) \geqslant 0$ |
| $x \geqslant 0$ | $y \geqslant 0$ |
| (2)  $\begin{cases} Ax \leqslant b \\ x \text{ unrestricted} \end{cases}$ | (2)  $\begin{cases} A'y - \nabla f(x_0) = 0 \\ y \geqslant 0 \end{cases}$ |
| (3)  $Ax = b$ | (3)  $A'y - \nabla f(x_0) \geqslant 0$ |
| $x \geqslant 0$ | $y$ unrestricted |
| (4)  $Ax = b$ | (4)  $A'y - \nabla f(x_0) = 0$ |
| $x$ unrestricted | $y$ unrestricted |

where $x_0$ is a solution to the primal problem. For ordinary linear programming $f(x) = c'x$ and the gradient vector is $c$ which is independent of $x$. Hence in linear programming, the dual problem may be stated only in terms of the vector $y$, but in NLP the dual has to be stated in terms of both the vector $x$ and $y$, where $x$ occurs in the primal problem.[2]

Other types of duality have been developed in respect to NLP. For example, Dennis [8] has developed an approach in which he defines

$$\nabla f(x_0) = y_c$$
$$y = y_L$$

and expresses the objective function in the dual (i.e. $Q$) in terms of the Legendre transformation of the function $f(x_0)$. Then he shows that the objective function $Q$ is a convex function of the variables $y_c, y_L$ provided $f(x)$ is a strictly concave function.

A different form of duality theorem was developed from the theory of conjugate functions presented by Fenchel. For a general set of restrictions $g(x) \geqslant 0$, $x \geqslant 0$ when both $f(x)$ and $g(x)$ are concave and differentiable, Wolfe [9] and Hanson [10] have derived some important duality results. Let $X$ denote the constraint set $(g(x) \geqslant 0; x \geqslant 0)$ and $Y$ the constraint set on $u$: $(\nabla f(u) + \nabla v'g(u) \leqslant 0; u \geqslant 0; v \geqslant 0)$. Then if $f(x)$ and $g(x)$ are concave and differentiable for all $x$ in the union set $XUY$, we have by the Kuhn-Tucker theorem that if

$$f(x_0) = \max f(x), x \in X, \tag{3.6}$$

and $v_0$ is a Lagrange multiplier associated with the constraints $g(x) \geqslant 0$, then,

$$v_0 \geqslant 0 \tag{3.7a}$$

$$(\nabla f(u) + \nabla v'g(u))_{(x_0, v_0)} \leqslant 0 \tag{3.7b}$$

$$x_0'(\nabla f(u) + \nabla v'g(u)) = 0 \tag{3.7c}$$

$$v_0'g(x_0) = 0 \tag{3.7d}$$

The following theorem can then be proved:

*Theorem 3.3* (Wolfe-Hanson) [10]

If there exists a vector $x_0$ such that

$$f(x_0) = \max_{x \in X} f(x), \tag{3.8}$$

---

[2] One exception to this statement is provided by concave homogeneous programming viz., Eisenberg, E., "Duality in homogeneous programming", *Proceedings of American Mathematical Society*, Vol. 12, October 1961, pp. 783–87.

then there exists a vector $v_0$ such that

$$K(x_0, v_0) - x_0' [K(u, v)]_{(x_0, v_0)} = \min [K(u, v) - u' \nabla K(u, v)]$$
$$u \in Y \qquad v \geqslant 0 \qquad (3.9)$$

and

$$f(x_0) = K(x_0, v_0) - x_0' [\nabla K(u, v)]_{(x_0, v_0)} \qquad (3.10)$$

where

$$K(u, v) = f(x) + v' g(u).$$

*Proof*: By definition, the vector $x_0$ belongs to the set $Y$ and $v_0 \geqslant 0$ that is, the point $(x_0, v_0)$ lies in the feasible solution set of the dual problem. Let $(u, v)$ be any point in this set. Then

$$K(x_0, v_0) - x_0' [\nabla K(u, v)]_{(x_0, v_0)} - [K(u, v) - u' \nabla K(u, v)]$$
$$= K(x_0, v_0) - [K(u, v) - u' \nabla K(u, v)] \qquad \text{by condition (3.7c)}$$
$$= f(x_0) - [f(u) + v' g(u) - u'(\nabla f(u) + \nabla v' g(u))] \qquad \text{by condition (3.7d)}$$
$$\leqslant (x_0 - u)' \nabla f(u) - v' g(u) + u'[\nabla f(u) + \nabla v' g(u)] \quad \text{since } f(x) \text{ is concave}$$
$$= x_0' \nabla f(u) - v' g(u) + u' \nabla v' g(u)$$
$$\leqslant x_0' \nabla v' g(u) - v' g(u) + u' \nabla v' g(u) \qquad \text{by condition (3.7c)}$$
$$= v' [- x_0' \nabla g(u) - g(u) + u' \nabla g(u)]$$
$$= - v' [(x_0 - u)' \nabla g(u) + g(u)]$$
$$\leqslant - v' g(x_0) \leqslant 0.$$

Hence the proof. Also, by conditions (3.7c), (3.7d) we get

$$f(x_0) = K(x_0, v_0) - x_0' [\nabla K(u, v)]_{(x_0, v_0)}.$$

That is, if the primal has a solution then so has the dual and the maximum of the primal is the minimum of the dual. Evidently the objective functions are then:

    *Primal*:    max $f(x)$

    *Dual*:      min $(K - u' \nabla K)$

               when $K = f(u) + v' g(u)$

                      $u = $ any solution to the primal.

With the respective objective functions the constraints are easily written down:

| *Primal*: | *Dual*: |
|---|---|
| (1) $g(x) \geqslant 0$ | (1) $\nabla v' g(u) + \nabla f(u) \leqslant 0$ |
| $\qquad x \geqslant 0$ | $\qquad v \geqslant 0$ |
| (2) $g(x) \geqslant 0$ | (2) $\nabla v' g(u) + \nabla f(u) = 0$ |
| $\qquad x$ unrestricted | $\qquad v \geqslant 0$ |

(3) $g(x) = 0$      (3) $\nabla v' g(u) + \nabla f(u) \leqslant 0$

     $x \geqslant 0$            $v$ unrestricted

(4) $g(x) = 0$      (4) $\nabla v' g(u) + \nabla f(u) = 0$

     $x$ unrestricted     $v$ unrestricted

Unlike the situation in linear programming, the dual formulation in NLP problems does not make the problems computationally any easier. However, perhaps because of the saddle point property, it has been reported that in most cases the arithmetic mean of the primal and dual solutions for any given iteration tends to be fairly good approximation (for that interation) to the optimum even when the individual solutions are bad approximations. It is still an open question how to define a good approximation and a good stopping rule in the iterative calculations. Since the computation methods for most NLP problems have to search for the saddle point of a Lagrangian function, they have to tackle the questions (a) how to determine the initial starting point and maintain feasibility later on, (b) how to define the rule of approximation, (c) how to establish the convergence of iteration, and lastly (d) when to stop in the iterative calculation.

The various duality results in NLP models are useful in several aspects. First, the dual prices in NLP models can be used either in specifying efficiency conditions or in various decomposition techniques and the associated rules of pricing. Second, in dynamic NLP models involving time, the stability characteristics (over time) of the optimal solution (i.e. optimal policy) in the primal can be inferred from the dual and thus the impact of various policy restrictions on the optimal solution can be measured in terms of imputed penalties (which can be adjoined to the original objective function sometimes to define improvements or revisions of optimal policies in different stages). Third, there are situations such as concave homogeneous NLP models in which the dual NLP can be specified only in terms of (the dual) vector $y$, whereas the primal problem is stated only in terms of vector $x$. This separability property is useful in establishing the so-called exhaustion theorem in economics, which states that if each factor is rewarded according to its marginal productivity, then under certain production conditions, the total product will be exactly exhausted with no deficit or surplus.

The following result is due to Eisenberg and Van Moeseke [11]:

*Theorem 3.4*

Let $f(x)$ and each $g_i(x) = b_i - h_i(x)$ be concave scalar and differentiable functions of vector $x$ satisfying the constraint qualification, such that each of the functions $f(x)$ and $h_i(x)$ are homogeneous of degree $n$. Then a solution vector $\bar{x}$ exists for the concave homogeneous NLP: max $f(x)$, $x \in X = \{x \mid g(x) = b - h(x) \geqslant 0; x \geqslant 0\}$, if and only if there exists a dual vector $\bar{y} \geqslant 0$ such that $f(\bar{x}) = \bar{y}'b$.

*Proof*: Consider the Lagrangian function $L(x, y) = f(x) + y'(b - h(x))$ and apply the KT necessary conditions for $\bar{x}, \bar{y}$ to get

  (i) $f_{x = \bar{x}} - h'_{x = \bar{x}} \cdot \bar{y} \leqslant 0$;

  (ii) $f'_{x = \bar{x}}\bar{x} - \bar{y}'h_{x = \bar{x}}\bar{x} = 0$

  (iii) $b - h(\bar{x}) \geqslant 0$

  (iv) $\bar{y}'b - \bar{y}'h(\bar{x}) = 0$.

Since $f(x)$ is homogeneous of degree $r$ (i.e. $f(\alpha x) = \alpha^r f(x)$, $\alpha$ is a positive constant), therefore by Euler's theorem

$$f'_x x = rf(x)$$

hence at $\bar{x}$, $rf(\bar{x}) = \bar{y}'h_{x = \bar{x}}$ by condition (ii); also by applying Euler's theorem to $h(x)$ at $\bar{x}$, $h_{x = \bar{x}} \cdot \bar{x} = rh(\bar{x})$; hence $f(\bar{x}) = \bar{y}'h(\bar{x}) = \bar{y}'b$ by condition (iv). These necessary conditions are also sufficient by concavity of $f(x)$ and $g(x)$.

### 3.1.3. Computational aspects [12]

Some of the most interesting features of different computational methods for NLP problems having some differentiability and smoothness conditions have been summarized by Wolfe [13].

The saddle point theory has provided the basis for many a computational method. It has been utilized by Arrow, Hurwicz and Uzawa [2] to define a system of differential equations for a steepest descent type of algorithm converging upon the solution in a large number of differentially small steps. There have been several attempts to define methods for descending in larger steps, e.g. the methods of Dennis and Zoutendijk [14] and the gradient projection method of Rosen [15]. While these methods are effective in maximizing the function to be maximized at every cycle of computation, many complications arise in keeping the approximations within the feasible region.

An interesting but quite different alternative method which approaches the maximum from outside the feasible region has been developed by Kelley [16] and others as the cutting plane method. This method avoids the complicated procedures required for keeping the argument point within the feasible region. On the other hand it requires the solution of an infinite sequence of

Features of NLP computational methods

| Method | Objective | Constraints | Convergence conditions | Termination if objective is | |
|---|---|---|---|---|---|
| | | | | linear | quadratic |
| 1. Direct differential gradient | N | N | not known | no | no |
| 2. Lagrangian differential gradient | N | N | strict convexity | no | no |
| 3. Simplex method for quadratic programming | Q | L | convexity | yes | yes |
| 4. Gradient projection I | N | L | – | yes | no |
| 5. Gradient projection II | N | N | convexity | yes | no |
| 6. Reduced gradient | N | L | – | yes | no |
| 7. Separable programming | N | N | | yes | no |
| 8. Decomposition | N | N | convexity | yes | no |
| 9. Cutting-plane | N | N | convexity | yes | no |
| 10. Accelerated cutting plane | N | L | convexity | yes | yes |

Note: N=nonlinear; Q=quadratic; L=linear.

linear programs with some uncertainty as to keeping the number of restrictions from becoming very very large.

Finally, there is an interesting method developed by Wegner [17] which is applicable when the feasible region is defined as the intersection of regions of smooth surfaces, i.e. vertices. But this method requires for each iteration the solution of sets of nonlinear simultaneous equations.

Recently Hartley [18] has developed a method which is very similar to the cutting plane method but utilizes a simplex routine. It is of some interest to characterize this formulation. For convenience the problem is written as

$$\max f(x) \tag{3.11}$$

under the conditions

$$_ig(x) \leqslant {}_ib; \qquad x \geqslant 0$$
$$(i = 1, 2, ..., m)$$

where $-f(x)$ and $_1g(x), _2g(x), ..., _mg(x)$ are convex differentiable functions, $_ib$ are constants and the constraint set is assumed to be bounded. Defining $x_{n+1} = f(x)$ the problem is easily seen to be equivalent to

$$\max x_{n+1} \tag{3.12}$$

under the conditions

$$_ig(x) \leqslant {}_ib; \qquad x_{n+1} \leqslant f(x); \qquad x_j \geqslant 0.$$

By imposing a grid point $x^*$ on the $n$-dimensional Euclidean space, each of the convex restrictions is then replaced by a set of linear restrictions by constructing tangent planes at each grid point. Hence

$$_ig(x^*) + \sum_{j=1}^{n} {}_ig_j^*(x_j - x_j^*) \leqslant {}_ib; \quad \text{where} \quad {}_ig_j = \frac{\partial_i g}{\partial x_j} \tag{3.13}$$

$$-f(x^*) - \sum_j f_j^*(x_j - x_j^*) + x_{n+1} \leqslant 0. \tag{3.14}$$

These two linear approximations may be summed up as

$$_iAx \leqslant {}_ic \tag{3.15}$$

$$_{m+1}Ax + x_{n+1}H \leqslant {}_{m+1}c \tag{3.16}$$

where

$$_ic = {}_ib - {}_ig(x^*) \sum_{j=1}^{n} {}_ig_j^* x_j^*$$

$$_{n+1}c = f(x^*) = \sum_j f_j^* x_j^*$$

$$H = \text{unit column vector}.$$

Now since the feasible region of the problem is bounded, one can postulate a large cube defined by $|x_j| \leqslant D$. The tangent planes to any of the $_i g(x)$ and $-f(x)$ are introduced only for such grid points $x^*$ which satisfy $|x_j^*| \leqslant D$; hence (3.15) and (3.16) define a finite but large number (say $N$) of linear inequalities. To these have to be added the $2n$ restrictions $|x_j| \leqslant D$. Hence the problem of maximizing $x_{n+1}$ subject to these $(N+2n)$ linear restrictions and $x_j \geqslant 0$ is a finite linear programming problem, and the dual simplex method can be applied (see Vajda [19]).

The gradient method as a procedure for successive approximations has the great advantage that under proper conditions it defines a very fast movement in the direction of the gradient vector and it satisfies conditions of local convergence. Let $\phi(x, y)$ be the Lagrangian or the saddle point scalar function

$$\phi(x, y) = \phi(x_1, ..., x_n; y_1, ..., y_m) \qquad (3.17)$$

then the first step is to choose a feasible nonnegative initial point $(x^{(1)}, y^{(1)})$. Then we define

$$\begin{cases} \delta_{x_j}^{(1)} = \phi_{x_j}(x^{(1)}, y^{(1)}) \\ \delta_{y_i}^{(1)} = \phi_{y_i}(x^{(1)}, y^{(1)}) \end{cases} \qquad (3.18)$$

where $\phi_{x_j}(x^{(1)}, y^{(1)})$ denotes the partial derivative of $\phi(x, y)$ with respect to $x_j$ evaluated at $(x^{(1)}, y^{(1)})$ and similarly for $\phi_{y_i}$. The next step is to compute the new values of $(x, y)$ by the following rule:

$$x_j^{(2)} = \begin{cases} 0, & \text{if } x_j^{(1)} = 0 \text{ and } \delta_{x_j}^{(1)} < 0 \\ x_j^{(1)} + k^{(1)} \delta_{x_j}^{(1)} & \text{otherwise} \end{cases}$$

$$y_i^{(2)} = \begin{cases} 0, & \text{if } y_i^{(1)} = 0 \text{ and } \delta_{y_i}^{(1)} > 0 \\ y_i^{(1)} - k^{(1)} \delta_{y_i}^{(1)} & \text{otherwise} \end{cases}$$

$$(j = 1, 2, ..., n; \qquad i = 1, 2, ..., m)$$

where $k^{(1)}$ is a small positive quantity.

And so on for other iterations. These restrictions are intended to make the successive approximating vectors $x$ and $y$ stay within feasibility along their paths to the saddle point.

At this stage some remarks may be made about the gradient method. First, one great advantage of a gradient method is that any feasible solution can be used to initiate the method and generally, in the interior movements, the movement in the direction of the gradient of $f(x)$ or $f(x) + y'g(x)$ specifies the maximum rate of increase. Second, the successive iterations in this method may be made only on the $x$-vector rather than on $x$ and $y$ both and in some cases the size of the step denoted by $k^{(1)}$ above may be determined in some optimizing manner.

For example, consider the case in which the constraints $g(x)$ are linear as follows:

$$g(x) = \begin{cases} b_i - \sum_{j=1}^{n} a_{ij}x_j \geq 0; & i \in I_1 \\ b_i - \sum_{j=1}^{n} a_{kj}x_j = 0; & i \in I_2 \end{cases}$$

$$x \geq 0$$

(3.19)

where the two index sets $I_1$ and $I_2$ are merely classifications of inequalities and strict equality restrictions. If the initial feasible vector is $x^{(1)}$ and the gradient vector $\nabla f(x^{(1)})$ of the nonlinear objective function $f(x)$ at $x^{(1)}$ is not identically zero, then we determine the next solution vector $x^{(2)}$ by the expression

$$x^{(2)} = x^{(1)} + k\nabla f(x^{(1)}); \quad k = \text{a positive scalar constant}$$

such that $f(x^{(2)}) > f(x^{(1)})$ with $x^{(2)}$ being feasible. In general, the optimal value of $k$ within $0 \leq k \leq \bar{k}$ where $\bar{k} > 0$ is a finite constant may be determined in principle by maximizing $f(x^{(2)}) = f(x^{(1)} + k\nabla f(x^{(1)}))$ with respect to $k$ within the range $0 \leq k \leq \bar{k}$, but this may be difficult to follow at each iteration, if the function $f(x)$ is nonlinear and complicated. In the case of linear constraints (3.19), another alternative is to note the largest value of the scalar constant $k$ for which $x^{(2)}$ will remain feasible, i.e. define two real numbers $r$ and $g$ as

$$r = \begin{cases} \min_{j}(-x_j^{(1)}/d_j^{(1)}), & \text{if } d_j^{(1)} = \nabla f(x^{(1)}) < 0 \\ \infty, & \text{if no } d_j^{(1)} < 0 \end{cases}$$

$$g = \begin{cases} \min_{i}\left(\dfrac{b_i - a_i'x^{(1)}}{a_i'd^{(1)}}\right), & \text{if } a_i'd^{(1)} > 0, i \in I_1 \\ \infty, & \text{if no } a_i'd^{(1)} > 0 \quad i \in I_1 \end{cases}$$

where $a_i'$ denotes the $i$th row of matrix $A = (a_{ij})$ and the vector $d^{(1)} = (d_j^{(1)})$. Then a value of $k$ may be determined by either $\min(r, g)$ or a number slightly less than that within $0 \leq k \leq \min(r, g)$. This method, however, may not be available in this simple form if the constraints $g(x)$ are nonlinear.

For the general NLP problems, since the saddle point of $\phi(x, y) = f(x) + y'g(x)$, when it exists $(x \geq 0, y \geq 0)$ under appropriate concavity and differentiability conditions, defines a maximum for $x$ (i.e. $\phi(x^0, y^0) \geq \phi(x, y^0)$) and a minimum for $y$ (i.e. $\phi(x^0, y^0) \leq \phi(x^0, y)$), the gradient method has been shown by Arrow, Hurwicz and Uzawa [2] to be equivalent for small steps to the following system of differential equations, where $t$ is computational time and the dot over a variable denotes its time derivative

$$\dot{x}_j = dx_j/dt = 0, \quad \text{if} \quad \phi_{x_j} < 0 \quad \text{and} \quad x_j = 0 \tag{3.20a}$$

$$\dot{x}_j = \phi_{x_j} \quad \text{otherwise}; \quad (j = 1, ..., n) \tag{3.20b}$$

$$\dot{y}_i = dy_i/dt = 0, \quad \text{if} \quad \phi_{y_i} > 0 \quad \text{and} \quad y_i = 0 \tag{3.20c}$$

$$\dot{y}_i = -\phi_{y_i} \quad \text{otherwise}; \quad (i = 1, ..., m). \tag{3.20d}$$

It is proved that these systems of equations have a continuous solution with respect to the starting point, if for the saddle point $(x^*, y^*)$, $x_j^* > 0$ and $y_i^* > 0$ for every interior index $i$ or $j$ (the interior indices are not corner indices). The corner indices satisfy $x_j = 0$, if $\phi_{x_j} < 0$. Let $x_{(1)}$ be the vector of components of $x$ with corner indices and $x_{(2)}$ that of interior components. Then the first order partial derivatives of $\phi$ with respect to $x_{(2)}^*$ vanish and under normal differentiability assumptions about $\phi$, we have that the matrix of partial derivatives

$$[\phi_{x_{(2)}x_{(2)}}] \quad \text{is negative semidefinite} \tag{3.21a}$$

and

$$[\phi_{y_{(2)}y_{(2)}}] \quad \text{is positive semidefinite}. \tag{3.21b}$$

Under these conditions the following theorem of local convergence and stability of iterations by the gradient method has been proved.

*Theorem 3.5* (Arrow-Hurwicz)

Let the scalar function $\phi(x, y)$ of vectors $x, y$ possess a saddle point $(x^*, y^*)$ satisfying conditions (3.21a) and (3.21b) above such that

$$x_j^* > 0 \text{ and } y_i^* > 0 \text{ for every interior index } i \text{ or } j$$

then, for *every initial position* in a sufficiently small neighborhood of $(x^*, y^*)$, there is a unique solution of the system of differential equations (3.20a) through (3.20d) such that

$$\lim_{t \to \infty} x(t) = x^*; \quad \lim_{t \to \infty} y = y^*$$

*Proof*: Since the saddle point $\phi(x^*, y^*)$ exists, therefore the vectors $p = x - x^*$ and $q = y - y^*$ are defined in a sufficiently small neighborhood of $(x^*, y^*)$ satisfying

$$\dot{p} = \phi_{xx}(x^*, y^*)' \, p + \phi_{xy}(x^*, y^*)' \, q$$

$$\dot{q} = -\phi_{yx}(x^*, y^*)' \, p - \phi_{yy}(x^*, y^*)' \, q \tag{3.22}$$

where the notation $\phi_{xy}(x^*, y^*)$ denotes the matrix of second partials of $\phi$ with respect to $x$ and $y$, evaluated at $(x^*, y^*)$. These equations follow from Taylor series expansions, e.g.

$$\phi_x = \phi_x(x^*, y^*) + \phi_{xx}(x^*, y^*)' \, p + \phi_{xy}(x^*, y^*)' \, q$$

applied to the original system (3.20b) and (3.20d). The system (3.22) may be simplified to

$$\dot{p} = (f_{xx}(x^*) + y^{*'} g_{xx}(x^*))' \, p + g_x(x^*)' \, q$$
$$\dot{q} = - g_x(x^*)' \, p. \qquad (3.23)$$

Now consider a Lyapunov function $V(p, q)$ along the solution path of (3.23) as follows:

$$V(p, q) = \tfrac{1}{2}(p'p + q'q).$$

Obviously this is the usual Euclidean distance function. If it can be shown that as computational time $t \to \infty$, $\mathrm{d}V(p, q)/\mathrm{d}t \leqslant 0$ along the solutions of the system (3.23), then the convergence of the gradient method can be established. Now by applying (3.23) to $V(p, q)$ we obtain

$$\frac{\mathrm{d}V}{\mathrm{d}t} = p'\dot{p} + q'\dot{q} = p' \left[ f_{xx}(x^*) + y^{*'} g_{xx}(x^*) \right] p = p' \phi_{xx}(x^*, y^*) \, p.$$

We find that $\mathrm{d}V/\mathrm{d}t \leqslant 0$, since by assumptions (3.21a) and (3.21b) the matrix $\phi_{xx}(x^*, y^*)$ is negative semi-definite (i.e. $\phi$ is concave with respect to $x$ for fixed $y = y^*$ and convex in $y$ for fixed $x = x^*$). The above proof holds for interior indices. But since there is an interior neighborhood around the saddle point $(x^*, y^*)$ by hypothesis, the local convergence holds if the initial starting point is appropriately chosen.

Other general proofs are also available [20]. For instance, Uzawa has shown that the above theorem on convergence holds for any feasible initial solution, if the saddle value function $\phi(x, y)$ is strictly concave with continuous second partial derivatives in $x$, for all feasible $y$. Also, the restrictions imposed by this theorem that the successive steps of iteration have to be differentially very small have been relaxed in some cases. The sufficient condition for local convergence requires that the saddle point function $\phi(x, y)$ be strictly concave in $x$ for each feasible vector $x$. As mentioned before, this theorem has important implications for decentralized planning, since it shows that successive iterations based on dual prices converge (i.e. sector optima converge to the overall optimum).

### 3.1.4. Quadratic programming methods

Problems of quadratic programming (i.e., problems having a quadratic objective function with linear restrictions) which are, of course, special cases of concave programming, have a simpler structure such that, after a little modification, the usual simplex method of computation is applicable and several algorithms [21] are available.

A usual quadratic programming problem may be defined as follows:

$$\text{maximize } f(x) = c'x + x'Dx \qquad c : n.1$$
$$x : n.1$$
$$\text{under the restrictions} \qquad D : m.n$$
$$A : m.n$$
$$Ax \leqslant b; \ x \geqslant 0 \qquad b : m.1.$$

The objective function $f(x)$ is strictly concave (only concave), only if the matrix $D$ is negative definite (negative semi-definite). This assumption about the matrix $D$ is required for the solution to be bounded, along with the assumption that the inequality restrictions above define a closed and bounded region containing the optimal solution. Define the Lagrangian function $L(x, y)$, which is identical with the notation $\phi(x, y)$ used at the outset of this chapter, as follows:

$$L(x, y) = c'x + x'Dx + y'(b - Ax); \qquad y : m.1.$$

If the objective function $f(x)$ is assumed strictly concave (i.e., the matrix $D$ is negative definite), then the Lagrangian function $L(x, y)$ is (strictly) concave in $x$ for all feasible $y$ and convex in $y$ for all feasible $x$. In such a case the Kuhn-Tucker conditions are both necessary and sufficient.

Applying the Kuhn-Tucker necessary conditions for optimality, we get

(i) $\partial L(x, y)/\partial x = L_x = c + 2Dx - A'y \leqslant 0$.

(ii) If $\partial L(x, y)/\partial x_j < 0$, then $x_j = 0$; $\quad j = 1, 2, ..., n$.

(iii) $\partial L(x, y)/\partial y = b - Ax \geqslant 0$.

(iv) If $\partial L(x, y)/\partial y_i > 0$, then $y_i = 0$; $\quad i = 1, 2, ..., m$.

Adding nonnegative slack vectors $v(v : n.1)$ and $w(w : m.1)$ and rearranging, this system reduces to

$$c + 2Dx - A'y + v = 0 \quad (n \text{ linear equations}) \tag{3.24}$$

$$b - Ax - w = 0 \quad (m \text{ linear equations}) \tag{3.25}$$

$$v'x = 0 \quad \text{(at least } n \text{ of the } 2n \text{ variables } v_j, x_j \text{ are zero)} \qquad (3.26)$$

$$w'y = 0 \quad \text{(at least } m \text{ of the } 2m \text{ variables } w_i, y_i \text{ are zero)}. \qquad (3.27)$$

The two equations (3.24) and (3.25) define a system of $(n+m)$ equations in $2(m+n)$ unknowns (i.e., $n$ of $v_j$'s and $x_j$'s and $m$ of $w_i$'s and $y_i$'s) but since the equations (3.26) and (3.27) imply that at least $n$ of the $2n$ variables (i.e., $x_j$'s and $v_j$'s) and at least $m$ of the $2m$ variables (i.e., $y_i$'s and $w_i$'s) must be zero, the system (3.24) through (3.27) reduces finally to a set of $n+m$) equations in $(n+m)$ unknowns. Thus if an initial solution to the original quadratic programming problem exists, it must be one of the basic solutions of the following system

$$\begin{bmatrix} 2D & -A' & I & 0 \\ A & 0 & 0 & I \end{bmatrix} \begin{bmatrix} x \\ y \\ v \\ w \end{bmatrix} = \begin{bmatrix} -c \\ b \end{bmatrix}. \qquad (3.28)$$

There are several computational algorithms available now, e.g. (a) the gradient method and its modifications, (b) two simplex algorithms proposed by Wolfe with slight modifications to take care of the nonlinear equations (3.26) and (3.27), and (c) other special methods developed by Lemke, Theil-Van de Panne and Beale.

The two algorithms proposed by Wolfe are most easily amenable to simplex routines. While the first method starts from the system (3.28), the second algorithm constructs an equivalent problem and develops a somewhat faster computing scheme. These two methods will be discussed briefly.

In the first method the computational steps are as follows:

*Step 1*: First determine a basic feasible solution to $Ax+w=b$ if it exists (this is the usual first phase of the simplex method). If it is found, then it is known that there exists at least one (and possibly more) basic feasible solution with nonnegative $x$ and $w$. Let this solution be denoted by $x_j^0$ $(j=1, 2, ..., m)$. Then choose a nonnegative value of the vector $v$ so that $x^{0'}v^0 = \sum_j x_j^0 v_j^0 = 0$ and hence the relation (3.26) is satisfied.

*Step 2*: In general $(x_j^0, v_j^0)$ will not satisfy (3.24). However, defining $s_j^0 = |\sum_{k=1}^{n} 2d_{jk} x_k^0 + c_j| \geqslant 0$ $(j=1, 2, ..., n)$ it follows that $(x_j^0, v_j^0, s_j^0)$ satisfy

$$A'y - 2Dx - c - v \pm s = 0 \qquad (3.29)$$

where $s$ is the $n$-dimensional column vector with a typical element $s_j$ defined above and where the sign in the last term $(\pm s_j)$ is chosen to be the same as the sign of the term enclosed in the absolute value for $s_j^0$. The vector $s$ actually augments (3.24) by adding the so-called artificial variables. Equation (3.28) replaces equation (3.24). Now our objective is to ensure that the negative of the sum of the artificial variables is maximized while maintaining the condition $x'v=0$, for it is apparent that if a solution for which $s_j=0$ can be generated, then the optimization problem is solved.

*Step 3*: To this end we proceed with the simplex algorithm to

$$\text{maximize} - \sum_{j=1}^{n} s_j$$

subject to (3.25), (3.29) and

$$s_j \geqslant 0, \, x_j \geqslant 0, \, v_j \geqslant 0$$
$$(j = 1, 2, ..., n).$$

This is a regular LP problem and a primal feasible solution is given by $(x_j^0, v_j^0, s_j^0)$. Generally, however, the sequence of primal feasible solutions arrived at through the ususal simplex algorithm will not satisfy the nonlinear condition (3.26) i.e., $v_j x_j = 0$ and hence an additional restriction is placed on the simplex procedure as follows: if for any index $j=1, 2, ..., m+n$ and any iteration the activity $x_j$ is a basic variable, then $v_j$ is not allowed to enter the basis (i.e., $v_j=0$) for that iteration, likewise, if any $v_j$ becomes a basic variable in any iteration, the corresponding $x_j=0$ for that iteration. Wolfe has shown that these simplex-type iterations converge in a finite number of steps, provided the original problem has bounded solutions; the iterations reach $\sum_{j=1}^{n} s_j = 0$ at the optimum solution, which implies $s_j = 0$ ($j = 1, 2, ..., n$), and the corresponding $x_j$ and $v_j$ satisfy the Kuhn-Tucker conditions (3.24) through (3.27).

In the second method, an equivalent problem to the given quadratic program is constructed as

$$\text{maximize } z = f_x' x - y' b$$

under the restrictions

$$Ax \leqslant b; \quad A'y \geqslant f_x; \quad y \geqslant 0, \, x \geqslant 0 \qquad (3.30)$$

where

$$f_x = c + 2Dx.$$

Note that from the restrictions it can be easily shown that $b'y \geqslant y'Ax \geqslant x'f_x$. Denote the slack vectors by $w=b-Ax$ and $v=A'y-f_x$. Then $z=-y'w-v'x$. Define vectors $q$ and $\bar{q}$ as $q=(x, w, y, v)'$, $\bar{q}=(v, y, w, x)'$; then the equivalent problem may be written as

$$\max z = -\tfrac{1}{2}\bar{q}'q$$

under the conditions

$$Tq = d, q \geqslant 0 \tag{3.31}$$

where

$$T = \begin{bmatrix} A & I & 0 & 0 \\ -2D & 0 & A' & -I \end{bmatrix}; \quad d = \begin{bmatrix} b \\ c \end{bmatrix}.$$

Note that at the optimal solution $q^*$ we must have $\bar{q}^{*\prime} q^* = 0$; otherwise for any feasible vector $q$, $-\bar{q}'q \leqslant 0$. Also note that the equivalent problem (3.31) is nonlinear in its objective function but that if $\bar{q}$ is given as a constant it becomes a regular LP problem.

Since the vector $\bar{q}$ is only the vector $q$ with components of $q$ (i.e. $(v, y, w, x)$) in reverse order, a successive method of computation can be built on the sequence that we start with any initial feasible basis vector $q$, compute $\bar{q}$ therefrom, then solve the LP problem (3.31) with $\bar{q}$ given from the earlier step; this yields a new vector $q$, and the iterations continue. The specific computational steps are as follows:

*Step 1*: Let $q = q_{(0)} = r_{(1)}$ be the initial feasible solution, then define $\bar{r}_{(1)}$ in the same way that $\bar{q}$ is defined from $q$ and set $\bar{q}_{(1)} = \bar{r}_{(1)}$. Then solve the LP problem:

$$\max - \tfrac{1}{2} \bar{r}_1' q \quad \text{with} \quad Tq = d; \quad q \geqslant 0$$

where $\bar{r}_{(1)}'$ is a row vector of known constants. The optimal solution of this LP problem is denoted by $q_{(1)} = r_{(2)}$ wherefrom we define $\bar{r}_{(2)} = \bar{q}_{(2)}$.

*Step 2*: Find a sequence of feasible vectors $q_{(1)}, q_{(2)}, \ldots, q_{(h)}$ such that $-\tfrac{1}{2} \bar{r}_{(1)}' q_{(1)} < -\tfrac{1}{2} \bar{r}_{(2)}' q_{(2)} < \cdots$

*Step 3*: Stop at first $q_{(h)}$ satisfying $\bar{q}_{(h)}' q_h = 0$. If the term $\max \bar{q}_{(h)}' q_{()h}$ is not zero, then set $\bar{r}_{(2)} = \bar{q}_{(h)}$ and repeat step 2.

At the $k$th stage of iteration we may have (if the objective function is concave and the optimal solution is attained in the convex linear constraint set) two cases:

either, $\bar{q}_{(k)}' q_{(k)} = 0$ in which case the optimal solution is reached

$$\text{or, } - \tfrac{1}{2} \bar{r}_{(k)}' q_{(k)} \geqslant -\tfrac{1}{2} \bar{r}_{(k)}' r_{(k)}.$$

In the latter case, set

$$q_{(k+1)} = q_{(k)} \quad \text{and} \quad r_{(k+1)} = \alpha q_{(k+1)} + (1 - \alpha) r_{(k)}$$

where the scalar quantity $\alpha$ $(0 < \alpha \leqslant 1)$ is determined by the rule mentioned in connection with the gradient methods, i.e.

$$\alpha = \min \left[ \frac{\bar{r}_{(k)}' (r_{(k)} - q_{(k+1)})}{(q_{(k+1)} - r_{(k)})' (\bar{q}_{(k+1)} - \bar{r}_{(k)})}, 1 \right].$$

Again the steps 2 and 1 are repeated with $q_{(k+1)}, \bar{r}_{(k+1)}$ till the optimal is reached.

Frank and Wolfe [21] have shown that $\bar{r}'_{(k)} r_{(k)}$ tends to zero as $k$ tends to infinity and hence this iterative method converges. Note also that convergence can be established by following the arguments mentioned in nonlinear fractional functional programming in ch. 2.2, since it can be easily shown that $-z = y'w + v'x$ is concave in $(x, w)$ for any fixed and feasible $(y, v)$ and convex in $(y, v)$ for any fixed and feasible $(x, w)$ and the function $-z$ is continuous in the closed, connected and bounded convex set $Tq \leqslant d, q \geqslant 0$.

A simple numerical example follws:

$$\text{maximize } z = 20x_1 + 10x_2 - 3x_1^2 - 2x_2^2$$

under the restrictions

$$2x_1 - x_2 \leqslant 6; \qquad -x_1 + x_2 \leqslant 10; \qquad x_1 \geqslant 0, \quad x_2 \geqslant 0.$$

Here $D = \begin{bmatrix} -3 & 0 \\ 0 & -2 \end{bmatrix}$ is negative definite. Denote $w_1 = x_3, w_2 = x_4, v_1 = y_3$ and $v_2 = y_4$. Then the restrictions are:

$$2x_1 - x_2 + x_3 = 6; \qquad -x_1 + x_2 - x_4 = 10;$$
$$6x_1 + 2y_1 - y_2 - y_3 = 20; \qquad 4x_2 - y_1 + y_2 - y_4 = 10.$$

Define $q = (x_1, x_2, x_3 = w_1, x_4 = w_2, y_1, y_2, y_3 = v_1, y_4 = v_2)'$. One initial feasible solution is $q = (0, 0, 6, 10, 30, 40, 0, 0)'$; then $\bar{q}'_{(1)} = \bar{r}'_{(1)} = (0, 0, 30, 40, 6, 10, 0, 0)'$ and the objective function is $-\frac{1}{2} \bar{r}'_{(1)} q_{(1)} = -15x_3 - 20x_4 - 3y_1 - 5y_2$. With the restrictions above, this is a regular LP problem, the optimal solution is found to be $x_2 = 5, x_3 = 11, x_4 = 5, y_1 = 10$. Since $\bar{r}'_{(1)} q_{(1)}$ at this optimal LP solution is not zero, the iteration is continued further. The final optimal vector is found to be

$$q^* = \left( \tfrac{10}{3}, \tfrac{5}{2}, \tfrac{11}{6}, \tfrac{65}{6}, 0, 0, 0, 0 \right)'.$$

A few remarks are in order for the other methods of quadratic programming. In Lemke's method the simplex algorithm (as in the first algorithm of Wolfe) is essentially applied to the dual of the original quadratic program, whereas in the method of Theil-Van de Panne systematic procedures are developed for specifically determining those constraints on which the optimal solution lies. The method of quadratic programming developed by Beale [22] is very similar to the computational algorithm developed for linear fractional functional programming in ch. 2.2. In this method, first a primal feasible solution $x_h$ $(h = 1, ..., m)$ is found for $Ax \leqslant b, x \geqslant 0$ where $(1, ..., m)$ is the index set for a basis; then the basic variables are expressed in terms of the nonbasic variables $\bar{x}_k = x_{m+k}$ $(k=1,...,n)$ as

$$x_h = \alpha_{h0} + \sum_{k=1}^{n} \alpha_{hk}\bar{x}_k; \quad h = 1,...,m. \tag{3.32a}$$

Also, the objective function $f = c'x + x'Dx$ is expressed in terms of the non-basic variables $\bar{x}_k$. Next we consider the partial derivatives

$$\tfrac{1}{2}\partial f/\partial \bar{x}_i = \gamma_{i0} + \sum_{k=1}^{n} \gamma_{ik}\bar{x}_k \tag{3.32b}$$

where $\alpha_{h0}$, $\alpha_{hk}$, $\gamma_{i0}$, $\gamma_{ik}$ are appropriate constants. If $\gamma_{i0} \leqslant 0$ for all $i = m+1$, ..., $n$ then optimality is reached. Otherwise $\max_i \gamma_{i0}$; $i = m+1,...,n$ defines the incoming activity, if at least for one $i$, $\gamma_{i0} > 0$; also the outgoing activity is selected by the criterion

$$\min_i (|\gamma_{i0}/\gamma_{hi}|, |\gamma_{i0}/\gamma_{ii}|) \quad \text{for } i = 1,...,m.$$

### 3.1.5. Applications to economic models

Three major types of application of NLP methods have been considered in economic models: (a) applications to nonlinear activity analysis models, e.g. a nonlinear extension of Von Neumann's model for the whole economy [23] and applications to problems of investment planning in underdeveloped countries [24]; (b) to spatial equilibrium models [25]; and (c) to optimal capital budgeting decision problems. Applications to operations research models are available in the fields of sensitivity analysis, probabilistic programming and portfolio analysis (discussed in some detail in ch. 5), project planning and production scheduling, and nonlinear inventory problems. Extended algorithms such as quadratic integer methods [26], conjugate gradient methods [20] and others are sometimes used for special problems in this area.

It may be useful at this stage to describe some economic situations for which NLP methods are the most suitable. For instance, consider a very important problem of multi-plant decisions, in the general strategy of investment planning for an underdeveloped economy. This problem frequently comes up in connection with the optimal expansion of capacity of a single manufacturing industry which has great economies of scale, e.g., fertilizers steel, chemicals, transport equipment and the generation of electric power, when the future rate of growth of demand is either known or can be estimated with considerable reliability. By itself, the existence of economies of scale implies that individual plants of large size should be built, and this means even building capacity much ahead of demand, if the given rate of growth of demand is very low. Other factors which tend to offset this economy of scale argument are the costs of transport and the costs of building capacity under budget restrictions. The decision problem is how to determine the optimal sequence of time of construction and size of plant, by analyzing the costs and benefits of alternative plant sizes and alternative locations if any.

The above problem has been considered as a single-phase optimization problem by Alan Manne [27], who showed that it is optimal to construct a plant at each point of a sequence of equally spaced points of time of size equal to the growth in demand during the time interval between any two such time points under the following simplified assumptions:

(i) the demand for the product is growing linearly over time and initially there is just enough capacity to meet the demand;

(ii) there are economies of scale in construction and operation of plant and the investment cost of installing a plant capacity of $x$ units of output is $kx^a$ where $k > 0$, $0 < a < 1$; all other costs are assumed to be proportional to capacity costs; and

(iii) finally the objective function is the minimization of the discounted stream of costs of all future time-intervals or cycles, when the rate of discount is given and the time-horizon of discounting is infinite.

Let the investment cost of installing a plant of size $x$ be $c(x)$ so that $c(x) = kx^a$ and let $r$ be the constant nonnegative rate of discount. Since the increase of demand is linear per unit time, we can fix a new unit of measurement by which the rate of increase of demand is one per unit time and the total capacity output available in any time-interval or cycle is $x$. If $T(x)$ be the sum total of costs of all future cycles discounted to the present time, then

$$T(x) = c(x)\left(1 + \exp(-rx) + \exp(-2rx) + \cdots\right)$$
$$= kx^a/(1 - \exp(-rx))$$

since the time points of expansion are all points (i.e., "the points of regeneration") at which demand and capacity are equal. In this formulation, demand is deterministic, shortages are not allowed and the cost of idle capacity is ignored.

It can be shown that the cost function $T(x)$ is convex near the minimizing value of $x = x_0$ which is given by $dT(x)/dx = 0$, i.e.,

$$\exp(rx_0) = (r/a)\, x_0 + 1.$$

For example, if $a = 0.77$, the growth rate of demand $= 1.0$ and the discount rate $r = 10\%$, then the optimal plant size is equal to 5 units of demand and the optimal time-interval is $t = 5$ years. It has been noted that, with this type of cost function, the computation of optimal plant size ($x$) is relatively insensitive to slight variations (or errors) in either the rate of discount or the estimate of demand increase.

However, when there are several alternative sites (location points) or regions at which expansion of an industry (location of a plant) can be realized, the determination of optimal capacity expansion depends on the transport costs and the spread of demand between different sites or regions. For example, assume that a country has a number of possible regions where fertilizer plants could be built; each region has its own growth of demand for fertilizers and each has its own advantages or disadvantages (i.e., availabilities of raw material, etc.) of location. For a region in which the growth of demand is very low, it may be more profitable not to build any fertilizer plant of its own but to allow neighboring regions to build larger sized plants and then acquiring its supplies from them by incurring transportation costs. Similarly over time, expansion of capacity in one region may be deferred, in one time-phase, if it achieves greater balance with the tempo of growth of demand for the whole multi-regional system. The alternatives are so many that a programming formulation is required.

An approximate formulation in linear programming terms has been given by Manne and Vietorisz [28], where they considered the following problem: given a fixed demand for synthetic ammonia fertilizers within individual countries, what combination of production plus imports would satisfy these requirements at a minimum cost to the Latin American region as a whole. There are four sets of decision variables in the model, i.e., $x_{ij}$ and $y_{jk}$ which must be nonnegative and $w_i$, $z_j$ which take only integer values of either zero or one. The subscripts $i$ and $j$ are used for production locations and $k$ is used for markets (i.e. demand points); the construction-cum-operation cost function is approximated by a linear function and the discounting problem is assumed away except as it is reflected in the approximating cost function. The variables are:

$x_{ij} =$ units of ammonia per year produced at location $i$ and shipped to fertilizer location $j$ at a cost $c_{ij}$ which includes both construction-cum-operation cost plus the cost of transportation;

$y_{jk} =$ number of ammonia-equivalent units of fertilizer produced at fertilizer location $j$ and shipped to market $k$ at a cost of $d_{jk}$ which includes both construction-cum-operation cost plus transportation;

$w_i$ = fraction of fixed charge (total annual fixed charge $= a_i$) incurred for an ammonia plant at $i$ ($w_i = 0$ or $1$);

$z_j$ = fraction of fixed charge (total annual fixed charge $= b_j$) incurred for a fertilizer plant at $j$ ($z_j = 0$ or $1$).

The optimizing problem is:

$$\text{minimize } [\sum_i a_i w_i + \sum_j b_j z_j + \sum_i \sum_j c_{ij} x_{ij} + \sum_j \sum_k d_{jk} y_{jk}] \qquad (3.33)$$

subject to

$$\sum_i x_{ij} = \sum_k y_{jk} \qquad \text{(all } j) \qquad (3.34)$$

$$\sum_j y_{jk} = R_k \qquad \text{(requirements of demand at } k). \qquad (3.35)$$

$$\text{If } w_i = \begin{cases} 1 \\ 0 \end{cases} \text{ then } \sum_j x_{ij} \begin{cases} \geqslant 0 \\ = 0 \end{cases} \qquad \text{(all } i). \qquad (3.36)$$

$$\text{If } z_j = \begin{cases} 1 \\ 0 \end{cases} \text{ then } \sum_k y_{jk} \begin{cases} \geqslant 0 \\ = 0 \end{cases} \qquad \text{(all } j) \qquad (3.37)$$

$$\text{and } x_{ij}, y_{jk} \geqslant 0; \qquad w_i, z_j = 0 \text{ or } 1.$$

Note that the objective function is the sum total of fixed and variable costs of production, plus transportation charges, plus import costs, and the coefficients $c_{ij}$ and $d_{jk}$ represent the parameters of linear approximation of the earlier scale coefficient $a$. The restriction (3.34) states that the sum of ammonia inputs from all primary locations $i$ should be equal to the total fertilizer distributed, since production is here measured in terms of ammonia-equivalents. $R_k$ denotes the total demand (i.e. requirement) at market $k$, assumed to be known. Restrictions (3.36) and (3.37) are self-evident. However this formulation is very complicated from the point of view of computation, since integer programming algorithms are required first of all and moreover the scale economies aspect is practically eliminated by the linear approximation of the cost function. However, approximate local optima can be more easily determined by methods of enumeration and the algorithms of dynamic programming.

A few comments may now be added about the single-phase optimization problem above. Abstracting from the locational problems altogether, it is necessary to point out that the Manne-model has not considered the time-path of optimal capacity expansion, i.e. once the optimal size $x_0$ is known, it is never changed between time intervals. A more general model in the line conceived by Arrow, Beckman and Karlin [29] would allow multiple phase optimization, since in this approach the choice of capacity expansion policies is limited by the initial capacity and also an upper bound, and by the restriction that capacity can never decrease over time. Further, the objective is the maximization of output rather than minimization of costs.

For example, let $d(t)$ be the demand function (i.e. quantity demanded) over time and $x(t)$ be the capacity at time $t$ in terms of cumulative output, and let the planning horizon extend from $t=0$ to $t=T$ and the unit price of the product be $p$, a constant. Further assume that the cost of capacity expansion at time $t$ is $c(\dot{x})=k\dot{x}^a$, where $\dot{x}=dx/dt=$ current output rate and $k>0$, $0<a<1$ as before. The sum of discounted profits is

$$\int_0^T [p \min(d(t), x(t)) - c(\dot{x})] \exp(-rt)\, dt \qquad (3.38)$$

if no other costs except those subsumed in capacity expansion costs are considered (otherwise more costs components such as inventory costs etc. are to be considered). The decision problem is then to choose the time function of cumulative output $x(t)$, i.e. the sequence of capacity expansions $x(1), x(2), ..., x(T)$, to maximize the discounted profit function (3.38) with $x(0)$ and $T$ given, subject to the restrictions of initial capacity and the maximum permissible rate of capacity expansion. Such a problem requires special treatment from the computational viewpoint, since the integrand of (3.38) involves the awkward problem of nondifferentiability and the usual Kuhn-Tucker conditions are not applicable without additional conditions. This problem is discussed in the next section (section 3.2) in some detail.

### 3.2. Control theory approach and variational programming

Methods of variational calculus are in a basic sense extensions of the techniques of point optimization of differentiable functions in differential calculus into the function space, in which the problem is to determine under certain conditions an optimum function rather than an optimum point. Intertemporal optimization problems are usually problems of variational calculus with or without some modifications. The modifications introduced by control theory are the classification of variables into state variables and control variables that may be subject to various types of inequality constraints [30]. Since the method of computation of adaptive feedback and optimal control which optimizes in some sense the overall performance of a system can be visualized as one in which distinct stages may be recognized such that decisions at later stages do not affect performance in the earlier ones, the control theory approach has a very close similarity to the technique of dynamic programming and its associated computational algorithms.

One of the simplest problems in classical variational calculus which has applications in many economic situations and problems of operations research is the following:

$$\text{maximize } J = \int_0^T F(x, \dot{x}, t)\, \mathrm{d}t \tag{3.40}$$

under the conditions $\qquad \dot{x} = \dfrac{\mathrm{d}x}{\mathrm{d}t} : n \cdot 1$

$x_0, x_T$ fixed, where $x_0 = x$ at $t = 0$, $x_T = x$ at $t = T$ $\tag{3.41}$

$F(x, \dot{x}, t)$, a scalar function of vectors, is concave
and differentiable in $x$, $\dot{x}$ and continuous in $t$. $\tag{3.42}$

Suppose the optimal function denoted by $x(t)$ is found. Consider a set of perturbed functions around the optimal function $x(t)$ defined by $x(t) + hy(t)$, where $h$ is a scalar constant (equal to a given small scalar number $\varepsilon$) and $y(t)$ is a vector function of scalar $t$ such that it vanishes at the two fixed points i.e. $y(0) = 0$, $y(T) = 0$. Now with the perturbed function, the integral $J$ in (3.40) becomes for any given function $y(t)$ dependent on $h$ only, i.e.

$$J(h) = \int_0^T F(x + hy, \dot{x} + h\dot{y}, t)\, \mathrm{d}t \qquad y : n \cdot 1$$

where $x(t)$, $y(t)$ are denoted here by $x$ and $y$. Now since by hypothesis $J(h)$ is maximum at $h = 0$ and since there are no corner points (i.e. no inequality restrictions), therefore its derivative with respect to $h$ must vanish at $h = 0$. But

$$\frac{\mathrm{d}J(h)}{\mathrm{d}h} = \int_0^T (F_x' y + F_{\dot{x}}' \dot{y})\, \mathrm{d}t;$$

where $F_x$ and $F_{\dot{x}}$ are partial derivatives of $F(x + hy, \dot{x} + h\dot{y}, t)$ with respect to $x$ and $\dot{x}$ respectively. The second term on the right hand side can now be integrated by parts and, noting that $F_{\dot{x}}' y \big|_0^T = 0$ since $y = 0$ at $t = 0$ and $T$, the derivative becomes finally,

$$\frac{\mathrm{d}J(h)}{\mathrm{d}h} = \int_0^T \left[ F_x' - \frac{\mathrm{d}}{\mathrm{d}t}(F_{\dot{x}}') \right] y\, \mathrm{d}t = 0. \tag{3.43}$$

Since the perturbation function $y = y(t)$ is quite arbitrary, so that condition (3.43) must hold identically for any $y$, therefore the integrand of (3.43) must be identically zero (otherwise a function $y(t)$ may be used with sufficiently small $h$ which would make $\mathrm{d}J(h)/\mathrm{d}h$ negative and hence $J(0)$ would not be the maximum). Hence we get the Euler-Lagrange necessary conditions for a maximum

$$F_x - \dot{F}_{\dot{x}} = F_{x_j} - \frac{\mathrm{d}}{\mathrm{d}t} F_{\dot{x}_j} = 0; \qquad j = 1, \dots, n \qquad (3.44a)$$

or,

$$F_x - (F'_{\dot{x}\dot{x}}\ddot{x} + F'_{\dot{x}x}\dot{x} + F_{\dot{x}t}) = F_{x_j} - \sum_{k=1}^{n} [F_{\dot{x}_j\dot{x}_k}\ddot{x}_k + F_{\dot{x}_j x_k}\dot{x}_k] - F_{\dot{x}_j t} = 0 \qquad (3.44b)$$

$j = 1, \dots, n$, where $\dot{F}_{\dot{x}}$ is the notation for $\dfrac{\mathrm{d}}{\mathrm{d}t}(\partial F/\partial \dot{x})$.

These necessary conditions are also sufficient if the integrand $F$ is concave in $x$, $\dot{x}$ and continuous in $t$, since the matrix $[\partial^2 F/\partial \dot{x}_i \partial \dot{x}_j]$ would in this case be negative (semi) definite (this is in fact the Legendre condition for a weak maximum).

Note that there may arise three types of problems in applying the Euler-Lagrange necessary conditions. First, the inequality restrictions on $x$ or $\dot{x}$ at any or all $t \in [0, T]$ would require a modification of (3.44a) in so far as the corner points or boundary points are concerned. Second, the system of nonlinear differential equations (3.44b) has to be solved subject to the two boundary restrictions and the computation of this solution has to be specified in discrete terms, since the successive iterations are to converge to the optimal solution. Third, the Kuhn-Tucker type constraint qualifications and the various sufficiency conditions must be analyzed, if the assumption of concavity of $F$ is not everywhere satisfied.

The first two types of modification can be easily incorporated by appropriately combining the Kuhn-Tucker necessary conditions with the Euler-Lagrange conditions, and these are called the ELKT-conditions of variational programming. We consider the two most frequent cases, continuous time and discrete time, and the results are presented as minimization rather than maximization problems, since the cost objective is more frequently used in operations research and control theory applications.

Now consider a continuous time optimal control problem with fixed end points, where $x$ is the state vector, $u$ is the control vector and the planning horizon $[0, T]$ is fixed and finite, i.e., $x_0$ and $x_T$ at $t = 0$, $T$ are given constant vectors. The problem is to

$$\text{minimize } C = \int_0^T F(x, u, t)\, dt \tag{3.45a}$$

under the restrictions

$$\dot{x} = g(x, u, t); \qquad x: n.1 \qquad \dot{x} = dx/dt \tag{3.45b}$$
$$\qquad\qquad\qquad u: m.1$$
$$h(x, u, t) \leqslant 0; \qquad h: k.1. \tag{3.45c}$$

Define the Lagrangian function

$$L = F + v'(g - \dot{x}) + w'h, \quad \text{where} \qquad F = F(x, u, t); \qquad g = g(x, u, t)$$
$$h = h(x, u, t)$$
$$v, w = \text{Lagrange multipliers}.$$

Then the following result [31] holds:

*Theorem 3.6*

If (i) the function $F$ and each component of the vector functions $g$ and $h$ are differentiable and convex in $(x, u)$, for all $t \in [0, T]$ and (ii) there exist Lagrange multipliers $\bar{v} = \bar{v}(t)$, $\bar{w} = \bar{w}(t)$ and the associated vectors $\bar{x} = \bar{x}(t)$, $\bar{u} = \bar{u}(t)$ with $\bar{x}(t)$, $\bar{v}(t)$ continuous and $\bar{w}(t)$ integrable such that they satisfy (3.45b) and (3.45c) and the following ELKT generalized necessary conditions

(iii)  (a) $L_{\bar{x}} = \dfrac{d}{dt}(L_{\dot{x}}) \Rightarrow F_{\bar{x}} + \nabla(v'g)_{x=\bar{x}} + \nabla(w'h)_{x=\bar{x}} = -\dot{\bar{v}}$

(b) $L_{\bar{u}} = \dfrac{d}{dt}(L_{\dot{u}}) \Rightarrow F_{\bar{u}} + \nabla(v'g)_{u=\bar{u}} + \nabla(w'h)_{u=\bar{u}} = 0$

(c) $\bar{w}(t) \geqslant 0$;     (d) $\bar{w}'h = 0$

(e) $\bar{v}(t) \geqslant 0$ (this need hold only for those components of $g$ which are nonlinear in $x$ or $u$ or both);

then the vectors $\bar{x}(t)$, $\bar{u}(t)$ are optimal in the sense that $C(x, u) - C(\bar{x}, \bar{u}) \geqslant 0$ for all other feasible $x, u$. (Here $\nabla(v'g)_{x=\bar{x}}$ denotes the gradient vector of $(v'g)$ with respect to $x$ evaluated at $\bar{x}$; the other expressions involving $\nabla$ have analogous interpretations; and $L_{\dot{x}}$ denotes $(\partial L/\partial \dot{x})_{x=\bar{x}}$.)
*Proof*:

$$C(x, u) - C(\bar{x}, \bar{u}) = \int_0^T (F(x, u, t) - \bar{F}(\bar{x}, \bar{u}, t))\, dt.$$

Since $F$ is convex,

$$\therefore F - \bar{F} \geqslant (x - \bar{x})' F_{\bar{x}} + (u - \bar{u})' F_{\bar{u}}$$

but from (iii)(a), (b)

$$F_{\bar{x}} = - [\nabla(v'g)_{\bar{x}} + \nabla(w'h)_{\bar{x}} + \dot{\bar{v}}]$$
$$F_{\bar{u}} = - [\nabla(v'g)_{\bar{u}} + \nabla(w'h)_{\bar{u}}].$$

Integrate by parts the expression

$$- \int_0^T (x - \bar{x})' \, \dot{\bar{v}} \, dt = - \left[ (x - \bar{x})' \, \bar{v} \Big|_0^T - \int_0^T (\dot{x} - \dot{\bar{x}}) \, \bar{v} \, dt \right]$$

$$= \text{zero} + \int_0^T (g - \bar{g})' \, \bar{v} \, dt \qquad \text{from (3.45b)}$$

where $\bar{g} = g(\bar{x}, \bar{u}, t)$ and $g = g(x, u, t)$.

Again, $g$ is by hypothesis convex,

$$\text{hence } g - \bar{g} \geqslant (x - \bar{x})' \, g_{\bar{x}} + (u - \bar{u})' \, g_{\bar{u}}.$$

Premultiplying both sides by the vector $\bar{v}$ which is nonnegative by (iii)(e),

$$(g - \bar{g})' \, \bar{v} \geqslant (x - \bar{x})' \, \nabla(\bar{v}'g)_{\bar{x}} + (u - \bar{u})' \, \nabla(\bar{v}'g)_{\bar{u}}.$$

Hence we get finally,

$$F - \bar{F} \geqslant (x - \bar{x})' \, F_{\bar{x}} + (u - \bar{u})' \, F_{\bar{u}} + (g - \bar{g})' \, v$$
$$\geqslant - (x - \bar{x})' \, \nabla(w'h)_{\bar{x}} - (u - \bar{u})' \, \nabla(w'h)_{\bar{u}}.$$

Since $h$ is convex, $h - \bar{h} \geqslant (u - \bar{u})' \, h_{\bar{u}} + (x - \bar{x})' \, h_{\bar{x}}$.

Premultiplying by $\bar{w}$ which is nonnegative by (iii)(c),

$$\bar{w}'h \geqslant \bar{w}'\bar{h} + (u - \bar{u})' \, \nabla(\bar{w}'h)_{\bar{u}} + (x - \bar{x})' \, \nabla(\bar{w}'h)_{\bar{x}};$$

hence

$$F - \bar{F} \geqslant \bar{w}'\bar{h} - \bar{w}'h = - \bar{w}'h \qquad \text{(from (iii) (d))}$$
$$\geqslant 0 \text{ since } h \leqslant 0 \text{ and } \bar{w} \geqslant 0.$$

Hence

$$C(x, u) - C(\bar{x}, \bar{u}) = \int_0^T (F - \bar{F}) \, dt \geqslant 0. \qquad \text{(Q.E.D.)}$$

The above theorem can also be presented in terms of Pontryagin's maximum principle [32] for an optimal control problem with a fixed time horizon. Using the vectors $\bar{u}, \bar{x}, \bar{w}$ as in theorem 3.6, the maximum principle would reinterpret theorem 1 as follows:

*Theorem 3.7* (Pontryagin's maximum principle)

There exist a scalar $\bar{p}_0(t)$ associated with the objective function (3.45a) and an $n$-element vector $\bar{p} = \bar{p}(t)$, not both zero, and vectors $\bar{w} = \bar{w}(t)$ such that the set $(\bar{x}, \bar{u}, \bar{p}_0, \bar{p}, \bar{w})$ satisfies (3.45b), (3.45c) and the following necessary conditions

(a) $\nabla_x \bar{p}_0 F(\bar{x}, \bar{u}) + \nabla_x \bar{p}' g(\bar{x}, \bar{u}) - \nabla_x(\bar{w}'h) + \dot{\bar{p}} = 0$

(b) $\nabla_u \bar{p}_0 F(\bar{x}, \bar{u}) + \nabla_u \bar{p}' g(\bar{x}, \bar{u}) - \nabla_u(\bar{w}'h) = 0$

(c) $\bar{p}_0 = \bar{p}_0(t) =$ a nonpositive constant

(d) $\bar{p}_0 F(\bar{x}, \bar{u}) + \bar{p}' g(\bar{x}, \bar{u}) \geqslant \bar{p}_0 F(\bar{x}, u) + \bar{p}' g(\bar{x}, u)$

for all $u$ satisfying (3.45b) and (3.45c), if the pair $(\bar{x}(t), \bar{u}(t))$ provides an optimal solution of the problem (3.45a) through (3.45c) (under the assumptions and sufficiency conditions mentioned in theorem 3.6). Here $\nabla_x(\cdot)$ denotes the gradient with respect to $x$.

Note that condition (d) specifies the usual version of Pontryagin's maximum principle, where the so-called Hamiltonian function $H$ is written as

$$H(\bar{x}, \bar{u}, \bar{p}) = \bar{p}_0 F(\bar{x}, \bar{u}) + \bar{p}' g(\bar{x}, \bar{u}) \geqslant H(\bar{x}, u, \bar{p}).$$

By fixing $\bar{p}_0 = -1$ and writing $\bar{p} = -\bar{v}$, where $\bar{v}$ is as in theorem 3.6, this theorem follows readily from theorem 3.6. It is easy to show that the two adjoint equations for the Hamiltonian $H$ hold at $(\bar{x}, \bar{p}_0, \bar{p})$, i.e.

$$\dot{\bar{p}}_i = -H_{\bar{x}_i}(i = 0, 1, \ldots, n) \quad \text{and} \quad \dot{\bar{x}}_i = H_{\bar{p}_i}(i = 1, \ldots, n), \quad \bar{p}_0 = -1$$

where the notation $H_{\bar{x}_i}$ is $(\partial H/\partial x_i)$ evaluated at $(\bar{x}, \bar{u}, \bar{p})$ and $H_{\bar{p}_i} = \partial H/\partial p_i$ evaluated at $(\bar{x}, \bar{u}, \bar{p})$.

Now we consider an optimal control problem for the discrete time case. For this purpose, let us restate the KT conditions by separating the constraints $g(x) \geqslant 0$ into two subsets $g_1(x) = 0$, $g_2(x) \geqslant 0$ according as there are equalities or inequalities, where the vector functions $g_1(x)$ and $g_2(x)$ may have $m_1$ and $m - m_1$ components. If $f(x)$ and $-g_1(x)$, $-g_2(x)$ are convex and differentiable in $x$, satisfying the so-called KT constraint qualifications, then in order that the vector $\bar{x}$ minimizes $f(x)$ subject to $g_1(x) = 0$, $g_2(x) \geqslant 0$ it is necessary that there must exist vectors (i.e., Lagrange multipliers) $\bar{v}$ with $m_1$ elements, $\bar{w}$ with $(m - m_1)$ components and the associated vector $\bar{x}$ satisfying the following, where $\phi = f(x) + v' g_1(x) - w' g_2(x)$:

$$\phi_{\bar{x}} = 0; \qquad \phi_{\bar{v}} = 0 \qquad\qquad (3.46a)$$

$$\phi_{\bar{w}} \leqslant 0; \qquad \phi_{\bar{w}}' \bar{w} = 0; \; \bar{w} \geqslant 0. \qquad (3.46b)$$

Note that because of the inequality constraints $g_2(x) \geqslant 0$, the conditions (3.46b) are written as they are, e.g. $\phi'_{\bar{w}} \bar{w} = 0$ and $\bar{w} \geqslant 0$. The sufficient condition that $\bar{x}$ provides a minimum is that the function $\phi = \phi(x, \bar{v}, \bar{w})$ is convex in $x$, i.e.

$$\phi(x, \bar{v}, \bar{w}) \geqslant \phi(\bar{x}, \bar{v}, \bar{x}) + (x - \bar{x})' \phi_{\bar{x}}(\bar{x}, \bar{v}, \bar{w}). \tag{3.46c}$$

Now consider the following discrete-time control problem:

$$\text{Minimize } C = G(x_N) + \sum_{i=0}^{N-1} f(x_i, u_i, i) \tag{3.47a}$$

under the restrictions

$$x_{i+1} = g(x_i, u_i, i); \ i = 0, 1, \dots, N-1 \tag{3.47b}$$

$$h(x_i, u_i, i) \geqslant 0 \tag{3.47c}$$

$$x_i : n.1$$
$$x_0 = c \text{ (constant)}, c \text{ and } N \text{ fixed.} \qquad u_i : m.1 \tag{3.47d}$$
$$h : r.1.$$

Here $i$ is the index for time, $x_i$ is the state vector and $u_i$ is the control vector at time $i$, $G(x_N)$ and $f(x_i, u_i, i)$ are scalar functions of vectors which represent costs associated with the terminal vector $x_N$ and other vectors $x_i$, $u_i$ ($i = 0, 1, \dots, N-1$). The optimal control problem is to determine a sequence $\{x_i, u_{i-1}; \ i = 1, \dots, N\}$ such that the cost $C$ defined in (3.47a) is minimized over all feasible sequences $\{x_i, u_{i-1}; i = 1, \dots, N\}$ satisfying (3.47b) through (3.47d), given that $G(x_N)$, $f(x_i, u_i, i)$ and $-h(x_i, u_i, i)$ are convex in $x_N$, $x_i$, $u_i$ and differentiable, satisfying the KT constraint qualifications.

Now define the $(n+m) N.1$ vector $y$, the $nN.1$ vector $g_1(y)$ and $rN.1$ vector $g_2(y)$ as follows:

$$y = (x_1, \dots, x_N, u_0, \dots, u_{N-1})'$$
$$g_1(y) = (g(x_0, u_0, 0) - x_1, \dots, g(x_{N-1}, u_{N-1}, N-1) - x_N)'$$
$$g_2(y) = (h(x_0, u_0, 0), \dots, h(x_{N-1}, u_{N-1}, N-1))'.$$

Also denote $f(y) = C = G(x_N) + \sum_{i=0}^{N-1} f(x_i, u_i, i)$ and define the Lagrangian function $\phi = \phi(y, v, w)$ as

$$\phi = G(x_N) + \sum_{i=0}^{N-1} [f(x_i, u_i, i) + v'_i(g(x_i, u_i, i) - x_{i+1}) - w'_i h(x_i, u_i, i)]$$

where $v_i : n.1$ and $w_i : r.1$ are Lagrange multiplier vectors. Now the original control problem can be rephrased as:
minimize $f(y) = C$ subject to $g_1(y) = 0$ and $g_2(y) \geqslant 0$ for which the necessary

and sufficient conditions (3.46a) through (3.46c) apply by replacing $x$ with $y$. Hence the following result [33]:

*Theorem 3.8*

The necessary conditions that the sequence of vectors $\{\bar{x}_i, \bar{u}_{i-1}\}$ provides an optimal solution to the discrete control problem (3.47a) through (3.47d) are that there exist Lagrange multiplier vectors $\{\bar{v}_i, \bar{w}_i\}$ satisfying

$$\phi_{\bar{x}_i} = f'_{\bar{x}_i} - \bar{v}'_{i-1} + \bar{v}'_i g_{\bar{x}_i} - \bar{w}'_i h_{\bar{x}_i} = 0, \ i = 1, ..., N-1$$

$$\phi_{\bar{x}_N} = G_{\bar{x}_N} - \bar{v}_{N-1} = 0$$

$$\phi_{\bar{u}_i} = f'_{\bar{u}_i} + \bar{v}'_i g_{\bar{u}_i} - \bar{w}'_i h_{\bar{u}_i} = 0, \ i = 0, 1, ..., N-1$$

$$\phi_{\bar{v}_i} = g\left(x_i, u_i, i\right) - x_{i+1} = 0, \ i = 0, 1, ..., N-1$$

$$x_0 = c, \quad N \text{ fixed}$$

$$\phi_{\bar{w}_i} = -h\left(\bar{x}_i, \bar{u}_i, i\right) \leqslant 0, \ i = 0, 1, ..., N-1$$

$$\bar{w}_i \geqslant 0, \ \bar{w}'_i h\left(\bar{x}_i, \bar{u}_i, i\right) = 0, \ i = 0, 1, ..., N-1.$$

Sufficient conditions for the optimal solution $\{\bar{x}_i, \bar{u}_{i-1}\}$ are that the Lagrangian function $\phi(y, \bar{v}, \bar{w})$ is a convex function of $y$ for values of $v$ and $\bar{w}$ fixed at $\bar{v}$ and $\bar{w}$ respectively. (The notation $f_{\bar{x}i}$ used here denotes $\partial f/\partial x_i$ evaluated at $\bar{x}_i, \bar{u}_i$ and so on for functions $\phi$ and $h$.)

In situations which are of some use in economic policy models [30], the functions $g(x_i, u_i, i)$ in (3.47b) are usually linear in $x_i$ and $u_i$, then if $G(x_N)$ and $f(x_i, u_i, i)$ are convex in $x_N$ and in $x_i, u_i$ respectively, the sufficient conditions certainly hold, as $\phi(y, \bar{v}, \bar{w})$ then becomes convex in $y$. For this case the analogy of this theorem to the discrete maximum principle can be shown, by virtue of the assumption of linearity of $g(x_i, u_i, i)$, i.e.

$$x_{i+1} = g\left(x_i, u_i, i\right) = A_i x_i + B_i u_i; \quad i = 0, ..., N-1 \qquad (3.48)$$

where $A_i, B_i$ are matrices independent of $x_i, u_i$.

For this case, if the conditions of theorem 3.8 hold for (optimal) vectors $(\bar{y}, \bar{v}, \bar{w})$, then by convexity of $\phi$

$$\phi(y, \bar{v}, \bar{w}) \geqslant \phi(\bar{y}, \bar{v}, \bar{w}). \qquad (3.49a)$$

Define the constraint set $R$ as

$$R = \left\{x_i, u_i \mid h(x_i, u_i, i) \geqslant 0; i = 0, 1, ..., N-1\right\}. \qquad (3.49b)$$

Using (3.49a) one could write for any feasible $(x_i, u_i) \in R$ that are not necessarily optimal,

$$f(\bar{x}_i, u_i, i) + \bar{v}'_i(A_i\bar{x}_i + B_iu_i - \bar{x}_{i+1}) - \bar{w}'_ih(\bar{x}_i, u_i, i)$$
$$\geqslant f(\bar{x}_i, \bar{u}_i, i) \qquad (3.49c)$$
$$i = 0, 1, ..., N - 1.$$

However, $\bar{w}'_ih(\bar{x}_i, u_i, i) \geqslant 0$ for all $(\bar{x}_i, u_i) \in R$.
Hence

$$f(\bar{x}_i, u_i, i) + \bar{v}'_i(A_i\bar{x}_i + B_iu_i) \geqslant f(\bar{x}_i, \bar{u}_i, i) + \bar{v}'_i(A_i\bar{x}_i + B_i\bar{u}_i) \qquad (3.49d)$$
$$i = 0, 1, ..., N - 1.$$

This inequality expresses the discrete maximum principle, since by defining the Hamiltonian function $H$ as

$$H = H(x_i, u_i, v_i, i) = f(x_i, u_i, i) + v'_i(A_ix_i + B_iu_i)$$

we could write the optimality condition (3.49d) alternatively as

$$H(\bar{x}_i, \bar{u}_i, \bar{v}_i, i) = \min_{\bar{x}_i, u_i \in R} H(\bar{x}_i, u_i, \bar{v}_i, i) \qquad i = 0, 1, ..., N - 1. \qquad (3.49e)$$

(Note that the maximum principle is stated as a minimum principle here.)
The adjoint equations become

$$\bar{v}'_{i-1} = H'_{\bar{x}_i} - \bar{w}'_ih_{\bar{x}_i}, \quad i = 1, ..., N - 1$$
$$x_{i+1} = H_{\bar{v}_i}, \quad i = 0, 1, ..., N - 1$$
$$H'_{\bar{u}_i} - \bar{w}'_ih_{\bar{u}_i} = 0, \quad i = 0, 1, ..., N - 1$$
$$h(x_i, u_i, i) \geqslant 0, \quad \bar{w}'_ih(x_i, u_i, i) = 0, \quad \bar{w}_i \geqslant 0$$
$$x_0 = c, \bar{v}_{N-1} = G_{x_N}; \quad \text{the notation} \quad H_{\bar{x}_i} = \partial H/\partial x_i \text{ at } \bar{x}_i, \bar{u}_i, \bar{v}_i.$$

Note that here the sufficiency conditions hold for the discrete maximum principle because of the linearity of the model, i.e. relation (3.48).

A few remarks may be made about the discrete maximum principle [34] for the case in which the equations (3.47b) are nonlinear but the functions $g(x_i, u_i, i)$ are continuous and well-defined for all $x_i$ and $u_i$ such that the Jacobian matrix $[\partial g(x_i, u_i)/\partial x_i]$ is continuous and bounded for all $x_i$ and further that $I + [\partial g(x_i, u_i)/\partial x_i]$ is nonsingular for all $x_i, u_i, I$ being the identity matrix. Let the end point $N$ be *free* rather than fixed such that $x_N \in S$ where $S$ is a smooth target set in the state space. Then a generalized discrete control problem may be formulated as:

$$\text{minimize } C = \sum_{i=0}^{N-1} f_i(x_i, u_i) \qquad (3.50a)$$

under the conditions

$$x_{i+1} - x_i = g(x_i, u_i) \qquad (3.50b)$$

$$x_0 = c \quad \text{at} \quad i = 0, \quad \text{at} \quad i = N, x_N \in S \tag{3.50c}$$

$$u_i \in U = \{h(x_i, u_i, i) \geqslant 0\} \quad \text{for all} \quad i = 0, 1, ..., N - 1 \tag{3.50d}$$

where $f_i(x_i, u_i)$ are scalar functions of vectors $x_i$, $u_i$, assumed continuous for all $x_i$, $u_i$ such that the Jacobian matrix $[\partial f_i / \partial x_i]$ is assumed continuous and bounded for all $x_i$ and for every fixed $u_i$. Still we require some assumptions concerning the target set $S$. If it is convex, then the problem (3.50) may have a solution. But a more generalized version of the requirement is what is called "directional convexity" in the control theory literature. This requirement is as follows: let $r, s, t$ be vectors belonging to the constraint set $U$ defined in (3.50c) and $\alpha$ ($0 \leqslant \alpha \leqslant 1$) a scalar; define

$$z_i = z_i(x, u) = (g(x_i, u_i), ..., f_i(x_i, u_i)'$$

where the last component is the scalar, while the other components are vectors. Then the directional convexity assumption is that for all $x = (x_i)$ and for any given vectors $r, s$ and scalar $\alpha(0 \leqslant \alpha \leqslant 1)$, there exists a scalar $\beta > 0$ and a vector $t \in U$ such that

$$z_i(x, t) = \alpha z_i(x, s) + (1 - \alpha) z_i(x, r) + k \tag{3.50e}$$

where $k$ is the column vector $(0, ..., 0, \beta)'$.
Now the Hamiltonian is defined by

$$H_i = H_i(x_i, p_{i+1}, u_i) = f_i(x_i, u_i) + p'_{i+1} g(x_i, u_i) \tag{3.50f}$$
$$\text{for} \quad i = 0, 1, ..., N - 1$$

where the notation $f_i(x_i, u_i)$ is used for the term $f(x_i, u_i, i)$ defined in (3.47a). Then, under the above assumptions, the *necessary conditions* for optimality are as follows:

*Theorem 3.9* (discrete maximum principle)

Let $(\bar{u}_0, \bar{u}_1, ..., \bar{u}_{N-1})$ be the optimal sequence of control vectors and $(\bar{x}_0, \bar{x}_1, ..., \bar{x}_N)$ be the associated optimal sequence of state vectors, then there exists a corresponding sequence of co-state (i.e. Lagrange multipliers) vectors $(\bar{p}_0, \bar{p}_1, ..., \bar{p}_N)$ such that the following conditions hold:
  (a) canonical difference equations

$$\bar{x}_{i+1} - \bar{x}_i = (\partial H / \partial p_{i+1})^*; \qquad \bar{p}_{i+1} - \bar{p}_i = - (\partial H / \partial x_i)^*$$

where the asterisk denotes that the partial derivatives are evaluated at $x_i, \bar{p}_i$
  (b) boundary conditions

$$\bar{x}_0 = c, \bar{x}_N \in S; \qquad \bar{p}_N \text{ normal to } S \text{ at } \bar{x}_N \quad \text{i.e.} \quad \bar{p}'_N \bar{x}_N = 0$$

(c) minimization of the Hamiltonian

$$H_i(\bar{x}_i, \bar{p}_{i+1}, \bar{u}_i) \leqslant H_i(\bar{x}_i, \bar{p}_{i+1}, u_i)$$

for all $u_i \in U$ and all $i = 0, 1, \ldots, N-1$.

### 3.2.1. Generalized methods of control under variational programming

A more generalized treatment of control theory under conditions of variational programming should include at least three other aspects, e.g. (a) specific implications of various different types of control particularly with regard to the sufficiency conditions and the corner points, (b) the methods of computation of optimal control policies, and (c) the analysis of time stability of feedback and optimal control systems. We will make a few remarks on each of these aspects.

Now consider the time continuous control problem presented in (3.45a) through (3.45c) and define $\dot{y} = u$, $y(t=0) = 0$ where $y$ is an $m$-dimensional vector; then the following Bolza-type problem may be presented as a generalization:

Bolza-problem: Find an arc $(x(t), y(t))$ in the $(n+m+1)$-dimensional space $(t, x, y)$ that minimizes

$$G(T, x(T)) + \int_0^T F(x, t, \dot{y}) \, dt \qquad (3.51a)$$

in the class of arcs that are piecewise twice differentiable and continuous, satisfying the system of differential equations

$$g(x, \dot{y}, t) - \dot{x} = 0 \quad x: n.1; u: \quad m.1; t: 1.1 \qquad (3.51b)$$

and the differential inequalities

$$R(x, t, \dot{y}) = -h(x, t, \dot{y}) \geqslant 0; \qquad h: k.1 \qquad (3.51c)$$

and the terminal conditions

$$x(t=0) = x_0, \quad y(t=0) = y_0 = 0; \qquad x(T) = x_T, \quad y(T) = y_T \quad (3.51d)$$

under the assumptions that the scalar functions $F$ and $G$ of vectors $x, u$ and scalar $t$ are real valued, continuous and twice differentiable and the vector functions $g$ and $R$ are continuous, real valued and twice differentiable, such that the constraint vector $R$ satisfies the following *constraint qualifications* [35]:

(i) if $k>m$ (where $k$ is the number of components of vector $R$ and $m$ is the number of components of the control vector $u$), then at most $m$ components of $R$ can vanish at each point of the feasible set $L = D \times U$ where $D$ is a bounded region of $(n+1)$ dimensional $(x, t)$ space and $U$ is the region of feasibility of the $m$-dimensional $u$-space; and

(ii) at each point of the feasible set $L$ the matrix $(\partial R_i / \partial u_j)$ where the index $i$ ranges over those components of $R$ which satisfy $R_i(x, t, u) = 0$ and $j = 1, ..., m$ has maximum rank. (Recall our previous discussion of the non-degeneracy condition in section 3.1.1.)

The Bolza-problem involving inequalities can be converted to an equivalent problem using Valentine's procedure as follows:

*Equivalent Bolza-problem*: Find an arc $(x(t), y(t), s(t))$ where $s = (s_1, ..., s_k)'$ that minimizes (3.51a) in the class of piecewise continuous, twice differentiable arcs satisfying (3.51b) and

$$R(x, t, \dot{y}) - (\dot{s})^2 = 0, \quad \text{where} \quad (\dot{s})^2 = (\dot{s}_1^2, s_2^2, ..., \dot{s}_k^2)' \quad (3.51c)'$$

(with dot denoting time derivative)
and the terminal conditions (3.51d) and

$$s(t = 0) = s_0 = 0, \quad s(T) = s_T. \quad (3.51e)$$

Assuming the existence of such types of control problems [36], let $\bar{u}$ be the optimal feasible control, $\bar{K}$ be the corresponding curve (i.e. arc) and $\bar{x}, \bar{y}, \bar{s}$ be the associated vectors, so that the arc defined by $(\bar{x}(t), \bar{y}(t), \bar{s}(t))$ where

$$\dot{\bar{s}}_i^2(t) = R_i(t, \bar{x}, \dot{y}), \quad \bar{s}_i(0) = 0 \quad (i = 1, ..., k)$$

provides a minimum of the equivalent Bolza problem. Denote this arc by $\bar{\bar{K}}$. Note that by the constraint qualifications, the equations (3.51b) and (3.51c)' are independent at every element $(\bar{x}, \bar{y}, \bar{s}, \dot{\bar{x}}, \dot{\bar{y}}, \dot{\bar{s}})$ of $\bar{K}$ (where, as usual, dot denotes the time derivative). Now since $\bar{\bar{K}}$ provides a minimum, the following necessary conditions must hold along $\bar{K}$ (proved by Berkovitz [35]):

*Theorem 3.10* (Berkovitz)

There exist a constant $\bar{v}_0 \geqslant 0$ and an $n$-dimensional vector $\bar{v}(t)$ and a $k$-dimensional vector $\bar{w}(t)$ defined on the real interval $0 \leqslant t \leqslant T$ such that $(\bar{v}_0, \bar{v}(t), \bar{w}(t))$ are never zero and $(\bar{v}(t), \bar{w}(t))$ are continuous except perhaps at values of $t$ corresponding to corners of $\bar{\bar{K}}$, where they possess unique right and left limits. Moreover the function

$$\bar{F}\left(t, \bar{x}, \bar{y}, \bar{s}, \dot{\bar{x}}, \dot{\bar{y}}, \dot{\bar{s}}, \bar{v}_0, \bar{v}, \bar{w}\right) = \bar{v}_0 F\left(\bar{x}, \bar{u}, t\right) + \bar{v}'\left(g\left(\bar{x}, \bar{u}, t\right) - \dot{\bar{x}}\right) \qquad (3.52a)$$
$$+ \bar{w}'\left(R\left(\bar{x}, \bar{u}, t\right) - (\dot{\bar{s}})^2\right)$$

satisfies the following conditions along the arc $\overline{\overline{K}}$

(i) (Euler-Lagrange conditions): Between corners of $\overline{\overline{K}}$,

$$\frac{\mathrm{d}}{\mathrm{d}t}\bar{F}_{\dot{x}} = \bar{F}_x; \qquad \frac{\mathrm{d}}{\mathrm{d}t}\bar{F}_{\dot{y}} = \bar{F}_y; \qquad \frac{\mathrm{d}}{\mathrm{d}t}\bar{F}_{\dot{s}} = \bar{F}_s, \qquad (3.52b)$$

while at a corner these equations hold for the unique one-sided limits;

(ii) (Weierstrass-Erdmann conditions): At a corner of $\overline{\overline{K}}$, the functions $\bar{F}_{\dot{x}}, \bar{F}_{\dot{y}}, \bar{F}_{\dot{s}}$ and $(\bar{F} - \dot{\bar{x}}'\bar{F}_{\dot{x}} - \dot{\bar{y}}'\bar{F}_{\dot{y}} - \dot{\bar{s}}'\bar{F}_{\dot{s}})$ have well-defined one-sided limits that are equal;

(iii) (Transversality conditions): At the terminal point

$(T, \dot{\bar{x}}_T, \bar{y}_T, \bar{s}_T)$ of $\overline{\overline{K}}$ the following must hold:
$$(\bar{F} - \dot{\bar{x}}'\bar{F}_{\dot{x}} - \dot{\bar{y}}' \bar{F}_{\dot{y}} - \dot{\bar{s}}'\bar{F}_{\dot{s}})\,\mathrm{d}T + \bar{F}'_{\dot{x}}\mathrm{d}x_T + \bar{v}_0\mathrm{d}G(T, \bar{x}_T) = 0 \qquad (3.52c)$$
$$\bar{F}'_{\dot{y}}\bar{y}_T = 0; \; \bar{F}'_{\dot{s}}\bar{s}_T = 0$$

(iv) (Weierstrass condition): For all $(t, \bar{x}, \bar{s}, \bar{y}, \dot{X}, \dot{Y}, \dot{S}) \neq (t, \bar{x}, \bar{s}, \bar{y}, \dot{\bar{x}}, \dot{\bar{y}}, \dot{\bar{s}})$ satisfying (3.51b) and (3.51c)'. The excess function $E \geqslant 0$, where

$$E = \bar{F}\left(t, \bar{x}, \bar{y}, \bar{s}, \dot{X}, \dot{Y}, \dot{S}\right) - \bar{F}\left(t, \bar{x}, \bar{y}, \bar{s}, \dot{\bar{x}}, \dot{\bar{y}}, \dot{\bar{s}}\right) \qquad (3.52d)$$
$$- (\dot{X} - \dot{\bar{x}})'\,\bar{F}_{\dot{x}} - (\dot{Y} - \dot{\bar{y}})'\,\bar{F}_{\dot{y}} - (\dot{S} - \dot{\bar{s}})'\,\bar{F}_{\dot{s}}$$

the functions $\bar{F}_{\dot{x}}, \bar{F}_{\dot{s}}$ being evaluated at $(t, \bar{x}, \bar{y}, \bar{s}, \dot{\bar{x}}, \dot{\bar{y}}, \dot{\bar{s}}, \bar{v}_0, \bar{v}, \bar{w})$, although the arguments $(\bar{v}_0, \bar{v}, \bar{w})$ are omitted throughout. (Here $X, Y, S$ may be regarded as perturbation vectors around $\bar{x}, \bar{y}, \bar{s}$.)

(v) (Clebsch condition): For every vector $(p, r, q) \neq 0$ where $p = (p_1, ..., p_n)'$, $r = (r_1, ..., r_m)'$ and $q = (q_1, ..., q_k)'$ that is a solution of the linear system (derived from (3.51b))

$$g'_y r - I_n p = 0; \qquad I_n = n\text{-order identity matrix}$$
$$R'_y r - 2\hat{\bar{S}}'q = 0 \qquad (3.52e)$$

(where $\hat{\bar{S}}$ is a $k.k$ diagonal matrix with diagonal elements $\dot{\bar{s}}_i$, $i = 1, ..., k$), the following inequality system holds:

$$p'\bar{F}_{\dot{x}\dot{x}}p + r'\bar{F}_{\dot{y}\dot{y}}r - 2\sum_{i=1}^{k} w_i(q_i)^2 \geqslant 0.$$

We note that the conditions of this theorem may be restated in terms of the Hamiltonian function $H$ which is now

$$H(t, x, u, v_0, v) = v_0 F(t, x, u) + v' g(t, x, u)$$

so that along the optimal arc $\bar{K}$ it holds that

$$H(t, \bar{x}, u, \bar{v}_0, \bar{v}) \geqslant H(t, \bar{x}, \bar{u}, \bar{v}_0, \bar{v})$$

for every feasible element $(u \in U)$.

### 3.2.2. *Computation of optimal control*

We have presented the problems of optimal control in such a way that the algorithms of nonlinear programming are directly applicable. However, in control problems which involve the time variable explicitly, special methods have sometimes been found useful. In most practical problems, the continuous version of Pontryagin's maximum principle has to be discretized in time in order to apply computational algorithms, since otherwise the problem of numerical solution of differential equations would have to be faced. Hence, assuming that the control problem has been appropriately discretized in time, we restrict ourselves to the three sets of necessary conditions stated previously in theorem 3.9 and mention several methods of computation of optimal control which have been operationally applied in the control literature:

(a) First group of methods: these methods, based on gradients in the function space, start from an initial solution satisfying conditions (a) and (b) of theorem 3.9 and iterate until condition (c) is satisfied. The basic idea is to make an initial guess as to a feasible control vector $u^{(1)}(t)$, say, such that when substituted in the canonical equations it defines a solution vector $x^{(1)}(t)$ satisfying the boundary conditions. The conjugate gradient method [37] and the gradient projection method [38] have found several applications here.

(b) Second group of methods: these iterative methods use condition (c) of theorem 3.9 to guess a vector of 'shadow prices' $p^{(1)}(t)$ satisfying the condition of minimization of the Hamiltonian and then compute $u^{(1)}(t)$. The vector $u^{(1)}(t)$ is then substituted in the canonical equations (i.e. condition (a)) and by eliminating $u^{(1)}(t)$ we get $(p^{(1)}(t); x^{(1)}(t))$; iterations continue till the boundary conditions (i.e condition (b) of theorem 3.9) are satisfied. Several such iterative methods have been discussed in a survey article by Paiewonsky [39]. Methods using the second variation of the objective functional $C = C(u)$ have proved very powerful here [40].

(c) Third group of methods: these methods, based on Newton-Raphson techniques otherwise known as quasi-linearization, take the same first step as in the second group of methods to guess a vector $p^{(1)}(t)$ and compute $u^{(1)}(t)$ satisfying condition (c) of theorem 3.9 and then eliminate $u^{(1)}(t)$ through the canonical equations to get a coupled system of difference (or differential in time-continuous cases) equations in $(p^{(1)}(t), x^{(1)}(t))$. Since these equations are generally nonlinear, they are linearized about some initial guessed values and this procedure is repeated till the generated trajectories $(p(t), x(t))$ satisfy the difference equations and the boundary conditions. Computational experiences [41] with these methods, which sometimes utilize the second variation of the objective functional $C = C(u)$, suggest that convergence (if it exists) is usually very fast near the optimal solution.

(d) Fourth group of methods: algorithms based on the functional equation technique of dynamic programming have also been applied [42]. Although this method initially blows up the dimensions of the original problem, it develops a sequential method of recursion to solve the optimum problem in stages and thereby obtains some economy in computation.

### 3.2.3. Stability aspects of control

In control problems a distinction is usually drawn between optimal (or adaptive) and feedback controls; whereas in the former there is an objective function which is a performance measure for the whole system, there is no explicit objective function for the latter. Hence, in the latter case the set of feasible control policies has to be evaluated by certain stability criteria rather than by an optimizing criterion.

For instance, consider a simple example of production control mentioned by Simon [43], where the scalars $x$, $u$ and $d$ denote respectively the inventory level, the rate of production and demand for a single product such that

$$\dot{x} = u - d$$
$$e = x - x_0,$$

where $x_0 =$ intended inventory assumed constant and hence zero. The problem is to determine a production policy $u = u(t)$ as a function of $e$ which represents in a sense deviations of actual inventory from the desired level. Possible feedback control policies are

(a) proportional feedback:    $u = -a_1 e + d$
(b) derivative control:    $u = -a_2 \dot{e} + d$
(c) integral control:    $u = -a_3 \int e \, dt + d$
(d) mixed control:    $u = -a_1 e - a_2 \dot{e} - a_3 \int e \, dt + d$

where $a_1, a_2, a_3$ are positive (or nonnegative) constants assumed known or estimated. Now given a forecast pattern of demand $d=d(t)$, these different feedback policies may be evaluated in terms of their impact on the time behavior of $x(t)$. For instance, the mixed control policy would generate oscillations unless

$$(1 + a_2)^2 \geqslant 4a_3(1 + a_2)$$

whereas the proportional and derivative control policies would not have this disadvantage at all.

However, sometimes it may be possible to combine the two apparently competitive objectives of stability and optimality in a control policy. Several applications of these ideas to stabilization policies under macrodynamic economic models have been made by Fox, Sengupta and Thorbecke [30]. Also some of the different types of stability in control theory are discussed in ch. 4.2.

Consider a dynamic model of control involving equalities only:

$$\dot{x} = g(x, u) \qquad x: n.1 \tag{3.53a}$$
$$u: m.1.$$

This control system would be feedback, if the control vector $u$ is a function of the state vector $x$ for all $t$, i.e. $\dot{x}=g(x, u)=g(x, u(x))=\bar{g}(x)$, say. To evaluate the stabilizing tendency of feedback controls of different sorts, one approach frequently used suggests adopting Lyapunov's (real valued) distance function $V(x)$ as a measure of error around the origin (or any other selected point) such that

$$V(x) = V(x - \bar{x}) > 0 \quad \text{for} \quad x - \bar{x} \neq 0, \quad \bar{x} = 0 \text{ (origin)}$$
$$V(0) = 0. \tag{3.53b}$$

Now if $x$ is a solution of the system $\dot{x}=\bar{g}(x)$, such that there exists a Lyapunov function (e.g. the square of the Euclidean length of the vector $x-\bar{x}$) satisfying (3.53b) and either

$$\frac{d}{dt}(V(x(t))) = \dot{V}(x) \leqslant 0 \tag{3.53c}$$

locally around $\bar{x}$ in the neighborhood $N$ of $\bar{x}$,

$$\frac{d}{dt}(V(x)) = \dot{V}(x) < 0 \quad \text{for all} \quad x \in N \text{ around } \bar{x} \quad \text{and} \quad x \neq 0 \tag{3.53d}$$

then the feedback control system at $\bar{x}$ is stable, if (3.53b) and (3.53c) are satisfied, asymptotically stable, if (3.53b) and (3.53d) hold and asymptotically stable in the large, if the neighborhood $N$ is large.

Now we consider the problem of improving the stability of a linearly controlled system subject to an optimizing criterion. Suppose the controlled system is given in the form:

$$\dot{x} = Ax + Bu; \quad x:n.1; \quad u:m.1; \quad A:n.n; \quad B:n.m \quad (3.54a)$$

where $A$ and $B$ are constant matrices and the uncontrolled system derived from (3.54a) i.e.

$$\dot{x} = Ax; \quad u = 0 \quad (3.54b)$$

is assumed to be stable asymptotically. Now consider a quadratic cost functional

$$C(x_0, u) = \int_0^\infty (x'Mx + u'Ru)\,dt \quad (3.54c)$$

as a performance measure of the controlled system, where $x_0 =$ the vector of initial values and the square matrices $M$ and $R$ are assumed to be positive definite and known (note that $x'Mx$ may represent cost of error and $u'Ru$ the cost of control). Our objective is to select a control vector $u$ that increases stability at and the same time reduces the cost functional (3.54c). Select a Lyapunov function $V(x)$ as

$$V(x) = x'Qx, \quad \text{where } Q \text{ satisfies} \quad A'Q + QA = -M \quad (3.54d)$$

since $\dot{V}(x) = \dot{x}'Qx + x'Q\dot{x} = x'AQx + x'QAx$ from (3.54b). Note that with no control ($u=0$), $\dot{V}(x) = -x'Mx$ and since the uncontrolled system is asymptotically stable, we can set

$$V(x_0) = C(x_0, 0), \quad \text{i.e.} \quad u = 0 \quad (3.54e)$$

where $V(x_0) = \int_0^\infty -\dot{V}(x)\,dt = \int_0^\infty x'Mx\,dt$.

Now for the system with control ($u \neq 0$), along its solution path

$$\dot{V}(x) = -x'Mx + u'BQx + x'QBu = -x'Mx + 2u'B'Qx \quad (3.54f)$$

$$= -x'Mx - u'Pu, \quad \text{where } P \text{ is any positive definite matrix } (m.m)$$

satisfying

$$-Pu = 2B'Qx. \quad (3.54g)$$

If there exists such a matrix $P$, then it can be shown that such a control $u$ has asymptotic stability and also improves under certain conditions the performance of the system. Obviously now

$$\dot{V}(x) = -x'Mx - u'Pu \leqslant 0 \tag{3.54h}$$

since $M$ and $P$ are positive definite matrices. To obtain the scalar quantity $V(x) = V(x, u)$ from (3.54f) note that $V(x)$ is a nonnegative quantity: we then obtain at $x = x_0$,

$$V(x_0, u) = \int_0^\infty x'Mx + \int_0^\infty u'Pu \, dt = C(x_0, 0) + \int_0^\infty u'Pu \, dt.$$

Therefore

$$C(x_0, u) = C(x_0, 0) + \int_0^\infty u'Ru \, dt$$

$$= V(x_0, u) - \int_0^\infty u'(P - R)u \, dt;$$

hence

$$V(x_0, u) - C(x_0, u) = \int_0^\infty u'(P - R)u \, dt \geqslant 0 \tag{3.54i}$$

if $(P - R)$ is positive definite. The positive definiteness of $(P - R)$ could be ensured for example, if there exists a scalar $h > 1$ such that $P = hR$, i.e. $P > R$. And since $V(x_0, u)$ could be interpreted as $V(x_0, 0) = V(x_0)$ if $u = u_0 = 0$ is fixed to satisfy the initial condition $x = x_0$ of the system, the inequality (3.54i) has the interpretation that the control vector $u$ which satisfies (3.54h) and (3.54i) with $h > 1$ increases stability and also reduces the cost functional (3.54c) compared to $V(x_0, u)$.

Note that the specifications (3.54i) and (3.54g) are only special cases of a more general formulation which is possible. For instance, other types of Lyapunov functions may be chosen; and even if there exists a positive definite matrix $P$, the condition $h > 1$ may be too strict. Another possible formulation would be to solve for the vector $u$ from the following nonlinear problem:

minimize $C(x_0, u) = V(x_0, u) - \int_0^\infty u'(P - R)u \, dt$
under the conditions
$P$ positive semi-definite, $x_0 =$ initial state vector
$u = u_0$ is the control vector associated with $x_0$ and,
$V(x_0, u) - \int_0^\infty u'(P - R)u \, dt \geqslant 0$.

However, this may give rise to a very complicated nonlinear problem and the solution may not always exist. Lee and Markus [36] and others [44] have studied the question of existence of a nonempty domain of controllability for the problem of optimal control for nonlinear processes.

Operationally speaking, a more generalized and useful formulation of the above control problem of combining stability with optimality is possible, if there is a single feedback control (i.e. $u$ is a scalar) intended. For instance, consider the problem of finding such a control $u \in U$ which satisfies

$$\dot{x} = f(x) + bu; \qquad\qquad x, \quad b: n.1$$
$$u: 1.1; f: n.1 \qquad (3.55a)$$

and minimizes the performance index $\qquad f:$ differentiable
(i.e. cost)

$$C = \int_0^T (u^2 + g(x)) \, dt \qquad (3.55b)$$

where $g(x)$ is a suitable scalar nonnegative and differentiable function of vector $x$, the initial state $x(0) = x_0$ is arbitrary and the desired terminal state $x(T)$ is assumed finite and attainable ($T$ could be $\infty$) and hence equated to zero without loss of generality. Denote by $V^*(x_0)$ the value of the performance index $C$ in (3.55b) for given initial state $x_0$ and the optimal control $u^*$, i.e.

$$V^*(x_0) = C(x, u^*) = \int_0^T (u^2 + g(x)) \, dt. \qquad (3.55c)$$

Denote the Hamiltonian function $H$ as

$$H(x, u, -\nabla V^*(x)) = -\nabla(V^*(x))' \cdot \dot{x} - (u^2 + g(x)) \qquad (3.55d)$$

where $\dot{x}$ satisfies (3.55a), $\nabla V(x)$ is the gradient of $V(x)$ and prime denotes transpose. A necessary condition of optimality if it exists and satisfies the so-called constraint qualifications is given by

$$-\max_u H(x, u, -\nabla V^*(x)) = 0; \, u \in U,$$

which implies

$$\tfrac{1}{4}(\nabla V^{*\prime} b)^2 - \nabla V^{*\prime} f(x) - g(x) = 0. \qquad (3.55e)$$

However, this differential equation may be difficult to solve except in very special cases when $f(x)$ and $g(x)$ take special forms. Two types of attempts have been made in this situation. First, an approximate solution to this problem has been sought [45] by expanding $f(x)$ (and sometimes $g(x)$) in a Taylor series and then solving the equation (3.55e) explicitly (and also checking to see that the sufficient conditions are satisfied locally for this approximate solution). Second, as in the arbitrary functional form of the Lyapunov function discussed in (3.54d) before, a positive definite function $V(x)$ is assumed to replace the optimal function $V^*(x)$ in (3.55c) and instead of maximizing the Hamiltonian function, the following equation is solved:

$$- H\big(x, u, - \nabla V(x)\big) = u^2 + \nabla V'(x) \cdot bu + \nabla V'(x) \cdot f(x) + g(x) = 0$$

which implies the following controls ($u^{(1)}$, $u^{(2)}$), since $V(x)$ is a positive definite quadratic form:

$$u^{(1)} = u_{00}(x) + \big(H_{00}(x)\big)^{\frac{1}{2}}; \; u^{(1)} \in U \qquad (3.55f)$$

$$u^{(2)} = u_{00}(x) - \big(H_{00}(x)\big)^{\frac{1}{2}}; \; u^{(2)} \in U \qquad (3.55g)$$

where, $u_{00}(x) = u_{max}(x) = -(\tfrac{1}{2})\nabla V'(x) \cdot b$

$$H_{00}(x) = H_{max}(x) = (\tfrac{1}{2}\nabla V'(x) \cdot b)^2 - \nabla V'(x) \cdot f(x) - g(x).$$

Note that $u^{(1)}$, $u^{(2)}$ are solved as feedback controls, i.e. as functions of the state vector $x = x(t)$. Also if $H_{00}(x) < 0$ for all real $x$, then from (3.55f), (3.55g) it follows that $u^{(1)}$, $u^{(2)}$ are imaginary numbers and hence such controls are not physically realizable. If $H_{00}(x) \geqslant 0$ for all real $x$, then the equations (3.55f) and (3.55g) suggest that any control $u(x)$ falling between the two controls $u^{(1)}$, $u^{(2)}$ (i.e. $u^{(2)} \leqslant u(x) \leqslant u^{(1)}$) is a better suboptimal control than either $u^{(1)}$ or $u^{(2)}$. This result can be stated [46] formally in a somewhat general context with $T = \infty$.

*Theorem 3.11*

Let the integrand $(u^2 + g(x))$ in (3.55b) be a stationary positive definite function of vector $x$; let the Lyapunov function $V(x_0)$ for (3.55a) with initial state $x_0$ and the controls $u(x)$ satisfying (3.55f) and (3.55g) be positive definite. If this Lyapunov function $V(x)$ for $x$ within its feasible domain yields a pair of controls $u^{(1)}$, $u^{(2)}$ defined in (3.55f), (3.55g) such that $H_{00}(x) \geqslant 0$ for $x$ in its feasible domain, then for any other control $u^{(3)} = u^{(3)}(x)$ satisfying the inequality $u^{(2)} \leqslant u^{(3)} \leqslant u^{(1)}$, the corresponding value of the Lyapunov function $V_3(x)$ satisfies the inequality $V_3(x) \leqslant V(x)$.

*Proof*: Define the Hamiltonian function $H$

$$- H(x, u, - \nabla V) = u^2 + \nabla V'(x) \cdot bu + \nabla V'(x) \cdot f(x) + g(x)$$

which equals zero by hypothesis as mentioned before. Then

$$\dot{V}(x)|_u = - u^2 - g(x) - H(x, u, - \nabla V)$$

where $\dot{V}(x)_u$ denotes the time derivative of $V(x)$ evaluated along (3.55a). By hypothesis, $H(x, u^{(1)} \text{ or } u^{(2)}, -\nabla V)=0$; also

$$\left(\frac{\partial H}{\partial u}\right)_{u=u^{(1)}} = 2(H_{\max}(x))^{\frac{1}{2}}; \left(\frac{\partial H}{\partial u}\right)_{u=u^{(2)}} = - 2(H_{\max}(x))^{\frac{1}{2}}$$

where $H_{\max}(x) \geqslant 0$ and $H(x, u^{(3)}, -\nabla V) \geqslant 0$ for all $u^{(2)} \leqslant u^{(3)} \leqslant u^{(1)}$ by hypothesis. Now the existence of a positive definite Lyapunov function $V(x)$ for the dynamic model (3.55a) satisfying $\dot{V}(x)|_u \leqslant 0$ implies asymptotic stability of the differential equation system (3.55a). Also evaluating $V(x)$ and $V_3(x)$ along $u^{(3)}$ separately,

$$\dot{V}(x)|_{u=u^{(3)}} = - (u^{(3)})^2 - g(x) - H(x, u^{(3)}, - \nabla V)$$
$$\geqslant - (u^{(3)})^2 - g(x) = \dot{V}_3(x)|_{u=u^{(3)}}.$$

Then, on integrating both sides of the above inequality between $t=0$ and $t=\infty$ and noting that $x(\infty)=0$ and $V_3(0)=V(0)=0$, one gets

$$V(x) \geqslant V_3(x) \geqslant 0. \qquad \text{(Q.E.D.)}$$

For economic and operations research models, this result is useful in several respects. First, it gives a method of generating a sequence of suboptimal controls which under certain conditions will converge to the exact optimal solution. Second, this result uses the class of feedback controls (e.g. $u$ as a function of the state vector $x$) to determine a sequence of suboptimal controls and hence the optimal control whenever it exists. (This procedure of combining feedback controls with optimizing properties is quite an ingenious device which may have several applications in short-term stabilization policies using a macrodynamic model, where $u$ could conceivably be government expenditure and $x$ could be the vector of sectoral outputs.) Third, some of the results of nonlinear stability analysis [47] could be conceived in the framework of nonlinear variational programming.

### 3.2.4. *Applications of variational programming and control*

One of the most interesting fields of application of continuous-time variational programming is in the theory of the firm, where it is required to determine the minimum cost production schedule [48] for a commodity over a fixed planning horizon $[0, T]$. Denote by scalar number $x(t)$ the cumulative output up to time $t$ (i.e. $X(t)=h_0+$cumulative production from

0 to $t$, where $h_0 =$ initial inventory assumed nonnegative), $\dot{X}$ the current rate of output per unit time, $f(\dot{X})$ the current production cost function assumed convex such that the marginal cost function $\partial f(\dot{X})/\partial \dot{X}$ is monotone increasing, differentiable, $S(t)$ the cumulative sales (i.e. quantity demanded) assumed exogenous (e.g. forecast) and the total inventory cost is assumed to be proportional to $\alpha(X - S)$ at any time $t$, where $\alpha$ is assumed to be a fixed nonnegative constant. The problem is then to

$$\underset{X(t)}{\text{minimize}} \; C = \int_0^T [\alpha(X - S) + f(\dot{X})] \, dt$$

under the following restrictions

$X(0) = h_0$ given, $X(T) = S(T)$, $T$ fixed and finite.
$X(t) \geqslant S(t)$ for $0 \leqslant t \leqslant T$; $S(t)$ given        (3.56)
$X(t)$ assumed continuous, nondecreasing with piecewise continuous derivatives.

This model, also known as the Modigliani-Hohn production model, could be solved by applying our earlier theorems on Kuhn-Tucker-Euler-Lagrange conditions, particularly theorem 3.10 of section 3.2.1. For the interior solutions, the Euler-Lagrange necessary conditions are:

$$\ddot{X} \cdot f_{\dot{X}\dot{X}} = \alpha; \quad \text{where} \quad \ddot{X} = d^2X/dt^2, \quad f_{\dot{X}\dot{X}} = \frac{\partial^2 f(\dot{X})}{\partial \dot{X} \cdot \partial \dot{X}}$$

whereas on the boundary solutions, where $X(t) = S(t)$, this becomes

$$\ddot{X} f_{\dot{X}\dot{X}} \geqslant \alpha.$$

At any corner point solution $X_c$, where $\dot{X}_c$ may not exist, although by assumption the left-hand $\dot{X}_{c-}$ and right-hand $\dot{X}_{c+}$ derivatives must exist, the following corner condition must also hold:

$$f(\dot{X}_{c+}) - f(\dot{X}_{c-}) = (\dot{X}_{c+} - \dot{X}_{c-}) \cdot f_{\dot{X}_{c-}}.$$

These three types of solutions (i.e. interior points, boundary points and corner points) exhaust all the possibilities here and since by the convexity of $f(\dot{X})$ and the monotone increasing property of the marginal cost function $\partial f(\dot{X})/\partial \dot{X}$ the sufficiency conditions for a minimum are fulfilled, therefore the problem is in principle solved.

Note that the above problem can be generalized even in the single product framework in two important directions. First, the cumulative demand $S(t)$ may be probabilistic rather than deterministic, in which case the objective function of model (3.56) has to be replaced by an expected cost function $EC$, i.e.

$$EC = \int_0^T \left[ \int_0^X \alpha(X - S)\, p(S)\, \mathrm{d}S + \int_X^\infty \beta(S - X)\, p(S)\, \mathrm{d}S + f(\dot{X}) \right] \mathrm{d}t$$

where $p(S)$ is the probability density function of $S$ and $\beta$ is a cost parameter per unit of excess demand; also the inequality $X(t) \geqslant S(t)$, $t \in [0, T]$ has now to be changed either by methods of probabilistic programming discussed in ch. 5 or by dropping it altogether by absorbing it in a very high positive value of the cost parameter $\beta$. A second line of extension of this model is to consider a discrete-time analogue of it.

For the discrete time case the concept of a linear decision rule for employment and production scheduling for a single product plant (firm) has been successfully applied by Holt, Modigliani, Muth and Simon [49]; also such methods have been applied to macrodynamic economic models of stabilization by Theil [50], Holt [51] and Sengupta [52]. The main objective of determining a linear decision rule for varying production and employment levels of a single product factory in order to adjust to fluctuations in orders is that it has certain optimal properties, if the errors in the equations are independent of the control variables and the objective function is quadratic (the concept of linear decision rules with such optimal properties is much emphasized in the context of what is called the certainty equivalence theorem in the theory of economic policy [53]). Consider the following cost components $(C_{it})$ comprising the total cost $C_T$ over the fixed planning horizon $[1, T]$ where

$$C_T = \sum_{t=1}^T (C_{1t} - C_{2t} + C_{3t} + C_{4t}). \tag{3.57a}$$

It is assumed that the firm operates under perfect competition, so that prices and sales are exogenous and cost minimization implies profit maximization. The decision rules are intended for the production manager, who on the basis of forecast demand or order rate $(r_t)$ plans to vary his employment schedule (i.e. $x_{1t} = $ work force in man-months) and production rate (i.e. $x_{2t} = $ volume of output in month $t$) so that the expected value of total cost $EC_T$ defined in (3.57a) is minimized under the inventory restrictions, e.g.

$$x_{2t} + x_{3t-1} \geqslant r_t \tag{3.57b}$$

where $x_{2t} \geqslant 0$ and $x_{3t} = $ net inventory at $t = $ gross inventory less back orders, i.e.

$$x_{3t} = x_{2t} + x_{3t-1} - r_t. \tag{3.57c}$$

It is assumed that decisions are made at regular time intervals, so that time series observations are available for estimating the cost components $C_{it}$ of (3.57a) through regression functions. The following regression estimates were obtained by Holt-Modigliani-Muth-Simon (HMMS) in a study relating to a paint factory:

$C_{1t}$ = regular payroll cost = $c_1 x_{1t} + u_{1t}$

$C_{2t}$ = cost of hiring and lay-off = $c_2 (x_{1t} - x_{1t-1})^2 + u_{2t}$

$C_{3t}$ = cost of overtime, approximated by

$\quad = c_3 (x_{2t} - x_{2t}^*)^2 + c_5 x_{2t} - c_6 x_{1t} + u_{3t}$

where $x_{2t}^*$ = desired production rate = $c_4 x_{1t}$

$C_{4t}$ = inventory, back order and set-up costs, approximated by

$\quad = c_7 (x_{3t} - x_{3t}^*)^2 + u_{4t}$, where $x_{3t}^*$ = desired inventory = $c_8 + c_9 r_t$.

Here the coefficients $c_1$ through $c_9$ (which are nonnegative) are parameters estimated by least squares and the $u_{it}$'s are equational errors assumed to be mutually independent with finite variances and zero means (and zero auto-correlation). Since this problem involves no essential inequalities except (3.57b), it can be solved without applying either the generalized ELKT conditions or the discrete maximum principle. The decision rule computed in the straight-forward manner requires for each month ($t$) a computation of the production rate and work force, e.g.

$$x_{2t} = \sum_{i=0}^{T-1} \alpha_i \hat{r}_{t+i} + \beta x_{1t-1} - \gamma x_{3t-1} + \delta$$

$$x_{1t} = \sum_{i=0}^{T-1} a_i \hat{r}_{t+i} + b x_{1t-1} - c x_{3t-1} - d$$

where $\alpha_i, \beta, \gamma, a_i, b, c, d$, are parameters and $\hat{r}_{t+i}$ is the forecast level of demand at $t+i$ months hence, made in month $t$. The advantage of this analytic linear decision rule is that it allows sequential revision of policies over time, as the precision of forecasting improves. As a matter of fact, even if substantial errors are made in estimating the parameters of the component cost functions, the factory performance in terms of linear decision rules will not be much affected, if the assumptions mentioned before are satisfied.

An interesting economic field in which methods of variational programming have recently been applied is in the theory of optimal growth and the associated problems of investment allocation over time [54]. Basically the problem here is to determine an optimal pattern of investment over time in physical and human capital subject to several constraints of production and distribution, the optimality being defined in terms of the specific form (or class) of the objective function. One possible formulation of this problem suggested by Dobell and Ho [55] is as follows:

$$\underset{s(t),\, e(t)}{\text{maximize}} \; J = \int_0^T (1 - s - e)\, wf \exp(-\gamma t)\, dt \qquad (3.58a)$$

subject to

$$\dot{r} = swf - (n + \delta)\, r;\; r(0) = r_0 \text{ preassigned}; \qquad f = f(r/w) \qquad (3.58b)$$

$$\dot{w} = (ewf/d) - (n + \mu)\, w;\; w(0) = w_0 \text{ preassigned} \qquad (3.58c)$$

$$s \geqslant 0,\, e \geqslant 0,\, 0 \leqslant s + e \leqslant 1 \qquad (3.58d)$$

$$0 \leqslant w \leqslant 1,\, r \geqslant 0 \qquad (3.58e)$$

and to terminal conditions

$$r(T) = r_T;\; w(T) = w_T. \qquad (3.58f)$$

Here the total output $Q$ of an economy is viewed as a function i.e., a regular and well-behaved production function of capital ($K$) and labor ($W$):

$$Q = F(K, W); \qquad \frac{\partial F}{\partial K} > 0, \quad \frac{\partial F}{\partial W} > 0; \qquad \frac{\partial^2 F}{\partial K^2} < 0, \quad \frac{\partial^2 F}{\partial W^2} < 0 \qquad (3.59a)$$

with $F$ assumed homogeneous of degree one in $K$ and $W$. This output is divided between consumption ($C$), investment in physical capital ($I = \dot{K} + \delta K$ where $\dot{K}$ = time derivative of $K$) and investment in training newly employed labor ($E = d_0(\dot{W} + \mu W)$ i.e.

$$C = F(K, W) - I - E = F(K, W) - (\dot{K} + \delta K) - d_0(\dot{W} + \mu W) \qquad (3.59b)$$

where, $\delta$ = depreciation rate, $d_0$ = cost of training, $\mu$ = proportion of existing labor requiring training – these are assumed constant. Define $s = I/Q$, $e = E/Q$; then the requirement of nonnegative consumption ($C \geqslant 0$) specifies the constraint (3.58d). Total labor force ($L$) whether employed or not is assumed to grow exogenously at an exponential rate $L = L_0 \exp(nt), L(0) = L_0$ and the assumption of full employment requires $W \leqslant L$. Define $r = K/L$, $w = W/L$ and, for finite time horizon, the terminal targets may be expressed as $W(T)/L(T) \geqslant w_T$ and $K(T)/L(T) \geqslant r_T$ with preassigned $w_T$ and $r_T$. The time rate of growth of $r$ and $w$ may be easily derived from (3.59a) and other substitutions as

$$\left.\begin{array}{l} \dot{r} = swf\,(r/w) - (n + \delta)\,r \\[2mm] \dot{w} = \dfrac{e}{d_0}\cdot wf\,(r/w) - (n + \mu)\,w \end{array}\right| \begin{array}{l} \text{here } f\,(r) \text{ denotes } F\,(r, 1) \\[2mm] \text{i.e. } f\,(r/w) = F\,(K/W, 1). \end{array}$$

These restrictions are in fact (3.58b) and (3.58c). With $\gamma$ as the fixed and positive discount rate, the objective function is the cumulative sum of discounted per capita consumption, i.e.

$$J = \int\limits_0^T (\exp(-\gamma t)\,C(t)/L(t))\,dt \text{ is as in (3.58a)}.$$

Here the planning problem is to determine the investment policy in terms of $s(t)$, $e(t)$ which maximizes $J$ in (3.58a) under the constraints above. One case which requires some analysis here is the case of singular controls, where the Hamiltonian may be independent in some sense of the decision variables. Hence, define the Hamiltonian function $H$ as

$$H = (1 - s - e)\,wf\,\exp(-\gamma t) + \lambda_r\big(swf - (n + \delta)\,r\big) + (\lambda_w + q) \qquad (3.59\text{c})$$
$$\left\{\frac{ewf}{d_0} - (n + \mu)\,w\right\}$$

where,

$$q = \begin{cases} 0, \text{ if } w < 1 \\ \leqslant 0, \text{ if } w = 1 \end{cases}$$

$\lambda_r$, $\lambda_w$ are Lagrange multipliers and not partial derivatives. Denote the partial derivative $\partial H/\partial x$ by $H_x$; then consider the case defined by

$$H_s - H_e = 0; \qquad H_s = H_e > 0 \qquad (3.59\text{d})$$

which implies $s + e = 1$ and from the Euler-Lagrange equations, i.e.

$$\dot{\lambda}_r = H_r, \; \dot{\lambda}_w = -H_w \text{ it follows that } \lambda_r = \lambda_w/d_0 \text{ along (3.59d)}$$

which defines a singular trajectory. Here using the notation $f = f\,(r/w)$,

$$H_e = \left(\frac{\lambda_w}{d_0} - \exp(-\gamma t)\right)\cdot wf\,; \; H_s = (\lambda_r - \exp(-\gamma t))\cdot wf$$

which shows that $H_e$ and $H_s$ do not involve the control variables $e$ and $s$ and hence the maximization of the Hamiltonian $H$ does not determine the optimal value of the control variables. In this case the singular control variables are determined by

$$\frac{d^2}{dt^2} H_s = 0, \qquad \frac{d^2}{dt^2} H_e = 0. \tag{3.59e}$$

Furthermore, on these 'singular trajectories' it is necessary to have

$$\frac{\partial}{\partial u_i} \frac{d^2}{dt^2} \left( \frac{\partial H}{\partial u_i} \right) \geqslant 0 \qquad u_i = s \text{ or } e \quad \text{(the control variables)}. \tag{3.59f}$$

Applying (3.59e) to the problem above we get after some computation

$$f \left( sw - \frac{er}{d_0} \right) - (\delta - \mu) r = 0$$

from which,

$$s = (wf - (\delta - \mu) r)/(f (w + r/d_0))$$
$$e = (f r/d_0 + (\delta - \mu) r)/(f (w + r/d_0)).$$

These relations can be used to specify differential equations for $r$, $w$, $\lambda_r$ and $\lambda_w$.

Consider another singular case defined by $H_s < 0$ (which implies $s = 0$) and $H_e = 0$ (which implies $\lambda_w = d_0 \exp(-\gamma t)$);
hence $\dot{\lambda}_w = -d_0 \cdot \gamma \exp(-\gamma t)$
which implies

$$f - \frac{r f_K}{w} = (n + \mu + \gamma) d_0, \quad \text{where} \quad f_K = \frac{\partial f (r/w)}{\partial K}$$

further differentiation yields

$$e = (\mu - \delta) \cdot d_0/f; \qquad s = 0,$$

which provide optimal singular controls. Similarly, other cases of singular control can be characterized.

Extensions of the above model for optimum growth have been made in several directions, of which three may be specially mentioned. First, there is the extension to Von Neumann type models with a nonlinear framework [23]. Second, the various methods of incorporating technical change in the production function (3.59e) and specifying the optimal rate of technical change [54] particularly with several capital goods with different vintages offer another useful approach. Third, some attempts have been made to link [54] the computational steps for optimal control with the decomposition techniques discussed in ch. 2, particularly the Arrow-Hurwicz type gradient methods. However, several basic issues are as yet unsolved in this area.

Another interesting field of application of variational programming and control is in aggregative and sectoral models of educational planning [56], where interesting issues are involved in imputing prices for nonmarket categories and activities.

### 3.3. Methods of dynamic programming

Dynamic programming may be viewed either as a computational technique or as a sequential approach towards optimizing the overall performance of a system characterized by distinct stages over which decisions may be made. For instance, as a computational technique the functional equation method of dynamic programming may be employed for solving nonlinear programming problems, in which for instance the objective function may not be differentiable or the constraint set may require integer values for some or all components of the solution. As a sequential approach, the method of dynamic programming may be closely related to the various decomposition and decentralization procedures mentioned in ch. 2.4. This sequential approach is particularly interesting in stochastic process models (e.g. the method of transition probability programming is discussed in ch. 5.1.), in which the decisions at later stages do not affect the performance of the earlier ones but nonetheless the expected penalty costs at any stage may be built into the original objective function (e.g. this is frequently done in a static context in two-stage linear programming under uncertainty, which is discussed in ch. 5.1).

Consider an $N$-stage discrete process with $x$ as the state vector and $u$ as the decision vector with their values after stage $n$ denoted by $x_n$ and $u_n$ $(n=1,\ldots, N)$. A model involving a sequence of decisions at different stages with their effects on the state variables may be generally viewed as a transformation $T_n$:

$$x_n = T_n(x_{n+1}; u_n) \tag{3.60a}$$

which means that given $u_n$ and $x_{n+1}$ it is possible to compute $x_n$ by means of the transformation $T_n$ which may be very simple or very complicated and nonlinear. Note that the decision vector $u_n$ at state $n$ affects only the subsequent states $x_n, x_{n-1}, \ldots, x_1$ and has no effect on preceding states $x_{n+1}$, $\ldots, x_N$. Such decision processes are processes without any feedback. For such processes an admissible policy is called optimal, if there exists a sequence of decision vectors $\{u_n\}$ satisfying all the constraints and optimizing an objective function which can be generally denoted by $J = \sum_{n=1}^{N} P_n (x_{n+1};$

$u_n$), $P_n(x_{n+1}; u_n)$ being a suitable function. The problem of determining such a sequence $\{u_{n-1}, x_n\}$ over discrete time periods we have already encountered in theorem 3.8 of section 3.2 but in those cases the functions $P_n(x_{n+1}; u_n)$ were assumed concave and differentiable everywhere. But if the functions $P_n$ are not differentiable and concave everywhere or some $x$'s are required to be integers or $J$ has a number of local maxima, it is extremely difficult to apply the Euler-Lagrange and gradient methods we have discussed before. In such cases if the optimum solution exists, the computational technique of dynamic programming developed very extensively by Bellman [57] provides an approach to finding such an optimum. This approach is based on the following principle of optimality: An optimal policy has the property that whatever the initial state and initial decision are, the remaining decisions must constitute an optimal policy with regard to the state resulting from the first decision.

To see how this optimality principle is applied to generate functional (recurrence) equations, assume that the $(n-1)$th stage optimal policy has been found at which $\sum_{k=1}^{n-1} P_k(x_{k+1}; u_k)$ is the maximum; denote this maximum value of the objective function by $f_{n-1}(x_n)$, since the maximum of the objective function will be a function of $x_n$ only. Now the objective functions for $n$ stages are

$$P_n(x_{n+1}; u_n) + \sum_{k=1}^{n-1} P_k(x_{k+1}; u_k)$$

where if $u_n$ is optimally selected, the optimal value of the objective function for $n$th stage policy will be

$$f_n(x_{n+1}) = \max_{\{u_n\}} [P_n(x_{n+1}; u_n) + f_{n-1}(x_n)] \qquad (3.60b)$$

where $x_n$ is related to $(u_n; x_{n+1})$ through (3.60a). For $n=1,\dots, N$ and with $f_0(x_1)=0$ the recurrence equation (3.60b), also called the functional equation, can be solved by successive iterations. In these iterations successive computations of optimal controls $u_n$ which can also be written as $u_n(x_{n+1})$ may not be unique; also these controls $u_n$ and state variables $x_n$ will be subject to restrictions at each stage of iteration.

Consider an example of stabilization policy in a macrodynamic model, due to Aris [58], where the state vector at any stage $n$ has three components $y_n$ =national income, $z_n = y_n - y_{n+1}$ and $h_n$ =cumulative sum of net govern- ment spending $(g_k)$ up to the $(n-1)$th stage$=\sum_{k=1}^{n-1} g_k = \bar{g} - \sum_n^N g_k$, with $\bar{g}$ being the total amount of government expenditures assumed to be fixed over the whole period, i.e. $\bar{g} = \sum_{n=1}^N g_n$. The only decision variable is government expenditure $g_n$ which is subject to the constraint

$$0 \leqslant g_n \leqslant h_{n+1} \leqslant \bar{g}; \quad n = 1, ..., N. \tag{3.61a}$$

The problem has the following objective function:

$$\text{maximize [the minimum of } \{y_1, ..., y_N\}] \tag{3.61b}$$

and the model involving the state and control variables is a typical multiplier-accelerator model of macroeconomic theory:

$$y_n = a y_{n+1} + ab z_{n+1} + g_n \tag{3.61c}$$

$$z_n = (a - 1) y_{n+1} + ab z_{n+1} + g_n \tag{3.61d}$$

$$h_n = h_{n+1} - g_n. \tag{3.61e}$$

In the notation of dynamic programming, define

$$f_N(y_{N+1}, z_{N+1}, h_{N+1}) = \max [\min \{y_1, ..., y_N\}] \tag{3.61f}$$

where the maximization is performed by suitable choice of the sequence $(g_1, ..., g_N)$. Consider the optimality principle for determining a $g_N$ which maximizes the lesser of the two quantities $y_N$ and $\min(y_1, ..., y_{N-1})$. This leads to the functional equation

$$f_N(y_{N+1}, z_{N+1}, h_{N+1}) = \max_{\{g_N\}} [\min \{y_N, f_{N-1}(y_N, z_N, h_N)\}]. \tag{3.61g}$$

Consider the following parameters $a = \frac{1}{2}$, $b = 1$ and $N = 4$ and $h_4 = 1$ for numerical purposes and see how the total government expenditure could be allocated among three years in order to maximize the minimum national income. Applying (3.61f) for $N = 1$,

$$f_1(y_2, z_2, h_2) = \max y_1$$
$$= \max (0.5(y_2 + z_2) + g_2); \quad \text{from (3.61c)} \tag{3.61h}$$
$$= 0.5(y_2 + z_2) + h_2, \quad \text{since} \quad h_n = \sum_{k=1}^{n-1} g_k$$

and the best policy is to spend all that is left, i.e.
$g_1 = h_2$ (since the coefficient of $h_2$ in (3.61h) is unity) and this follows from $h_n = \sum_{k=1}^{n-1} g_k$ with $n = 2$.

Now consider two years $N = 2$; then

$$f_2(y_3, z_3, h_3) = \max_{\{g_2\}} [\min \{y_2, f_1(y_2, z_2, h_2)\}]$$
$$= \max_{\{g_2\}} [\min \{0.5(y_3 + z_3) + g_2; 0.5(y_2 + z_2) + h_2\}]. \tag{3.61i}$$

But by definition of $h_n$ it satisfies $h_{n+1} = h_n + g_n$; therefore

$$0.5(y_2 + z_2) + h_2 = 0.5z_3 + h_3, \text{ from (3.61c) through (3.61e)}$$
$$= \text{independent of } g_2.$$

Now $[0.5(y_2 + z_2) + h_2]$ is a constant independent of $g_2$, but we have to know whether the other term $[0.5(y_3 + z_3) + g_2]$ is above or below or equal to it; hence we have three cases depending on the level of $y_3$, i.e.

(i) $y_3 \leqslant 0$, $f_2(y_3, z_3, h_3) = 0.5(y_3 + z_3) + h_3$ and $g_2 = h_3$;

(ii) $0 \leqslant y_3 \leqslant 2h_3$, $f_2(y_3, z_3, h_3) = 0.5z_3 + h_3$ and $g_2 = h_3 - 0.5y_3$; and

(iii) $2h_3 \leqslant y_3$, $f_2(y_3, z_3, h_3) = 0.5z_3 + h_3$ and $g_2 = 0$.

Consider now the three year plan with $N = 4$ and with the following values $y_4 = 1 = h_4$, $z_4 = 0.5$. Then the values of $y_3, z_3$ and $h_3$ are $y_3 = 0.75 + g_3$, $z_3 = 0.25 + g_3$ and $h_3 = 1 - g_3$. Since $g_3$ is positive, we cannot have $y_3 \leqslant 0$, but we have to consider other cases; it is easy to show that $y_3 \leqslant 2h_3$ if $g_3 \leqslant \frac{5}{12}$; therefore as in case (ii) above,

$$0 \leqslant y_3 \leqslant 2h_3, \; f_2(y_3, z_3, h_3) = 0.5z_3 + h_3$$
$$= 1.125 - 0.5g_3;$$

also we have $y_3 = 0.75 + g_3$. The two lines $y_3$ and $f_2(y_3, z_3, h_3)$ intersect at $g_3 = 0.25$ and it is easy to show that this value of $g_3$ makes the lesser of $f_2(y_3, z_3, h_2)$ and $y_3$ as large as possible. With $g_3 = 0.25$ optimally determined along with $y_3 = 0.75 + g_3 = 1$, $z_3 = 0.25 + g_3 = 0.5$, $h_3 = 1 - g_3 = 0.75$ and $f_3(1, 0.5, 1) = 1$. Since in this case $g_3 < \frac{5}{12}$ and $y_3 < 2h_3$, the optimal policy for year 2 is $g_2 = h_3 - 0.5y_3 = 0.25$. Then $y_2 = 1$, $z_2 = 0$, $h_2 = 0.5$ and similarly with third year $g_1 = h_2 = 0.5$ and $y_1 = 1$, given the optimal solution of the second year.

This example shows that national income has been maintained at the level 1 by following this optimizing procedure; if on the other hand government spending had been equally divided between the three years $g_1 = g_2 = g_3 = 0.333$, the levels of national income would have fluctuated as $y_1 = 1.416$, $y_2 = 0.916$ and $y_3 = 0.541$.

Several remarks may be made about the computational economy of the method of dynamic programming. First, it is to be noted that although the dimensionality of the original problem is significantly increased because at any stage the optimal value of the decision vector has to be determined by enumerating several feasible policies, the storage of information about earlier optimal calculations may be helpful and lead to substantial economies. Second, there are available several special techniques [59] when a variational calculus problem in continuous time is involved and a discrete time transformation is required in order to apply the dynamic programming algorithm. Also, for economic problems involving indivisibilities of some sort (e.g. optimal investment allocation between projects or optimal routing of integer-valued quantities within a given network system), the computational load of dynamic programming may be considerably reduced. Third, one should note that for cases in which there is a strong interdependence between investment projects and the interactions between different projects (i.e. through transportation or otherwise) are nonlinear but not of the concave or quasi-concave form, there is as yet no general all-purpose algorithm, although the dynamic programming algorithm could give us good enough approximate solutions. As a matter of fact, the burden of computation of dynamic programming can be considerably reduced if instead of the optimal solution, suboptimal solutions (i.e. second best, third best solutions, etc.) defined in some sense are acceptable.

We will not enumerate the host of diverse fields in which dynamic programming algorithms have been applied [57] in both deterministic and stochastic contexts. Because of their applicability to economic models, two areas will be briefly referred to; (1) the relation of dynamic programming to Pontryagin's maximum principle in variational control theory and (2) the interpretation of dynamic programming as a sequential approach of decomposition or decentralization as discussed in ch. 2.4.

Consider an optimal control problem for the system

$$\dot{x}_i = dx_i/dt = g_i(x, u, t); \qquad i = 1, \ldots, n; \qquad x: n.1$$
$$u: m.1 \qquad (3.62a)$$
$$\text{with } u(t) \in U, \ U \text{ being the constraint set} \qquad t: 1.1$$

where the control vector $u$ has to be determined from the set $U$ satisfying (3.62a) such that a given function $F[x(T)]$ of the terminal state of the system at a fixed time $T$ is minimized, given the initial state $x^0$ of the system at $t_0$. Assuming the existence, denote the optimal control vector by $\bar{u} = \bar{u}(t_0, x^0, t)$ and the corresponding optimal state trajectory by $\bar{x} = x(t_0, \bar{x}^0, t)$ and the minimal value of the objective functional by $S_T(x^0, t_0) = F[\bar{x}(t_0, x^0, t)]$. By varying the initial data $(x^0, t_0)$ of the problem, we obtain a function $S_T(x^0, t_0)$ which will also be denoted by $S_T(x, t)$ when there are no ambiguities.

Now consider a point $x^{(1)} = \bar{x}(x^0, t_0, t_1)$ on the optimal trajectory at some point of time $t_1, t_0 < t_1 < T$, and consider the same control problem as before with only the initial values $(t_0, x^0)$ changed to $(t_1, x^{(1)})$. Denote the optimal (control) solution of the latter problem by $\bar{\bar{u}} = \bar{\bar{u}}(x^{(1)}, t_1, t)$. Now by virtue of the optimality principle of dynamic programming, optimal controls $\bar{u}(t)$ and $\bar{\bar{u}}(t)$ on the segment $(t_1, T)$ must give the same optimal value of the criterion functional equalling $S_T(x^{(1)}, t_1)$. But since the functional is defined only by the terminal state vector, hence

$$S_T(x^0, t_0) = S_T(x^{(1)}, t_1). \tag{3.62b}$$

Also by definition, since $\bar{u}(t)$ is the optimal control on the segment $[t_0, t_1]$, it is necessary that at the point $x^{(1)}$ at time $t_1$ there corresponds a least value of the function $S_T(x^{(1)}, t_1)$, i.e.

$$S_T(x^0, t_0) = \min_{u \in U} S_T(x^{(1)}, t_1) \tag{3.62c}$$

$$t_0 \leqslant t \leqslant t_1$$

where $x^{(1)}$ is a functional on $u(t)$ and depends on $x^0, t_0$.

Now set $t_1 = t_0 + h$ where $h$ is very small and write $x_i^{(1)}$ as

$$x_i^{(1)} = \bar{x}_i(t_0 + h) = x_i^0 + hg_i[x^0, t_0, \bar{u}(t_0)] + \alpha, \tag{3.62d}$$

since $\bar{x}(t_0) = x^0$ and $\bar{x}_i(t_0) = f_i[x^0, t_0, \bar{u}(t_0)]$ and $\alpha$ is a small quantity of higher order smallness than $h$. Assuming the existence and continuity of the partial derivatives, we then expand $S_T(x^{(1)}, t_1)$ in a Taylor series as

$$S_T(x^{(1)}, t_1) = S_T(x^0, t_0) + \sum_{i=1}^{n} \frac{\partial S_T(x^0, t_0)}{\partial x_i^0} \cdot (x_i^{(1)} - x_i^0)$$

$$+ \frac{\partial S_T(x^0, t_0)}{\partial t_0} \cdot (t_1 - t_0) + \delta \tag{3.62e}$$

where $\delta$ is smaller than $h$. Substitute this expression (3.62e) in the right hand side of (3.62c) to get

$$S_T(x^0, t_0) = \min_{u(t) \in U} \left[ S_T(x^0, t_0) + h \sum_{i=1}^{n} \frac{\partial S_T(x^0, t_0)}{\partial x_i^0} \cdot g_i[x^0, t_0, \bar{u}(t_0)] \right.$$

$$\left. + h \frac{\partial S_T(x^0, t_0)}{\partial t_0} + \gamma \right]$$

where $\gamma$ is smaller than $h$.

Since the terms $S_T(x^0, t_0)$, $h \, \partial S_T(x^0, t_0)/\partial t_0$ do not involve $u(t)$, they can be taken out and then, by simplifying and dividing by $h$, we get

$$\frac{\partial S_T(x^0, t_0)}{\partial t_0} = - \min_{\substack{u(t) \in U \\ t_0 \leqslant t \leqslant t_0 + h}} \left[ \sum_{i=1}^{n} \frac{\partial S_T(x^0, t_0)}{\partial x_i^0} \, g_i[x^0, t_0, \bar{u}(t_0)] + \frac{\gamma}{h} \right].$$

Letting $h \to 0$ so that $(\gamma/h) \to 0$ and denoting $\bar{u}(t_0)$ by $u^0$, we get for the control $\bar{u}(t)$ at $t = t_0$:

$$\frac{\partial S_T(x^0, t_0)}{\partial t_0} = \min_{u \in U} \sum_{i=1}^{n} \frac{\partial S_T(x^0, t_0)}{\partial x_i^0} \cdot g_i(x^0, t_0, u^0)$$

$$= \max_{u \in U} \sum_{i=1}^{n} - \left( \frac{\partial S_T(x^0, t_0)}{\partial x_i^0} \right) \cdot g_i(x^0, t_0, u^0).$$

This relationship is valid for any $t_0$, $x^0$ but since $t_0$, $x^0$ are arbitrary, this relation must hold for any $t$ and $x$ if they are on the optimal trajectory, i.e.

$$\frac{\partial S_T(x, t)}{\partial t} = \max_{u \in U} \sum_{i=1}^{n} \left( \frac{- \partial S_T(x, t)}{\partial x_i} \right) \cdot g_i(x, u, t). \tag{3.62f}$$

This partial differential equation can be integrated by using the corresponding boundary conditions. This equation (3.62f) is structurally similar to Pontryagin's maximum principle and this can be shown by taking the following linear objective functional $F[x(T)] = \sum_{i=1}^{n} c_i x_i(T)$ and defining the Hamiltonian $H$ as

$$H = \sum_{i=1}^{n} p_i g_i(x, u, t).$$

Rozonoer [60] has proved the following result in this context:

*Theorem 3.12*

In the problem of maximizing $\sum_{i=1}^{n} c_i x_i(T)$, let the function $S_T(x, t)$ defined before be continuous and continuously differentiable in the region $R$; then for all $t$ for which $(\bar{x}(t), t) \in R$ the min-optimal control $\bar{u}(t)$ satisfies Pontryagin's maximum condition with respect to $p(t) = (p_1(t), \ldots, p_n(t))'$ where

$$p_i(t) = - \frac{\partial S_T[\bar{x}(t), t]}{\partial x_i}, \quad i = 1, \ldots, n; \quad (\bar{x}(t) \text{ is associated with } \bar{u}(t))$$

and

$$\frac{\partial S_T[\bar{x}(t), t]}{\partial t} = H[\bar{x}(t), p(t), \bar{u}(t), t] = \sum_{i=1}^{n} p_i(t)\, g_i[\bar{x}(t), \bar{u}(t), t].$$

Also, the function $S_T(x, t)$ satisfies in $R$ the following partial differential equation derived by Bellman's optimality principle:

$$\frac{\partial S_T(x, t)}{\partial t} = \max_{u \in U} \sum_{i=1}^{n} \left( \frac{-\partial S_T(x, t)}{\partial x_i} \right) g_i(x, u, t)$$

where

$$S_T(x, T) = \sum_{i=1}^{n} c_i x_i, \text{ if } (x, T) \in R.$$

This result shows the basic structural similarity of the maximum principle of Pontryagin and the optimality principle of Bellman.

We may now consider another illustration of the optimality principle in two-level planning techniques of decomposition. Consider the overall central problem of allocating a given investment budget (scalar) $y$ between different regions ($i = 1, ..., N$ where $N$ = total number of regions) with net returns $g_i(y_i)$ for an allocation of $y_i$ to region $i$ such that total return $z = \sum_{i=1}^{N} g_i(y_i)$ is maximized under the conditions $y_i \geqslant 0$ and $\sum_{i=1}^{N} y_i \leqslant y$ where $y$ is fixed. Since the maximum of $z = z(y_1, ..., y_N)$ depends only on $y$ (i.e. its appropriate partitions) and $N$, therefore define a function $f_N(y)$ as

$$f_N(y) = \max z(y_1, ..., y_N) \quad \text{with} \quad f_N(0) = 0, \quad f_1(y) = g_1(y).$$

Suppose in the first stage that a quantity $x$ out of a total of $y$ is allocated to the $R$th region which yields $g_R(x)$, with the remaining resource $(y - x)$ allocated to the remaining $(R - 1)$ regions with total returns denoted by $f_{R-1}(y - x)$. By definition of $f_R(y)$,

$$f_R(y) = \max_{0 \leqslant x \leqslant y} [g_R(x) + f_{R-1}(y - x)], \qquad R = 2, 3, ..., N \qquad (3.63)$$

with $f_1(x) = g_1(x)$.

This functional equation can be constructed systematically and solved sequentially (provided the functions $g_i(y_i)$ or $z$ are such that the maximum exists) by the method illustrated before. The central authority at any stage would utilize the regional net return figures $g_R(x)$ to combine them into a composite plan according to the functional equation (3.63) and would continue the iterations between different regions till the overall maximum is reached. In principle this is basically similar to a pricing process whereby a provisional value $\lambda = \lambda^{(1)}$, say, of the Lagrange multiplier is associated with the restriction $\sum_{i=1}^{N} y_i \leqslant y$ by the central authority and each region maximizes $g_i(y_i)$ subject to $y_i \geqslant 0$ and $y_i \leqslant y$ such that $y_i^{(1)}$ denotes its optimal solution; then $\lambda^{(1)}$ is successively revised by the central authority according to the following rule:

$$\lambda^{(2)} = \lambda^{(1)} + k \left( \sum_{i=1}^{N} y_i^{(1)} - y \right), \qquad k = \text{a small positive quantity}$$

i.e.

at any stage $t$,

$$\lambda^{(t)} = \lambda^{(t-1)} + k \left( \sum_{i=1}^{N} y_i^{(t-1)} - y \right).$$

This pricing rule implies that $\lambda^{(t)} > \lambda^{(t-1)}$ if $\sum_i y_i^{(t-1)} > y$ and $\lambda^{(t)} \leqslant \lambda^{(t-1)}$ if $\sum_i y_i^{(t-1)} \leqslant y$. This is essentially the logic of the gradient methods also.

Sometimes when the functions $g_i(y_i)$ are complicated, e.g. nonlinear with integer requirements for $y_i$, second best optimal solutions in the form of local optimals may be selected and this will reduce the load of computation somewhat. However, for problems of reasonable size the dimensionality factor may sometimes be very great, resulting in a very large memory requirement for the computer calculations.

## REFERENCES

[1] Kuhn, H. W. and A. W. Tucker, "Nonlinear programming". In: J. Neyman (ed.), *Proceedings of Second Berkeley Symposium on Mathematical Statistics and Probability.* Berkeley: Univ. of California Press, 1951, 481–492.

[2] Arrow, K. J. and A. C. Enthoven, "Quasi-concave programming", *Econometrica*, Vol. 29, 779–800.

[3] Arrow, K. J., L. Hurwicz and H. Uzawa (eds.), *Studies in linear and nonlinear programming.* Stanford: Stanford University Press, 1958.
Arrow, K. J., L. Hurwicz and H. Uzawa, "Constraint qualifications in maximization problems", Office of Naval Research Technical Report No. 64, Department of Economics, Stanford University, 1958.

[4] Slater, M., "Lagrange multipliers revisited: a contribution to nonlinear programming", Cowles Commission Discussion Paper, Math. 403, November 1950.
Hadley, G., Nonlinear and dynamic programming. Reading, Mass.: Addison-Wesley, 1964.

[5] Karlin, S., *Mathematical methods and theory in games, linear programming and economics*, Vol. I. Cambridge, Mass.: Addison-Wesley, 1960.

[6] Arrow, K. J. and L. Hurwicz, "Decentralization and computation in resource allocation". In: R. W. Pfouts (ed.), *Essays in Economics and Econometrics.* Chapel Hill: University of North Carolina Press, 1960.

[7] Dorn, W. S., "A duality theorem for convex programs", *IBM Journal of Research*, Vol. 4, 1960, 407–413.

Mangasarian, O. L., "Duality in nonlinear programming", *Quarterly Journal of Applied Mathematics*, Vol. 20, 1962, 300–302.

[8] Dennis, J. R., *Mathematical programming and electrical networks*. New York: Wiley, 1959.

[9] Wolfe, P., "A duality theorem for nonlinear programming", *Rand Report*, P. 2028, 1960.

[10] Hanson, M. A., "A duality theorem in nonlinear programming with nonlinear constraints", *Australian Journal of Statistics*, Vol. 3, 1961, 64–72.

[11] Eisenberg, E., "Duality in homogeneous programming", *Proceedings of American Mathematical Society*, Vol. 12, 1961, 783–787.

Van Moeseke, P., "A duality theorem for convex homogeneous programming", *Metroeconomica*, Vol. 16, 1964, 32–40.

[12] Zoutendijk, G., "Nonlinear programming: a numerical survey", *SIAM Journal on Control*, Vol. 4, No. 1, 1966.

Abadie, J. (ed.), *Nonlinear programming*. Amsterdam: North-Holland, 1967.

[13] Wolfe, P., "Methods of nonlinear programming". In: R. L. Graves and P. Wolfe (eds.), *Recent advances in mathematical programming*. New York: McGraw-Hill, 1963.

[14] Zoutendijk, G., *Methods of feasible directions*. Amsterdam: Elsevier Publishing, 1960.

[15] Rosen, J. B., "The gradient projection method for nonlinear programming: I, II", *SIAM Journal*, Vol. 8, 1960, 181–217 and Vol. 9, 1961, 514–532.

[16] Kelley, J. E., "The cutting plane method for solving convex programs", *SIAM Journal*, Vol. 8, 1960, 703–712.

[17] Wegner, P., "A nonlinear extension of the simplex method", *Management Science*, Vol. 7, 1960, 43–55.

[18] Hartley, H. O. and R. Hocking, "Convex programming by a dual simplex method", *Dittoed Report*, Department of Statistics, Iowa State University, 1964.

[19] Vajda, S., *Mathematical programming*. Reading, Mass.: Addison-Wesley, 1961.

[20] Fletcher, R. and C. M. Reeves, "Function minimization by conjugate gradients", *British Computer Journal*, 1964, 149–154.

Fiacco, A. V. and G. P. McCormick, "The sequential unconstrained minimization technique for nonlinear programming, a primal dual method", *Management Science*, Vol. 10, 1964, 360–366.

Lasdon, L. S., S. K. Mitter and A. D. Waren, "The conjugate gradient method for optimal control problems", *IEEE Transactions on Automatic Control*, Vol. Ac-12, No. 2, April 1967, 132–138.

[21] Frank, M. and P. Wolfe, "An algorithm for quadratic programming", *Naval Research Logistics Quarterly*, Vol. 3, 1956, 95–110.

Lemke, C. E., "A method for solution of quadratic programs", *Management Science*, Vol. 8, 1962, 442–453.

Houthakker, H. S., "The capacity method of quadratic programming", *Econometrica*, Vol. 28, 1960, 62–87.

Boot, J. C. G., *Quadratic Programming*. Amsterdam: North-Holland, 1964.

[22] Beale, E. M. L., "On quadratic programming", *Naval Research Logistics Quarterly*, Vol. 6, 1959, 227–244.

Hartley, H. O., "Nonlinear programming by the simplex method", *Econometrica*, Vol. 29, 1961, 223–237.

Hildreth, C., "A quadratic programming procedure", *Naval Research Logistics Quarterly*, Vol. 4, 1957, 79–85.

[23] Morishima, M., *Equilibrium, stability and growth*. Oxford: Clarendon Press, 1964.

Haque, W., "Intertemporal optimality and von Neumann equilibrium in nonlinear activity analysis", *Metroeconomica*, Vol. 16, 1964, 15–31.

[24] Chenery, H. B. and H. Uzawa, "Nonlinear programming in economic development".

In: K. J. Arrow, L. Hurwicz and H. Uzawa (eds.), *Studies in linear and nonlinear programming*, op. cit.

[25] Smith, V., "Minimization of economic rent in spatial price equilibrium", *Review of Economic Studies*, Vol. 30 (1), No. 82, 1963.

[26] Kunzi, H. P. and W. Oettli, "Integer quadratic programming". In: R. L. Graves and P. Wolfe (eds.), *Recent advances in mathematical programming, op. cit.*

[27] Manne, A. S., "Capacity expansion and probabilistic growth", *Econometrica*, Vol. 29, 1961, 632–649.
Manne, A. S., *Investments for capacity expansion*. Cambridge, Mass.: MIT Press, 1966.

[28] Vietorisz, T. and A. S. Manne, "Chemical processes, plant location and economies of scale". In: A. S. Manne and H. M. Markowitz (eds.), *Studies in process analysis*. New York: John Wiley, Cowles Foundation Series, Vol. 18, 1963.

[29] Arrow, K. J., S. Karlin and H. Scarf (eds.), *Studies in the mathematical theory of inventory and production*. Stanford: Stanford University Press, 1958.

[30] Fox, K. A., J. K. Sengupta and E. Thorbecke, *The theory of quantitative economic policy with applications to economic growth and stabilization*. Amsterdam: North-Holland, 1966.

[31] Mangasarian, O. L., "Sufficient conditions for the optimal control of nonlinear systems", *SIAM Journal on Control*, Vol. 4, No. 1, 1966, 139–152.

[32] Oldenburger, R., *Optimal and self-optimizing control*. Cambridge, Mass.: MIT Press, 1966.
Pontryagin, L. S., "Optimal regulation processes", *American Mathematical Society Translations*, Series 2, Vol. 18, 1961, 295–339.

[33] Ho, Y. and P. B. Brentani, "On computing optimal controls with inequality constraints", *SIAM Journal on Control*, Vol. 1, No. 3, 1963, 319–347.
Athans, M., "The status of optimal control theory and applications for deterministic systems", *IEEE Transactions on Automatic Control*, Vol. AC-11, No. 3, 1966, 580–596.
Pearson, J. B. and R. Sridhar, "A discrete optimal control problem", *IEEE Transactions on Automatic Control*, Vol. AC-11, No. 2, April 1966, 171–174.

[34] Holtzman, J. M., "Convexity and the maximum principle for discrete systems", *IEEE Transactions on Automatic Control*, Vol. AC-11, No. 1, January 1966, 30–35.

[35] Berkovitz, L. D., "Variational methods in problems of control and programming", *Journal of Mathematical Analysis and Applications*, Vol. 3, 1961, 145–169.

[36] Lee, E. B. and L. Markus, "Optimal control for nonlinear processes", *Archiv for Rational Mechanics and Analysis*, Vol. 8, No. 1, 1961, 36–58.

[37] Lasdon, L. S. and S. K. Mitter, "The conjugate gradient method for optimal control problems", *IEEE Transactions on Automatic Control*, Vol. AC-12, No. 2, April 1967, 132–138.
Denham, W. F. and A. E. Bryson, "Optimal programming problems with inequality constraints", *AIAA Journal*, Vol. 2, January 1964, 25–34.

[38] Balakrishnan, A. V. and L. W. Neustadt (eds.), *Computing methods in optimization problems*. New York: Academic Press, 1964.

[39] Paiewonsky, B., "Optimal control: a review of theory and practice", *AIAA Journal*, Vol. 3, 1965, 1985–2006.

[40] Bryson, A. E. and W. F. Denham, "A steepest ascent method for solving optimum programming problems", *Journal of Applied Mechanics*, Vol. 29, 1962, 247–257.

[41] McGill, R., "Optimal control, inequality state constraints and the generalized Newton-Raphson algorithm", *SIAM Journal on Control*, Vol. 3, 1965, 291–98.
Kopp, R. E. and R. McGill, "Several trajectory optimization techniques". In: A. V. Balakrishnan and L. W. Neustadt (eds.), *Computing methods in optimization problems, op. cit.*

Merriam, C. W., "An algorithm for the iterative solution of a class of two-point boundary value problems", *SIAM Journal on Control*, Series A, Vol. 2, No. 1, 1964, 1–10.

Faulkner, F. D., "A comparison between some methods for computing optimum paths in the problem of Bolza". In: A. V. Balakrishnan and L. W. Neustadt (eds.), *Computing methods in optimization problems, op. cit.*

[42] Dreyfus, S. E., *Dynamic programming and the calculus of variations*. New York: Academic Press, 1965.

[43] Simon, H. A., "On the application of servomechanism theory in the study of production control", *Econometrica*, Vol. 20, April 1952, 247–268.

[44] Wang, P. K. C., "Invariance, uncontrollability and unobservability in dynamical systems", *IEEE Transactions on Automatic Control*, Vol. AC-10, July 1965, 366–367.

[45] Letov, A. M., *Stability in nonlinear control systems*. Princeton: Princeton University Press, 1961.

La Salle, J. P., "Stability and control", *SIAM Journal on Control*, Vol. 1, No. 1, 1962, 3–15.

[46] Rekasius, Z. V., "Suboptimal design of intentionally nonlinear controllers", *IEEE Transactions on Automatic Control*, Vol. AC-9, October 1964, 380–386.

[47] Brockett, R. W., "The status of stability theory for deterministic systems", *IEEE Transactions on Automatic Control*, Vol. AC-11, No. 3, 1966, 596–606.

[48] Modigliani, F. and F. Hohn, "Production planning over time and the nature of the expectation and planning horizon", *Econometrica*, Vol. 23, No. 1, 1955, 46–66.

Morin, F., "Note on an inventory problem", *Econometrica*, Vol. 23, No. 4, 1955, 447–450.

[49] Holt, C., F. Modigliani, J. Muth and H. Simon, *Planning production, inventories and work force*. Englewood Cliffs, N. J.: Prentice Hall, 1960.

[50] Theil, H., *Optimal decision rules for government and industry*. Amsterdam: North-Holland, 1965.

[51] Holt, C. C., "Linear decision rules for economic stabilization and growth", *Quarterly Journal of Economics*, Vol. 76, 1962, 20–45.

[52] Sengupta, J. K., "A simple generalization of the Phillips-type model of economic stabilization", *Zeitschrift für die gesamte Staatswissenschaft*, Vol. 122, October 1966.

[53] Theil, H., "A note on certainty equivalence in dynamic planning", *Econometrica*, Vol. 25, 1957, 346–349.

[54] Shell, K. (ed.), *Essays on the theory of optimal economic growth*. Cambridge, Mass.: MIT Press, 1967.

[55] Dobell, A. R. and Y. C. Ho, "Optimal investment policy: an example of a control problem in economic theory", *IEEE Transactions on Automatic Control*, Vol. AC-12, No. 1, February 1967, 4–14.

[56] Fox, K. A. and J. K. Sengupta, "The specification of econometric models for planning educational systems: an appraisal of alternative approaches", *Kyklos*, Vol. 21, No. 4, 1968, 665–694.

[57] Bellman, R., *Adaptive control processes: a guided tour*. Princeton: Princeton University Press. 1961.

Bellman, R. and S. Dreyfus, *Applied dynamic programming*. Princeton: Princeton University Press. 1962.

[58] Aris, R., *Discrete dynamic programming*. New York: Blaisdell Publishing Co., 1965.

[59] Hadley, G., *Nonlinear and dynamic programming, op. cit.*

[60] Rozonoer, L. I., "Pontryagin's maximum principle in the theory of optimum systems", I, II and III, *Automation and Remote Control*, Vol. 20, Nos. 10, 11, 12. Also reprinted in R. Oldenberger, *Optimal and self-optimizing control, op. cit.*

# Chapter 4

# SENSITIVITY ANALYSIS IN PROGRAMMING

## 4.1. Sensitivity analysis in linear programming

Methods of analyzing the sensitivity of solutions to a static or dynamic problem of linear programming may be classified into two broad groups: (a) sensitivity analysis in deterministic (i.e., without probabilities in a basic sense) LP problems and (b) sensitivity analysis through models of probabilistic programming. In this chapter we discuss the first group of methods only, which may be further subdivided into the following subgroups: (1) methods of parametric programming; (2) perturbation analysis; (3) stability analysis (through sensitivity measures); (4) error analysis; (5) sensitivity analysis through equivalent nonlinear programs; and (6) sensitivity analysis in dynamic LP models (commonly used in control theory applications).

### 4.1.1. Parametric programming

For a standard LP problem with parameters $(A, b, c)$ the most usual question posed in parametric linear programming is to analyze the effects on the optimal basis which would be induced by variations in parameters $(\delta A, \delta b, \delta c)$ (e.g. to analyze the conditions of variations in parameters under which the old optimal basis still remains optimal or does not).

In the usual notation of ch. 2 consider the augmented system of restrictions

$$Bx_B + Nx_N = b \qquad B: m \cdot m \text{ (basis)} \qquad (4.1a)$$
$$N: m \cdot n.$$

Premultiply by a row vector $y'(1 \cdot m)$ of simplex multipliers

$$y'Bx_B + y'Nx_N = y'b \qquad (4.1b)$$

and add to the objective function $z$ where

$$c'_B x_B + c'_N x_N = z \qquad (4.1c)$$

to obtain

$$(y'B + c'_B) x_B + (y'N + c'_N) x_N = y'b + z. \qquad (4.1d)$$

149

Since $x'_B = 0$ (i.e., nonbasic activities are zero), if we choose $y' = -c'_B B^{-1}$ then $y'B + c'_N = 0$ and hence

$$z = -y'b = -\sum_{i=1}^{m} y_i b_i. \tag{4.1e}$$

From (4.1a)

$$x_B = B^{-1}b - B^{-1}Nx_N \quad (\text{i.e., } x_i = b_{i0} - \sum_{j=m+1}^{n} \beta_{ij}x_j \tag{4.2}$$

where $[\beta_{ij}] = (B^{-1}N)$ and $b_{i0} = i$th element of $(B^{-1}b)$.
Denote

$$z'_N = c'_B B^{-1}N \tag{4.3a}$$

$$\Delta'_N = c'_N - z'_N. \tag{4.3b}$$

We have seen before that the given basis $B$ is optimal if $\Delta'_N \leqslant 0$ for all activities not in the basis. Now consider the various types of parametric variations.

(i) *Changes in vector b* (i.e. $b \to b + \delta b$).
If the new solution vector

$$x_B = B^{-1}(b + \delta b) \tag{4.4}$$

remains nonnegative, then since the optimality criterion $\Delta'_N$ in (4.3b) is independent of $\delta b$, the old set of optimal activities still remains optimal. If however, any of the components of $x_B$, i.e. $x_i$ ($i$ in $B$), say, becomes negative due to the variation $\delta b$ in (4.4), then the corresponding row of the standard simplex tableau is multiplied by $-1$ and an artificial variable to replace the infeasible $x_i$ with a very large negative price coefficient $(-M)$ in the objective function is introduced in order to eliminate the negative activity $(x_i)$ from the basis. The new artificial variable along with other (old) basis variables provide the new initial feasible solution in the usual simplex algorithm (or the revised simplex routine).

Note that rewriting (4.4) as

$$\delta x_i = \sum_{k=1}^{m} \beta_{ik} \delta b_k; \quad (i = 1, 2, ..., m) \tag{4.5}$$

it is possible to determine the range of variation of $b_k$ up to which the old optimal basis would still remain optimal.

(ii) *Changes in vector c* (i.e. $c \to c + \delta c$).
Here the optimality criterion

$$\Delta'_N = c'_N - c'_B B^{-1}N \tag{4.6a}$$

reduces itself to

$$\bar{\Delta}'_N = c'_N + \delta c'_N - (c'_B + \delta c'_B) B^{-1} N. \tag{4.6b}$$

If the changes are made in the $c_j$ values satisfying

$$\bar{\Delta}'_N \leqslant 0 \text{ for all nonbasic activities} \tag{4.6c}$$

then the old optimal basis still remains the optimal; the value of the new objective function will be changed, however. If changes are made in the $c_j$ coefficients of the nonbasic variables only satisfying (4.6c), then the old optimal basis still remains optimal, with no change in the optimal value of the old objective function. But if the changes in $c_j$ variables violate the optimality criterion (4.6c), this is an indication that an improvement (barring degeneracy) can be made in the objective function by bringing that activity into the basis which violates the optimality criterion (4.6c). This can be done by using further iterations from the old optimal tableau.

In the single parameter case, when only one parameter, say, $c_k$ is varied at a time satisfying (4.6c), then the whole range of such variations (i.e. the lower and the upper limit) can be determined by the usual simplex routine with very little modification. However, a generalization to several parameters varying simultaneously, although theoretically feasible, has not been computationally explored in any detail.

(iii) *Changes in input-coefficients* $(a_{ij})$.
Denote the new set of input coefficients by $\bar{a}_{ij}$ where

$$\bar{a}_{ij} = a_{ij} + \delta a_{ij}. \tag{4.7a}$$

Now a typical activity $x_i$ in the old optimal basis may or may not be in the new basis with input coefficients $\bar{a}_{ij}$. If the typical activity $x_i$ is not in the new basis, then define

$$\bar{P}_i = B^{-1} \begin{bmatrix} \bar{a}_{1i} \\ \vdots \\ \bar{a}_{mi} \end{bmatrix} \tag{4.7b}$$

where $B =$ (old) optimal basis and replace the column vector $P_i$ in the old (simplex) optimal tableau by $\bar{P}_i$ and start the iterations by noting the following points:

(a) introduce a new activity $\bar{x}_i$ with a price coefficient $c_i$;

(b) introduce a new column vector $\bar{P}_i$ defined by (4.7b) to replace the column $P_i$ in the old optimal tableau; and

(c) now since the variables $x_i$ and $\bar{x}_i$ have the same price coefficients $c_i$ and since with the new set of coefficients $\bar{a}_{ij}$ the new variable of interest is $\bar{x}_i$, we associate a very high negative price coefficient $(-M)$ with $x_i$ replacing its old coefficient $c_i$ in order to eliminate $x_i$ from the old optimal basis.

This model could obviously be generalized when more than one activity leaves the old basis due to a change-over of coefficients; however, convenient computational methods are not yet available to handle the simultaneous exit of several unwanted activities from the old optimal basis.

(iv) *Introducing new activities.*

Let $(a_{1, n+1}, \ldots a_{m, n+1})$ be the coefficients associated with the new activity of variable $x_{n+1}$ and $c_{n+1}$ be its price coefficient in the objective function. Denote a new column vector $P_{n+1}$ by

$$P_{n+1} = B^{-1} \begin{bmatrix} a_{1, n+1} \\ \vdots \\ a_{m, n+1} \end{bmatrix}; \qquad B = \text{old optimal basis} \qquad (4.8)$$

and introduce this column in the original optimal simplex tableau and carry on the usual simplex procedures till an optimal solution is obtained.

(v) *Adjoining new constraints.*

Let the constraint adjoined to the system be

$$a_{m+1, 1} x_1 + \cdots + a_{m+1, n} x_n \leqslant b_{m+1}. \qquad (4.9a)$$

From the original optimal basis $(B)$,

$$x_B = B^{-1} b - B^{-1} N x_N \qquad (4.9b)$$

i.e.

$$x_i = b_{i0} - \sum_{j=m+1}^{n} \beta_{ij} x_j; \qquad (i \text{ in optimal basis}) \qquad (4.9c)$$

where $b_{i0} = i$th element of vector $(B^{-1}b)$ and $[\beta_{ij}] = B^{-1}N$.

Substituting these values of $x_i$ from (4.9c) into the new constraint (4.9a), one gets

$$\sum_{i=1}^{m} a_{m+1, i} \left[ \sum_{j=m+1}^{n} \beta_{ij} x_j \right] - \sum_{j=m+1}^{n} a_{m+1, j} x_j \geqslant \sum_{i=1}^{m} a_{m+1, i} b_{i0} - b_{m+1}$$

i.e.

$$\sum_{j=m+1}^{n} \bar{a}_{m+1, j} x_j \geqslant \bar{b}_{m+1} \qquad (4.9d)$$

$$\bar{a}_{m+1, j} = \sum_{i=1}^{m} (a_{m+1, i} \beta_{ij}) - a_{m+1, j}$$

where

$$\bar{b}_{m+1} = \sum_{i=1}^{m} a_{m+1, i} b_{i0} - b_{m+1}.$$

Now depending on whether $\bar{b}_{m+1}$ is nonnegative or nonpositive we introduce an artificial or slack variable. Denote the slack variable by $x_{n+1}$ and the artificial variable by $x_{n+2}$ and rewrite (4.9d) as an equated constraint

$$\sum_{j=m+1}^{n} \bar{a}_{m+1, j} x_j - x_{n+1} + x_{n+2} = \bar{b}_{m+1}. \tag{4.9e}$$

We adjoin the columns associated with (4.9e) to the old optimal basis. Now the initial new basis consists of the old optimal basis and the column corresponding to $x_{n+2}$ and the usual simplex iterations continue. (As usual we have to associate a very high negative price coefficient $(-M)$ with the artificial variable $x_{n+2}$, since the artificial variable should take the value zero, if the overall problem with the new constraints is feasible.)

In a LP problem with a very large number of constraints and variables, the computational cost may be very large and in that case approximate solutions may be desired for savings in computational costs. The approximation problem in this case is one of solving LP problems with the same objective function relative to a subset of the constraints. Assume there are $k = 1, 2, ..., K$ partition LP problems, each with the same (max-type) objective function but with different subsets of restrictions and denote by $z^*_{(k)}$ the maximum value of the objective function for the $k$th partition problem. Then the following result due to Saaty [1] holds:

$$\min_k z^*_{(k)} \geqslant z^*; \quad k = 1, 2, ..., K \tag{4.10a}$$

where $z^*$ is the maximum value of the objective function for the entire problem over the whole set of restrictions, which contains all the subsets of restrictions. Thus for any finite $k$, an upper bound to the overall optimal value of the objective function is provided by the left hand term of relation (4.10a). Similarly for a minimization-type objective function with notations $w^*_{(k)}$ and $w^*$ it holds that

$$w^* \geqslant \max_k w^*_{(k)}; \quad (\text{note } w^* = z^*). \tag{4.10b}$$

Several other situations in parametric linear programming have been investigated in the literature. A case important for investment planning problems in economics, due to Courtillot [2], considers adjoining to the given LP model a relation between the components of resource vector $b$ and a supplementary variable. For instance, let the relation

$$\sum_{i=1}^{m} k_i(\bar{b}_i - b_i) \leqslant D; \quad \bar{b}_i \geqslant b_i \tag{4.11}$$

be added to the initial problem, where $(\bar{b}_i - b_i)$ may represent the increase of resources $\bar{b}_i$ of unit value $k_i$ and $D$ denotes the total increase in the investment budget. The solution of the original problem is then found as a function of $D$ by solving the following LP problem:

$$\text{maximize } z = \sum_{j=1}^{n} c_j x_j$$

under the restrictions

$$\sum_{j=1}^{n} a_{ij}x_j + x_{n+i} \geqslant b_i; \qquad i = 1, 2, ..., m$$

$$\sum_{i=1}^{m} \sum_{j=1}^{n} k_i(a_{ij}x_j + x_{n+i}) \leqslant D + \sum_{i=1}^{m} k_i b_i \qquad \text{all } x_j \geqslant 0$$

where $x_{n+1}$ is the auxiliary variable of the $i$th equation in the initial LP problem. If a solution is available for $D=0$ (i.e. $\bar{b}_i - b_i$), then this problem can be transformed to the case (v) discussed before.

Another type of parametric LP problem seeks to determine the entire region in the parameter space (and its characteristics) in the neighborhood of the original set of parameters in which the optimality and feasibility properties are retained. For instance, the following theorem is proved by Saaty [3].

*Theorem 4.1*

A solution vector $x^* = (x_1^*, ..., x_n^*)'$ of the original maximization-type LP problem which yields a maximum corresponding to the price vector $c^* = (c_1^*, ..., c_n^*)'$ also yields a maximum over a convex region in parameter space containing the optimal price vector $c^*$.

*4.1.2. Perturbation analysis*

In perturbation analysis, conditions are investigated under which the parameters may be perturbed in general without affecting the choice of optimal basis. In economic applications the most important perturbations occur in the input-coefficients and one type of perturbation analysis in this line has been investigated by Barnett and others [4] as follows:

Denote the basis vectors by $P_k$ $(k=1, 2, ..., m)$ and let the vector $P_s$ of the basis $(P_1, ..., P_m)$ be changed to a new vector $\bar{P}_s$. Now the problem is: what are the conditions under which the perturbed basis $(P_1, ..., \bar{P}_s, ..., P_m)$ is the optimal feasible basis for the new perturbed problem?

Since $(P_1, ..., P_s, ..., P_m)$ provides a basis, therefore

$$\bar{P}_s - P_s = h_{1s}P_1 + \cdots + h_{ms}P_s \tag{4.12a}$$

i.e.

$$P_s = - (1 + h_{ss})^{-1} [h_{1s}P_1 + \cdots - \bar{P}_s + \cdots + h_{ms}P_m]. \qquad (4.12b)$$

For $(P_1, \ldots, \bar{P}_s, \ldots, P_m)$ to be the new basis (i.e. linearly independent) it must hold that

$$(1 + h_{ss}) \neq 0. \qquad (4.12c)$$

Now substitute the value of $P_s$ in terms of $\bar{P}_s$ from (4.12b) into the old basis equalities $b = P_1 x_1 + \cdots + P_m x_m$ to get

$$b = P_1 \left( x_1 - \frac{h_{1s}x_s}{1 + h_{ss}} \right) + \cdots + \bar{P}_s \left( \frac{x_s}{1 + h_{ss}} \right) \cdots + P_m \left( x_m - \frac{h_{ms}x_s}{1 + h_{ss}} \right). \qquad (4.12d)$$

Since the new basis (with $\bar{P}_s$ replacing $P_s$) is feasible, therefore

$$x_i - \frac{h_{is}x_s}{1 + h_{ss}} \geqslant 0 \quad \text{for all} \quad i = 1, \ldots, m \text{ except } i = s \qquad (4.12e)$$

$$x_s/(1 + h_{ss}) \geqslant 0 \quad \text{but since} \quad x_s > 0, \quad \text{therefore} \quad 1 + h_{ss} > 0. \qquad (4.12f)$$

These provide the conditions of feasibility of the new basis. To derive the conditions of optimality of the new basis, consider the original optimal basis where any vector $P_j$ whether in the basis or not can be expressed as a linear combination of the basis vectors, i.e.

$$P_j = \sum_{i=1}^{m} x_{ij}P_i; \qquad j = 1, \ldots, n; \qquad i \text{ in optimal basis}. \qquad (4.13a)$$

Substituting the value of $P_s$ from (4.12b) into (4.13a) and rearranging

$$P_j = \left( x_{1j} - \frac{h_{1s}x_{sj}}{1 + h_{ss}} \right) P_1 + \cdots + \left( \frac{x_{sj}}{1 + h_{ss}} \right) \bar{P}_s + \cdots. \qquad (4.13b)$$

Let

$$\bar{x}_{ij} = x_{ij} - \frac{h_{is}x_{sj}}{1 + h_{ss}}; \qquad \left( \text{note } \bar{x}_{sj} = x_{sj}/(1 + h_{ss}) \right) \qquad (4.13c)$$

$$\bar{z}_j = \sum_{i=1}^{m} \bar{x}_{ij}c_i = z_j - \left( \frac{x_{sj}}{1 + h_{ss}} \right) \sum_{i=1}^{m} h_{is}c_i \qquad (4.13d)$$

where $z_j = \sum_{i=1}^{m} x_{ij}c_i$ from the old optimal basis

$$\bar{\Delta}_j = c_j - \bar{z}_j = \Delta_j + \left( \frac{x_{sj}}{1 + h_{ss}} \right) \sum_{i=1}^{m} h_{is}c_i \qquad (4.13e)$$

where $\Delta_j = c_j - z_j$ from the old optimal basis.

Then the conditions for optimality for the new perturbed basis are that

$$\bar{\Delta}_j \leqslant 0 \text{ for all } j \text{ and in particular for } j = m+1, ..., n. \qquad (4.14a)$$

Since (4.14a) can also be written as

$$\left(\sum_i h_{is} c_i / (1 + h_{ss})\right) \leqslant (-\Delta_j / x_{sj}) \qquad (4.14b)$$

therefore further bounds on the coefficients $h_{is}$ can be specified in terms of, say, $M_s^*$ and $M_s^{**}$ where

$$\max_j (-\Delta_j / x_{sj}) = \begin{cases} + M_s^* > 0 & \text{for } x_{sj} > 0 \\ +\infty, & \text{if no } x_{sj} \text{ is positive} \end{cases}$$

$$\min_j (-\Delta_j / x_{sj}) = \begin{cases} - M_s^{**} < 0 & \text{for } x_{sj} < 0 \\ -\infty, & \text{if no } x_{sj} \text{ is negative}. \end{cases}$$

In other words, the following bounds must hold for the new basis to be optimal:

$$M_s^* \geqslant \sum_{i=1}^m h_{is} c_i / (1 + h_{ss}) \geqslant - M_s^{**}. \qquad (4.14c)$$

Note that since $(-\Delta_j)$ is nonnegative and since the LP problem is a maximization type of problem, we consider $x_{sj} \geqslant 0$ to define $M_s^*$.

A situation which is not uncommon for economic problems arises in the special case when there is equal relative change in the input coefficients, i.e.

$$\delta a_{js} = k a_{js} (j = 1, ..., m); \qquad k = \text{constant} \qquad (4.15a)$$

then

$$h_{is} = 0 (i \neq s); \qquad h_{ss} = k$$

and

$$\delta a_{js} = \sum_{i=1}^m h_{is} a_{ji} = h_{ss} a_{js} = k a_{js}$$

(Note that $\delta a_{js} = \bar{P}_s - P_s$).
The conditions of feasibility and optimality of the perturbed basis are:

$$x_i > 0; \qquad (4.15b)$$

$$1 + h_{ss} = 1 + k > 0 \qquad (4.15c)$$

$$M_s^* \geqslant \frac{\sum_i h_{is} c_i}{1 + h_{ss}} = \frac{c_s k}{1 + k} \geqslant - M_s^{**}. \qquad (4.15d)$$

Conditions (4.15c) and (4.15d) are to be interpreted in relation to the price coefficient $c_s$. For instance if $c_s > 0$ and $c_s < M_s^*$ then from (4.14c),

$$k(M_s^* - c_s) + M_s^* \geqslant 0$$

i.e.

$$k \geqslant - M_s^* / (M_s^* - c_s).$$

For arbitrary changes in input-coefficients $\delta a_{js}$ we have

$$\delta a_{js} = \sum_{i=1}^{m} h_{is} a_{ji};$$

then

$$h_{is} = \sum_{j=1}^{m} \beta_{ij} \delta a_{js}; \quad (i = 1, \ldots, m) \quad \text{and} \quad [\beta_{ij}] = B^{-1}.$$

Applying the conditions of feasibility and optimality we essentially define an $m$-space such that every point in it has coordinates $\delta a_{js}$.

Another type of perturbation analysis, useful for comparative static methods in economic models, seeks to specify the direction in which a specific optimal activity (activities) should change when a specific (set of) parameter (parameters) changes in a specific direction. Denote the saddle point (or the Lagrangian) function for two nonnegative vectors $u$, $v$ by

$$L(u, v) = c'u + v'(b - Au);$$

then the optimal primal $(x)$ and dual $(y)$ nonnegative vectors associated with a LP problem with parameters $(A, b, c)$ may be viewed as

$$L(x, y) = \max_{u \geqslant 0} L(u, y) = \min_{v \geqslant 0} L(x, v). \tag{4.16a}$$

Now suppose the parameters $(A, b, c)$ change to $(A + \delta A, b + \delta b, c + \delta c)$, giving rise to a change in the optimal primal-dual vectors from $(x, y)$ to $(x + \delta x, y + \delta y)$. Denote the Lagrangian function for the perturbed problem by an $L(\cdot)$ function. Then the relation (4.16a) implies the following inequalities:

$$L(x, y) - L(x + \delta x, y) \geqslant 0 \tag{4.16b}$$

$$L(x, y) - L(x, y + \delta y) \leqslant 0 \tag{4.16c}$$

$$L_\delta(x + \delta x, y + \delta y) - L(x, y + \delta y) \geqslant 0 \tag{4.16d}$$

$$L_\delta(x + \delta x, y + \delta y) - L(x + \delta x, y) \leqslant 0. \tag{4.16e}$$

Since the expression $[(4.16b) + (4.16d) - (4.16c) - (4.16e)]$ is nonnegative, the following relation must hold:

$$(\delta c' - y' \delta A) \delta x - \delta y' (\delta b - \delta A . x) \geqslant 0. \tag{4.17a}$$

This implies three interesting propositions:

$$\text{if } \delta A = 0 = \delta b, \quad \text{then} \quad \delta c' \delta x \geqslant 0; \tag{4.17b}$$

in other words, optimal activities in this case tend to move in the same direction as the generating changes in profitabilities;

$$\text{if } \delta A = 0 = \delta c, \quad \text{then} \quad \delta b' \delta y \leqslant 0; \tag{4.17c}$$

in other words, the efficiency (or dual) prices (i.e. marginal productivities) in this case tend to move in a direction opposite to changes in resources or capacities;

$$\text{if } \delta A = 0, \quad \text{then} \quad \delta c' \delta x - \delta b' \delta y \geqslant 0; \tag{4.17d}$$

in other words, at least one of the two sets of optimal variables $\delta x$ and $\delta y$ must change in the expected optimizing direction.

The above results have been derived by Beckmann and others [5] more specifically. From the inequalities of the dual (minimization) LP problem $A'y \geqslant c$ define a net revenue vector $p$ whose typical term is

$$p_k = c_k - \sum_{i=1}^{m} y_i a_{ki}. \tag{4.18a}$$

Since $(x, y)$ is an optimal pair, hence $p_k \leqslant 0$. Further from (4.18a),

$$\delta p_k = \delta c_k - \sum_{i=1}^{m} \delta y_i a_{ki} - \sum_{i=1}^{m} y_i \delta a_{ki}. \tag{4.18b}$$

By the standard duality theorem of LP

if for any $k$th activity, $p_k < 0$, then $x_k = 0$;                    (4.19a)

if for any $k$, $p_k + \delta p_k < 0$, then $x_k + \delta x_k = 0$;                    (4.19b)

if $x_k > 0$ and $x_k + \delta x_k > 0$, then

$$p_k = 0 = p_k + \delta p_k; \text{i.e.} \delta p_k = 0 \quad (4.19c)$$

if $p_k < 0$ and $p_k + \delta p_k < 0$, then $\delta x_k = 0 = x_k$.                    (4.19d)

Hence if both $\delta x_k \neq 0$ and $\delta p_k \neq 0$ for any $k$, then for that $k$ it must be true that

*either* $x_k = 0$ (i.e. $p_k < 0$) *and* $\delta x_k > 0$     (i.e. $p_k + \delta p_k = 0$)   (4.19e)

*or* $x_k + \delta x_k = 0$     (i.e. $p_k + \delta p_k < 0$) *and* $\delta x_k < 0$ (i.e. $x_k > 0$
                                                        i.e. $p_k = 0$)   (4.19f)

Note that both (4.19e) and (4.19f) imply

$$\delta p_k \delta x_k \geqslant 0 \tag{4.19g}$$

i.e.

$$\delta\left(c_k - \sum_{i=1}^{m} y_i a_{ki}\right) \delta x_k \geq 0; \quad (k = 1, 2, ..., n). \tag{4.19h}$$

A symmetrical argument using the primal problem inequalities $b \geq Ax$ and $(1+\delta)\, b \geq (1+\delta)\, Ax$ and the result that

$$\text{if } b_i \geq \sum_{k=1}^{n} a_{ki} x_k \text{ then } y_i \geq 0$$

can be used to prove that for every index $i$ in the optimal basis,

$$\delta y_i \delta\left(b_i - \sum_{k=1}^{n} a_{ki} x_k\right) \leq 0; \quad (i = 1, 2, ..., m) \tag{4.19i}$$

combining (4.19h) and (4.19i) in vector-matrix notation

$$\delta(c' - y'A)\,\delta x \geq 0 \geq \delta y'\delta(b - Ax). \tag{4.19j}$$

Expansion of the $\delta$-operator leads to the same result derived before in (4.17a).

This type of perturbation analysis is of some help in computing approximate changes in the level of an optimal activity, when its price coefficient is known to have changed in a certain direction by a certain amount.

### 4.1.3. Stability analysis

For deterministic LP problems with nonrandom variations in parameters two types of stability may be distinguished, e.g. (a) static stability where the parameter variations are not essentially dependent on time and (b) dynamic stability where the parameters in $(A, b, c)$ tend to vary as functions of a scalar variable, time, $t$. Questions of dynamic stability are discussed in section 4.2 later.

Investigations about the static stability of a LP model generally center around the problem of characterizing the neighborhood of the optimal solution with a specified set of parameters.

Let $S = (A, b, c)$ and $\bar{S} = (\bar{A}, \bar{b}, \bar{c})$ be two conformable parameter sets associated with two given LP problems each having a primal and a dual. Denote the optimal values of the objective functions in the two cases by $z(S)$ and $z(\bar{S})$ respectively. Now consider a new set $(S + h\bar{S})$ where $h$ is a scalar and the corresponding LP problem, the optimal objective function value of which is denoted by $z(S + h\bar{S}) = f(h)$, say. We are interested in the behavior of $f(h)$ near $h = 0$, since for any arbitrary set $\bar{S}$ for which optimal feasible solutions exist, the local stability or sensitivity of the optimal objective function for the set $S$ with respect to the set $\bar{S}$ is indicated thereby.

Note that the set $\bar{S}$ can be interpreted as perturbations of the orignal set $S$. As a measure of such sensitivity to local perturbations, H. Mills [6] has proposed the concept of 'marginal value' of a LP problem as

$$\dot{f}(0) = \lim_{h \to 0^+} \left( \frac{z(S + h\bar{S}) - z(S)}{h} \right),$$  (4.20a)

provided such a limit exists. The necessary and sufficient condition for the existence of such a limit (as found by Williams [6]) is that both the primal and dual optimal sets of the LP problem with $S$ be bounded both from below and above. If the existence condition is fulfilled, then there is a direct method of calculating marginal value by using

$$\dot{f}(0) = \max_{x} \min_{y} L(\bar{S}, x, y)$$  (4.20b)

where $(x, y)$ is the *optimal* pair of primal dual variables and $L(\cdot)$ is the usual Lagrangian function, e.g.

$$L(S, x, y) = c'x + y'b - y'Ax.$$

Note that if the existence condition for (4.20a) holds, then one can write approximately

$$f(h) \doteq f(0) + h\dot{f}(0); \qquad h \in [0, h_0]$$  (4.20c)

for small perturbations, provided of course certain regularity conditions are satisfied. This relation can be used in specifying approximate size of the neighborhood containing a given optimal solution.

A second type of specification of the neighborhood around the optimal value of the objective function has been suggested by Saaty [7]. Let $v = z^* = w^*$ be the optimal value of the objective function with optimal primal and dual variables $x^*$ and $y^*$ respectively; then

$$\partial v / \partial c^* = x^*;$$  (4.21a)

$$\partial v / \partial b^* = y^*$$  (4.21b)

$$\partial v / \partial a_{ij} = -x_j^* y_i^* \quad \text{at the optimal basis}$$  (4.21c)

provided of course such expansions around the optimal point $(x^*, y^*)$ are valid, i.e. the vector $c$ has to be in the *interior* of the cone associated with the solution vertex. These sensitivity indices, particularly (4.21c), have been further generalized by considering the optimal value $v = z^* = w^*$ as a function of a vector of parameters, say time $t$ in different phases. Averaging of such indices over a series of steady-state time periods gives a method of evaluating changes in the neighborhood of the optimal value of the objective function. Practical applications of these sensitivity indices to oil refinery models have been reported by Saaty and Webb [8].

A third type of sensitivity measure can be developed by using extreme points which are neighbors, so to say, to the optimal extreme point. Denote the optimal extreme point (i.e., the first best solution) by $(z^{(1)}, x^{(1)})$, the second best by $(z^{(2)}, x^{(2)})$ and the third best by $(z^{(3)}, x^{(3)})$ such that $z^{(1)} > z^{(2)} > z^{(3)}$. Now suppose that only the parameter $c$ (i.e., the net prices vector) is liable to vary, whereas the constraints are fixed. Then the Euclidean distance between $x^{(1)}$ and $x^{(2)}$, $x^{(2)}$ and $x^{(3)}$ and also the area of the triangle made by these three extreme vector points $x^{(1)}, x^{(2)}, x^{(3)}$ provide a measure of sensitivity of the overall program. (Empirical applications of some of these measures and their economic implications are reported in ch. 5.) In the general case when any parameters in $S = (A, b, c)$ can vary, use may be made of the active approach of Tintner [9] to define additional decision variables $u_{ij}$ such that

$$b_i = \sum_{j=1}^{n} u_{ij} b_i; \; u_{ij} \geqslant 0; \; \sum_{j=1}^{n} u_{ij} \leqslant 1 \qquad (4.22a)$$

when the sensitivity coefficient $R$ may be defined as

$$R = \min_k \frac{z^{(1)}(S, u_{ij}^{(1)}) - z^{(k)}(S, u_{ij}^{(k)})}{z^{(1)}(S, u_{ij}^{(1)})}; \qquad (k \neq 1, k = 2, 3, ...) \qquad (4.22b)$$

where $u_{ij}^{(1)}$ denotes the optimal allocation ratio associated with $x^{(1)}$ and $u_{ij}^{(k)}$ $(k \neq 1)$ denotes any other allocation ratio resulting in a value of the objective function less than $z^{(1)}$.

### 4.1.4. *Error analysis*

A satisfactory analysis of errors in a LP model must consider the probability structure of the errors (e.g. whether normal or other distributions would be the most appropriate). However, in this section variation of parameters is considered as an error, the effects of which on the optimal solution vector are analyzed in terms of expected value and variance, without introducing very specific probabilistic assumptions regarding the probability generating mechanism. Errors play the role of approximations and the purpose is not to discuss probabilistic programming but to analyze the extent of sensitivity of the optimal solution vectors due to observational or measurement errors in the coefficients around the optimal basis.

Let the optimal basis equations with errors be

$$(B + \delta B)(x_B + \delta x_B) = b + \delta b \qquad (4.23a)$$

while the $\delta$-operator denotes small errors such that the optimal basis equations still remain optimal. From (4.23a) it is easy to derive that

$$\delta x_B = B^{-1}\delta b + \left( \sum_{i=1}^{\infty} (-1)^i (B^{-1}\delta B)^i \right) (x_B + B^{-1}\delta b) \qquad (4.23b)$$

noting that $x_B = B^{-1}b$.

Following Hanson [10], let us make the following simplifying assumptions that

(i) the errors $\delta B$, $\delta b$ are *mutually* independent with expected values zero i.e. $E\delta B = 0 = E\delta b$ where E is the expected value operator;

(ii) higher moments beyond the second are assumed negligible; and

(iii) the infinite sum on the right hand side of (4.23b) truncated at $i = 2$ results in negligible approximation error.

Under these assumptions the expected value of the perturbed optimal solution vector in (4.23b) may be written as

$$E\delta x_B = E[(B^{-1}\delta B)(B^{-1}\delta B) x_B]. \qquad (4.23c)$$

Also,

$$\text{Var } x_B = E\delta x_B \delta x_B' = E(B^{-1}\delta b \delta b' B'^{-1}) + E(B^{-1}\delta B x_B x_B' \delta B' B'^{-1}). \qquad (4.23d)$$

Denote

$$B^{-1} = [\beta_{ij}]; \qquad (i, j = 1, ..., m: \text{the optimal basis})$$

$$\rho_{is} = \sum_{j=1}^{m} \beta_{ij}\delta a_{js}; \qquad (s = 1, ..., m: \text{optimal basis})$$

$$q_{sk} = \sum_{t=1}^{m} \beta_{st}a_{tk}; \qquad (t, k = 1, ..., m: \text{optimal basis})$$

$$r_{ik} = \sum_{s=1}^{m} \rho_{is}q_{sk}; \qquad (i, s, k, j, t = 1, ..., m: \text{optimal basis}).$$

Then for any index $i$ belonging to the optimal basis, the expected value solution in (4.23e) may be written as

$$E\delta x_i = \sum_{k=1}^{m} r_{ik}x_k = \sum_{k=1}^{m} \sum_{s=1}^{m} E[\rho_{is}q_{sk}x_k].$$

Because of the first two assumptions, this reduces further to

$$E\delta x_i = \sum_{k=1}^{m} \beta_{ik}^2 E(\delta a_{ki}^2) x_k = \sum_{k=1}^{m} \beta_{ik}^2 x_k \text{ Var}(a_{ki}). \qquad (4.23e)$$

Similarly var $x_i$ for $i$ in the optimal basis can be expressed as

$$\operatorname{Var} x_i = \sum_{k=1}^{m} A_{ki}^2 \operatorname{Var}(b_k) + \sum_{k=1}^{m} \sum_{j=1}^{m} A_{ki}^2 x_j^2 \operatorname{Var}(a_{kj}) \qquad (4.23f)$$

where $A_{ij}$ is the reduced co-factor of $a_{ij}$ in the optimal basis matrix $B$ and $\operatorname{Var}(a_{ij})$ denotes the variance of $a_{ij}$, etc.

Note that the expected value and variance of the change in optimal solution can be computed, provided assumptions or stipulations are made about the coefficient of variation of the parameters and it could be reasonably assumed that errors are independent and small enough that cross products of (unlike elements of) errors are negligible. In one small example considered by Hanson, the maximum expected value of the objective function (note: $E\delta z = c_B' E\delta x_B$) increased by nearly 50 percent with considerable changes in the levels of optimal basic activities, when the input coefficient $a_{ij}$ was allowed to vary with a coefficient of variation of 2 percent. This fact is of course dependent on the structure of the particular optimal basis considered but the point remains it may sometimes be extremely risky to accept the results of linear programming without an analysis of the errors involved.

A more specific analysis of the effects of error on the stability of basic feasible solutions is possible in the context of a LP model with errors. Let us specify a LP problem under error as follows:

$$\text{maximize } z = (c + r)' x$$

under the conditions

$$(A + \alpha) x \leqslant b + \beta$$
$$x \geqslant 0.$$

We assume the error variables to satisfy certain regularity conditions and denote by the superscript $k$ the finite set of basic feasible solutions for any given sample observation of the triplet $(A + \alpha, b + \beta, c + r)$.

*Theorem 4.2*

Let $F^{(k)}(z)$ be the objective function value for the $k$th basic feasible solution at the point $z$ with $k = 1, 2, \ldots$ up to at most $\binom{m+n}{m}$. Assume the errors $\alpha = [\alpha_{ij}]$ to be distributed over an interval small enough that any set of column vectors from the coefficient matrix $(A + \alpha)$ that are linearly independent with error terms all zero (i.e., $\alpha = 0$) remain linearly independent under error. Suppose there is a selection $k_1$ (in particular this may be the optimal solution) such that $F^{(k_1)}(z) > F^{(k)}(z)$ for $k \neq k_1$. Then there is a general neighborhood $N(z)$ of $z$ defined by the errors throughout which $F^{(k_1)}(y) > > F^{(k)}(y)$ for all points $y$ belonging to the neighborhood $N(z)$.

The proof [11] follows from the observation that for all $k$ the objective function $F^{(k)}$ is a continuous function of the coefficients, if and only if the appropriate determinant of the coefficient matrix for the $k$th selection is nonsingular. If the LP problem is interpreted as a method of selecting an operating policy in some sense, one interpretation of this theorem is the following: an operating policy which is selected at its optimum under the assumption that the coefficient matrix is fixed and known, will still remain the best operating policy even though there might be some error made in specifying the coefficients or even though the value of the coefficients change slightly after the policy is put into effect. Some application of this type of analysis is reported by Sengupta, Millham and Tintner [11].

Analysis of errors due to approximation through rounding using appropriate norms of vectors and matrices is sometimes found useful especially for large LP models with coefficients ranging from very low to very high values. To fix ideas, define the norm of a vector $y$ of $n$ components as $\|y\|$:

$$\|y\| = \sum_{i=1}^{n} |y_i|,$$

where $|\cdot|$ denotes absolute values; similarly the norm of a square matrix $H$ is denoted by $\|H\|$:

$$\|H\| = \max_{j} \sum_{i=1}^{n} |h_{ij}|.$$

Further, to relate the vector and matrix norms the following compatibility condition is imposed:

$$\|Hy\| \leqslant \|H\| \cdot \|y\|.$$

Now consider a special case of the optimal basis equation (4.23a) with no variation in the resource vector (i.e., $\delta b = 0$), i.e.

$$(B + \delta B)(x_B + \delta x_B) = b. \tag{4.24a}$$

Denote $B^{-1}\delta B$ by $K$ and write $B + \delta B = B(I + K)$; then a necessary and sufficient condition for the inverse $(B + \delta B)^{1-}$ to exist (i.e. for the solution of (4.24a) to exist) after perturbations can be easily shown to be

$$\|K\| = \text{norm of } K < 1. \tag{4.24b}$$

Assuming this condition satisfied for admissible perturbations, (4.24a) can be rewritten as

$$\delta x_B = [(I + K)^{-1} - I] \, x_B. \tag{4.24c}$$

On taking norms on both sides of (4.24c) and applying the compatibility conditions for norms, we obtain

$$\frac{\|\delta x_B\|}{\|x_B\|} \leqslant \|B^{-1}\delta B\| / [1 - \|B^{-1}\delta B\|]. \tag{4.24d}$$

This inequality specifies the relative change in the optimal solution vector as a function of the perturbations in the optimal basis matrix. Again, since we have further

$$\|B^{-1}\delta B\| \leqslant \|B^{-1}\| \cdot \|\delta B\|, \tag{4.24e}$$

the inequality (4.24d) may be replaced by

$$\frac{\|\delta x_B\|}{\|x_B\|} \leqslant \frac{\|B^{-1}\| \cdot \|\delta B\|}{1 - \|B^{-1}\| \cdot \|\delta B\|}. \tag{4.24f}$$

However this inequality may provide a gross overestimate of the true error if $(\|B^{-1}\| \cdot \|\delta B\|)$ is considerably greater than $\|B^{-1} \delta B\|$. Denote

$$\|B\| \cdot \|B^{-1}\| = k_0$$
$$\|\delta B\| / \|B\| = r.$$

Then (4.24f) becomes

$$\|\delta x_B\| / \|x_B\| \leqslant k_0 r / (1 - k_0 r). \tag{4.24g}$$

The quantity $r$ is clearly a measure of the relative perturbation in matrix $B$ and the quantity $r$ is often taken as a condition number of the matrix $B$. In estimating an upper bound for the relative error in the optimal solution vector, the condition number of the matrix $B$ plays a significant role. These results are useful in determining to what extent relative errors in the optimal solution vector may be tolerated.

Note that in case $\delta b$ is not zero so that the right hand side of (4.24a) is $b + \delta b$ and the other conditions are satisfied, it is possible to derive an upper bound of the error as:

$$\|\delta x_B\| \leqslant \frac{\|B^{-1}\| \cdot \|\delta B\| \cdot \|x_B\| + \|B^{-1}\| \cdot \|\delta b\|}{1 - \|B^{-1}\| \cdot \|\delta B\|} \tag{4.24h}$$

i.e. as

$$\|\delta x_B\| \leqslant \frac{k_0 r \|x_B\| + k_0 \|\delta b\| / \|B\|}{1 - k_0 r}. \tag{4.24i}$$

Two comments may be added about these upper bounds. First, it is possible to use other simpler norms like

$$\|x\| = \max_i |x_i|; \qquad i = 1, 2, ..., n$$

$$\|B\| = \max_i \sum_{j=1}^{m} a_{ij}; \qquad (i, j = 1, 2, ..., m)$$

which are much easier to calculate and then use the above upper bounds to determine the tolerance level for the change in the optimal solution vector. Second, the above inequalities are all in scalar numbers, so that the effect of errors on the entire LP model can be easily evaluated (and sometimes it may be useful to consider this type of sensitivity measure along with chance-constraints in a chance-constrained LP model, which will be discussed in the next chapter).

### 4.1.5. Equivalent nonlinear programs

In the various types of sensitivity approaches considered before, we have implicitly assumed that variations or perturbations $\delta A$, $\delta b$, $\delta c$ in parameters are independent in some sense of the optimal decision variables. But in practical applications this assumption of relative independence is not likely to be always fulfilled. It is easy to illustrate this by assuming that variations in parameters are statistically random. Then instead of having the following problem which is linear

> Maximize $(\text{E}c)'x$
> under the conditions     E: expectation operator     (4.25a)
> $(\text{E}A)\,x \leqslant \text{E}b$
> $x \geqslant 0$

we have in general the following nonlinear programming problem:

> Maximize $\text{E}(c'x)$
> under the conditions                     (4.25b)
> $\text{E}(Ax \leqslant b)$
> $x \geqslant 0.$

The nonlinear viewpoint of the problem presupposes that errors are jointly likely in $(A, b, c, x)$ and not simply in $(A, b, c)$ independently of $x$. However it is easily noted that the LP model (4.25a) can be viewed as a special case (i.e., an approximation) of the more general problem (4.25b). But the point remains that various other special cases can be derived from the general model (4.25b). In the next chapter on probabilistic programming some of these aspects will be discussed in detail. In the present context it is assumed we have only one sample value of the triplet $(A, b, c)$ which is observed. Still one can outline two different lines of attack through equivalent programs.

The first line of attack is to generate hypothetical sample observations around the given observation and then construct a nonlinear problem in order to test the sensitivity of the optimal solution of the LP problem. For instance, consider the price coefficient $c_j$; if it could be assumed that it follows a Poisson-type distribution where mean equals variance, then the standard deviation of $c_j$ can be computed by taking the positive square root of $c_j$. Assuming mutual independence of different $c_j$'s, the variance of total profit $z$ can then be computed as

$$\text{Var } z = \sum_{j=1}^{n} c_j x_j^2; \qquad \text{Mean of } z = \sum_{j=1}^{n} c_j x_j.$$

An alternative way, suggested by Talacko (see Vajda), is to consider the ranges of variation of each parameter $(a_{ij}^{-} \leqslant a_{ij} \leqslant a_{ij}^{+}; b_i^{-} \leqslant b_i \leqslant b_i^{+}; c_j^{-} \leqslant c_j \leqslant c_j^{+})$ where the upper and lower bounds are fixed and then consider a sequence of LP problems by appropriate selection of parameters within the prescribed ranges such that the optimal objective function $z^{(k)}$ for the $k$th selection can be viewed as an increasing sequence

$$z^{(1)} \leqslant z^{(2)} \leqslant \cdots$$

For instance, $z^{(1)}$ may arise from the following LP problem

$$\text{Maximize } \sum_{j=1}^{n} c_j^{-} x_j$$

under the restrictions

$$\sum_{j=1}^{n} a_{ij}^{+} x_j \leqslant b_i^{-}$$

$$x_j \geqslant 0$$

whereas $z^{(2)}$ may arise from

$$\text{maximize } \sum_{j=1}^{n} c_j^{+} x_j$$

under the restrictions

$$\sum_{j=1}^{n} a_{ij}^{-} x_j \leqslant b_i^{+}$$

$$x_j \geqslant 0$$

and so on. A third method of constructing a nonlinear program to test the sensitivity of a linear program is sometimes available, if for example it can be assumed that the $c_j$ values are linear functions of activities; e.g. in economic models $c_j$ values depend on prices $(p_j)$, and prices may be viewed as in some sense dependent on supply. Similarly through reinvestment of profits, a relation between the resource $b_i$ and the past level of activities can be set up in a recursive LP model.

The second line of attack is to apply repricing theorems developed by Charnes and Cooper [12] to test the sensitivity of a LP model. To fix ideas, consider the following transportation-type LP model:

$$\min w = \sum_{i=1}^{m} \sum_{j=1}^{n} c_{ij} x_{ij}$$

under the restrictions

$$\sum_{j=1}^{n} x_{ij} = a_i \qquad\qquad (4.26a)$$

$$\sum_{i=1}^{m} x_{ij} = b_j$$

$$x_{ij} \geqslant 0.$$

Further, denote the minimum value of the objective function of this LP problem (4.26a) by $w^* = \sum_i \sum_j c_{ij} x_{ij}^*$ which represents the least total shipment cost satisfying all constraints. Charnes and Cooper have proved the following result:

*Theorem 4.3*

The optimal objective function $w^*$ is a concave function of the elements $c_{ij}$ and it is finitely piecewise linear in $c_{ij}$.

This theorem can be used to induce alternate optima around $w^*$ for a particular route, say, from origin $p$ to destination $q$. Consider for example the behavior of $w^*$ as a function of a particular coefficient $c_{pq}$. At some sufficiently low value, say $c_{pq}^L$, the maximum amount permitted is equal to the minimum of $(a_p, b_q)$, so that the smaller of these two amounts fixes the slope of the curve of $w^*$ as a function of $c_{pq}$. Let $c_{pq}^{(1)}$ be the largest value of $c_{pq}$ for which any amount is shipped over this route so that for all $c_{pq} \geqslant c_{pq}^{(1)}$ the value of $w^*$ is independent of $c_{pq}$. Between $c_{pq}^{(1)}$ and $c_{pq}^{(2)}$, say, the same optimal basis can be maintained so that the slope of this piece of the $w^* = f(c_{pq})$ graph is equal to $x_{pq}^{(1)}$, i.e. the amount shipped from $p$ to $q$ at a cost per unit of $c_{pq}^{(1)}$.

Hence, the method of inducing alternate optima with respect to this route $p$ to $q$ may be formulated as a problem in which it is desired to determine the maximum value of $c_{pq}$ which will produce a decrease of at least $\alpha w^*$ in the present best total shipment costs, where $\alpha$ is the preassigned proportionality factor $(0 < \alpha < 1)$. The the following problem results:

$$\max c_{pq} \tag{4.27a}$$

under the conditions

$$\sum_j x_{ij} = a_i; \sum_i x_{ij} = b_j \tag{4.27b}$$

$$\sum_{i^*} \sum_j c_{ij} x_{ij} + c_{pq} x_{pq} \leqslant w^* (1 - \alpha) \tag{4.27c}$$

$$x_{ij} \geqslant 0; \qquad i = 1, ..., m; \qquad j = 1, ..., n \tag{4.27d}$$

where $i^*$ denotes that the index $i$ runs from 1 to $m$ exluding the $p, q$ route in the double sum over $i$ and $j$. Now this problem is nonlinear, since the term $c_{pq} x_{pq}$ involves a product of two variables. This nonlinearity can however be transferred to the objective function by making the change of variables

$$y_{pq} = c_{pq} x_{pq}$$

which provides an equivalent problem

$$\max y_{pq} / x_{pq}$$

under the restrictions (4.27b), (4.27d) and

$$\sum_{i^*} \sum_j c_{ij} x_{ij} + y_{pq} \leqslant w^* (1 - \alpha). \tag{4.27e}$$

This equivalent problem is easily seen to be a special case of linear fractional functional programming, already discussed in ch. 2. An extension of this method of repricing to nonlinear convex (or concave) objective functions is also available.

Apart from its usefulness in sensitivity analysis, this theorem provides an interesting operational method for comparing LP solutions with different vectors of net prices, one of which may be the reference or the control vector.

### 4.2. Sensitivity in dynamic models

In control theory applications [13] the most common form of dynamic model seeks to determine a vector of control variables $u(t)$ as a function of time $t$ satisfying the dynamic equations and the constraints

$$\dot{x}(t) = Ax(t) + Bu(t) + v(t); \qquad\qquad A: n.n \tag{4.28a}$$
$$B: n.m; u(t): m.n$$

$u(t)$ belongs to a closed convex set                                    (4.28b)
i.e. $u_i(t)$ is bounded by all $t \geqslant 0$ with preassigned upper
and lower bounds;

the elements of the parameters, $A$, $B$, $v$ are bounded with
preassigned upper and lower bounds;                                      (4.28c)

initial values $x(0)$, $u(0)$ are preassigned;                           (4.28d)
and also optimizing a performance integral, i.e.

$$\text{optimize } W = \int_0^T F\big(x(t), u(t)\big)\, dt \tag{4.28e}$$

where the integrand $F(x(t), u(t))$ is a scalar function of the state vector
$x(t)$ and the control vector $u(t)$. By our notation here the dot over a variable
denotes its time derivative. With discrete time $\dot{x}(t)$ is usually approximated
by $x(t) - x(t-1)$.

Note that if the integrand in (4.28e) is a linear function and the upper
bound, lower bound restrictions on the control vector (4.28b) and the parameter vector (4.28c) are linear, then this is a problem in the continuous time
LP approach. Compared to the static LP problems considered before, at
least two additional facets of the sensitivity problem now become apparent,
e.g. (a) time-stability of the optimal solution as the time horizon extends to
infinity, for example, and (b) the sensitivity of the optimal solution with
respect to the optimal control vector.

Since the literature on control theory analysis of sensitivity [14] in dynamic
models is quite extensive, it is not possible to treat it comprehensively in this
section; hence, only a few selected results will be reported here.

Assume that the linear dynamic model (4.28) has been solved to obtain
an optimal control vector $u$ and the corresponding output-vector $\underline{x}$ with
coordinates $u_i(t)$ and $x_i(t)$ respectively for a fixed time horizon $0 \leqslant t \leqslant T$.
Now suppose there are perturbations introduced through the forcing term
$v(t)$ in (4.28a) satisfying certain regularity conditions such that the new
optimal solution is $\bar{u}$ and $\bar{x}$ with coordinates $\bar{u}_i(t)$ and $\bar{x}_i(t)$. Then the
following concepts of stability of the optimal solution vector $\underline{x} = x_i(t)$ may
be distinguished:

(i) An optimal solution trajectory $x_i(t)$ belonging to vector $\underline{x}$ is *stable*,
if for any given positive number $N$ and initial time $t_0 \geqslant 0$, a positive number
$M$ depending on $N$ and in general on $t_0$ can be found such that for any

perturbed trajectory $\bar{x}_i(t)$ belonging to $\bar{x}$, the initial distance inequality

$$d_0 < M, \text{ where } d_0 = d_t \text{ at } t = 0$$

implies for all time $t \geqslant t_0$ the inequality

$$d_t < N.$$

Here $d_t$ represents the Euclidean distance between the two trajectories $\underline{x} = \underline{x}(t)$ and $\bar{x}(t) = \bar{x}$.

(ii) An optimal solution trajectory $x_i(t)$ belonging to $\underline{x} = \underline{x}(t)$ is *asymptotically stable*, if it is stable and in addition a positive number $M_1 \geqslant M$ exists such that starting from any initial distance $d_0$ for which

$$d_0 < M_1$$

the limiting condition

$$\lim_{t \to \infty} d_t = 0$$

holds uniformly till the initial quantities $t_0$ and $x_i(t_0)$ are reached.

(iii) An optimal solution trajectory $x_i(t)$ belonging to $\underline{x} = \underline{x}(t)$ is *asymptotically stable in the large*, if it is asymptotically stable and the number $M_1$ is also very large.

(iv) An optimal solution trajectory $x_i(t)$ belonging to $\underline{x}$ is said to be structurally stable in a parameter space $S_0$, if the stability of $x_i(t) = \underline{x} = \underline{x}(t)$ is invariant in that space $S_0$ (also called Lefschetz stability).

(v) If the perturbations $v_i(t) = v_i(t; x_1, ..., x_n)$ in (4.28a) are constantly acting in such a manner that the optimal basis equations (4.28a) have unique solutions under given initial conditions, then an optimal solution trajectory $x_i(t)$ belonging to $\underline{x} = \underline{x}(t)$ is said to be *stable under persistent perturbances*, if in addition to stability conditions mentioned in (i) above, $x_i(t)$ for $t = t_0$ satisfies some appropriate restrictions on the magnitude of $v_i(t)$. For instance, if the magnitude of perturbations satisfies the condition

$$\int_0^\infty \max_{x_i} |v_i(t, x_1, ..., x_n)| \, dt < Q \tag{4.29a}$$

where $Q$ is an appropriate positive number, then the optimal solution $\underline{x} = \underline{x}(t)$ is said to have the property of integral stability. If (4.29a) is replaced by

$$\int_t^{t+\tau} \max_{x_i} v_i(t, x_1, ..., x_n) \, dt < Q \tag{4.29b}$$

where $\tau$ is a small time interval,

then the system is said to have '*stability in the mean*'. Again if

$$\max_{x_i} |v_i(t, x_1, ..., x_n)| < Q \tag{4.29c}$$

then the optimal solution $x_i(t)$ is called *totally stable* in respect of perturbations (e.g. Vrkov, Letov [14]).

Note that in case of total stability the perturbations must be small in magnitude but in case of stability in the mean, they may be large but the interval of time must then be small. Further note that we have referred all the time to the optimal solution vector $\underline{x} = \underline{x}(t) = (x_i(t))$. This implicitly assumes that the perturbations are such that the indices of the optimal basis are preserved over all $t \geq t_0$; otherwise the above stability discussions would have to relate to any feasible solution of the continuous LP system. Also, it is to be noted that the above discussions on stability are useful for inter-temporal models of investment planning for the whole economy based on dynamic input-output models of the Leontief type, using a difference equation version of (4.28a) for instance.

### 4.2.1. Sensitivity of optimal control policy

Apart from stability analysis, an important line of approach in control theory is concerned with developing indices or measures of relative sensitivity to serve as a standard for acceptance of an optimal control policy. A brief reference to this line of approach may be worthwhile. First, consider the control problem (4.28) and assume that the objective function (4.28e) is a minimization problem; further, let $r$ denote any of the elements of the parameter set $A$, $B$, and let $U$ be the closed set containing the feasible control vector $u(t)$. Let $R$ be the closed convex set containing all the $r$ parameters and let the asterisk over a variable denote its optimum value. Then the following measures (i.e. indices) of relative sensitivity ($S^R$), system sensitivity ($S^M$) and probabilistic sensitivity ($S^E$) can be usefully distinguished and applied:

$$S^R = \text{Relative Sensitivity} = \frac{W(r, u(t)) - W(r, u^*(t))}{W(r, u^*(t))} \tag{4.30a}$$

$$S^M = \text{System Sensitivity} = \max_{r \in R} [S^R(r, u(t))] \tag{4.30b}$$

$$S^E = \text{Probabilistic Sensitivity} = E[S^R(r, u(t))] \text{ over } r \in R \tag{4.30c}$$
$$(E \text{ is the expected value}).$$

The last measure (4.30c) is meaningful when the parametric variations could be assumed to be random either subjectively or objectively.

These sensitivity indices are useful either as a basis for comparison among alternative choices of parameters and the coefficients of the objective functional or as a method of accounting for incomplete specification of the system parameters.

Second, an alternative measure of system sensitivity considers the relative sensitivity of the eigenvalues of the system (4.28a) for the optimal control $u^*(t)$ in respect of variations in the parameters. For instance, the $n$ characteristic roots of matrix $A$ in (4.28a) solved from the characteristic equation $A - \lambda I = 0$ may also be written as

$$A\lambda_i = \lambda_i X_i; \qquad \lambda_i = i\text{th eigenroot}, \; X_i = \text{corresponding eigenvector}$$
$$i = 1, 2, ..., n. \tag{4.31a}$$

Consider the transpose $A'$ of matrix $A$: its eigenroots will be the same as those of $A$ but its eigenvectors will be different. Denote the eigenvectors of $A'$ by $V_i$. Then it can be shown that

$$\frac{\partial \lambda_i}{\partial \alpha} = \frac{X_i' \, (\partial A/\partial \alpha)' \, V_i}{X_i' V_i}; \qquad (i = 1, ..., n) \tag{4.31b}$$

where $\alpha$ is any parameters, i.e. any element of the matrix $A$, provided the eigenroots are distinct.

Equations of sensitivity become more complicated if there is a multiplicity of eigenroots. This formula (4.31b) is often used in numerical computation analysis as a satisfactory method of finding the sensitivities of the eigenroots. Once the eigenvectors $X_i$ and $V_i$ have been found for a given eigenroot, the denominator can be evaluated and the matrix $\partial A/\partial \alpha$ will in general be very sparse. In case the problem has elements of randomness, this line of work lends itself to a generalization in terms of the statistical distribution of the latent roots as functions of random elements. A recent application of these ideas to simultaneous econometric equation systems has been made by Neudecker and Van de Panne [15].

Third, measures of sensitivity based on norms of appropriate vectors and matrices have also been found very useful in certain types of control systems. Consider a special case of equation (4.28a) assuming $y(t) = \dot{x}(t) - Ax(t)$ and $v(t) = 0$, e.g.,

$$y(t) = Bu(t)$$

which is written for simplicity as

$$y = Bu. \tag{4.32a}$$

The restrictions on $u$ are that $u$ is contained in a closed set $U$. Then if there are parameter variations in $B$, the system becomes

$$y + \delta y = (B + \delta B)\, u \,. \tag{4.32b}$$

It is apparent from this that $\delta y = (\delta B \cdot u)$ is a characterization of the failure of the system to act like $B$ at the control level $u$. (Without loss of generalization the level of $u$ may be the optimal level itself.) Denote the norm of a vector or matrix by $\|\cdot\|$ and let $r$ be any free parameter which allows a degree of freedom in the specification of the system sensitivity measure $M = M(\delta B, u, r)$ as

$$M = \left[ \frac{\|\delta B \cdot u\|^2}{\|u\|^2 + r\,\|Bu\|^2} \right]^{\frac{1}{2}} ; 0 \leqslant r < \infty \,. \tag{4.32c}$$

In case the control level $u$ in (4.32c) is not optimal, then the measure becomes

$$\operatorname*{Sup}_{u \in U} M \,. \tag{4.32d}$$

An important defect of such a measure is that it does not consider in a basic sense the relative structures of the two matrices $\delta B$ and $B$. To remedy this defect, assume that the set of admissible variations in the optimal control vector $u$ is contained in the Hilbert space $H_u$ and the corresponding variations in $y$ belong to the Hilbert space $H_y$. Further assume that $P_1$, $P_2, \ldots, P_m$ denote the orthogonal projections of $H_u$ *onto* the pairwise orthogonal subspaces $H_u^1, H_u^2, \ldots, H_u^m$ and $Q_1, Q_2, \ldots, Q_n$ the orthogonal projections of $H_y$ *onto* the pairwise orthogonal subspaces $H_y^1, \ldots, H_y^n$ such that

$$P_i P_j = 0, \; i \neq j \text{ and } I = P_1 + \cdots + P_m$$
$$Q_i Q_j = 0, \; i \neq j \text{ and } I = Q_1 + \cdots + Q_n \,.$$

Then a matrix sensitivity indicator can be defined by $M_{ij} = M_{ij}(\delta B, H_u, r)$ where

$$M_{ij} = \operatorname*{Sup}_{u \in H_u} \left[ \frac{\|\delta B_{ij} \cdot u\|^2}{\|u\|^2 + r\,\|B_{ij} \cdot u\|^2} \right]^{\frac{1}{2}} \tag{4.32e}$$

where

$$B_{ij} = Q_j B P_i$$
$$\delta B_{ij} = Q_j \cdot \delta B \cdot P_i \,.$$

This measure (4.32e) is based on the relative structures of the matrices $\delta B$ and $B$ and hence more fundamental than the measure (4.32c). Moreover, a scalar-valued sensitivity measure can be easily built out of this matrix measure. Noting that the Euclidean norm of a matrix $[a_{ij}]$ is defined by

$$\|[a_{ij}]\|_E = \left[\sum_{i=1}^{n} \sum_{j=1}^{n} |a_{ij}|^2\right]^{\frac{1}{2}}$$

the scalar valued sensitivity measure $S_{\delta B}$ may be defined as

$$S_{\delta B} = \|[M_{ij}]\|_E \quad \text{where} \quad M_{ij} \text{ is defined in (4.32e)}. \tag{4.32f}$$

Two general comments about these measures may be added. First, some of these measures are computationally very expensive, especially for large models; however, if the sensitivity with respect to only a few critical parameters is required, then it may be still worthwhile. Second, almost all the above sensitivity measures except a very few are based on nonstochastic variations of the parameters. Stochastic variations are considered in the next chapter.

### 4.2.2. Sensitivity in nonlinear models

Broadly speaking, for a sufficiently general nonlinear (programming) model we do not have adequate tools or even the theory for sensitivity analysis. Here by a sufficiently general nonlinear model is meant a model in which the nonlinear functions have regions of convexity, concavity or otherwise simultaneously. However, if the nonlinear functions have appropriate concavities (i.e. if the problem is to maximize $f(x)$ subject to $g(x) \geqslant 0$, $x \geqslant 0$, and both $f$ and $g$ are concave and continuous functions of $x$ and the constraint set is well-behaved), then linear approximations around selected points can be defined and so the various techniques of sensitivity analysis discussed before can be applied to the equivalent linear approximate model. Note that in this case the sensitivity analysis techniques would be valid only *locally* around the selected point (or grid) and this conditional nature of local sensitivity analysis could be generalized by considering several selected points rather than one; in fact, there are methods of sequential selection [16] using the techniques of steepest ascent (i.e. in the direction of the gradient vector).

The fact that a local maximum may not be the global maximum constitutes one great difficulty in a general nonlinear program, e.g. computation may have to be terminated at some step before the optimal solution is reached and some evaluation of the truncation error has to be made. The relations between an optimal solution and the set of suboptimal solutions following a given algorithm (e.g. dynamic programming, gradient method, etc.) have not been much explored and we do not have as yet a good set of operational criteria for comparing the relative power, and hence efficiency, of different computational algorithms in this regard.

However, in special cases of nonlinear programs containing random parameters in the objective function only, several results are available [17] for computing bounds for optimal solutions whenever the random elements are replaced by their expected values. For instance, let the scalar (nonlinear) objective function $f(x, d)$ of the decision vector $x$ and the set of parameters $d$ be assumed convex and continuous in $d$ in region $R$ of the Euclidean space for every vector $x$ satisfying the linear constraints $Ax \leqslant b, x \geqslant 0$; then the following inequalities can be easily proved [18] by using Jensen's probabilistic inequality,

$$\mathrm{E} \max_x f(x, d) \geqslant \max_x f(x, \mathrm{E}d) \qquad (4.33)$$

where $x \in X$: $\{x \mid Ax \leqslant b, x \geqslant 0\}$, $f(x, d)$ is assumed concave and continuous in $x$ for any fixed $d$ and E denotes expectation. These results are useful in analyzing the implications for optimal deterministic solutions when, for a nonlinear program, the parameters in the objective function are varied or sequentially improved.

*An empirical application*

An interesting economic example of nonlinear optimization in macro-dynamic models is provided by the optimal growth path computation problem analyzed by Ramsay [19] and more recently by various turnpike theorems [20]. We consider a very special case of this formulation [21], in which the optimization problem is to

$$\text{maximize} \int_0^T \log(C - C_0) \, \mathrm{d}t$$

under the restrictions

$$Y = C + I; \qquad I = \mathrm{d}K/\mathrm{d}t = \dot{K} \qquad (4.34)$$
$$Y = f(K, L); \qquad L = L_0 \exp(rt)$$

where the time horizon $[0, T]$ is fixed, $C, I, K, Y$ and $L$ refer respectively to aggregate levels of consumption, investment, stock of capital, net national product and labor demand, $C_0$ is initial consumption taken as a function of initial period population, and $L_0$ is the initial employment level. The function $f(K, L)$ is the production function in the model and for estimation purposes two types of functions were specified, e.g.

$$Y = a_0 + a_1 K + a_2 L; \qquad \text{(linear case)} \qquad (4.35a)$$

$$Y = \exp(m_0 t) \cdot K^{m_1} L^{m_2}; \qquad \text{(Cobb-Douglas case)}. \qquad (4.35b)$$

This model was applied to analyze the empirical specification of optimal growth-paths using long run statistical data for the United States economy (1900–1953). Obviously, the purpose was illustrative, since the model is highly aggregative. The least squares estimates of parameters in (4.35a) and (4.35b) were as follows:

$$a_0 = 49\,786\,533; \quad a_1 = 0.1940; \quad a_2 = 1.7084; \quad (R^2 = 0.9164)$$
$$m_0 = 0.0131, \quad m_1 = 0.2639; \quad m_2 = 1.8678; \quad (R^2 = 0.9913).$$

Now the optimal solution of problem (4.34) combined with (4.35b) cannot be solved quite generally in a closed form, since the final Euler-Lagrange condition reduces here to a complicated nonlinear differential equation; however, if in this case the integrand of the objective function of (4.34) is approximated by

$$C - C_0 \approx (\log Y - \dot{K}/Y)$$

then the resulting Euler-Lagrange equations become linear differential equations. The optimal solutions in this case are termed approximate optimal paths and denoted by $Y_t^*, C_t^*, I_t^*$. These paths may be compared with the optimal solutions $Y_t^0, C_t^0, I_t^0$ of the model (4.34) combined with the linear production function (4.35a), if the two initial conditions are identically imposed for the two problems (e.g. $Y_t$ at $t=0$ is taken to be $\$595.1 \times 10^9$ for 1963 and $\dot{Y}_t$ at $t=0$ as 0.03).

The results are then as follows (in units of $\$10^9$):

| $t$ | $Y_t^*$ | $C_t^*$ | $I_t^*$ | $Y_t^0$ | $C_t^0$ | $I_t^0$ |
|---|---|---|---|---|---|---|
| 0 | 595.1 | 381.5 | 213.6 | 595.1 | 503.1 | 92.0 |
| 1 | 641.8 | 411.4 | 230.4 | 616.9 | 505.1 | 111.8 |
| 2 | 691.8 | 443.4 | 248.4 | 646.0 | 510.3 | 135.7 |
| 3 | 744.8 | 477.4 | 267.4 | 682.4 | 517.6 | 164.8 |
| 4 | 800.8 | 513.3 | 287.5 | 726.2 | 526.2 | 200.0 |
| 5 | 860.1 | 551.3 | 308.8 | 778.5 | 535.8 | 242.7 |
| 10 | 1203.3 | 771.3 | 432.0 | 1222.5 | 582.2 | 640.3 |

These results show how different orders of approximation can affect the predicted speed of growth along the optimal path. More work is needed in this area before actual policy recommendations can be made on the basis of such macrodynamic models. Some simulation studies along this line are available [22] in control theory applications.

### 4.3. Policy models and sensitivity analysis

The theory of economic policy models [23] usually classifies variables as targets (i.e. state variables), instruments (i.e. control variables) and data (i.e. exogenous variables) and the objective function is usually viewed as a function of target variables (and sometimes also control variables). If the condition of optimization of the objective function is required to be satisfied, then the policy model is said to be a flexible target model; otherwise it is a fixed target policy model. Whereas in the first case the policy model may be viewed essentially as a programming problem, in the second case the emphasis is more on forecasting rather than optimizing and hence more use is made here of econometric models rather than programming models.

Several interesting applications of both macro and microeconometric models are available now [24] which specifically discuss the various technical and operational problems of statistical estimation under various conditions of interdependence, simultaneity and the boundary conditions imposed by policy constraints. Decision rules derived from econometric, models of various types have considerable operational implications for policy making at different levels and hence sensitivity analysis methods applied to decision rules derived from econometric models are potentially very important. However, since this field has been critically surveyed by Fox, Sengupta, and Thorbecke [25], we will not discuss this aspect in any detail.

### 4.3.1. Applications in LP models

Since a flexible target linear policy model with inequalities as boundary conditions may be viewed generally as an LP model, it will be worthwhile to discuss in this section a few empirical applications of some of the sensitivity measures discussed in section 4.1. We investigate here[1] the application of three different methods of sensitivity analysis to the empirical crop-mix problem of a farmer who has to allocate his fixed resources such as land, labor and capital among different crops, when their marginal profitability coefficients have variations due to variations in market prices.

The first method considers perturbation of data around the optimal basis under the assumption of a preassigned coefficient of variation for the elements of the resource vector and the coefficient matrix and computes the variability of the optimal solution vector and the objective function measured in terms of variance. The second method is suitable for analyzing the marginal

---

[1] This illustration is discussed in more details in section 5.2.2 of ch. 5.

variation of the optimal objective function due to changes in the individual input coefficients. The third method applies the fractile criterion by which the $\alpha$-fractile of the cumulative statistical distribution of the objective function is maximized with the value of $\alpha$ assumed to be preassigned. In this case the transformed problem is usually nonlinear in the activity vector and the solution may be compared with the linear programming solutions analyzed before.

The empirical formulation of our problem is based on annual statistical data relating to a single farm enterprise in Hancock County, Iowa for the years 1928–1952, which were developed and utilized initially by Tintner and Babbar in their studies on stochastic linear programming. These data show quite interestingly the role of short-term variations in weather and other random elements in agricultural production and resource use. Babbar and Tintner found for these data that the input coefficients did not have any trend; hence, to specify an optimal product-mix in the face of observed variations in market prices and therefore in net returns presents an interesting choice problem, for the solution of which our different sensitivity analyses should be useful.

Five activities are considered, $x_1$ growing corn, $x_2$ oats, $x_3$ soybeans, $x_4$ flax and $x_5$ wheat. The resource vector $b$ has the components $b_1 = 148$ (land in acres), $b_2 = 1,800$ (capital in dollars), $b_3 = 182$ (manhours available in May only), and $b_4 = 182$ (minimum of manhours available for different months). The input coefficients are derived as an average over 25 years and the resulting coefficient matrix $A = (a_{ij})$ is taken as fixed:

|  | $x_1$ | $x_2$ | $x_3$ | $x_4$ | $x_5$ |  |
|---|---|---|---|---|---|---|
| | 0.0227 | 0.0277 | 0.0586 | 0.0925 | 0.0908 | land |
| $A =$ | 0.3177 | 0.2787 | 0.7081 | 0.9696 | 1.0036 | capital |
| | 0.0256 | 0.0752 | 0.0549 | 0.2119 | 0.4232 | May labor |
| | 0.0525 | 0.0000 | 0.1168 | 0.0000 | 0.0000 | other labor |

Two new considerations were added to the empirical data provided by the Babbar-Tintner studies. First, in order to get more diversified solutions, two additional restrictions, e.g., $x_3 \geqslant 200$ and $x_5 \geqslant 100$ were added, so that the sensitivity of optimal solutions could be perceived under several inequality constraints. Second, the vector of net prices $c$ was not taken to be fixed but assumed to be probabilistic, varying directly in proportion to market prices, for which quarterly and monthly data are available.

Denote the set $R$ of restrictions as

$$R = \{x \mid Ax \leqslant b; x_3 \geqslant 200, x_5 \geqslant 100, x \geqslant 0\};$$

then the following linear programs are computed and solutions compared whenever they are meaningful:

$$\text{Problem P1: } \max c'x, \ x \text{ in } R \tag{4.36}$$

where the vector $c$ is the same as Babbar and Tintner's;

$$\text{Problems P2 to P9: } \max c_q'x, \ x \text{ in } R \tag{4.37}$$

where the subscript $q$ denotes quarterly prices for the two years 1964 and 1965 (i.e., a set of eight problems);

$$\text{Problems P10 to P16: } \max \bar{c}_s'x, \ x \text{ in } R \tag{4.38}$$

where $\bar{c}_s$ is an estimate of the maxima of quarterly prices which are assumed to be generated by independent normal distributions and the estimate uses simulated values $E\bar{c} \pm k\sigma_{\bar{c}}$ for $k = 0, 0.1, 0.2$ and $0.3$, where E is expectation and $\sigma_{\bar{c}}$ is the estimated standard deviation;

$$\text{Problems P17 to P23: } \max(\underline{c})_s'x, \ x \text{ in } R \tag{4.39}$$

where $(\underline{c})_s$ is an estimate of the minima of quarterly prices using simulated values $E\underline{c} \pm k\sigma_{\underline{c}}$ for $k = 0, 0.1, 0.2$ and $0.3$ assuming independence and mutual normality;

$$\text{Problems P24 to P29: } \max \bar{c}_r'x, \ x \text{ in } R \tag{4.40}$$

where the subscript $r$ in $\bar{c}$ denotes the maxima of quarterly prices for six years 1960–1965; and

$$\text{Problems P30 to P35: } \max(\underline{c})_r'x, \ x \text{ in } R \tag{4.50}$$

where the subscript $r$ in $\underline{c}$ denotes the minima of quarterly prices for different crops for six years (1960–1965) available in U.S.D.A. Reports.

*Perturbation analysis*

In this approach errors are admitted around a specific optimal basis with the condition that they preserve the indices of the optimal basis and therefore the errors must necessarily be small and specially structured so that they preserve feasibility and optimality. Denote the system of optimal basis equations by $Bx = b$, which under errors gets transformed to

$$(B + \delta B)(x + \delta x) = b + \delta b \qquad \begin{matrix} B: m.m; & b: m.1; \\ x: m.1 \end{matrix} \tag{4.51a}$$

where the operator $\delta$ denotes small errors preserving the original optimal basis. From this it can be shown [10] that

$$\delta x = B^{-1}\delta b + \left( \sum_{i=1}^{\infty} (-1)^i (B^{-1}\delta B)^i (x + B^{-1}\delta B) \right) \quad (4.51b)$$

where $x = B^{-1}b$.

Following Hanson [10], if we make the following simplifying assumptions that the errors $\delta B$, $\delta b$ are mutually independent with zero expected values, the higher moments beyond the second are negligible and the infinite series on the right hand-side of (4.51b) can be truncated at $i=2$ with negligible error on the average, then the expected value and variance of the perturbation vector $\delta x$ can be explicitly computed as

$$E\delta x_i = \sum_{k=1}^{m} r_{ik}^2 x_k \, \text{Var}\,(a_{ki}) \quad (4.51c)$$

$$\text{Var}\,x_i = E\delta x_i^2 = \sum_{k=1}^{m} A_{ki}^2 \, \text{Var}\,(b_k) + \sum_{k=1}^{m} \sum_{j=1}^{m} A_{ki}^2 x_j^2 \, \text{Var}\,(a_{kj}) \quad (4.51d)$$

where $r_{ik}$ is an element of the inverse matrix $R = B^{-1}$, $A_{ij}$ is the reduced co-factor of $a_{ij}$ in the optimal basis matrix $B$, and $\text{Var}(a_{ij})$ denotes the variance of $a_{ij}$.

These computations are helpful in showing how the optimal solution vector $(x)$ and hence the optimal function vary with preassigned small perturbations in the parameters contained in $B$ and $b$. For our empirical problem we assumed a coefficient of variation of 1 percent for each element of $B$ and $b$ in the optimal basis. The matrix $B$ for problems P2–P6, P9–P11, P14–P18, P21–P28 and P30–P35 is the same, i.e.,

$$B = \begin{bmatrix} 0.0586 & 0.0925 & 0.0908 & 1 & 0 \\ 0.7081 & 0.9696 & 1.0036 & 0 & 1 \\ 0.0549 & 0.2119 & 0.4232 & 0 & 0 \\ 0.1168 & 0.0000 & 0.0000 & 0 & 0 \\ 0.0000 & 0.0000 & -1.0000 & 0 & 0 \end{bmatrix}$$

and its inverse $R = B^{-1} = (r_{ij})$ is

$$R = \begin{bmatrix} 0 & 0 & 0.0000 & 8.5617 & 0.0000 \\ 0 & 0 & 4.7192 & -2.2182 & 1.9972 \\ 0 & 0 & 0.0000 & 0.0000 & -1.0000 \\ 1 & 0 & -0.4365 & -0.2965 & -0.0939 \\ 0 & 1 & -4.5757 & -3.9117 & -0.9329 \end{bmatrix}.$$

Denote the above two sets of values of $B$ and $R$ as case I and case II respectively. Then the following values may be obtained by applying the relation (4.51c):

| Case I | Case II |
|---|---|

*Case I*

$\bar{x}_1 = 1558.2$; $\bar{x}_2 = 255.5$; $\bar{x}_3 = 100$

$E\delta\bar{x}_1 = 0.0024$; $E\delta\bar{x}_2 = 0.0100$; $E\delta\bar{x}_3 = 0.0349$

$\bar{x}_4 = 24.0$; $\bar{x}_5 = 348.6$

*Case II*

$E\delta x_1 = 0.01$; $E\delta\bar{x}_2 = 0.0036$

$E\delta\bar{x}_3 = 0.0242$;

$E\delta\bar{x}_4 = 0.0363$; $E\delta\bar{x}_5 = 0.3022$

$E\delta\bar{x}_6 = 0.0200$

where it should be mentioned that in case I, activities $\bar{x}_4$, $\bar{x}_5$ are slack, $\bar{x}_1$ corresponds to $x_3$ of the original problem, $\bar{x}_2$ to original $x_4$ and $\bar{x}_3$ to original $x_5$ and in case II, $\bar{x}_1$ corresponds to original $x_1$, $\bar{x}_2$ to original $x_3$, $\bar{x}_3$ to original, $x_4$, $\bar{x}_4$ to original $x_5$, $\bar{x}_5$ to original $x_6$ and $\bar{x}_6$ to original $x_7$ whereas $\bar{x}_6$ and $\bar{x}_7$ here are slack.

The computation of $\text{Var}\, x_i$ is more complicated. For case I problems, we need to compute 25 co-factors and for case II 36 co-factors before we can apply the formula (4.51d). The following two tables (tables 4.1 and 4.2) summarize the effect of perturbation around the optimal basis in terms of both optimal activities and the maximand. For this purpose we define the following indicators:

$$D_i^+ = (x_i + E\delta x_i)/(\text{Var}\, x_i)^{\frac{1}{2}}; \quad \begin{array}{l} i = 1, ..., 5 \text{ for case I} \\ = 1, ..., 6 \text{ for case II} \end{array} \quad (4.51e)$$

$$D_i^- = (x_i - E\delta x_i)/(\text{Var}\, x_i)^{\frac{1}{2}}; \quad i = \text{as above} \quad (4.51f)$$

$$E\delta z = \sum_{i=1}^{m} c_i E\delta x_i; \quad i \in \text{optimal basis (as above)} \quad (4.51g)$$

$$\text{Var}\, z = \sum_{i=1}^{m} c_i^2\, \text{Var}\, x_i; \quad i \in \text{optimal basis (as above)} \quad (4.51h)$$

$$D_k^-(z) = (z^{(k)} - E\delta z^{(k)})/(\text{Var}\, z^{(k)})^{\frac{1}{2}}; \ k = 1, 2, ..., 35 \quad (4.51i)$$

where $z$ is the maximand (i.e., optimal value of the objective function), $z^{(k)}$ is the maximand for the $k$th problem, and for any fixed $k$th problem the quantities $E\delta z^{(k)}$, $\text{Var}\, z^{(k)}$ are estimated by applying (4.51g) and (4.51h) with (4.51c) and (4.51d). Also the crop-wise breakdown of total variance of optimal profits is presented in table 4.3.

Several comments are in order for the perturbation characteristics reported in tables 4.1 through 4.3. First, note that this scheme of calculation does not require any prior assumption about probabilities of the original parameters. Table 4.1 shows that the soybeans activity has the highest variance around the optimal solution and wheat has the least in case I problems, whereas in case II

TABLE 4.1

Characteristics of perturbation around the optimal solution for case I and case II problems.

| Crop | $E\delta x_i$ | $\mathrm{Var}\, x_i$ | $D_i^+$ | $D_i^-$ |
|------|------|------|------|------|
| | | *Case I* | | |
| Soybeans | 0.0024 | 0.2974 | 2857.00 | 2856.99 |
| Flax | 0.0100 | 0.0864 | 869.28 | 869.21 |
| Wheat | 0.0349 | 0.0012 | 2863.78 | 2861.78 |
| | | *Case II* | | |
| Corn | 0.0100 | 0.2691 | 5825.40 | 5825.40 |
| Soybeans | 0.0036 | 0.0259 | 1242.29 | 1242.25 |
| Flax | 0.0242 | 0.0164 | 1892.69 | 1892.31 |
| Wheat | 0.0363 | 0.0006 | 4353.03 | 4349.87 |

problems corn has the highest variability and wheat the least. Second, although the neighborhood around the optimal solution defined in this way is very small in size, because of the simplifying approximations made, yet since this neighborhood preserves the indices of the optimal basis, approximate or asymptotic normality may hold under certain regularity conditions (which are mentioned in ch. 5 in detail):

$$\mathrm{Prob}\quad [(\delta x_i - E\delta x_i)/(\mathrm{Var}\, x_i)^{\frac{1}{2}} < t] \to N(t)$$
$$\mathrm{Prob}\quad [(\delta z^{(k)} - E\delta z^{(k)})/(\mathrm{Var}\, z^{(k)})^{\frac{1}{2}} < t] \to N(t)$$

where $N(t)$ is the cumulative distribution of a unit normal variate. These asymptotic probabilities could be utilized in setting confidence intervals or otherwise as in the work of Babbar and Tintner. Third, a comparison of the two sets of problems P24–P29 and P30–P35 based on two extreme sets of prices (maxima and minima) shows that it cannot generally be stated that the optimistic approach of taking quarterly maximum prices will necessarily result in higher variance of optimal profits, although the average value of $E\delta z$ for P24–P29 is higher than that for P20–P35. Note further, however, that our calculations are all constrained by the assumption that the coefficient of variation is only 1 percent.

*Sensitivity coefficient approach*

This approach suggests a method of specification of the neighborhood around the optimal solution vector and the maximand in terms of the partial derivatives with respect to the various parameters. For instance, let $v$ be the maximand of a primal linear programming problem at its optimal basis;

TABLE 4.2

Expected perturbation and variance of the maximand around the optimal solution.*

| Problem | $E\delta z^{(k)}$ | $\mathrm{Var}\,z^{(k)}$ | $D_{k}^{-}(z)$ | $\dfrac{(\mathrm{Var}\,z^{(k)})^{\frac{1}{2}}}{E\delta z^{(k)}}$ |
|---|---|---|---|---|
| *P1* | 0.1955 | 1.0973 | 6118.23 | 5.3574 |
| P2 | 0.0864 | 2.9628 | 2998.88 | 19.9328 |
| P3 | 0.0826 | 2.8931 | 2992.14 | 20.6001 |
| P4 | 0.0819 | 2.5682 | 2982.04 | 19 5766 |
| P5 | 0 0825 | 2.3170 | 2971.72 | 18.4566 |
| P6 | 0 1015 | 2.6499 | 3008.60 | 16.0413 |
| P7 | 0.1539 | 0.6097 | 6011.97 | 5.0746 |
| P8 | 0.1365 | 0.5842 | 5943.78 | 5.5976 |
| *P9* | 0.0856 | 2.6835 | 2982.23 | 19.1432 |
| P10 | 0.1002 | 2.6708 | 2974.23 | 16.3051 |
| P11 | 0.1042 | 2.8419 | 2977.96 | 16.1825 |
| P12 | 0.1722 | 0.7673 | 5987.50 | 5.0875 |
| P13 | 0.1784 | 0.8454 | 6027.35 | 5.1551 |
| P14 | 0.0963 | 2.5050 | 2970.23 | 16.4379 |
| P15 | 0.0923 | 2.3447 | 2965.97 | 16.5818 |
| *P16* | 0.0884 | 2.1896 | 2961.34 | 16.7390 |
| P17 | 0.0905 | 2.1634 | 2976.88 | 16.2534 |
| P18 | 0.0944 | 2.3178 | 2980.89 | 16.1206 |
| P19 | 0.1562 | 0.6229 | 5979.68 | 5.0538 |
| P20 | 0.1623 | 0.6934 | 6024.46 | 5.1291 |
| P21 | 0.0866 | 2.0144 | 2972.55 | 16.3986 |
| P22 | 0.0826 | 1.8710 | 2967.87 | 16.5579 |
| *P23* | 0.0787 | 1.7327 | 2962.76 | 16.7332 |
| P24 | 0.0864 | 2.9683 | 2998.96 | 19.9513 |
| P25 | 0.1016 | 2.6853 | 3009.27 | 16.1245 |
| P26 | 0.1042 | 2.6453 | 3014.55 | 15.6132 |
| P27 | 0 1062 | 2.5853 | 2915.21 | 15.1440 |
| P28 | 0.1041 | 3.3946 | 2984.63 | 17.6981 |
| *P29* | 0.1578 | 0.5340 | 6016.04 | 4.6324 |
| P30 | 0.0846 | 2.3169 | 2970.45 | 18.0017 |
| P31 | 0.0834 | 2.3028 | 2967.28 | 18.1902 |
| P32 | 0.1013 | 2.3658 | 3000.89 | 15.1790 |
| P33 | 0.1021 | 2.2200 | 2974.58 | 14.5948 |
| P34 | 0.0970 | 2.1341 | 2996.24 | 15.0653 |
| P35 | 0.0945 | 1.6907 | 2939.83 | 13.7624 |

* Here the problems P1, 7, 8, 12, 13, 19, 20 and 29 show values of approximately 6000 for $D_{k}^{-}(z)$ and 5.0 for $(\mathrm{Var}\,z^{(k)})^{\frac{1}{2}}/E\delta z^{(k)}$, while the others show values of approximately 3000 and 15.0 or more. This is due to the special data structure of this problem.

TABLE 4.3
Crop-wise variance of optimal profits.

| Problem | Corn | Soybeans | Flax | Wheat | Max Row | Total variance |
|---|---|---|---|---|---|---|
| P1 | 0.6549 | 0.2016 | 0.2381 | 0.0027 | 0.6549 (corn) | 1.0973 |
| P2 | – | 2.2491 | 0.7166 | 0.0026 | 2.2491 (soybeans) | 2.9683 |
| P3 | – | 2.1841 | 0.7067 | 0.0022 | 2.1841 (soybeans) | 2.8931 |
| P4 | – | 1.8886 | 0.6774 | 0.0023 | 1.8886 (soybeans) | 2.5682 |
| P5 | – | 1.6564 | 0.6582 | 0.0024 | 1.6564 (soybeans) | 2.3170 |
| P6 | – | 1.9338 | 0.7117 | 0.0044 | 1.9338 (soybeans) | 2.6499 |
| P7 | 0.3316 | 0.1430 | 0.1332 | 0.0019 | 0.3316 (corn) | 0.6097 |
| P8 | 0.3139 | 0.1443 | 0.1249 | 0.0012 | 0.5842 (corn) | 0.5842 |
| P9 | – | 1.9643 | 0.7166 | 0.0025 | 1.9643 (soybeans) | 2.6835 |
| P10 | – | 1.8613 | 0.8055 | 0.0040 | 1.8613 (soybeans) | 2.6708 |
| P11 | – | 1.9874 | 0.8501 | 0.0044 | 1.9874 (soybeans) | 2.8419 |
| P12 | 0.4104 | 0.1844 | 0.1700 | 0.0024 | 0.4104 (corn) | 0.7673 |
| P13 | 0.4677 | 0.1961 | 0.1790 | 0.0026 | 0.4677 (corn) | 0.8454 |
| P14 | – | 1.7392 | 0.7621 | 0.0036 | 1.7392 (soybeans) | 2.5050 |
| P15 | – | 1.6215 | 0.7199 | 0.0033 | 1.6215 (soybeans) | 2.3447 |
| P16 | – | 1.5077 | 0.6789 | 0.0030 | 1.5077 (soybeans) | 2.1896 |
| P17 | – | 1.5123 | 0.6479 | 0.0033 | 1.5123 (soybeans) | 2.1634 |
| P18 | – | 1.6262 | 0.6879 | 0.0036 | 1.6262 (soybeans) | 2.3178 |
| P19 | 0.3306 | 0.1519 | 0.1384 | 0.0020 | 0.3306 (corn) | 0.6229 |
| P20 | 0.3822 | 0.1625 | 0.1465 | 0.0022 | 0.3822 (corn) | 0.6934 |
| P21 | – | 1.4025 | 0.6090 | 0.0030 | 1.4025 (soybeans) | 2.0144 |
| P22 | – | 1.2970 | 0.5714 | 0.0027 | 1.2970 (soybeans) | 1.8710 |
| P23 | – | 1.1954 | 0.5349 | 0.0024 | 1.1954 (soybeans) | 1.7327 |
| P24 | – | 2.2491 | 0.7166 | 0.0026 | 2.2491 (soybeans) | 2.9683 |
| P25 | – | 1.9643 | 0.7166 | 0.0044 | 1.9643 (soybeans) | 2.6853 |
| P26 | – | 1.9338 | 0.7067 | 0.0048 | 1.9338 (soybeans) | 2.6453 |
| P27 | – | 1.6284 | 0.9523 | 0.0045 | 1.6284 (soybeans) | 2.5853 |
| P28 | – | 2.4497 | 0.9409 | 0.0041 | 2.4497 (soybeans) | 3.3946 |
| P29 | 0.2800 | 0.0965 | 0.1556 | 0.0020 | 0.2800 (corn) | 0.5340 |
| P30 | – | 1.6564 | 0.6582 | 0.0023 | 1.6564 (soybeans) | 2.3169 |
| P31 | – | 1.6424 | 0.6582 | 0.0022 | 1.6424 (soybeans) | 2.3028 |
| P32 | – | 1.6988 | 0.6629 | 0.0041 | 1.6988 (soybeans) | 2.3658 |
| P33 | – | 1.5190 | 0.6969 | 0.0041 | 1.5190 (soybeans) | 2.2200 |
| P34 | – | 1.5900 | 0.6113 | 0.0037 | 1.5900 (soybeans) | 2.1341 |
| P35 | – | 1.0849 | 0.6022 | 0.0036 | 1.0849 (soybeans) | 1.6907 |

then one can derive

$$\partial v/\partial c = x; \qquad \partial v/\partial b = y; \qquad \partial v/\partial a_{ij} = - x_j y_i$$

where $x$, $y$ denote optimal primal and dual vectors with components $x_j$, $y_j$, provided of course such expansions around the optimal pair $(x, y)$ are valid, e.g., the vector $c$ has to be in the interior of the cone associated with the solution vertex.

Practical applications of these sensitivity measures to oil refinery models have been reported by Saaty and Webb, who have suggested that averaging of such indices (i.e., proper scaling) over a series of steady-state time periods gives a method of evaluating changes in the neighborhood of the maximand. Sometimes, of course, when the changes are small in the sense that they preserve the indices of the optimal basis, use could be made of the formula

$$\Delta v \equiv \Delta z = \sum_j (\partial v/\partial c_j) \, \Delta c_j + \sum_i (\partial v/\partial b_i) \, \Delta b_i + \sum_i \sum_j (\partial v/\partial a_{ij}) \, \Delta a_{ij}$$

to analyze changes in the maximand $(\Delta v)$, in terms of the various components, $\Delta c_j$, $\Delta b_i$, $\Delta a_{ij}$ and their contributions.

However, the most important component is the marginal variation of the maximand with respect to the input-output coefficients $(\partial v/\partial a_{ij})$. Denoting by $k_{ij}$ the absolute value of these marginal variations (i.e., $k_{ij} = x_i y_j$), one can analyze how this sensitivity coefficient $k_{ij}$ varies for the three best maximands, i.e., $z_1, z_2$ and $z_3$, using the same data which underly tables 4.1, 4.2 and 4.3. The median values of $k_{ij}$ for $i=3, 4, j=1,...,5$ (for all the problems) are as follows (since the first two shadow prices $y_1$, $y_2$ are zero, $i=1, 2$ are omitted):

Median values of the sensitivity coefficient $(k_{ij})$
(Unit: $10^4$ dollars)[2]

|  | $x_1 y_3$ | $x_1 y_4$ | $x_2 y_3$ | $x_2 y_4$ | $x_3 y_3$ | $x_3 y_4$ | $x_4 y_3$ | $x_4 y_4$ | $x_5 y_3$ | $x_5 y_4$ |
|---|---|---|---|---|---|---|---|---|---|---|
| Maximand: $z_1$ | 4.261 | 4.594 | 0 | 0 | 2.029 | 2.095 | 0.341 | 0.360 | 0.135 | 0.1 |
| second best: $z_2$ | 3.997 | 3.913 | 0.763 | 1.657 | 0.271 | 0.266 | 0.328 | 0.315 | 0.135 | 0.1 |
| third best: $z_3$ | 2.478 | 4.523 | 0.581 | 1.030 | 0.178 | 0.317 | 0 | 0 | 0.088 | 0.1 |

(Note: The first best (maximand), second best and third best are defined in ch. 5 in more detail.)

---

[2] Note that these median values of $k_{ij}$ are not scaled. For instance, the median value $k_{31} = x_1 y_3$ when scaled should be written as $y_3 a_{31} x_1 = a_{31} \; x_1 y_3 = 0.0256 \times 4.261 \times 10^4 = $ = \$1090.82$, where $a_{31} =$ May labor input for corn, with its marginal profitability $y_3 = \$14.10$. Similarly other values would be changed.

Theoretically, one of the most satisfactory ways to utilize these sensitivity coefficients $(k_{ij})$ would be to estimate their statistical distributions which would naturally be functions of the distributions of $x_j$ and $y_i$ around the optimal basis, since then one could specify the cumulative probability $P(k_{ij} \leqslant k_0)$, where $k_0$ is a fixed preassigned number, and ask for optimal solutions satisfying this probabilistic condition in a specified manner, as is done in the methods of chance-constrained programming. Short of these distributional computations, we have followed two operational methods. First, we have evaluated the coefficient of elasticity $E_{ij} = k_{ij}a_{ij}/z_1$ of the maximand with respect to the input-coefficients in the optimal basis for all the 35 samples P1–P35, of which the median values are

$$E_{31} = 0.2216, \qquad E_{33} = 0.2438, \qquad E_{34} = 0.1560$$
$$E_{35} = 0.1224, \qquad E_{43} = 0.5484, \qquad E_{41} = 0.4928.$$

These imply that on the average the maximand has in this case the highest degree of elasticity with respect to the soybeans activity involving other labor and the least degree of elasticity with respect to the wheat activity involving May labor. However, if, as in price theory, elasticity coefficients greater (less) than one are termed elastic (inelastic), then the maximand here is inelastic with respect to all input coefficients, on the average.[3]

Second, we have computed the sample values of the expectation $(m_{ji} = = Ek_{ij})$ and standard deviation $(s_{ji} = (\text{Var}(k_{ij}))^{\frac{1}{2}})$ of the sensitivity coefficients $k_{ij}$ in table 4.4 for five groups of problems P2–P9, P10–P16, P17–P23, P24–P29 and P30–P35. As before, it appears from this table that the coefficient $a_{43}$ (soybeans activity with other labor) contributes to the highest variance $s_{34}^2$ in all the five groups of problems, whereas the coefficient $a_{35}$ (wheat activity with May labor) contributes to the least variance $s_{53}^2$ in all the five groups of problems. However, it does not hold either that the soybeans activity with other labor contributes to the highest average value of $k_{ij}$ or that the wheat activity with May labor contributes to the least average value of $k_{ij}$. A comparison of the two sets of problems P24–P29 and P30–P35 further shows that there is higher variance of the sensitivity coefficients for all the coefficients in P30–P35, which are based on averages of quarterly minimum prices. In this sense, the problems P24–P29 based on quarterly maximum prices have higher stability in their sensitivity measures. Hence, it is not always true that a pessimistic solution defined in the sense of problems P30–P35 has more stability in terms of sensitivity measures.

---

[3] An economic criterion of the instability of an input coefficient may be easily formulated on this basis, e.g., the case $E_{ij} > 1$ defines instability, $E_{ij} < 1$ defines stability and $E_{ij} = 1$ defines a type of neutral stability.

*Fractile approach of risk-programming*

This approach, which is essentially probabilistic and is discussed in some detail in ch. 5, adopts the criterion of maximizing the $\alpha$-fractile of the cumulative distribution of the objective function with the value of $\alpha$ preassigned by the decision maker. Assuming the vector $c$ in the objective function $z = c'x$ to follow a multivariate normal distribution with mean vector $m$ and variance-covariance matrix $V$, the fractile criterion which preassigns the tolerance measure $\alpha(0 < \alpha < 1)$, e.g.,

$$\text{Prob }(z \leqslant f) = 1 - \alpha$$

where $z = c'x$, can be converted to the following concave programming problem:

$$\max f = m'x - q \cdot (x'Vx)^{\frac{1}{2}}$$
$$\text{under the constraints } Ax \leqslant b, \; x \geqslant 0$$

where $q$ is a constant, $q = -F^{-1}(w)$, positive if $\alpha > 0.5$ and $F(w)$ is the cumulative probability $\text{Prob}(y \leqslant w)$ of the unit normal variate $y$. From the vectors

TABLE 4.4

Sample estimates of expectation and standard deviation of the sensitivity coefficients ($k_{ij}$).

| Group | Type of estimate | P2–P9 | P10–P16 | P17–P23 | P24–P29 | P30–P35 * |
|---|---|---|---|---|---|---|
| $x_1, y_3$ | $m_{13}$ | 40391.36 | 43540.28 | 39048.22 | 43540.58 | – |
| | $s_{13}$ | 734.06 | 2567.97 | 2568.11 | 3059.39 | – |
| $x_1, y_4$ | $m_{14}$ | 46589.78 | 44984.65 | 40477.79 | 45588.39 | – |
| | $s_{14}$ | 3435.68 | 4640.39 | 4300.46 | 6451.35 | – |
| $x_3, y_3$ | $m_{33}$ | 16289.82 | 16860.82 | 15121.29 | 19190.78 | 20136.31 |
| | $s_{33}$ | 8409.43 | 9601.10 | 8621.79 | 8102.70 | 551.08 |
| $x_3, y_4$ | $m_{34}$ | 18789.63 | 17420.15 | 15674.88 | 20093.36 | 20358.57 |
| | $s_{34}$ | 9792.76 | 10028.55 | 9032.63 | 8835.53 | 2057.14 |
| $x_4, y_3$ | $m_{43}$ | 3371.18 | 3627.21 | 3252.99 | 3649.88 | 3301.78 |
| | $s_{43}$ | 102.10 | 233.19 | 229.56 | 267.97 | 90.36 |
| $x_4, y_4$ | $m_{44}$ | 3388.52 | 3747.54 | 3372.08 | 3821.54 | 3338.29 |
| | $s_{44}$ | 301.83 | 398.29 | 368.50 | 546.90 | 337.31 |
| $x_5, y_3$ | $m_{53}$ | 1336.71 | 1440.92 | 1292.26 | 1440.93 | 1292.28 |
| | $s_{53}$ | 24.29 | 84.98 | 84.99 | 101.25 | 35.37 |
| $x_5, y_4$ | $m_{54}$ | 1541.84 | 1488.72 | 1339.57 | 1508.70 | 1306.56 |
| | $x_{54}$ | 113.70 | 153.57 | 142.32 | 213.50 | 132.02 |

* The value of $x_1$ in group P30–P35 was zero. Also note that the $m_{ij}$ and $s_{ji}$ values are not scaled. For instance, the value of $m_{13} = 40391.36$ for P2–P9 when scaled should be multiplied by $a_{31} = 0.0256$, the May labor input requirement per unit of corn activity. Hence $a_{31} m_{13} = \$1034.02$ and $a_{31} s_{13} = \$18.79$. Similarly the other values would be changed when scaled.

of net prices in problems P24–P29 we estimate the mean vector $\bar{m}$ and variance-covariance matrix $\bar{V}$ (which is assumed for simplicity to be diagonal):

$$\bar{m} = E\bar{c} = (1.0683,\ 0.6683,\ 2.5017,\ 3.0533,\ 1.8250)'$$
$$\text{diag } \bar{V} = (0.00602,\ 0.00014,\ 0.11146,\ 0.04602,\ 0.03578).$$

Similarly for problems P30–P35 with quarterly minimum prices, the mean vector $\underline{m}$ and the variance-covariance matrix $\underline{V}$ (assumed to be diagonal) are

$$\underline{m} = E\underline{c} = (0.9417,\ 0.6167,\ 2.2550,\ 2.7383,\ 1.6533)$$
$$\text{diag } \underline{V} = (0.00634,\ 0.00054,\ 0.03146,\ 0.00562,\ 0.04894).$$

Using these estimated parameters, the following eight concave programming problems are set up:

Problem Q1:     max $\bar{m}'x$, $Ax \leqslant b$, $x \geqslant 0$
Problem Q2:     max $\underline{m}'x$, $Ax \leqslant b$, $x \geqslant 0$
Problems Q3–Q5:     max $(\bar{m}'x - q \cdot (x'\bar{V}x)^{\frac{1}{2}})$, $Ax \leqslant b$, $x \geqslant 0$
for $q = 1.28,\ 1.64,\ 2.33$ corresponding to $\alpha = 0.90,\ 0.95$ and 0.99

Problems Q6–Q8: max $(\underline{m}'x - q \cdot (x'\underline{V}x)^{\frac{1}{2}})$, $Ax \leqslant b$, $x \geqslant 0$ for $q$ as in Q3–Q5.

Note that while the first two problems Q1–Q2 are linear, the remaining problems are much different from a typical quadratic program because of the square root term $(x'Vx)^{\frac{1}{2}}$, where $V$ is either $\bar{V}$ or $\underline{V}$. However, a computational algorithm essentially based on the Gauss-Newton type of approximation has been developed by Kataoka and others [26].

This method, which has very high rates of convergence, has four essential steps. First, consider problem Q3 and, neglecting the term $q(x'\bar{V}x)^{\frac{1}{2}}$, solve the linear program and denote the optimal solution vector by $x_0$. Use this $x_0$ at the second step to define the quantity $R_0 = x_0'\bar{V}x_0$; then, treating this $R_0$ as a constant, formulate the standard quadratic program as

$$\text{maximize } \bar{m}'x - \tfrac{1}{2}q\,(R_0^{-\frac{1}{2}} \cdot x'\bar{V}x)$$
$$\text{under the restrictions } Ax \leqslant b,\ x \geqslant 0$$

and denote its optimal solution vector by $x_0^{(1)}$. Third, use the optimal solution vector $x_0^{(1)}$ from the second step to compute a new value of $R_0$, denoted by $R_0^{(1)}$, as $R_0^{(1)} = x_0^{(1)'}\bar{V}x_0^{(1)}$; then, using this new constant $R_0^{(1)}$, formulate a new quadratic program as in the second step, except that $R_0^{(1)}$ replaces $R_0$. Fourth, continue the process of iteration until $R_0^{(k)}$ converges in the sense that $R_0^{(k)}$ becomes approximately equal to $R_0^{(k+1)}$ for some $k$.

For most practical purposes, however, the iterations are terminated as soon as the successive values of the optimal objective function tend to differ by a very small fraction for any $k$th iteration. Further, degeneracy situations at the optimal may be checked by the usual methods of perturbation around the neighborhood of $R_0^{(k)}$.

Now the solutions of the two linear problems Q1–Q2 are given by the same optimal activity vector ($x_1 = 0$, $x_2 = 0$, $x_3 = 1558.2$, $x_4 = 255.5$, $x_5 = 100.0$), although the maximand takes a value of \$4860.72 in Q1 (with maxima of quarterly prices) and \$4378.60 in Q2 (with minima of quarterly prices). The characteristics of the solution for problems Q3–Q8 are reflected in tables 4.5–4.7.

Several points may be noted here. First, the rate of convergence to the optimal solution is very rapid and the functional values of the optimal objective function in its successive approximations are very close on and after the fourth stage of iteration for all the three levels of significance

TABLE 4.5

Convergence to optimal values for concave programs Q3–Q5.

| Stage of iteration | $R_0{}^{\ddagger}$ | $f^0$ | $x_1$ (corn) | $x_3$ (soybeans) | $x_4$ (flax) | $x_5$ (wheat) |
|---|---|---|---|---|---|---|
| | | *Case* $\alpha = 0.90$ *i.e.,* $q = 1.28$ | | | | |
| 0 (LP Prob.) | – | 4860.72 | – | 1558.20 | 255.50 | 100.00 |
| 1 | 523.44 | 4631.76 | 1739.26 | 776.45 | 247.90 | 100.00 |
| 2 | 297.65 | 4560.80 | 2170.74 | 582.50 | 246.01 | 100.00 |
| 3 | 263.30 | 4541.59 | 2235.68 | 553.31 | 245.73 | 100.00 |
| 4 | 259.52 | 4539.28 | 2243.31 | 549.88 | 245.69 | 100.00 |
| 5 | 259.10 | 4539.13 | 2244.89 | 549.20 | 245.69 | 100.00 |
| | | *Case* $\alpha = 0.95$ *i.e.,* $q = 1.64$ | | | | |
| 0 | – | 4860.72 | – | 1558.20 | 255.50 | 100.00 |
| 1 | 523.44 | 4603.56 | 1958.98 | 677.69 | 246.93 | 100.00 |
| 2 | 278.31 | 4507.53 | 2323.62 | 513.79 | 245.34 | 100.00 |
| 3 | 252.89 | 4488.58 | 2362.19 | 496.45 | 245.18 | 100.00 |
| 4 | 253.35 | 4488.75 | 2360.74 | 497.10 | 245.18 | 100.00 |
| 5 | 253.41 | 4488.75 | 2360.70 | 497.10 | 245.18 | 100.00 |
| | | *Case* $\alpha = 0.99$ *i.e.,* $q = 2.33$ | | | | |
| 0 | – | 4860.72 | – | 1558.20 | 255.50 | 100.00 |
| 1 | 523.44 | 4555.79 | 2188.01 | 574.74 | 245.94 | 100.00 |
| 2 | 262.26 | 4413.71 | 2462.90 | 451.18 | 244.74 | 100.00 |
| 3 | 247.63 | 4396.57 | 2478.74 | 444.06 | 244.67 | 100.00 |
| 4 | 249.16 | 4398.21 | 2476.73 | 444.96 | 244.68 | 100.00 |
| 5 | 249.22 | 4398.21 | 2476.70 | 444.96 | 244.68 | 100.00 |

considered. Also, as the tolerance level $\alpha$ increases form 0.95 to 0.99 the optimal value of the objective function denoted by $f_0$ is reduced from \$4182.9 to \$4039.0, both at the fifth stage of iteration. Second, compared to the linear program (at the zero stage of iteration) in which corn was at zero level, the concave programs have corn as an optimal activity at a very high level. This is, of course, expected on an economic basis, since the above concave programs allow substitution possibilities. Third, it appears from table 4.7 that both the variance and the coefficient of variation of optimal profits decrease as the expected values of optimal profits decrease, thus implying a direct relation between expectation and variance of optimal profits. Note also that optimal profits have higher variance (and higher coefficient of variation) for problems Q3–Q5 (which are based on quarterly maximum prices) than those of Q6–Q8. Further, the critical ratio [4] shows

TABLE 4.6

Convergence to optimal values for concave programs Q6–Q8.

| Stage of iteration | $R_0$[‡] | $f_0$ | $x_1$ (corn) | $x_3$ (soybeans) | $x_4$ (flax) | $x_5$ (wheat) |
|---|---|---|---|---|---|---|
| | | *Case* $\alpha=0.90$ *i.e.,* $q=1.28$ | | | | |
| 0 (L.P.) | – | 4378.60 | – | 1558.20 | 255.50 | 100.00 |
| 1 | 277.92 | 4203.46 | 302.60 | 1422.21 | 254.15 | 100.00 |
| 2 | 255.08 | 4190.46 | 420.74 | 1369.10 | 253.64 | 100.00 |
| 3 | 246.87 | 4185.48 | 462.32 | 1350.41 | 253.45 | 100.00 |
| 4 | 243.98 | 4183.78 | 482.65 | 1341.27 | 253.37 | 100.00 |
| 5 | 242.74 | 4182.85 | 484.27 | 1340.54 | 253.36 | 100.00 |
| | | *Case* $\alpha=0.95$ *i.e.,* $q=1.64$ | | | | |
| 0 (L.P.) | – | 4378.60 | – | 1558.20 | 255.50 | 100.00 |
| 1 | 277.92 | 4165.07 | 616.95 | 1280.91 | 252.78 | 100.00 |
| 2 | 234.26 | 4136.26 | 792.55 | 1201.98 | 252.02 | 100.00 |
| 3 | 224.23 | 4128.42 | 833.09 | 1183.76 | 251.84 | 100.00 |
| 4 | 222.10 | 4126.71 | 842.03 | 1179.74 | 251.80 | 100.00 |
| 5 | 221.65 | 4126.25 | 844.52 | 1178.62 | 251.79 | 100.00 |
| | | *Case* $\alpha=0.99$ *i.e.,* $q=2.33$ | | | | |
| 0 (L.P.) | – | 4378.60 | – | 1558.20 | 255.50 | 100.00 |
| 1 | 277.92 | 4102.79 | 948.30 | 1131.97 | 251.34 | 100.00 |
| 2 | 216.47 | 4049.11 | 1122.90 | 1053.49 | 250.58 | 100.00 |
| 3 | 212.70 | 4044.89 | 1132.83 | 1049.03 | 250.53 | 100.00 |
| 4 | 206.40 | 4037.60 | 1151.12 | 1040.81 | 250.45 | 100.00 |
| 5 | 208.14 | 4039.01 | 1138.09 | 1046.66 | 250.51 | 100.00 |

[4] This term is defined in table 4.7, later.

TABLE 4.7

Expected optimal profits and their variability in problems Q1–Q8.

| Problem | Optimal profits | | Coefficient of variation | Critical ratio* | Optimal activities other than $x_5 = 100$ | | | |
|---------|-----------------|-----------|--------------------------|-----------------|-------------------------------------------|-----------|-----------|-----------|
| | Expectation | (Variance)‡ | | | $x_1$ | $x_3$ | $x_4$ | |
| Q1 | 4860.7 | 523.44 | 0.1077 | 1.0124 ($x_3$) | – | 1558.2 | 255.5 | |
| Q2 | 4378.6 | 277.92 | 0.0635 | 1.0112 ($x_3$) | – | 1558.2 | 255.5 | |
| Q3 | 4539.1 | 259.01 | 0.0571 | 1.9958 ($x_1$) | 2244.9 | 549.2 | 245.7 | |
| Q4 | 4488.8 | 253.41 | 0.0565 | 1.9141 ($x_1$) | 2360.7 | 497.1 | 245.2 | |
| Q5 | 4398.2 | 249.21 | 0.0580 | 1.6819 ($x_1$) | 2476.7 | 445.0 | 244.7 | |
| Q6 | 4182.9 | 242.64 | 0.0580 | 1.0413 ($x_3$) | 484.3 | 1340.5 | 253.4 | |
| Q7 | 4126.3 | 220.41 | 0.0546 | 1.1116 ($x_3$) | 844.5 | 1178.6 | 251.8 | |
| Q8 | 4039.0 | 208.61 | 0.0516 | 1.2627 ($x_3$) | 1138.1 | 1046.7 | 250.5 | |

‡ If $x_i$ ($i = 1, \ldots, m$) is an optimal activity and the total variance of optimal profit is $T = \sum_i c_i x_i^2 \operatorname{Var} c_i$, then the ratio of $T$ to $(x_k^2 \operatorname{Var} c_k)$ is called the critical ratio, where $x_k^2 \operatorname{Var} c_k = \max_i (x_i^2 \operatorname{Var} c_i: i = 1, \ldots, m)$.

that corn contributes the most to total variance of optimal profits in Q3–Q5, whereas soybeans does so in problems Q6–Q8.

However, more theoretical work is needed on the distribution of optimal profits in the concave programming cases, particularly when the mean vector and the variance-covariance matrix are estimated from sample data based on extreme values. The extremes of sample values do not ordinarily tend to normality [27]; hence, the concave programs we have considered have to be taken only as first approximations, the small sample distribution problems still remaining unexplored.

### 4.3.2. *Systems approach and simulation in policy models*

For econometric models, in which the structural equations are generally estimated on the basis of past statistical data, specification error is all the more likely, since the true form of the structural equations is generally unknown and for ease of estimation the equations are usually taken to be linear or approximately linear with time-lagged variables. Here the methods of simulation and Monte Carlo techniques have frequently been applied. These methods essentially generate parametric variations in various parts of the econometric model but, unlike programming, they have the advantage here of using partly at least the analytic equations of the econometric model which are much easier to handle than inequalities.

From a broad viewpoint, the application of simulation methods in economic policy models of various types has been motivated by three objectives. First, there is the need for forecasting the values of endogenous and exogenous variables and thereby predicting the consequences of alternative policies. Several interesting applications of different methods of forecasting to macroeconomic models are available in the literature now [28, 29]. Second, the need for sensitivity analysis for econometric models with regard to various types of control and stabilization policies has led to several interesting applications of simulation methods, e.g. to short-term econometric models [30], to alternative control policies in macrodynamic models [31], and to price and output policies of a firm in imperfect competition (or oligopoly) where there are multiple goals (e.g. profit, production and sales goals) and there are multiple feasible strategies for each firm [32]. Third, since one of the basic objectives of simulation is to afford insights into the pattern of behavior of several economic variables, it is essential to take account of the uncertain components as far as possible through incorporating probabilistic characteristics and variations into the simulation model. (A discussion of some of the essential characteristics of probabilistic programming is presented in the next chapter.) The simulation method here is generally based on samples drawn from a particular type of stochastic process (which is nothing but a family of random variables) and the deterministic model is viewed as a specific realization of the more generalized stochastic process model. Applications of such probabilistic methods of simulation have been very frequent in inventory control models [33], queuing models and other stochastic process models [34]; applications to economic models have been made e.g. in firm size behavior and growth [35], the pattern of stock market price behavior [36], models of growth of a national economy [37], econometric models of higher educational systems [38], and the systems used in water-resource planning for a nonmarket enterprise. It should be stressed that the probabilistic elements are essentially due to a multiplicity of deterministic factors such as the inadequacy of aggregation or disaggregation, the neglect of jointness and interdependence between different policies (or outputs) and the various implicit assumptions behind any classification of variables in a model.

## REFERENCES

[1] Saaty, T. L., *Mathematical methods of operations research*. New York: McGraw-Hill, 1959.
[2] Courtillot, M., "On varying all parameters in a linear programming problem", *Operations Research*, Vol. 10, 1962.
[3] Saaty, T. L., op. cit..
[4] Barnett, S., "Stability of the solution to a linear programming problem", *Operational Research Quarterly*, Vol. 13, No. 3, 1962.
     Enrick, N. L., "Control applications in linear programming", *Management Science*, Vol. 11, June 1965, Series B.
[5] Beckmann, M. J., "Comparative statics in linear programming and the Giffen paradox", *Review of Economic Studies*, Vol. 33, 1955–1956, 232–235.
[6] Bailey, M. J., "A generalized comparative statics in linear programming", *Review of Economic Studies*, Vol. 33, 1955–1956, 236–240.
     Mills, H. D., "Marginal values of matrix games and linear programs". In: H. W. Kuhn and A. W. Tucker (eds.), *Linear inequalities and related systems*. Princeton: Princeton University Press, 1956, 183–193.
     Williams, A. C., "Marginal values in linear programming", *Journal of Society of Industrial and Applied Mathematics*, Vol. 11, No. 1, March 1963.
[7] Saaty, T. L., "Coefficient perturbation of a constrained extremum", *Operations Research*, Vol. 7, 1959.
[8] Saaty, T. L. and K. W. Webb, "Sensitivity and renewals in scheduling aircraft overhaul", *Proceedings of Second International Conference on Operations Research*, 1961, 708–715.
[9] Tintner, G., "A note on stochastic linear programming", *Econometrica*, Vol. 28, 1960, 490–495.
[10] Hanson, M. A., "Errors and stochastic variations in linear programming", *Australian Journal of Statistics*, Vol. 2, 1960, 41–46.

[11] Sengupta, J. K., C. Millham and G. Tintner, "On the stability of solutions under error in stochastic linear programming", *Metrika*, Vol. 9, 1965, 47–60.

[12] Charnes, A. and W. W. Cooper, "Systems evaluation and repricing theorems", *Management Science*, October 1962.

[13] Fox, K. A., J. K. Sengupta and E. Thorbecke, *Theory of quantitative economic policy with applications to economic growth and stabilization*. Amsterdam: North-Holland, 1966.
Zadeh, L. and C. A. Desoer, *Linear system theory*. New York: McGraw-Hill, 1963.

[14] Tomovic, R., *Sensitivity analysis of dynamic systems*. New York: McGraw-Hill, 1963, translated by D. Tornquist.
Krasovskii, N. N., *Stability of motion*. Stanford: Stanford University Press, 1963, translation of 1959 Russian edition.
Popov, V. M., "Absolute stability of nonlinear systems of automatic control", *Automation and Remote Control*, Vol. 21, March 1962, 857–875.

[15] Neudecker, H. and C. van de Panne, "Note on the asymptotic standard errors of latent roots of econometric equation systems", *Review of International Statistical Institute*, Vol. 34, No. 1, 1966, 43–47.

[16] Wetherill, G. B., *Sequential methods in statistics*. London: Methuen and Co., 1966.

[17] Mangasarian, O. L., "Nonlinear programming problems with stochastic objective functions", *Management Science*, Vol. 10, No. 2, January 1964, 353–359.
Fromovitz, S., "Nonlinear programming with randomization", *Management Science*, Vol. 11, No. 9, Series A, July 1965, 831–846.

[18] Mangasarian, O. L. and J. B. Rosen, "Inequalities for stochastic programming problems". In: R. L. Graves and P. Wolfe (eds.), *Recent advances in mathematical programming*, op. cit.

[19] Ramsey, F. P., "A mathematical theory of saving", *Economic Journal*, Vol. 38, 1928, 543–559.

[20] Morishima, M., *Equilibrium, stability and growth*. Oxford: Clarendon Press, 1964.
Samuelson, P. A., "Efficient paths of capital accumulation in terms of calculus of variations". In: K. J. Arrow and others (eds.), *Mathematical methods in the social sciences, 1959*, Stanford: Stanford University Press, 1960.

[21] Sengupta, J. K. and D. A. Walker, "On the empirical specification of optimal economic policy for growth and stabilization under a macrodynamic model", *The Manchester School*, Sept. 1964, 215–238.

[22] Kopp, R. E. and R. McGill, "Several trajectory optimization techniques". In: A. V. Balakrishnan and L. W. Neustadt (eds.), *Computing methods in optimization problems*. New York: Academic Press, 1964.

[23] Tinbergen, J., *Economic policy: principles and design*. Amsterdam: North-Holland, 1956.

[24] Theil, H., *Economic forecasts and policy*. Amsterdam: North-Holland, 1961, revised ed.

[25] Fox, K. A., J. K. Sengupta and E. Thorbecke, *The theory of quantitative economic policy with applications to economic growth and stabilization*. Amsterdam: North-Holland, 1966.

[26] Kataoka, S., "A stochastic programming model", *Econometrica*, Vol. 31, 1963.

[27] Kendall, M. G., *The advanced theory of statistics*, Vol. 1. London: C. Griffin and Co, 1943.
Sengupta, J. K., "The extremes of extreme value solutions under risk programming", 1967, author, sent for publication.

[28] Fox, K. A., J. K. Sengupta and E. Thorbecke, *The theory of quantitative economic policy*, op. cit., chapter 6.
Duesenberry, J. S., G. Fromm, L. R. Klein and E. Kuh (eds.), *The Brookings quarterly econometric model of the United States*. Amsterdam: North-Holland and Chicago: Rand McNally, 1965.

[29] Theil, H., *Economic forecasts and policy*, op. cit.

[30] Duesenberry, J. S. and others, "A simulation of the U.S. economy in recession", *Econometrica*, Vol. 28, 1960, 749–809.

Adelman, I. and F. L, "The dynamic properties of the Klein-Goldberger model", *Econometrica*, Vol. 27, October 1959, 596–625.

Orcutt, G., M. Greenberger, J. Korbel and A. Rivlin, *Micro analysis of socio-economic systems: a simulation study*. New York: Harper, 1961.

[31] Phillips, A. W., "Stabilization policy in a closed economy", *Economic Journal*, Vol. 64, 1954, 290–324.

Fox, K. A., J. K. Sengupta and E. Thorbecke, *Theory of quantitative economic policy*, op. cit.

Shell, K. (ed.), *Essays on the theory of optimal economic growth*. Cambridge, Mass.: MIT Press, 1967.

[32] Cohen, K. J., R. M. Cyert, J. B. March and P. O. Soelberg, "A general model of price and output determination". In: A. C. Hoggatt and F. E. Balderston (eds.), *Symposium on simulation models: methodology and applications to behavioral sciences*. Chicago: South-Western Publishing Co., 1963.

[33] Hansmann, F., "A survey of inventory theory from the operations research viewpoint". In: R. L. Ackoff (ed.), *Progress in operations research*. New York: John Wiley, 1961.

[34] Morse, P. M., *Queues, inventories and maintenance*. New York: John Wiley, 1958.

Sengupta, S. S., *Operations research in Sellers' competition*. New York: John Wiley, 1967.

Bharucha-Reid, A. T., *Elements of the theory of Markov processes and applications*. New York: McGraw-Hill, 1960.

[35] Steindl, J., *Random processes and the growth of firms*. New York: Hafner, 1965.

[36] Cootner, P. H. (ed.), *The random character of stock market prices*. Cambridge, Mass.: MIT Press, 1964.

[37] Sengupta, J. K. and G. Tintner, "An approach to a stochastic theory of economic development with applications". In: *Problems of economic dynamics and planning: essays in honor of M. Kalecki*. Warsaw: PWN Polish Scientific Publishers, 1964.

[38] Fox, K. A. and J. K. Sengupta, "The specification of econometric models for planning educational systems: an appraisal of alternative approaches", *Kyklos*, 1968.

OECD, *Mathematical models in educational planning*. Paris: OECD, 1967.

OECD, *Econometric models of education: some applications*. Paris: OECD, 1965.

# Chapter 5
# PROBABILISTIC PROGRAMMING METHODS

The need for developing methods of probabilistic programming in the context of LP models arose from at least three different sources, e.g. (a) the errors and variations in parameters which sometimes can be associated with probability measures, (b) the presence of risk and uncertainty which sometimes allow a meaningful numerical representation of the utility function of a decision-maker (e.g. Von Neumann's axiomatic systems), and finally (c) the requirement of developing optimal decision rules, which is essentially related to the theory of statistical decision functions.

A typical problem in the first kind of situation is the specific characterization of the way the errors enter randomly into the model. For instance, if the errors are small and they preserve the indices of the optimal basic activities for all admissible perturbations, then the problem becomes very simple. A more difficult problem would arise on the other hand, if the errors are such that they do not preserve the indices of a suitably selected optimal basic set of activities; as a matter of fact they may even violate the conditions of feasibility of a LP model. Hence, there arises the problem of constructing suitable approximations to a given LP model under the presence of parametric errors. Sometimes these approximations are called *deterministic equivalents*, since essentially they define a method of transforming the probabilistic problem into a larger dimensional deterministic problem. Also, it is broadly true that such transformations applied to a given LP problem with probabilistic errors tend to convert the linear problem into a nonlinear one and generally with increased dimensions.

A typical problem in the second kind of situation (which is also termed risk programming) is the specification of the risk element; it may be adjoined to the original objective function (e.g. through maximizing expected profit or minimizing variance of profit around a preassigned level, etc.), or it may be separately introduced through a specific utility function with the original objective function as its argument. Also, compared to the first situation it is far more important here to characterize the specific probability distributions of the random variations in parameters, due to errors or otherwise.

This is so, because optimal decision rules (i.e., optimal solutions) now depend on the parameters of a statistical distribution. However, it holds very broadly in this situation, as in the first, that a deterministic equivalent type of approximation introduces higher dimensions and also nonlinearity.

A typical problem in the third kind of situation is to decide *ex ante* on an optimal decision rule with possibly error-adjusting properties, when it is known that data variations will occur *ex post* after the decision rule or operating policy is in action for some time. Over and above the requirements of specification of probabilistic variations in risk as mentioned for the second type of situation, it is all the more necessary now to introduce rules of adjustment (e.g. rules of learning) when expectations are not realized for any part of the model (e.g. certain parameters). However, these rules of adjustment can be very diverse, e.g. they may be in terms of an interaction between prior and posterior statistical distributions, or in terms of sequential revision of forecast estimates of parameters of the problem, or in terms of a recursive link through appropriately constructed submodels, each dependent on information sets recursively generated.

### 5.1. Approaches to probabilistic programming

In terms of our classification it may be convenient to subdivide the alternative approaches to probabilistic programming as follows:
A.  Probabilistic sensitivity analysis
B.  Risk programming in LP Models
    1.  Chance-constrained programming (CCP)
    2.  Two-stage programming (TSP)
    3.  Stochastic linear programming (SLP)
    4.  Transition probability programming (TPP)
C.  Decision-theoretic programming models
    1.  Adaptive programming
    2.  Other alternative approaches.
Perhaps it is worth mentioning at the outset that the term 'probabilistic' in probabilistic programming does not imply that some of the results developed here are not applicable in deterministic situations. On the one hand, the concept of subjective probability may be easily conceivable in deterministic situations where only one sample observation is available; on the other hand, simulated sample observations around the given observation can be generated by random sampling from tables of random numbers and/or specific probability distributions. What is important is to impose appropriate

restrictions on the neighborhood around which additional samples are simulated and Monte Carlo methods applied.

Further, the view that a deterministic LP model can be considered as a special case of a probabilistic programming model appropriately constructed has several far-reaching implications, few of which have been investigated in any detail. For instance, two of the biggest unsolved problems in this area are: (a) how rational is the 'rational approach' of maximizing the mathematical expectation of utility under the utility axioms of Von Neumann and Morgenstern, particularly under the LP type of constraints? In particular the work of Milnor, who showed that any optimal decision rule contradicts at least one reasonable criterion in a reasonable set of utility axioms, may be referred to in this connection. (b) Secondly, how can one specify an operational procedure, in some sense the best, for testing the sensitivity of the optimal solution of a given LP problem by utilizing the properties of statistical distributions of solutions of those probabilistic programming models which contain the optimal solution of the given LP problem?

### 5.1.1. Probabilistic sensitivity analysis

One of the simplest types of probabilistic sensitivity analysis in static LP problems arises when the random variations in parameters $(\delta A, \delta b, \delta c)$ preserve the indices of the optimal basic activities in the LP problem with parameters $(A, b, c)$. In this case, depending on the specific statistical distribution of $\delta B$ and $\delta b$ in the optimal basis equation

$$(B + \delta B)(x_B + \delta x_B) = b + \delta b \qquad (5.1a)$$

the statistical distribution of the optimal solution vector $x_B$ can be determined either exactly in some cases or approximately by numerical methods.

For instance, consider the equations of the optimal basis when each random variable has been replaced by its expected value

$$\bar{B}\,\bar{x}_B = \bar{b}; \qquad \text{(bar denotes expected value)}. \qquad (5.1b)$$

For any set of parameters $(B, b, c)$ different from $(\bar{B}, \bar{b}, \bar{c})$ or not, we have the relations

$$B x_B = b; \qquad z = c'_B B^{-1} b = c'_B R b \quad \text{where} \quad R = B^{-1}. \qquad (5.1c)$$

For simplicity, it may be assumed that $B$, $b$, $c$ are mutually independent statistically. Neglecting for a while the random nature of the parameters, we consider first a finite Taylor expansion of $z$ around the expected values $\bar{z} = \bar{c}'_B \bar{R} \bar{b}$ where $\bar{R} = \bar{B}^{-1}$. Suppose in the $(i, k)$th element of matrix $B$ of (5.1c), a quantity $h$ is added; then the inverse of the modified (i.e., new) matrix is known to be [1]

$$R - \frac{h}{1 + r_{ki}h} \cdot \begin{pmatrix} r_{1i} \\ \vdots \\ r_{mi} \end{pmatrix} \cdot (r_{k1} \ldots r_{km}) \tag{5.1d}$$

where $R$ is the inverse of the original matrix $B$. Then

$$z(a_{ik} + h) - z(a_{ik}) = -\frac{h}{1 + r_{ki}h} \, y_i x_k$$

where

$$y_i = \sum_{j=1}^{m} c_j r_{ji}.$$

From this it follows that

$$\partial z / \partial a_{ik} = -y_i x_k; \qquad (i, k = 1, \ldots, m \text{ at optimal basis}).$$

Again, by applying the rule (5.1d) twice we obtain

$$z(a_{ik} + h) + z(a_{ik} - h) - 2z(a_{ik}) = h^2 y_i x_k \frac{r_{ki}}{1 - h^2 r_{ki}^2} \tag{5.1e}$$

from which it follows that

$$\frac{\partial^2 z}{\partial a_{ik}^2} = \lim_{h \to 0} \frac{z(a_{ik} + h) + z(a_{ik} - h) - 2z(a_{ik})}{h^2}$$

$$= y_i x_k r_{ki}; \quad i, k = 1, \ldots, m; \quad \text{provided } |i - p| + |k - q| > 0, \tag{5.1f}$$

where $p, q$ belong to the index sets of $i$ and $k$ respectively. Similarly one can determine

$$\frac{\partial^2 z}{\partial a_{ik} \partial a_{pq}} = x_k y_p r_{qi} + x_q y_i r_{kp}$$

$$\frac{\partial^2 z}{\partial a_{ik} \partial c_j} = x_k r_{ji}; \qquad \frac{\partial^2 z}{\partial a_{ik} \partial b_j} = y_i r_{kj};$$

$$\partial z / \partial c_j = x_j; \qquad \partial z / \partial b_i = y_i; \qquad \frac{\partial^2 z}{\partial c_i \partial b_j} = r_{ij}$$

$$(\text{all } i, j, k = 1, 2, \ldots, m).$$

Now denote

$$B - \bar{B} = D = [d_{ij}]; \qquad c - \bar{c} = \gamma = [\gamma_j]; \qquad b - \bar{b} = \beta = [\beta_i].$$

Then the objective function $z$ can be expanded around the expected solution up to second order terms as follows:

$$z = \bar{z} - \sum_{i,k} \bar{y}_i d_{ik} \bar{x}_k + \sum_i \bar{y}_i \beta_i + \sum_k \bar{x}_k \gamma_k + \tfrac{1}{2} \sum_{i,k} y_i d_{ik}^2 r_{ki} x_k$$

$$+ \sum_{i,k,j} x_k r_{ji} d_{ik} \gamma_j + \sum_{|i-p|+|k-q|>0} (x_k y_p r_{qi} + x_q y_i r_{kp}) d_{ik} d_{pk} \qquad (5.1\text{g})$$

(all indices run from 1, 2, ..., $m$).

Or, in vector-matrix notation

$$z - \bar{z} = \bar{y}'D\bar{x} + \bar{y}\beta + \bar{x}'\gamma + e$$

where $e$ is the error term representing the following terms, i.e.,

$$e = -\tfrac{3}{2}x'\hat{D}y + 2y'DRDx + \gamma'RDx + y'DR\beta$$

and $\hat{D}=$ the matrix with entries $d_{ik}^2 r_{ki}$. The above Taylor series expansions are derived by Prekopa [1]. Note that in the above Taylor series development, $(x, y, R)$ which are functions of $(b, c, B)$ are considered at a point $(\bar{b}_i + t\beta_i, \bar{c}_i + t\gamma_i, \bar{a}_{ij} + td_{ij})$ where $0 < t < 1$.

Neglecting the error term $e$ in (5.2a), the expectation of $(z - \bar{z})$ is zero and its variance $\sigma_z^2$ is

$$\sigma_z^2 = \sum_{i,k} \bar{x}_i \bar{y}' V_{ik} \bar{y} \bar{x}_k + \bar{y}'G\bar{y} + \bar{x}'F\bar{x} \qquad (i, k = 1, 2, ..., m) \qquad (5.2\text{b})$$

where $V_{ik} = \mathrm{E}[(a_i - \bar{a}_i)'(a_k - \bar{a}_k)]$ where $a_i$ is the $i$th column of $B$

$$G = \text{covariance matrix of } \beta, \text{ i.e., } \mathrm{E}\beta\beta' = G$$
$$F = \text{covariance matrix of } \gamma, \text{ i.e., } \mathrm{E}\gamma\gamma' = F.$$

If the columns of the optimal basis $B$ are independent and also the vectors $b$, $c$ have statistically independent components, then $\sigma_z^2$ can be further simplified as

$$\sigma_z^2 = \sum_{i,k=1}^m (\bar{y}_i)^2 v_{ik}^2 (\bar{x}_k)^2 + \sum_{i=1}^m (\bar{y}_i)^2 s_i^2 + \sum_{k=1}^m (\bar{x}_k)^2 t_k^2 \qquad (5.2\text{e})$$

where

$$v_{ik}^2 = \mathrm{E}(d_{ik}^2) = \mathrm{E}(a_{ik} - \bar{a}_{ik})^2$$
$$t_k^2 = \mathrm{E}(c_k - \bar{c}_k)^2 = \mathrm{E}\gamma_k^2$$
$$s_i^2 = \mathrm{E}(b_i - \bar{b}_i)^2 = \mathrm{E}\beta_i^2.$$

Under certain conditions which are not very restrictive, Prekopa [1] has proved the following interesting theorem:

*Theorem 5.1*

In the neighborhood of $(\bar{B}, \bar{b}, \bar{c})$ for a given LP problem if the subscripts of the optimal feasible basis $B$ are preserved by the admissible perturbations in the parameters, then the optimum value $z$ of the (stochastic) LP problem has an asymptotic normal distribution with expectation $\bar{z}$, i.e.,

$$\text{Prob}\left[(z - \bar{z})/\sigma_z \leqslant t\right] \rightarrow \phi(t)$$

where $\phi(t) = (\sqrt{2\pi})^{-1} \int_{-\infty}^{t} e^{-\frac{1}{2}x^2} dx = \text{cdf}$ (cumulative density function) of a normal variate. Two interesting implications of the theorem may be noted. First, on an asymptotic basis at least, confidence intervals can be placed on a particular solution $z$ of the random LP problem and in this sense it provides a measure of probabilistic sensitivity. Second, computation of the variance $\sigma_z^2$ in (5.2b) shows that in case the perturbations in parameters are not normal, and especially in nonasymptotic cases, even then the errors of approximations to nonnormal distributions through a combination of normal variates can be evaluated and these can be used to determine the bounds for attaining a safety level of profits.

There are several other ways in which the above measures of sensitivity can be used. For example, consider for any given set of parameters $(A, b, c)$, the optimal solutions $x^*$, $y^*$ and let the sensitivity measure with respect to the optimal objective function $z^*$ be

$$S^* = -\partial z^*/\partial a_{ik} = y_i^* x_k^*. \tag{5.3a}$$

When $a_{ik}$ is perturbed, let $S$ be the sensitivity measure defined in the same manner as (5.3a) and assume that it is desirable to reduce the sensitivity of the system to parameter perturbations (i.e., random variations) by setting tolerance levels, i.e.,

$$\text{Prob}\left(|S^* - S| \leqslant r\right) \geqslant \alpha; \qquad 0 \leqslant \alpha \leqslant 1 \tag{5.3b}$$

where $\alpha$ denotes the preassigned level of probability that sensitivity decreases by at least the amount $\alpha$ and $r$ denotes the difference in sensitivity measure considered to be significant. By Tchebycheff's inequality

$$\text{Prob}\left(|S^* - S| \leqslant r\right) \geqslant 1 - \text{E}\left(|S^* - S|^2\right)/r^2.$$

Also

$$\text{Prob}\left(|S^* - S| \leqslant r\right) \leqslant 1 - \alpha.$$

Hence, combining

$$1 - \alpha \geqslant 1 - \text{E}\left(|S^* - S|^2\right)/r^2$$

i.e.,

$$r^2 \alpha \leqslant E(|S^* - S|^2) \tag{5.3c}$$

where E is the expectation operator. Now to evaluate the right hand side term of (5.3c), the expression $|S^* - S|^2$ can be expanded in a Taylor series about the mean value of $a_{ik}$ and the first two terms used as an approximation. For instance, let

$$g(a_{ik}) = |S^* - S|$$

then

$$Eg^2(a_{ik}) \simeq g^2(Ea_{ik}) + [(g_{(1)}(Ea_{ik}))^2 + g(Ea_{ik})g_{(2)}(Ea_{ik})](\text{Var } a_{ik})$$

where $g_{(1)}$, $g_{(2)}$ are the first and the second partials of $g(a_{ik})$ with respect to $a_{ik}$ and evaluated at $Ea_{ik}$. On substituting in (5.3c) we get

$$r^2 \alpha \leqslant g^2(Ea_{ik}) + [(g_{(1)}(Ea_{ik}))^2 + g(Ea_{ik})g_{(2)}(Ea_{ik})](\text{Var } a_{ik}). \tag{5.3d}$$

Thus, if the distribution of $a_{ik}$ in the domain of random perturbations is known or estimable, the value of the tolerance level $r$ in sensitivity difference can be found from (5.3d) for any preassigned probability $\alpha$. Since for any fixed statistical distribution of the random parameter $a_{ik}$ in its domain of variations around $Ea_{ik}$ the right hand side of (5.3d) is a constant, it is easily seen that $r^2$ and $\alpha$ are inversely related, i.e., the higher the value of $\alpha$ in the range $0 \leqslant \alpha \leqslant 1$, the lower the value of $r^2$. The graph of the hyperbola $r^2\alpha = k_0$, where $k_0$ denotes the right hand side of (5.3d), can be used as a sensitivity frontier for determining an appropriate safety-level combination of $r$ and $\alpha$. (Note that in these derivations $S^*$ is defined for any arbitrary set of parameters, although an appropriate choice for this is perhaps $(EA, Eb, Ec)$ resulting in an optimal value of sensitivity $S^* = ES$.)

Another type of application of the sensitivity measure $S^*$ defined in (5.3a), when the element $a_{ik}$ in the optimal basis is random, would be to analyze the exact or approximate statistical distribution of the random quantity $S^*$ as a product of two nonnegative random quantities $y_i^*$, $x_k^*$. There is some scope here for attempting log normal and other related statistical distributions as possible approximations.

A somewhat more difficult problem arises when the random variations $(\delta A, \delta b, \delta c)$ in parameters do not necessarily preserve the indices of the optimal basic activities in the LP problem with parameters $(A, b, c)$. Two different approaches are possible in this case, e.g. (a) methods of risk programming in general, i.e., chance-constrained, two-stage and stochastic programming, etc. and (b) methods of adjoining to the given LP problem additional cost (or disutility) functions due to those random variations. In the latter group of methods, the simpler cases arise when the input-output coefficients represented by matrix $A$ are fixed (i.e., $\delta A = 0$), so that random variations are possible only in the vectors $c$ or $b$.

Assuming for simplicity that vector $c$ only is random, the methods of adjoining an additional cost or disutility function may be of several types: (a) the method of utility functions $U(z)$, where $z = c'x$ is the value of the objective function and $U(z)$ specifies certain types of utility functions with properties of diminishing marginal utility, nonsatiety and certain other reasonable conditions; (b) the method of satisficing behavior according to which, whenever the random vector $c$ differs from any desired level $c^0$ preassigned, a cost (or disutility) $Q = Q(c_1 - c_1^0, ..., c_n - c_n^0)$ is incurred and the objective of minimizing this cost in some (average) sense is adjoined to the objective function of the original LP model; and (c) the method of second best and third best solutions, according to which we consider for each admissible sample vector $c$, not only the optimal solution $x^{(1)}$ with the maximal profit $z^{(1)}$ but also the second best and third best *basic* feasible solutions $x^{(2)}$ and $x^{(3)}$ leading to profit levels $z^{(2)}$, $z^{(3)}$ respectively such that $z^{(1)} > z^{(2)} > z^{(3)}$; as the random vector $c$ varies in its own domain, the solutions $(x^{(1)}, z^{(1)})$, $(x^{(2)}, z^{(2)})$, $(x^{(3)}, z^{(3)})$ also vary, so that by observing such variations, their mean, variance, etc., one could decide whether to accept the second best, the third best or the first best as the optimal decision rule.

Perhaps the simplest case in the utility function approach arises when the profit level $z = c'x$ is defined in monetary units, subject to a continuous probability distribution $f(z)$, and the utility function $U(z)$ is a continuous analytic function in the domain of variations of $z$. In this case, the utility function $U(z)$ can be expanded around the mean value $\bar{z}$ in a Taylor series; retaining up to quadratic terms,

$$\bar{U}(z) = U(\bar{z}) - k(\text{Var } z)$$

where

$$k = -\tfrac{1}{2}U_{\bar{z}\bar{z}}, \quad U_{\bar{z}\bar{z}} = [\partial^2 U(z)/\partial z^2] \text{ at } z = \bar{z}$$

$$\bar{U}(z) = EU(z): \quad \text{expected value of utility.} \tag{5.4a}$$

If $k$ could be taken to be approximately constant, then a positive value of this parameter $k$ (i.e., $U_{\bar{z}\bar{z}} < 0$) would reflect a risk-averting (i.e., conservative) attitude based on the diminishing marginal utility assumption, whereas a negative value would indicate a risk-taking (i.e., gambling) attitude on the part of the decision-maker (note that $k = 0$ specifies the level of indifference with respect to risk).

Three different types of operational specialization of the result (5.4a) are conceivable, when maximization of expected utility is accepted as a criterion of decision making, e.g.
(i) a preassigned quantity $z_0$ is specified such that $\bar{U}(z) = U(z_0)$, in which case one obtains from (5.4a):

$$U(\bar{z}) = U(z_0) + k \operatorname{Var} z.$$

Since $U(z_0)$ is a known number, this problem reduces to minimizing var $z$ if $k$ is negative.
(ii) a specific form of the utility function $U(z)$ may be used, e.g. consider a squared disutility function as

$$U(z) = (z^0 - z)^2$$

where $z^0$ is a preassigned constant representing a very high desired level of profits. Then by applying (5.4a) and noting that $z = c'x$ where $c$ only is random, we get the following nonlinear program:

Minimize $\bar{U}(z) = \bar{U}(z^0 - z) = x'\bar{c}\bar{c}'x - 2\bar{c}'xz^0 + (z^0)^2 + x'(\operatorname{E}cc')x$

under the restrictions

$$Ax \leqslant b; x \geqslant 0.$$

(iii) a specific form of the probability distribution of the random variable $z = c'x$ induced by the random elements of vector $c$ may be introduced. For instance, Freund [2] considered the case in which the profit level $z$ follows a normal distribution $N(m, v)$ with mean $m$ and standard deviation $v$, and used the following utility function: $U(z) = 1 - \exp(-rz)$, where the positive parameter $r$ indicates the element of risk-proneness. In this case it can be easily shown that

$$EU(z) = \bar{U}(z) = 1 - \exp\left[-rm + \tfrac{1}{2}r^2v^2\right] \tag{5.4b}$$

so that maximizing $\bar{U}(z)$ is equivalent to

maximizing $\bar{c}'x - \tfrac{1}{2} \cdot r \cdot x' \operatorname{E}(c - \operatorname{E}c)(c - \operatorname{E}c)'x$

under the restrictions
$$Ax \leqslant b; \quad x \geqslant 0.$$

Consider now the method of satisficing behavior which has several possible lines of interpretation. According to one interpretation, the decision-maker has the idea of a desired level of profits $z^0 = c^{0'}x$, where the price coefficients $c^0$ are preassigned accordingly. In the event, however, that the level $z$ of stochastic profits differs from the desired level $z^0$, penalty costs are incurred, i.e. a penalty of $p_1$ for $z \leqslant z^0$ and a penalty of $p_2$ for $z > z^0$, and the expected total penalty cost (EPC) is then given as:

$$\text{EPC} = p_1 \int_0^{z^0} (z^0 - z) f(z) \, dz + p_2 \int_{z^0}^{\infty} (z - z^0) f(z) \, dz; \qquad 0 \leqslant z \leqslant \infty. \tag{5.4c}$$

Here $f(z)$ is the probability density function of $0 \leqslant z \leqslant \infty$ and the penalty costs $p_1, p_2$ are assumed to be known constants. This expected penalty cost function (5.4c) is adjoined to the original LP problem. Hence the transformed problem becomes:

$$\text{Maximize } \bar{c}'x - \text{EPC}$$

under the restrictions

$$Ax \leqslant b; \qquad c^{0\prime}x = z^0; \qquad x \geqslant 0$$

($\bar{c} = Ec$, E is the expectation operator).

The implicit costs of specifying a very high value of desired profits become an endogenous part of this type of model specification, since it can be shown from (5.4c) that the value of $z^0$ which minimizes EPC in (5.4c) must satisfy the condition

$$F(z^0) = \text{Prob}(z \leqslant z_0) = p_2/(p_1 + p_2). \tag{5.4d}$$

Note, however, that it is possible to define other types of interpretation for satisficing behavior. Consider the following problem:

$$\text{Max Prob}(c'x \geqslant f) = \alpha$$

under the restrictions

$$Ax \leqslant b; \qquad x \geqslant 0$$

where the tolerance measure $\alpha$ is preassigned but the satisficing level of profits $f$ is not a deterministic quantity but subject to a randomized decision rule. For instance, if $f_0$ is a desired level of profits expected by the decision-maker, the penalty costs of the probabilities of $f \leqslant f_0$ and $f > f_0$ have to be evaluated over the admissible range of variations of $f$ and these costs have to be adjoined to the original LP model.

Now consider the method of second best and third best solutions, according to which we may compute the means and variances of the objective functions corresponding to the three best solutions, before deciding on which type of best solution is to be accepted as a decision rule. Denote the expected values and variances of the three best solutions by $(f_i, V_i)$, $i=1$, 2, 3 and define $h$ by

$$z^{(1)} = hz^{(2)} \quad \text{where} \quad f_1 > f_2 \tag{5.5a}$$

then the following result may be derived (Sengupta [3]):

*Theorem 5.2*

If the random variable $h$ defined in (5.5a) be such that the function $g = g(h, z^{(2)}) = h^2(z^{(2)})^2$ is analytic around the expected values $Eh$ and $f_2$ for all possible variations in the admissible space, then under very mild conditions it holds that $V_1 > V_2$, i.e., the first best solution has higher variability of its objective function compared to the second best solution.

This theorem is useful in two directions. First, it implies that the second (or the third) best solution may have advantages over the first best, particularly if the decrease in variance $(V_2 - V_1)$ overcompensates the decrease in expected profit $(f_2 - f_1)$. In other words, the marginal variance of expected return $(\lambda)$

$$\lambda = \frac{\Delta V}{\Delta f} = \frac{V_2 - V_1}{f_2 - f_1} \tag{5.5b}$$

provides the crucial level for risk measurement, which represents the barter terms of trade between the two facets of optimization, e.g. expectation and variance. Second, the optimal choice between the different best solutions may be viewed as a problem in optimization between vectors, the elements of which may be the different order moments of $z^{(k)}$, of the Euclidean distance between $x^{(k)}$ and $x^{(k+1)}$ for $k=1$, 2, 3 and of the area of the triangle of the first best, second best and third best points. (Note that only partial ordering is defined here.)

The idea that the choice between alternative risky solutions or policies may be specified through utility functions per se, where the utility function has arguments in the form of expected profit, its variance, etc., is of considerable importance. The main exponent of this approach is Markowitz [4], who has applied this model for specifying efficient portfolio investment. As an example of this approach, assume that the total available investment fund is $x_T$ which is to be invested in $j=1$, 2, ..., $n$ securities in amounts $x_j$ in some optimal manner, when the unit net return $r_j$ per $j$th security is a random variable with expected value $m_j$ and covariance $v_{ij}$ ($i, j = 1$, 2, ..., $n$). Then the expected net return of the entire portfolio investment is $\sum_j m_j x_j = E_T$ with variance $\sum_{i,j} x_i x_j v_{ij} = V_T$. One type of specification of the utility function is to minimize $V_T$ under a preassigned lower bound constraint on the net expected total return, e.g.

$$\text{minimize } V_T = \sum_{i,\,j=1}^{n} x_i x_j v_{ij}$$

under the conditions

$$\sum_j m_j x_j \geqslant E_0$$

$$\sum_j x_j \leqslant x_T$$

$$x_j \geqslant 0; \qquad i, j = 1, 2, \dots, n; \qquad\qquad (5.6a)$$

$m_j$ and $v_{ij}$ are required to be estimated from statistical data on net returns for various securities by the methods of regression or other stochastic process methods. Further, note that the quadratic problem (5.6a) allows at its *optimal solution* the following interpretation of the two Lagrange multipliers $y_1$ and $y_2$:

$$y_1 = \partial V_T / \partial(-E) = -\partial V_T / \partial E = \text{marginal variance of expected return}$$

$$y_2 = \partial V_T / \partial x_T = \text{marginal risk of increased or decreased investment.}$$

Two brief comments on the Markowitz approach, which is also termed the E-V approach may be added. First, Markowitz has shown that, if in respect of problem (5.6a), given a preassigned value of $E_0$ the optimal (minimum) value of the objective function is denoted by $V_T^0$, then a quadratic problem equivalent to the quadratic problem (5.6a) can be formulated as

$$\text{maximize } E_T = \sum_j m_j x_j$$

under the restrictions

$$\sum_{i,\,j} x_i x_j v_{ij} \leqslant V_T^0$$

$$\sum_j x_j \leqslant x_T$$

$$x_j \geqslant 0 \qquad\qquad (5.6b)$$

such that the two problems have identical optimal solution vectors. Second, the E-V approach may be basically viewed as a special case of the statistical theory of decision functions developed by Wald and others, since the expected loss ($L$) can be written as

$$L = \mathrm{E}(z - \mathrm{E}z)^2 \quad \text{where} \quad z = c'x \qquad\qquad (5.6c)$$

where the optimal decision variables $x$ are selected by minimizing the expected loss $L$ under specified restrictions in the form $Ax \leqslant b$, $x \geqslant 0$. However, the interaction between prior and posterior statistical distribution of parameters provides an interesting field which has not been much explored in this context.

We have so far considered probabilistic sensitivity analysis in the context of static LP models. In dynamic (continuous or discrete time) LP models with or without control variables, almost all of our previous discussion is applicable. Further, the time-oriented stability properties can now be given a probabilistic interpretation, e.g. an optimal time path $x^*(t)$ may be defined to be probabilistically stable, if it has a neighborhood for all $t \geqslant 0$ in which the Liapunov type distance is preserved for $t \to \infty$.

Similarly consider the E-V approach model (5.6a). If the parameters $m_j$ and $v_{ij}$ can be viewed as functions of time, generated through a stochastic process model, and further the activities $x_j$ have recursive relations such as

$$x_j(t) = a_j x_j(t - 1) + u_j(t) \tag{5.6d}$$

then the LP model is essentially a dynamic one and its time-stability properties can be analyzed by using various methods mentioned in the previous chapter. Note that the equality relation of (5.6d) can be converted into weak inequalities, whenever it is meaningful.

### 5.1.2. Risk programming methods

Methods of risk programming essentially convert a probabilistic LP model into a nonlinear deterministic form, since most operational decision rules have to be specified in nonrandom terms. However, it is in principle possible to specify randomized decision rules in the context of probabilistic programming, and the techniques of simulation have ample scope here. The various methods of risk programming discussed in the following sections are limited mostly to probabilistic LP models of the static variety, under simplifying assumptions regarding the statistical distributions of the parameters of the problem which are $(A, b, c)$.

### 5.1.2.1. Chance-constrained programming.

The simplest case of chance-constrained programming (CCP) developed by Charnes, Cooper and others [5] arises when the resource vector $b$ is assumed normally distributed; the inequalities are chance-constrained

$$\text{Prob}(a_i'x \leqslant b_i) \geqslant \alpha_i; \qquad i = 1, 2, \ldots, m \tag{5.7a}$$

where $a_i$ is the $i$th column of matrix $A$, $\alpha_i$ is a measure of probability pre-assigned, and the decision rules are restricted within the linear class, e.g.

$$x = Db; \qquad D: n.m \tag{5.7b}$$
$$b: m.1.$$

Further, if the objective function $z = c'x$ has random components in the elements of $c$, three types of deterministic transformations are considered, e.g. maximizing the expected value of profits, $Ez$ (also called, E-model), minimizing the variance of profits, Var $z$ (also called, V-model) and maximizing the probability of profits being at or above specified levels, (also called, P-model). These three types of transformation are combined with (5.7a) and (5.7b) to develop three nonlinear programming models, each of which is nonstochastic.

Consider the chance-constrained relations (5.7a) and (5.7b) and express $b$ as $\bar{b} + \hat{b}$ (i.e., $b_i = \bar{b} + \hat{b}_i$), $\hat{b}_i = $ random deviations for $i = 1, 2, ..., m$. Using (5.7b) and (5.7a) and after appropriate normalization of the random terms,

$$\text{Prob}(T_i \geqslant K_i) \geqslant \alpha_i; \qquad i = 1, ..., m \tag{5.7c}$$

where

$$T_i = (\hat{b}_i - a_i'D\hat{b}_i)/\sqrt{[E(\hat{b}_i - a_i'D\hat{b})^2]} \sim N(0, 1)$$
$$K_i = (-\bar{b}_i + a_i'D\bar{b})/\sqrt{[E(\hat{b}_i - a_i'D\hat{b})^2]}.$$

Since $T_i$ is seen to be a unit normal variate by the assumption that each $b_i$ is normal, the inequality (5.7c) may be rewritten as

$$F_i\left(\frac{-\bar{b}_i + a_i'D\bar{b}}{\sqrt{[E(\hat{b}_i - a_i'D\hat{b})^2]}}\right) \geqslant \alpha_i \tag{5.7d}$$

where

$$F_i(w) = (\sqrt{2\pi})^{-1} \int_w^\infty e^{-\frac{1}{2}y^2} \, dy.$$

Usually for normal distributions we consider $\alpha_i \geqslant 0.50$, since this satisfies the constraints at least 50% of the times. Then the relation (5.7d) becomes

$$\frac{-\bar{b}_i + a_i'D\bar{b}}{\sqrt{[E(\hat{b}_i - a_i'D\hat{b})^2]}} \leqslant F_i^{-1}(\alpha_i) = -q_i, \quad \text{say, when } q_i > 0$$

$$\text{for all} \quad i, \quad \text{if} \quad \alpha_i > 0.5. \tag{5.7e}$$

These inequalities, which involve nonrandom variables only, can be further simplified to a convex programming problem by introducing new nonrandom nonnegative variables $v_i$ and writing the system (5.7e) as

$$-\bar{b}_i + a_i'D\bar{b} \leqslant -v_i \leqslant -q_i\sqrt{[E(\hat{b}_i - a_i'D\hat{b})^2]} \leqslant 0$$

i.e., as

$$-a_i'D\bar{b} - v_i \geqslant -\bar{b}_i \tag{5.7f}$$

$$v_i^2 - q_i^2 E[\hat{b}_i - a_i'D\hat{b}]^2 \geqslant 0. \tag{5.7g}$$

Hence, taking the expected value of profit as the deterministic transformation of the stochastic objective function $z = c'x$ where the vector $c$ is assumed to have random elements, the CCP model in its deterministic form may be written (in one version) as:

$$\text{minimize} - \bar{c}'D\bar{b}$$

under the conditions (5.7f), (5.7g)

$$\text{and} \quad v_i \geqslant 0, x \geqslant 0$$

which is a convex programming problem in the variables $v$ and $D$. Similarly, the other two cases of the CCP model based on the V-model and the P-model may be derived.

An interesting case of the CCP model has been constructed by Kataoka [6], in which the chance-constrained relation (5.7a) is combined with the following type of objective function

$$\text{Prob}(c'x \leqslant f) = \beta, \qquad 0 < \beta < 1 \tag{5.7h}$$

where $c$ is assumed to have a multivariate normal distribution with mean $\bar{c}$ and dispersion matrix $C = E(c - \bar{c})(c - \bar{c})'$ and $\beta$ is assumed to be less than or equal to 0.50. The objective function (5.7h) implies that instead of maximizing the expected value of profits, the lower allowable limit $f$ is maximized with a specified probability level $\beta \leqslant 0.50$. Note that $f$ can be written as

$$f = \bar{c}'x + F^{-1}(\beta) \cdot (x'Cx)^{\frac{1}{2}}$$

where

$$F(w) = (\sqrt{2\pi})^{-1} \int_{-\infty}^{w} e^{-\frac{1}{2}y^2} \, dy. \tag{5.7i}$$

$(x'Cx)^{\frac{1}{2}}$ can be shown to be a convex function and if $\beta \leqslant 0.50$, then $F^{-1}(\beta) = -s, s \geqslant 0$; then the function $f$ of (5.7i) is a concave function in $x$, if the parameters $(\bar{c}, C)$ are known or estimated and $\beta \leqslant 0.50$. Now the chance-constrained relation (5.7a), without using (5.7b), can be transformed as

$$Ax \leqslant b^*; \qquad x \geqslant 0 \tag{5.7j}$$
$$b_i^* = \bar{b}_i - q_i\sigma_{b_i}$$
$$q_i = -F_i^{-1}(\alpha_i) \text{ defined in (5.7e)}$$
$$\sigma_{b_i} = \text{standard deviation of } b_i;$$
$$\bar{b}_i = \text{expected value of } b_i.$$

Since the concave programming problem defined by (5.7i) and (5.7j) is not quadratic, Kataoka considered a subsidiary quadratic program as

$$\text{maximize } \bar{c}'x - (s/2R)\cdot x'Cx$$

under the conditions

$$Ax \leqslant b^*; \quad x \geqslant 0, R = \text{a positive parameter}, \quad (5.8)$$

and proved the following result.

*Theorem 5.3*

If there exists an optimal solution $x(R)$ of the quadratic programming problem (5.8) satisfying the condition

$$R = \left(\hat{x}(R)' \, C\hat{x}(R)\right)^{\frac{1}{2}} \quad (5.9a)$$

then $x(R)$ is also an optimal solution for the concave programming problem defined by (5.7i) and (5.7j), and vice versa. (Note that $\hat{x}(R)$ denotes an optimal solution for any fixed $R$ and the equality sign in (5.9a) should be viewed in the sense of a limiting tendency.)

The above result is useful in developing an iterative algorithm as follows: *Step 1*: Solve the LP problem consisting of (5.7j) and the linear part of (5.7i) in which $f = \bar{c}'x$ is maximized and thereby obtain an initial value of $R$, called $R_0$

$$R_0 = \left(\hat{x}_0' \, C\hat{x}_0\right)^{\frac{1}{2}}$$

where $\hat{x}_0$ is the optimal solution of the LP problem.

*Step 2*: Using this value of $R_0$ as the value of the parameter $R$ in (5.8), solve the quadratic programming problem (5.8) and denote its optimal solution by $\hat{x}(R_0)$. Now compute $\left(\hat{x}'(R_0) \, C\hat{x}(R_0)\right)^{\frac{1}{2}}$ and denote it by $R_1$. So long as the final optimal solution is not reached, $R_1$ is used to replace $R$ in (5.8) and then the quadratic program (5.8) is solved, thereby obtaining optimal solutions $\hat{x}(R_1)$ and so on. If at the $k$th iteration ($k \geqslant 1$) with $\hat{x}(R_k)$ as the optimal solution, it happens that

$$\left(\hat{x}(R_k)' \, C\hat{x}(R_k)\right)^{\frac{1}{2}} = R_{k+1} \doteq R_k$$

then the final optimal solution is reached. Note that the symbol $\doteq$ stands for approximate equality, which suggests a finite termination for most practical purposes.

*Step 3*: If the final optimal solution is reached at the $k$th iteration with a value of the parameter $R$ denoted by $R_k$, then in order to check the degeneracy of the optimal solution $\hat{x}(R_k)$, we should test it for a small decrement $(\Delta R_k)$ of $R_k$ (note: $R_{k+1} \leqslant R_k$) to see whether there is degeneracy, i.e., whether there is an intersection on the line $\varDelta R_k = \varDelta R_{k+1}$. If there is degeneracy, the method of perturbation can be applied for a sufficiently small neighborhood of $R_k$. If the intersection $\varDelta R_k = \varDelta R_{k+1}$ cannot be found for a sufficiently small change in $R$, we have a trivial optimal solution $\hat{x} = 0$.

Several types of extension of the CCP approach are conceivable. First, the assumption of normality needs to be relaxed, since for several economic elements such as price, negative ranges of values are not meaningful. Second, the use of deterministic transformations which are distribution-free or non-parametric in nature is another important line of generalization. Third, the role of the safety first principle in relation to the CCP approach is as yet not fully explored. Considering the chance-constrained relation (5.7h) for instance, the safety first principle would utilize the Tchebycheff inequality

$$\text{Prob}(c'x = z \leqslant f) \leqslant \frac{\text{Var } z}{(\text{E}z - f)^2} \qquad (5.9b)$$

and would minimize the right-hand side of this inequality. The CCP approach on the other hand specifies the probability $\beta$ in (5.7h) and then maximizes $f$. A method which combines both the CCP and the safety first approaches would convert (5.9b) as

$$\text{Prob}\left(\frac{c'x - \bar{c}'x}{\sqrt{[\text{E}(c'x - \bar{c}'x)^2]}} \leqslant \frac{f - \bar{c}'x}{\sqrt{[\text{E}(c'x - \bar{c}'x)^2]}}\right) \leqslant \frac{\text{Var } z}{(\text{E}z - f)^2}$$

and then solve for $f$ from the inequality

$$F\left(\frac{f - \bar{c}'x}{\sqrt{[\text{E}(c'x - \bar{c}'x)^2]}}\right) \leqslant \frac{\text{Var } z}{(\text{E}z - f)^2} \,.$$

However, this form is very complicated and difficult to solve except approximately in numerical terms. Some of these extensions have been considered by Sengupta [7] both theoretically and empirically.

*5.1.2.2. Two-stage programming.* Consider any LP problem written as: $[\min c'x, a_i'x \geqslant b_i; \ x \geqslant 0]$ $(i = 1, 2, \ldots, m)$, where the element $b_i$ of the resource vector $b$ is random with a known or estimable distribution function. The random parameter space of each $b_i$ can then be divided into two disjoint classes, one satisfying the constraints and the other not satisfying the constraints. If the latter class is nonempty, then there is a finite probability of the $i$th constraint being violated and if a finite (constant) penalty cost $f_i$ per unit can be associated with each $i$th constraint violation, then the mean total penalty cost is $\sum_i \mathrm{E} f_i y_i$ where E is expectation and $y_i$ is defined as:

$$a_i'x + y_i = b_i; \qquad y_i \geqslant 0; \qquad i = 1, 2, ..., m. \tag{5.10a}$$

Hence, one could adjoin the mean total penalty cost to the original objective function and rewrite the two stages of the problem as:

$$\text{minimize } c'x + \mathrm{E}f'y \tag{5.10b}$$

under the restrictions

$$Ax + By = b; \qquad x \geqslant 0, y \geqslant 0. \tag{5.10c}$$

In this case $B = I$, where $I$ is the identity matrix of order $m$. It can easily be shown that if for each $i$, $b_i$ is uniformly distributed within $[\bar{b}_i - m_i, \bar{b}_i + m_i]$ and $\bar{y}_i$ denotes $(\bar{b}_i - a_i'x)$, then the mean penalty cost $\mathrm{E}f_i y_i$ for each $i$th constraint can be shown to be the sum of three component costs $p_{i1}, p_{i2}, p_{i3}$ where $\qquad p_{i1} = 0$, if $\bar{y}_i \geqslant m_i$

$$p_{i2} = \int_0^{m_i - \bar{y}_i} (f_i t / 2m_i)\,\mathrm{d}t, \quad \text{if} \quad -m_i < \bar{y}_i < m_i$$

$$p_{i3} = \int_{-m_i - \bar{y}_i}^{m_i - \bar{y}_i} (f_i t / 2m_i)\,\mathrm{d}t, \quad \text{if} \quad \bar{y}_i \leqslant -m_i.$$

Hence

$$\mathrm{E}f_i y_i = p_i = p_{i1} + p_{i2} + p_{i3} = (f_i / 4m_i)(m_i - \bar{y}_i)^2 - f_i \bar{y}_i$$

which is a convex quadratic function in nonstochastic variables $\bar{y}_i = \bar{b}_i - a_i'x$, where a bar over a variable denotes its expected value.

To convert the problem to a fully deterministic (convex quadratic) one, the probabilistic constraints (5.10c) should be written either in a nonstochastic form, e.g. $\bar{y}_i = \bar{b}_i - a_i'x$ or interpreted as a two-stage problem as follows: first $x$ is to be decided upon (on the basis of any estimate or guess of $b$), then $b$ is to be observed (and its discrepancy from the prior guessed estimate noted), and then at the second and final stage $y = y(b, x)$ is to be decided upon in an optimal manner. In this two-stage formulation, the selection of vector $x$ is judged optimal if it leads to the smallest expected cost including the penalty cost of $y$. Note that the problem of finding an optimal $y$ vector after $x$ has been decided upon and $b$ observed is a straight-forward LP problem. Hence, in the two-stage LP problem under uncertainty, the central emphasis is on the problem of finding an optimal $x$ given the penalty costs of violation and the sequential observations of the random structure of the elements $b_i$.

A general specification of the two-stage primal problem is as follows:

$$\text{minimize } c'x + \text{E min } f'y \tag{5.11a}$$

under the restrictions

$$Ax + By \geqslant b, \quad \text{all} \quad b$$
$$x \geqslant 0, \quad y \geqslant 0$$

where $A$ and $B$ are known $m.n_1$ and $m.n_2$ matrices, $x$ and $y$ are $n_1$ and $n_2$-dimensional vectors and $b$ is a random $m$-dimensional vector with known distribution $g = g(b)$ with probability density $dg(b)$.

Two basic assumptions are generally made for solving such problems: (i) there exists a nonempty convex set $K$ consisting of nonnegative solution vectors $x$ such that for each $b$ there exists a solution vector $y(b)$ such that the pair $(x, y(b))$ is feasible (this is otherwise called the assumption of permanent feasibility), and (ii) the penalty cost vector $f$ is known with certainty.

Now introduce the following notation:

$$D = [A, B], e' = (c', f'), h'(b) = (x', y'(b)) \tag{5.11b}$$

then the primal problem (5.11a) becomes:

$$\text{minimize } \int e'h(b) \, dg(b) = \text{expected cost}$$

under the restrictions                                                                    (5.11c)

$$Dh(b) \geqslant b; \quad h(b) \geqslant 0 \quad \text{for all} \quad b.$$

This has the following dual problem:

$$\text{maximize } \int b'r(b) \, dg(b) = \text{expected profit}$$

under the restrictions                                                                    (5.11d)

$$D'r(b) \leqslant e; \quad r(b) \geqslant 0 \quad \text{for all} \quad b$$

where $r(b)$ is an $m$-dimensional vector of dual variables. On the basis of this primal and dual formulation, Madansky [8] has proved some interesting theoretical results.

*Theorem 5.4*

Let $\bar{h}(b)$ and $\bar{r}(b)$ be optimal solution vectors for the primal (5.11c) and dual (5.11d) problems respectively; then

$$\int e'\bar{h}(b) \, dg(b) = \int b'\bar{r}(b) \, dg(b) = \int \bar{r}'(b) \, D\bar{h}(b) \, dg(b)$$

and

$$\bar{r}'(b)\,[D\bar{h}(b) - b] = 0; \qquad \bar{h}'(b)\,[D'\,\bar{r}\,(b) - e] = 0$$

almost everywhere. Also conversely, if the collections $\bar{h}(b)$, $\bar{r}\,(b)$ satisfy feasibility and the conditions

$$\bar{r}'(b)\,[D\bar{h}(b) - b] = 0$$
$$\bar{h}'(b)\,[D'\,\bar{r}(b) - e] = 0$$

almost everywhere, then they are optimal for the primal and dual problems respectively.

*Proof*: Denote the Lagrangian expressions $L(h(b),\, r\,(b))$ and $L(h(b),\, r\,(b))$ for the primal problem (5.11c) and the dual problem (5.11d) respectively as

$$L\big(h\,(b),\, r(b)\big) = \int\,(-\,e')\,h\,(b)\,dg\,(b) + r(Dh(b) - b)$$

$$= -\int e'h\,(b)\,dg\,(b) + \int h'\,(b)\,D'r\,(b)\,dg\,(b) - \int b'r\,(b)\,dg\,(b)$$

with $h(b)\geqslant 0$, $r\,(b)\geqslant 0$ being feasible, and

$$-\,L\big(h\,(b),\, r(b)\big) = \int b'r\,(b)\,dg\,(b) - \int h'\,(b)\,D'r\,(b)\,dg\,(b) + \int e'h\,(b)\,dg\,(b)$$

with $h(b)\geqslant 0$; $r\,(b)\geqslant 0$ being feasible.

Then it follows by the saddle point theorem that if there exists a collection of vectors $\bar{h}(b)$ belonging to the set $\bar{H}$ which is feasible for the primal problem, then this vector is optimal if and only if there exists another collection of dual vectors $\bar{r}\,(b)$ belonging to the set $\bar{R}$ satisfying the Lagrangian inequality

$$L\big(h\,(b),\, \bar{r}(b)\big) \leqslant L\big(\bar{h}\,(b),\, \bar{r}(b)\big) \leqslant L\big(\bar{h}\,(b),\, \bar{r}(b)\big)$$

for all feasible solution vectors $h(b)$, $r\,(b)$ belonging to their respective feasible sets $H$ and $R$ where $\bar{H}$ and $\bar{R}$ are respective subsets of $H$ and $R$.

Now for the feasible vectors $h(b)$ in $H$ and $r\,(b)$ in $R$ it follows from (5.11d) and (5.11c) that

$$\int h'\,(b)\,[D'\bar{r}(b) - e]\,dg\,(b) \leqslant 0$$

and this implies

$$L\big(\bar{h}\,(b),\, \bar{r}(b)\big) \geqslant L\big(b\,(b),\, \bar{r}(b)\big) \tag{5.11e}$$

where

$$L\big(\bar{h}(b), \bar{r}(b)\big) = - \int b'\bar{r}(b)\,dg(b)$$

$$L\big(h(b), \bar{r}(b)\big) = - \int b'\bar{r}(b)\,dg(b) + \int h'(b)\,[D'\bar{r}(b) - e]\,dg(b).$$

Similarly from (5.11c) and (5.11d)

$$\int r'(b)\,[D\bar{h}(b) - b]\,dg(b) \geqslant 0$$

which implies

$$L\big(h(b),\, \bar{r}(b)\big) \leqslant L\big(\bar{h}(b),\, \bar{r}(b)\big) \tag{5.11$f$}$$

where

$$L\big(\bar{h}(b), \bar{r}(b)\big) = - \int e'\bar{h}(b)\,dg(b)$$

$$L\big(\bar{h}(b), r(b)\big) = - \int e'\bar{h}(b)\,dg(b) + \int r'(b)\,[D\bar{h}(b) - b]\,dg(b).$$

From (5.11e) and (5.11f) it follows by the saddle point theorem that the vectors $\bar{h}(b)$, $\bar{r}(b)$ are optimal.                                            Q.E.D.

Consider now the second-stage program:

$$\text{minimize } f'y$$

under the restrictions

$$By \geqslant b - Ax; \qquad y \geqslant 0 \tag{5.12a}$$

and its dual

$$\text{maximize } s'(b - Ax)$$

under the restrictions

$$B's \leqslant f; \qquad s \geqslant 0. \tag{5.12b}$$

Let $\bar{y}(b, x)$ and $\bar{s}(b, x)$ denote optimal primal and dual vectors for this problem for given $b$ and $x$. To fix ideas let us fix $x = \bar{x}$. Then the following result has been proved by Dantzig and Madansky [9]:

*Theorem 5.5*

If there exist optimal dual vectors $\bar{s}(b, \bar{x})$ for the second stage program (5.12a) such that

$$[c' - \bar{s}'(b, \bar{x}) \cdot A]\,\bar{x} = 0$$
$$[c' - \bar{s}'(b, \bar{x}) \cdot A] \geqslant 0 \quad \text{for almost all } b$$

then $\bar{r}(b) = \bar{s}(b, \bar{x})$ and $\bar{h}(b) = [(\bar{x}', \bar{y}'(b, \bar{x})]$ are optimal vectors for the original program.

*Proof*: From (5.12b) it follows that the vectors in $\tilde{s}(b, \tilde{x})$ satisfy (e.g. the Kuhn-Tucker conditions)

$$[f' - \tilde{s}'(b, \tilde{x}) \cdot B] \geqslant 0; \qquad [f' - \tilde{s}'(b, \tilde{x}) \cdot B] \cdot \tilde{y}(b, \tilde{x}) = 0 \quad \text{for all } b.$$

Then by theorem 5.4, $\tilde{r}(b) = \tilde{s}(b, \tilde{x})$ and $\tilde{h}'(b) = (\tilde{x}', \tilde{y}'(b, \tilde{x}))$ are optimal vectors.

These results are useful in characterizing the optimal solutions of a TSL problem and in specifying the requirements for an optimal solution to exist.

Consider now a very simple example of a TSP problem due to Dantzig, which is concerned with determining the optimal level of factory production $(x_{11})$, storage $(x_{22})$ and outside purchase $(x_{21})$ of a single commodity, for which the market demand $r$ is random with a uniform probability density $p(r) = (80 - 70)^{-1}$ and the constraints are such that the total supply, made up of production $(x_{11})$ plus the amount purchased in the open market $(x_{21})$ at a unit cost of two dollars, is never allowed to fall short of demand $(r)$ and further, due to storage space and other considerations, the amount produced $(x_{11})$ within the factory plus the amount stored $(x_{12})$ must equal 100. The unit cost of factory production is one dollar per unit of $x_{11}$. Hence the model is

$$\text{minimize } w = x_{11} + 2x_{21}$$

under the conditions

$$x_{11} + x_{12} = 100$$
$$x_{11} + x_{21} - x_{22} = r;$$
$$x_{ij} \geqslant 0; \qquad p(r) = 1/(80 - 70)$$

where the objective function is to minimize the cost of buying outside and producing at the factory (neglecting the cost or value aspects of excess stock). Permanent feasibility of the second constraint is assumed here, which implies that it is possible to choose $x_{21}$ (outside purchase) and $x_{22}$ (excess supply), whatever be the feasible values of $x_{11}$ (factory production) and $x_{12}$ (factory stock).

Now it is clear from this model that if $x_{11} > r$ for a fixed $r$, then $x_{21} = 0$ gives minimum cost but if $x_{11} \leqslant r$ then $x_{21} = r - x_{11}$ gives minimum cost, since $x_{21}$ is more costly per unit than $x_{11}$; hence

$$\text{minimum cost: } \min_{x_{21}} w = \begin{cases} x_{11}, & \text{if } x_{11} > r \\ x_{11} + 2(r - x_{11}), & \text{if } x_{11} \leqslant r \end{cases}.$$

But since market demand $(r)$ is probabilistic with density function $p(r) = \frac{1}{10}$

there are three cases to consider:

I. $x_{11} \geqslant 80$: E min $w = x_{11}$, since $Ex_{21} = 0$ (E = expectation),

II. $x_{11} \leqslant 70$: E min $w = \int_{70}^{80} [x_{11} + 2(r - x_{11})] p(r) \, dr = -x_{11} + 150$,

III. $70 \leqslant x_{11} \leqslant 80$: E min $w = \int_{70}^{x_{11}} x_{11} p(r) \, dr + \int_{x_{11}}^{80} [x_{11} + 2(r - x_{11})]$
$\times p(r) \, dr = \frac{1}{10} (75 - x_{11})^2 + 77.5$.

Hence the total expected cost function is quadratic and its minimum value is attained at $x_{11} = 75$; since this value is feasible for the first restriction $x_{11} + x_{12} = 100$, hence the optimal solution is: $x_{11} = Er = 75$, $x_{12} = 25$, $x_{21} = = r - 75$ where $Ex_{21} = 0$.

Two concluding comments about the TSP approach may be added. First, an extension of the case where the coefficient matrix $A$ is also random has been attempted by a number of authors, although this appears to be a harder problem. One direction of effort has been the search for a certainty equivalent, i.e., the replacement of all random elements by nonrandom values satisfying the two-stage problem. It is to be noted that the expected value of the random vector $b$ is not always a certainty equivalent, but there are some special situations under which it is. For instance, Madansky has shown that if $C(b, x) = c'x + \min_y f'y$ has the form

$$C(b, x) = A_1(x) + A_2(b) + A_3(x) \cdot b$$

where $A_1(x)$, $A_3(x)$ are functions of $x$ only, $A_2(b)$ a function of $b$ only, then replacing the random vector $b$ by its expected value and solving the resulting nonstochastic problem will also solve the two-stage problem. A typical example of such a function $C(b, x)$ is a quadratic function in both $x$ and $b$.

Second, the TSP approach has not yet been successful in developing optimal decision rules in any sequential fashion, when the distribution of the random vector $b$ is other than uniform. Extension to more general situations requires an analysis of the statistical distribution of the objective function $(c'x + E \min f'y)$ as a function of $x$. Simulation studies have some scope here.

### 5.1.2.3. Stochastic linear programming.

Methods of stochastic linear programming (SLP) may be divided into three broad types, e.g.
(a) the passive approach in which the distribution of the optimal solution vector and the optimal objective function is derived under the simplifying assumptions that the random errors around the optimal basis are specially

structured. This is the method developed by Babbar and Tintner [10] and recently extended by Bereanu, Prekopa and others [11];

(b) the active approach developed by Tintner and extended by Sengupta and Tintner [12], in which each resource vector is decomposed in terms of additional decision variables $u_{ij}$, where $u_{ij} \geqslant 0$, $\sum_j u_{ij} \leqslant 1$ and

$$b_i = \sum_j b_i u_{ij}; \qquad j = 1, ..., n; \qquad i = 1, ..., m$$

and the distribution of the optimal solution vector and the optimal objective function is truncated or conditioned by a specific choice of the allocation ratios $(u_{ij})$; and

(c) the other distributional approaches to stochastic linear programming in which any of the following aspects are analyzed: (i) the extreme value aspects, according to which each $c_j$ coefficient is replaced over the sample values $s = 1, 2, ..., N$ by $\max_s c_{js}$ or $\min_s c_{js}$ and the distribution behavior of solutions with the most optimistic and the most pessimistic set of parameters is analyzed (here the extreme value approach in statistics is relevant); (ii) the relation between the distribution problems of the SLP, CCP and TSP approaches, particularly with regard to their deterministic equivalents; (iii) methods of analyzing the effects on the optimal deterministic solution of any departure from the assumptions of normality, independence and other simplifying conditions for the random elements of the problem; and (iv) the distribution of the utility function $U(z)$ defined on the set of values of the objective function $z = c'x$ subject to the usual convex set of linear restrictions $Ax \leqslant b$, $x \geqslant 0$.

It would not be possible to discuss all the different aspects of the SLP methods; hence only a few selected methods will be presented here. Consider first the earliest problem of the passive approach, in which the *optimal* basis equations are written as

$$(A + \alpha)x = b + \beta \qquad A, \alpha: m \cdot m$$
$$b, \beta: m \cdot 1 \qquad (5.13a)$$

where the random errors $\alpha_{ij}$ and $\beta_i$ are assumed to satisfy the following conditions

$$\mathrm{E}(\alpha_{ij}) = 0 = \mathrm{E}\beta_i; \qquad \mathrm{E}\alpha_{ij}^2 = \sigma_{ij}^2 < \infty; \qquad \mathrm{E}\beta_i^2 = t_i^2. \qquad (5.13b)$$

From (5.13a), the $k$th optimal activity $x_k$ can be solved for as

$$x_k = |D^k + d^k| / |A + \alpha|; \qquad k = 1, ..., m \qquad (5.13c)$$

where $|D^k + d^k|$ is the determinant of matrix $(A + \alpha)$ when its $k$th column is replaced by the column vector $(b + \beta)$.

Also

$$z = \sum_{r=1}^{m} (c_r + \gamma_r)\, x_r, \quad \text{where} \quad E\gamma_r = 0; \qquad E\gamma_r^2 = w_r^2 < \infty$$

and the index set $r = 1, \ldots, m$ is defined for the optimal basic activities only.

Now limiting to first order errors and neglecting cross product terms of *unlike* random elements, the following approximate expressions can be derived:

$$|D^k + d^k| \doteq |D^k| + \sum_{i=1}^{m} s_{ik}\beta_i + \sum_{i=1}^{m} \sum_{\substack{j=1 \\ j \neq k}}^{m} d_{ij}^k \alpha_{ij} = N(x_k), \quad \text{say;}$$

$$|A + \alpha| \doteq |A| + \sum_{i}\sum_{j} s_{ij}\alpha_{ij} = D(x), \quad \text{say;}$$

$$\sum_{r=1}^{m} (c_r + \gamma_r)\,|D^r + d^r| = \sum_{r} c_r |D^r| + \sum_{r} c_r\Big(\sum_{i} s_{ir}\beta_i\Big) + \sum_{\substack{j=1 \\ j \neq r}} c_r \sum d_{ij}^r \alpha_{ij}$$

$$+ \sum_{r} |D^r|\,\gamma_r = N(z), \quad \text{say;}$$

$$E\,|D^k + d^k| = |D^k| = d_k, \quad \text{say;}$$

$$\text{Var}\,|D^k + d^k| = \sum_{i} s_{ik}^2 t_i^2 + \sum_{i}\sum_{j} (d_{ij}^k)^2 \sigma_{ij}^2 = \sigma_k^2, \quad \text{say;}$$

$$E\,|A + \alpha| = |A| = a_0, \quad \text{say;}$$

$$\text{Var}\,|A + \alpha| = \sum_{i}\sum_{j} s_{ij}^2 \sigma_{ij}^2 = \sigma_A^2, \quad \text{say;}$$

$$\text{Cov}\big(|D^k + d^k|, |A + \alpha|\big) = \sum_{i}\sum_{j} d_{ij}^k s_{ij} \sigma_{ij}^2 = \sigma_{Ak}, \quad \text{say;}$$

$$EN(z) = \sum_{r} |D^r|\, c_r = d_{N(z)}, \quad \text{say;}$$

$$\text{Var}\,N(z) = \sum_{r=1}^{m} \Big(\sum_{i=1}^{m} c_i s_{ri}\Big)^2 t_i^2 + \sum_{r=1}^{m} c_r^2 \Big[\sum_{i=1}^{m} \sum_{j=1}^{m} (d_{ij}^r)^2 \sigma_{ij}^2\Big]$$

$$+ \sum_{r} |D^r|^2 w_r^2 = \sigma_{N(z)}^2, \quad \text{say;}$$

$$z = N(z)/D(z) \quad \text{where} \quad |A + \alpha| = D(x) = D(z), \text{say;}$$

with $\quad ED(z) = |A| = a_0 \quad$ and $\quad \text{Var}\,D(z) = \sigma_A^2; \quad$ and

$$\text{Cov}\big(N(z), D(z)\big) = \sum_{r} c_r \sum_{\substack{i,j \\ j \neq r}} d_{ij}^r s_{ij} \sigma_{ij}^2 = \sigma_{A.N(z)}^2, \quad \text{say,}$$

where $s_{ik}$ is the co-factor of element $a_{ik}$ in $|A|$ and $d_{ij}^k$ is the co-factor of $(i, j)$th element of $|D^k|$, and $|D^k|$ is the determinant of $A$ with its $k$th column replaced by the resource vector $b$.

Now the distribution problem for the optimal solution $x_k = N(x_k)/D(x)$ and the optimal objective function $z = N(z)/D(z)$ is seen to be reduced to the problem of finding the distribution of the ratio of two random variables. If we interpret or assume the approximations of the original set of random elements as normally distributed, then the problem is one of finding the distribution of the ratio of two random variables, each of which is normally distributed. Even in this form the distribution problem is complicated, unless certain simple (although asymptotic) results can be utilized. Babbar and Tintner have utilized the following result due to Geary [13]:

*Theorem 5.6*

If $N$ and $D$ are two normally distributed variables with means $\bar{N}$, $\bar{D}$ and covariance $\sigma_N^2$, $\sigma_D^2$, $\sigma_{ND}$ and $z = N/D$, then the transformed variable $y$

$$y = \frac{\bar{D} \cdot z - \bar{N}}{(\sigma_D^2 z^2 - 2z\sigma_{ND} + \sigma_N^2)^{\frac{1}{2}}}$$

tends to be approximately normally distributed as a unit normal variate, provided the effective range of variation of the denominator $D$ is such that $\bar{D} - 3\sigma_D \leqslant D \leqslant \bar{D} + 3\sigma_D$, whereby $D$ is nonnegative if $\bar{D} \geqslant 3\sigma_D$.

If the nonnegativity condition for $D$ is satisfied (which it is in some cases), then this theorem is useful in deriving the density function of the random variable $z$ and setting up confidence intervals. For instance, let

$$v = \sigma_D^2 z^2 - 2z\sigma_{ND} + \sigma_N^2;$$

then

$$z = (\bar{N}/\bar{D}) + v^{\frac{1}{2}} y/\bar{D}$$

$$dz = (\bar{D})^{-1} \left[ v^{\frac{1}{2}} dy + \frac{\bar{D}z - \bar{N}}{v} \cdot (\sigma_D^2 z - \sigma_{ND}) \, dz \right]$$

since $dv = 2\sigma_D^2 z \, dz - 2\sigma_{ND} dz$;

hence define

$$dy = Q \, dz$$

where

$$Q = v^{-\frac{3}{2}} \cdot [\bar{D}\sigma_N^2 - \bar{N}\sigma_{ND} + z(\bar{N}\sigma_D^2 - \bar{D}\sigma_{ND})].$$

The probability density function (pdf) of $z$, denoted by $f(z) \, dz$, becomes therefore

$$f(z) \, dz = (2\pi)^{-\frac{1}{2}} Q \exp\left[ -\frac{1}{2} \left\{ \frac{(\bar{D}z - \bar{N})^2}{\sigma_D^2 z^2 - 2z\sigma_{ND} + \sigma_N^2} \right\} \right]. \quad (5.13d)$$

This probability density function can be used now to set confidence limits in the usual manner. For instance, let us set $100 \, \delta$ percent limits on the probability

$$\text{Prob}(|y| \leqslant \varepsilon) = \delta$$

i.e.,

$$\text{Prob}\left[(\bar{D}z - \bar{N})^2 \leqslant \varepsilon^2 \cdot (\sigma_D^2 z^2 - 2z\sigma_{ND} + \sigma_N^2)\right] = \delta$$

i.e.,

$$\text{Prob}\left[g_1 z^2 - 2g_2 z + g_3 \leqslant 0\right] = \delta$$

where

$$g_1 = \bar{D}^2 - \varepsilon^2 \sigma_D^2$$

$$g_2 = \bar{D}\bar{N} - \varepsilon^2 \sigma_{ND} \quad \text{and} \quad g_3 = \bar{N}^2 - \varepsilon^2 \sigma_N^2.$$

The roots of the quadratic equation in $z$, i.e.,

$$g_1 z^2 - 2g_2 z + g_3 = 0$$

will specify two numbers say, $z_{(1)}$ and $z_{(2)}$, $(z_{(1)} < z_{(2)})$, such that there will be approximately a 100 $\delta$ percent probability that the optimal profit $z$ lies between $z_{(1)}$ and $z_{(2)}$, i.e.,

$$\text{Prob}\left[z_{(1)} \leqslant z \leqslant z_{(2)}\right] = \delta.$$

Several comments may be added about the applicability and extension of this distribution approach of SLP. First, the asymptotic approximations implied by Geary's theorem are unlikely to be very useful in small sample situations. Moreover, the normality assumption for the original random elements has the unrealistic consequence that it is not very suitable for economic models in which prices, resources and input coefficients are generally required to be nonnegative. An extension to situations where each component of the set $(A, b, c)$ follows an independent chi-square distribution has been made by Sengupta [14], who has shown that in this case the problem reduces itself to finding the distribution of a ratio, the numerator of which is a mixture of chi-square distributions and the denominator is a central chi-square variate. An appropriate approximation for this case has been suggested in the form of a noncentral $F$-distribution, for which standard statistical tables are available.

Second, it is to be noted that the quantity

$$t_i = b_i - a_i' x; \qquad a_i = i\text{th column of } A \tag{5.14a}$$

for the original set of restrictions $Ax \leqslant b$ (before the slack variables are introduced) where $A$, $b$ have random components, follows a normal distribution $N(m_i, v_i)$ with mean $m_i$ and variance $v_i$

$$m_i = \text{E}b_i - (\text{E}a_i)' x$$

$$v_i = \text{Var } b_i + x' \left[\text{E}(a_i - \text{E}a_i)(a_i - \text{E}a_i)'\right] x$$

whenever the random components of $A$ and $b$ follow mutually independent normal distributions. Now the feasibility restrictions require that $t_i \geqslant 0$. This implies that the negative range of values of $t_i$ (i.e., for $t_i < 0$) is discarded. Hence the feasible set of values of the random variable $t_i$ satisfying $t_i \geqslant 0$ for all $i$ defines a truncated normal distribution, the density function (pdf) of which is given by $f(t_i)\,dt_i$ where

$$f(t_i)\,dt_i = [\sqrt{v_i} \cdot 2\pi \{1 - \phi(- m_i/\sqrt{v_i})\}]^{-1} \cdot \exp\left[\frac{-(t_i - m_i)^2}{2v_i}\right] dt_i, \qquad t_i \geqslant 0$$

(5.14b)

with

$$\phi(w) = (\sqrt{2\pi})^{-1} \int\limits_{-\infty}^{w} e^{-\frac{1}{2}t^2}\,dt.$$

Various methods of estimating the parameters of truncated normal distributions from observed sample data are available. Further, the approximations for truncated normal distributions can also be utilized to improve the distribution analysis of the passive approach of SLP.

Third, the role of the active approach of SLP consists primarily in varying the additional decision variables $u_{ij}$ where $b_i = \sum_{j=1}^{n} b_i u_{ij}$ in such a fashion that the variance or other measure of the optimal activity or the optimal objective function is reduced. This is sometimes possible, because the mean or variance of $b_i$, for example, which enters as a parameter of the distribution problem, is itself made a function of the nonstochastic decision variables $u_{ij}$ which are essentially the relative proportions or weights. (For some of the mathematical results and empirical economic applications in this direction see Sengupta [15] and Sengupta, Millham and Tintner [16].)

*5.1.2.4. Transition probability programming.* System analysis through transition probabilities has frequently been found useful, especially for formulating sequential decisions over time, when the stochastic element can be viewed as a Markov process (Howard, Blackwell, Bellman, Wolfe and Dantzig, and others [17]). Such situations may be found, for instance, in queuing models, certain types of inventory models, machine replacement problems and in diffusion process analysis applied to the introduction of a new product or invention.

Consider a simple problem in which a system at any given point of time $t$ ($t = 0, 1, 2, \ldots$) can be identified as being in one of $N$ possible states ($j = 1, 2, \ldots, N$). Given that the system is in state $i$ at discrete time $t$, a decision $k$ is selected from a nonempty finite set $K_i$, where for each $k$ there is

(i) a Markovian transition probability matrix $p_{ij}^{(k)}$ $(j=1,...,N)$ with $p_{ij}^{(k)} \geqslant 0$, $\sum_j p_{ij}^{(k)} = 1$ and $i, j = 1, 2, ..., n$;

(ii) a 'cost factor' $c_i^{(k)}$ which is assumed constant; and

(iii) a discount factor $r$, $0 \leqslant r < 1$ which is constant for all states and all time points.

Now a feasible policy may be defined as any rule that selects for any time $t$ and any state $i$ a unique decision $k$ from the finite set $K_i$. An optimal policy is then one which results in minimizing the total discounted expected cost when the constant discount factor $r$ is used.

Define for any $t$, $s_i^{(k)}(t)$ as the joint probability of being in state $i$ and making a decision $k$; since the transition probabilities are assumed to be Markovian (i.e., only one period-lag, the recent past counts), the joint probabilities $s_i^{(k)}(t)$, also called state probabilities, may be written as a recursive relation

$$\sum_{k \in K_j} s_j^{(k)}(t) = s_j(0), \quad \text{for} \quad t = 0; \tag{5.15a}$$

$$= \sum_{i=1;\, k \in K_i}^{n} p_{ij}^{(k)} s_i^{(k)}(t-1), \quad \text{for} \quad t = 1, 2, ...,$$

$$j = 1, 2, ..., N \tag{5.15b}$$

where $s_j(0)$, the probability of the system in state $j$ at time zero, is assumed known such that $\sum_{j=1}^{N} s_j(0) = 1$. It can be easily proved that the sequence $s_j^{(k)}(t)$ defines a well-behaved probability distribution provided the conditions (5.15a) and (5.15b) are satisfied. Further, the total expected discounted cost over an infinite time horizon $(t \to \infty)$ must be bounded since $r < 1$, i.e.

$$\frac{c_L}{1-r} \leqslant \sum_{t=0}^{\infty} r^t \sum_{i=1;\, k \in K_i}^{N} c_i^{(k)} s_i^{(k)}(t) \leqslant \frac{c_U}{1-r} \tag{5.15c}$$

where

$$c_L = \min_{i,k} c_i^{(k)}; \qquad c_U = \max_{i,k} c_i^{(k)}.$$

The infinite-horizon optimization model in one version may be presented therefore as follows:

$$\text{minimize} \sum_{t=0}^{\infty} r^t \sum_{i=1;\, k \in K_i}^{N} c_i^{(k)} s_i^{(k)}(t) \tag{5.15d}$$

under the constraints (5.15a), (5.15b) and

$$s_i^{(k)}(t) \geqslant 0; \qquad \sum_{j=1}^{N} s_j(0) = 1, \, s_j(0) \text{ given}$$

$$i, j = 1, 2, ..., N; \qquad k \in K_i; \qquad t = 0, 1, 2, ..., \infty.$$

Since the sequences $s_j^{(k)}(t)$ are bounded for all $t$, therefore a new set of variables $x_j^{(k)}$ may be defined as

$$x_j^{(k)} = \sum_{t=0}^{\infty} r^t s_j^{(k)}(t) \qquad (5.15e)$$

and the problem (5.15d) may also be rewritten as

$$\text{minimize} \sum_{j=1;\ k \in K_j}^{N} \sum c_j^{(k)} x_j^{(k)}$$

under the conditions

and
$$\sum_{k \in K_j} x_j^{(k)} - r \sum_{i=1;\ k \in K_i}^{N} \sum p_{ij}^{(k)} x_i^{(k)} = s_j(0); \qquad j = 1, 2, ..., N \qquad (5.15f)$$

$$x_i^{(k)} \geq 0; \qquad i = 1, 2, ..., N; \qquad k \in K_i.$$

It can be seen that the transform $x_j^{(k)}$ of any nonnegative sequence $s_j^{(k)}(t)$ which is a solution of (5.15a) and (5.15b) is itself a solution of the problem (5.15f). Now define a *stationary policy* by a function which for each state $i$ selects exactly one variable $x_i^{(k)}$, where $k$ is selected from the nonempty set $K_i$. Then the following results [18] can be easily proved.

*Theorem 5.7*

If the equality restrictions of the problem (5.15f) define solutions $x_i^{(k)}$ selected by a stationary policy only, then

(i) the subsystem $x_j^{(k)} - r \sum_{i=1}^{N} p_{ij}^{(k)} x_i^{(k)} = s_j(0); (j = 1, ..., N)$ for a fixed $k$ has a unique solution (i.e., the coefficient matrix has rank $N$);

(ii) if $s_j(0) \geq 0$, then $x_j^{(k)} \geq 0, (j = 1, ..., N)$;

(iii) whenever $s_j(0) > 0$ $(j = 1, ..., N)$, then a stationary policy has a corresponding unique solution to $x_j^{(k)} - r \sum_{i=1}^{N} p_{ij}^{(k)} x_i^{(k)} = s_j(0)$ which has $N$ positive variables (i.e., this solution is a basic feasible solution); and

(iv) with a positive value for $s_j(0)$, the LP problem (5.15f) has a unique optimal basic solution and there is an optimal stationary policy associated with it.

The implications of this theorem are two-fold. First, the sequence of optimal stationary policies can be easily characterized. This offers an indirect way of evaluating slight deviations from the optimal policy sequence by means of the dual solutions. Second, the implications of a finite-horizon model can also be compared with those of an infinite-horizon model.

Note, however, that the cost factor $c_i^{(k)}$ can be given the broader interpretation of negative returns (or rewards) and instead of a minimization type decision model it may sometimes be more convenient to specify a maximization-type model with a slightly different orientation. Denote by

$v_i(t)$ the expected value of total returns at time $t$, if the system now is in state $i$; let $q_{ij}$ be the constant amount of return per transition of the system from state $i$ to state $j$ and let $p_{ij}$ be the transition probabilities assumed to follow a simple Markov process. Then the following recursive relation can be derived as before

$$v_i(t) = \sum_{j=1}^{N} p_{ij}(q_{ij} + v_j(t-1)); \qquad i = 1, ..., N; \qquad t = 1, 2, ... \qquad (5.16a)$$

If there is a constant discount factor $r(0 \leqslant r < 1)$ to be applied to compute the discounted value of total expected returns and there are $K_i$ alternative decisions out of which any decision $k$ may be selected with transition probabilities $p_{ij}^{(k)}$ and unit returns $q_{ij}^{(k)}$, then the recursive relation (5.16a) can be rewritten as

$$v_i(t+1) = \max_{k \in K_i} \left( \sum_{j=1}^{N} p_{ij}^{(k)}(q_{ij}^{(k)} + rv_j(t)) \right), \qquad (5.16b)$$

provided an optimal decision is made out of the set $K_i$ of possible alternative decisions. The objective function (5.16b) may be maximized under the boundary conditions

$$\sum_{j} p_{ij}^{(k)} = 1, \qquad p_{ij}^{(k)} \geqslant 0 \quad \text{and given} \quad v_j(0);$$

this would define a well behaved LP problem from which the expected optimal future returns of the system at each stage of the process may be computed for as many discrete values of $t$ as required. Note however that the relation (5.16b) is an application of the principle of optimality developed by Bellman in connection with dynamic programming.

Two comments may be added by way of general remarks. First, the above types of optimization model may be constructed for more general types of Markov processes known as stochastic birth and death processes involving difference-differential equations (i.e., continuous time, discrete number of states) but the solutions are generally more complicated and the iterative methods of dynamic programming have to be applied (some applications of these ideas to economic models specifying optimal growth paths have been investigated by Sengupta and Tintner [17]). Second, the usefulness of the above types of optimization models is still very limited due to the difficulty of (i) actually estimating or evaluating the parameters $(c_i^{(k)}, q_{ij}^{(k)})$ specific to each decision, (ii) characterizing the level of performance of a system defined by more than one or two key variables and (iii) specifying the type of Markov process relevant to each specific problem.

### 5.1.3. Decision-theoretic programming models

Some of the decision-theoretic aspects of probabilistic LP models have already been discussed in different forms before, in this section some special emphasis is given to those decision-theoretic aspects which involve some specific features of sequential decision-making, e.g. prior and posterior distributions of parameters, imputed penalty functions for infeasibility, introduction of aspiration levels through fractile criteria, etc.

First, consider a penalty function approach (due to W. H. Evers and others [19]) in the 'here and now' version of the two-stage programming model under uncertainty. Here the LP problem is

$$\text{minimize } c'x \qquad (5.17a)$$
$$x$$

under the restrictions

$$A_1 x \geqslant b_1 \qquad A_1 : k \,.\, n \text{ matrix (random)} \qquad (5.17b)$$

$$A_2 x \geqslant b_2 \qquad A_2 : (p - k) \,.\, n \text{ matrix (deterministic)} \qquad (5.17c)$$

$$x \geqslant 0 \qquad c, x : n \,.\, 1$$

where the rows of the matrix $A_1$ only have random elements. Denote by $S$ the set $(s_1, s_2, ..., s_k)$ of indices corresponding to the stochastic rows of matrix $A_1$ and let the superscript $s$ denote a specific element of this set. Further define a chance-constrained set $T$ for given $\alpha$ (a scalar) as

$$T = \{x : \text{Prob}[(A_1 x \geqslant b_1)] \geqslant \alpha; \qquad 0 \leqslant \alpha \leqslant 1, x \geqslant 0\}. \qquad (5.17d)$$

Let $x_1$ be a vector in $T$, $x_2$ be a deficiency variable and $x_3$ a slack variable $(x_3 \geqslant 0)$ such that

$$x_2^{(s)} = \begin{cases} b_1^{(s)} - A_1^{(s)} x_1, & \text{if } A_1^{(s)} x_1 < b_1^{(s)} \text{ for all } s \text{ in } S \\ 0 \text{ otherwise} \end{cases}$$

then the constraints become

$$A_1^{(s)} x_1 + x_2^{(s)} \geqslant b_1^{(s)}$$
$$A_2 x_1 - x_3 = b_2$$
$$x_1 \geqslant 0, x_2 \geqslant 0, x_3 \geqslant 0.$$

Note that the probability of infeasibility of a particular restriction may be computed from

$$\text{Prob}(x_2^{(s)} > 0) = 1 - \alpha_s, \qquad s \in S$$

where $\alpha_s$ is a tolerance measure for the $s$th constraint.

Assuming the rows of $A_1$ to be independent

$$\alpha = \prod_{s \in S} \alpha_s. \tag{5.17e}$$

Denote by $k_s$ the constant penalty per unit violation of the $s$th constraint, then the expected total penalty cost for shortage of all constraints is

$$K'\mathrm{E}(x_2^{(s)}), \qquad x_2 \geqslant 0 \tag{5.17f}$$

where $K'$ is the row vector with elements $k_s$ and E is expectation. In addition to penalty costs for shortage there may be a cost for obtaining any infeasibility at all. From (5.17d), $\alpha$ is the probability that all constraints are satisfied and thus $(1 - \alpha)$ is the probability that at least one constraint is violated. Let $N$ be the constant cost for this infeasibility with total expected cost on this account as $N(1 - \alpha)$, which is sometimes called the set-up cost. Hence the reduced form of the nonstochastic program which incorporates the expected penalty costs of shortage and expected set-up costs becomes:

$$\underset{x_1}{\text{minimize}}\, c'x + K'\mathrm{E}(x_2^{(s)}) + N\big(1 - \alpha(x)\big)$$

subject to

$$A_2 x \geqslant b_2, \qquad x \geqslant 0$$

where $\alpha(x)$ is a function which specifies the probability for every $x \geqslant 0$.

As a second type of problem consider the deterministic approach to probabilistic programming through aspiration or fractile criteria (Geoffrion (1967), Sinha (1963), Roy (1952) and others [20]). Assume that the vector $c$ of net prices in the objective function ($c'x$, $x \in X$ where $X$ is the feasible set) has a multinormal distribution with mean vector $m$ and covariance matrix $V$, so that the objective function defines a multinormal variate $\mathrm{N}(m'x, x'Vx)$. Consider three deterministic reformulations of the objective function (max $c'x$, $x \in X$):

$$\max \mathrm{E}c'x; \qquad x \in X; \qquad \text{E is expectation;} \tag{5.18a}$$

$$\max F_\alpha(c'x); \qquad x \in X; \qquad \alpha \text{ is a predetermined constant} \tag{5.18b}$$

$0 < \alpha < 1$ such that $F_\alpha(c'x)$ is the $\alpha$-fractile of the distribution of $c'x = z$; and

$$\max P_k(c'x); \qquad x \in X \quad \text{and} \quad P_k(c'x) = \mathrm{Prob}(c'x \geqslant k) \tag{5.18c}$$

where $k$ is a predetermined 'aspiration level' pay-off.

Note that there are several apparent relations between the three objective functions, e.g.

(i) If $\alpha = 0.5$, then (5.18b) is equivalent to (5.18a), since the median (i.e., 0.5 fractile) of a normal variate is equal to the mean;

(ii) the functions $F_\alpha(c'x)$, $P_k(c'x)$ can be respectively written as

$$F_\alpha(c'x) = m'x + \phi^{-1}(\alpha)\cdot(x'Vx)^{\frac{1}{2}} \tag{5.18d}$$

where $\phi[.]$ is the standardized normal distribution function;

$$P_k(c'x) = 1 - \phi[(k - m'x)/\sqrt{x'Vx}] \equiv \phi[(m'x - k)/\sqrt{x'Vx}] \tag{5.18e}$$

hence, if $0 < \alpha < 0.5$, then $\phi^{-1}(\alpha) < 0$ and therefore $F_\alpha(c'x)$ becomes concave (however, if $x'Vx$ vanishes at some points, this concave function may not have differentiability). Again, since $\phi[.]$ is a strictly increasing function of its arguments, maximization of (5.18e) is equivalent to

$$\max_{x \in X} \frac{m'x - k}{\sqrt{x'Vx}}. \tag{5.18f}$$

If the aspiration level $k$ is equated to max $Ec'x$ in (5.18a), then (5.18f) is easily seen to have the optimal value zero, which is achieved for those feasible $x$ for which $m'x = v$, where $v = $ max $Ec'x$, $x \in X$. In this case the maximum probability defined by (5.18c) is 0.5, since $\phi(0) = 0.5$. A conservative policy-maker would naturally want to choose aspiration levels $k < v$, since by lowering his expected return he may achieve less variance of his return (i.e., more stability).

(iii) If (5.18b) and (5.18c) are termed the fractile criteria and the aspiration criteria respectively, then these programming models can be interpreted as methods of adaptive programming, since they adapt the expectation criteria defined in (5.18a) in relation to the aspiration or fractile levels. (Other types of adaptive programming are also conceivable.) Geoffrion has noted the following reciprocity relation between the fractile and the aspiration criteria (for any appropriate distribution function on $c$):

(a) For each fixed $\alpha$, every optimal solution of the fractile model (5.18b) is also optimal for the aspiration model (5.18c) with $k$ equal to the optimal value of the fractile model (5.18b);

(b) For each fixed aspiration level $k$, every optimal solution of aspiration model (5.18c) is also optimal for the fractile model (5.18b) with $\alpha$ equal to one minus the optimal value of the aspiration model (5.18c).

Note that the fractile and aspiration models can be reduced to parametric quadratic programs of the type

$$\max_x \theta \cdot (m'x) - (1 - \theta)\, x'Vx; \qquad x \in X \tag{5.19}$$

where the parameter $\theta(0 \leqslant \theta \leqslant 1)$ is varied successively, starting from $\theta = 1$ and decreasing $\theta$ until the fractile function $F_\alpha(c'x^*(\theta))$ where $x^*(\theta)$ denotes optimal solution for a specific $\theta$ say $\theta = \theta_\alpha$, reaches its maximum on $[0, 1]$. A trade-off curve $(E_{z/\alpha}, F_\alpha(z))$ could thus be generated, where $E_{z/\alpha}$ is the expected maximand $E(c'x^*(\theta)) = m'x^*(\theta)$ and $F_\alpha(c'x^*(\theta))$ for a given $\theta$, when $x^*(\theta)$ is an optimal solution of (5.19a) and $\theta$ is varied from 1 to $\theta_\alpha$.

Similarly, one may solve (5.19a) by varying $\theta$ from $\theta = 1$ and then reducing till the value $\theta = \theta_k$, say, $(\theta_k \geqslant 0)$ at which the function $(m'x^*(\theta)/\sqrt{x^*(\theta)\,'Vx^*(\theta)})$ reaches its maximum on the interval $[0, 1]$. Here also a trade-off curve $(E_{z/k}, P_k(z))$ can be generated, where $E_{z/k}$ denotes $m'x^*(\theta)$, $P_k(z) = \text{Prob}\ (c'x^*(\theta) \geqslant k)$ for a specific $\theta$ and $\theta$ is varied from 1 to $\theta_k$.

These trade-off curves help to specify the risk attitudes of the decision-maker and suggest a method for determining an operational policy consistent with his risk attitudes. The specification of a particular type of risk attitude is determined either exogenously or through separate utility functions; neither of these procedures, however, is satisfactory or realistic for several practical situations.

Consider a third type of LP model [21] where the vector $c$ only is random, the feasible set is $X = (x \mid Ax \leqslant b; x \geqslant 0)$ and the basic feasible set is $S$ i.e., it is the set of all extreme points of the set $S$. Now the vector $c$ is considered as the unknown mean vector of a multivariate stochastic process. A *prior statistical distribution* on $c$ is then conceived as a prior distribution on the mean of the multivariate stochastic process and sampling from this process enables one to arrive at a *posterior distribution* on $c$. The decision problem now is to make an optimal choice in some sense of a terminal action or solution vector $x$ when $x \in X$ and when a prior or posterior distribution on $c$ is given.

Let the vector $c$ be assigned a prior measure $_t p(c)$ by the decision-maker with a mean vector $_t\bar{c}$. Under $_t\bar{c}$ let the optimal terminal decision vector be $_t x$ (where the left subscript $t$ denotes prior measure) so that the expected value of this optimal terminal action is:

$$_t E_c(c'_t x) = {_t\bar{c}'} \quad _t x = \max_{x \in X}({_t\bar{c}'x}) = \max_{x \in S}({_t\bar{c}'x}) \tag{5.20a}$$

where

$$\max_{x \in S}({_t\bar{c}'x}) \geqslant [{_t E_c(c'x)}, \quad \text{all} \quad x \in X] \tag{5.20b}$$

where $_t E_c$ denotes expectation with respect to the prior distribution on $c$.

Now if the decision-maker through a sampling experiment (or observation) with outcome $u$ substitutes for the prior measure $_t p(c)$ the posterior measure

$p_t(c \mid u)$ with mean vector $\bar{c}_t$, his optimal terminal decision vector will be $x_t$, for which the expected value of the optimal terminal action is

$$E_{t,\,c|u}(c'x_t) = \bar{c}_t'x_t = \max_{x \in X}(\bar{c}_t'x) = \max_{x \in S}(\bar{c}_t'x) \qquad (5.20c)$$

where

$$\max_{x \in S}(\bar{c}_t'x) \geqslant [E_{t,\,c|u}(c'x), \quad \text{all} \quad x \in X] \qquad (5.20d)$$

where $E_{t,\,c\mid u}$ denotes expectation with respect to the posterior distribution on $c$ given the outcome $u$.

To compare these two situations with that of perfect information, assume that the decision-maker's optimal terminal action vector is $x^*$ when he has perfect information on $c$. The conditional value of perfect information (CVPI) given $c$ would then be

$$\text{CVPI} = c'x^* - c_t'x \qquad (5.21a)$$

and the expected value of perfect information (EVPI) can be computed with respect to the prior distribution on $c$ as

$$\text{EVPI} = {}_t E_c(c'x^* - c_t'x) = {}_t E_c(\max_{x \in X}(c'x)) = {}_t \bar{c}_t'x$$
$$= {}_t E_c[\max_{x \in S}(c'x) - {}_t \bar{c}_t'x]. \qquad (5.21b)$$

Similarly the conditional value of sample information (CVSI), given the observed outcome $u$ of the sampling experiment and the expected value of sample information (EVSI) based on the posterior measure $p_t(c \mid u)$, may be computed respectively as:

$$\text{CVSI} = \bar{c}_t'x_* - \bar{c}_t x_t \qquad (5.21c)$$

$$\text{EVSI} = E_{t,\,c|u}[\bar{c}_t'x_* - \bar{c}_{t\,t}x] = E_{t,\,c|u}[\max_x c_t'x - \bar{c}_{t\,t}x]$$

$$= [E_{t,\,c|u}[\max(\bar{c}_t'x)] - {}_t\bar{c}_t'x] \qquad (5.21d)$$

where $x_*$ is the optimal terminal decision vector selected by the decision-maker, if the outcome $u$ of the sampling experiment replaces the prior measure ${}_t p(c)$ by the posterior measure $p_t(c \mid u)$, i.e.

$$\bar{c}_t'x_* = \max_{x \in X}(\bar{c}_t'x) = \max_{x \in S}(\bar{c}_t'x).$$

Note that $x_*$ and $x_t$ could be identical. Further note that both in (5.21b) and (5.21d) the expected value of a maximum has to be evaluated, which involves the statistical distribution of an extreme (i.e., maximal) variate. In this respect the statistical theory of extreme values has an important role to play in the area of stochastic linear programming (some interesting illustrative attempts in this direction have been made by Bracken and Soland [21], Clark [22], Balinski, the proponents of the Monte Carlo methods, and others [23]. However this field is wide open for useful research.

## 5.2. Applications to operational models

A number of empirical and illustrative applications of some of the methods of probabilistic programming will be briefly discussed in this section.

To mention a very simple but operational example [24], we consider first a typical decision problem of an individual farmer who has to allocate his fixed and limitational resources to the production of different crops under a fairly fixed set of input coefficients but with fluctuating market prices and hence fluctuating returns. If the market prices of different crops are available for several years by quarters and it is known that there has been no systematic change in the structure of the system, how might the individual farmer utilize this set of information to define a plan of resource allocation which is in some sense optimal, given the observed set of variations in prices and hence returns? If the problem is cast in the form of a linear programming framework, then the question is how to define an optimal solution (i.e., an optimal rule of action or resource allocation), when the coefficients of the objective function representing net return per acre of each crop are observed to be probabilistically varying rather than fixed. Note that these variations are assumed probabilistic in the sense that the systematic sources are already assumed to have been taken into account deterministically.

Various partial solutions to the above-type decision problem under risk have been discussed in the literature and, from the viewpoint of simplicity and operationalism, the following three types of decision rules are analyzed in this section:

(i) the expectation criterion by which the expected value of the objective function is maximized;

(ii) the fractile criterion by which the $\alpha$-fractile of the cumulative distribution of the objective function is maximized with the value of $\alpha$ $(0<\alpha<1)$ preassigned by the decision-maker; and

(iii) the safety-first type portfolio criterion by which the variance of total profit is minimized under suitable restrictions (i.e., discounting) on the total expected profit and on the crop-specific estimate of (sample) variance. (This will be called the discounted portfolio criterion.)

For a standard linear programming problem let $X$ denote the set of feasible solutions $x$ where $Ax \leqslant b$; $x \geqslant 0$ and let $z = c'x$ be the objective function, where the $n$-component vector of net returns $c$ is assumed to be probabilistic with estimated means and covariances. The above three sets of criteria may then be reformulated as follows, where in each case maximization is to be performed with respect to $x$ over the set of feasible variations $X$:

(1) max $Ec'x = \max (Ec)'x$; $E$ is the expectation;

(2) max $F_\alpha(z) = \max F_\alpha(c'x)$, where $F_\alpha(z)$ denotes the $\alpha$-fractile of the cumulative distribution of the objective function $z$; and

(3) max $-x'Vx$ with $\bar{c}'x \geqslant z_0$, where the vector $\bar{c}$ represents a discounted estimate of net returns (i.e. with no discounting $\bar{c} = Ec$) and the covariance matrix $V$ denotes a discounted estimate of variances and covariances (i.e. with no discounting $V = Ecc' - (Ec)(Ec)'$) and $z_0$ specifies a preassigned level of total profits, below which solutions are not tolerated. The concept of discounting refers here to the sample information, e.g. a pessimistic discounting of $c_j$ may consider for each year the quarter at which returns (prices) for that crop were the lowest and then average over several years; similarly for the discounted estimates of variances.

Our object here is to analyze the nature of optimal solutions derived under the above set of criteria and their possible usefulness in specifying optimal production plans. A practical empirical problem of crop-planning is considered as the basis of application, since on the one hand the agricultural data satisfy very closely some of the regularity conditions required for probabilistic variations and on the other hand it is possible to identify the source of variations in agricultural yields, prices and returns in terms of a multiplicity of factors such as weather, conditions of perfect competition, etc., none of which can be easily separated.

*Logic of the criteria of choice*

Without entering into the whole discussion of alternative approaches to the theory of choice under risk, it would be of some interest to mention the generality and the limitations of the above set of criteria.

About the generality the following points may be noted. First, the expected value criterion requires the very minimum of information from the observed data, i.e. only the first moment of the probability distribution, and if the view is taken that the observed values on each $c_j$ are coming from a population with parameter $\theta_j$, then the sample mean $Ec_j$ provides perhaps the best linear estimate. Further, if the parameters $\theta_j$ themselves are supposed to have specific prior probability distributions, so that the expectation operator $E$

can be considered with respect to either the prior probability distribution conditional on a set of observed $c_j$ values or the posterior probability distribution of $c_j$ values, then the relative value of sample information on the average can be analyzed and incorporated.

One interesting extension of the expected value criterion is possible, if the probability distribution of each $c_j$ can be known or estimated. For instance, assume that there are $N$ sample values $c_{js}$ $(s=1, 2, ..., N)$ for each $c_j$ all coming from a known probability density function $p(c_j)$; then a new set of quantities called extreme values

$$c_j^* = \min_s c_{js} \qquad (s = 1, ..., N) \qquad (5.22a)$$

$$c_j^{**} = \max_s c_{js} \qquad (s = 1, ..., N) \qquad (5.22b)$$

can be defined and the expectation operator can be applied over $c_j^*$ values (which would be most appropriate for pessimistic and safety-minded decision-makers) or over $c_j^{**}$ values (which would be most appropriate for optimistic and risk-taking decision-makers). This type of two-point extreme value analysis is quite important, since for certain very general cases of distributions it can be shown that the variance of $c_j^* x_j$ would be much less than that of $c_j^{**} x_j$ relative to the excess of $Ec_j^{**} x_j$ over $Ec_j^* x_j$. This line of approach has not been given much attention by economists, although its importance in situations in which the reserve withholding power of farmers is slender could be substantial.

Second, the fractile criterion which generally considers the first two moments and hence is most suitable for the case in which the vector $c$ follows a multivariate normal distribution with mean vector $m = Ec$ and covariance matrix $V$, preassigns the tolerance measure $\alpha$, $(0 < \alpha < 1)$

$$\text{Prob}(z \leqslant f) = \alpha$$

and solves for that level of profits $(f)$ which attains the $100 \, \alpha$ percent level of probability. Assuming normality for the vector $c$, the $100 \, \alpha$ percent level of profits $f$ becomes

$$f = m'x - k(x'Vx)^{\frac{1}{2}} \qquad (5.23)$$

where the constant $k = -F^{-1}(\alpha)$ and $F(w)$ is the cumulative distribution Prob$(y \leqslant w)$ of the unit normal $N(0, 1)$ variate $y$. With $\alpha = 0.99$, the value of $k$ is 2.33 from the standard normal tables. The fractile criterion maximizes with respect to $x$ the $100 \, \alpha$ percent level of profits $f$ defined in (5.23).

There are three general aspects of the fractile criterion which are very appealing in many practical applications:

(a) Even when the profit level $z$ is not normally distributed, since the elements $c_j$ may not be so distributed, there are many cases in which normality may hold as a limiting distribution by the well-known central limit theorem in mathematical statistics, and in that case the fractile criterion may still be applicable. The errors made in approximating a nonnormal distribution through a limiting normal distribution can in most cases be evaluated by using the so-called Hermite polynomials, which in effect consider expanding the nonnormal distribution around the unit normal distribution in a Taylor series.

(b) For cases in which the population density function $g(z)$ of profits $z$ is known to depend only on a location parameter $\mu$ and a scale parameter $\sigma$, i.e. when $g(z)$ is expressible in the form

$$g(z) = \frac{1}{\sigma} f\left(\frac{z - \mu}{\sigma}\right)$$

the limiting distribution of the sample quantiles can be very easily derived. For instance, let the $\alpha$-quantile of the standardized population be $u$, i.e.

$$\int_{-\infty}^{u} f(t)\, dt = \alpha;$$

then since

$$\alpha = \int_{-\infty}^{(z-\mu)/\sigma} f(t)\, dt = \int_{-\infty}^{u} f(t)\, dt$$

it holds under very general conditions on the frequency function $f(z)$ that

$$z = \mu + u\sigma.$$

These results suggest the potential use of the fractile criterion of maximization in the area of nonparametric statistics, where specific assumptions about any particular distribution are not generally admitted.

(c) The fractile criterion has a very close relation to the safety-first principle of holding assets advocated by Roy [20]. According to the latter principle, if the profit level $z$ has probabilistic variations such that the specific form of probability distribution is not known with sufficient precision, the decision-maker 'should' try to minimize the chance of a disaster level (or bankruptcy level) of profits. If $r$ is the preassigned disaster level of profits, below which the decision-maker may not survive, then by Tchebycheff inequality it follows that

$$\text{Prob}(z \leqslant r) \leqslant (\text{Var}\,z)\,(\text{E}z - r)^{-2}.$$

In default of minimizing the unknown probability Prob $(z \leqslant r)$ with pre-assigned $r$, the safety-first principle recommends minimizing its upper bound, i.e. $(\text{Var}\,z)\,(\text{E}z-r)^{-2}$. Note that in the notation of equation (5.23), $r=f$, $\text{E}z = m'x$ and $\text{Var}\,z = x'Vx$ and $\alpha = \text{Prob}\,(z \leqslant r)$. Hence it follows that

$$\alpha(m'x - f)^2 \leqslant x'Vx.$$

For given $\alpha$, the tolerance measure, the fractile criterion solves for $f$ and maximizes it; the safety-first principle on the other hand assumes $f$ to be given and then solves for the quantity $(m'x-f)^2/(x'Vx)$ and maximizes it. Naturally, a more general approach should consider the simultaneous variation of $\alpha$ and $f$ at different rates of trade-off through an indifference diagram on the $\alpha$-$f$ axes, i.e.

$$I(\alpha, f) \geqslant 0, \quad \text{where} \quad I(\alpha, f) = x'Vx - \alpha(m'x - f)^2.$$

Third, consider the discounted portfolio criterion where the tolerance level of probability or the concept of a disaster level or a satisficing level is not explicitly introduced at all. However, the 'best' methods of estimating the parameters, e.g. the mean vector $\text{E}c$ and the dispersion matrix $V$ are to be applied. Further, the most appropriate level of minimum profit $(z_0)$, below which solutions are not tolerated at all (i.e. there is an infinitely high penalty cost for profits below the level $z_0$) has to be carefully preassigned, since a too high value may preempt feasibility and a too low value may imply an unduly pessimistic degree of risk aversion. Note, however, that the portfolio criterion developed in its original form by Markowitz and others, especially in the framework of programming, can be generalized in several important directions:

(a) first of all, the estimates of mean and covariance parameters may be appropriately discounted in relation to the standard errors of those sample estimates; this risk discounting is particularly necessary if the presence of nonnormality in the parent population is suspected. One operational way of analyzing the effects of such risk-discounting particularly in small sample situations is to consider a range estimate based on the mean and covariance estimates. For instance, if quarterly data on market prices and hence returns are available for several years but the portfolio model is applied for annual decisions, then for any parameter (say the mean or the variance of crop $j$)

$\theta_j$ three different estimates are possible

(a) $\max_q \hat{\theta}_{j,t/q}$;  (b) $\min_q \hat{\theta}_{j,t/q}$;  (c) $\hat{\theta}_{j,t,q}$

where $t = 1, 2, ..., T$ (the number of years), $q = 1, 2, 3, 4$ (the number of quarters) and $\hat{\theta}_{j,t/q}$ denotes an unbiased estimate of $\theta_j$ for a fixed quarter over all the years and $\hat{\theta}_{j,t,q}$ denotes an estimate based on pooled data. A pessimistic decision-maker who considers safety first above other things, may find it reasonable to use $\min_q \hat{\theta}_{j,t/q}$ for the expected gross return for the $j$th crop.

(b) Secondly, the Markowitz model essentially characterizes a normal-type probability distribution model, since it considers only the first two moments; although this may be very reasonable for large sample situations, when the central limit theorem may be presumed to hold, the small sample nature of most economic data requires us to consider relatively distribution-free results. For example, if the random profit level $z = c'x$ is assumed to be generated by a continuous population distribution function and the observed sample values define a numerical step-polygon kind of approximation, then use could be made of the Kolmogorov-Smirnov statistic based on the maximum distance between empirical and the population distributions to define small sample probabilities of the profit level lying in a certain specified non-empty range. Some work in this line is available [25].

(c) A third important line of extension of the Markowitz portfolio model is possible, in which the sample values of $c_j$ denoted by $c_{js}$ ($s = 1, 2, ..., N$) are arranged in an ascending order, e.g.

$$c_{j1} \leqslant c_{j2} \leqslant \cdots \leqslant c_{jr} \leqslant \cdots \leqslant c_{jN}; \qquad (j = 1, ..., n)$$

and then the probability distribution of the $r$th order-statistic is considered to compute its expected value and variance. Note that in this case for $r = 1$ or $N$ we get the extreme values defined in (5.22a) and (5.22b) and, generally speaking, the expectation and variance of extreme values have several peculiar characteristics not shared by ordinary values (for instance, the extreme value distributions have in general high degrees of skewness and therefore normal approximations are very, very imprecise if not completely inapplicable).

It is necessary at this stage to say a few words about the limitations of the three criteria of choice under risk, e.g. the expected value criterion, the fractile criterion and the discounted portfolio criterion.

First, the expected value criterion, which is most popular, is known to be very suitable and appropriate when the random error components of the model are additive and independent of the decision variables and the objective function is at most quadratic. This is the framework in which the certainty-equivalence theorem developed by Holt, Theil and Simon [26] applies most appropriately and the knowledge of variance or other moments is practically of no use for determining the optimal decision rule. Indirectly this serves to indicate its basic weakness as an optimization criterion in several respects if the above assumptions are not (known to be) exactly satisfied, e.g.

(a) the random elements of the vector $c$ may not be independent of the decision vector $x$ in its entire domain of variability. However, if the interdependence has to be explicitly introduced in the model, this invariably becomes a nonlinear programming problem more complicated than a quadratic one;

(b) the expected value criterion is generally likely to give different results according as the prior or the posterior probabilities are considered. The scope of minimax and other decision rules is open in this area; and

(c) the expected value criterion is also unsuitable for a decision-maker who is a risk-taker rather than a risk-averter, since the concept of an average may be less appealing to him compared to the gambling prospect of a high return. The view has been taken by Shackle and others [27] that most economic decisions are nonrepetitive, so that the very concept of an average is meaningless. One interpretation of this criticism could be that one should pay more attention to the subjective probabilities and also to the extreme values defined in (5.22a) and (5.22b).

Second, the fractile criterion, which is comparable to the method of chance-constrained programming developed by Charnes, Cooper and others, has the basic difficulty also shared by chance-constrained programming that the statistical distribution of the objective function $z = c'x$ becomes very complicated, if the vector $c$ of net prices is not distributed like a multivariate normal vector. Since in economic models the nonnegative distributions are more relevant and since a linear sum of nonnegative variates such as $c_j x_j$ when $c_j$ is random is generally a mixture of original distributions, it is generally not possible to get a quadratic-type concave function as in (5.23). For instance, if each $c_j$ has a mutually independent chi-square distribution, the linear sum $z = c'x$ has a mixture of chi-square distributions which can only be very roughly approximated by a noncentral chi-square distribution.

Third, the discounted portfolio criterion has the basic limitation that it seeks to construct a certainty equivalent $v$, so to say, from an exogenous specification of the decision-maker's utility function $f(\mu, \sigma)$ where $\mu =$ mean of $z = c'x$ and $\sigma =$ standard deviation of $z$, i.e.

$$v = f(\mu, \sigma).$$

In other words, it seeks to collapse the two dimensions of probable profits, the expected value ($\mu$) and the risk of variability ($\sigma$), into a single scalar quantity ($v$) which is like the certainty equivalent, from which all uncertainty is purged. Further, the usual conditions imposed on the utility function $f(\mu, \sigma)$, i.e.

$$\partial v/\partial \mu > 0, \ \partial v/\partial \sigma < 0 \quad \text{and} \quad d\sigma/d\mu > 0$$

imply risk aversion and guarantee in most cases the attainment of the classical equilibrium of the deterministic theory of consumer choice. The point that the expected value ($\mu$) and risk ($\sigma$) may not be collapsible into a scalar, so that the problem remains one of vector optimization rather than scalar optimization, seems to be neglected in the literature. Of course, in a vector optimization problem the optimal solution may not be as simply and uniquely derivable as in a scalar case.

### 5.2.1. Empirical applications of fractile programming

In order to evaluate the alternative optimization criteria so far discussed, we consider the empirical decision problem for a single farm enterprise in Hancock County, Iowa for which detailed input-output studies were made by Babbar and Tintner previously in their models of stochastic linear programming. The input-output restrictions which are common to all our empirical models are taken from the Babbar-Tintner study, in which the five activities are: corn ($x_1$), oats ($x_2$), soybeans ($x_3$), flax ($x_4$) and wheat ($x_5$). The resource vector $b$ has the following components: $b_1 = 148$ (land in acres), $b_2 = 1800$ (capital in dollars), $b_3 = 234$ (manhours of labor for July), $b_4 = 234$ (manhours of farm labor available for August), $b_5 = 182$ (manhours of farm labor for May). The input-output coefficient matrix $A$ in the relation $Ax \leqslant b$ is taken from their study as:

$$A = \begin{bmatrix} 0.02274 & 0.02770 & 0.05862 & 0.09249 & 0.09081 \\ 0.31772 & 0.27870 & 0.70812 & 0.96956 & 1.00356 \\ 0.02555 & 0.07523 & 0.05485 & 0.21186 & 0.42324 \\ 0.00000 & 0.08370 & 0.00000 & 0.30910 & 0.08650 \\ 0.05253 & 0.00000 & 0.11681 & 0.00000 & 0.00000 \end{bmatrix}. \quad (5.24a)$$

However, unlike the Babbar-Tintner study which used fixed $c_j$ values, we assume $c_j$ values varying directly with market prices for which we consider six years' (1960-1966) quarterly data. Assuming that $c_j$ values are coming from a normal parent population, the unbiased estimates of the mean and variance of each $c_j$ value are computed as follows from all of the data:

$$\text{mean } c = \text{E}c = (1.0025, 0.6455, 2.3690, 2.9143, 1.7408)' \qquad (5.24\text{b})$$

diagonal elements of $V = \text{Var } c = (0.00276, 0.00030, 0.00334, 0.00125, 0.00306)$. It is assumed that the $c_j$ values are statistically independent for different crops.

Our first two problems (hereafter abbreviated as P1, P2 respectively) are built out of these parameter values as follows:

$$\text{Problem P1:} \quad \max (\text{E}c)'x, \, Ax \leqslant b, \, x \geqslant 0 \qquad (5.25)$$

$$\text{Problem P2:} \quad \max [(\text{E}c)'x - 2.33(x'Vx)^{\frac{1}{2}}], \, Ax \leqslant b, \, x \geqslant 0 \qquad (5.26)$$

where $V$ is given by the matrix of Var $c$ in (5.24b) and the value 2.33 corresponds to $\alpha = 0.99$ in (5.23).

The problem P1 is solved and its optimal objective function value is denoted by $z_0$. Given this value of $z_0$, the third problem (P3) is constructed as follows:

$$\text{Problem P3:} \quad \min x'Vx, \, Ax \leqslant b, \, x \geqslant 0, \, (\text{E}c)'x \geqslant z_0 \qquad (5.27)$$

where $V$ is the same as in (5.26) and $\text{E}c$ is taken from (5.24b).

The next four problems have the same structure as P3, except that the variance matrix $V$ and expectation vector $\text{E}c$ are computed for a given quarter over the six years. Denoting $V_q$ and $(\text{E}c)_q$ as the estimate for quarters $q = 1, 2, 3, 4$ the problems may be stated as follows:

$$\text{P4} - \text{P7:} \min x'V_q x, \, Ax \leqslant b, \, x \geqslant 0, \, (\text{E}c'_q x \geqslant z_0; \, (q = 1, 2, 3, 4). \qquad (5.28)$$

Here for our empirical problem the unbiased estimates are:

$$(\text{E}c)_{q=1} = \begin{bmatrix} 0.960 \\ 0.660 \\ 2.400 \\ 2.945 \\ 1.798 \end{bmatrix}; \quad (\text{E}c)_2 = \begin{bmatrix} 1.038 \\ 0.660 \\ 2.435 \\ 2.942 \\ 1.770 \end{bmatrix}; \quad (\text{E}c)_3 = \begin{bmatrix} 1.057 \\ 0.625 \\ 2.323 \\ 2.898 \\ 1.672 \end{bmatrix}; \quad (\text{E}c)_4 = \begin{bmatrix} 0.955 \\ 0.637 \\ 2.318 \\ 2.872 \\ 1.723 \end{bmatrix}.$$

The diagonal elements of $V_q$ denoted by $\hat{V}_q$ are:

$$\hat{V}_1 = (0.00976, 0.00092, 0.07448, 0.05143, 0.03062);$$
$$\hat{V}_2 = (0.00686, 0.00052, 0.10735, 0.03102, 0.04864);$$
$$\hat{V}_3 = (0.00439, 0.00039, 0.04631, 0.04822, 0.05446);$$
$$\hat{V}_4 = (0.00587, 0.00083, 0.05846, 0.05090, 0.05567).$$

The next four problems are constructed on the basis of the discounted portfolio criterion as follows:

Problem P8:  $\min_x x' (\max_q V_q) x,\ Ax \leqslant b,\ x \geqslant 0,\ (\min_q (Ec)'_q) x \geqslant z_0;$

$$(5.29)$$

Problem P9:  $\min_x x' (\min_q V_q) x,\ Ax \leqslant b,\ x \geqslant 0,\ (\max_q (Ec)_q)' x \geqslant z_0;$

$$(5.30)$$

Problem P10:  $\min_x x' (\min_q V_q) x,\ Ax \leqslant b,\ x \geqslant 0,\ (\min_q (Ec)_q)' x \geqslant z_0;$

$$(5.31)$$

Problem P11:  $\min_x x' (\max_q V_q) x,\ Ax \leqslant b,\ x \geqslant 0,\ (\max_q (Ec)_q)' x \geqslant z_0.$

$$(5.32)$$

Note that the optimal value of the objective function of the linear programming problem P1, i.e. $z_0$, is set as a lower bound of the constraints in P7 through P11. Note further that whereas problems P3 through P11 could be solved by the standard quadratic programming (Frank-Wolfe) algorithm whenever feasible solutions exist, the fractile quadratic problem P2 requires special algorithms because of the standard deviation term $(x' Vx)^{\frac{1}{2}}$.

Fortunately, for this type of fractile quadratic programming problem Kataoka has developed a simple computational algorithm which has a very high rate of convergence. This algorithm has four essential steps:

First, solve the linear programming problem by neglecting the term (2.33 $(x' Vx)^{\frac{1}{2}}$) and denote the optimal solution vector by $x_0$.

Second, compute a quantity $R_0$ on the basis of $x_0$ as $R_0 = x'_0 V x_0$ and then, treating this $R_0$ as a constant, formulate the standard quadratic programming problem:

$$\max_x (Ec)'x - 2.33 (R_0^{-\frac{1}{2}} \cdot x'Vx)$$

under the restrictions $Ax \geqslant b$ ;  $x \geqslant 0$ ;

and let the optimal solution vector of this quadratic programming problem be denoted by $x_0^{(1)}$.

Third, using $x_0^{(1)}$ from the earlier stage, define a new value of the quantity $R_0$, denoted by $R_0^{(1)}$ as

$$R_0^{(1)} = x_0^{(1)'} V x_0^{(1)}$$

and, using this new constant $R_0^{(1)}$, formulate a new quadratic problem as in the second stage except that $R_0^{(1)}$ replaces $R_0$.

Fourth, continue the process of iteration until $R_0^{(k)}$ converges as $k$ takes a limiting value. Practically speaking the iterations are terminated, however, as soon as the values of the objective function $f_0$ in the successive quadratic programs tend to differ by a very, very small fraction (which may be pre-assigned).

In our problem the results of applying the Kataoka method of fractile quadratic programming are as follows: see tables 5.1 and 5.2.

TABLE 5.1.

Results of Kataoka method for problem P2.

| stage of iteration | $R_0{}^\ddagger$ | $f_0$ | $x_1$(corn) | $x_3$(soybeans) | $x_4$(flax) |
|---|---|---|---|---|---|
| LP problem | – | 5581.20 | 2041.50 | 639.90 | 692.60 |
| 1 | 116.137 | 5459.55 | 1413.88 | 922.26 | 668.02 |
| 2 | 94.466 | 5439.83 | 1275.32 | 984.57 | 662.60 |
| 3 | 91.005 | 5435.96 | 1252.19 | 994.52 | 661.73 |
| 4 | 90.507 | 5435.39 | 1250.01 | 995.95 | 661.61 |
| 5 | 90.187 | 5435.01 | 1247.96 | 996.87 | 661.53 |
| 6 | 90.392 | 5435.25 | 1249.27 | 996.28 | 661.58 |

TABLE 5.2

Optimal solutions for P1 through P11.

| problem | expected optimal profits ($z$) | optimal activities | | |
|---|---|---|---|---|
| | | $x_1$ | $x_3$ | $x_4$ |
| P1 | 5581.19 | 2041.5 | 639.9 | 692.6 |
| P2 | 5540.61 | 1249.3 | 996.3 | 661.6 |
| P3 | not feasible | | | |
| P4 | not feasible | | | |
| P5 | 5581.19 | – | 1558.1 | 607.5 |
| P6 | 5408.28 | 1480.5 | 892.2 | 670.6 |
| P7 | not feasible | | | |
| P8 | not feasible | | | |
| P9 | 5581.19 | – | 1558.1 | 606.9 |
| P10 | not feasible | | | |
| P11 | 5581.19 | – | 1558.1 | 606.9 |

Note that the functional values of the optimal objective function of the quadratic programming problems are very, very close at and after the fourth stage of iteration. Further, if we compute an expected level of optimal profits using the optimal solution vector at the sixth stage of iteration with the corresponding net prices ($Ec_1$, $Ec_3$, $Ec_4$), then one obtains a quantity 5540.61, which has a 99 percent probability of being realized under the assumptions and which falls short of the optimal objective function value under the linear program by about 40.59, i.e. about 0.7 percent of 5540.61. This shows incidentally a very interesting result that the fractile quadratic program can be used as a method of measuring the sensitivity of the optimal solution of a linear programming problem. In our case it is seen that the optimal linear programming solution is very stable in terms of the optimal objective function value.

Now for the problems P3 through P11, a lower-bound constraint $z_0 = 5581.20$ is adjoined for each. The general structure of the optimal solutions and expected optimal profits is indicated in table 5.2.

Two simple ways for evaluating the optimal solutions for the different feasible problems are available. One way is to analyze the relative variability of optimal profits through such measures as variance or coefficient of variation (i.e., the ratio of standard deviation to expected value) and the second way is to analyze the contribution of each crop to the expectation and variance of total optimal profits. Tables 5.3, 5.4 and 5.5 present the results of evaluation by these two methods.

TABLE 5.3

Relative variability of optimal profits.

| Problem | Mean | Standard deviation | Coefficient of variation | Critical ratio $(K)$ |
|---------|------|-----------|-------------|---------------|
| P1 | 5581.19 | 114.506 | 0.0205 | 1.176 (corn) |
| P2 | 5540.61 | 89.641 | 0.0162 | 1.925 (corn) |
| P5 | 5581.19 | 521.588 | 0.0934 | 1.044 (soybeans) |
| P6 | 5408.28 | 261.113 | 0.0483 | 1.849 (soybeans) |
| P9 | 5581.19 | 351.955 | 0.0631 | 1.101 (soybeans) |
| P11 | 5581.19 | 528.723 | 0.0947 | 1.073 (soybeans) |

TABLE 5.4

Crop-wise expected optimal profits.*

| Problem | Crop 1 (corn) | Crop 3 (soybeans) | Crop 4 (flax) | Max (row) | Total expected profits |
|---------|---------------|-------------------|---------------|-----------|------------------------|
| P1 | 2406.8 | 1515.9 | 2018.5 | 2046.8 | 5581.2 |
| P2 | 1252.4 | 2360.2 | 1928.0 | 2360.2 | 5540.6 |
| P5 | – | 3793.9 | 1787.2 | 3793.9 | 5581.2 |
| P6 | 1413.9 | 2068.3 | 1926.1 | 2068.3 | 5408.3 |
| P9 | – | 3793.9 | 1787.2 | 3793.9 | 5581.2 |
| P11 | – | 3793.9 | 1787.2 | 3793.9 | 5581.2 |
| min (column) | 1252.4 | 1515.9 | 1787.2 | – | 5408.3 |

* Decimal values are rounded.

TABLE 5.5

Crop-wise variance of optimal profits.*

| Problem | Crop 1 (corn) | Crop 3 (soybeans) | Crop 4 (flax) | Max (row) | Total variance |
|---------|-------|-------|-------|-------|-------|
| P1 | 11144.5 | 1367.6 | 599.6 | 11144.5 | 13111.7 |
| P2 | 4173.2 | 3315.2 | 547.1 | 4173.2 | 8035.6 |
| P5 | – | 260606.2 | 11448.1 | 260606.2 | 272054.3 |
| P6 | 9622.9 | 36870.1 | 21687.0 | 36870.1 | 68180.0 |
| P9 | – | 112447.9 | 11424.7 | 112447.9 | 123872.6 |
| P11 | – | 260606.2 | 11424.7 | 260606.2 | 279548.0 |
| min (column) | 4173.2 | 1367.6 | 547.1 | – | 8035.6 |

\* Decimal values are rounded.

It is evident from table 5.3 that the fractile criterion (P2) shows the smallest coefficient of variation of optimal profits; the 99 percent level of which is given by the value of 5540.61 dollars. Next to that, the linear programming problem (P1) with the expected value criterion shows a very similar degree of stability, and the standard deviation of optimal profits is also very small, in fact the smallest if P2 is excepted. Further, note that in table 5.2 the problems P3, P4, P7, P8 and P10 turn out to be infeasible because of the high value of the lower bound constraint denoted by the minimum expected profit level $z_0 = 5581.20$. Of the solutions that are feasible under the discounted portfolio criterion, the problem P6 specifies a lower coefficient of variation of optimal profits and almost the same level of profits as P1, which applies the expected value criterion. However, one should note that the optimal crop-mix is much different between the cases P9 and P1, and since P1 shows a much lower standard deviation and coefficient of variation of optimal profits, its optimal output-mix is most likely to maintain a greater degree of stability and hence safety.

Note that in table 5.3 the last column denotes a critical ratio $K$ which is defined for any given problem by the ratio of total variance of optimal profits to the maximum variance contribution by a single crop. In other words, if $x_1$, $x_3$, $x_4$ turn out to be the optimal activities, then

total variance $= (\mathrm{Var}\, c_1)\, x_1^2 + (\mathrm{Var}\, c_3)\, x_3^2 + (\mathrm{Var}\, c_4)\, x_4^2$

maximum variance for a crop $= \max$ of $((\mathrm{Var}\, c_1)\, x_1^2,$

$$(\mathrm{Var}\, c_3)\, x_3^2, (\mathrm{Var}\, c_4)\, x_4^2)$$

critical ratio $= (\text{total variance/maximum variance for a crop}).$

It is evident from table 5.3 that the expected value and fractile criteria (P1, P2) have an interesting difference from the portfolio models (P5, P6, P9, P11) in that different crops provide the critical ratio in the two situations, corn in the first and soybeans in the second.

Tables 5.4 and 5.5 provide an optimal crop calendar for the farmer in the sense that they summarize the relevant information about expected profit and its variability (risk) be each specific crop that enters into the optimal solution. Several lines of application of this crop calendar can be envisaged, e.g.,

(a) In the planning sense, the calendar provides the farmer the knowledge that certain specific crops may contribute more to the variability of his total optimal net returns (profits) than others and accordingly this may help him to specify his risk-taking or risk-averting attitude more explicitly.

(b) In the event the farmer considers one specific crop to be highly unstable in terms of its contribution to the total variance of optimal profits, he may decide to give as low an importance to that crop as possible and accordingly he may select different optimal plans from P1 through P11. Alternatively, if his resources are divisible, he can convert the resource inequality $Ax \leqslant b$ by redefining each resource limit $b_i$ as

$$b_i = \sum_{j=1}^{n} b_i u_{ij} \qquad (n = \text{number of crops})$$
$$u_{ij} \geqslant 0, \qquad \sum_j u_{ij} \leqslant 1$$

where $u_{ij}$ is the proportional (relative) allocation of the $i$th resource to the $j$th activity, and then rewriting the original resource constraints as

$$a_{ij}x_j \leqslant b_i u_{ij} \qquad (i = 1, 2, ..., m; m = \text{number of resources}).$$

The relative allocation ratios $u_{ij}$ are now the new decision variables the levels of which the farmer can decide and manipulate so as to obtain a pre-assigned safety-level of optimal profits. This method of truncating the original statistical distribution of optimal profits has been called the active approach in the theory of stochastic linear programming developed by Tintner, Sengupta and others. Note that by manipulating these decision variables appropriately, a specific crop which was contributing a very high degree of instability (or variance) to the expected total optimal profits may be eliminated altogether.

(c) Further, a predictive application of the above type of crop calendar is possible, if there are reasons to believe that farmers tend to select one of the optimization criteria considered above and that the outcomes of their decisions over years are actually reflected in the empirical data about land and other resource allocation in a region or a district. Then the values predicted by our models could be compared with the empirically observed values by a chi-square or other suitable statistic, to determine which of the optimization criteria comes nearest to reality.

### 5.2.2. *An alternative application*

The same set of empirical data were used [28] with some modifications in order to analyze the empirical statistical distribution of the three best optimal values of the objective function and its economic implications. Here the five crops are exactly the same as before but the coefficient matrix $A$ taken from the Babbar-Tintner studies is:

$$
A = \begin{array}{c}
\begin{array}{ccccc} x_1 & x_2 & x_3 & x_4 & x_5 \end{array} \\
\begin{bmatrix}
0.0227 & 0.0277 & 0.0586 & 0.0925 & 0.0908 \\
0.3177 & 0.2787 & 0.7081 & 0.9696 & 1.0036 \\
0.0256 & 0.0752 & 0.0549 & 0.2119 & 0.4232 \\
0.0525 & 0.0000 & 0.1168 & 0.0000 & 0.0000
\end{bmatrix}
\begin{array}{l} \text{land} \\ \text{capital} \\ \text{May labor} \\ \text{other labor.} \end{array}
\end{array}
$$

Two new considerations were added to the empirical data provided by the Babbar-Tintner studies. First, in order to get more diversified solutions, two additional restrictions, e.g., $x_3 \geqslant 200$ and $x_5 \geqslant 100$ were added, so that the sensitivity of optimal solutions could be perceived under several inequality constraints. Second, the vector of net prices $c$ was not taken to be fixed but assumed to be probabilistic, varying directly in proportion to market prices for which quarterly and monthly data are available.

Denote the set $R$ of restrictions as

$$ R = \{x \mid Ax \leqslant b; x_3 \geqslant 200, x_5 \geqslant 100, x \geqslant 0\} $$

then the following linear programs are computed and solutions compared whenever they are meaningful:

$$ \text{problem P1:} \quad \max c'x, \; x \text{ in } R \tag{5.33} $$

where the vector $c$ is the same as Babbar and Tintner's.

$$ \text{problem P2 to P9:} \quad \max c_q'x, \; x \text{ in } R \tag{5.34} $$

where the subscript $q$ denotes quarterly prices for the two years 1964 and 1965 (i.e., a set of eight problems).

$$ \text{problems P10 to P16:} \quad \max \bar{c}_s'x, \; x \text{ in } R \tag{5.35} $$

where $\bar{c}_s$ is an estimate of the maxima of quarterly prices which are assumed to be generated by independent normal distributions and the estimate uses simulated values $E\bar{c} \pm k\sigma_{\bar{c}}$ for $k = 0$, 0.1, 0.2 and 0.3 where E is expectation and $\sigma_{\bar{c}}$ is the estimated standard deviation.

$$\text{Problems P17 to P23:} \quad \max (\underline{c})'_s x, \ x \text{ in } R \tag{5.36}$$

where $(\underline{c})_s$ is an estimate of the minima of quarterly prices using simulated values $E\underline{c} + k\sigma_{\underline{c}}$ for $k = 0$, 0.1, 0.2 and 0.3 assuming independence and mutual normality.

$$\text{Problems P24 to P29:} \quad \max \bar{c}'_r x, \ x \text{ in } R \tag{5.37}$$

where the subscript $r$ in $\bar{c}$ denotes the maxima of quarterly prices for six years 1960–1965.

$$\text{Problems P30 to P35:} \quad \max (\underline{c})'_r x, \ x \text{ in } R \tag{5.38}$$

where the subscript $r$ in $\underline{c}$ denotes the minima of quarterly prices for different crops for six years 1960-1965 [29].

These six sets of $c_j$ values for different crops are reproduced in table 5.6. It should be mentioned that the simulation estimates of $\bar{c}$ and $\underline{c}$ in the third and fourth set of problems (i.e., P10 to P16 and P17 to P23) are derived using the distribution of extreme values from a unit normal distribution. For example, denote $\bar{c}_j$ by $\bar{m}_j + \bar{u}_j$, where $\bar{m}_j$ is the systematic part (i.e., an average estimate of maxima of quarterly prices) and $\bar{u}_j$ is the random component. Let the sample values of $\bar{c}_j$ denoted by $\bar{c}_{js}$ ($s = 1, 2, ..., N$) be arranged in an ascending order $\bar{c}_{j1} \leqslant \bar{c}_{j2} \leqslant \bar{c}_{jk} \leqslant \cdots \leqslant \bar{c}_{jN}$ and so also the random components $\bar{u}_{j1} \leqslant \bar{u}_{j2} \leqslant \cdots \leqslant \bar{u}_{jN}$. Assuming the ordered set of random elements $\bar{u}_{js}$ to come from a unit normal population, the density function $p(\bar{u}_{jk})$ of $\bar{u}_{jk}$ is known to be computable as

$$p(\bar{u}_{jk}) = \left( \frac{N! \sqrt{2\pi}}{(k-1)!(N-k)!} \right) \cdot I(k-1, \bar{u}_{jk}) \cdot I(N-k, -\bar{u}_{jk}) \cdot \exp\left(-\tfrac{1}{2}\bar{u}_{jk}^2\right)$$

where a set of tables are available for computing the functions $I(k-1, \bar{u}_{jk})$, $I(N-k, -\bar{u}_{jk})$ and the associated coefficients. In our case $N = 4$ and $k =$ either 4 (for P10 to P16) or 1 (for P17 to P23). We used this distribution $p(\bar{u}_{jk})$ to compute estimates of the variance of $\bar{u}_{j4}$ (or of $\bar{u}_{j1}$) and denoted them as $\sigma_{\bar{c}}^2$ (or $\sigma_{\underline{c}}^2$), whereas the expected values $E\bar{c}$ (or $E\underline{c}$) are estimated as averages over sample extremes.

Note that in the last four sets of problems we are using in some form or other extreme values (or estimates) in the sample space of net returns. Two special reasons for using extreme statistics in a linear program may be added. First, the implications of extreme value indicators in economic models have been very little explored. Second, there is the additional point that sometimes the optimal solutions using extreme sample values (minima or maxima) may have less variability of optimal profits than those using averages of sample values. Hence, if only the first two moments of the distribution are taken to characterize the risk attitudes, the extreme value approach might sometimes indicate the existence of more stable solutions.

TABLE 5.6

Estimated and actual prices ($c_j$ values) for different crops (in dollars per bushel).

| (1)<br>Problem | (2)<br>$x_1$<br>(corn) | (3)<br>$x_2$<br>(oats) | (4)<br>$x_3$<br>(soybeans) | (5)<br>$x_4$<br>(flax) | (6)<br>$x_5$<br>(wheat) |
|---|---|---|---|---|---|
| *P1*  | 1.56   | 0.84   | 2.79   | 3.81   | 2.14   |
| P2    | 1.10   | 0.68   | 2.75   | 2.88   | 1.46   |
| P3    | 1.16   | 0.68   | 2.71   | 2.86   | 1.36   |
| P4    | 1.12   | 0.64   | 2.52   | 2.80   | 1.37   |
| P5    | 1.01   | 0.64   | 2.36   | 2.76   | 1.41   |
| P6    | 1.03   | 0.67   | 2.55   | 2.87   | 1.91   |
| P7    | 1.11   | 0.66   | 2.35   | 2.85   | 1.80   |
| P8    | 1.08   | 0.62   | 2.36   | 2.76   | 1.39   |
| *P9*  | 1.05   | 0.64   | 2.57   | 2.88   | 1.45   |
| P10   | 1.0683 | 0.6683 | 2.5017 | 3.0533 | 1.8250 |
| P11   | 1.1517 | 0.7517 | 2.5851 | 3.1367 | 1.9084 |
| P12   | 1.2350 | 0.8350 | 2.6684 | 3.2200 | 1.9917 |
| P13   | 1.3184 | 0.9184 | 2.7518 | 3.3034 | 2.0751 |
| P14   | 0.9849 | 0.5849 | 2.4183 | 2.9699 | 1.7416 |
| P15   | 0.9016 | 0.5016 | 2.3350 | 2.8866 | 1.6583 |
| *P16* | 0.8182 | 0.4182 | 2.2516 | 2.8032 | 1.5749 |
| P17   | 0.9417 | 0.6167 | 2.2550 | 2.7383 | 1.6533 |
| P18   | 1.0251 | 0.7001 | 2.3384 | 2.8217 | 1.7367 |
| P19   | 1.1084 | 0.7834 | 2.4217 | 2.9050 | 1.8200 |
| P20   | 1.1918 | 0.8668 | 2.5051 | 2.9884 | 1.9034 |
| P21   | 0.8583 | 0.5333 | 2.1716 | 2.6549 | 1.5699 |
| P22   | 0.7750 | 0.4500 | 2.0883 | 2.5716 | 1.4866 |
| P23   | 0.6916 | 0.3666 | 2.0049 | 2.4882 | 1.4032 |
| P24   | 1.16   | 0.68   | 2.75   | 2.88   | 1.46   |
| P25   | 1.11   | 0.67   | 2.57   | 2.88   | 1.91   |
| P26   | 1.14   | 0.68   | 2.55   | 2.86   | 1.99   |
| P27   | 0.98   | 0.67   | 2.34   | 3.32   | 1.93   |
| P28   | 1.00   | 0.65   | 2.87   | 3.30   | 1.84   |
| P29   | 1.02   | 0.58   | 1.93   | 3.08   | 1.82   |
| P30   | 1.01   | 0.64   | 2.36   | 2.76   | 1.39   |
| P31   | 1.03   | 0.62   | 2.35   | 2.76   | 1.36   |
| P32   | 0.99   | 0.64   | 2.39   | 2.77   | 1.84   |
| P33   | 0.89   | 0.62   | 2.26   | 2.84   | 1.85   |
| P34   | 0.90   | 0.60   | 2.26   | 2.66   | 1.76   |
| P35   | 0.83   | 0.58   | 1.91   | 2.64   | 1.72   |

Now we divide the set of basic feasible solutions for a given linear programming problem into two disjoint subsets, the first containing the optimum solution vector leading to a maximal value of the objective function and the second containing other basic feasible solutions leading to a value of the objective function less than the maximal value. With a given linear objective function it is always possible to order the basic feasible solutions belonging to the second subset in an increasing order according to objective function values. Thus, if $z_1^{(k)}$ denotes the maximal value of the objective function (i.e., the first-best value) with its solution vector $x_1^{(k)}$, where the superscript $k$ indicates a particular set of data $(A, b, c)_k$, then $z_2^{(k)}$ might represent the next highest value of the objective function (i.e., second-best value) with its solution vector $x_2^{(k)}$ and $z_3^{(k)}$ the next highest value (i.e., the third-best value) with its solution vector $x_3^{(k)}$. Note that we are restricting ourselves to *basic* feasible solutions only in defining the three best solutions. Generally, for a non-degenerate set of linear programming problems, it should be possible to obtain the second-best and third-best basic feasible solutions satisfying $z_1^{(k)} > z_2^{(k)} > z_3^{(k)}$ by a slight modification of the simplex routine [30].

Now for a given problem with a fixed value of $k$, there is no reason for selecting the second-best and third-best solutions, since the first best is available. But when there are perturbations in the data (i.e., the superscript $k$ takes different sample values implying that there are several sample values of the parameters $(A, b, c)$), two new elements enter into the decision problem. First, the variability of $z_2^{(k)}$ or $z_3^{(k)}$ in terms of variance, say, may be far lower compared to that of $z_1^{(k)}$ over the sample space $k = 1, 2, ..., K$. As a matter of fact, under very mild restrictions it holds [31] that the variance of $z_1$ tends to be larger than that of $z_2$ and so forth. In terms of portfolio analysis language, the three best solution vectors $x_1$, $x_2$ and $x_3$ may represent three different investment portfolios having unequal means and variances of net returns. Second, since $z_2$ and $z_3$ are suboptimal values of the objective function corresponding to the suboptimal solutions $x_2$ and $x_3$, the average distance (and its variability) between $z_1$ and $z_2$ and $z_1$ and $z_3$ should provide important guide lines for the decision problem. For instance, if the second-best solution is very close to the first best in terms of both mean and variance of $z_1$ and $z_2$ (i.e., $\mathrm{E}z_1 - \mathrm{E}z_2 \leqslant h$ and $\mathrm{Var}\, z_1 - \mathrm{Var}\, z_2 \leqslant h$ for a small value of $h$ in some normalized scale), then the first-best solution may still be the first candidate to be chosen. However, if the second best is not so close, other choices may seem more plausible.

In our empirical application, where only the vector $c$ takes different values, two different methods are followed to emphasize the characteristics of the three best solutions and the three best maximands (i.e., maximum values of the objective function). First, the statistical distributions of the three maximands are estimated by using the method of moments due to Karl Pearson [32]. Although it is known that this method is not very efficient compared to maximum likelihood methods, yet the fact that maximum likelihood estimates are more complicated to compute in the presence of inequality constraints, not to mention their unstable behavior in small sample situations, forced us to rely only on the method of moments, which however has to be taken as an approximation. Further, we had intended to improve the approximate estimates provided by the method of moments by using maximum likelihood methods of scoring after the form of the distribution was indicated by the method of moments, but this was dropped, since the estimated statistical distribution was found to be a Pearsonian Type I distribution for the three best maximands and application of maximum likelihood in this case would have required several approximations for the digamma and other functions. Second, the distances between the three maximands are measured in terms of the Euclidean distance between $(x_1, x_2)$, $(x_2, x_3)$ and $(x_1, x_3)$ denoted by $d_{12}$, $d_{23}$ and $d_{13}$ and by the area of the triangle formed by the vectors $(x_1, x_2, x_3)$ denoted by $D$. For any fixed and admissible $k$th sample, the distance $d_{ij}^{(k)}$ and the area of the triangle $D^{(k)}$ are defined as follows:

$$d_{ij}^{(k)} = [(x_i^{(k)} - x_j^{(k)})' (x_i^{(k)} - x_j^{(k)})]^{\frac{1}{2}}, \qquad i \neq j; \qquad i, j = 1, 2, 3 \qquad (5.39a)$$

$$D^{(k)} = \tfrac{1}{2} [(d_{12}^{(k)})^2 (d_{32}^{(k)})^2 - \{(x_1^{(k)} - x_2^{(k)})' (x_3^{(k)} - x_2^{(k)})\}]^{\frac{1}{2}} \qquad (5.39b)$$

where the index $k$ takes values $k = 1, 2, ..., 35$ corresponding to 35 linear programming problems we have mentioned in relations (5.33) through (5.38). For purpose of presentation, these indicators $d_{ij}^{(k)}$ and $D^{(k)}$ are normalized as

$$e_{ij}^{(k)} = d_{ij}^{(k)} / (z_i^{(k)} + z_j^{(k)}), \qquad i, j = 1, 2, 3 \quad \text{and} \quad i \neq j \qquad (5.40a)$$

$$t^{(k)} = D^{(k)} / (z_1^{(k)} + z_2^{(k)} + z_3^{(k)}), \qquad k = 1, 2, ..., 35. \qquad (5.40b)$$

These indicators are presented in table 5.9 below. Ideally, one would like to compute statistical distributions either exactly or approximately for these measures of distance and triangular area, so that one could ask for those solutions which satisfy the condition that their mutual distances and the triangular area do not exceed on the average a prescribed constant. However, such distributional computations are very complicated even on an approximate basis.

The statistical distribution of the three maximands (i.e., the three best objective function values) was estimated by following Pearson's method of moments and in each case the estimated distribution turned out to be Pearsonian Type I, in which the frequency function of a scalar random variable $y$ is given by $p(y)$ where

$$p(y) = y_0 \left( 1 + \frac{y}{a_1} \right)^{m_1} \left( 1 - \frac{y}{a_2} \right)^{m_2}, \quad - a_1 \leqslant y \leqslant a_2, \quad y_0 = \text{a constant}$$

(5.41)

with origin taken at the modal value and $m_1/a_1 = m_2/a_2$. The estimates of the parameters of the distribution of the three maximands are presented below in tables 5.7 and 5.8 for the three groups of problems, P2 to P9, P24

TABLE 5.7

Estimates of parameters of the distribution (5.41) of the three maximands.

| | Parameter | P2 to P9 | P24 to P29 | P30 to P35 |
|---|---|---|---|---|
| | $z_1$ (first best) | 101647.613 | − 8669.818 | − 38.892 |
| $a_1$ | $z_2$ (second best) | − 5292.430 | − 3445.151 | − 1626.374 |
| | $z_3$ (third best) | − 4110.533 | − 4912.931 | − 1197.509 |
| | $z_1$ (first best) | − 100889.624 | 10281.976 | 858.840 |
| $a_2$ | $z_2$ (second best) | 6192.893 | 4525.630 | 2387.247 |
| | $z_3$ (third best) | 4878.054 | 6152.459 | 1949.554 |
| | $z_1$ (first best) | − 0.06645 | − 0.16156 | 0.01546 |
| $m_1$ | $z_2$ (second best) | − 0.54202 | 0.26271 | 0.13362 |
| | $z_3$ (third best) | − 0.51016 | 0.23626 | 0.10878 |
| | $z_1$ (first best) | 0.06595 | 0.19160 | − 0.34144 |
| $m_2$ | $z_2$ (second best) | 0.63423 | − 0.34510 | − 0.19614 |
| | $z_3$ (third best) | 0.60541 | − 0.29587 | − 0.17709 |

to P29 and P30 to P35. Reasons for excluding problems P10 to P23 are twofold. First, these represented simulated estimates of the net price vector, which in general differed markedly from the observed set of quarterly maxima and minima of prices; one reason for this may be that the normality assumption may not have been very good especially with small sample sizes. Second, the parameters of the distribution of the three maximands estimated from the simulated data were somewhat different and relatively unstable compared to those for the other groups of problems.

TABLE 5.8

Characteristics of the distribution of the three maximands $z_1$, $z_2$ and $z_3$.

| Characteristic | | P2–P9 | P24–P29 | P30–P35 |
|---|---|---|---|---|
| Mean | $z_1$ (1st best) | 4822.46 | 4930.71 | 4378.67 |
| | $z_2$ (2nd best) | 4595.14 | 4581.15 | 4125.28 |
| | $z_3$ (3rd best) | 4351.87 | 4285.02 | 3882.81 |
| Mode | $z_1$ (1st best) | 6561.52 | 4874.90 | 4028.16 |
| | $z_2$ (2nd best) | 4567.06 | 3818.60 | 3859.16 |
| | $z_3$ (3rd best) | 4273.96 | 3464.10 | 3663.39 |
| Variance | $z_1$ (1st best) | $0.4813 \,(10)^5$ | $0.1207 \,(10)^6$ | $0.6735 \,(10)^5$ |
| | $z_2$ (2nd best) | $0.2400 \,(10)^5$ | $0.9889 \,(10)^5$ | $0.6006 \,(10)^5$ |
| | $z_3$ (3rd best) | $0.2528 \,(10)^5$ | $0.1358 \,(10)^6$ | $0.6187 \,(10)^5$ |
| Skewness $\sqrt{\beta_1}$ | $z_1$ (1st best) | 0.1169 | 0.1188 | 1.4647 |
| | $z_2$ (2nd best) | 0.2053 | 0.9023 | 0.5102 |
| | $z_3$ (3rd best) | 0.3735 | 0.7202 | 0.4816 |
| Kurtosis $\beta_2 - 3$ | $z_1$ (1st best) | $-1.1907$ | $-0.7984$ | 0.6530 |
| | $z_2$ (2nd best) | $-0.5299$ | $-0.4302$ | $-1.1171$ |
| | $z_3$ (3rd best) | $-0.6228$ | $-0.7474$ | $-1.1846$ |
| Coefficient of variation | $z_1$ (1st best) | 0.04549 | 0.07046 | 0.05927 |
| | $z_2$ (2nd best) | 0.03371 | 0.06864 | 0.05941 |
| | $z_3$ (3rd best) | 0.03653 | 0.08601 | 0.06406 |

Note: Denoting second, third and fourth sample moments about the mean by $\mu_2$, $\mu_3$ and $\mu_4$, the coefficients $\beta_1$ and $\beta_2$ underlying skewness and kurtosis are defined as $\beta_1 = \mu_3^2/\mu_2^3$ and $\beta_2 = \mu_4/\mu_2^2$.

Two implications of tables 5.7 through 5.10 may be mentioned briefly. First, it appears that the first-best maximand $(z_1)$ does not have minimum variance in any of the three sets of problems P2-P9, P24-P29 and P30-P35; as a matter of fact the second-best maximand $(z_2)$ has minimum variance in all the three groups of problems and almost the minimum coefficient of variation. Note further that the two groups of problems P24-P29 and P30-P35, the one using maxima of quarterly prices and the other minima of quarterly prices, show on comparison that the first-best and the second-best maximands have higher variance and higher coefficient of variation for P24-P29 than the third-best, implying that higher prices have higher risk in terms of variability. Second, it may be observed from table 5.3 that the two groups of problems P24-P29, P30-P35 have one basic differential characteristic in that the latter group shows on the average greater distance measured in terms of $e_{ij}$ coefficients between the first-best and second-best solution vectors and also greater variability measured in terms of larger

TABLE 5.9

Selected indicators measuring the spread of the three best solution vectors using (5.40a) and (5.40b).

| Problem | $e_{12}$ | $e_{13}$ | $e_{23}$ | $t$ |
|---------|---------|---------|---------|--------|
| P1  | 0.0582 | 0.2936 | 0.2951 | 68.18  |
| P2  | 0.3351 | 0.3515 | 0.0788 | 83.68  |
| P3  | 0.3324 | 0.3484 | 0.0762 | 82.28  |
| P4  | 0.3493 | 0.3671 | 0.0791 | 86.22  |
| P5  | 0.3740 | 0.3933 | 0.0860 | 92.78  |
| P6  | 0.3522 | 0.3700 | 0.0826 | 87.91  |
| P7  | 0.3575 | 0.3771 | 0.0861 | 295.19 |
| P8  | 0.3654 | 0.3859 | 0.0871 | 300.81 |
| P9  | 0.3518 | 0.3706 | 0.0825 | 87.87  |
| P10 | 0.3483 | 0.3676 | 0.0804 | 86.63  |
| P11 | 0.3323 | 0.3489 | 0.0752 | 81.96  |
| P12 | 0.3178 | 0.3331 | 0.0754 | 260.62 |
| P13 | 0.3044 | 0.3177 | 0.0729 | 249.97 |
| P14 | 0.3658 | 0.3884 | 0.0866 | 91.87  |
| P15 | 0.3853 | 0.4116 | 0.0935 | 97.77  |
| P16 | 0.4069 | 0.4378 | 0.1018 | 104.49 |
| P17 | 0.3895 | 0.4106 | 0 0906 | 97.07  |
| P18 | 0.3697 | 0.3875 | 0.0840 | 91.24  |
| P19 | 0.3518 | 0.3679 | 0.0830 | 287.66 |
| P20 | 0.3355 | 0.3491 | 0.0799 | 274.75 |
| P21 | 0.4116 | 0.4367 | 0.0983 | 103.69 |
| P22 | 0.4364 | 0.4663 | 0.1075 | 111.27 |
| P23 | 0.4643 | 0.5002 | 0.1186 | 120.05 |
| P24 | 0.3291 | 0.3450 | 0.0758 | 81.62  |
| P25 | 0.3491 | 0.3590 | 0.0782 | 84.65  |
| P26 | 0.3398 | 0.3563 | 0.0766 | 83.68  |
| P27 | 0.3635 | 0.3869 | 0.0853 | 91.13  |
| P28 | 0.3287 | 0.3489 | 0.0824 | 84.07  |
| P29 | 0.3956 | 0.4247 | 0.1009 | 334.66 |
| P30 | 0.3742 | 0.3935 | 0.0860 | 92.83  |
| P31 | 0.3726 | 0.3924 | 0.0851 | 92.27  |
| P32 | 0.3705 | 0.3896 | 0.0862 | 92.27  |
| P33 | 0.3922 | 0.4146 | 0.0934 | 98.59  |
| P34 | 0.3958 | 0.4170 | 0.0936 | 99.15  |
| P35 | 0.4403 | 0.4659 | 0.1013 | 109.48 |

triangular area ($t$). Short of any knowledge of the exact or approximate distribution of the distance measures, one possible way to use them is to take sample estimates of their means and variances and set up confidence intervals in terms of Tchebycheff inequalities. This is followed in the safety first approach. Another way of looking at the situation is that, given probabilistic variations in vector $c$ with probabilities unknown, an optimal decision rule

TABLE 5.10

Values of the objective function: the optimal, the second best and the third best (the three maximands) for the 35 problems (in dollars).

| (1)<br>Problem | (2)<br>Optimal ($z_1^{(k)}$) | (3)<br>Second best ($z_2^{(k)}$) | (4)<br>Third best ($z_3^{(k)}$) |
|---|---|---|---|
| *P1* | 6409.043 | 6059.391 | 5166.113 |
| P2 | 5166.848 | 5717.715 | 4484.160 |
| P3 | 5089.406 | 4876.164 | 4647.457 |
| P4 | 4779.016 | 4703.758 | 4462.277 |
| P5 | 4523.488 | 4333.680 | 4101.891 |
| P6 | 4897.648 | 4508.766 | 4270.809 |
| P7 | 4694.664 | 4569.898 | 4316.922 |
| P8 | 4543.203 | 4521.481 | 4262.703 |
| *P9* | 4885.367 | 4529.625 | 4268.762 |
| P10 | 4860.715 | 4650.754 | 4367.219 |
| P11 | 5020.316 | 4947.988 | 4701.188 |
| P12 | 5244.875 | 5179.723 | 4958.199 |
| P13 | 5542.117 | 5339.324 | 5156.531 |
| P14 | 4701.109 | 4353.516 | 4033.250 |
| P15 | 4541.703 | 4056.634 | 3699.677 |
| P16 | 4382.102 | 3759.398 | 3365.705 |
| P17 | 4378.660 | 4125.367 | 3882.930 |
| P18 | 4538.258 | 4422.606 | 4216.902 |
| P19 | 4719.488 | 4697.668 | 4519.473 |
| P20 | 5016.731 | 4857.266 | 4717.801 |
| P21 | 4219.059 | 3828.136 | 3548.965 |
| P22 | 4059.653 | 3531.256 | 3215.393 |
| *P23* | 3900.051 | 3234.016 | 2881.419 |
| P24 | 5166.848 | 4899.020 | 4665.465 |
| P25 | 4931.367 | 4756.925 | 4516.543 |
| P26 | 4903.090 | 4846.727 | 4618.020 |
| P27 | 4687.383 | 4426.719 | 4079.725 |
| P28 | 5499.133 | 4579.309 | 4223.504 |
| P29 | 4396.438 | 3976.204 | 3606.883 |
| P30 | 4521.488 | 4331.684 | 4099.895 |
| P31 | 4502.902 | 4387.113 | 4141.668 |
| P32 | 4615.789 | 4324.672 | 4090.463 |
| P33 | 4432.102 | 4014.461 | 3749.636 |
| P34 | 4377.121 | 3992.067 | 3757.200 |
| P35 | 3822.635 | 3701.704 | 3458.028 |

should consider not the scalar optimization problem of maximizing a concave function with mean and variance as arguments but rather the vector optimization problem, in which a vector with elements comprising the mean and variance of $z_i$, the average distance $E e_{ij}$ and the average area of the neighborhood $E t$ defined by the three best solution vectors is optimized subject to restrictions.

## 5.2.3. Other applications

The case of chance-constrained linear programming in which the resource vector has a multivariate normal distribution has found several interesting applications, e.g., (a) Van de Panne and Popp [33] have applied it to determine the minimal cost cattle feed-mix under probabilistic protein constraints, (b) Charnes and Cooper [34] have made several applications to optimal shipment problems under probabilistic demand requirements, in PERT (program evaluation and review technique) formulations of network analysis and in developing different types of decision rules (optimal to different degrees), and (c) Naslund [35] (also Naslund and Whinston) have made interesting applications to the capital budgeting problems of a single firm involving multi-period investment decisions.

The method of stochastic linear programming in its active approach has been frequently applied in economic planning for optimal allocation of investment between sectors [36]. Problems of optimal capital accumulation have also been considered in terms of transition probabilities in the specification of stochastic process models of overall economic growth [37]. However, what are known as turnpike theorems [38] in optimal growth theory are not sufficiently generalized yet to incorporate the various stochastic aspects referred to before.

## 5.3. Simulation methods in risk programming

By simulation methods in risk programming [39] we refer to those non-analytic rules and techniques by which we try to estimate or predict some of the essential components of risk under situations in which the probabilities involved are either unknown or estimable in a very partial sense. These situations are also termed situations of uncertainty as opposed to risk. Although not many operational rules are available in this area, yet through the use of the computer it is possible to have some limited characterization of uncertainty, which may be present either in the parameter set $(A, b, c)$ or in the constrained inequalities or in the linear approximations to what are supposedly nonlinear relations in the real world.

Two types of simulation methods may be distinguished from an operational viewpoint. First, there is a set of criteria for characterizing optimal decision rules, if the probability distribution of the parameters $(A, b, c)$ in an LP model is either unknown or unestimable. Second, there exist a number of techniques for exploring the sequential revision of optimal (i.e. suboptimal) solutions when either the sample observations are available or the appropriate tables of random numbers can be used to develop a sequential approximation to real world sample observations.

To give an example of the first type of simulation method, consider the three best maximands $z_1^{(k)} > z_2^{(k)} > z_3^{(k)}$ defined in section 5.2.2 and the associated basic feasible solution vectors $x_1^{(k)}$, $x_2^{(k)}$, $x_3^{(k)}$ where $k = 1, 2, ..., K$ denotes the number of admissible samples. In the general case in which the parameter set is $S = (A, b, c)$ and any elements of the set may be random with unknown probabilities, a specific sample $S^{(k)} = (A^{(k)}, b^{(k)}, c^{(k)})$ leading to the above ordering of $z$'s can be defined to be admissible. Now if $K$ samples are admissible, say that nature has $K$ strategies available; on the other hand, the decision-maker has available in this case the choice of three strategies, the first best, second best and third best solution vectors. If the probabilities associated with the sets $S^{(k)}$ are unknown, but a nonnegative pay-off matrix $(u_{ij})$ with finite elements where $i = 1, 2, 3$ for the three best strategies of the decision-maker and $j = 1, 2, ..., K$ for the $K$ admissible states of nature can be defined satisfying the ordinary ordering conditions of a real-valued preference function, then several criteria for decisions under uncertainty may be applied. (Note that the pay-off matrix elements $u_{ij}$ must have functional dependence on resulting profits $z_i$ when the state of nature is at $j$ and the decision-maker's strategy is at $i$). For instance, the following criteria are available for characterizing the best strategy, the best in a specific sense:

Wald:      minimax criterion: $\max_i \min_j u_{ij}$,

Laplace:    equal probability criterion: $\max_i \text{average}_j u_{ij}$,

Hurwicz:   optimism-pessimism index: $\max_i (\alpha \max_j u_{ij} + (1 - \alpha) \min_j u_{ij})$ with $0 < \alpha < 1$,

Savage:    minimax regret criterion: $\max_i \min_j r_{ij}$; where
$$r_{ij} = (u_{ij} - \max_i u_{ij}).$$

Naturally there is no single criterion which would define the best strategy under all circumstances. However one of the principal operational uses of these criteria is to have a starting decision and then successively improve on it in a sequential manner as the empirical data or observations become available. Several applications of this line of work have been reported in the literature [40].

As an example of the second type of simulation method in risk programming, consider the following specification of a programming model: the decision vector $x$ belongs to the closed and bounded set $X = (x \mid Ax \leq b, x \geq 0)$ with known parameters but the scalar objective function $z = z(x) = z(x_1, ..., x_n)$, which may be nonlinear is very incompletely known; however, a series of simulated experiments or computations can be performed in order to determine either exactly or approximately the value of the vector $x$ for which the expected value of profit $Ez = Ez(x)$ is a maximum. Several different methods are available in this case for determining an optimal vector $\bar{x}$ at which $Ez(\bar{x})$ is the maximum.

Economic examples of such situations occur very frequently in estimating the maximum of a response surface (e.g. an agricultural production function) for different inputs (e.g. fertilizers) on the basis of experimental data obtained through experimental plots [41]. Hufschmidt [42] in his simulation study of a multipurpose water-resource system has reported the case where 'the net benefit response surface' is some function of several design components but not completely known. Some of the different methods available may be mentioned here very briefly. First, a nonsequential method may be used to vary different levels of the vector $x$ within all feasible sets of values and explore the whole region in which the maximum of $Ez(x_1, ..., x_n)$ may lie. However, since this may be very expensive, the search for the maximum may be made through a set of randomly selected levels of each $x_j$ ($j = 1, ..., n$). Second, a steepest ascent type method based on gradients may be used, in which a small set of feasible observations is first used to make a rough guess of the maximum and the successive revisions of the initial levels are made in the direction of steepest ascent by using a gradient method and approximating the response surface as a quadratic. If the unknown function $Ez(x_1, ..., x_n)$ is concave and the steepest ascent method is used with the restriction that the feasibility conditions are satisfied, then such a sequential method is known to have local convergence to the optimal solution [43].

A few remarks may now be made briefly about other types of simulation procedures applied to probabilistic LP models. First, several attempts have been reported in which artificial and simulated data have been generated around a specific set of parameter values ($A, b, c$) (one example of which has already been mentioned in section 5.2.2). Such types of simulated estimates of parameters provide interesting insights into the effects of departures from normality upon the optimal solution. Several such experiments in LP problems have been reported by Kuhn and Quandt and others [44].

Second, the propagation of errors from various sources in an LP framework is as yet unexplored. Some of the common sources which are neglected are: (a) the specification error when an LP model is viewed as an approximation to a nonlinear model, (b) the errors involved in arbitrary definitions of activities ignoring their interdependence and jointness, and (c) the errors involved in ignoring various adjustments and learning phenomena implicit in any decision-making process over time, e.g. the revision or adaptation of goals and subgoals [45]. In this respect, simulation techniques have yet to develop interesting insights into the probable behavior of optimal LP solutions when the model is deformed, partitioned or even aggregated.

REFERENCES

[1] Prekopa, A., "On the probability distribution of the optimum of a random linear program", *SIAM Journal on Control*, Vol. 4, 1966.
[2] Freund, R. J., "The introduction of risk into a programming model", *Econometrica*, Vol. 24, 1956, 253–263.
[3] Sengupta, J. K., "The stability of truncated solutions of stochastic linear programming", *Econometrica*, Vol. 34, 1966, 77–104.
[4] Markowitz, H., *Portfolio selection*. New York: Wiley, 1959.
[5] Charnes, A. and W. W. Cooper, "Deterministic equivalents for optimizing and satisficing under chance constraints", *Operations Research*, Vol. 11, 1963, 18–39.
[6] Kataoka, S., "A stochastic programming model", *Econometrica*, Vol. 31, 1963, 181–196.
[7] Sengupta, J. K., "Stochastic linear programming with chance constraints", accepted for publication in *International Economic review*.
Sengupta, J. K., "A generalization of chance-constrained programming with applications" (author: sent for publication).
Sengupta, J. K., "Distribution problems in stochastic and chance-constrained programming" (accepted for publication in essays in honor of G. Tintner).
Sengupta, J. K., "Econometric models of risk programming", Annual Econometric Number, *Indian Economic Journal*, Vol. 15, No. 4, 1968.
[8] Madansky, A., "Dual variables in two-stage linear programming under uncertainty", mimeographed report of the Center for Advanced Study in the Behavioral Sciences, December 1, 1961.
[9] Dantzig, G. B. and A. Madansky, "On the solution of two-stage linear programs under uncertainty", *Proceedings of Fourth Berkeley Symposium on Mathematitcal Statistics and Probability*, Vol. I. Berkeley: University of California Press, 1961.
[10] Babbar, M. M., "Distribution of solutions of a set of linear equations with applications to linear programming", *Journal of American Statistical Association*, Vol. 50, 1955, 155–164.
Tintner, G., "Stochastic linear programming with applications to agricultural economics", *Proceedings of Second Symposium on Linear Programming*, National Bureau of Standards, Washington, D.C., 1955.
[11] Bereanu, B., "On stochastic linear programming: the Laplace transform of the distribution of the optimum and applications", *Journal of Mathematical Analysis and Applications*, Vol. 15, 1966.
Sengupta, J. K., G. Tintner and C. Millham, "On some theorems of stochastic linear programming with applications", *Management Science*, Vol. 10, 1963, 143–159.
Sengupta, J. K., "The extremes of extreme value solutions under risk programming", (sent for publication).
[12] Sengupta, J. K. and G. Tintner, "The approach of stochastic linear programming: a critical appraisal" (sent for publication).
[13] Geary, R. C., "The frequency distribution of the quotient of two normal variates", *Journal of Royal Statistical Society*, Vol. 93, 1930, 442–446.

[14] Sengupta, J. K., "Chance-constrained programming with chi-square type deviates" (sent for publication: July 1967).

[15] Sengupta, J. K., "On the active approach of stochastic linear programming", to be published in *Metrika*.

[16] Sengupta, J. K., G. Tintner and C. Millham, "On some theorems of stochastic linear programming with applications", *Management Science*, Vol. 10, 1963.

[17] Howard, R. A., *Dynamic programming and Markov processes*. Cambridge, Mass.: MIT Press, 1960.

Bellman, R., *Dynamic programming*. Princeton: Princeton University Press, 1957.

Blackwell, D. H. and M. A. Girshick, *Theory of games and statistical decisions*. New York: John Wiley, 1954.

Bharucha-Reid, A. T., *Elements of the theory of Markov processes and applications*. New York: McGraw-Hill, 1960.

Sengupta, J. K. and G. Tintner, "The flexibility and optimality of Domar-type growth models", *Metroeconomica*, Vol. 17, 1965, 3–16.

Sengupta, J. K. and G. Tintner, "An approach to a stochastic theory of economic development with applications", In: *Problems of economic dynamics and planning: essays in honor of M. Kalecki*. Warsaw, PWN Polish Scientific Publishers, 1964.

[18] Ghellinck, G. T. and G. D. Eppen, "Linear programming solutions for separable Markovian decision problems", *Management Science*, Vol. 13, No. 5, January 1967, 371–394.

[19] Zangwill, W. I., "Nonlinear programming via penalty functions", *Management Science*, Vol. 13, No. 5, January 1965, 344–358.

[20] Geoffrion, A. M., "Stochastic programming with aspiration or fractile criteria" *Management Science*, Vol. 13, 1967, 672–679.

Sinha, S. M., "Programming with standard errors in the constraints and the objective". In: R. L. Graves and P. Wolfe (eds.), *Recent advances in mathematical programming*. New York: McGraw-Hill, 1963.

Roy, A. D., "Safety first and the holding of assets", *Econometrica*, Vol. 20, 1952, 431–449.

Sengupta, J. K., "Safety first rules under chance-constrained linear programming", Operations Research, Vol. 17, No. 1, January-February 1969, 112–132.

[21] Bracken, J. and R. M. Soland, "Statistical decision analysis of stochastic linear programming problems", *Naval Research Logistics Quarterly*, Vol. 13, 1966, 205–226.

[22] Clark, C. E., "The greatest of a finite set of random variables", *Operations Research*, Vol. 9, No. 2, March-April 1961, 145–162.

[23] Kushner, H. J., *Stochastic stability and control*. New York: Academic Publishers, 1967.

Sworder, D., *Optimal adaptive control systems*. New York, Academic Press, 1966.

[24] Sengupta, J. K., "Econometric models of risk programming", to be published in *Indian Economic Journal:* Annual Econometric Number, Vol. 15, No. 4, 1968.

Sengupta, J. K. and J. H. Portillo-Campbell, "A fractile approach to linear programming under risk" (sent for publication).

[25] Sengupta, J. K., "Distribution problems in stochastic and chance–constrained programming", accepted for publication in Essays in honor of G. Tintner.

Sengupta, J. K. and G. Tintner, "The approach of stochastic linear programming: a critical appraisal", to be published.

[26] Theil, H., *Economic forecasts and policy*. Amsterdam: North-Holland, 1961, revised edition.

[27] Shackle, G. L. S., *Uncertainty in economics*. Cambridge: Cambridge University Press, 1955.

[28] Sengupta, J. K. and B. C. Sanyal, "Sensitivity analysis methods for a crop-mix problem in linear programming" (authors: sent for publication).

[29] U.S. Department of Agriculture, *Agricultural prices*. Crop Reporting Board, Washington, D.C.; 1960–1966.

[30] Balinski, M. L., "An algorithm for finding all vertices of convex polyhedral sets", *Journal of Society of Industrial and Applied Mathematics*, Vol. 9, 1961, 72–88.

[31] Sengupta, J. K., "The stability of truncated solutions of stochastic linear programming", *Econometrica*, Vol. 34, January 1966, 77–104.

[32] Kendall, M. G., *The advanced theory of statistics*, Vol. I. London: C. Griffin and Co., 1943.

[33] Van de Panne, C. and W. Popp, "Minimum cost cattle feed under probabilistic protein constraints", *Management Science*, Vol. 9, April 1963, 405–430.

[34] Thompson, G. L., W. W. Cooper and A. Charnes, "Characterizations by chance-constrained programming". In: R. L. Graves and P. Wolfe (eds.), *Recent advances in mathematical programming*. New York: McGraw-Hill, 1963.

[35] Naslund, B. and A. W. Whinston, "A model of multi-period investment under uncertainty", *Management Science*, Vol. 8, 1962.
Naslund, B., *Decisions under risk*, Stockholm ,Economic Research Institute, Stockholm School of Economics, 1967.

[36] Tintner, G. and J. K. Sengupta, "Stochastic linear programming and its application to economic planning". In: *Essays in honor of O. Lange on political economy and econometrics*. Warsaw: PWN Polish Scientific Publishers, 1964, 601–617.

[37] Sengupta, J. K. and G. Tintner, "The flexibility and optimality of Domar-type growth models", *Metroeconomica*, Vol. 17, 1965, 3–16.

[38] Morishima, M., *Equilibrium, stability and growth*. Oxford, Clarendon Press, 1964.

[39] Meyer, H. A. (ed.), *Symposium on Monte Carlo methods*. New York: Wiley, 1956.
Hoggatt, A. C. and F. E. Balderston (eds.), *Symposium on simulation models*. Chicago: South-Western Publishing Co., 1963.

[40] Sengupta, J. K., "A computable approach to risk programming in linear models", Paper presented at the Joint Symposium on Theoretical and Applied Economics at the University of Iowa, May 1968, published in *Papers in Quantitative Economics*, University Press of Kansas, Lawrence, 1968, pp. 543–566.
Weiss, L., *Statistical decision theory*. New York: McGraw-Hill, 1961.

[41] Heady, E. O. and J. L. Dillon, *Agricultural production functions*. Ames: Iowa State University Press, 1961.

[42] Hufschmidt, M. M., "Simulating the behavior of a multi-unit, multi-purpose water resource system". In: A. C. Hoggatt and F. E. Balderston (eds.), *Symposium on simulation models, op. cit.*

[43] Wetherill, G. B., *Sequential methods in statistics*. London: Methuen and Co., 1966.

[44] Kuhn, H. W. and R. E. Quandt, "An experimental study of the simplex method". In: Mathematica: *decomposition principles for solving large structured linear programs*. Princeton, N. J.: Mathematica, 20 Nassau Street, 1963.
Wolfe, P. and L. Cutler, "Experiments in linear programming". In: R. L. Graves and P. Wolfe (eds.), *Recent advances in mathematical programming, op. cit.*

[45] Ijiri, Y., *Management goals and accounting for control*. Amsterdam: North-Holland, 1965.

# Chapter 6

# MODELS OF FIRM BEHAVIOR AND OTHER APPLICATIONS

Some broad applications of the theory of optimization developed in chs 2 through 5 are illustrated in this chapter and the next. Whereas the applications reported in ch. 7 refer to the various decision procesess of a nonmarket institution and the associated problems of imputing appropriate prices to the relevant quantities, this chapter discusses the decision problems of a firm or enterprise with definite market variables such as prices and quantities. The concept of firm used here is very broad, ranging from the concept of a plant to a single industry or a project. Our purpose is to present not a comprehensive review of firm behavior models but only a select number of decision models in this area, e.g. (a) a selected set of production-inventory models which are in our opinion the most interesting from the viewpoints of both the economist and the operations researcher; (b) a few models of optimal capacity expansion for the firm when it is planning its investment expansion under conditions of known demand and significant economies of scale in production; (c) a selected number of queuing models applicable to either a group of firms comprising an industry or a single firm viewed as a population of customers; and (d) the methods of project analysis and critical path techniques applicable to a project with interrelated activities.

## 6.1. Optimization in production-inventory models

There is an extensive literature [1–3] on inventory systems in various contexts, statistical, economic and other. Methods of inventory control in theory and practice have become a very important field, in which operations research has combined with some success statistical techniques such as stochastic processes and various forecasting procedures with the methods of control, optimization and simulation.

The economist's approach to production-inventory models appears to have several differentiating characteristics from that of the operations researcher. First, the economist is more concerned with developing the deterministic part of the theory of the firm's behavior and that is why he emphasizes the various types of deviations from perfect competition and their implications for demand and other variables. Second, because of data limitations in the context of individual firms and his interest in aggregative economic behavior and the associated macroeconomic models, the economist feels the need to explain the short-term fluctuations in aggregate investment by sectors or industries and the role of inventory holdings and other associated factors which may offer possible explanations. What types of production-inventory decision rules, if followed by individual firms within an industry, may lead to fluctuations in inventory investment at different levels? Does the concept of a desired level (or a normal level) of inventory in relation to output have the same explanatory implication for an aggregate of firms as for a single firm which operates under given prices?

An operations researcher, on the other hand, is more interested in specifying optimal production-inventory decision rules for a single firm with a given pattern of demand and state of competition under varying objectives of cost minimization (or profit maximization) with or without probabilistic components. Hence, an operations researcher emphasizes in detail the various aspects characterizing an optimal decision rule, e.g. the single period vs. multiperiod decision cases, single item vs. multi-item cases, fixed vs. variable lead time (i.e., the time interval between order and delivery), single station vs. parallel station problems, static vs. transition probabilities, and the various costs associated with ordering 'lost sales' (i.e., shortage of supply) and the penalty cost of supply shortages when backlogging of demand is not possible.

From an economic viewpoint, we find the following classification of production-inventory models to be useful and convenient:

*A.* Cost minimization models for an individual firm under static conditions, when the possible interdependence of different firms is excluded from the analysis;

*B.* Dynamic optimization models for an individual firm under conditions of perfect and imperfect competition but with no product differentiation explicitly introduced;

*C.* Static and dynamic optimization models for an individual firm under various types of oligopolistic interdependence with product differentiation; and

*D.* Econometric models at an industry level for specifying the response of manufacturers' inventory holdings to changes in several explanatory variables, e.g. sales volume, backlog of unfilled orders, market expectations, the degree of industrial concentration, and others.

Our objective will be to present typical models in each of the four categories mentioned above and thereby to emphasize the salient characteristics of various production-inventory models which are available in the fields of operations research, economics and industrial engineering.

### 6.1.1. Static cost minimization models

One of the simplest models in this category which assumes a deterministic case (i.e., a single product with its demand fixed over time and known) is provided by the classical lot-size model based on a square-root formula. This model is appropriate for a manufacturer who has to supply a total demand of $D$ units during the time period $T$ at a constant rate per unit time $t$, where shortages are not allowed (i.e., the cost of shortage is infinite) and the variable costs associated with the manufacturing process are: $a =$ the cost of one unit in inventory per unit time (assumed constant), and $b =$ the set-up cost per production run, where $x$ is the quantity produced per run. The policy problem is to determine an optimal value of $x$, which will minimize total variable costs over the time period $T$. (If the product is not produced by the manufacturer but ordered outside, $x$ will represent the size of the order rather than the size of the production run and $b$ will represent ordering cost per lot rather than set-up cost per run; note that $b$ is a fixed cost per lot but a variable cost per unit.)

Now denote by $t$ the interval of time between production runs (or orders with the lead time assumed zero); then over the total planning period $T$ there are $m = D/x$ production runs (or numbers of orders) and the rerun or reorder time interval is $t = T/m = Tx/D$. Since demand is at an even and constant rate, therefore $\frac{1}{2}x$ is the size of the average inventory during the reorder time interval $t$ and $\frac{1}{2}atx$ provides the total inventory cost per production run. Hence the total variable cost per production run (or per order) is $(\frac{1}{2}atx + b)$ and therefore total variable cost (TVC) over the planning horizon $T$ is

$$\text{TVC} = \text{TVC}(x) = (b + \tfrac{1}{2}atx)m = bD/x + \tfrac{1}{2}aTx. \qquad (6.1a)$$

By equating $d(\text{TVC})/dx$ to zero, the optimal quantity to produce per run (or the optimal quantity to order by lot) is given by $\bar{x}$:

$$\bar{x} = \left(\frac{2bD}{aT}\right)^{\frac{1}{2}} \qquad (6.1b)$$

the corresponding optimal values of $t$, $m$ and TVC are

$$\bar{t} = \left(\frac{2bT}{aD}\right)^{\frac{1}{2}}; \quad \bar{m} = D/\bar{x}; \quad \text{TVC}(\bar{x}) = (2abDT)^{\frac{1}{2}}. \quad (6.1c)$$

Although the above model is admittedly very simple, several interesting realistic modifications may be made in it without much complication.

(1) If there are errors in estimating the parameters $a$, $b$ or $D$ the effects on the optimal solution $\bar{x}$ can be easily worked out. For instance, if the true values of $a$, $b$ and $D$ were mistakenly taken to be $k_1a$, $k_2b$ and $k_3D$, then the estimated optimal quantity and optimal cost would be

$$\bar{x}(\text{est.}) = \left(\frac{2k_2bk_3D}{k_1aT}\right)^{\frac{1}{2}} = \bar{x}.\sqrt{k}, \quad \text{where} \quad k = k_2k_3/k_1$$

$$\text{TVC}(\bar{x}(\text{est.})) = (abDT)^{\frac{1}{2}}\left(\frac{k+1}{\sqrt{2k}}\right).$$

The ratio of $\text{TVC}(\bar{x}(\text{est.}))$ when one attempts to minimize cost with incorrect data to these costs $\text{TVC}(\bar{x})$ with correct data is $(k+1)/2\sqrt{k}$ and this expression provides a measure of the effect of errors in measurement of the parameters. By using this measure it can be shown that the optimal cost calculations are not unduly sensitive to errors in the estimation of relevant cost and demand parameters.

(2) Demand relations can be introduced in the model, if the manufacturer can affect demand through price variations as in monopoly or in imperfect competition. Assuming a linear demand function

$$D = \alpha p + \beta, \quad p = \text{price per unit}; \quad \alpha < 0 \quad (6.2a)$$

and the following TVC

$$\text{TVC}(x) = bD/x + \tfrac{1}{2}axT + cD \quad (6.2b)$$

where $c$ is a parameter (assumed constant) reflecting the unit costs associated with a unit of sales, the optimal lot size $\bar{x} = \bar{x}(p)$ can be computed by formula (6.1b) as before for each given level of price $p$. Now if price can be used as a control variable by the firm, a second degree of freedom is introduced into the classical model: both price $p$ and the order size (or run size) $x$ become decision variables. Denoting fixed cost of production by $A$ and total profits by $Q$,

$$Q = pD - \text{TVC}(\bar{x}) - A$$
$$= \alpha p^2 + \beta p - (2abT(\alpha p + \beta))^{\frac{1}{2}} - c(\alpha p + \beta) - A.$$

The optimal value $\bar{p}$ of price $p$ can be determined by equating $dQ/dp$ to zero, i.e. by solving the following cubic equation in $\bar{p}$ by numerical methods:

$$8\alpha^3\bar{p}^3 + (16\alpha^2\beta - 8c\alpha^3)\bar{p}^2 + (10\alpha\beta^2 - 12c\alpha^2\beta + 2c^2\alpha^3)\bar{p} + q_0 = 0,$$

where

$$q_0 = 2\beta^3 - 4c\alpha\beta^2 + 2c^2\alpha^2\beta - baT\alpha^2.$$

However, if the demand function is not linear as in (6.2a), the equation $dQ/dp=0$ may be very difficult to solve by approximate and numerical methods.

(3) The economic lot-size model can incorporate several products (i.e., several items) for which inventories are maintained, provided they are more or less independent. Assume there are $n$ products, with $x_i$, $b_i$, $\bar{a}_i=a_iT$, $D_i$ $(i=1,...,n)$ replacing $x$, $b$, $a$, $D$ in equation (6.1a) and that there is perfect competition in each market so that the prices $p_i$ are given. The firm (or company) operates in different items (some of the items may be goods in process or raw materials, for which demand has to be conceived as derived demand, i.e. derived from the demand for final output) and is assumed to operate under the working capital constraint that it cannot exceed the average inventory investment of amount $I_0$. Further, it is assumed that the following objective function is still reasonable for the firm to optimize:

$$\text{TVC}(x_1,...,x_n) = \sum_{i=1}^{n} \left[ b_iD_i/x_i + \tfrac{1}{2}\bar{a}_in_ix_i \right] \tag{6.3a}$$

where $n_i=$ per unit cost or value of item $x_i$.

The optimal policy problem is then to minimize (6.3a) under the restrictions

$$\sum_{i=1}^{n} \tfrac{1}{2}(n_ix_i) \leqslant I_0. \tag{6.3b}$$

This is a typical convex programming problem in $x_i$ $(i=1,...,n)$ and hence it could be solved by the numerical methods discussed in ch. 5. In some cases, in which the $n$ products sold by the firm have interrelations on the demand and cost sides in a specific form, i.e.

$$D_i = \beta_i + \sum_{j=1}^{n} \alpha_{ij}p_j \qquad p_j = \text{unit price} \tag{6.3c}$$

(demand function)

$$f(x_1,...,x_n) = 0 \tag{6.3d}$$

(output transformation or production possibility map)

such that the total profit $(Q)$

$$Q = \sum_{i=1}^{n} \left[ p_i D_i - \frac{b_i D_i}{x_i} - \frac{\bar{a}_i n_i x_i}{2} - c_i D_i \right] \tag{6.3c}$$

is a quasi-concave function in $x_i$ and $p_i$, then $Q$ in (6.3c) can be maximized under the restrictions (6.3c) and (6.3d) and the optimal decision variables $\bar{x}_i, \bar{p}_i$ $(i = 1, ..., n)$ determined. However, this view of the multiproduct firm [4] is very special, since the problems of indivisibility, joint products and capacity constraints are assumed away when we specify that $Q$ is quasi-concave in each $x_i$ and $p_i$.

Nevertheless, a very interesting specification of the multi-item economic lot-size model in linear programming terms has been made [5, 6] by Dzielin-ski, Baker and Manne (DBM model). This model incorporates in its deterministic framework three important characteristics which are absent in the classical lot-size formula, e.g. the DBM model allows the presence of capacity constraints in production which generate interdependence between lot sizes, reduces the fluctuations in capacity and labor utilization rates in alternative production set-up sequences, and considers a planning horizon suitable for job-shop scheduling. Define the following terms: $x_{ij}$ = fraction of total requirements for the $i$th item or part $(i = 1, 2, ..., I)$ produced with the $j$th alternative production set-up sequence $(j = 1, ..., J)$, $q_{ijt}$ = number of parts $i$ produced in sequence $j$ during period $t$, $L_{ft}^{(1)}$, $L_{ft}^{(2)}$ = number of workers assigned to first shift operation in facility (or activity) $f$ without and with overtime, $L_{ft}^{(3)}$, $L_{ft}^{(4)}$ = number of workers for the second shift operation in facility $f$ without and with overtime, $F_{ft}^{+}$, $F_{ft}^{-}$ = increase or decrease in total number of workers employed in facility $f$ from period $(t-1)$ to $t$, $M_{ijft}$ = labor input during period $t$ to carry out the $j$th alternative set-up sequence on the facility $f$ for item or part $i$ such that

$$M_{ijft} = \begin{cases} 0, & \text{if } q_{ift} = 0 \\ a_{if} + b_{if} q_{ift} & \text{if } q_{ift} > 0; \end{cases} \quad (a_{if}, b_{if} = \text{constant}),$$

$L_f$ is the maximum number of workers assigned to facility $f$ during a single shift, $H^{(s)}$ $(s = 1, ..., 4)$ is the total number of shift hours per period without $(s = 1, 3)$ and with overtime $(s = 2, 4)$, $w_{ft}^{(s)}$ is the shift wage for facility $f$ discounted over periods between first and second shift, $c_{ot}$ is the cost of laying off one worker, $c_{ht}$ is the cost of hiring one worker, and $c_{it}$ is the unit material cost of part $i$, where all these costs are appropriately discounted over preceding periods. The DBM model then considers the chance-independent part of forecast demand and assuming it known solves the following production-scheduling LP model:

$$\text{minimize } J = \sum_{i,f,t} \left\{ \sum_{s=1}^{4} [w_{ft}^{(s)} L_{ft}^{(s)} + c_{ot} F_{ft}^{-} + c_{ht} F_{ft}^{+}] + \sum_{j} x_{ij} c_{it} q_{it} \right\} \qquad (6.4a)$$

subject to

$$\sum_{j} x_{ij} = 1; \qquad i = 1, \dots, I \qquad (6.4b)$$

$$\sum_{i,j} M_{ijft} x_{ij} \leqq \sum_{s=1}^{4} H^{(s)} L_{ft}^{(s)}; \qquad f = 1, \dots, F_0; \qquad t = 1, \dots, T \qquad (6.4c)$$

$$\sum_{s=1}^{4} L_{ft}^{(s)} = \sum_{s=1}^{4} L_{f,t-1} + F_{ft}^{+} - F_{ft}^{-}; \qquad t = 1, \dots, T \qquad (6.4d)$$

$$L_{ft}^{(1)} + L_{ft}^{(2)} \leqslant L_f; \qquad L_{ft}^{(3)} + L_{ft}^{(4)} \leqslant L_f \qquad (6.4e)$$

$$x_{ij} \geqslant 0, \quad L_{ft}^{(s)} \geqslant 0, \quad F_{ft}^{+}, \quad F_{ft}^{-} \geqslant 0. \qquad (6.4f)$$

This type of model, however, becomes very complicated as soon as the integral requirements for some variables are considered and the linearity assumption ceases to hold. Simulation methods offer an interesting alternative approach in this area.

(4) The lot-size formula can be easily modified to incorporate shortages and shortage costs. Consider the relation (6.1a) for $\text{TVC}(x)$ defined before and denote by $S$ the inventory level at the beginning of each interval. It is assumed that the output rate equals the demand rate as long as $S > 0$. Let $t$ be the reorder time interval and let $t_1$, $t_2$ be subintervals such that $t_1 + t_2 = t$ with the average number of units in inventory being $\frac{1}{2}S$ during $t_1$ and the average shortage being $\frac{1}{2}(x - S)$ during subinterval $t_2$. If $t_1 = t$, then $t_2 = 0$ which implies no shortage, i.e. $x = S$, since the order size equals the inventory level at the beginning of each interval $t = t_1$. Now so long as $t_2 > 0$ and $t_1 < t$ with $t_1 + t_2 = t$, the initial stock will hold out up to the end of $t_1$ and the average stock level during $t$ will be $\frac{1}{2}S$, since demand is assumed to be at a constant uniform rate; then during $t_2$ the inventory level may fall short of the order size (i.e. demand requirement) by an average amount $\frac{1}{2}(x - S)$, per unit shortage cost being assumed $h$. Note however that for the $t_1$ interval it must hold that

$$xt_1 = St \quad \text{i.e.} \quad t_1 = St/x; \qquad t_1 < t \qquad (6.5a)$$

since at this stage there is no shortage. Then by the condition $t_1 + t_2 = t$ it follows that

$$t_2 = (x - S)t/x, \quad \text{where} \quad t = Tx/D. \qquad (6.5b)$$

Hence the $TVC = TVC(x, S)$ during the period $T$ now becomes

$$TVC(x, S) = (\tfrac{1}{2} S \cdot at_1 + \tfrac{1}{2}(x - S) \cdot ht_2 + b) D/x, \qquad (6.5c)$$

i.e. the cost per cycle is composed of the cost of carrying an average inventory of $\tfrac{1}{2}S$ for $t_1$ time units, the cost of tolerating an average shortage of $\tfrac{1}{2}(x-S)$ for $t_2$ time units and the cost of one set-up. Substituting (6.5a), (6.5b) and $t = Tx/D$ in (6.5c) and equating $d\,TVC(x, S)/dS$ and $d\,TVC(x, S)/dx$ to zero we obtain the optimal values

$$\bar{x} = \left(\frac{2Db}{aT}\right)^{\frac{1}{2}} \left(\frac{a+h}{h}\right)^{\frac{1}{2}}; \qquad\qquad \bar{t} = \left(\frac{2Tb}{aD}\right)^{\frac{1}{2}} \left(\frac{a+h}{h}\right)^{\frac{1}{2}}$$

$$\bar{S} = \left(\frac{2Db}{aT}\right)^{\frac{1}{2}} \left(\frac{h}{a+h}\right)^{\frac{1}{2}}; \qquad TVC(\bar{x}, \bar{S}) = \left[(2TDab)\left(\frac{h}{a+h}\right)\right]^{\frac{1}{2}}.$$

Note that $TVC(\bar{x}, \bar{S})$ is smaller than $TVC(\bar{x})$ of (6.1c) by the factor $(h/(a+h))^{\frac{1}{2}}$.

Another way to get the same result is to consider the time interval $t$ between production runs and introduce the continuous demand rate $r$ (i.e. $r = D/T$) such that the output rate $x$ is held equal to the demand rate $r$, as long as the inventory level is positive. Then the subintervals $t_1$ and $t_2$ are

$$t_1 = S/r; \qquad t_2 = t - S/r = (rt - S)/r$$

and the cost $C$ per inventory cycle is

$$C = \frac{1}{t}\left(b + \tfrac{1}{2}aS \cdot t_1 + \frac{x - S}{2} \cdot ht_2\right)$$

$$= \frac{b}{t} + \frac{aS^2}{2rt} + \frac{h(rt - S)^2}{2rt}.$$

Equating $dC/dS$ and $dC/dt$ to zero we get the optimal values:

$$\bar{t} = \left(\frac{2b}{ra}\right)^{\frac{1}{2}} \left(\frac{a+h}{h}\right)^{\frac{1}{2}}; \qquad \bar{S} = \left(\frac{2rb}{a}\right)^{\frac{1}{2}} \left(\frac{h}{a+h}\right)^{\frac{1}{2}}$$

$$\bar{C} = (2rba)^{\frac{1}{2}} \left(\frac{h}{a+h}\right)^{\frac{1}{2}}.$$

An important new consideration is introduced into the static model if probabilistic variations in demand are admitted. We still assume the size of order to be the only control variable, with known and constant reorder cycle time, thus eliminating price or selling cost variations; only one product (or item) is involved. The problem is to determine the stock level $S$ at the beginning of a period $t$ given that the lead time is insignificant and the demand rate $r$ is random with cumulative distribution $F(y) = \text{Prob}(r \leqslant y) = \int_{-\infty}^{y} f(r)\,dr$. Expected profit (EQ) defined as expected revenue (ER) less expected cost (EC) is maximized in the model to determine an optimal value $\bar{S}$ of inventory. Revenue is assumed to be a linear function of quantity sold, i.e. $R = a_0 + a_1 q$ where $q$ is the amount sold; hence

$$\text{ER} = a_0 + a_1 S(1 - F(s)) + a_1 \int_0^s r\,dF(r); \qquad a_0, a_1 = \text{constant}. \qquad (6.6a)$$

The following cost components may be introduced:

$C_1 = $ purchasing cost for $S$ units $= S(b_0 - b_1 S) + b_2$; $b_0 > 0$, $b_1 \geqslant 0$ where $(b_0 - b_1 S)$ denotes price per unit; $b_0, b_1 = $ constant

$C_2 = $ carrying cost $= c_0 + c_1 S$; $c_0, c_1 = $ constant

$C_3 = $ depletion penalty function $h = h(r - S)$ is assumed to be given as

$$h = \begin{cases} d_0 + d_1(r - S) > 0, & \text{if } r > S \\ 0, & \text{if } r \leqslant S \end{cases} \qquad \begin{array}{l} d_0, d_1 = \text{nonnegative constants,} \\ \text{not both zero} \end{array}$$

the expectation of which is

$$Eh = (d_0 - d_1 S)\,[1 - F(S)] + d_1 \int_S^\infty r\,dF(r). \qquad (6.6b)$$

Net expected loss $L = L(S) = \text{EC} - \text{ER} = -\text{EQ}$ can now be written as

$$L(S) = \left[ q_0 + (c_1 + b_0 - b_1 S)S + d_0[1 - F(S)] - (d_1 + a_1) \right.$$
$$\left. \left\{ S[1 - F(S)] - \int_0^s r\,dF(r) \right\} \right] \qquad (6.6c)$$

where

$$q_0 = b_2 + c_0 + d_0 - a_0.$$

The inventory level $\bar{S}$ is optimal if $L(\bar{S}) \leqslant L(S)$ for every $S$. If the cumulative distribution $F(r)$ of demand has a density function $f(r) = dF(r)/dr$, then if the absolute minimum of $L(S)$ is not at $S = 0$, it will be at some point $\bar{S}$ satisfying

$$\left( \frac{dL(S)}{dS} \right)_{S = \bar{S}} = 0 \quad \text{and} \quad \left( \frac{d^2 L(S)}{dS^2} \right)_{S = \bar{S}} > 0 \qquad (6.6d)$$

since it can be easily shown that the function $L(S)$ is convex in $S$. The conditions in (6.6d) imply

$$c_1 + b_0 - 2b_1\bar{S} = d_0 f(\bar{S}) + (d_1 + a_1)[1 - F(\bar{S})] \tag{6.6e}$$

i.e. marginal expected cost = marginal expected return and

$$(d_1 + a_1) f(\bar{S}) - 2b_1 - d_0 \cdot \left(\frac{df(S)}{dS}\right)_{S=\bar{S}} > 0. \tag{6.6f}$$

For instance, if $b_1 = 0 = d_1 = a_1$ then (6.6e) and (6.6f) become

$$f(\bar{S}) = (c_1 + b_0)/d_0 \quad \text{and} \quad (df(S)/dS)_{S=\bar{S}} < 0.$$

Another special case of this problem occurs when only the penalty cost function $h$ is considered but in a somewhat more general form as

$$h = \begin{cases} d_1(r - S), & \text{if } r > S; \quad d_1 = \text{a positive constant} \\ d_2(S - r), & \text{if } r \leqslant S; \quad d_2 = \text{a positive constant}. \end{cases}$$

Then the total expected cost TEC($S$) is

$$\text{TEC}(S) = d_1 \int_S^\infty (r - S) f(r)\, dr + d_2 \int_0^S (S - r) f(r)\, dr \tag{6.6g}$$

provided the distribution of demand $F(r)$ has a density function $f(r)$ which is continuous. The optimal value of $S$, denoted by $\bar{S}$, which minimizes TEC($S$) is easily computed as:

$$F(\bar{S}) = \int_0^S f(r)\, dr = d_1/(d_1 + d_2). \tag{6.6h}$$

If the distribution of demand $F(r)$ is discrete, then (6.6g) can be written as

$$\text{TEC}(S) = d_1 \sum_{r=S+1}^\infty p(r)(r - S) + d_2 \sum_{r=0}^S p(r)(S - r) \tag{6.6i}$$

where $p(r)$ is the discrete probability of occurrence of each value of $r$. In this case the optimal value of inventory is that value $\bar{S}$ which satisfies the condition

$$p(r \leqslant \bar{S} - 1) \leqslant \frac{d_1}{d_1 + d_2} \leqslant p(r \leqslant \bar{S}), \tag{6.6j}$$

where $p(r \leqslant \bar{S} - 1)$ denotes the probability of $r$ being equal to or less than

$(\bar{S}-1)$. If there exists a value of $\bar{S}$ such that $p(r \leqslant \bar{S}) = d_1/(d_1 + d_2)$ then $\bar{S}+1$ and $\bar{S}$ are both optimal; similarly if $p(r \leqslant \bar{S}-1) = d_1/(d_1 + d_2)$ then both $\bar{S}$ and $(\bar{S}-1)$ are optimal.

The above model can be easily generalized to include a nonzero lead time (i.e. time lag between order and delivery) during the reorder period, if the lead time is known with certainty, for a buffer inventory for the lead time period will need to be maintained. To characterize this situation analytically, assume the cost situation given in (6.6g). Let $n$ be the number of order cycle periods in the order lead time $(n \geqslant 1)$, $r_i$ be the demand requirement during the $i$th order cycle period so that $r = \sum_{i=1}^{n} r_i$ is the total demand over the total lead time and $S_0$ be the stock level at the end of the period preceding placing of the order. Further, let $q_1, q_2, ..., q_{n-1}$ denote the quantities ordered which arrive in periods $1, 2, ..., n-1$ such that the inventory $S_n$ at the end of the $n$th period can be calculated as

$$S_n = S_0 + \sum_{i=1}^{n-1} q_i + q_n - \sum_{i=1}^{n} r_i = s - r, \quad \text{say,}$$

where

$$s = S_0 + \sum_{i=1}^{n-1} q_i + q_n, \qquad r = \sum_{i=1}^{n} r_i.$$

Substituting these quantities $s$ and $r$ in place of $S$ and $r$ in (6.6g) we get the optimal solution $\bar{s}$ from the equation

$$F(\bar{s}) = \frac{d_1}{d_1 + d_2},$$

where $f(r) = $ density of $r$ assumed continuous and $F(\bar{s}) = \text{Prob}(r \leqq \bar{s})$. The optimal value $\bar{q}_k$ of $q_k$ is then recursively generated from the relation

$$\bar{q}_k = \bar{s} - \left(S_0 + \sum_{i=1}^{k-1} \bar{q}_i\right); \qquad k = 2, ..., n.$$

This method of providing safety levels for random demand during the reorder lead time should be distinguished from the method usually considered in the Wilson lot-size formula, in which the safety stock level is selected as being some multiple of the standard deviation of demand during the lead time.

Two comments may be made about the probabilistic static models we have so far considered. First, the models consider only single period problems in a basic sense. Second, only very simple cases of probabilistic variations are analyzed (e.g. situations involving random lead times, multiple reorder points and reorder quantities, and multiple products are not considered at all). However, it is possible through these simple cases to get some insight into the $N$-period dynamic models.

To illustrate this point, consider the simple model (6.6g) specifying TEC$(S)$ for a given period, denote by $S_0$ the initial inventory, and introduce the proportional ordering cost function $c_1 S$; then the optimal amount to order may be determined from the following cost formula $C(S_0)$, i.e.

$$C(S_0) = \min_{S \geq S_0} \left( c_1 S + \text{TEC}(S) \right).$$

This implies the optimal solution $\bar{S}_0$ such that

(i)　if $S_0 \leq \bar{S}_0$, then $S = \bar{S}_0$, i.e. buy up to $\bar{S}_0$, and

(ii)　if $S_0 > \bar{S}_0$, then $S = S_0$, i.e. buy none.

This optimal solution is still valid if the unit costs $d_1$ and $d_2$ are convex functions rather than constants, still maintaining the convexity of TEC$(S)$. Further, if the proportional ordering cost is replaced by a more general ordering cost of the form

$$c(z) = \begin{cases} k + c \cdot z, & \text{if } z > 0 \\ 0, & \text{if } z = 0 \end{cases} \tag{6.6k}$$

where $z$ is the amount ordered, $k$ is the set up cost, $c$ is the unit price (constant), and $c(z)$ is the ordering cost function, then the optimal solution is indicated again by two critical numbers $\hat{s}, \hat{S}$ such that

(i)　if the initial stock $S_0 \leqslant \hat{s}$, then order $(\hat{S} - S_0)$, and

(ii)　if the initial stock $S_0 > \hat{s}$, then do not order.

The specification of these two critical numbers is usually termed an $(s, S)$ type inventory policy. A very general formalization of this type of policy is considered in the Arrow-Harris-Marschak (AHM) model [6].

The AHM model assumes equidistant checking points, identical probability distributions of demand $r$ (which we now denote by $g(r)$) during checking intervals, zero lead time and carry over of shortages to the next period. We adopt now a different set of notations to present the model. Let $x$ be stock on hand before ordering, $y = y(x)$ be an ordering policy at a given checking point, $(y - x)$ be the amount to be ordered $(y \geqslant x)$ and the cost per period be $C(x, y, r)$. The AHM model considers minimization of long run expected cost through a dynamic programming algorithm. This requires us to derive for a finite process of $N$ periods, $N$ optimal ordering functions denoted by $y_k(s)$ $(k = 1, ..., N)$ for the $N$ checking points.

Define expected cost $L(x, y)$ in any period, given $x$ and $y$, as

$$L(x, y) = EC(x, y, r); \qquad E \text{ is expectation.} \tag{6.7a}$$

Clearly, $y_k(s)$ can be found by minimizing $L(x, y)$ with respect to $y$ for each value of $x$. Hence if $f_N(x)$ denotes the minimum value of the expected cost in the $N$th period, then we must have

$$f_N(x) = \min_{y \geqslant x} L(x, y). \qquad (6.7b)$$

Similarly, $f_{N-1}(x)$ will denote the minimum expected cost for the last two periods $N-1$ and $N$, given the stock level $x$ at the beginning of period $N-1$. The relation between $f_N(x)$ and $f_{N-1}(x)$ and their recursive derivation requires a series of one-dimensional minimizations with respect to $y$, one for each value of $x$. To show this, assume that we have ordered tentatively up to the level $y$ at the beginning of period $N-1$; then the stock level before ordering at the beginning of period $N$ will be $(y - r_{N-1})$ where $r_{N-1}$ is demand during $(N-1)$th period. This provides our $x = y - r_{N-1}$, the stock on hand before ordering during the beginning of period $N$. Hence the optimal ordering policy $y_N(x)$ for period $N$ is $y_N(y - r_{N-1})$ which denotes $y_N$ as a function of $(y - r_{N-1})$. Now the total cost for the combined policy, which starts with a tentative ordering decision $y$ at the beginning of period $N-1$ and thereafter makes the optimal decision $y_N(y - r_{N-1})$ becomes:

$$C(x, y, r_{N-1}) + C(y - r_{N-1}, y_{N-1}(y - r_{N-1}), r_N).$$

The expected value of this expression relative to the joint density $g(r_{N-1})$ $g(r_N)$ is easily computed as

$$L(x, y) + \int_0^\infty f_N(y - r_{N-1}) \, g(r_{N-1}) \, dr_{N-1}.$$

Hence $f_{N-1}(x)$, which by definition is the minimum expected cost for periods $N$ and $N-1$ given the stock level $x$ in the beginning of period $N-1$, is as follows:

$$f_{N-1}(x) = \min_{y \geqslant x} \left[ L(x, y) + \int_0^\infty f_N(y - r) \, g(r) \, dr \right], \qquad (6.7c)$$

since $g(r)$ is the density function of $r$ independent and identical for different periods and $y$ was taken to be a tentative ordering policy at the beginning of period $N-1$.

The relation (6.7c) defines a set of recurrence relations used in dynamic programming:

$$f_{k-1}(x) = \min_{y \geqslant x} \left[ L(y, x) + \int_0^\infty f_k(y - r) \, g(r) \, dr \right]; \qquad k = 2, ..., N. \qquad (6.7d)$$

For an infinite stage ($N \to \infty$) process it is necessary to discount the cost of all future $k$ periods by a factor $\alpha^k$ where $0 < \alpha < 1$ in order to keep the total future costs bounded. In this case the functional equation (6.7d) becomes

$$f(x) = \min_{y \geq x} \left[ L(y, x) + \alpha \int_0^\infty f(y - r) g(r) \, dr \right] \qquad (6.7e)$$

where $f(x)$ denotes the minimum cost for $k \to \infty$ and $y(x)$ denotes the corresponding optimum ordering policy. For a large but finite $N$ with the discount factor $\alpha$ and with the following specification of the $L(y, x)$ function,

$$L(y, x) = c(z) + \int_y^\infty p(r - y) g(r) \, dr = c(z) + L(y), \quad \text{say}, \qquad (6.7f)$$

where $c(z)$ is the cost of ordering $z = y - x$ items initially to increase the stock level and $p(r-y) = $ the penalty cost as a function of the excess demand $(r-y)$, the functional equation (6.7d) becomes

$$f_k(x) = \min \left[ c(y - x) + L(y) + \alpha \int_0^\infty f_{k-1}(y - r) g(r) \, dr \right], \qquad 0 \leq r \leq \infty.$$
$$(6.7g)$$

If the ordering cost function $c(y - z)$ and the expected penalty function $L(y)$ are convex, then it can be shown [7] from (6.7g) recursively that, owing to the convexity of the functions $f_1(x), \ldots, f_{N-1}(x)$ and $f_N(x)$, the optimal policy in each time period is a single critical number. Thus we get $\bar{x}_N, \bar{x}_{N-1}, \ldots, \bar{x}_2, \bar{x}_1$ as the critical or optimal numbers characterizing an optimal policy for an $N$-period problem. It has also been shown that $\bar{x}_k \geq \bar{x}_{k-1}$ ($k = 2, \ldots, N$), if the unit costs of ordering and penalty are constant; further with $N \to \infty$, there exists a critical number $\bar{x}_\infty$ satisfying

$$c(1 - \alpha) + \left( \frac{\partial L}{\partial x} \right)_{x = \bar{x}_\infty} = 0.$$

A simple proof for the case in which the unit ordering cost $c$ and the unit penalty cost $p$ are constant and the time horizon $N$ is finite with no discounting is instructive [8, 9].

*Theorem 6.1*

Let $f_N(x)$ denote the expected cost over an $N$-stage period starting with an initial quantity $x$ and using an optimal policy such that

$$f_1(x) = \min_{y \geqslant x} \left[ c(y - x) + p \int_y^\infty (r - y) g(r) \, dr \right] \tag{6.8a}$$

$$f_{k+1}(x) = \min_{y \geqslant x} \left[ c(y - x) + p \int_y^\infty (r - y) g(r) \, dr + f_k(0) \int_y^\infty g(r) \, dr \right.$$
$$\left. + \int_0^y f_k(y - r) g(r) \, dr \right]; \tag{6.8b}$$

then for each $k = 1, \ldots, N$ the optimal ordering policy has the form

(i) $y = \bar{x}_k$ $(k = 1, \ldots, N)$, if $x \leqslant \bar{x}_k$

(ii) $y = x$, if $x > \bar{x}_k$ $(k = 1, \ldots, N)$

where the sequence $\{\bar{x}_k\}$ is monotone increasing.

*Proof*: An inductive proof will be outlined. From the definition of $f_1(x)$, equate to zero the first derivative of the expression in parenthesis on the right-hand side of (6.8a), with respect to $y$ to get the critical stock level from the integral equation

$$c = p \int_y^\infty g(r) \, dr; \tag{6.8c}$$

this solution exists if $p > c$ and is unique. Denote this value by $\bar{x}_1$. Then for the first period $(k = 1)$, the optimal policy is:

(i) $y = \bar{x}_1$ for $x \leqq \bar{x}_1$

(ii) $y = x$ for $x > \bar{x}_1$.

When $x < \bar{x}_1$, then $df_1(x)/dx = \dot{f}_1(x) = -c$, from (6.8a) and when $x \geqq \bar{x}_1$, then

$$f_1(x) = p \int_x^\infty (r - x) g(r) \, dr; \qquad \dot{f}_1(x) = -p \int_x^\infty g(r) \, dr \geqslant -c;$$

also

$$\ddot{f}_1(x) = d\dot{f}_1(x)/dx = p \, g(x) > 0;$$

hence

$$\dot{f}_1(x) + c \geqslant 0 \quad \text{for all} \quad x \geqslant 0.$$

With $k=2$,

$$f_2(x) = \min_{y \geqslant x} \left[ c(y - x) + p \int_y^\infty (r - y) g(r) \, dr + f_1(0) \int_y^\infty g(r) \, dr \right.$$

$$\left. + \int_0^y f_1(y - r) g(r) \, dr \right].$$

The critical value of $y$ is attained by setting the partial derivative with respect to $y$ equal to zero,

$$c = p \int_y^\infty g(r) \, dr - \int_0^y f_1(y - r) g(r) \, dr = F_1(y), \quad \text{say.} \qquad (6.8d)$$

Since $g(r)$ is continuous, the function $F_1(y)$ is absolutely continuous and has the derivative

$$\dot{F}_1(y) = dF_1(y)/dy = - pg(y) - \dot{f}_1(0) g(y) - \int_0^y \ddot{f}_1(y - r) g(r) \, dr.$$

Since $\ddot{f}_1 > 0$ and $p + \dot{f}_1(0) > c + \dot{f}_1(0) = 0$, the function $F_1(y)$ is seen to be monotone decreasing; hence there can be at most one root of the equation (6.8d). Again, $F_1(0) = p$ and $F_1(\infty) = 0$ from (6.8d) with $0 \leqslant r \leqslant \infty$. Hence there is precisely one root of the integral equation (6.8d). Denote this root by $\bar{x}_2$. For $k = 2$, the optimal policy is then

(i)   $y = \bar{x}_2$,   for   $0 \leqq x \leqq \bar{x}_2$
(ii)   $y = x$,    for   $\bar{x}_2 < x$.

Now $\bar{x}_2 > \bar{x}_1$, since $-\dot{f}_1 \geqslant 0$ and the right hand side of (6.8d) (which determines $\bar{x}_2$) lies above that of (6.8c) (which determines $\bar{x}_1$) for any $y > 0$. Also $-\dot{f}_2(x) \geqslant -\dot{f}_1(x)$, since

$$- \dot{f}_1(x) = \begin{cases} c, & \text{for} \quad 0 \leqslant x \leqslant \bar{x}_1 \\ p \int_x^\infty g(r) \, dr, & \text{for} \quad x \geqslant \bar{x}_1 \end{cases}$$

and

$$- \dot{f}_2(x) = \begin{cases} c, & \text{for} \quad 0 \leqslant x \leqslant \bar{x}_2 \\ p \int_x^\infty g(r) \, dr - \int_0^x \dot{f}_1(x - r) g(r) \, dr, & \text{for} \quad x \geqq \bar{x}_2, \end{cases} \qquad (6.8e)$$

and also $x_2 > x_1$ and the function $(c - p \int_x^\infty g(r) \, dr)$ is monotonic and zero at $x = x_1$. Again the function $f_2(x)$ is convex, since in the range $[0, \bar{x}_2]$, $\ddot{f}_2(x) \geqslant 0$ and in the range $[\bar{x}_2, \infty]$ using the relations (6.8e)

$$\ddot{f}_2(x) = pg(x) + \dot{f}_1(0) g(x) + \int_0^x \ddot{f}_1(x - r) g(r) \, dr > 0,$$

$$\text{since} \quad \dot{f}_1(0) + p > 0, \quad \ddot{f}_1 \geqslant 0$$

and since $\dot{f}_2(x)$ is continuous with $\ddot{f}_2(x) > 0$, therefore $f_2(x)$ is convex. This completes the proof.

Two remarks may be made about the specification of the AHM model. First, the optimal ordering policy of the AHM model which is of the $(s, S)$ type, where the reorder point is $s$, the reorder quantity is $(S, s)$, i.e.,

(i)  if in period $k$, $x \leqslant s_k$, order $S_k - x$, $(S_k = \bar{x}_k)$

(ii)  if in period $k$, $x > s_k$, do not order,

may be difficult to compute empirically in an explicit form, unless the probability distribution $g(r)$ is very simple (e.g. a uniform distribution) and the unist costs of shortage $(p)$ and ordering $(c)$ are constant. Second, the sensitivity [10] of such $(s_k, S_k)$ types of optimal policy with respect to errors in estimating the parameters such as $p$ and $c$ may be difficult to determine except in very simple cases; simulation studies and probabilistic nonlinear programming are as yet unexplored for such cases.

However, the $(s, S)$ type policies have been generalized in several respects in recent years [11]. An important modification in the dynamic programming formulation is required if there is a set-up cost in the ordering cost function. In this case the notion of $k$-convexity is introduced by Scarf [12] to treat the ordering cost of the form mentioned in (6.6k) before, i.e.

$$c(z) = \begin{cases} 0, & \text{if} \quad z = 0 \\ k + cz, & \text{if} \quad z > 0. \end{cases}$$

With $k \geqslant 0$, a differentiable function $f(x)$ is called $k$-convex if

$$k + f(a + x) - f(x) - af'(x) \geqslant 0 \quad \text{for all positive } a \text{ and all } x.$$

For such $k$-convex functions, Scarf has shown that if the expected shortage and holding cost functions (i.e. $L(y)$ in (6.7g) for example) are convex but the ordering cost function is $k$-convex, even then the optimal policy is of the $(s, S)$ type for each period.

Again, we have so far considered zero lead time cases. With a lead time of $j$ periods, orders placed in $t-j$ are delivered in $t$. If we assume backlogging of demand and the lead time $j$ known, then the problem with a nonzero lead time has again the structure of an $(s, S)$ policy. However the problem is still unresolved in several respects when the lead time is random [13], or there are multiple reorder points [14], or backlogging is not permitted. Also the extension of the $(s, S)$ type policies to more than one product, when there is interdependence between them on the cost and demand sides still offers a challenging problem. Because of these operational difficulties, the two-bin type $(s, S)$ policies are sometimes given less attention in the practical applications to inventory management problems.

### 6.1.2. Dynamic inventory models

Inventory models are called dynamic, when the time variable enters essentially into the model. This is possible in various ways, e.g. through shifting planning horizons, through variations of demand over time both deterministically (e.g. seasonal variations) and stochastically (e.g. demand is viewed as a time-dependent stochastic process), and through time-interdependence between several interrelated stations (or branches) of a single enterprise (e.g. decomposition problems in dynamic control). The static models discussed in the earlier section are in our view special cases of the more general dynamic models and, as we have mentioned before, the static models of the AHM type have several dynamic features. From the viewpoint of operational applications, the dynamic inventory models involving multiple orders may be usefully categorized [15] into three systems: (a) the Q-system, in which the order size is fixed but the frequency of ordering (i.e. reorder point) is determined by the pattern of fluctuations in demand, (b) the P-system, in which the order period is fixed but the size of the order is allowed to vary with fluctuations in demand, and (c) a mixed system, in which features of the two systems may be combined (e.g. the inventory policy for a seasonal product with peak and slack demands may combine both P- and Q-systems through a fixed review period for inventory monitoring).

As an example of the Q-system model, consider a very special case which can be derived from the AHM model; this is a dynamic version of the classical lot-size formula developed by Wagner and Whitin [16]. Consider a fixed and finite planning horizon of $N$ periods with known demands $r_i$ for a single product in period $i=1,\ldots, N$. Denote by $q_i$ the quantity produced with a positive set up cost $k_i$ if $q_i>0$ and by $I_i$ the level of inventory at the and of period $i$ with $h_i I_i$ as the total inventory holding cost. With $I_0$ as the initial starting inventory at the beginning of the horizon (assumed known), the closing inventory in period $i$ is defined as

$$I_i = I_0 + \sum_{j=1}^{i} (q_j - r_j); \qquad i = 1, \ldots, N.$$

The problem of determining an optimal set $(q_1, \ldots, q_N)$ may then be formulated as one of minimizing the total set-up costs and inventory costs over the fixed horizon subject to the requirements of nonnegativity of production $(q_i \geqslant 0)$ and inventory $(I_i \geqslant 0$, i.e. shortages are to be avoided) for each $i = 1, \ldots, N$.

$$\text{Minimize } C_N = \sum_{i=1}^{N} (k_i x_i + h_i I_i)$$
$$\{q_i\}$$

$$\text{subject to } q_i, I_i \geqslant 0 \quad (i = 1, \ldots, N), \qquad (6.9)$$

where

$$x_i = \begin{cases} 0, & \text{if } q_i = 0 \\ 1, & \text{if } q_i > 0. \end{cases}$$

This problem can be solved by the dynamic programming algorithm outlined before. Several modifications of this type of model have been considered in the literature. First, this type of linear programming formulation to balance the costs of inventories and shortages with those of changing production and marginal production costs have been extended [17] to additional cost components [18] such as the regular payroll, hiring, lay-off, overtime and the deviations from desired inventory and production rates (e.g. the HMMS model discussed in ch. 3.2) and to alternative forms of the inventory cost function (e.g. the inventory cost is proportional to the time integral of the positive inventory level rather than to the closing inventory level) and to more than one product and one production sequence [19].

A convex programming formulation of a production-inventory model analogous to the system (6.1) has been formulated and applied by Charnes, Cooper and Symonds [20]. This model does not have set-up costs but introduces instead general production cost functions $c_i(q_i)$ for each period $i = 1, \ldots, N$ which are assumed to be convex and twice differentiable (i.e. $dc_i(q_i)/dq_i > 0$ and $d^2c_i(q_i)/dq_i^2 > 0$) and the demand rate $r_i$ is assumed probabilistic with a constant probability density $g_i(r_i)$ which is assumed independent for different periods $i = 1, \ldots, N$. Also, the total inventory carrying cost $(\bar{I}_i)$ is assumed proportional to the average inventory level, i.e.

$$\bar{I}_i = \tfrac{1}{2}(I_i + I_{i-1}); \qquad \begin{array}{l} I_i = \text{closing inventory at the end of period } i \\ i = 1, \ldots, N. \end{array}$$

The CCS model then minimizes the total expected cost over the fixed horizon to determine the set of optimal quantities $(\bar{q}_1, \ldots, \bar{q}_N)$ under certain chance-constrained restrictions.
The model is as follows:

$$\text{minimize}_{\{q_i\}} \text{EC}_N = \int_{r_1} \cdots \int_{r_N} \left[ \left\{ \sum_{i=1}^N [c_i(q_i) + h\bar{I}_i] \right\} g_1(r_1) \ldots g_N(r_N) \, dr_1 \ldots dr_N \right]$$
(6.10a)

where $\quad I_i = I_0 + \sum_{j=1}^i (q_j - r_j), \quad i = 1, \ldots, N,$

and $\quad h = \text{constant unit cost associated with } \bar{I}_i,$

subject to the

shortage restriction: $\quad \text{Prob} \left[ I_0 + \sum_{j=1}^i (q_j - r_j) \geqslant I_{min} \right] \geqslant \alpha_i$ (6.10b)

and the

storage restriction: $\quad \text{Prob} \left[ I_0 + \sum_{j=1}^i (q_j - r_j) \leqslant I_{max} \right] = 1,$ (6.10c)

where $i = 1, \ldots, N$; $\alpha_i = $ a set of preassigned (e.g. 95 percent level) confidence levels and $I_{min}, I_{max}$ are the desired minimum and maximum levels of inventory respectively (assumed preassigned). The CCS model seeks optimal decision rules in the form

$$q_1 = y_1 \quad \text{and} \quad q_i = r_{i-1} + y_i \quad (i = 2, \ldots, N)$$ (6.10d)

where $y_i$ $(i = 1, \ldots, N)$ is a set of constants to be determined optimally. Once the optimal, $y_i$'s, are known, the decision rules (6.10d) are used to determine each output rate $q_i$ after the demand levels $r_1, \ldots, r_{i-1}$ have materialized and are known. (Note, however, that decision rules of type (6.10d) are not the only ones possible; others are conceivable as in the HMMS decision rules discussed in ch. 3.2.)
Substituting (6.10d) in (6.10b) the shortage restriction becomes

$$\text{Prob} \left[ r_i \leqslant I_0 - I_{min} + \sum_{j=1}^i y_j \right] = F_i \left[ I_0 - I_{min} + \sum_{j=1}^i y_j \right] \geqslant \alpha_i$$

where $F_i(w_i) = \text{Prob}(r_i \leqslant w_i)$ and this can be written as

$$I_0 - I_{min} + \sum_{j=1}^i y_j \geqslant F_i^{-1}(\alpha_i) \quad (i = 1, \ldots, N)$$ (6.10e)

where $F_i^{-1}(\alpha_i)$ is a set of constants. Similarly the storage restriction (6.10c) can be written as

$$I_0 - I_{max} + \sum_{j=1}^{i} y_j \leqslant \min r_i \qquad (i = 1, ..., N). \qquad (6.10\text{f})$$

Further, since $q_i$ must be nonnegative, it is necessary to impose the further restrictions

$$y_1 \geqslant 0 \quad \text{and} \quad \text{Prob}\,[r_{i-1} + y_i \geqslant 0] = 1 \qquad (i = 2, ..., N)$$

which can be written as

$$y_1 \geqslant 0 \quad \text{and} \quad \min r_{i-1} - y_i \geqslant 0 \qquad (i = 2, ..., N). \qquad (6.10\text{g})$$

Now we have to substitute our decision rules (6.10d) into the objective function (6.10a). The production cost component $c_i(q_i)$ becomes

$$c_1(y_1) + \sum_{i=2}^{N} (r_{i-1} + y_i),$$

the expected value of which is

$$c_1(y_1) + \sum_{i=2}^{N} \int_{r_i-1} c_i(r_{i-1} + y_i)\, g_{i-1}(r_{i-1})\, \mathrm{d}r_{i-1}.$$

This expected value function is a separable convex function of $y_i$, since the function $c_i(q_i)$ is convex in each $q_i$; also $I_i$ depends linearly on $y_i$ and the demand rates and hence it is separable convex in each $y_i$. Therefore the objective function (6.10a) can be written as a sum of separable convex functions $f_i(y_i)$ i.e.

$$\underset{\{y_i\}}{\text{minimize}}\, EC_N = \sum_{i=1}^{N} f_i(y_i), \quad \text{where} \quad \mathrm{d}^2 f_i(y_i)/\mathrm{d}y_i^2 > 0. \qquad (6.10\text{h})$$

The final reduced form model is then a convex programming problem in $y_i$ $(i=1, ..., N)$, where the separable convex function $EC_N$ in (6.10h) is minimized under the linear restrictions (6.10e) through (6.10g), where min $r_i$ are constants determined in a manner analogous to the determination of terms such as $F_i^{-1}(\alpha_i)$. Such convex programming problems can be solved by the various methods discussed in ch. 3.

Two comments may be made about this general model. First, the objective function specified here as the minimization of expected cost may be generalized to include the variance or fractiles of the distribution and if the demand rates $r_i$ are subject to stochastic processes over time such that $Er_i$ is a specified function of time, then the objective function may need appropriate modification. Second, it is important to note that this CCS model seeks optimal solutions in the class of linear decision rules (6.10d) i.e. optimal $q_i$ is computed and known only after the demands $(r_1, ..., r_{i-1})$ have materialized and are known. So long as the basic structure of the convex program is unchanged, other types of decision rules may obviously be considered, e.g. $q_i$ as a linear function of $q_{i-j}, r_{i-j}$ and $y_{i-k}$ with $j = 1, 2, ..., (i-1)$ and $k = 1, 2, ..., i$ with known weights.

Our survey of selected models of the Q-system would be incomplete if we did not mention a generalized ordering model developed by Dvoretzky, Kiefer and Wolfowitz (DKW model), which in many ways generalizes the theoretical structure of the AHM model. In one of the simpler versions, the DKW model [21] considers a dynamic single product situation with zero lead time and with a finite number of decision intervals. The demand in period $i$ is described by a conditional probability distribution function (assumed known)

$$g_i(r \mid B_i); \qquad i = 1, ..., N$$

where the vector $B_i = (x_1, ..., x_i; \; y_1, ..., y_i; \; r_1, ..., r_{i-1})$ specifies the past history in the form of past demand $(r_1, ..., r_{i-1})$ up to period $i-1$ and stock levels before ordering $(x_i)$ and after ordering $(y_i)$ up to period $i$. Define the following quantities related to the past history of demands and stock levels, i.e.

$$\bar{B}_i = (x_1, ..., x_i; \qquad y_1, ..., \underline{y_{i-1}}; \qquad r_1, ..., r_{i-1})$$
$$\bar{\bar{B}}_i = (x_1, ..., x_i; \qquad y_1, ..., y_i; \qquad r_1, ..., \underline{r_i})$$

where any specific values (i.e. realizations) of $\bar{B}_i$ and $\bar{\bar{B}}_i$ are denoted by $\bar{\beta}_i$ and $\bar{\bar{\beta}}_i$ respectively. Note that the quantities $(x_2, ..., x_N)$ are functions of variables such as $y_i$ and $r_i$ which are random. Thus $x_2$ is a function of at least $y_1$ and $r_1$, $x_3$ a function of at least $y_2$ and $r_2$ and so on. Now the expected cost in period $i$ is a function of the form

$$C_i(x_i, y_i \bar{\bar{B}}_{i-1} = \bar{\bar{\beta}}_{i-1}) \quad \text{also denoted as} \quad C_i(x, y)$$

where

$$\bar{\bar{B}}_{i-1} = (x_1, ..., x_{i-1}; \qquad y_1, ..., y_{i-1}; \qquad r_1, ..., - r_{i-1}).$$

An ordering policy is defined by a set of functions

$$\{Y_i(x) \mid \bar{\bar{B}}_{i-1} = \bar{\bar{\beta}}_{i-1}\}; \qquad i = 1, ..., N,$$

which is also denoted by $Y(x)$, such that in the $i$th interval when the past history is $\bar{\bar{B}}_{i-1} = \bar{\beta}_{i-1}$ one orders the amount

$$y_i = Y_i(x_i \mid \bar{\bar{B}}_{i-1} = \bar{\beta}_{i-1}) - x_i; \qquad i = 1, ..., N$$

where $Y_i(x) \geqslant x$ for all $i$ and $x$; $\bar{\bar{B}}_0 = \bar{\beta}_0$ means that there is no restriction and $x_i$ is always of the form

$$x_i = \max(y_{i-1} - r_{i-1}, 0).$$

It is now possible to define the expected cost associated with a given policy and hence an optimal policy. Starting with the last period, the optimal solution is constructed by means of a dynamic programming algorithm using a series of one-dimensional minimizations with respect to $y_i$, e.g. at the $i$th stage of the process a one-dimensional minimization must be performed for each combination of the initial conditions specified by $(\bar{\bar{B}}_{i-1}, x_i)$. Sometimes the computational burden can be reduced by performing one-dimensional minimization at any stage $j$ within $\varepsilon$ for a given constant $\varepsilon > 0$. For instance, assume that the optimal quantities (denoted by asterisks) $Y_{j+1}^*, ..., Y_N^*$ ($j \geqslant 1$) have been determined such that with a given (scalar) number $\varepsilon > 0$ and the $N$th stage, the optimal policy is

$$y_N = Y_N^*(x_N \mid \bar{\bar{B}}_{N-1} = \bar{\beta}_{N-1})$$

with

$$C_N(x_N, y_N) \leqslant \inf_y C_N(x_N, y) + \varepsilon/N$$

where inf denotes infimum (or minimum). Now after the optimal policies $(Y_{j+1}^*, ..., Y_N^*)$ are known for any $j \geqslant 1$, then we can choose an optimal policy by the optimality principle of dynamic programming as

$$y_j = Y_j^*(x_j \mid \bar{\bar{B}}_{j-1} = \bar{\beta}_{j-1})$$

so that

$$C_j(x_j, y_j; Y_{j+1}^*, ..., Y_N^*) \leqslant \inf_y C_j(x_j, y; Y_{j+1}^*, ..., Y_N^*) + \frac{\varepsilon}{N}.$$

This gives us a recursive method of constructing functional equations for computing optimal policies for different stages. This method of finding optimal policies may be simple only in very special cases, e.g. when the expected cost function $C_i(x, y)$ is independent of $i$ and $\bar{\bar{B}}_{i-1}$ for all $i$ and the demand levels $r_i$ are independently and identically distributed (in which case this method essentially reduces to the functional equation (6.7g) in section 6.1.1 which can be explicitly computed by assuming specific probability distributions for demand $r_i$). Yet as a general method which in principle is computable, this characterization of the DKW model is of great analytic importance. This is especially true since this method has been extended to include cases of infinitely many time intervals, several commodities, finite lead times and cases of unknown distributions of demand.

Now we consider some cases of the P-system of inventory control, in which a fixed order period is optimally determined while the order size is allowed to vary in response to fluctuations in demand. The P-system is completely determined when it is known what the optimal order period is and what the amount in stock and on order should be. Two important characteristics of the P-system of inventory control which are different from the Q-system should be noted, although in actual empirical cases considerations such as convenience of administrative management of inventory rules and other noneconomic factors may sometimes render it very difficult to determine which system is the most realistic. First, in the P-system it is necessary to have safety reserve stock both for the order period (i.e. the reorder time point or time interval) and the lead time period, since there is no flexibility in order period once it is determined (in the Q-system, safety reserve stock needs be carried only for the lead time period). Second, the fact that variables such as demand and order for any given period have interactions with those variables over subsequent periods requires more attention in the P-system of inventory control to the cumulative and sequential effects of time. In particular this may require sequential revision of policies and more simulation-type analysis, because it may be difficult to determine from time-series data on demand the specific form of interdependence. However, we should note that so far as mathematical techniques of optimization (e.g. nonlinear programming) are concerned, those we have discussed before in the various static and dynamic models are still applicable in appropriate situations. The dynamic programming algorithm is a general tool, which is readily applicable to the case in which demand for different periods follows any specified stochastic process. Hence, we will not analyze the P-system models in any detail.

The time-pattern of fluctuations of demand, which requires special attention in the P-system models, can be characterized by various methods, including the Markov-process type of transition probability analysis and the non-Markovian stochastic processes. An important special case of the Markov process analysis is the convolution method of incorporating interactions between demand distributions for different periods (when the probability distribution is constant over periods). Since the stochastic process methods in general are discussed in section 6.3, we consider here only the method of convolutions.

Consider $r_1$ and $r_2$ as two continuous independent random variables $(0 \leqslant r_1, r_2 \leqslant \infty)$ representing demand levels in two periods with continuous probability densities $(f_1(r_1), f_2(r_2))$ and the moment-generating functions $F_1(s)$ and $F_2(s)$ defined as

$$F_i(s) = \int_0^\infty \exp(-sr_i) f_i(r_i) \, dr_i; \qquad i = 1, 2. \tag{6.11a}$$

We intend to determine the moment-generating function of the sum $y = r_1 + r_2$, since this will enable us to characterize the distribution of the sum $(r_1 + r_2)$ and hence its different moments. Now since $r_2 = y - r_1$ is nonnegative, $r_1$ has to range from 0 to $y$ so that the probability density of $y = r_1 + r_2$ is

$$f(y) = \int_0^y f_1(r_1) f_2(y - r_1) \, dr_1.$$

Its moment-generating function using formula (6.11a) is

$$F(s) = \int_0^\infty \int_0^y f_1(r_1) f_2(y - r_1) \exp(-sy) \, dr_1 \, dy = F_1(s) \cdot F_2(s).$$

This result holds quite generally for $n$ independent random variables $r_i$ with moment generating functions $F_i(s)$, where the sum $y = (r_1 + \cdots + r_n)$ has the moment generating function

$$F(s) = F_1(s) \dots F_n(s) \tag{6.11b}$$

from which the density function $f(y)$ of $y$ can be computed. In the special case in which each $r_i$ has the same density $f(r_0)$, say, the formula (6.11b) becomes $F(s) = F_0^n(s)$ and in this case the density $f(y)$ of $y$ is called the $n$-fold *convolution* of $f(r_0)$ and is usually denoted by $f^{(n)}(r_0)$.

Now consider the following simple representation of total cost (TC) in a P-system model, in terms of $x$, the amount ordered, and $v$, the amount of reserve stock, due to Starr and Miller [15], where total cost for a single commodity is computed over a one-year planning horizon, unit costs of carrying (reserve) stock ($h$), ordering ($c$) and of running out of stock ($k$) are fixed, the lead time is $m$ and the average weekly demand is $\bar{r}$ (i.e. the annual average demand is $52\,\bar{r}$):

$$TC = \frac{52\,\bar{r}c}{x} + \tfrac{1}{2}x \cdot h + v \cdot h + \frac{52\,\bar{r}}{x} \cdot k \int_{t\bar{r}+v}^\infty f^{(t)}(y) \, dy \tag{6.11c}$$

where it is assumed that the demand distribution is known for a basic one-week period and

$t = m + x/\bar{r}$, i.e. lead time + order period in weeks,

$f^{(t)}(y)\,dy = t$-th convolution of the basic demand distribution $f(y)$ for a week,

$h$ = carrying cost assumed to be measured on a yearly basis.

The four components of annual costs specified in equation (6.11c) are respectively (a) the annual ordering cost, (b) the annual carrying cost for the stock to meet average demand, (c) the annual carrying cost of the reserve stock and (d) the annual cost of running out of stock. Note that when the sum of demand over any $m$ periods exceeds $(m\bar{r} + x)$, we have shortage and this explains the component of annual out-of-stock cost in (6.11c).

The optimal solutions $x^*$ and $v^*$ are obtained by minimizing total cost TC in (6.11c) with respect to both variables $x$ and $v$ simultaneously, i.e. $x^*$ and $v^*$ must satisfy the first order necessary conditions

$$(\partial TC/\partial x)_{x=x^*} = 0; \quad (\partial TC/\partial v)_{v=v^*} = 0. \tag{6.11d}$$

However, these equations may be very difficult to solve without some knowledge about the specific form of the convolution of the demand distributions. Assuming a basic normal distribution for weekly demand with mean $\bar{r}$ and standard deviation $s$, an approximate interative method of solving (6.11d) may be indicated. For in this case

$$f^{(t)}(y)\,dy = \left[\frac{\bar{r}}{s^2(x + m\bar{r})2\pi}\right]^{\frac{1}{2}} \exp\left[\frac{-(y - \bar{r})^2\sqrt{\bar{r}}}{2(x + m\bar{r})s^2}\right]dy. \tag{6.11c}$$

Using this expression in the total cost equation TC in (6.11c) we may minimize total cost with respect to $v$ (the amount of reserve stock), which gives

$$f\left(\frac{v\sqrt{\bar{r}}}{s\sqrt{x + m\bar{r}}}\right) = \frac{h(x + m\bar{r})^{\frac{3}{2}} \cdot s}{52k(\bar{r})^{\frac{3}{2}}}. \tag{6.11e}$$

Again, equating the derivative of TC with respect to $x$ to zero gives

$$\frac{h}{104\bar{r}}\left[1 + \frac{v}{x + m\bar{r}}\right] = \frac{c}{x^2} + \frac{k}{(x + m\bar{r})^2}\left[1 - F\left(\frac{v\sqrt{\bar{r}}}{s\sqrt{x + m\bar{r}}}\right)\right]. \tag{6.11f}$$

The iterative calculations may start with any trial estimate for a value of $x = x^{(1)}$, say, determined by the optimal lot-size formula; then we may solve for $v = v^{(1)}$ from (6.11e) by using $x^{(1)}$. Using $v^{(1)}$ in (6.11f) we solve for an $x = x^{(2)}$, say, and so the iterations continue. If the TC function is concave and differentiable, then this method can be shown to converge very fast to the pair of optimal values $(v^*, x^*)$ satisfying (6.11e) and (6.11f) simultaneously.

Some comments are in order. First, if the basic demand distribution is not normal, the convolution $f^{(t)}(y)\,dy$ of demand distributions may be very difficult to determine in a form suitable for operational calculations; hence approximations of nonnormal distributions by means of a combination of normal distributions are sometimes attempted. Nonparametric and distribution-free methods are yet to be applied in this field. Second, the problem of estimating (i.e., forecasting) the parameters of the convolution of demand distributions through sample values is a separate problem which has to be solved before an empirical application of such inventory rules is considered.

All the dynamic models of production-inventory decisions discussed so far have assumed implicitly that the firm operates in a market which is perfectly competitive. The economists' theory of different types of competition and its implications for dynamic stability of the market as a whole may now be related. We will analyze now some models of production and inventory policy for a firm under perfect and imperfect competiton with alternative patterns of expectation. This analysis is due to Mills [22] and others [23] who have initiated the basic approach of integrating the economists' theory of the firm with that of the operations researcher.

Consider first a simple deterministic model of a single product firm under perfect competition with a finite horizon of $N$ periods with no discounting, in which production costs $(c(z_n))$ in one period are assumed independent of the volume of production in other periods and production cost functions $(c(z_n))$ and inventory cost functions $(r(I_n))$ are assumed unchanged over time, although prices may change in the future. Total profits $Q_N$ of the firm over the entire discrete horizon $[1, N]$ may be written

$$Q_N = \sum_{n=1}^{N} \left[ \bar{p}_n x_n - c(z_n) - r(I_n) \right] \qquad (6.12a)$$

where $\bar{p}_n$ is the unit price expected by the firm in period $n$ (this expected price is assumed nonstochastic), $x_n = $ sales (i.e. quantity sold) and $z_n = $ production (i.e. quantity produced), both during the $n$th period, $c(z) = $ total cost of producing $z$ units in any period and $r(I) = $ total cost of storing $I$ units between any two consecutive periods. Both $c(z)$ and $r(I)$ are assumed strictly convex and differentiable functions of their arguments.

In the simplest case the firm's decision problem is to determine the optimal values $(z_n^*, x_n^*, I_n^*)$ of $z_n$, $x_n$ and $I_n$ which maximize total profits

$Q_N$ in (6.12a) under the restrictions

$$x_n, z_n, I_n \geq 0; \qquad (n = 1, ..., N) \qquad (6.12b)$$

$$I_n = I_{n-1} + z_n - x_n; \qquad n = 1, ..., N; \qquad I_0 \text{ given.} \qquad (6.12c)$$

Eliminating $x_n$ from (6.12a) by using (6.12c) and then applying the necessary conditions of the Kuhn-Tucker theorem, it is seen that the optimal values $(z_n^*, x_n^*, I_n^*; n = 1, ..., N)$ when they exist must satisfy

$$\bar{p}_n - c_n(z_n^*) \leq 0, \quad \text{where} \quad c_n(z_n) = \partial c(z_n)/\partial z_n; \qquad n = 1, ..., N \qquad (6.12d)$$

$$\bar{p}_{n+1} - \bar{p}_n - r_n(I_n^*) \leq 0; \qquad n = 1, ..., N-1;$$

$$\text{where} \quad r_n(I_n) = \partial r(I_n)/\partial I_n \quad \text{with} \quad z_n^*, I_n^* \geq 0. \qquad (6.12e)$$

The assumptions of convexity of the cost functions imply that any solution of the system (6.12d), (6.12e) if feasible (i.e. nonnegative) must provide at least a local maximum of (6.12a) rather than a minimum. Taking the interior solutions only (or disregarding the restriction (6.12b)) the conditions (6.12d) and (6.12e) may be written

$$\bar{p}_n - c_n(z_n^*) = 0, \qquad n = 1, ..., N \qquad (6.12f)$$

$$r_n(I_n^*) = \bar{p}_{n+1} - \bar{p}_n, \qquad n = 1, ..., N - 1 \qquad (6.12g)$$

which state the familiar marginal cost conditions in the economists' theory of the firm, i.e. price must equal marginal cost for every period $n$ and the marginal storage cost must equal the change in expected prices between the two consecutive periods. More generally it is possible to combine (6.12d) and (6.12e) since production cost functions $c(z_n)$ are independent over time, i.e.

$$c_n(z_n^*) + r_n(I_n^*) \geq c_{n+1}(z_{n+1}^*); \qquad n = 1, ..., N - 1 \qquad (6.12h)$$

which states that it is never worthwhile to produce in period $(n+1)$ an amount whose marginal production cost exceeds the marginal cost of producing a unit in the previous period and storing it at a marginal storage cost of $r_n(I_n^*)$.

Now consider linear marginal cost functions

$$\partial c(z)/\partial z = c_1 z, \quad \partial r(I)/\partial I = r_1 I, \quad \text{where} \quad c_1, r_1 \text{ are positive constants.}$$
$$(6.12i)$$

Denote a nonnegative (feasible) solution of the system (6.12d) and (6.12e) by

$(z_n^0, I_n^0)$, which can be explicitly written down in this case as

$$z_n^0 = \bar{p}_n/c_i \quad \text{and} \quad I_n^0 = \max(\bar{p}_{n+1} - \bar{p}_n, 0). \tag{6.12j}$$

Now consider the whole industry as an aggregate of single-product firms, of which the typical firm's cost functions and feasible decision variables are given in (6.12h) and (6.12j). Assume that all firms within the industry have marginal production costs proportional to output as in (6.12i), though the coefficient $c_1$ may be different for different firms. Under this assumption the total industry output $z_n^T$ would be

$$z_n^T = \sum_{k=1}^{T} z_n^{(k)} = \bar{p}_n \sum_{k=1}^{T} (1/c_1^{(k)}); \quad \text{superscript } k \text{ denotes } k\text{th firm}$$

$$k = 1, \ldots, T \text{ (number of firms)}$$

$$= \bar{p}_n/c \quad \text{say}, \quad 1/c = \sum_{k} (1/c_1^{(k)}). \tag{6.12k}$$

Similarly,

$$I_n^T = \max\left[\frac{\bar{p}_{n+1} - \bar{p}_n}{r}, 0\right], \quad 1/r = \sum_{k} (1/r_1^{(k)}). \tag{6.12l}$$

Hence the industry supply $(x_n^S)$ function in period $n$ is

$$x_n^S = z_n^T + I_{n-1}^T - I_{n-1}^T. \tag{6.12m}$$

The industry demand $(x_n^D)$ curve is assumed to be linear in current actual price $(p_n)$ rather than the expected price $(\bar{p}_n)$:

$$x_n^D = a - bp_n; \quad a, b \text{ are nonnegative constants.} \tag{6.12n}$$

The market clearing condition is also introduced for each period $n$

$$x_n^D = x_n^S. \tag{6.12o}$$

Now the stability behavior of the competitive industry characterized by (6.12k) through (6.12o) can be analyzed under alternative assumptions about the relationship between the actual and expected price for each period, e.g. (i) all price expectations are correct in the sense that $p_n = \bar{p}_n$ for all $n = 1, \ldots, N$ and (ii) price expectations are on the average correct in the sense $p_n = \bar{p}_n + u_n$ where $u_n$ is a random variable independently and identically distributed from period to period with a zero expected value.

Considering the first case $p_n = \bar{p}_n$ for all $n$, we get from (6.12k) through (6.12o)

$$a - bp_n = p_n/c + \max\left(\frac{p_n - p_{n-1}}{r}, 0\right) - \max\left(\frac{p_{n+1} - p_n}{r}, 0\right). \tag{6.13a}$$

This nonlinear second-order difference equation in price must be satisfied if price expectations are to be fulfilled each period. The equilibrium price in the market is the stationary solution of (6.13a) obtained by putting $p_n = \bar{p}$ for all $n$ ($\bar{p} = $ a constant), i.e.

$$\bar{p} = ac/(1 + bc). \tag{6.13b}$$

At this equilibrium price firms in the competitive industry hold no inventories and the price that clears the market is unaffected by the cost of carrying inventory.

The second order nonlinear difference equation (6.13a) must have two initial conditions, say $p_0$ and $p_1$, and since the equation (6.13a) is piecewise linear, different initial conditions imply different linear equations. For instance, if the two initial prices $p_0$ and $p_1$ both equal the equilibrium price $\bar{p}$ in (6.13b), then this equilibrium price will continue until exogenous factors disturb the market. But if this equilibrium is disturbed, the price behavior implied by (6.13a) becomes explosive in an upward direction. Mills [22] has proved an important theorem in this regard:

*Theorem 6.2*

For any initial conditions $p_0$ and $p_1$, neither of which is equal to the equilibrium price $\bar{p}$ in (6.13b) but for which a solution to the second order equation (6.13a) exists, price is unstable in an upward direction.

To obtain a heuristic proof of this result, consider the following difference equation derived from (6.13a):

$$p_{n+1} - (2 + r/c + rb)\, p_n + p_{n-1}\, ar = 0 \tag{6.13c}$$

the homogenous part of which has the characteristic equation in $\lambda$

$$\lambda^{n+1} - k_1 \lambda^n + \lambda^{n-1} = 0, \qquad k_1 = 2 + r/c + rb > 2$$

with two characteristic roots

$$\lambda_1 = k_1 - \varepsilon, \quad \lambda_2 = \varepsilon \quad \text{where} \quad k_1 - 2\varepsilon = \sqrt{(k_1^2 - 4)} > 0 \quad \text{and} \quad 0 < \varepsilon < 1.$$

Hence the complete solution of (6.13c) is

$$p_n = A_1 \lambda_1^n + A_2 \lambda_2^n + \bar{p}, \quad \text{where } \bar{p} \text{ is given in (6.13b)} \tag{6.13d}$$

and

$$A_1 = (\lambda_2 - \lambda_1)^{-1} \left[ (p_0 - \bar{p})\, \lambda_2 - (p_1 - \bar{p}) \right],$$
$$A_2 = (\lambda_2 - \lambda_1)^{-1} \left[ (p_0 - \bar{p}) - \lambda_1 (p_0 - \bar{p}) \right]$$

where the constants $A_1$, $A_2$ depend on $p_0, p_1, \lambda_1$ and $\lambda_2$. Note that $\lambda_1 > 1$ and

$\lambda_2 > 0$, hence the solution of (6.13d) is explosive, for some set of initial constants $A_1, A_2$ determined by the initial values $p_0, p_1$. If we assume $p_1 > p_0$, then it can be shown that the cases $p_1 > \bar{p} > p_0$, $p_0 > \bar{p}$ and $\bar{p} > p_1 > p_0$ would contradict either (6.13a) or (6.13c) and (6.13d).

This result has two important implications concerning the perfectly competitive system. First, the instability associated with the competitive industry may be present in different intensities depending on the divergence between $p_n$ and $\bar{p}_n$ and this fact should be given some importance in the analysis of macroeconomic stabilization policies and industrial price control measures. Second, as soon as uncertainty concerning price is introduced in the form of less than perfect equality between $p_n$ and $\bar{p}_n$, e.g.

$$p_n = \bar{p}_n + u_n; \qquad u_n \sim \text{zero mean, independent} \qquad (6.13e)$$

we get an equation analogous to (6.13a), namely

$$a - bp_n + v_n = \bar{p}_n/c + \max\left(\frac{\bar{p}_n - p_{n-1}}{r}, 0\right) - \max\left(\frac{\bar{p}_{n+1} - p_n}{r}, 0\right) \qquad (6.13f)$$

where $v_n$ is a random variable having the same properties as $u_n$, i.e. an identical and independent distribution from period to period and a zero mean, where $v_n$ occurs in the industry demand function

$$x_n^D = a - bp_n + v_n.$$

The solution of the system (6.13f) has the features of price instability we have observed before in (6.13c), but it has additional features stemming from the variance around the equilibrium price. The instability due to variance may be reduced sometimes by postulating a price expectation pattern different from that mentioned in (6.13e).

Now consider the case of imperfect competition under which a firm is assumed to face a demand curve of the form (assuming a static case first)

$$x = X(p) + u \qquad (6.14a)$$

where $x$ is the quantity demanded, $p$ is the price set (which now is another decision variable for the firm) and $u$ is a random term. The firm is assumed to know the distribution function $f(u, p)$, such that when it sets the price $p$, it can compute the expected amount of demand and other estimates. It will be assumed that $u$ is independent of $p$. Let $z$ be the quantity produced; then the revenue $R(z, p)$ realized is

$$R(z, p) = \begin{cases} px, & \text{if} \quad x \leqslant z \\ pz, & \text{if} \quad x \geqslant z \end{cases} \qquad (6.14b)$$

and assuming a continuous distribution for demand, the expected revenue is

$$ER(z, p) = pX(p) F(z - X(p)) + p \int\limits_{-\infty}^{z - X(p)} uf(u) \, du$$

$$+ pz \left[ 1 - F(z - X(p)) \right] \qquad (6.14c)$$

where

$$u = z - X(p) \quad \text{and} \quad F(w) = \int\limits_{-\infty}^{w} f(u) \, du.$$

Denoting by $c(z)$ the total production cost, the expected value of profits is

$$EQ = ER(z, p) - c(z) = pX(p) - pD(z, p) - c(z);$$

$$D(z, p) = \int\limits_{z - X(p)}^{\infty} (u - z + X(p)) f(u) \, du. \qquad (6.14d)$$

The firm's decision variables are those values of $p$ and $z$ which jointly maximize expected profits in (6.14d). The necessary conditions give

$$F(z - X(P)) = (p - \partial c(z)/\partial z)/p$$

which states that the firm's price and output policy should make the probability of shortage $u = z - X(p)$ equal to the ratio of marginal cost to price. When there are nonnegativity restrictions on some variables, again the Kuhn-Tucker conditions may be applied.

In the dynamic model with multiperiod horizon we have to incorporate the effects of current operations on future profitability by some means; one possible method is to define the total available supply $y_n$ in period $n$ as $y_n = z_n + I_{n-1}$ and then to introduce a cost function $h(y_n - x_n)$ associated with the $n$th period's terminal inventory $(y_n > x_n)$ or shortage $(y_n < x_n)$. The expected profit $EQ_n$ in the $n$th period can then be written as

$$EQ_n = p_n X(p_n) - p_n D(y_n, p_n) - c(y_n - I_{n-1})$$

$$+ \int\limits_{-\infty}^{\infty} h(y_n - X(p_n) - u_n) f(u_n) \, du_n - g(y_n - I_{n-1} - z_{n-1}).$$

This is the dynamic analogue of equation (6.14d), where the function $g(z_n - z_{n-1})$ denotes the costs of changing the production rates between periods. Again we have to obtain the equilibrium price and output of the firm by the simultaneous solution of

$$\frac{\partial EQ_n}{\partial p_n} = 0 \quad \text{(or more generally, } \frac{\partial EQ_n}{\partial p_n} \leqslant 0\text{)} \qquad n = 1, ..., N \qquad (6.15b)$$

and

$$\partial EQ_n/\partial y_n = 0 \quad \text{(or more generally, } \partial EQ_n/\partial y_n \leqslant 0\text{)} \qquad n = 1, ..., N. \quad (6.15c)$$

Sometimes it may be possible to write the approximate solutions in terms of decision rules of the form

$$p_n = H_1(z_{n-1}, I_{n-1}), \quad z_n = H_2(z_{n-1}, I_{n-1}) \qquad (6.15d)$$

where $H_1$ and $H_2$ are certain functions appropriately approximating the above two equations (6.15b) and (6.15c). Whenever this approximation (6.15d) is possible, statistical estimation through regression techniques may be applied (e.g. HMMS decision rules). If the approximations (6.15d) could be taken to be linear and the firms could be aggregated into an imperfectly competitive industry, then these functions could be given an aggregative industry-wide interpretation, e.g.

$$p_n = H_1(z_{n-1}^T, I_{n-1}^T), \quad z_n^T = H_2(z_{n-1}^T, I_{n-1}^T) \qquad (6.15e)$$

where the superscript $T$ denotes the aggregate of firms. Several empirical calculations and simulated studies have been done by Mills using this type of argument and the results are of great interest.

Two comments may be added. First, the empirical testing of such a hypothesis as (6.15e) on the basis of industry-wide data is very difficult and the methodology is yet to be improved in this regard. Cross-section applications would be more useful in our opinion. Second, the aggregate inventory behavior over time should be related to other basic variables such as investment, capacity changes and the general pattern of inter-industry fluctuations.

### 6.1.3. Inventory models with interdependence of sales

We consider in this section a few models of production-inventory decisions under both static and dynamic conditions when there is oligopolistic inter-dependence of sales between firms through product differentiation and selling cost. This offers another basic approach attempted by S. S. Sengupta [23] and others towards integrating the economists' theory of monopolistic competition with the operations researchers' models of the production and inventory decisions of a firm. Our analysis in this section is based mostly on the work of S. S. Sengupta.

Consider the static case of a firm's decision problem, where the market is oligopolistic and the product is differentiated. The individual firm's decision variables are the price $p$ to set for its product and the selling cost $c$ to incur in a given period under the market situation characterized by the following assumptions:

(i) sellers advertise only the characteristics of their products; they do not communicate with respect to their prices and selling costs and the competition between sellers is only over sales, i.e. over the money spent by the customers;

(ii) every buyer has his own maximum demand price $P^*$ and the buyers compare the prices of those firms they approach (buyers approach the sellers directly with no intermediaries);

(iii) the product-differentiation is of such a nature that the buyers have roughly equal preferences for the products of all the sellers they approach;

(iv) the seller quotes an identical price to every unit of buying inquiry (i.e. a unit of demand is a unit of buying inquiry that materializes as a sale at the price quoted) that arrives during a planning period and a customer with $k$ units of inquiry is treated by the seller as $k$ customers, each with one unit of inquiry; and

(v) the sellers all produce on order so that there is no inventory holding (this assumption is relaxed later on).

Now we ask how to determine the likelihood of a sale by the individual firm in question when the customers may randomly choose between different firms. Let $p$ be the unit price of the firm and $q(j)$ be the maximum demand price of the $j$th customer for the product of the firm in question. Let $\bar{q}(j) = \{q_1(j), ..., q_r(j)\}$ denote the $j$th customer's maximum demand prices for the $r$ other firms approached, where $\bar{p} = \{p_1, ..., p_r\}$ denotes the price quotations of $r$ other firms. It is assumed that the customer decides to buy according to the criterion: $\min[p - q(j), p_1 - q_1(j), ..., p_r - q_r(j)]$. Note that from the viewpoint of the firm in question, the variables $\bar{p}$, $q(j)$ and $\bar{q}(j)$ are random. Now since the seller with the lowest price will obtain the sales, the likelihood of a sale (denoted by $\mu_s(p)$) by the firm in question to a randomly arriving inquiry depends upon the joint likelihood of two events,

$$\text{Prob}(p < \min(p_1, ..., p_r)) \quad \text{and} \quad \text{Prob}(p \leqslant q(j)); \quad \text{i.e.,}$$

$$\mu_s(p) = \left[ \int_p^\infty \cdots \int_p^\infty f_1(p_1, ..., p_r) \, dp_1 ... dp_r \right] \left[ \int_p^\infty f_2(q) \, dq \right] \qquad (6.16a)$$

where

$f_1(p_1, ..., p_r)$ = probability density of the joint distribution of competitors' prices,

and

$f_2(q(j)) = f_2(q)$ = probability density of the maximum demand price for a given customer.

Averaging this likelihood $\mu_s(p)$ over the ensemble (or aggregate) of customers would define the probability $\mu(p)$ of acceptance $0 < \mu(p) < 1$.

Since each unit of inquiry is forced to reject or accept a quotation by a given firm, the probability $\Pr(S; v, p)$ that $S$ units are sold in $v$ inquiries is given by

$$\Pr(S; v, p) = \binom{v}{S} [\mu(p)]^S [1 - \mu(p)]^{v-S} \qquad (6.16b)$$

where $v$, the number of inquiries, is a random variable. A simple model for determining the probability distribution of $v$ is a Poisson process

$$\Pr(v = n) = \lambda^n \exp(-\lambda)/n! \qquad (6.16c)$$

which allows the average number $\lambda$ of units of inquiry per period (where the period may be chosen to coincide with the firm's planning period) to determine its parameters. This 'average rate of arrival' of inquiry is assumed to depend on selling efforts of all the firms, i.e. $\lambda = \lambda(c)$, where $c$ is the selling cost per unit of sale. Hence combining (6.16b), (6.16c) and $\lambda = \lambda(c)$ we get

$$\Pr(S; c, p) = \sum_{n=0}^{\infty} \left[ \binom{n}{S} [\mu(p)]^S [1 - \mu(p)]^{n-S} \frac{[\lambda(c)]^n}{n!} \exp(-\lambda(c)) \right] \qquad (6.16d)$$

where $\lambda = \lambda(c)$ is to be understood as the expected number of arrivals of customers per period as a function of selling cost $c$ per unit of sale. The relation (6.16c) may be written more simply as

$$\Pr(S; c, p) = \frac{[A(c, p)]^S}{S!} \exp[-A(c, p)] = g(S; c, p), \quad \text{say}, \qquad (6.16e)$$

where $A(c, p) = \lambda(c) \mu(p)$ is the average rate of sales with a price quoted at $p$ and unit selling cost $c$.

Now the total profit $Q$ may be easily defined by introducing a production cost function $K(S)$ related to the level of sales, as a function of $S$, the number of units sold, i.e.

$$Q = Q(p, c) = pS - K(S) - cS; \qquad cS = \text{total selling cost}. \qquad (6.16f)$$

Hence the expected profit is

$$EQ = \sum_{S=0}^{\infty} [pS - K(S) - cS] \, g(S; c, p)$$

$$= [pA(p, c) - cA(p, c)] - E[K(S)] = R - C, \quad \text{say,} \quad (6.16g)$$

where $R = pA(p, c) - cA(p, c)$ is expected gross revenue and $C = EK(S)$ is the expected cost. The decision variables are $p$ and $c$. If the gross revenue function $R$ is strictly concave and the expected cost function $C$ is convex, so that $EQ$ is strictly concave, then this problem can be uniquely solved. Again the Kuhn-Tucker theorem and its various extensions could be applied. If the solutions exist and the functions $R$ and $C$ are differentiable, then the following necessary conditions should hold at a stationary interior point:

$$\frac{\partial EQ}{\partial p} = \frac{\partial R}{\partial p} = \lambda(c) \left[ p \frac{d\mu}{dp} + \mu(p) \right] = 0$$

note: $A(c, p) = \lambda(c) \mu(p)$

$$\frac{\partial EQ}{\partial c} = \frac{\partial R}{\partial c} - \frac{\partial C}{\partial c} = \mu(p)(p - L - c) \frac{d\lambda}{dc} - A(p, c)$$

where

$$L = \sum_{t=1}^{\infty} M(t, t-1) \cdot \frac{[A(p, c)]^{t-1}}{(t-1)!} \exp(-A(p, c)),$$

and

$M(t, t-1) = K(t) - K(t-1)$ is marginal production cost of $t$-th unit.

However in a very general case with inequalities as boundary conditions, these equations would in general be complicated and some numerical methods would be necessary.

Now inventory holdings may be introduced in the model in the same way as was followed in equations (6.14b) and (6.15a) in Mills' models. For instance, one way would be to redefine equation (6.16f) as

$$Q = -K(z) - cS + \begin{cases} pS, & \text{if } S \leqslant z \\ pz, & \text{if } S \geqslant z \end{cases} \qquad (6.16h)$$

where $z$ is the quantity produced and $S$ is the quantity sold.

A dynamic analogue of this representation is possible by noting first that the sales probabilities could be viewed in the multiperiod case in terms of transition probabilities and secondly that a dynamic model of the profit equation developed in equation (6.15a) could be easily applied.

For instance, assume that the sales variable $S(p, c)$ can be represented by a Markovian stochastic process and further that the sequence in which price and selling expenses are varied has no effect on the probabilistic behavior of the sales process. Then since for large $S$ the density function $g(S; c, p)$ in (6.16e) tends to be normal, $S(p, c)$ may be represented as a normalized variable, i.e.

$$S(p, c) = A(p, c) + \varepsilon_1 \sqrt{A(p, c)}, \qquad \varepsilon_1 : N(0, 1)$$

where $\varepsilon_1$ is a unit normal random variable. Similarly the effect of variations in $p$ and $c$ on sales can be represented in the large $S$ case as

$$S(p + h, c) = A(p + h, c) + \varepsilon_2 \sqrt{A(p + h, c)}; \qquad \varepsilon_2 : N(0, 1)$$

$$S(p, c + k) = A(p, c + k) + \varepsilon_3 \sqrt{A(p, c + k)}; \qquad \varepsilon_3 : N(0, 1)$$

$$S(p + h, c + k) = A(p + h, c + k) + \varepsilon_4 \sqrt{A(p + h, c + k)}; \qquad \varepsilon_4 : N(0, 1)$$

where $p, h, c, k$ are given quantities. Now consider the conditional probability of sales due to a change of policy, given the sales under the current policy. If this conditional probability distribution has finite first two moments, i.e.

$$m[p, c, S(p, c)] = \lim_{\substack{h \to 0 \\ k \to 0}} E\left[ \frac{S(p + h, c + k) - S(p, c)}{|h| + |k|} \right., \quad \text{given that}$$

$$\left. S(p, c) = a \right] \qquad (6.16i)$$

$$\sigma^2[p, c, S(p, c)] = \lim_{\substack{h \to 0 \\ k \to 0}} E\left[ \frac{\{S(p + h, c + k) - S(p, c)\}^2}{|h| + |k|} \right., \quad \text{given that}$$

$$\left. S(p, c) = a \right] \qquad (6.16j)$$

when it is given that sales $S(p, c)$ equal the value $a$, then it is possible by Doob's theorem [24] to represent the stochastic process of a change in sales $dS(p, c)$ as

$$dS(p, c) = m_1 \, dp + m_2 \, dc + \sigma_1 \, dY_1(p) + \sigma_2 \, dY_2(c) \qquad (6.16k)$$

where $m_1, \sigma_1$ denotes the quantities defined in (6.16i) and (6.16j), when only $p$ (also $h$) is varied and $m_2, \sigma_2$ when only $c$ (hence $k$) is varied; further, $Y_1(p)$ and $Y_2(c)$ represent interval valued stochastic processes whose increments $dY_1, dY_2$ are mutually independent normal random variables. This representation (6.16k) may now be used either in equation (6.15a) before, as in Mills' model, to compute expected net profits in each period or in equation (6.15e) in section 6.1.1 to compute the expected sum of discounted net profits over a planning horizon. These expected profits may then be optimized with respect to price ($p$), unit selling cost ($c$) and quantity produced ($z$).

A few comments may be made about the production-inventory models under oligopolistic interdependence considered in this section. First, the dynamic multiperiod models have yet to be empirically tested over actual industrial data before the optimal decision rules derived therefrom can be recommended for policy. Second, the role of nonprice offers and conjectural variations, familiar in the theory of duopoly and oligopoly, is yet to be incorporated in the theoretical framework. Third, the role of mergers and possible cooperative game-theoretic rules is yet to be explored in a basic sense in this field. Once again, simulation studies [22] offer an interesting challenge in this area.

### 6.1.4. *Econometric models of manufacturers' inventories*

In this section we present a few econometric models which attempt to specify through sets of regression equations some of the major factors influencing industrial investment in inventories. These econometric models are essentially empirical and based on industry-level aggregate data. If an industry fulfilled reasonably well the conditions of pure competition and there was not much product differentiation, then knowledge of the market share of a typical firm could be used to specify the time behavior of aggregate production and inventories within the industry by appropriate rules of aggregation. In this sense the aggregative econometric models offer indirect though not conclusive evidence about the major decision variables identified as optimizing variables in the single firm models of inventory control discussed in ealier sections. Further, the aggregative econometric models of manufacturers' inventories help to identify the major explanatory factors responsible not only for fluctuations in aggregate inventories but also for other variables such as investment and capacity changes.

As an illustration of the first type of econometric model, we may refer to the interesting application of Mills' approach [22] to the published quarterly statistical data on the United States cement industry from 1927 (2nd quarter) through 1941 (fourth quarter) comprising wholesale prices ($p_n$), production ($z_n$), sales ($x_n$), inventories ($I_n$) and also expected sales, i.e. forecast sales in period $n$, ($\bar{x}_n$). There is a strong seasonal pattern in the production, sales and inventory series for cement for the period considered and the actual monthly data are aggregated to form a quarterly series. Questions may of course be raised about the validity of the time series of published sales expectations ($\bar{x}_n$), the characterization of seasonality in the time series data and the best methods of specifying and estimating a model using such long run data. Although several alternative models are now available, yet from the point of view of simplicity the following linear model estimated by Mills using single equation least-squares estimation methods is of great interest:

$$\hat{z}_n = 68.8^* + 0.791^* x_n + 0.156^* z_{n-1} - 0.234^* I_{n-1}; \qquad R^2 = 0.964$$
$$(6.179)(0.068) \qquad (0.026) \qquad (0.068) \qquad\qquad d = 1.98$$
$$(d = \text{Durbin-}$$
$$\text{Watson}$$
$$\text{statistic})$$

$$(6.17a)$$

$$\hat{p}_n = 47.7^* + 0.015 x_n - 0.016 z_n - 0.032^* I_{n-1} + 0.560^* p_{n-1};$$
$$(9.988)(0.012) \quad (0.013) \quad (0.014) \qquad (0.100)$$
$$R^2 = 0.571$$
$$d = 2.27$$

$$(6.17b)$$

and

$$\hat{z}_n = -48.8^* + 0.255^* \bar{x}_n + 0.478^* z_{n-1} + 0.553^* I_{n-1};$$
$$(20.27) \ (0.102) \qquad (0.121) \qquad (0.132)$$
$$R^2 = 0.531$$
$$d = 1.82$$

$$(6.17c)$$

$$\hat{p}_n = 43.9^* + 0.008 \bar{x}_n - 0.010 z_n - 0.031^* I_{n-1} + 0.601^* p_{n-1};$$
$$(9.85) \ (0.007) \qquad (0.007) \quad (0.014) \qquad (0.105)$$
$$R^2 = 0.572$$
$$d = 2.22$$

$$(6.17d)$$

$^*$ = significant at the 5% level.

Several remarks may be made about these estimates. First, the price equations (6.17b) and (6.17d) have all their coefficients with correct signs, although the lagged price term ($p_{n-1}$) appears to be more important than any other explanatory variable in explaining the total variance of $p_n$. Also, the inventory coefficients are both significant. Second, the production relation (6.17a) appears to be better than (6.17c), in terms of both higher $R^2$ and the negative sign of the inventory coefficient which is expected on theoretical grounds. Comparisons of regression forecasts with naive forecasts, not reported here, also show that the published data on expected sales ($\bar{x}_n$)

provide less accuracy of forecast in general than do the implicit expectations represented by $x_n$ and $p_{n-1}$.

Several other applications to industries such as pneumatic tires, Southern pine lumber and department store shoes have been made by Mills [22]. If anything, these applications suggest the need for further empirical work in this field. On the one hand, the dynamics of inventory holdings are influenced in the real world by a host of factors, e.g. the time lags between output and sales, the rate of unfilled orders and backlogs, the different motives for holding inventories, market expectations and ownership patterns. On the other hand, there is a definite need for analyzing overall business cycle fluctuations into their components, and investment in inventories is one of the most dynamic components in the short run cyclical framework.

Using changes in deflated goods output (i.e. GNP less services and construction) during the intervals between peaks and troughs to measure the cycle periods, Darling and Lovell [25] find for the United States data on income and output (from the *Survey of Current Business*) that shifts from investment to disinvestment in business inventories accounted for about 60 percent of the shrinkage in aggregate demand for goods output during the four recessions 1948–1949, 1953–1954, 1957–1958 and 1960–1961, whereas during the first year of four periods of business expansion, shifts from disinvestment to investment in stocks accounted for about 58 percent of the increase in total demand for goods. This shows how the success of any short-run stabilization policy would depend on the precision of its inventory investment equations.

Lovell [26] has considered several regression models based on quarterly data in billions of 1954 dollars with changes in inventory investment ($\Delta I$) as the dependent variable and several explanatory variables for both durable and nondurable manufacturing sectors. Denoting the equilibrium (or desired) inventory level by $\bar{I}$, the lagged inventory by $I_{-1}$, the constant ratio of equilibrium inventory ($\bar{I}$) to sales volume ($S$) by $b$ and using a flexible accelerator sort of adjustment, i.e.

$$\Delta I = d_0 \cdot (\bar{I} - I_{-1}); \qquad 0 < d_0 < 1$$
$$= d_0 bS - d_0 I_{-1}. \tag{6.18a}$$

The influence of other explanatory variables can be brought into this framework. Taking the ratio of unfilled orders ($O_U$) to sales volume as a rough measure of the delivery lag, one may hypothesize that the desired inventory to sales ratio depends on the delivery lags and other factors of market tightness, as in

$$I/S = b + c(O_U/S) + gK_M,$$ (6.18b)

where $K_M$ denotes manufacturing output as a percent of capacity (i.e. it is a measure of capacity developed by Frank de Leeuw which may be taken as a proxy for other factors reflecting market uncertainties). Combining (6.18a) and (6.18b),

$$\Delta I = d_0 bS + d_0 cO_U + d_0 gK_M - d_0 I_{-1}.$$ (6.18c)

Using quarterly data from 1950 (third quarter) to 1961 (fourth quarter) the following selected estimates may be presented here:

*Durable manufacturing sector*: (1950(III) to 1961(IV))

$$\Delta I^M = -3.54 - 0.077 I^M_{-1} + 0.180 S^M_R - 0.239 G_R + 0.181 D + 0.088 K_M S_R$$
$$(0.029) \quad (0.049) \quad (0.131) \quad (0.045) \quad (0.021)$$

$R^2 = 0.733$, standard error $= 0.370$; $d =$ Durbin-Watson statistic $= 1.70$ (6.19a)

$$\Delta I^M = -1.075 - 0.238 I^M_{-1} + 0.107 S^M_R - 0.402 G_R + 0.013 D$$
$$(0.052) \quad (0.047) \quad (0.149) \quad (0.059)$$
$$+ 0.074 \Delta O^M_{RU} + 0.065t + 0.064 K_M S^M_R$$
$$(0.020) \quad (0.016) \quad (0.021)$$

$R^2 = 0.808$, standard error $= 0.323$; $d = 1.68$ (6.19b)

where, $I^M =$ inventory stock in durable manufacturing in billions of dollars, $S^M_R =$ shipment by manufacturers of durable goods in billions of dollars deflated by the wholesale price index of manufacturers' durable goods with base year 1954, $G_R =$ Department of Defense net expenditures on development, research, test and evaluation in billions of dollars deflated by the wholesale manufacturers' price index, $D =$ Department of Defense obligations in billions of dollars, $O^M_{RU} =$ unfilled orders of durable goods industries deflated by the wholesale manufacturing price index and $t =$ time in quarters.

*Nondurable manufacturing sector*: (1950(III) to 1961(IV))

$$\Delta I^N = -1.169 - 0.050 I^N_{-1} + 0.042 S^N_R - 0.417 \Delta O^N_{RU} + 0.329 O^N_{RU}$$
$$(0.049) \quad (0.020) \quad (0.077) \quad (0.074)$$

$R^2 = 0.582$, standard error $= 0.176$; $d = 1.87$ (6.20a)

$$\Delta I^N = 1.543 - 0.116 I^N_{-1} + 0.008 S^N_R - 0.431 \Delta O^N_{RU} + 0.320 O^N_{RU}$$
$$(0.062) \quad (0.078) \quad (0.082) \quad (0.094)$$
$$+ 0.004 K_M S^N_R + 0.0005t S^N_R$$
$$(0.037) \quad (0.0004)$$

$R^2 = 0.626$, standard error $= 0.171$; $d = 1.85$, (6.20b) where the superscript N denotes nondurable manufacturing for those variables already defined above.

Note that these estimates show the correct signs for the marginal desired inventory coefficients (i.e. $d_0$ in the coefficient $d_0b$ in (6.18c)), the significant role of the order variable $O_{RU}$ (which appears to be more important for the nondurable manufacturing finished goods) and the use of the capacity utilization factor as an explanatory variable in the durable manufacturing sector. However, more work is still needed on methods of incorporating the various motives for holding inventories [27] through indirect estimates of opportunity costs for holding inventories of different types (e.g. purchased materials and goods in process, buffer stock inventories of finished goods, and unintended inventories).

More econometric work is also needed to analyze the process of transmission of inventory fluctuations from the retailers to the manufacturers' level. A study of inventory fluctuations in department stores in the United States by Mack [28] for selected periods during 1947–1961 showed that orders placed by retailers for merchandise led retail sales by an average of seven months at peaks and were nearly synchronous at troughs. This suggests an asymmetry in transmission of the pattern of demand (i.e. order) magnification and contraction which seems to require more investigation and research.

## 6.2. *Optimal capacity expansion policies* [1]

This section presents an analytical appraisal of the various theories of optimal capacity expansion policies for an individual firm. Here, as in the theory of inventory models, there is a need to integrate the approaches of the economist and the operations researcher and our objective will be to present in the light of such needs the operational implications of some of the recent growth models of the firm and to suggest some lines of generalization. However, we will exclude for the most part probabilistic variations in demand and other variables, so that our models will all be deterministic; also, the problems of peak-load pricing [29], production-scheduling and econometric estimation will not be considered here.

We begin with a general outline of capacity expansion models, which are divided into three broad groups: (a) static capacity models, (b) capacity expansion models with scalar optimization over time, and (c) capacity models

---

[1] This section is based on a paper by J. K. Sengupta and A. Sen [30] with some modifications.

with optimal intertemporal paths. Then we present a technical appraisal of the models and consider their generalization from an operational viewpoint.

### 6.2.1. General outline of capacity models

Consider a single-product firm with only two inputs: (a) the stock of one indivisible factor which determines the plant size and (b) the flow of current input that is utilized contemporaneously with the output produced. Denote the following variables:

$p$        = price per unit of output;

$d(p, a(t))$ = demand function with $a(t)$ a shift variable over time;

$[k]$      = a vector $(k_1, k_2, ..., k_T)$, where $k_t$ measures the size of plant at time period $t = 1, 2, ..., T$;

$[q]$      = the output vector $(q_1, q_2, ..., q_T)$, where $q_t$ denotes output produced in period $t = 1, 2, ..., T$;

$T$        = the span of the planning horizon;

$x_t$      = the physical dimension of the current input at period $t = 1, 2, ..., T$;

$q_t$      = $q_t(x_t, k_t)$ the production function; and

$r$        = given discount rate.

Some of the assumptions which are common to most of the models surveyed here are as follows:

(i) the prices of both current and stock inputs are fixed over time and there is no change in technology, so that the production function is invariant over time and the form of the function is known in advance; hence the corresponding short-run cost function $E_t = \min_{x_t} E(k_t, q_t(x_t, k_t))$ is completely specified in each period;

(ii) the shift-factor $a(t)$ is a single-valued known function of time, so that the total revenue function $R_t$ can be written as $R_t = p \cdot d(p, a(t))$;

(iii) the efficiency of a plant is in no way affected in subsequent periods by its rate of use in any of the $t$ periods. This assumes away user cost and makes the distribution of $[k]$ independent of $[q]$; and

(iv) only a single nonstorable product is produced. This assumes away problems of optimal inventory holding and those of product-mix considerations.

Given these assumptions (some of which may be relaxed in later stages) there are essentially three decision vectors, $[x]$, $[k]$ and $[q]$, and the problem of optimal capacity expansion of the firm may be characterized in several ways, of which the following two are especially important [31]:

(a) For each vector $[q]$ we determine the optimum (i.e., least cost) combination of [x] and [k] by minimizing the total discounted cost over the fixed planning horizon subject to the restrictions set by the production function. Then at the second stage an optimum output vector [q] is chosen by maximizing the total discounted profit over the planning horizon, given the demand conditions; and

(b) for each vector [k] in the feasible region, we determine the optimum time path of [q] by equating at each time $t$ the partial derivatives of $R_t$ and $E_t$ with respect to output. (If at any $t$, they are equated at negative output, the $q_t$ programmed for that period would be zero.) We then compare the optimum output programs for different [k] and choose that [k] with corresponding [x] and [q] that maximizes total discounted profits.

The two approaches lead to the same result, for they are equivalent two-stage formulations of a more general one-step constrained maximization problem, in which [x], [k] and [q] are optimized to subject the restraints of the production function and the given demand function. Historically, the first line of approach is associated with the theory of production, while the second line of approach is resorted to in the theory of capital.

Now of the three decision variables $x_t$, $q_t$ and $k_t$, the first two are continuously variable while $k_t$ is discontinuously variable. In the theory of capital, several different types of variability of a given capital equipment are considered [32]:

(i) There is only one capital equipment, of a constant efficiency type and with a given technically determined life $L$. We can distinguish two subcases: (a) $L = \infty$ (infinite durability). Hence [k] is determined by one parameter, the size of capital equipment $\bar{k}$ say, and $[k] = [\bar{k}, \bar{k}, ..., \bar{k}]$, since $k_1 = k_2 = = ... k_T = \bar{k}$ whatever may be the value of $T$; and (b) $L \geqslant T$ (sufficient durability). Here also [k] assumes the same form as in (a) above but the cost of [k] will be determined by both $\bar{k}$ and $L$.

(ii) A constant efficiency, identical capital equipment is installed at $t = L$, $2L, 3L, ...$ up to $nL$ where $nL \leqslant T \leqslant (n+1) L$. When $T$ is finite $n$ will also be finite and this is called a 'finite chain', while when $T \to \infty$, $n \to \infty$, and we have an 'infinite chain'. The vector [k], however, retains the same form, but here the cost of [k] will be determined by $\bar{k}$ (the identical size), $L$ (the fixed life) and $r$ (the discount rate).

(iii) The capital equipment is of a decreasing efficiency type with a given durability, $L$. Here again we distinguish two subcases: (a) $L \geqslant T$, i.e., no replacement is contemplated. Here $k_t$ will be determined by two parameters, $k_0$, the size of capital equipment at the time of installation, and $t$, the age of the machine; and (b) $L < T$. We do not consider this case.

(iv) All capital equipments are of a constant efficiency type and one of in-finite durability (or of sufficient durability to maintain constant efficiency up to the end of $T$) and a finite or infinite chain of capital units of the same size are installed at equally spaced intervals; $[k]$ will then be determined by (a) the size of the capital unit and (b) the time period between two successive building dates. If we assume that size is additive, then $[k] = [\bar{k}, \bar{k}, \ldots; 2\bar{k}, 2\bar{k}, \ldots; 3\bar{k}, 3\bar{k}, \ldots; \ldots; n\bar{k}, n\bar{k} \ldots, n\bar{k}]$ where $n\hat{\imath} \leqslant T \leqslant (n+1)\hat{\imath}$, $\hat{\imath}$ being the equally spaced time interval.

Note that if all capital equipments are of a constant efficiency type and of infinite (or sufficient) durability, $k_t$ will be nondecreasing over time. When they have a fixed life but are of a constant efficiency type, the vector $[k]$ will depend not only on the new value of $\bar{k}$ (the size variable) but also on the new value of $L$ that may be chosen.

Now consider the variability of the other two variables, $q_t$ and $x_t$. In our general model the demand function is determined by two variables. If we drop the shift variable, our demand function looks more like the usual demand function under static (or simple) expectation. Alternatively, we may introduce a once-for-all shift in the demand function. Such a once-shifting demand function is used for comparing two positions of steady-state equilibria in the comparative static analysis. If this once-for-all shift is related to the entry of firms in the open period, we have a demand function under polypolistic expectation in the Hicksian sense [33]. But so long as we want to retain the shift variable as a single-valued function of time, the clas-sical analysis of market structures does not fit in with our general optimiza-tion model, for in the classical theory, the shift variable is related not only to the entry and exit of firms producing identical or similar products (the so-called 'industry effects') but also to the structure of the market and the price-output strategy of the firm. Even when we assume away oligopolistic expectation to arrive at the classical long-run equilibrium, the marginal conditions of equilibrium for each firm must be supplemented by the total condition of equilibrium for the industry as a whole.

What happens if we drop the price variable instead of the shift variable from our demand function? On the face of it the demand function looks like the type that is now increasingly used in the operations research literature, especially in the inventory models, in which the output requirement (or the order rate) is often shown as a single-valued function of time alone. But the exclusion of the price variable may mean different things. Thus in Chenery type models [34], in which demand can neither be backlogged, nor met from inventory accumulated from previous production, the optimum output program [q] collapses to the demand function $d(t)$, so that the optimization problem reduces to the usual cost-minimization problem. Chenery justifies such an approach by the possibility of price-inelasticity of demand, desire to maintain market share and public service motivation. In the Arrow, Beckmann and Karlin model [35], the $d(t)$ function only provides the upper limit of the optimum output program, [q]. In Manne type models [36–38] demand can be backlogged at a finite (penalty) cost, which is equivalent to assuming that the deficit can be met by importing from abroad. In Smith type models [39], the $d(t)$ function has the same role as in the Chenery model, specifying fixed output requirements over time.

As regards the specific form of the $d(t)$ function, the simplest assumption is that it is constant over time. Such an assumption may be extremely useful in the theory of production for finding the optimal time path solution of $x_t$ and $k_t$. A more useful form of $d(t)$ for a capacity-expansion policy model is one in which its first derivative (or as in Srinivasan's model [40], its logarithmic first derivative) is constant over time. In some of the models, $d(t)$ is distributed as a sine law over time and in one model, the only restriction on $d(t)$ is that it is nondecreasing over time [38]. Lastly, the geometric rate of growth of demand is the decision variable in Baumol's growth equilibrium decision model [41].

As regards the variability of $x_t$ we note that it is generally ignored. Chenery's reason is the assumption that the cost of $x_t$ is negligible in relation to the cost of $k_t$. Manne assumes $x_t$ to be strictly proportional to $q_t$, so that the total expenditure on current output has the same discounted value for a given [q] and thus can be regarded as a fixed charge for the optimization problem. The only decision variable is [k] and only the cost associated with it appears in the objective function of the policy-maker. Thus, we are here at the opposite pole from the textbook theory of the firm, in which the cost associated with the capital input is a fixed charge and the only variable item in the cost function is on account of $x_t$. In the Arrow, Beckmann and Karlin model also, strict proportionality between output and current input is assumed. Only in Smith type models does $x_t$ retain the pride of place and what is sought there is the optimum level of $x_t$ relative to $\bar{k}$, for in the usual Smith type model, [k] assumes the steady-state form $[\bar{k}, \bar{k}, ..., \bar{k}]$.

A brief outline of the types of models considered may now be presented. Not all the models surveyed in this paper are strictly capacity expansion policy models. In Smith type models the ultimate interest is in the relative levels of $x_t$ and $k_0$ or $\bar{k}$. Following the Lutzes, Smith calls such models 'the choice of technique models'. We refer to them as 'static capacity models'.

Of the capacity expansion policy models, some use classical optimization techniques to obtain the optimal values of the decision variables, others use the functional equation approach of Bellman to determine the optimal capacity schedule over time. The following classification of models is adopted from now on for convenience:

A. Static capacity models:

1. Single plant: { (a) Smith model (M1)
                   { (b) Miller model

2. Chain of plants:    Smith model (M2)
3. Exponential life case: Haavelmo model

B. Capacity expansion models with scalar optimization:
   (a) Chenery model
   (b) Manne-Erlenkotter model
   (c) Srinivasan model
   (d) Baumol model

C. Capacity expansion models with an optimal path approach:
   (a) Arrow-Beckmann-Karlin model
   (b) Manne-Vienott model
   (c) Zabel model

Since in none of the above models except Miller's does price appear as an explicit variable, the major departure of the above models from the usual microeconomic models is in assuming away price. In capital theory we aggregate over different operational periods. If we want to retain price as a variable, classical optimization techniques can be applied only under the assumption that all these operational periods are alike, so that maximization of profit in one operational period will maximize total discounted profit also. Alternatively we have to assume that maximization of profit in one operational period is independent of the maximization of profit in other periods. In Carlson's [42] celebrated monoperiodic production theory, this assumption is made explicit by assuming that all inputs are of the same order of variability.

The introduction of period-dichotomy, by which Harrod [43] in his famous 1934 paper tried to solve the problem, is misleading in its simplicity. According to his two-fold marginal conditions of equilibrium for a source of supply, short-period marginal cost is equated to short-period marginal revenue for determining the rate of utilization of a given lay-out and long-period marginal cost is equated to long-period marginal revenue for determining the appropriate long-run lay-out or the long-run output of a source of supply. But nowhere does he make clear what he means by long-period marginal revenue. Presumably its value will depend on the short-period outputs produced in each operational period. But the latter are determined, assuming a given lay-out, by the scale of the plant which is tangential to the long-run (or envelope) cost curve at the hypothetical long-run output. We are thus involved in a simultaneity problem of the worst sort.

As the Lutzes [32] have shown, it is possible to rescue the classical long-period theory from this mess if the planning period is subsumed within the lifetime of a plant and all capital expenditures are made in the initial period. The most profitable plant size will then be determined by maximizing the good will $G(k_0)$ of the plant with respect to $k_0$, the size of the plant, i.e.

$$G(k_0) = \int_0^T [R(p, t, q) - E(q; k)]\, e^{-rt}\, dt + S(T)\, e^{-rt} - C(k_0) \tag{6.21}$$

where $S(T)$ = the scrap value of the plant at $T$.

In each period $q_t$ is determined by equating the partial derivatives of $R(t)$ and $E(q, k)$ with respect to output. For a finite chain of plants of the same size $\bar{k}$, the maximand is (assuming $S(t)$ is the same at $t = L, 2L, ..., nL$)

$$G(\bar{k}) = \left[ \left\{ \int_0^L [R(p, q, t) - E(q; \bar{k})]\, e^{-rt}\, dt - C(\bar{k}) + S\, e^{-rL} \right\} \right.$$
$$\left. \{1 + e^{-rL} + \cdots + e^{-nrL}\} \right] \tag{6.22}$$

where $nL \leqslant T \leqslant (n+1)\, L$.

If $t = \infty$, then

$$G(\bar{k}) = \frac{1}{1 - e^{-rL}} \left[ \int_0^L [R(p, q, t) - E(q; \bar{k})]\, e^{-rt}\, dt - C(\bar{k}) + S\, e^{-rL} \right]. \tag{6.23}$$

Once again $q_t$ is determined in the same way as in (6.21).

It does not make much of a difference in the formulation whether the capital equipment is of a constant-efficiency or a decreasing-efficiency type. In the latter case, the only change will be in the $E$ function which must be rewritten as $E(q, \bar{k}, t)$, where $t$ allows for the decrease in efficiency owing to the age of the equipment.

If the sizes of plants installed at different dates are not the same but not more than one capital unit exists at a given time, an analogous formulation to (6.23) will be

$$G([k]) = \int_0^T [R(p, q, t) - E(q, t, k)]\, e^{-rt}\, dt - C([k]) + S[k]. \tag{6.24}$$

However, now the decision variable is no longer a scalar but a vector and the only way to solve the problem is by some kind of iterative procedure.

Another common feature of the policy models considered here is the assumption that all capital equipments are of a constant efficiency, given durability type. In the usual capital theory, the crucial variable is the optimal durability of the capital equipment. By bypassing the question of durability, the optimal scale of plant and its time-phasing is uniquely determined in equations (6.21), (6.22), (6.23) and (6.24). But since in real life most capital is of a 'decreasing efficiency' type, the economic life of equipment is often a decision variable.

### 6.2.2. *Structure of models*

*A.    Single plant static capacity model*:

The crucial assumption of this type of model is that all capital expenditures are made in the initial period so that the decision variable is the size of plant at the time of initial installation. The major work in this field has been done by Smith [39]. We shall present here a generalized version of the Smith type model. The assumptions are:

 (i) the output requirements over time, $d(t)$, are given up to $T$;

 (ii) only one plant is built at the time of initial installation;

 (iii) there is only one current input $x$. The price of $x$ at time $t$ is $w_t$ and this function is known at the beginning of the planning period for all $t$, $0 < t < T$; and

 (iv) the rate of discount $r$ is given ($r > 0$).

Then $q = q(x, k)$ and from this function the $E$ function, i.e. the short-run cost function, can be derived by minimizing current cost $E_t$, i.e. $E_t = \min_x E(q, k_t, w_t)$ where $k_t$ is uniquely determined by $k_0$ (the size of the initial installation) and $t$ (the age of the machine).

The object of the entrepreneur is to minimize $Z$

$$Z = \int_0^T \left[ w(t)\,x(t)\,e^{-rt}\,dt - \lambda \{ q(x_t, k_t - d(t)) \}\,dt \right] + C(k_0) \qquad (6.25)$$

where $C(k_0)$ is the cost of building a plant of size $k_0$.

The optimal path of $x_t$ is derived by applying Euler's condition for minimizing $Z$. By substituting in (6.25), the reduced cost function is minimized with respect to $k_0$. We can then derive

$$\frac{\int_0^T w_t q_2(x_t; k_0) e^{-rt} dt}{q_1(x_t, k_0)} = C'(k_0) = dC(k_0)/dk_0 \qquad (6.26)$$

where

$$q_1 = \partial q(x_t, k_0)/\partial x_t \quad \text{and} \quad q_2 = q_2(x_t, k_0) = \partial q(x_t, k_0)/\partial k_0.$$

The above relation can be simplified by making additional assumptions, such as,

(v) $w_t = w$ for all $t$, i.e., $x$ has a fixed price;

(vi) the plant is of a constant efficiency type, i.e., $k_t = k_0$ for all values of $t$ up to $T$;

(vii) $T$ can be taken as infinity; and

(viii) $C(k_0) = ck_0$, where $c$ is a constant, i.e., the cost of installation is strictly proportional to size.

Assumptions (v) and (vi) reduce (6.26) to

$$\frac{wq_2(x, k_0)}{q_1(x, k_0)} = \frac{1 - e^{-rT}}{r} = C'(k_0). \qquad (6.26a)$$

(Since $w_t = w$ and the $E$ function is invariant over time, $x_t = x$ for all $t$.) Lastly the assumptions (v), (vi), (vii) and (viii) reduce (6.26) to

$$\frac{wq_2(x, k_0)}{q_1(x, k_0)} = rc. \qquad (6.26b)$$

More interesting results are obtained if we assume a more specific form of the production function.

$$q_t = Ax_t^{\frac{1}{2}} k_0^{\frac{1}{2}} \qquad A, x_t, k_0 \geqslant 0. \qquad (6.27)$$

We can now compare (a) the optimal production plan when the output requirement is constant at $d$ with (b) the optimal production plan when the output requirements $d(t)$ oscillate according to a sine law about $d$ with a period of $2\pi/\theta$ and an amplitude of $\gamma$.

Retaining the assumptions (i) to (viii), the optimum size of installation $k_0$ under a static production level is $(d\sqrt{w})/Ar$, while the optimum size of plant under the sine wave pattern demand curve $d(t) = d(1 + \gamma \sin \theta t)$ is

$$k_0^{**} = \frac{d\sqrt{w}\sqrt{B}}{Ar} = k_0^* \sqrt{B} \qquad (6.28)$$

where

$$B = 1 + \frac{2r\theta\gamma}{r^2 + \theta^2} + \frac{2\theta^2\gamma^2}{r^2 + 4\theta^2}.$$

Consider a similar model formulated by Miller [44]. In this model price as well as the shift variable $a(t)$ enters into the demand function. The specific form of the demand function is

$$d(t) = \frac{1}{g}a(t) - \frac{1}{g}p(t); \quad a(t), g > 0. \tag{6.29}$$

Retaining the assumptions (i) to (viii) and the form of the production function (6.27), the problem before the firm is to choose $k_0$ such that $G$ is maximized, where

$$G = \int_0^\infty [p(t)\hat{q}_t - wx_t] \, e^{-rt} \, dt - ck_0. \tag{6.30}$$

In the above relation $\hat{q}_t$ is chosen by equating marginal revenue and marginal current cost. This gives

$$\hat{q}_t = a(t)/2(g + w/A^2k_0). \tag{6.31}$$

The output program thus depends on $a(t)$ as well as on $k_0$. Next, Miller specifies the $a(t)$ function such that

$$a(t) = a_0(1 + \gamma \sin \theta t). \tag{6.32}$$

When $\gamma = 0$, the optimum output program will be constant and the corresponding optimum level of $k_0$ is given by

$$k_0^* = [Aa_0(w/rc)^{\frac{1}{2}} - 2w]/2A^2B; \quad \text{and} \tag{6.33}$$

when $\gamma \neq 0$,

$$k_0^{**} = (Aa_0(Bw/rc)^{\frac{1}{2}} - 2w)/2A^2g. \tag{6.34}$$

Once again it can be shown that $k_0^{**} \gtreqless k_0^*$ according as $B \gtreqless 1$. But then the average level of output $\hat{\hat{q}}_t$ when $\gamma \neq 0$ will also be greater than, equal to or less than $\hat{q}$, according as $B \gtreqless 1$. When $k_0^*$ is built under a demand curve (6.32), the average output $\hat{\hat{q}}_t = \hat{q}_t$. But with demand curve (6.32), it can be shown that $k_0^*$ is nonoptimal.

A few general remarks about the single plant models may be added. First, none of the above models contains a trend. With a single machine case, it would be unrealistic to assume that demand is growing over time and nothing is done to expand capacity by building a parallel facility.

Second, it may be mentioned here that $d_t = d$ for all $t$ does not simplify (6.26b), for $d(t)$ does not enter into (6.26). However, such an assumption provides a sort of rationale for models with a single machine of constant efficiency. It may be appropriate for a plant of the decreasing efficiency type only when no replacement is contemplated either because $T$ is too short or because of the nature of the demand curve.

**B.    *A chain of plants model* [39]**

The assumptions of this model are:
(i) all capital goods have a fixed technically determined life and have no salvage value. Furthermore, they are identical and of the constant efficiency type;
(ii)  output requirements are constant (i.e., at $d$) over time; and
(iii) the price of the current input is fixed at $w$.

The decision variables are $\bar{k}$, the size of plant, $\bar{L}$, its fixed life, and $x$, the rate of current input.

The object of the entrepreneur is to minimize

$$Z = \int_0^T wx\, \mathrm{e}^{-rt}\, \mathrm{d}t + C(\bar{k}, \bar{L})(1 + \mathrm{e}^{-rL} + \mathrm{e}^{-2rL} + \cdots \mathrm{e}^{-nrL}) +$$

$$\gamma\{d - q(x, \bar{k}, \bar{L})\}, \qquad (6.35)$$

where $n = T/L$ is assumed to be an integer.
If we let $T$ be infinity (6.35) reduces to

$$Z = \frac{wx}{r} + \frac{C(\bar{k}, \bar{L})}{1 - \mathrm{e}^{-rL}} + \gamma\{d - q(x, \bar{k}, \bar{L})\}. \qquad (6.36)$$

Suppose we have fixed $\bar{L}$, i.e., we consider different values of $\bar{k}$ all having a fixed life $\bar{L}$. Then corresponding to (6.26a) of the single machine case we get

$$\frac{C(\bar{k}, \bar{L})}{1 - \mathrm{e}^{-rL}} = \frac{w \cdot q_k(w, \bar{k}; \bar{L})}{r q_x(x, \bar{k}; \bar{L})} \qquad (6.37)$$

where $q_{\bar{k}}$, $q_x$ are partial derivatives of $q$ with respect to $\bar{k}$ and $x$. Similarly we can fix $\bar{k}$, and consider the optimum value of $\bar{L}$.

Under static assumptions, i.e., the demand curve remaining the same, an infinite chain of replacements at equidistant time intervals may be optimum if the output per unit of time is constant over the lifetime of the plant. This is because when the chain is infinite, the capitalized value of the future goodwills will be constant over time and the optimum durability of the successive machines in the chain will be the same. So a chain of plants model is appropriate only under a static continuous flow demand condition.

The Lutzes [32] have shown that even when the plant is of the decreasing efficiency type the optimal durabilities of successive plants will be the same when the chain is infinite. The length of life will then be determined (as in the finite chain case) by the condition that the plant should be discarded as soon as it ceases to earn a quasi-rent which covers interest on its scrap value plus interest on the capitalized value of all the future goodwills – the latter being constant, once again, when the chain is infinite. We have to assume that the demand curve remains the same.

### C.  Exponential life case [45]

An interesting and mathematically tractable case is that in which each capital item is subject to a constant percentage rate of depreciation. This may be realistic if time wears upon the quantity of capital at a constant relative rate, regardless of the intensity of use, and when this wear simply means a corresponding reduction in the volume of physical capital. Alternatively the reduction in efficiency may be due to technical change, and this will show up in the size (amount) of capital when measured by some constant-quality index.

Haavelmo [45] in particular, has considered this type of model. The assumptions of the simplest Haavelmo type model are:

(i) only a particular kind of capital is used and there is no other variable factor of production;

(ii) the amount of capital $k_t$ depreciates at a constant rate $\delta$ per year;

(iii) the cost per unit of capital is fixed at $c$; and

(iv) the production function $q_t = q_t(k_t)$ is the same over time.

The object of the producer is to maximize $G$, where

$$G = \int\limits_{0}^{T} e^{-rt} \left[ pq_t(k_t) - c(r + \delta) k_t \right] dt. \tag{6.38}$$

The necessary condition for a maximum is

$$pq_t'(k_t) - c(r + \delta) = 0, \quad 0 \leqslant t \leqslant T. \tag{6.39}$$

where $q_t'(k_t)$ denotes the partial derivative of $q_t$ with respect to $k_t$.

Hence if capital is perfectly mobile, it will be adjusted instantaneously at $t=0$ and kept constant over the whole horizon $T$. Thus if all prices and the interest rate are going to stay constant, there is no reason for any finite demand for capital. Haavelmo also considers the effects of changes in the rate of interest, and of speculative elements based on expected changes in prices, on the demand for capital.

### D.  Capacity-expansion models

So far in all the models considered, there is only one plant (or capital unit) in any given time period. One crucial feature of the capacity-expansion policy models is that capacity can be expanded by building a parallel plant. This introduces some ambiguity in the concept of the size of $k$. When all plants are identical (i.e., replicas of one another), size can be measured unambiguously only if it is additive, i.e., the efficiency of two identical capital units is the same as the efficiency of a double-sized unit. However, this does not imply that the construction cost of a double-sized unit will be the same as the construction cost of two identical units. In fact, the shape of the (long-run) cost function (e.g. with declining marginal cost) implies that the cost of the doubled size unit will be less.

It may be mentioned here that the term 'efficiency' used in this section need only imply a quasi-ordering. If for all outputs, $E_t(k'_t) = E_t(k''_t)$, then $k'_t = k''_t$ in efficiency. If for some outputs $E_t(k'_t) > E_t(k''_t)$ and for other outputs $E_t(k'_t) < E_t(k''_t)$, then efficiency is not defined. A plant is of constant efficiency if (assuming there is only one plant) $E_1(\bar{k}) = E_2(\bar{k}) = \cdots E_T(\bar{k})$ for all levels of output. Similarly it is of decreasing efficiency if $E_1(\bar{k}) \leqslant E_2(\bar{k}) \leqslant E_3(\bar{k}) \cdots$ $\cdots \leqslant E_T(\bar{k})$, where at least in one case the strict inequality holds.

Henceforth we shall assume that plant size is additive and all plants are of the constant efficiency, infinite durability type. We can now introduce a new variable 'capacity of the firm' which is simply the sum of sizes of plants at any given point in time. The increment in capacity will then be determined by the rate of building plants over time and their scales. The concept of capacity has therefore the following characteristics:

 (i) it is defined for a firm (i.e., not for a plant);

 (ii) it is additive;

(iii) it is nondecreasing over time; and

(iv) it is uniquely determined by the number of plants of each size and the scale of these plants.

We shall also assume that only one plant will be built in any time period. This is quite legitimate if economies of scale exist, so that marginal construction cost is decreasing. With constant returns to scale, the number of plants built is a matter of indifference since both size and cost are additive.

How does the above concept of capacity compare with its usual sense? Different writers at different dates have tried to give a comprehensive list of various shades of meaning attached to the concept of capacity [46–51]. Ignoring such nuances, the concept of capacity in microtheory has generally been related to cost curves in such a way that it serves as an index of an optimal rate of output in the welfare-theoretic sense [48, 52]. On the other hand in macrotheory the concept has been related to an output limit determined by the characteristics of the plant – the limit being determined by pure engineering principles adjusted by some practical considerations regarding operating conditions. The latter concept was first evolved by empirical research on capacity, i.e., by the people who took up the task of measuring capacity, whether for a firm, an industry or a national economy as a whole [53]. But even this concept, like the previous one, amounts to nothing but renaming of certain things that are implicit in the production function – the cost function being only the reduced form of the production function, obtained by applying marginal conditions [45].

Another distinction that is made is between the concept of capacity as measured by inputs and the concept as measured by output. In this paper capacity is an integral over plants of different size, so it is measured by input. But under certain conditions, we can also measure it in terms of output. The general procedure is to define an optimum output for a given scale of plant and to measure capacity output of the plant by that hypothetical output. The difficulty with this procedure is that the cost-minimizing output of a given scale of plant (i.e., the lowest point of the short-run cost curve) does not generally coincide with the level of output at which that scale of plant is optimal (i.e., at which the short-run cost curve is tangential to the envelope or the long-run cost curve). An alternative procedure is to assume fixed proportions, so that the cost curve will be (reversed) L-shaped, and to define the capacity output of a plant at the corner point of the (short-run) cost curve. Similarly, if the cost curve of a firm is stair-step, capacity points occur at the corner points.

Lastly it may be mentioned here that the concept of capacity used in this section has no welfare implications. It is a decision variable, which is at the same time an index of cumulative capital expenditures on plant and equipment made up to that date and also a factor determining a closed and bounded set of paths of demand requirements that can be satisfied. Similarly the cost of construction is purely a cost to the firm and does not involve any kind of concept of social cost.

Now we can discuss some specific capacity expansion models.

*Chenery model* [34].

The assumptions of the Chenery model are:
(i) $d(t)$ is given such that its time derivative $\dot{d}(t) = g$, where $g$ is a constant $(g > 0)$;
(ii) all capital units are of the constant efficiency type up to the end of the planning period $T$, $(T < \infty)$; and
(iii) demand at time 0, $d_0 = 0$.

The production function of the Chenery model can be written as

$$q = q(x, X, k_{ij})$$

where $q$ is the output produced, $x$ is the physical dimension of variable costs (flow inputs), $X$ is the number of capital inputs of divisible nature (e.g. different types of machines with a fixed process) and $k_{ij}$ denotes an indivisible factor where $i$ is the physical size of the factor and $j$ is the number of units of the factor; $j$ can assume only integral (nonnegative) values.

From this production function (which is invariant over time and hence can be written without time subscripts), we can derive a series of cost curves: $C_1$ is the long-run cost function showing the minimum cost of producing any given $q$ by varying $x$, $X$, $i$ and $j$ (as there are economies of scale, $j = 1$ so long as we move on $C_1$);
$C_I$ is the intermediate cost for curve varying $x$ and $X$, given $i$ and $j$;
$C(i)$ is the intertemporal cost curve showing the minimum cost of producing $q$, by varying $x$, $X$ and $j$, given $i$; and one may define that a plant curve is the similar cost function obtained by varying $x$ alone, given $X$, $i$ and $j$.

Now, owing to the nature of the demand curve, profit maximization will require installation of the same size of plant as that previously existing and at equally spaced time intervals. Hence, the only relevant decision variable is the size of plant which, in turn, will be uniquely related to the time interval between two subsequent installations. Since $C(i)$ corresponds to a given value of $i$, the objective of the entrepreneur is to minimize total discounted cost with respect to $i$ under the constraint of given output requirements.

In his more specific model, Chenery made the additional assumptions:
(iv) variable costs, i.e., costs associated with $x$, can be ignored; and
(v) $X$ is assumed to be fixed (i.e., no process flexibility), so that $C(i)$ will consist of a series of stair steps. Also, the long-run cost function is specified by the relation

$$C_1 = bs^\alpha$$

where $\alpha$ and $b$ are constants $(b > 0, 0 < \alpha < 1)$, and $s$ is the scale of the plant of size $i$ measured in terms of output. (This output is the same as capacity.) Maximum output of the plant is uniquely determined, for $X$ is now fixed and $j$ must be one since $\alpha < 1$, the only variable being $x$. Next, Chenery approximates the stair-step cost function $C(i)$ as a linear function of $s$, i.e., by $C_t$, say:

$$C_t = a_0 + \tfrac{1}{2}a_1 s + a_1 tg \qquad (6.40)$$

where $a_0$ is the portion of total cost that does not depend on output, and $a_1 = (C_1 - a_0)/s$ and $g = s/\sigma$ where $\sigma$ is the scale of plant measured in years. The minimizing condition for total discounted cost is then

$$\tfrac{1}{2}b\alpha(\sigma)^{\alpha-1} + b(\alpha-1)t(\sigma)^{\alpha-2} + a_1 t/\sigma^2 = 0 \qquad (6.41)$$

where $\sigma$ is the scale of plant measured in years so that $\sigma g = s$.

Assuming $a_1$ and $b$ are given constants, (6.41) gives a relation among $\alpha$, $r$, $T$ and $\hat{\sigma}$, the optimum scale of plant. The first three of these are parameters and the last one is the decision variable. Keeping any two of the parameters fixed, it is possible to show the parametric variation of $\hat{\sigma}$ due to the changes in any one of the three parameters. Specifically, it can be shown that $\hat{\sigma}$ is a decreasing function of $\alpha$, given $r$ and $T$. Since a lower value of $\alpha$ indicates greater economies of scale, the Chenery model provides theoretical support to the policy of building capacity ahead of demand when substantial economies of scale exist. Chenery has also shown that with process flexibility (i.e., when $X$ is variable), the profitability of building capacity ahead of demand is increased and under fluctuating demand conditions the optimal capacity expansion policy will be biased in favor of overexpansion.

*Manne-Erlenkotter model* [36, 37, 54]

The assumptions of the model are:

(i) $d(t)$ is growing at a constant annual rate $g$ (also, denote $d_0 =$ initial capacity);

(ii) all capital units are of the constant efficiency infinite-durability type;

(iii) the planning period is infinite;

(iv) all operating costs are proportional to output;

(v) the $C$ function (i.e., capacity-construction cost function) is stationary; and

(vi) there is a penalty (shortage) cost for the failure to meet $d(t)$ and the rate of penalty cost is strictly proportional to the size of the backlog $z$, measured in years.

The object of the entrepreneur is to minimize

$$C(\sigma, \bar{z}) = \frac{1}{1 - e^{-r\sigma}} \left[ p \int_0^{\bar{z}} z\, e^{-rz}\, dz + e^{-r\bar{z}} C(\sigma) \right] \tag{6.42}$$

where $p$ is the penalty cost per unit of backlog $z$ and $\bar{z}$ is the optimum trigger level for backlog in demand, so that whenever $z$ grows to $\bar{z}$, a new facility is built. Both $z$ and $\bar{z}$ are like $\sigma$, expressed in years, so that $zg$ is the amount of backlog and $\bar{z}g$ is the maximum amount of backlog that is permitted, both in terms of output; $C(\sigma)$ is the construction cost of building a plant of scale $\sigma$. The decision variables are $\sigma$ and $\bar{z}$.

Erlenkotter has shown the following:
(1) An admissible plant size $\sigma$ must satisfy the relation

$$C(\sigma)\Big|_{t=0} \leqslant \int_0^\infty \sigma p\, e^{-rt}\, dt = \frac{\sigma p}{r}. \tag{6.43}$$

If no value of $\sigma$ satisfies (6.43), no plant will be built. (A similar lower limit can be found for any nondecreasing demand function.)
(2) For all admissible plant sizes

$$\bar{z}(\sigma) = \frac{rC(\sigma)}{pg} \leqslant \sigma. \tag{6.44}$$

Using these results and simplifying, it can be shown that an equivalent problem to (6.42) is to minimize

$$C[\sigma, \bar{z}(\sigma)] = \frac{p \cdot g}{r} \cdot \frac{1 - e^{-r\bar{z}}}{1 - e^{-r\sigma}}. \tag{6.45}$$

Taking the log of (6.45), differentiating with respect to $\sigma$, and setting the result equal to zero gives

$$\frac{e^{r\bar{z}} - 1}{e^{r\sigma} - 1} = \frac{rC'(\sigma)}{p}. \tag{6.46}$$

An important special case is when $C(\sigma) = b\sigma^\alpha$, where as before $b > 0$ and $0 < \alpha < 1$.
The minimum admissible plant size will then be

$$\min(\bar{k}) = \left( \frac{rb}{p} \right)^{1/(1-\alpha)}. \tag{6.47}$$

The minimizing condition is

$$\frac{\alpha r \bar{z}}{\sigma(e^{r\bar{z}} - 1)} - \frac{r}{e^{r\sigma} - 1} = 0,$$  (6.48)

i.e.,

$$\frac{r\sigma}{e^{r\sigma} - 1} \bigg/ \frac{r\bar{z}}{e^{r\bar{z}} - 1} = \alpha.$$  (6.49)

If the penalty cost is very high $(p \to \infty)$, $\bar{z}$ drops out and (6.49) reduces to

$$\alpha = \frac{r\sigma}{e^{r\sigma} - 1}.$$  (6.50)

This is an alternative version of Chenery's specific model with an infinite planning horizon and continuous discounting. Since the planning period, $T$, is no longer a parameter, we are left with only two parameters, $r$ and $\alpha$. A higher $r$ leads to lower $\hat{\sigma}$ and a higher $\alpha$ to a higher $\hat{\sigma}$.

An important feature of the Manne-Erlenkotter model is its regeneration point property, which states that between any two building dates there is a point at which demand equals capacity installed up to that point. In other words, no plant will be constructed when excess capacity exists. Also from (6.47) it is evident that for all admissible plant sizes the temporary phase for which demand is backlogged is less in duration than the number of years required for the growth of demand to equal the optimum scale of a plant. Thus the assumption of finite penalty cost makes building capacity ahead of demand profitable under more general cost conditions (i.e., concavity of $C_1$ need not be assumed) and at the same time stipulates the condition that demand will catch up to capacity before any further addition to capacity is made.

### Srinivasan's model [40]

The assumptions of this model are similar to the continuous discounting, infinite horizon version of the Chenery model described earlier. The only difference is in the nature of the demand function, namely $(i')$ $d(t)$ grows at a constant geometric rate, so that $\dot{d}(t)/d(t) = g'$ for all $t$. Also, as before, $d(0)$ is the initial capacity. Srinivasan then establishes the result that it is optimal to construct plants at each point of a sequence of equally spaced time points, but now the size of plants to be constructed will grow exponentially.

The decision variable is taken as $\bar{t}$, the time interval between any two successive plant-installations, and the objective is to minimize

$$C(\bar{t}) = \sum_{n=0}^{\infty} e^{-nr\bar{t}} b \cdot \{d(0) (e^{g'\bar{t}} - 1) e^{ng'\bar{t}}\}^{\alpha}. \tag{6.51}$$

Assuming $r > \alpha g'$ and dropping the constant term, an equivalent problem to (6.51) is to choose $\bar{t}$ so as to minimize

$$[e^{g'(\bar{t})} - 1]^{\alpha} / [1 - e^{-(r-\alpha g')\bar{t}}]. \tag{6.52}$$

The optimum $\bar{t}$, which can be shown to be unique, is given by

$$\alpha g' (e^{h\bar{t}} - 1) = h (1 - e^{-g'\bar{t}}) \tag{6.53}$$

where $h = r - \alpha g' > 0$ by assumption.

It hardly needs mentioning that Srinivasan, like Chenery, assumes that demand requirements must be met, which is equivalent to assuming an infinite penalty cost.

*Baumol's growth-equilibrium model* [41]

The decision variable of this model is the rate of growth of the firm which maximizes profit. The assumptions of this model are:
(i) costs are of two types: (a) output costs, i.e. ordinary production and operating costs, are constant per unit of output owing to fixity of input prices and constant returns to scale (linear homogeneity of the production function); (b) expansion costs, on the other hand are an increasing function of $g'$, the rate of growth of output;
(ii) since the price of output is also fixed, net revenue (i.e., net of output costs) is constant per unit of output.

The objective of the decision maker is to maximize the growth profit function $(\bar{G})$:

$$\bar{G} = R_0 \frac{1+r}{r-g'} - C(g') \tag{6.54}$$

where $R_0$ is the initial net revenue at $t = 0$, and $g' < r$, by assumption; $C(g')$ is the total discounted expansion costs.

The profit maximizing condition (assuming the second-order condition is satisfied) is (here $C'(g')$ denotes the marginal expansion cost)

$$C'(g') = \frac{1+r}{(r-g')^2}. \tag{6.55}$$

The expansion costs of the Baumol model arise mainly due to four factors:
(i) a physical limit to the rate of growth of capacity;

(ii) a financial limit due to the imperfection of the capital market;

(iii) an internal limit due to increasing administrative and organization cost; and

(iv) a risk cost.

Baumol considers the effects of changes in $r$ and various types of tax-subsidy schemes on stimulating growth.

Now a few remarks may be added. First, note that all the above models employ classical optimization procedures to determine the structure of the optimum values. In the Chenery and Manne-Erlenkotter models the optimum size of plant is the decision variable and, since it is independent of the initial capacity, by applying renewal theory (or the idea of regeneration points) it can be shown that the same scale of plant will be built at equidistant time intervals. In the Srinivasan model the decision variable is the timing of installation of new plants and, since in this model also the optimum size of plant is independent of initial capacity, the time-phasing will be the same, though the size of plant will be growing. Second, due either to the concavity of the cost function (Chenery and Srinivasan cases) or to the assumption of finite penalty cost for backlogging (Manne-Erlenkotter case) the optimum sequence of time points at which plants are added must be discrete, i.e., separated from one another by finite time intervals. In every case the optimum time interval has an upper limit, i.e. it is not profitable to build capacity infinitely ahead of demand. If the cost of construction of capacity were strictly proportional to incremental capacity and if the penalty cost were infinite, it would always be profitable to wait for demand to increase before any further addition to capacity was made and there would be a continuous addition to capacity at the rate of increase of demand.

In Baumol's model the decision variable is the equilibrium rate of growth. The main departure of Baumol's model from the other models considered here lies in the fact that the $d(t)$ function plays no role in his model. In fact, if there were no expansion cost, an infinite rate of growth would be profitable. So while in other models the demand function $d(t)$ provides the upper limit to the growth of revenue and hence to the rate of growth of capacity, in Baumol's model, the $C(g')$ function limits the rate of profitable growth and hence that of net revenue.

### 6.2.3. Capacity expansion models with optimal path approaches

We shall now consider the capacity-expansion policy models which aim to develop algorithms for finding out the optimal path of capital expansion. We shall, however, discuss here only the economic aspects of these models rather than their computational aspects. (The computational techniques discussed in ch. 3 are relevant here.)

*Arrow, Beckmann and Karlin model* [35]

The assumptions of this model are:

(i) $d(t)$ is given as a function of time but its time rate of change $\dot{d}(t)$ is not constant;

(ii) all capital units are of the constant efficiency type with infinite durability (strictly speaking, they assumed that maintenance costs are proportional to output);

(iii) $y_t$, the maximum (capacity) output at $t$, is uniquely determined by $k_t$, the aggregate size of capital equipments at $t$;

(iv) $E_t = mq_t$ is defined only for values of $q_t \leqslant y_t$; $m$ is a constant ($m > 0$);

(v) $y_0 =$ capacity at time $t = 0$; and

(vi) $0 \leqslant \dot{y}(t) \leqslant M$ for all $t$, where $M$ is a given constant ($M < \infty$) and $\dot{y}(t)$ is the rate of change of capacity at $t$.

Since capacity and cost are both additive we have

$$y_t = y_0 + \int_0^t \dot{y}(\tau)\, d\tau \tag{6.56}$$

and

$$C = \int_0^T c\dot{y}(t)\, e^{-rt}\, dt, \tag{6.57}$$

where $c$ is a constant ($c > 0$) and $C$ is total discounted cost over the planning horizon.

In this system $q_t = \min(d_t, y_t)$ is measured in units of net profitability. The object of the entrepreneur is to choose an optimum capacity schedule $(y_1, y_2, \ldots, y_T)$ such that

$$G = \int_0^T [q_t\, e^{-rt} - c\dot{y}_t\, e^{-rt}]\, dt \text{ is maximized.}$$

An equivalent way to write the objective function is

$$\max_v \min_u H(v, u) \quad \text{where}$$

$$H(v, u) = \int_0^T [d_t(1 - u(t)) + y_t u(t) - c\dot{y}_t]\, e^{-rt}\, dt \tag{6.58}$$

subject to the following constraints
(i) $\dot{y}_t \leqslant M$
(ii) $0 \leqslant u(t) \leqslant 1$.
Let

$$\phi(t) = \int_t^T u(\tau) e^{-r\tau} d\tau - c e^{-rt}. \tag{6.59}$$

Then the optimal capacity expansion policy would be
(1) $\dot{y}_t = 0$ for all $t$, i.e., $\bar{y}(t) = y_0$ if $rc \geqslant 1$; and
(2) if $0 < rc < 1$, the optimal path $(0, T)$ can be divided into sub-intervals of the following types:
(a) $\phi(t) > 0$; $\dot{y}_t = M$, i.e., maximum expansion.
(b) $\phi(t) < 0$; $\dot{y}_t = 0$, i.e., no expansion.
(c) $\phi(t) = 0$; $\dot{y}_t = d_t$; so that $\bar{y}_t = d_t$ throughout this subinterval.

The economic meaning of the results is that when $rc \geqslant 1$, the interest on the cost of expansion of capacity by one unit is as large as or greater than unit profitability. Hence the condition (1) holds. Also, $u(\tau)$ will be one when demand exceeds capacity and zero when capacity expands demand. So the integral $\int_t^T u(\tau) d\tau$ is a measure of the set of times at which the firm will produce at capacity from $t$ to $T$. Hence, the present value of returns from adding one more unit to capacity at $t$ is given by the integral in (6.59) and its cost is $c e^{-rt}$; $\phi(t)$ is therefore the marginal profitability or the (discounted) profitability at $t$ of adding a marginal unit to capacity, and hence we have 2(a) and 2(b). Lastly, when $0 < \dot{y}_t < M$, $u(t) = rc < 1$ and $y_t = d_t$ and $\dot{y}_t = d_t$ as in 2(c).

In this model $d(t)$ is given as a function of time but the optimum output program does not coincide with it. In other words, the model allows for negative excess capacity in the sense that for some periods, $d(t)$ may exceed the output produced and there is no penalty cost associated with this situation. Also, negative excess capacity may exist even when marginal profitability is positive, since it is impossible to add new capacity above a certain level. This restraint is similar to the expansion cost associated with the first of the four factors in Baumol's model. But here this expansion cost is infinite when $\dot{y}_t = M$ and zero below that level. This restraint is necessary, for otherwise there would be an infinite expansion of capacity if marginal profitability is positive. Since the cost function, $C$, is linear, there is no building ahead of demand.

Since in this model, output is measured in units of profitability (i.e., net revenue), the existence of a maintenance cost, proportional to output, does not make any difference. We have only to redefine a unit of output so that it is also net of maintenance cost of capital per unit of output. So assumption (ii) is not really necessary. We need only to assume that the capital unit has no fixed lifetime and that its service period can be extended up to the end of the planning period by incurring maintenance cost which is proportional to output.

*Manne-Veinott model* [38]

The assumptions of this model are:

(i) $d(t)$ is given subject to the condition that $d(t) \geqslant 0$ for all $t$, up to $T$ and $\sum_{t=0}^{T-1} d(t) > 0$;

(ii) all capital equipments are of the constant efficiency and infinite durability type;

(iii) $C_t = c_t \dot{y}_t$ where $C_t$ is the cost of the increment in capacity at $t$ and $\dot{y}_t$ is the increment in capacity; this function is assumed to be concave for all $t$;

(iv) $y_0 = d_0$, i.e., initial capacity is equal to initial demand; and

(v) $\dot{y}_t \geqslant 0$.

Once again additivity of capacity, i.e. (6.56), holds. The objective of the firm is to find an optimal feasible capacity-expansion schedule defined by the vector $\dot{y}_t = (\dot{y}_0, \dot{y}_1, \ldots, \dot{y}_{T-1})$, to minimize

$$C([\dot{y}_t]) = \sum_{t=0}^{T-1} c_t \left( \dot{y}_t + \sum_{t=0}^{T-1} p_t \max(0, -z_t) \right) \tag{6.60}$$

where $p_t$ is the (temporary) penalty cost proportional to negative excess capacity.

Let $\Omega_t$ be the end of period excess capacity at $t$, i.e., the difference between the cumulative values of $\dot{y}_t$ and $d_t$. The feasibility requirements on the $\dot{y}_t$ vector are given by $\dot{y}_t \geqslant 0$ and $\Omega_T = 0$.

A point of regeneration of capacity on the expansion schedule, $\dot{y}_t$ is said to occur at those points at which $\Omega_t = 0$. It is then proved that there is an optimal capacity schedule which has the regeneration point property as defined previously and that of the several feasible schedules with that property one could apply a dynamic programming algorithm to find one feasible schedule that is optimal.

In many respects the above model is a generalization of the Manne-Erlenkotter model. While it generalizes the specific forms of demand and cost functions, it also arrives at less economically meaningful results.

*Zabel's model* [55]

The assumptions of Zabel-type models are:

(i) $d(t)=d$ $(d>0)$ and this demand (output requirement) must be satisfied;
(ii) all capital units are of the same type and additive, so that $k_t$ is the simple sum of capital units of various ages at $t$;
(iii) the maintenance charge per period per unit of $k_t$ is fixed at $u$ and is independent of the age structure of $k_t$;
(iv) a unit of capital has no fixed life;
(v) $E_t(q_t, k_t)$ is differentiable and strictly convex-increasing in $q_t \geqslant 0$ for each $k_t>0$ and differentiable and strictly convex-decreasing in $k_t>0$ for each $q_t>0$ (an alternative way of arriving at the same cost function would be to assume that for each capital unit, the marginal operating cost function starts at the origin and is decreasing throughout its range); and
(vi) a fraction $\delta$ $(0<\delta<1)$ of the available capital stock $(k_t)$ wears out at the end of the $t$-th period, where $\delta$ is a random variable with a differentiable and known density function $\Psi(\delta)$; this worn out capital has no scrap value.

The objective of the entrepreneur is to produce the quantity demanded $d$, at least cost by choosing an efficient "ordering rate" for capital. In his constant-stock policy model the cost of capital is given by (for $k_t>k_{t-1}$),

$$C(k_t - k_{t-1}) = c(k_t - k_{t-1}), \qquad (6.61)$$

where $c$ is a constant for all time periods.

Assume further that $T=\infty$. Since $d>0$, $k_t$, i.e. capital equipment in any period, must be positive, while $k_{t-1} \geqslant 0$. Let $\varepsilon>0$ be the minimal $k_t$ required to produce $d$. Then $k_t \geqslant \varepsilon$ for all values of $t$. Let $G(k_{t-1})$ be the maximum present value of returns over the (infinite) horizon for any initial stock $k_{t-1}$ at the beginning of the $t$-th production period. Then

$$G(k_{t-1}) = \max_{k_t \geqslant \max(\varepsilon,\, k_{t-1})} [c \cdot k_{t-1} - J(k_t)] \qquad (6.62)$$

where $J(k_t)$ is independent of $k_{t-1}$, i.e.

$$J(k_t) = ck_t + E_t(d, k_t) + uk_t - p \cdot d - \frac{1}{1+r} \int_0^1 G(k_t - \delta k_t)\, \Psi(\delta)\, d\delta. \qquad (6.63)$$

It can be shown that $J(k_t)$ has a unique minimum at $\hat{k}_t$. The optimal policy is, therefore, to order up to $\hat{k}_t$ (i.e., add $\hat{k}_t - k_{t-1}$) in the $t$-th period if $k_{t-1} < \hat{k}_t$

and order zero if $k_{t-1} \geqslant \hat{k}_t$. So the optimal level of $k_t$ is given by

$$k_t^* = \hat{k}_t \quad \text{if} \quad \hat{k}_t - k_{t-1} > 0$$
$$k_t^* = k_{t-1} \quad \text{if} \quad \hat{k}_t - k_{t-1} \leqslant 0. \tag{6.64}$$

An alternative version of the above constant stock policy model is obtained when the $C$ function in (6.61) is modified by adding to it a positive constant, $c_0$, whenever $(k_t - k_{t-1})$ is positive and making $T$ finite. The $C$ function then becomes

$$C(k_t - k_{t-1}) = c(k_t - k_{t-1}) + c_0; \quad k_t \geqslant k_{t-1}. \tag{6.61a}$$

The corresponding $J_{(T)}(k_t)$ function will still have a unique minimum $\hat{\hat{k}}_t$. An optimal policy is then an $(S_T, s_T)$ policy, i.e. order up to $S_T = \hat{\hat{k}}_t$ if $k_{t-1}$ is less than $s_T$ and order zero otherwise. The value of $S_T$ is given by the following relations:

$$s_T = \varepsilon \quad \text{if} \quad J_{(T)}(\varepsilon) \leqslant c_0 + J_{(T)}(\hat{\hat{k}}_t)$$
$$s_T = \tilde{k}_t \quad \text{if} \quad J_{(T)}(\varepsilon) > c_0 + J_{(T)}(\hat{\hat{k}}_t) \tag{6.65}$$

where $\tilde{k}_t$ is that value of $k_t$ at which $J_{(T)}(s_T) = c_0 + J_{(T)}(\hat{\hat{k}}_t)$.

It can be shown that when $T \to \infty$, there is an analogous $(S, s)$ policy so that the nature of optimal policies remains unchanged.

A peculiar feature of the Zabel model is the nature of $\delta$ function. As a first approximation he assumes it to be a known constant. Further, he assumes that a unit of capital has no fixed life. Since $\delta$ is not a function of the age-structure of the capital stock ($k_t$), nor a function of the rate of output, the logical way to interpret it may be as a dummy variable for the rate of obsolescence due to technical change which may be assumed to affect all capital units at the same rate. Such an assumption underlies dynamic equipment policy models of the Terborgh type [56]. But Zabel assumes that there is no technical change. Also, we have a fixed maintenance charge per period per unit of capital, yet all capital units are subject to a constant rate of physical depreciation independent of the level of maintenance charges.

Zabel considers the case in which the lifetime of capital units is predetermined or when the lifetime is one of the decision variables but only to the extent of arriving at the negative conclusion that under such circumstances the optimal capital policy has a complex form, i.e. it cannot be shown to be dependent on a single specified variable.

Zabel's constant stock policy model is very similar to Haavelmo's model. The main difference is that while output produced is a decision variable in

Haavelmo's model, the output requirement is given in Zabel's model. But in both cases they are static at a given or preassigned level appropriately chosen.

### 6.2.4. General appraisal

In recent years a number of capacity expansion policy models have appeared and it is not possible to give a comprehensive account of all these models. The purpose of several models not considered here is to extend the basic models presented above to more general conditions and to undertake either a kind of sensitivity analysis to show the variations of the optimal plant size and its time phasing as one or another of the parameters is changed or to evolve a computing procedure to find the optimal capacity expansion path. Some of these extensions are quite straightforward. Thus, instead of a deterministic demand function, a probabilistic growth of demand function was considered by Manne even in his 1961 article. Zabel also adds a probabilistic component to his constant level demand function. In both cases the extensions do not alter the nature of optimal policies though they may require some additional conditions.

Another line that has been explored by Manne and his associates is the case of more than one producing area, instead of a single producing area [57–59]. In this case, however, the extensions generally give less definite results and the computing procedure is only combinatorial, enumerative and less efficient.

Smith has considered, within a static framework the variable life capital equipment models in which the life of capital equipment is a decision variable, i.e. it is determined by the optimal economic considerations. Zabel also considers a technically or economically determined life, but since in his system the capital equipment is not of a decreasing efficiency type, the economic interpretation of his results is not very clear.

All the models considered here assume a constant discount rate. (Smith considers the effects of capital rationing but once again in a static framework.) In real life the marginal borrowing rate often rises sharply if a given capital budget is exceeded. It is one component of expansion costs in the Baumol model. In the Arrow, Beckmann and Karlin model, presumably the constraint on the rate of growth of capacity is due to the physical impossibility of accelerating the rate of growth of capacity above a certain level and has no connection with capital rationing considerations. Zabel considers the possibility of a delay in the supply of capital and Haavelmo also considers the possibility of delayed adjustment due to immobility of capital.

However, the assumption of a constant discount rate may be justified on the grounds that without such an assumption capital theory has a great tendency to get meshed into a theory of finance rather than in the technology of the production process. For the same reason, the exclusion of price as a variable may be justified.

The major limitation of the capital expansion policy models is the assumption of nonstorable output. This assumption is crucial since in real life the substitutability of size of plant and the stock of finished product severely limits the usefulness of the policy models to those extreme cases of service industries (such as the shipping industry or electricity generating plants) or those luxury industries (such as working rough diamonds to produce commercial gems) in which cost per unit of plant capacity is very low in relation to cost per unit of stock [60]. But in some of these industries, high transportation cost makes the assumption of a single producing area very unrealistic. Therefore it is surprising that of the writers considered here only Smith shows awareness of the possibility of inventory accumulation as a substitute for scaling of plant by extending the Modigliani-Hohn type model [61] to the case of production planning. (Zabel also mentions the ubiquity of the nonstorability assumption in capital theory.)

For a majority of manufacturing industries, the possibility of storage at a finite cost exists. But if we allow inventory accumulation we cannot apply period by period optimization over the planning horizon and investment and output decisions are made interdependent once again. The possibility of inventory accumulation has been considered in the Manne-type framework but at the expense of retaining some of its more stringent conditions on the nature of demand curve and the cost function. The policy of building ahead of demand still remains profitable [62].

One major difficulty in integrating the capacity expansion policy models and inventory policy models lies in their different assumptions about the cost curve. In inventory policy models the cost function is usually convex, while in capacity expansion policy models it is usually concave. Also, in the inventory policy model the cost function is a function only of current output and (the cumulative value of) past outputs, while in the capacity expansion policy models the cost function is mainly dependent on the future level of output.

Another usual feature of the manufacturing industries that is systematically ignored by the policy models considered here is the fact that very few firms produce a single output. Especially when extra capacity exists, it can be utilized by adding one more product to the list of products of the firm. The role of technological change is also frequently unspecified.

However, with all these limitations, the capacity expansion policy models open up a new and fruitful line of inquiry for prospective planning of size and time phasing of investments for capacity expansion. For a public undertaking the rate of discount can often be equated with a social rate of time preference and, given a target rate of output set by planners, the above policy models can provide clear-cut answers to many questions which are not being treated properly in conventional capital theory.

A few remarks may now be made about the empirical estimation of economies of scale in plant operation, which has important implications for optimal growth. First, note that even if it is approximately reasonable to consider the plant operating cost $(C)$ functions of the type

$$C = bx^{\alpha}; \qquad 0 < \alpha < 1; \qquad x = \text{capacity output}$$

which are included in the Manne-type models, empirical evidence gathered by Bruni [63] and Haldi [64] suggests that the scale coefficient $\alpha$ varies considerably from under 0.41 to over 0.90 between the different plant units and the entire plants and also that cost economies for the various petrochemical categories studied can be separately attributed to capital and labor. From these empirical considerations Bruni sought to generalize the long-run operating cost function as

$$C = b_1 L^{\alpha_1} + b_2 K^{\alpha_2}$$

where $L$ is labor and $K$ is capital at the capacity level of output. However this function is very difficult to operate with in any optimization problem.

Second, there have been some empirical attempts at estimating the expansion paths for selected industries by analyzing the relationship between economies of scale and the growth of plants along these expansion paths. For instance, Shen [65] has attempted to estimate the expansion path from the long-run annual data on manufacturing establishments covering about 10 000 manufacturing plants from the census annually conducted by the Department of Labor and Industries of Massachusetts. Let $Q$ be output, $L$ labor and $K$ capital. After logarithmic transformation, each variable (over the cross-section of plants) is further standardized by setting its mean zero and variance unity and the new variables are denoted by $q, l$ and $k$. The expansion path $s$ (i.e. the scale of operation) is then fitted over a roughly homogeneous sample of plants by a weighted regression of the form

$$S = a_1 q + a_2 k + a_3 l.$$

Some of the estimated coefficients are

| Industry | Selected years | No. of observations | $\hat{a}_2$ | $\hat{a}_3$ | Total variance explained % |
|---|---|---|---|---|---|
| Food | 1935–41 | 2068 | 0.78 | 1.12 | 89 |
| | 1947–53 | 1522 | 0.92 | 1.13 | 90 |
| | 1954–59 | 993 | 0.92 | 1.13 | 92 |
| Chemicals | 1947–53 | 476 | 0.94 | 1.17 | 94 |
| | 1954–59 | 298 | 0.95 | 1.22 | 93 |
| Machinery | 1947–53 | 974 | 1.00 | 1.07 | 97 |
| | 1954–59 | 702 | 1.01 | 1.09 | 97 |
| Leather goods | 1935–41 | 644 | 0.96 | 1.09 | 88 |
| | 1947–53 | 696 | 0.97 | 1.09 | 93 |
| | 1954–59 | 428 | 0.93 | 1.10 | 95 |

These estimates, although very rough, serve to indicate that in most industries the expansion path has shifted in such a way that there is a continuous improvement in returns to scale; also along the expansion path the estimates evidence increasing returns to scale for labor and decreasing returns to scale for capital. If anything, these computations suggest that the trend of economies of scale internal to the firm may have significant feedback from the overall industry performance and dispersion of plants within the industry which account for increases in the average (industry's) economies of scale. Hence, the spatial and locational factors should be given some weight in the specification of optimal capacity expansion paths for an enterprise or firm, in case it is a part of an overall industrial framework.

## 6.3. Stochastic process and queuing models

Broadly viewed, a stochastic process is a family of random variables interrelated in a sequence. A time series of demand, for example, is a stochastic process. Let $T$ denote a set of points on a time axis such that at point $t$ in $T$ an observation is made of a random variable $X(t, w)$ occupying a point $w$ in the entire state space $W$; then a stochastic process is completely specified by the family of random variables $\{X(t); t \in T, w \in W\}$. One of the most important types of stochastic processes which is of great operational use is provided by the stationary Markov process. A stationary stochastic process is one in which the statistical distribution of the random variables is independent of the translation of time and a Markov process (or chain) is one in which the complete specification of the transition probabilities associated with the present state determines the future stochastic behavior of the system completely. Therefore, a stochastic process which has after-effects such that a specification of the future stochastic behavior of a system cannot be completely made from observing the present system alone is termed non-Markovian.

We will be concerned in this section with only a brief description of some aspects of the stationary Markovian stochastic processes in order to illustrate some applications. The applications of stochastic processes in different fields are quite numerous and there is an extensive literature in the subject [66–68]. Applications to economic models are, however, less extensive, although in production-inventory models in operations research the sequence of demand variations in time with the associated structure of transition probabilities has received considerable attention, particularly the case in which the lead time is varying in a probabilistic manner. The theory of queues, which is concerned with the formulation of mathematical models to predict (or optimize) the behavior of a given system that provides services for randomly arriving demands offers another very interesting field of application. Again, the literature on the theory of queues is quite extensive [69, 70], and there is a very wide range of applications (e.g. to problems of telephone traffic, machine breakdown and repair, inventory control, storage and servicing problems in supermarkets, etc.).

Our objective in this section will be to illustrate the applications of Markovian stochastic processes in three selected models which can be used in economic decision making. The first model analyzes the stochastic process implications of aggregate growth models built by the economists and shows how investment allocation decisions could be optimized in this context. The implications of such models for the growth of firms are also mentioned in this case. The second model considers the problem of specifying an optimal inventory policy under conditions in which demand is described by a stationary Markovian stochastic process. The third model considers a few applications of queuing theory to problems of servicing and repairing.

### 6.3.1. Applications to models of economic growth and planning

Modern theoretical analysis of economic growth by means of specific aggregative models [71], although very helpful in characterizing the process of development in its different aspects, has been quite restrictive in one respect.

This is because the recent growth models, with the exception of Haavelmo's theory [72], neglect the influence of stochastic elements. It is not difficult, however, to show that the most important growth variables such as population, investment and output are probabilistic in nature, since the economic decisions underlying demand and capacity variations are made in a world of imperfect knowledge and uncertainty. Recently attempts have been made by Tintner and others [73] to develop a stochastic theory of growth and investment planning with several empirical applications.

Consider the simplest assumption that economic development is measured by a single (scalar) variable $X(t)$ which may denote real per capita national income. This is assumed here to be a discrete variable, as it simplifies the initial mathematical development. Let $p_x(t)$ denote the probability that $X(t)$ will have a given value $x$, i.e.

$$p_x(t) = \text{Prob}\{X(t) = x\} \quad \text{for} \quad x = 0, 1, 2, \ldots$$

The following assumptions are now made about the possible changes in the value of $X(t)$ during a small time interval between $t$ and $(t+\Delta t)$:
(i) assumptions about stationary independent increments which postulate (a) the probability of transition of the system $X(t)$ from $x$ to $x+1$ in the small interval $(t, t+\Delta t)$ is given by $\lambda_x \Delta t + O(\Delta t)$, where $O(\Delta t)$ denotes a value of smaller order of magnitude than $\Delta t$ and $\lambda_x$ denotes a certain function of $x$ ($x=0, 1, \ldots$) and $t$; (b) the probability of transition of the system from $x$ to $x-1$ in the same interval $(t, t+\Delta t)$ is $\mu_x(t) + O(\Delta t)$ where $\mu_x$ denotes a certain function of $x$ and $t$; and (c) the probability of transition between any two values (or states) $x$ and $x+s$ is independent of the initial position;
(ii) the probability of no transition to a neighboring value (or state) is given by $1 - (\lambda_x + \mu_x)\,\Delta t + O(\Delta t)$; and
(iii) the probability of a transition to a value other than a neighboring value is $O(\Delta t)$ which tends to zero in the limit, as $\Delta t$ tends to zero.

Now if the system $X(t)$ is at $x$ during the current time period $t$, it may be due to either a transition from $(x-1)$ to $x$ or from $x+1$ to $x$ or from $x$ to $x$ during $\Delta t$. This specifies the following recurrence relation for the transition probabilities:

$$p_x(t + \Delta t) = \lambda_{x-1} p_{x-1}(t) \cdot \Delta t + \mu_{x+1} p_{x+1}(t)\,\Delta t + (1 - \lambda_x - \mu_x)$$
$$p_x(t) \cdot \Delta t + 0(\Delta t). \quad (6.66a)$$

Taking the limit $\Delta t \to 0$, this becomes

$$dp_x(t)/dt = \dot{p}_x(t) = \lambda_{x-1} p_{x-1}(t) + \mu_{x+1} p_{x+1}(t) - (\lambda_x + \mu_x) p_x(t). \quad (6.66b)$$

The initial conditions governing equation (6.66b) are assumed as

$$p_x(0) = \delta_{xx_0} = \begin{cases} 1 \text{ for } x = x_0 \\ 0 \text{ otherwise} \end{cases}$$

when the system takes the value $x = x_0$ $(0 < x_0 < \infty)$ at time zero. Let us further extend the notation for transition probabilities as

$$p_{jk}(t) = \text{Prob}\left[X(t + s) = k \mid X(s) = j\right] \qquad (6.66c)$$

where $p_{jk}(t)$ denotes the conditional probability of $X(t+s)$ taking a specific value $k$, given that $X(s)$ has been observed at time point $s$ to take the value $j$. Then the functions $\lambda_x$, $\mu_x$ can be interpreted as follows:

$$\lim_{\Delta t \to 0} (1/\Delta t)\left[p_{x, x+1}(t + \Delta t)\right] = \lambda_x(t) \quad \text{for} \quad x \geqslant 0; \qquad (6.67a)$$

$$\lim_{\Delta t \to 0} (1/\Delta t)\left[p_{x, x-1}(t + \Delta t)\right] = \mu_x(t) \quad \text{for} \quad x \geqslant 0; \quad \text{and} \qquad (6.67b)$$

$$\lim_{\Delta t \to 0} (1/\Delta t)\left[1 - p_{x, x}(t + \Delta t)\right] = \lambda_x(t) + \mu_x(t) \quad \text{for} \quad x \geqslant 0. \qquad (6.67c)$$

By making specific assumptions about the transition probabilities $\lambda_x = \lambda_x(t)$, $\mu_x = \mu_x(t)$ it is possible to generate alternative probabilistic models of economic growth as follows:

*Case A*: linear birth process model: here it is assumed that $\mu_2(t) = 0$ and $\lambda_x(t) = \lambda \cdot x(t)$ for all $t$ and $x$, where $\lambda$ is a positive constant. In this case the solution [74] of the difference-differential equation (6.66b) is

$$p_x(t) = \binom{x - 1}{x - j} \exp(-j\lambda t)\left[1 - \exp(-\lambda t)\right]^{x-j} \quad \text{for} \quad x > j \geqslant 1, \qquad (6.68a)$$

where $j$ denotes the value of $x$ at time zero. Since by appropriate choice of units one can take $j = 1$, the solution (6.68a) may be written more simply as:

$$p_x(t) = \exp(-\lambda t)(1 - \exp(-\lambda t))^{x-1} \quad \text{for} \quad x = 1, 2, 3, \ldots, \infty$$

from which the mean $M(t)$ and variance $V(t)$ can be computed,

$$M(t) = \sum_{x=0}^{\infty} x p_x(t) = j \exp(\lambda t)$$

$$V(t) = \sum_{x=0}^{\infty} (x - M(t))^2 \, p_x(t) = j \exp(\lambda t)\left[j \exp(\lambda t) - 1\right]$$

where $j$ may be taken to be unity.

To consider the economic meaning of the proportional growth rate (or "birth rate") $\lambda$ in terms of economic models, one may interpret $\lambda$ as the product of two structural coefficients of the Harrod-Domar type growth model, i.e. the marginal output-capital ratio ($\sigma$) and the savings-income ratio ($\alpha$), i.e. $\lambda = \alpha\sigma$. The deterministic growth model of the Harrod-Domar type may be formulated as

$$\dot{x} = \mathrm{d}x/\mathrm{d}t = \lambda x, \quad \text{Solution}: x(t) = j\exp(\lambda t), \quad j = x(t = 0).$$

*Case B*: linear birth and death process: here it is assumed that $\mu_x(t) = \mu \cdot x(t)$ and $\lambda_x(t) = \lambda \cdot x(t)$ where $\lambda$, $\mu$ are positive constants. The rate $\mu$, which is termed the death rate in stochastic process language, may represent the average rate of decline in real national income attributable to such factors as obsolescence and scrapping of equipment and buildings, unrealized investment and unutilized capacity and so on. Defining $\bar{\lambda} = \lambda - \mu$ as the net birth rate, assuming it to be positive, the formulas above in case A can all be derived except that $\bar{\lambda}$ replaces $\lambda$.

*Case C*: linear nonhomogeneous growth: here it is assumed that $\lambda_x = \lambda_0 + \lambda_1 x$, $\mu_x = \mu_0 + \mu_1 x$ where $\lambda_0$, $\lambda_1$, $\mu_0$, $\mu_1$ are positive constants. Then the solution [74] of the equation (6.66b) is found to be

$$p_x(t) = \left(\frac{\lambda_0 + \lambda_1 M(t)}{\lambda_0}\right)^{-\lambda_0/\lambda_1} \cdot \frac{\lambda_0(\lambda_0 + \lambda_1)(\lambda_0 + 2\lambda_1)\ldots(\lambda_0 + (x-1)\lambda_1)}{x!}$$
$$\times \left[\frac{M(t)}{\lambda_0 + \lambda_1 M(t)}\right]^x$$

where $M(t) = EX(t)$ is the mean value function.

It can be shown [74] that if $(\lambda_0/\lambda_1)$ is not fixed but tends to infinity, then this solution defines a Poisson process, i.e.

$$p_x(t) = \exp(-M(t))\,[M(t)]^x/x!$$

On the other hand, if $(\lambda_0/\lambda_1)$ tends to $-1$, we get a geometric distribution with probability function as

$$p_x(t) = [1 + M(t)]^{-1}\,M(t)/[1 + M(t)]^x; \quad M(t) > 0 \quad \text{for} \quad t \geqslant 0.$$

*Case D*: nonlinear process: one specific form of a nonlinear stochastic growth model which has a very close relation to the deterministic logistic-type growth model formalized by Haavelmo [45] is obtained by assuming the birth ($\lambda$) and death ($\mu$) rates as

$$\lambda_x(t) = \lambda x \quad \text{with} \quad \lambda = a(k_2 - x)$$
$$\mu_x(t) = \mu x \quad \text{with} \quad \mu = b(x - k_1) \quad \text{with} \quad k_1 < k_2$$

where $a$, $b$, $k_1$, $k_2$ are constants such that $x(t=0)$ lies in the closed interval $[k_1, k_2]$. In this case the difference-differential equation (6.66b) becomes very complicated and its explicit solution is not yet known. However it has been shown by Kendall and others [75] that the mean value function $M(t)$ in this case satisfies the following differential equation

$$\mathrm{d}M(t)/\mathrm{d}t = (ak_2 + bk_1) M(t) - (a + b) m_2(t),$$

where $m_2(t)$ is an unknown function representing the second moment about the origin for the process $\{X(t)\}$. Denoting the variance of the process $\{X(t)\}$ by $V(t)$ this equation may be written as

$$\mathrm{d}M(t)/\mathrm{d}t = (a + b) \left[ \frac{ak_2 + bk_1}{a + b} \cdot M(t) - M^2(t) - (a + b) V(t) \right]. \qquad (6.68b)$$

Now the deterministic analogue of this model (6.68b) can be written in terms of the nonstochastic variable $x(t)$ representing the permanent component of real per capita national income as

$$\mathrm{d}x(t)/\mathrm{d}t = (a + b) \left[ \frac{ak_2 + bk_1}{a + b} \cdot x(t) - x^2(t) \right]. \qquad (6.68c)$$

By comparing (6.68b) and (6.68c) it is apparent that for any positive value of the variance function $V(t)$, the mean solution of the logistic stochastic model of income growth given in (6.68b) would be less than the exact solution of the deterministic model (6.68b).

Several empirical applications to economic models of more generalized stochastic processes (e.g., log-normal diffusion processes) and particularly the methods of estimation through maximum likelihood and least squares under several restrictions have been discussed by Tintner and others [73]. Applications to intertemporal growth models with capital accumulation have been discussed by Sengupta and Tintner [76]. To illustrate the application of our stochastic process growth models to problems of investment planning through resource allocation, consider the following linear two sector growth model [76] with $x_1(t)$, $x_2(t)$ denoting net real outputs of two sectors in period $t$, the consumption goods and the capital goods sectors, such that the second sector produces additional capacity (i.e. capital goods) for expansion of output in both sectors and $u$ denotes the allocation of additional capacity,

$$\mathrm{d}x_1/\mathrm{d}t = a_1 x_1(t) + b_1 u x_2(t); \qquad 0 \leqslant u \leqslant 1 \qquad (6.69a)$$

$$\mathrm{d}x_2/\mathrm{d}t = b_2(1 - u) x_2(t); \qquad 0 \leqslant u \leqslant 1 \qquad (6.69b)$$

where $a_1$, $b_1$, $b_2$ are positive constants and $x(t) = x_1(t) + x_2(t)$ can be interpreted as net national output. Note that the allocation ratio $u$ representing allocation of additional investment may be interpreted as a decision variable which influences the future course of output growth and in this respect the second sector is more dominant in the model, since its growth determines the growth of the other sector.

Now given a set of values for $a_1$, $b_1$, $b_2$, $u$ the solution of this deterministic model is easily found to be

$$x_2(t) = C_0 \exp[tb_2(1 - u)];$$

$$x_1(t) = \left(\frac{b_1 C_0}{b_2(1 - u) - a_1}\right) \exp[tb_2(1 - u)] + D_0 \exp(ta_1) \tag{6.69c}$$

where the initial constants $C_0$, $D_0$ are determined by the initial composition of national output at $t = 0$. Now from our case A of the linear birth process model, it is easy to show from the second sector output solution in (6.69c) that a linear birth and death process type of stochastic model can be constructed. Assuming that such processes (i.e. 6.68a) apply, the mean size of the second sector output denoted by $M_2(t)$ and its variance $V_2(t)$ can be computed as

$$M_2(t) = \exp(tb_2(1 - u));$$

$$V_2(t) = \left(\frac{u - 1}{u + 1}\right) \exp(tb_2(1 - u)) [\exp(tb_2(1 - u) - 1] \tag{6.69d}$$

where it is assumed that $x_2(t) = 1$ for $t = 0$.

Similarly the mean $M_1(t)$ and variance $V_1(t)$ of the first sector output may be computed as

$$M_1(t) = \frac{b_1 u}{b_2(1 - u) - a_1} \exp(tb_2(1 - u)) - \exp(a_1 t) \tag{6.69e}$$

$$V_1(t) = \frac{-b_2(1 + u)(b_1 u)^2}{(b_2 - b_2 u - a_1)^2} \left[\frac{\exp(2tb_2(1 - u))}{b_2(1 - u)} - \frac{\exp(2a_1 t)}{b_2(1 - u) - 2a_1}\right.$$
$$\left. - \frac{2 \exp\{t(b_2(1 - u) + a_1)\}}{a_1}\right] + \frac{b_1 u \exp(a_1 t)}{b_2(1 - u) - a_1}$$
$$+ b_1 u \exp(t(b_2(1 - u))) \left[\frac{1}{b_2(1 - u) - a_1}\right.$$
$$\left. + \frac{2b_1 u b_2(1 + u)}{a_1(b_2 - b_2 u)(b_2 - b_2 u - 2a_1)}\right] \tag{6.69f}$$

where $x_1(0) = 1 = x_2(0)$ so that the constants $C_0$, $D_0$ of the deterministic solution (6.69c) are satisfied. Now the decision variable $u$ can be selected either by optimizing $M_1(t) + M_2(t)$, which would then imply optimizing $x_1(t) + x_2(t)$ of the deterministic solution (6.69c), or by optimizing a scalar preference functional $F = F(M_1(t), M_2(t), V_1(t), V_2(t))$ giving weights to both expected values and variances. Note that the second type of optimal allocation would consider not only the expected output increment resulting from investment allocation to a specific sector but also its variability measured by variance (either over a planning horizon or for each $t$). The implications of including such features in a general investment allocation model are discussed by Sengupta and Tintner [76].

Note that our growth models are discussed in such a manner that could be related to any other growth phenomena. For instance, if $X(t)$ denotes the size of a firm then the birth and death process model above could be easily applied to the growth of a firm. Viewing a firm as a population of customers, Steindl [77] has applied such birth and death process models with the additional consideration that he allows the entry of new firms by means of the probability of survival of firms having different age distributions.

### 6.3.2. Applications to inventory models

Consider the $(s, S)$ type Q-system of inventory control, where the replacement order is made at regular intervals of time and reordering is done only when the stock level is less than $s$. We consider here the backlog case in which demand occurring in excess of the current amount of inventory on hand is backlogged until supply becomes available. Denote by $X_t$ the amount of inventory on hand and on order prior to any order in period $t$ (and subsequent to any demand and delivery in period $t$), and by $r$ the quantity of demand for the (single) product with the density function $g(r)$ which is assumed to satisfy the conditions of a stationary and discrete Markov process [2]. The objective here is to derive the stationary distribution $p_{X_t}(x)$ of the variable $X_t$ with $t \to \infty$, where $X$ denotes the amount of inventory on hand or backlogged and on order before the end of the period. Then the $(s, S)$ policy may be specified by

$$X_{t+1} = X_t - r, \quad \text{if} \quad s + 1 \leqslant X_t \leqslant S \qquad (6.70a)$$

$$X_{t+1} = S - r, \quad \text{if} \quad X_t \leqslant s \qquad (6.70b)$$

where $X_{t+1}$ may be negative if demand is backlogged, i.e. back orders are possible. Now by enumeration of possibilities of transition for the discrete demand, the transition probabilities $p_{X_{t+1}}(x)$ associated with (6.70a) and (6.70b) (i.e. the probability that $X_{t+1}$ takes a value $x$) may be written as

$$p_{X_{t+1}}(x) = g(S - x) \sum_{j=-\infty}^{s} p_{X_t}(j) + \sum_{j=x}^{S} g(j - x) p_{X_t}(j), \quad \text{if} \quad s + 1 \leqslant x \leqslant S$$

(6.71a)

and

$$p_{X_{t+1}}(x) = g(S - x) \sum_{j=-\infty}^{s} p_{X_t}(j) + \sum_{j=s+1}^{S} g(j - x) p_{X_t}(j), \quad \text{if} \quad x \leqslant s.$$

(6.71b)

The stationary probabilities are derived from these equations by dropping the time subscript and then obtaining an infinite set of linear equations in the stationary probabilities $p_X(x)$, i.e.

$$p_X(x) = g(S - x) \sum_{j=-\infty}^{s} p_X(j) + \sum_{j=x}^{S} g(j - x) p_X(j), \quad \text{if} \quad s + 1 \leqslant x \leqslant S,$$

(6.72a)

and

$$p_X(x) = g(S - x) \sum_{j=-\infty}^{s} p_X(j) + \sum_{j=s+1}^{S} g(j - x) p_X(j), \quad \text{if} \quad x \leqslant s. \quad (6.72b)$$

If demand is not discrete but continuous, then these stationary probabilities become

$$p_X(x) = g(S - x) \int_{-\infty}^{s} p_X(t) \, dt + \int_{x}^{S} g(t - x) p_X(t) \, dt, \quad \text{if} \quad s \leq x \leq S,$$

(6.73a)

and

$$p_X(x) = g(S - x) \int_{-\infty}^{s} p_X(t) \, dt + \int_{s}^{S} g(t - x) p_X(t) \, dt, \quad \text{if} \quad x < s, \quad (6.73b)$$

where $g(r)$ is now a continuous (stationary) density function.

Note that the solution of the equations (6.71), (6.72) or (6.73) may be obtained in a recursive fashion by assuming a specific form of the density function $g(r)$ for demand, although this process may be complicated in some cases [78] and Monte Carlo methods of simulation are therefore unavoidable in very general cases. Consider for illustration that demand $r$ has a discrete uniform distribution

$$g(r) = m, \, r = 0, 1, \ldots, n \quad \text{and} \quad Er = \tfrac{1}{2}n;$$

then it is easy to show from (6.72a) and (6.72b) that for

$$s + 1 \leqslant x \leqslant S, \qquad p_X(x) = m(1 - m)^{x-s-1},$$

and for

$$S - (1/m) - 1 \leqslant x \leqslant s, \qquad p_X(x) = m,$$

and for

$$x \leqslant s - (1/m), \qquad p_X(x) = 0.$$

For illustration, take the case $s+1 \leqslant x \leqslant S$. The stationary equation (6.72a) becomes

$$p_X(x) = m \sum_{j=-\infty}^{s} p_X(j) + m \sum_{j=x}^{s} p_X(j).$$

Writing this equation for $x+1$ when $s+1 \leqslant x+1 \leqslant S$ and computing the quantity $p_X(x+1) - p_X(x) = \Delta p(x)$, we get

$$\Delta p(x) = - m p(x) \quad \text{where} \quad p(x) \text{ is another notation for } p_X(x).$$

This first order difference equation has the solution

$$p(x) = A_0(1 - m)^x,$$

where $A_0$ is a constant of summation which can be determined by the require-ment that at the lower limit of $x=s+1$, the probability $p_X(s+1)$ should equal $m$, i.e.

$$p(x = s + 1) = A_0(1 - m)^{s+1} = m, \quad \text{whence} \quad A_0 = m(1 - m)^{-s-1}.$$

Again, if the density function $g(r)$ of demand is continuous and uniform, i.e. $g(r) = m$, $0 \leqslant r \leqslant (1/m)$, then it can be easily shown by applying the equa-tions (6.73a) and (6.73b) for transition probabilities that for

$$s \leqslant x \leqslant S, \qquad p_X(x) = m \exp(- m(x - s)),$$

for

$$S - (1/m) \leqslant x \leqslant s, \qquad p_X(x) = m,$$

and for

$$s - (1/m) \leqslant x \leqslant S - (1/m), \qquad p_X(x) = m - m \exp[- 1 - m(x - s)]$$

with

$$p_X(x) = 0 \quad \text{for} \quad x \leqslant s - (1/m).$$

Note that once these transition probabilities $p_{X_t}(x)$ or $p_X(x)$ are calculated either exactly or approximately, they have to be incorporated in an overall cost function (of the type mentioned in equation (6.7g) for example in section

6.1.1) to compute the expected cost (and the variance function whenever computable) for following such an $(s, S)$ type inventory policy, which may then be minimized over a fixed or infinite horizon. This would generate the optimal sequence of decision variables.

Several extensions of the above type inventory policy model under stationary transition probabilities have been made in the literature. The model has been extended to include (a) more than two phases or two bins [79] as in the characterization of (6.70a) and (6.70b), (b) the cases of lagged delivery [80], and (c) the possibility of variable and random lead time. However, the computational aspects of these models are as yet very complicated, due to the basic difficulty of solving the stochastic nonlinear equations (6.71) or (6.72) with arbitrary density functions for demand. Also there is some problem of statistically estimating the parameters of the stationary Markovian processes from the observed time series of demand, although some work is now available to help in the operational computation [81].

### 6.3.3. Selected queuing models

Queuing models under Markov process conditions were originally developed in connection with the equilibrium behavior of telephone exchanges by Erlang [82] as early as 1908. They can be viewed mainly as specific characterizations of the equation (6.66b) for transition probabilities, which is also termed the equilibrium form of the Kolmogorov equations for Markov processes with a countable number of discrete states. A queuing or waiting line model characterizes the stochastic behavior of any system which may be interpreted as providing "services" to "customers" arriving randomly. A queuing system is characterized therefore by (a) the probability law governing the arrival of the customers (i.e. this is called the *input process*) which is specified by the sequence of arrival times $\{t_n\}$, $n = 1, 2, \ldots$ and the sequence of interarrival times $\{h_n\}$ where $h_n = t_{n+1} - t_n$, with $0 < t_1 < t_2 < \cdots < t_n < \infty$, (b) the *queue discipline* which gives the rule by which customers are served (e.g. a possible rule is: "first come, first served" which will be assumed here in our discussion), and (c) the probability law $\{g_n\}$ governing the time required to serve the $n$th customer (i.e. this is called the service time distribution mechanism).

Queuing models are in general non-Markovian, unless specific assumptions are made about the probability distributions of arrival times $\{t_n\}$ and the service times $\{g_n\}$, $n = 1, 2, \ldots$ However, if the distributions $\{t_n\}$ and $\{g_n\}$ satisfy a Poisson process with mutually independent increments, then the resulting stochastic process is Markovian. This type of Markovian queuing system is frequently denoted by $M/M/1$, where the first $M$ specifies that the input-process is random and of the Poisson type, the second $M$ indicates that the service time distribution is random and Poisson and the third term 1 indicates that there is only one serving station. Assuming that the service times $g_1, g_2, ..., g_n, ...$ are statistically independent of one another and of the interarrival times $\{h_n\}$, denote the cumulative statistical distribution of inter-arrival times by $F(h)$ and its density by $f(h)$. Erlang assumed a chi-square distribution for $f(h)$ which may be denoted by $E_n$

$$f(h)\, dh = \frac{(\mu n)^n}{n!} h^{n-1} \exp(-\mu n h)\, dh : E_n \qquad (6.74a)$$

where $\mu$ is the parameter denoting the expected service time. Hence a queuing system written as $M/E_n/1$ denotes Poisson arrival times, chi-square service time distributions and a single server (or a single station). A general Markovian queuing system is of the type $M/M/s$, where there are $s$ serving stations.

Consider now a simple queuing system of the $M/M/1$ type, where during the interval $(t, t+\Delta t)$ the following probability structure is assumed:

(i) the probability of one customer arriving at the service station is $\lambda \Delta t + O(\Delta t)$, $\lambda > 0$;

(ii) the probability of service being completed for one customer is $\mu \Delta t + O(\Delta t)$, $\lambda > 0$;

(iii) the probability of no arrivals or no service is $1 - (\lambda + \mu)\Delta t + O(\Delta t)$; and

(iv) the probability of more than one arrival during $(t, t+\Delta t)$ is $O(\Delta t)$,

where in each case $O(\Delta t)$ tends to zero as $\Delta t \to$ zero. Denoting by $p_x(t)$ the probability that there are $x$ units (or customers) in the queue or waiting line at time $t$ (where $x$ is assumed discrete), the queuing system may now be characterized under the above assumptions as follows:

$$p_x(t + \Delta t) = \lambda p_{x-1}(t) \cdot \Delta t + \mu p_{x+1}(t) \cdot \Delta t + (1 - \lambda - \mu)\, p_x(t) \cdot \Delta t + O(\Delta t). \qquad (6.74b)$$

Letting $\Delta t \to 0$ this implies

$$dp_x(t)/dt = \lambda p_{x-1}(t) + \mu p_{x+1}(t) - (\lambda + \mu)\, p_x(t); \qquad x = 1, 2, ... \qquad (6.74c)$$

$$dp_0(t)/dt = -\lambda p_0(t) + \mu p_1(t); \qquad x = 0$$

with the common requirement:

$$\sum_{x=0}^{\infty} p_x(t) = 1. \qquad (6.74d)$$

Note that these equations (6.74b) through (6.74d) are special cases of the birth and death process type models discussed earlier in equations (6.66a) through (6.68b). A more general specification of the single station queuing problem is to assume that the rates of arrival ($\lambda$) and servicing ($\mu$) are not constants but dependent on the length of the queue. The transition probability equations then become

$$\frac{dp_x(t)}{dt} = \lambda_{x-1} p_{x-1}(t) + \mu_{x+1} p_{x+1}(t) - (\lambda_x + \mu_x) p_x(t); \qquad (x = 1, 2, \ldots)$$

(6.74e)

$$\frac{dp_0(t)}{dt} = -\lambda_0 p_0(t) + \mu_1 p_1(t); \qquad x = 0.$$

(6.74f)

In a more general case in which there are $s$ servicing stations (or servers) where $s > 1$ and the process $\{X(t)\}$ characterized by $X(t)$, the number of customers in the queue at time $t$, is a Markov process with a countable number of discrete states, the transition probability equations may be more generally written as

$$\frac{dP_x(t)}{dt} = \lambda_{x-1} P_{x-1}(t) + \mu_{x+1} P_{x+1}(t) - (\lambda_x + \mu_x) P_x(t)$$

(6.74g)

$$\frac{dP_0(t)}{dt} = -\lambda_0 P_0(t) + \mu_1 P_1(t); \qquad x = 0$$

(6.74h)

where $P(t) = [p_{ij}(t)]$ denotes the matrix of transition probabilities and $P_x(t) = \mathrm{Prob}\{X(t) = x\}$, $x = 0, 1, \ldots$ denotes the probability that $X(t)$ takes on the value $x$ at time $t$ (i.e. the probability that at time $t$ the queue is of length $x$). If the equations (6.74g) and (6.74b) can be solved explicitly, then the exact probability of satisfying $x$ customers for any given $x$ can be computed and the queue length can be appropriately fixed. On the other hand, this information may also be used to design an optimal number of serving stations, by associating various penalty costs for net servicing a given number of customers. Further, sometimes it is easier to get solutions in the form of stationary probabilities $Q_x = \lim_{t \to \infty} P_x(t)$, although for a finite $t$ it may be difficult to get explicit solutions.

The theory of queues, a brief sketch of which is outlined above, has been extended in recent years in several directions [83], some of which include (a) the various types of arrival time and waiting time distributions (e.g. the so-called hyperexponentia ldistributions [83], (b) various "phases" of delay and the notion of busy periods and the possibility of bulk service [84], and (c) also some interesting methods of estimation of the parameters such as $\lambda$ and $\mu$ particularly under the restriction that these have to be nonnegative [81].

Applications of queuing models have been very extensive also. Problems in which there are $m$ machines and $r$ repairman for servicing and the machine running time $(t)$ and the service or repair time $(g)$ each have exponential cumulative distributions $A(t)$ and $B(g)$ respectively

$$A(t) = 1 - \exp(-\lambda t), \quad t \geqslant 0, \quad \lambda > 0 \tag{6.75a}$$

$$B(g) = 1 - \exp(-\mu g), \quad g \geqslant 0, \quad \mu > 0 \tag{6.75b}$$

have been applied to various industrial production situations which are of great interest for the economist and the operations researcher. This problem can again be put in the form of the equations (6.74g) and (6.74h) developed before, if the Markov process conditions are satisfied, provided $x = 0, 1, \ldots, m$ is interpreted as the number of machines and a transition from state $x$ to state $x + 1$ is due to a breakdown of one among the $(m - x)$ working machines. The case in which the queuing system is in state $x$ with $x \leqslant r$ is to be interpreted as one in which $x$ machines are being serviced, while $r - x$ are idle; if $x > r$, the interpretation is that $r$ machines are being serviced, while $(x - r)$ machines are waiting. In this case the transition probabilities during $(t, t + \Delta t)$ are

$$\text{Prob}(x \to x + 1) = \lambda_x \Delta t + 0(\Delta t),$$
$$\text{Prob}(x \to x - 1) = \mu_x \Delta t + 0(\Delta t), \quad \text{and}$$
$$\text{Prob}(x \to x) = 1 - (\lambda_x + \mu_x) \Delta t + 0(\Delta t)$$

where the birth rates $\lambda_x$ and death rates $\mu_x$ are given in view of (6.75a), (6.75b) by

$$\lambda_x = \begin{cases} m\lambda, & \text{if } x = 0 \\ (m - x)\lambda, & \text{if } 1 \leqslant x \leqslant r, \quad r \leqslant x \leqslant m. \end{cases}$$

$$\mu_x = \begin{cases} 0, & \text{if } m = 0 \\ \mu \cdot x, & \text{if } 1 \leqslant x \leqslant r \\ r \cdot \mu, & \text{if } r \leqslant x \leqslant m \end{cases}$$

where $\lambda$ and $\mu$ are positive constants. The Kolmogorov equations such as (6.74g) and (6.74h) become

$$\frac{dP_x(t)}{dt} = (m - x + 1)\lambda \cdot P_{x-1}(t) - \{(m - x)\lambda + x\mu\} P_x(t)$$
$$+ (x + 1)\mu P_{x+1}(t), \quad \text{if } 1 \leqslant x \leqslant r, \tag{6.75c}$$

$$\frac{dP_0(t)}{dt} = -m\lambda P_0(t) + \mu P_1(t), \quad \text{with } 1 \leqslant x \leqslant r, \tag{6.75d}$$

and

$$\frac{dP_x(t)}{dt} = (m - x + 1) \lambda \cdot P_{x-1}(t) - \{(m - x) \lambda + r\mu\} P_x(t)$$

$$+ r\mu P_{x+1}(t), \quad \text{if} \quad r \leqslant x \leqslant m. \qquad (7.65e)$$

The solutions of these equations would determine the average number of machines in the waiting line and, if costs could be associated with the transition probabilities (this situation is discussed in some detail in ch. 5 in transition probability programming), then the condition of minimizing the expected cost appropriately defined would determine one possible type of optimal solution (i.e. optimal decision). Again the role of Monte Carlo methods of simulation is very important in obtaining approximate solutions of equations (6.75c) through (6.75e).

### 6.4. Critical path methods and project analysis

In this section we consider situations in which variables are required to be nonnegative integers and decisions relate essentially to a project or a set of projects; the project may be viewed either very broadly as a set of interrelated budgeting programs as in investment projects or very specifically as a single scheme comprising a very large number of successive activities which are arranged in a complex network. Our objective here is to discuss very briefly the specific methods of project analysis known as PERT (program evaluation review technique) and CPM (critical path methods), followed by a short discussion of the problem of optimal project selection amongst a set of interrelated projects. The latter problem was mentioned before in ch. 2, section 3 in connection with integer linear programming; the reason we discuss these problems once again is to illustrate that in real life decision problems require a combination of several techniques (such as quadratic integer programming or chance-constrained linear programming with integer requirements for decision variables) rather than one.

### 6.4.1. Network methods

Consider a project comprising a large number of successive "activities" as a complex network represented by a graph with points in a plane called "nodes" connected by lines called arcs or edges. Attach to each arc connecting a given pair of nodes a number representing its "length". This number defines the flow capacity of the arc. A "chain" (or "path") is defined as a succession of arcs without a gap between two selected nodes, which are usually called the "source" and the "sink". A "chain flow" is defined by the number attached to a chain from the source to the sink which is not larger than a flow capacity of any arc forming part of the chain. A "network flow" is defined by a collection of chain flows such that the sum of the chain flows through any arc does not exceed its capacity.

Now consider a problem of sending the maximal flow through the network of $2(n+1)$ nodes from the source to the sink formulated as an integer linear program. Denote the flow from node $i$ to node $j$ by $x_{ij}$ where $x_{ij}$ is required to be a nonnegative integer and the capacity of the $(i, j)$ arc by $r_{ij}$. Also let $x_{ii}$ denote the flow through node $i$, $r_{ii}$ its flow capacity both measured in integer numbers and let $x_{00}$ denote the total flow from the source to the sink. Then the problem is to

$$\text{maximize } x_{00} \qquad (6.76a)$$

subject to

$$\sum_{\substack{j \\ j \neq i}} x_{ij} \leqslant x_{ii} \quad (i = 0, 1, \ldots, n) \qquad (6.76b)$$

$$\sum_{\substack{i \\ i \neq j}} x_{ij} \leqslant x_{jj} \quad (j = 0, 1, \ldots, n) \qquad (6.76c)$$

$$0 \leqslant x_{ij} \leqslant r_{ij}; \quad x_{ij}, r_{ij} \text{ integers } (i, j = 0, 1, \ldots, n). \qquad (6.76d)$$

Given a preassigned set of values for $x_{ii}$, $x_{jj}$ and $r_{ij}$, the optimal solution of this problem when it exists characterizes a maximal flow (which is also termed a "minimal cut" in the theory of Ford and Fulkerson [85] by invoking the duality property which holds for integer LP problems).

Now a PERT network is one in which each activity commences at a particular "node" of the network but not until all activities terminating at that node are completed. The arcs become now the "tasks" which provide the links between nodes. The source now becomes the starting point usually labeled zero and the remaining nodes are numbered in such a way that if there is a link (i.e. an arc) directed from node $i$ to node $j$ then the activities terminating at node $i$ must be completed before the activities which terminate at node $j$. This implies that the task $(i, j)$ can start as soon as all the tasks directed towards node $i$ have been completed. Also we introduce dummy nodes so that the arc $(i, j)$ can represent a unique task in which some of the $i$ and $j$ may be dummy nodes (just like dummy activities in LP models) and let the arc length be substituted for by task times (i.e. times to complete a given task).

Consider a simple example of a PERT network in which the tasks are $A$ through $D$ and the nodes are 0 through 4 as follows:

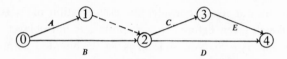

Here the task $(1, 2)$ indicated by the dotted arc is a dummy task and the assumed (or estimated) task times in days are $A=20$, $B=7$, $C=10$, $D=14$ and $E=5$. Given the above project network and the task times, we have to determine the minimum time in which the project can be completed and also identify the critical tasks which may delay the project.

Denote by $t_i$ the minimum (i.e. earliest) time for node $i$ (assuming $t_0=0$ i.e. the start is immediate) and by $t_{ij}$ the time required for task $(i, j)$ with $t_{ij}=0$ for dummy nodes. Now from the above diagram and the sequential relations indicated by the directed arcs, we may compute for nodes $i=1, 2, 3, 4$ the minimum time $t_i$:

$$t_1 = t_0 + t_{01} = 20$$
$$t_2 = \max\{t_0 + t_{02}, t_1 + t_{12}\} = \max(0 + 7, 20 + 0) = 20$$
$$t_3 = \max\{t_2 + t_{23}\} = 20 + 10 = 30$$
$$t_4 = \max\{t_2 + t_{24}, t_3 + t_{34}\} = \max(20 + 14, 30 + 5) = 35$$

Hence the entire project can be completed in 35 days. Note that the earliest time $t_2$, for example, is computed as the longer of the times for the two routes with nodes 0, 2 and 1, 2 (since $t_2 \geqslant t_0 + t_{02} = 7$ and $t_2 \geqslant t_1 + t_{12} = 20$ and by feasibility $t_2$ equals 20) and the rules for computing time $t_i$ are simply that

$$t_0 = 0 \quad \text{and} \quad t_i = \max_k\{t_k + t_{ki}\} \tag{6.77a}$$

where $k$ ranges over all nodes for which tasks $(k, i)$ exist. Now denote by $T_i$ the latest time at which node $i$ could be reached without any delay, i.e.

$$T_i = \min_j\{T_j - t_{ij}\} \tag{6.77b}$$

where $j$ ranges over all nodes for which tasks $(i, j)$ exist. Note again that if $j=2, 3$ and $(i, 2), (i, 3)$ exist, then $T_i \leqslant T_2 - t_{i2}$ and $T_i \leqslant T_3 - t_{i3}$ and by feasibility we get (6.77b). Denote slack times by

$$T_i - t_j \geqslant 0 \quad (i, j = 1, 2, \ldots) \tag{6.77c}$$

and let $E_{ij}$ denote the earliest time of completion of task $(i, j)$. Then

$$E_{ij} = t_i + t_{ij} \quad \text{where } t_i \text{ is defined in (6.77a).} \qquad (6.77\text{d})$$

In order to fix our ideas, consider the computation of $T_1$ from (6.77b) from our network given before. Now if node 2 is not delayed, it must be completed in time $T_2 = 20$. Now so long as we reach node 1 before $T_2 - t_{12} = 20 - 0$, there will be no delay in node 2, hence $T_1 = 20$. Hence at node 1, the slack time is $T_1 - t_1 = 0$ and $E_{12} = t_1 + t_{12} = 20 + 0 = 20$. Now for the task $(i, j)$, the difference $T_j - E_{ij}$ is called the task slack time, e.g. for task $(1, 2)$ in our example $T_2 - E_{12} = 20 - 20 = 0$. Any task that has a zero slack time is called a critical task, since its delay in completion can delay the entire project completion time (i.e. if a critical task is completed at time $T_j + \alpha$ ($\alpha > 0$), then the entire project with the sink at node $n$ will not be completed until time $T_n + \alpha$. A path or a chain of the network which links the nodes with zero slack time is called a critical path.

Now consider a PERT network with source node 0 and sink node $n$, where the completion time $t_i$ at node $i$ defined in (6.77a) is random, i.e.

$$\text{earliest time } t_0 = 0 \quad \text{and} \quad t_i = \max_k \{t_k + t_{ki}\} \quad \text{where } (k, i) \text{ is a task} \quad (6.78\text{a})$$

$$\text{latest time } T_n = t_n \quad \text{and} \quad T_i = \min_j \{T_j - t_{ij}\} \quad \text{where } (i, j) \text{ is a task} \quad (6.78\text{b})$$

$$\sigma_0^2 = 0 \quad \text{for} \quad t_0 = 0 \quad \text{and} \quad \sigma_i^2 = \sigma_r^2 + \sigma_{ri}^2 \qquad (6.78\text{c})$$

where $\sigma_i^2$ denotes the variance of $t_i$, $\sigma_{ri}^2$ the variance of task time $t_{ri}$ for the task $(r, i)$ and $r$ is the node such that

$$t_i = \max_k \{t_k + t_{ki}\} = t_r + t_{ri}, \quad \text{where } (k, i) \text{ is a task.}$$

If there is more than one value of $k$ which maximizes $t_k + t_{ki}$ in computing $t_i$, we choose that value (which then is called $r$) which gives the largest $\sigma_i^2$. These variances $\sigma_i^2$ of $t_i$ are computed generally under the assumption that the task time of completion $t_i$ follows a univariate beta distribution which has the density function $f(x) \, dx$, i.e.

$$f(x) \, dx = K (x - a)^{m_1} (b - x)^{m_2} \, dx; \qquad a \leqslant m \leqslant b$$

$\text{E}x = (1/3) [2m + \tfrac{1}{2}(a + b)]$ where $m$ is the mode, E is the expectation, although other distributions [86] are sometimes proposed.

Now since the task completion time $t_i$ has some variance, one may introduce the notion of a penalty cost as a function of the deviation between the desired (or scheduled) completion time $\theta_i$ and $t_i$, where $\theta_i$ may be pre-assigned before from prior experience. A more direct way to introduce costs is to assume that a cost $c_{ij}$ is incurred when a task $(i, j)$ is completed in time $t_{ij}$, i.e.

$$c_{ij} = g_{ij} - t_{ij}h_{ij}, \qquad m_{ij} \leqslant t_{ij} \leqslant M_{ij}, \qquad (6.78d)$$

where $g_{ij}$ and $h_{ij}$ are nonnegative constants such that $c_{ij} \geqslant 0$ and $(m_{ij}, M_{ij})$ are the preassigned minimum and maximum times to completion of task $(i, j)$. Denote by $L_m$ and $L_M$ the total project time from source 0 to sink $n$ when for *all* $(i, j)$ in a chain from 0 to $n$ we have $t_{ij} = m_{ij}$ and $t_{ij} = M_{ij}$ respectively. In other words $L_m(L_M)$ provides the most optimistic (most pessimistic) estimate of total project time. Let $L$ be the total project time if it is feasible, i.e.

$$L_m \leqslant L \leqslant L_M. \qquad (6.78e)$$

Now the optimum decision problem which the CPM (critical path method) seeks to solve is to

$$\underset{\{t_{ij}\}, \{t_i\}}{\text{minimize}} \sum_i \sum_j [g_{ij} - h_{ij}t_{ij}] = \underset{\{t_{ij}\}, \{t_i\}}{\text{maximize}} \sum_i \sum_j h_{ij}t_{ij} \qquad (6.79a)$$

under the restrictions

$$t_i \geqslant t_k + t_{ki}, \quad (k, i) \text{ being a task,} \quad i = 1, ..., n \qquad (6.79b)$$

$$m_{ij} \leqslant t_{ij} \leqslant M_{ij}, \quad L_m \leqslant L \leqslant L_M \qquad (6.79c)$$

$$t_i \geqslant 0, t_{ij} \geqslant 0, \quad t_i \text{ is given by (6.78a)}. \qquad (6.79d)$$

Also two more constraints are generally added. First, each $t_i$ satisfying (6.79b) and (6.78a) has to be the smallest possible; this point may be incorporated by rewriting the objective function as

$$\text{maximize} \sum_i \sum_j h_{ij}t_{ij} - \sum_i t_iC_i$$

where $C_i$ is a very large positive constant (like the $-M$ pricing technique in linear programming methods when a particular activity is not to enter the optimal basis). Second, the restriction (6.79b) may be so written that it reflects the variances $\sigma_i^2$ of $t_i$. This can be done either by following the methods of the chance-constrained model [20] as applied in equation (6.10e) in section 6.1.2 in connection with dynamic inventory models or by the various techniques discussed in ch. 5. Several special algorithms for solving problems of the type given in (6.79a) through (6.79d) are also available [87].

Several general remarks may now be made about the CPM methods which in different forms are now applied in administrative organizations also. First, note that the total of completion times along the critical path is a statistical variable, if the task completion times $t_i$ have a specified distribution and the expected value of this statistical variable specifies the expected time to complete the entire project. More detailed analysis of the distribution of this statistical variable as a function of the distributions of each $t_i$ is yet needed, although some very useful work [88] has been done recently in computing the bias and other characteristics by classifying projects into different categories and developing several Monte Carlo type procedures of sequential revision of estimates. Second, if the decision variables $\{t_i\}, \{t_{ij}\}$ are required to be nonnegative integers and the cost function $c_{ij}$ in (6.78d) is not linear, then the problem specified by (6.79a) through (6.79d) becomes a nonlinear integer programming problem and the only computational method which would still apply is the algorithm of dynamic programming. An application of this idea and also the computation of next best policies is available in Aris [89].

### 6.4.2. Capital budgeting in interrelated projects

The problem of allocating capital budgets over a set of interrelated investment projects has already been discussed very briefly in connection with the applications of integer linear programming (see ch. 2, section 3.2). In this section we propose to discuss very briefly some additional characteristics of interdependence between projects when there is a budget constraint at each period.

Consider the following integer linear programming problem [90] of budget allocation between $n$ projects:

$$\text{maximize } \sum_{j=1}^{n} c_j x_j \qquad (6.80\text{a})$$

under the restrictions

$$\sum_{j=1}^{n} a_{tj} x_j \leqslant b_t; \qquad t = 1, ..., T \text{ (fixed)} \qquad (6.80\text{b})$$

$$0 \leqslant x_j \leqslant 1, \qquad (6.80\text{c})$$

$$x_j = \text{an integer.} \qquad (6.80\text{d})$$

Here $x_j$ is the fraction of project $j = 1, ..., n$ accepted with $x_j$ being either zero or one; $c_j$ is the net discounted present value of project $j$, when discounting is assumed to be done [91] by an appropriate rate of interest, $a_{tj}$

is the expenditure required for the $j$th project in period $t$ and $b_t$ is the pre-assigned budget limit for $t = 1, ..., T$ with $T$ fixed and finite. The optimal solution of the above model when it exists will be denoted by $\bar{x} = (\bar{x}_j)$ and although the models of computation of such optimal solutions are already mentioned in ch. 2 (section 3.2), it may be emphasized again that as yet, no very efficient method of integer linear programming is available.

Weingartner [90] has discussed several modifications (or extensions) of the constraints (6.80c) and (6.80d) to include various types of interdependence between projects. (1) If there is a set $J$ of *mutually exclusive* projects from which at most one is to be selected then this could be expressed by the constraint

$$\sum_{j \in J} x_j \leqslant 1, \ x_j \geqslant 0, \quad x_j \text{ integer.} \tag{6.81a}$$

(2) If two projects $i$ and $j$ are *contingent* in the sense that project $i$ may be undertaken only if project $j$ is accepted, while project $j$ is independent, then this can be specified by the following constraints

$$x_i \leqslant x_j \quad \text{and} \quad x_j \leqslant 1, x_i, x_j \geqslant 0 \text{ (integers).} \tag{6.81b}$$

Thus if project $j$ is accepted in the optimal solution (i.e. $\bar{x}_j = 1$) then $x_i \leqslant 1$ becomes the effective constraint. Otherwise if project $j$ is not in the optimal solution $\bar{x}$ (i.e. $x_j = 0$, $x_j$ is not in $\bar{x}$), then $x_i \leqslant 0$; but also we have $x_i \geqslant 0$, hence $x_i$ is forced to be zero. Again a chain of contingent projects can be built in a similar manner.

An interesting generalization to include all pair-wise second-order effects involving pairs of projects has been made by Reiter [92]. A triangular pay-off matrix $B$ is defined for the set of $n$ investment projects.

$$B = \begin{bmatrix} b_{11} & b_{12} & \cdot & \cdot & \cdot & b_{1n} \\ 0 & b_{22} & \cdot & \cdot & \cdot & b_{2n} \\ \cdot & \cdot & \cdot & \cdot & \cdot & \cdot \\ 0 & 0 & \cdot & \cdot & \cdot & b_{nn} \end{bmatrix} = [b_{ij}] \tag{6.82a}$$

such that the pay-off (e.g. net discounted present value) from the acceptance of project $i$ alone is $b_{ii}$ ($i = 1, ..., n$) and the additional pay-off from the acceptance of both projects $i$ and $j$ is $b_{ij}$ plus $b_{ii}$ and $b_{jj}$. An optimal partitioning of the set of project indices into two mutually exclusive and exhaustive subsets is sought such that the total pay-off from one subset (called the optimal subset) is a maximum. Now the dependence of project $i$ on project $j$ is introduced by letting $b_{ii}$ be the cost (i.e. a negative quantity) while $b_{ij}$ represents the benefit (i.e. a positive quantity) from having project $i$ in addition to $j$. It is apparent now that Reiter's method actually defines an integer quadratic programming model as follows:

$$\text{Maximize } x'Bx = \sum_{i=1}^{n} \sum_{j=1}^{n} b_{ij}x_i x_j \qquad (6.82b)$$

under the restrictions

$$x_j = 0 \quad \text{or} \quad 1, \quad B = [b_{ij}] \text{ is given in (6.82a).} \qquad (6.82c)$$

Several algorithms [93] including an algorithm developed by Reiter are now available for computing such problems, along with the all-purpose algorithm of dynamic programming. Note that only if, in the optimal solution $\bar{x}$, both $\bar{x}_i = 1$ and $\bar{x}_j = 1$ is the pay-off $b_{ij}$ realized; otherwise $b_{ij}\bar{x}_i\bar{x}_j = 0$ for either $\bar{x}_i = 0$, $\bar{x}_j = 1$, or $\bar{x}_i = 1$, $\bar{x}_j = 0$ or $\bar{x}_i = 0 = \bar{x}_j$.

Now a budget restriction of the type (6.80b) for each period $t$ may be built into the Reiter format as follows. Consider the simple case in which equation (6.80b) is written for one period only as

$$\sum_{j=1}^{n} a_j x_j \leqslant b; \qquad (6.82d)$$

then define $\lambda$ as the Lagrange multiplier and denote $\bar{B}$ as:

$$\bar{B} = \begin{bmatrix} b_{11} - \lambda a_1 & b_{12} & & b_{13} & \cdot & \cdot & \cdot & b_{1n} \\ 0 & b_{22} - \lambda a_2 & b_{23} & \cdot & \cdot & \cdot & b_{2n} \\ \vdots & & & & & & \\ 0 & \cdots\cdots\cdots & & \cdot & & \cdot & \cdot & \cdot & b_{nn} - \lambda a_n \end{bmatrix}. \qquad (6.82e)$$

Substituting this $\bar{B}$ into $B$ of (6.82b), we solve the optimization problem given in (6.82b) and (6.82c) with varying values of $\lambda$ (a scalar) till the budget condition in (6.82d) is satisfied. Otherwise we may also adjoin restrictions (6.82d) or (6.80b) to the quadratic integer program specified by (6.82b) and (6.82c).

The above formulation may be easily interpreted to hold when the net discounted present value $c_j$ of project $j$ given in (6.80a) is not fixed but random with $\mu_j$ and covariances $\sigma_{ij}$. Then the model (6.80a) through (6.80d) can be written as

$$\text{maximize } \sum_{i=1}^{n} \mu_i x_i - \lambda \sum_{i=1}^{n} \sum_{j=1}^{n} x_i \sigma_{ij} x_j$$

under the restrictions

$$x_i = 0, 1 \quad (i = 1, ..., n) \quad \text{and} \quad (6.80b),$$

where $\lambda$ is a measure of risk aversion. Note that this problem has the same structure as the Reiter model given in (6.82b) and (6.82c), provided (6.80b) is not introduced and $B$ is interpreted as follows:

$$
B = \begin{bmatrix}
\mu_1 - \lambda\sigma_1^2 & -2\lambda\sigma_{12} & . & . & . & -2\lambda\sigma_{1n} \\
0 & \mu_2 - \lambda\sigma_2^2 & . & . & . & -2\lambda\sigma_{2n} \\
\vdots & & & & & \\
0 & 0 & . & . & . & \mu_n - \lambda\sigma_n^2
\end{bmatrix} .
$$

Hence the algorithms developed by Reiter could be applied. However one should note that these algorithms have not yet been tested for their sensitivity to specific perturbations and hence the need for developing new algorithms and suitable Monte Carlo methods of simulation and approximation is all the greater.

## REFERENCES

[1] Wagner, H. M., *Statistical management of inventory systems*. New York: John Wiley, 1962.
Hanssmann, F., *Operations research in production and inventory control*. New York: John Wiley, 1962.
[2] Hadley, G. and T. M. Whitin, *Analysis of inventory systems*. Englewood Cliffs, N. J.: Prentice Hall, 1963.
Prabhu, N. U., *Queues and inventories*. New York: John Wiley, 1965.
[3] Arrow, K. J., S. Karlin and H. Scarf, *Studies in the mathematical theory of inventory and production*. Stanford: Stanford University Press, 1958.
[4] Dhrymes, P. J., "On the theory of the monopolistic multiproduct firm under uncertainty", *International Economic Review*, Vol. 5, September 1964, 239–257.
[5] Dzielinsky, B. P., C. T. Baker and A. S. Manne, "Simulation tests of lot-size programming", *Management Science*, January 1963.
Banerjee, B. P., "On a linear programming model of production-inventory situations", *Arthaniti*, January 1965, 69–82.
[6] Arrow, K. J., T. Harris and J. Marschak, "Optimal inventory policy", *Econometrica*, Vol. 19, No. 3, 1951, 250–272.
[7] Bellman, R. and S. E. Dreyfus, *Applied dynamic programming*. Princeton: Princeton University Press, 1962.
[8] Bellman, R., "The theory of dynamic programming", *Bulletin of American Mathematical Society*, Vol. 60, 1954, 503–516.
[9] Bellman, R., I. Glicksberg and O. Gross, "On the optimal inventory equation", *Management Science*, Vol. 2, 1955, 83–104.
[10] Levy, J., "Loss resulting from the use of incorrect data in computing an optimal inventory policy", *Naval Research Logistics Quarterly*, Vol. 5, No. 1, March 1958, 75–81.
[11] Karlin, S. and A. J. Fabens, "A stationary inventory model with Markovian demand". In: K. J. Arrow, S. Karlin and P. Suppes (eds.), *Mathematical methods in the social sciences*, 1959, Stanford: Stanford University Press, 159–175.
[12] Scarf, H., "The optimality of *(S, s)* policies in the dynamic inventory problem". In:

K. J. Arrow, S. Karlin and P. Suppes (eds.), *Mathematical methods in the social sciences*, 1959, *op. cit.* 196–202.

[13] Bramson, M. J., "The variable lead-time problem in inventory control: survey of the literature, Part I", *Operational Research Quarterly*, Vol. 13, No. 1, 41–53.

[14] Geisler, M. A., *Some statistical properties of simulation models used in studying inventory problems*, Washington, D.C., U.S. Gov't. Research Reports, Dept. of Commerce, Document No. AD270-817, 1961.

[15] Starr, M. K. and D. W. Miller, *Inventory control: theory and practice*. Englewood Cliffs, N.J.: Prentice Hall, 1962.

Naddor, E., *Inventory systems*. New York: John Wiley, 1966.

[16] Wagner, H. M. and T. M. Whitin, "Dynamic version of the economic lot-size model", *Management science*, Vol. 5, No. 1, October 1958, 89–96.

[17] Johnson, S. M., "Sequential production planning over time at a minimum cost", *Management Science*, Vol. 3, No. 4, 1957, 435–437.

Holt, C. C., F. Modigliani and J. F. Muth, "Derivation of a linear decision rule for production and employment scheduling", *Management Science*, Vol. 2, January 1956, 159–177.

[18] Bowman, E. H., "Production scheduling by a transportation method of linear programming", *Operations Research*, Vol. 4, No. 1, February 1956, 100–103.

Dannerstedt, G., "Production scheduling for an arbitrary number of periods, given the sales forecast in the form of a probability distribution", *Operations Research*, Vol. 3, No. 3, August 1955, 300–318.

Veinott, A. F., "The status of mathematical inventory theory", *Management Science*, Vol. 12, No. 11, Series A, July 1966, 745–777.

[19] Eilon, S., "Economic batch-size determination for multi-product scheduling", *Operational Research Quarterly*, Vol. 9, December 1958, 217–227.

Manne, A. S., "Programming of economic lot-sizes", *Management Science*, Vol. 4, No. 2, January 1958, 115–135.

[20] Charnes, A., W. W. Cooper and G. G. Symonds, "Cost horizons and certainty equivalents: an approach to stochastic programming of heating oil", *Management Science*, Vol. 4, No. 3, 1958, 235–263.

[21] Dvoretzky, A., J. Kiefer and J. Wolfowitz, "The inventory problem", *Econometrica*, Vol. 20, No. 2, April 1952, 187–222, and No. 3, July 1952, 450–466.

Dvoretzky, A., J. Kiefer and J. Wolfowitz, "On the optimal character of the *(S, s)* policy in inventory theory", *Econometrica*, Vol. 21, No. 4, October 1953, 586–596.

[22] Mills, E. S., *Price, output and inventory policy*. New York: John Wiley, 1962.

[23] Sengupta, S. S., *Operations research in Sellers' competition*. New York: John Wiley, 1967.

[24] Doob, J. L., *Stochastic processes*. New York: John Wiley, 1953.

[25] Darling, P. G. and M. C. Lovell, "Factors influencing investment in inventories". In: J. S. Duesenberry, G. Fromm, L. R. Klein and E. Kuh (eds.), *The Brookings quarterly econometric model of the United States*. Chicago: Rand McNally, 1965.

[26] Lovell, M., "Manufacturers' inventories, sales expectations and the acceleration principle", *Econometrica*, Vol. 29, No. 3, July 1961, 293–314.

Metzler, L. A., "The nature and stability of inventory cycles", *Review of Economics and Statistics*, Vol. 3, August 1941, 113–129.

Lovell, M. C., "Buffer stocks, sales expectations and stability: a multi-sector analysis of the inventory cycle", *Econometrica*, Vol. 30, April 1962, 267–296.

[27] Modigliani, F., "Business reasons for holding inventories and their macro-economic implications". In: *Problems of capital formation: concepts, measurement and controlling factors*, Studies in Income and Wealth, Vol. 19. Princeton: Princeton University Press, 1957.

[28] Mack, R. P., *Information, expectations and inventory fluctuations: a study of materials stock on hand and on order*, National Bureau of Economic Research. New York: Columbia University Press, 1967.

[29] Boiteux, M., "La tarification des demandes en point: application de la théorie de la vente au cout marginal", *Revue Générale de l'Electricité*, Vol. 58, August 1949, 321–340; translated as "Peak-load pricing", *Journal of Business*, Vol. 33, April 1960, 157–179.

[30] Sengupta, J. K. and A. Sen, "Models of optimal capacity expansion for the firm: an appraisal" (authors: Department of Economics, Iowa State University, 1967).

[31] Masse, P., *Optimal investment decisions*. Englewood Cliffs, N.J.: Prentice Hall, 1962.

[32] Lutz, F. and Vera Lutz, *The theory of investment of the firm*. Princeton: Princeton University Press, 1951.

[33] Hicks, J. R., "The process of imperfect competition", *Oxford Economic Papers*, February 1954.

[34] Chenery, H. B., "Overcapacity and the acceleration principle", *Econometrica*, January 1952.

[35] Arrow, J. K., M. J. Beckmann and S. Karlin (eds.), "The optimal expansion of the capacity of a firm", In: *Studies in the mathematical theory of inventory and production*. Stanford: Stanford University Press, 1958.

[36] Manne, A. S., "Capacity expansion and probabilistic growth", *Econometrica*, Vol. 29, October 1961, 632–649.

[37] Manne, A. S., "Calculation for a single producing area". In: A. S. Manne (ed.), *Investment for capacity expansion*. Cambridge, Mass.: MIT Press, 1967.

[38] Manne, A. S. and A. F. Veinott, "Optimal plant size with arbitrary increasing time path of demand". In: A. S. Manne (ed.), *op. cit.*, Ch. 11.

[39] Smith, V. L., *Investment and production*. Harvard: Harvard University Press, 1961.

[40] Srinivasan, T. N., "Geometric rate of growth of demand". In: A. S. Manne (ed.), *Investment for capacity expansion*, op. cit.

[41] Baumol, W. J, *Business behavior, value and growth*. Princeton: Princeton University Press, 1966.

[42] Carlson, S. A., *A study on the pure theory of production*. London: P. S. King and Sons, 1965.

[43] Harrod, R. F., "Doctrines of imperfect competition", *Quarterly Journal of Economics*, May 1934.

[44] Miller, R., "A note on the theory of investment and production", *Quarterly Journal of Economics*, November 1959.

[45] Haavelmo, T., *A Study in the theory of investment*. Chicago: University of Chicago Press, 1961.

[46] Bowman, R. T. and A. Phillips, "The capacity concept and induced investment", *Canadian Journal of Economics and Political Science*, May 1955.

[47] Ferguson, C. E., "A social concept of excess capacity", *Metroeconomica*, April, 1956.

[48] Klein, L. R., "Some theoretical issues in the measurement of capacity", *Econometrica*, April 1960.

[49] Klein, L. R. and R. S. Preston, "The measurement of capacity", *American Economic Review*, March 1967.

[50] Koyck, L. M., *Distributed lags and investment analysis*. Amsterdam: North-Holland Publishing Co., 1954.

[51] Leeuw, F. de, "The concept of capacity", *Journal of the American Statistical Association*, December 1962.

[52] Cassels, J. M., "Excess capacity and monopolistic competition", *Quarterly Journal of Economics*, 1937.

[53] Nourse, E. G. and associates, *America's capacity to produce*. Washington, D.C.: Brookings Institution, 1934.

[54] Erlenkotter, D., "Optimal plant-size with time-phased imports". In: A. S. Manne (ed.), Investment for capacity expansion, Ch. 10. Cambridge, Mass.: MIT Press, 1967, *op. cit.*

[55] Zabel, E., "Efficient accumulation of capital for the firm", *Econometrica*, Vol. 31, Jan.–April, 1963, 131–150.

[56] Terborgh, G., *Dynamic equipment policy*. New York, McGraw-Hill, 1949.

[57] Erlenkotter, D., "Two producing areas – dynamic programming solutions". In: *Investment for capacity expansion*, Ch. 13, *op. cit.*

[58] Manne, A. S., "Two producing areas – constant cycle time policies", Ch. 12, *op. cit.*

[59] Manne, A. S., "Calculations for multiple producing areas", Ch. 4, *op. cit.*

[60] D'Alessandro, L., *Plant and stock in the production of goods in seasonal demand.* Oxford: Basil Blackwell, 1963.

[61] Modigliani, F. and F. E. Hohn, "Production planning over time and the nature of the expectation and planning horizon", *Econometrica*, Vol. 23, 1955, 46–66.

[62] Krishnan, K. S., T. K. Sarkar and S. K. Gupta, "Optimal capacity expansion", unpublished monograph of the Indian Institute of Management, Calcutta, 1966 (cyclostyled).

[63] Bruni, L., "Internal economies of scale with a given technique", *Journal of Industrial Economics*, Vol. 12, No. 3, July 1964, 175–190.

[64] Haldi, J., *Economies of scale in economic development*. Stanford: Stanford University Press, 1960.

[65] Shen, T. Y., "Economies of scale, expansion path and growth of plants", *Review of Economics and Statistics*, Vol. 47, November 1965, 420–428.

[66] Takacs, L., *Stochastic processes*. London: Methuen and Co., 1960.

Bartlett, M. S., *An introduction to stochastic processes*. Cambridge: Cambridge University Press, 1955.

[67] Feller, W., *An introduction to probability theory and its applications*. New York: John Wiley, 1957; 2nd ed.

[68] Doob, J. L., *Stochastic processes*. New York: John Wiley, 1953.

[69] Kendall, D. G., "Stochastic processes occurring in the theory of queues", *Annals of Mathematical Statistics*, Vol. 24, 1953, 338–354.

Kiefer, J. and J. Wolfowitz, "The general queueing process", *Annals of Mathematical Statistics*, Vol. 27, No. 1, 1956.

Lindley, D. V., "The theory of queues with a single server", *Proceedings of Cambridge Philosophical Society*, Vol. 48, Part 2, 1952, 277–289.

Smith, W. L., "On the distribution of queueing times", *Proceedings of Cambridge Philosophical Society*, Vol. 49, 1953, 449–461.

[70] Moran, P., *The theory of storage*. New York: John Wiley, 1959.

Prabhu, N. U., *Queues and inventories, op. cit.*

Saaty, T. L., *Elements of queueing theory*. New York: McGraw-Hill, 1961.

[71] Allen, R. G. D., *Macro-economic theory: a mathematical treatment*. New York: St. Martin's Press, 1967.

[72] Haavelmo, T., *A study in the theory of economic evolution*. Amsterdam: North-Holland Publishing Co., 1954.

[73] Tintner, G., J. K. Sengupta and E. J. Thomas, "Applications of the theory of stochastic processes to economic development". In: I. Adelman and E. Thorbecke (eds.), *The theory and design of economic development*. Baltimore: Johns Hopkins Press, 1966, 99–110.

Tintner, G. and R. C. Patel, "A log-normal diffusion process applied to the economic development of India", *Indian Economic Journal*, Vol. 13, 1965, 465–474.

[74] Bharucha-Reid, A. T., *Elements of the theory of Markov processes and their applications*. New York: McGraw-Hill, 1960.

[75] Kendall, D. G., "Stochastic processes and population growth", *Journal of the Royal Statistical Society*, Series B, Vol. 11, 1949, 230–264.

[76] Sengupta, J. K. and G. Tintner, "An approach to a stochastic theory of economic development with applications". In: *Problems of economic dynamics and planning: essays in honor of M. Kalecki*. Warsaw: Polish Scientific Publishers, 1964.

Sengupta, J. K. and G. Tintner, "The flexibility and optimality of Domar-type growth models", *Metroeconomica*, Vol. 17, 1965, 3–16.

[77] Steindl, J., *Random processes and the growth of firms*. New York: Hafner Publishing Co., 1965.

[78] Morse, P. M., *Queues, inventories and maintenance*. New York: John Wiley, 1958.

Little, J. D. C., "The use of storage water in a hydroelectric system", *Operations Research*, Vol. 3, 1955, 187–197.

Meyer, H. A. (ed.), *Symposium on Monte Carlo methods*. New York: John Wiley, 1956.

[79] Pitt, H. R., "A theorem on random functions with applications to a theory of provisioning", *Journal of London Mathematical Society*, Vol. 21, 1946, 16–22.

[80] Beckmann, M. and R. Muth, "An inventory policy for a case of lagged delivery", *Management Science*, Vol. 2, 1956, 145–155.

[81] Billingsley, P., *Statistical inference for Markov processes*. Chicago: University of Chicago Press, 1961.

Theil, H. and G. Rey, "A quadratic programming approach to the estimation of transition probabilities", *Management Science*, Vol. 12, May 1966, 714–721.

[82] Brockmayer, E., H. L. Halstrom and A. Jensen, "The life and works of A. K. Erlang". Copenhagen: Copenhagen Telephone Company, 1948.

[83] Jackson, R. and R. Adelson, "A critical survey of queueing theory", *Operational Research Quarterly*, Vol. 13, No. 4, 1962, 299–307.

[84] Jaiswal, N. K., "Time dependent solution of the bulk service queueing problem", *Operations Research*, Vol. 8, 1960, 773–781.

[85] Ford, L. R. and D. R. Fulkerson, *Flows in Networks*. Princeton: Princeton University Press, 1962.

[86] Grubbs, E. F., "Attempts to validate certain PERT statistics, or picking a PERT", *Operations Research*, Vol. 10, 1962, 912–915.

[87] Kelley, J. E., "Critical path panning and scheduling: mathematical basis", *Operations Research*, Vol. 9, 1961, 296–320.

[88] Hartley, H. O. and A. W. Wortham, "A statistical theory for PERT critical path analysis", *Management Science*, Vol. 12, No. 10, June 1966, B469–481.

Miller, R. W., *Schedule, cost and profit control with PERT*. New York: McGraw-Hill, 1963.

[89] Aris, R., *Discrete dynamic programming*. New York: Blaisdell Publishing, 1963.

[90] Weingartner, H. M., "Capital budgeting of interrelated projects: survey and synthesis", *Management Science*, Vol. 12, March 1966, 485–516.

[91] Baumol, W. J. and R. E. Quandt, "Investment and discount rates under capital rationing", *Economic Journal*, Vol. 75, June 1965, 317–329.

[92] Reiter, S., "Choosing an investment program among interdependent projects", *Review of Economic Studies*, Vol. 30, 1963, 32–36.

[93] Kunzi, H. P. and W. Oettli, "Integer quadratic programming". In: R. L. Graves and P. Wolfe (eds.), *Recent advances in mathematical programmming*. New York: McGraw-Hill, 1963.

# Chapter 7

# MODELS OF RESOURCE ALLOCATION AND PLANNING IN EDUCATIONAL INSTITUTIONS AND SYSTEMS

Educational systems, government agencies and voluntary organizations of various types (churches, labor unions, service clubs, professional associations, trade associations and others) are often referred to as nonmarket institutions. Economic theory has concerned itself primarily with market-oriented institutions such as business firms. A firm buys inputs and sells outputs at market prices, and the allocation of resources within a firm is said to be price-guided.

In this chapter we will limit our attention to educational institutions and systems, with particular attention to universities. In this field, the absence of readily available prices for some inputs and most outputs constitutes an initial difficulty in formulating an objective function and applying optimizing techniques.

It is clear enough that a university has (*de facto*) a technology matrix relating vectors of specified inputs to specified outputs. It is also subject to budgetary and other resource constraints. Some major university outputs (notably the career income consequences of university educations) can be priced approximately in dollar terms; so can a major input not included in the university budget, namely income foregone by students in attending the university rather than working at the kinds of jobs which would have been open to them as high school graduates. Thus, the teaching function of the university links it to the national economy and a pricing system for professional skills.

In allocating resources between teaching and research, university administrators act as if they were making judgments concerning the values of research outputs relative to the values of teaching outputs. Hence, in the models presented in this chapter we will assume that the relevant policy maker (department chairman or dean) is capable of assigning objective function weights to various outputs. Only the relative levels of these weights affect the optimal solutions in terms of activity levels and resource allocation, so we do not require the policy maker to identify his objective function weights with career income contributions or other market-like magnitudes.

On these assumptions, we will review, present and appraise a number of optimizing methods and models that have been applied in very recent years to educational systems and to university departments and colleges.

## 7.1. Models of educational planning: a review

An educational system can be defined at various levels, at the national level, at the level of a particular university, and at the level of a particular department or discipline in a specific university. At each level there arise fundamental problems of planning which are no less interesting and important than those of national economic planning which are usually discussed in the context of economic growth models and policy-making. The process of planning an educational system at any level is understood here to include any or all of the following aspects:

(a) An analysis of basic variables, both quantitative and qualitative, characterizing an educational system, in terms of exogenous (or instrument) and endogenous (or target) variables, so that the incidence on the endogenous variables of a variation in the set of exogenous variables can be analyzed, predicted and optimized whenever possible through using an objective function of the policy maker [1, 2].

(b) An analysis of the overall goal and its components, the various subgoals of the set of feasible policies pursued by the educational system, and the implicit costs of achieving these subgoals and the overall goal through the various methods of decomposition or decentralization of activities appropriately defined.

(c) A prognosis of the trend of growth (or decline) and its structural aspects characterizing the evolution of an educational system over time, so that the sequential effects and constraints of feasible policies in one period on those of other periods and hence the recursive interdependence of means and objectives can be analyzed with a view to changing the orientation of the trend whenever desired by one or multiple policy makers.

(d) A systematic investigation in the context of educational planning of the uncertain components in evaluation of demand and supply, price and cost or intangible aspects of return and outlay with appropriate choice of discounting factors, so that appropriate levels of policy can be postulated to insulate the system to various degrees from the elements of risk and miscalculation and the consequent inoptimal allocation of resources, whenever it is feasible to do so.

In this chapter we can present only a limited number of models and applications. A broader review of models available as of 1967 is contained in Fox and Sengupta [3]. More extended discussions of the specific examples used in section 7.3 will be found in Fox, McCamley and Plessner [4] and Plessner, Fox and Sanyal [5]. A wider range of literature (through mid-1968) is being surveyed and many new results are being presented in a book, *Operations analysis of higher education* [6], by Fox, Sengupta, Bose, Kumar and Sanyal which should be completed in manuscript form by December 1969. Section 7.3 is based largely on a paper by Sengupta and Fox [7]. Special mention should be made of a 1967 doctoral dissertation by McCamley [8] which implemented the most detailed and realistic activity analysis model of a set of university departments that has so far come to our attention.

### 7.1.1. Aggregative models

Aggregative models of educational systems at the national level may be classified into at least four different groups, the common link between which appears to be provided by the specification of a production function whereby education provides the skills and manpower for overall economic growth measured in terms of real output trends:

A. Models with few sectors (usually two sectors) with national output as an exogenous variable [9, 10];

B. Models with several sectors based on open-dynamic input-output models [11, 12];

C. Programming models with investment in education as a component of aggregate national investment [13, 14]; and

D. Recursive models with specific variables relating to a particular component of the overall educational system [15, 16], e.g. the allocation of scientific personnel between teaching, research and other work or the investment needs of a planned change in the scale of higher education in an economy to attain a desired level of formation of skills of appropriate types.

Perhaps the simplest model in category A is specified by means of a one-input production function and an equilibrium relation for the growth of labor force with a certain education level (e.g., a third-level or a secondary-level education). Denote by $N_t$ the stock of labor force with a given education level, by $Y_t$ the total volume of real income or production of a given economy, by $m_t$ the number of those who have entered the labor force within the previous six years (for example) and by $n_t$ the total number of students at that given education level attending classes, then the basic model [9] is as follows:

$$N_t = a_1 Y_t + a_2 n_t; \qquad \text{(production function)} \qquad (7.1)$$

$$N_t = (1 - d_1) N_{t-1} + m_t; \qquad \text{(growth of labor force)} \qquad (7.2)$$

$$m_t = g n_{t-1}. \qquad \text{(supply of labor)} \qquad (7.3)$$

Here $d_1$ represents drop-out rates (assumed to be an estimated constant) due to various factors such as retirement, death, etc., and the coefficient $g$ represents a factor of proportionality between $m_t$, the gross increase in the stock of manpower $N_t$ during the last six years, and $n_{t-1}$ (i.e., the total number of students attending classes at that education level during period $t-1$).

Equation (7.1) says that the labor force with a given education level consists of those currently employed in production (assumed proportional in numbers to the volume of national output) and of those teaching at that level of education (assumed proportional to the current number of students). Since the model has one degree of freedom [1], one can close the model by postulating an exogenously determined relation. For example, if real national output is growing at a rate of $r$ percent per year, then the requirement of a balanced growth of student population at the given education level is specified from the system as

$$n_t = (g/a_2) n_{t-1} + Y_0 (1 + r)^{t-1} (1 - d_1 - a_1 - a_1 r), \qquad (7.4)$$

given the initial levels $n_0$, $Y_0$ and $N_0$ at $t=0$. Here the balanced growth concept is one of regular growth of skill formation through student training parallel to the desired growth of the economy in terms of real output. If the balanced growth rate specified by (7.4) is not satisfied, then we have either insufficient or excessive supply in relation to the requirement level over time.

There is another interesting way of closing the model if one introduces cost of training, i.e. investment cost of skill formation $(c_t)$, which is assumed for simplicity to be linearly proportional to the number of students trained, e.g.,

$$c_t = i n_t; \qquad (i = \text{constant of proportionality}) \qquad (7.5)$$

then by combining (7.1) through (7.3) with (7.5)

$$Y_t = (1 - d_1) Y_{t-1} + (a_2 + g) c_{t-1}/(a_1 i) - a_2 c_t (a_1 i). \qquad (7.6)$$

By means of this relation (7.6) and given the initial values $Y_0$, $c_0$ and $N_0$, one can derive a partial optimum rate of growth of investment cost of skill formation by maximizing the end-period income level with a planning horizon of (say) a decade or so (or maximizing the sum total of incomes over the given planning horizon). The rate of investment cost (and hence the rate of growth of skill formation) so computed is called partially optimum, because the model does not incorporate in a basic sense the rest of the economy and the investment activity therein. Further, it has only one input in the production function and it does not include other technological constraints due to the interdependence of the education sector with the rest of the economy and the restrictions imposed by the overall fiscal capacity of the economy.

Two obvious lines of extension of the above model are readily apparent. First, the production function in the model could be generalized to incorporate curvilinear relationships, the result of capital and technology, which may be determined outside the model but their restrictions must remain implicit behind the partial equilibrium setup of this education model. Second, the various types of education generating different types of skills could be distinguished, along with an appropriate breakdown of the overall national economy (and its output) into "sectors", so that the student population and labor force could be conceived as vectors, where each component of the vector may be age-specific and skill-specific.

The second line of extension is basically equivalent to the multisectoral model of the educational system developed by Stone [11], which may be viewed as a typical model in category B. In this model, the educational system is defined to be a system of connected processes and the model includes all forms of education, training and retraining. The flow equation of the system is basically similar to that of an open-dynamic input-output model in that a given year's activity levels expressed in terms of students are shown as functions of future vectors of graduate leavers who are potential entrants to the labor force.

As in the input-output model, this type of formulation enables us to calculate the requirements for activity levels in the educational system corresponding to a desired rate of change in the structure of output and in the structure of skill formation. Let the column vector $s_t$ denote the stock of students of specified age-groups in various levels (or processes) of education at the beginning of year $t$, and $\hat{h}$ be a diagonal matrix of age-specific survival rates (i.e. school continuation rates as distinct from dropouts), then $\hat{h}s_t$ denotes the surviving student population at the beginning of year $t$. Out of this a proportion (i.e., $\hat{p}\hat{h}s_t$ where $\hat{p}$ is a diagonal matrix with proportions in the diagonal) continues in the system from one education level (or process) to another and the remaining (i.e., $(I-\hat{p})\hat{h}s_t$ which is denoted as $g_t$) are graduate leavers at the end of year $t$. It is assumed that the numbers of students who stay in the various processes can be expected in terms of next year's initial stock of students, i.e.,

$$\hat{p}\hat{h}s_t = Js_{t+1}, \tag{7.7}$$

where $J$ denotes a matrix with ones in the diagonal immediately above the leading diagonal and zeros everywhere else (since the matrix $\hat{p}$ can be interpreted to denote the probability that a surviving student who was in process (level) $j$ this year will be found in process (level) $j+1$ next year). Hence it follows that

$$\hat{h}s_t = Js_{t+1} + g_t,$$

where $g_t = (I-\hat{p})\,\hat{h}s_t$ which implies that

$$s_t = (\hat{h}^{-1}J)\,s_t + (\hat{h}^{-1}J)\,\Delta s_t + \hat{h}^{-1}g_t, \tag{7.8}$$

where $\Delta s_t = s_{t+1} - s_t$ and $I$ = identity matrix. The equation (7.8) which shows the recursive relationship between present numbers of students in different processes (or levels) and the future numbers of graduate leavers from the different processes is basically similar to the flow equation of an open-dynamic input-output model [17] in which the output levels are the elements of vector $s_t$ and the final products are the elements of $\hat{h}^{-1}g_t$.

According to this interpretation, the input structure behind the output vector $s_t$ has now to be introduced. Denote by $X$ a matrix whose rows relate to different economic inputs (e.g., number of teachers of different skill-groups, building space, research equipment, etc.) and whose columns refer to different educational levels or processes (e.g., secondary level, undergraduate college level, graduate level, Ph.D. level, postdoctoral research, etc.). Then by dividing the elements in each column by the corresponding activity levels, we obtain a coefficient matrix $U$, i.e.

$$U = X\hat{s}_t^{-1}, \tag{7.9}$$

where $\hat{s}_t$ denotes a diagonal matrix whose diagonal elements are composed of the corresponding elements of the vector $s_t$. Any change in the elements of the coefficient matrix $U$ reflects changes in the structure (qualitative or quantitative) of economic inputs into various educational processes. Thus the "technology" of the educational system is reflected in the coefficient matrices $U$ and $\hat{h}^{-1}J$ where the latter reflects mainly the changes in the normal time to complete different learning processes at different levels. Denoting the vector of row-sums of matrix $X$ by $x_t$, one could compute the required supply of economic inputs corresponding to any preassigned level of output vector $s_t$, i.e.,

$$x_t = Us_t. \tag{7.10}$$

As in the model of category A discussed before, our model now can be closed in several ways. First of all, assume that the structure of growth of $s_t$ is solved from (7.8) and plugged into (7.10) to compute the vector of required input levels $x_t$; then by comparing the existing supply-of-inputs structure with the required one, we may find the deficiency or otherwise of the present supply and estimate its consequences (e.g., a deficient supply system has to be reflected in any of the following: a lowering of standards, a postponement of the present rate of improvement, and so on). The evaluation of consequences for the overall output or income components may be facilitated by postulating an impact relation, e.g.,

$$\bar{y}_t = \bar{y}_{t-1} + Rv_{t-1}, \tag{7.11}$$

$$v_t = Cx_t + b, \tag{7.12}$$

where $\bar{y}_t$ is a vector of those components of national output which are relevant, $v_t$ is a vector of cost components associated with the structure of inputs $x_t$, and the matrices $R$, $C$ and vector $b$ are constants the estimates of which are assumed to be known. In this setup any deficiency in the supply-of-inputs structure would be reflected in its effects on the components of national output $\bar{y}_t$, since the matrix $R$ represents the output-creating effects of investment in education. A second way of closing the model is to introduce social welfare functions, e.g., minimize

$$\text{either:} \quad (w'v_T + \bar{w}'\bar{y}_T) \tag{7.13}$$

$$\text{or:} \quad W(v_0, v_1, v_2, ..., v_T; \ \bar{y}_0, \bar{y}_1, ..., \bar{y}_T), \tag{7.14}$$

and determine the optimal levels of $x_t$ and $\bar{y}_t$ subject to the constraints

$$\bar{y}_t \geq \bar{y}_{t-1} + Rv_{t-1},$$
$$s_t \geq (\hat{h}^{-1}J) s_t + (\hat{h}^{-1}J) \Delta s_t + \hat{h}^{-1} g_t,$$
$$x_t = Us_t; \quad v_t = Cx_t + b; \quad s_t, x_t, v_t, \bar{y}_t \geq 0,$$

where $w$ and $\bar{w}$ are vectors of nonnegative weights for the terminal cost, $W(\cdot)$ indicates a weighted combination of the components of $v_t$ and $\bar{y}_t$, and $T$ is the end year of the planning horizon.[1]

Another interesting aspect of the model presented by relations (7.8) through (7.10) is that it allows a decomposition of the overall system into

---

[1] This type of closing is quite conventional in the theory of linear dynamic input-output models characterizing an intertemporally optimal path of capital accumulation [17], although other types of closure are easily conceivable [18, 19].

subsystems, for each of which a demand-supply analysis and for that matter the conditions for equilibrium growth can be specified. Suppose we consider the teaching input into the educational processes and partition the matrix $U$ of (7.9) to define a submatrix $A$ taking only the set of rows relating to teachers in the various educational processes. Then the demand for teachers $D_t$ can be presumed to depend mainly on the activity levels of different educational processes measured by the size of student population, i.e.,

$$D_{t+1} = As_{t+1}. \tag{7.15}$$

Further, the supply of teachers $S_{t+1}$ could be related to the number of the existing stock $(S_t)$ of teachers who remain active and the number of graduate leavers (B.S. through Ph.D.'s) who enter into teaching careers, i.e.,

$$S_{t+1} = (I - \hat{d}) S_t + Bg_t; \qquad I = \text{identity matrix} \tag{7.16}$$

where $\hat{d}$ is a diagonal matrix whose diagonal elements refer to the wastage rates (i.e., retirements, deaths and transfers into other occupations) of different kinds of teachers and the elements of the matrix $B$ denote the proportion of different kinds of graduates taking up teaching as a career. Again, if the estimated supply computed from (7.16) tends to be deficient in relation to estimated demand from (7.15), then several policy alternatives (e.g., increasing the prospects of return in teaching occupations, decreasing the intensity of demand for teachers at undergraduate levels by changes in curricula or methods of teaching or lowering of standards, etc.) have to be conceived to reduce the gap between demand and supply.

Two comments are in order about the model in category B presented above. First, although the flow equation of an open-dynamic input-output model provides a very close analogy to the basic equations derived in (7.8) through (7.10), there is some need in the latter system to distinguish between "capacity" variables and current account variables. For instance, the development of a good faculty in one department of a university has at least two effects: (1) it raises the quality of teaching and research training provided to its students so that the current rate of formation of skills in students is increased, and (2) it stimulates further improvement and professional development within the faculty itself through mutual interaction among faculty members in the given department and in other related departments and through the development of teamwork in research. An appropriate stock of faculty members engaged in teaching and research is essential for maintaining a given level of educational output but for upgrading the level of educational performance (e.g., upgrading the professional excellence of an academic department) a far more essential factor may be the catalytic role played by a few "eminent" or highly creative faculty members in providing the core of an improved environment in which accelerated research output and professional growth are easily achievable. Similarly it is essential to recognize the role of external benefits to other departments when a given department such as Mathematics attains a higher level of excellence and thereby acquires the potential for giving better training to students of other departments.

The identification of indivisible elements in the variables characterizing an educational system is a task of primary importance which needs to be carefully performed before the scale effects (i.e., the economies and dis-economies) of the overall evolution of an educational system can be incor-porated in the above-type linear dynamic difference equations. A closely related aspect is the evaluation of implicit costs of activities such as research and educational administration, which cannot most appropriately be fitted into the strait jackets of demand and supply because of the lack of a so-called common denominator, price. Hence, decomposition with respect to such activities has to be treated, at the least, at a level different from the rest.[2]

Secondly, the sequential aspects of educational policies affecting the educational system and its quality of excellence, so to say, need to be in-corporated into the model structure in a basic sense; in other words, the implicit opportunity costs of alternative educational policies pursued by multiple policy makers and their sequential effects over time are not amenable to analysis within the confines of the aggregative model above. The degree to which the elements of the matrices $\hat{p}$, $\hat{s}_t$, $R$, $A$, and $B$ are amenable to influence through deliberate policies pursued by policy makers at different stages is a subject of considerable importance in educational planning. Further, it must be noted that most of these coefficients are average estimates with a margin of uncertainty around them and therefore it is all the more necessary to emphasize the role of adaptive and/or self-correcting decision rules.

Even at the aggregate level, the dynamic input-output type model in

---

[2] The concept of decomposition of an overall model into several submodels has different variants of interpretation [20, 21] e.g., (a) a method of two-level planning by linking the submodel solutions through a two-facet objective function in each submodel, of which one facet reflects the external effects of the submodel on the other sectors, (b) a method of allocating resources on the basis of suboptimal solutions and (c) a recursive linking of submodels.

category B can be easily extended to incorporate the details of investment planning in the education sector and in the rest of the economy, viewing the total allocable investible resource at any period as having two outlets, one of which is the education sector and the other is the rest of the economy. This viewpoint readily takes us into models of category C.

A model in this category [13] uses a dynamic programming approach with a planning horizon of a decade or more, with investment in education optimized simultaneously with investment in real capital for different sectors of the economy. The optimal time patterns of production, imports and exports for each of the several sectors of the economy are also determined concurrently. An appropriate objective function, e.g. the maximization of the economy's rate of growth (i.e., maximization of the discounted sum of GNP over the given horizon) is set up and optimized subject to a set of linear constraints of several types: (a) constraints for the educational system specifying the initial supply of teachers, the supply of school buildings, etc., along with the "technological" conditions for the transformation of students at a given level (undergraduate) to a higher level (graduate) whenever feasible; (b) sociocultural constraints stipulating that the enrollments in each type of school are nondecreasing through time; (c) labor force change equations which stipulate the differential productivity contributions of graduates and dropouts from schools and colleges of a given type to the supply of labor of a particular skill (it is to be noted that these equations provide the principal link between the educational system and the productive sectors of the economy); (d) constraints for the productive sectors of the economy specifying the technological conditions of production and investment and limiting the economy's use of primary resources to available stocks of productive capacity (by sector), manpower (by skill), and foreign exchange and saving; and (e) a set of behavioral constraints about certain minimum levels of domestic consumption and the maximum absorptive capacity of investment in each sector. Finally, the terminal requirement is that the sectoral investment in the last period of the planning horizon must at least cover that period's depreciation charges.

The optimal solution of such a model specifies the optimal levels of two sets of decision variables: (1) for the noneducational part, the optimal sectoral levels of domestic production, imports, fixed capital formation, net foreign capital inflow, etc.; and (2) for the educational system, the optimal number of graduates and dropouts in each time period to be allocated to a particular type of employment (i.e., labor of a given skill or retention within the school either as a student or as a teacher).

About the relative usefulness of such a type of formulation, two claims are generally made. First, the shadow prices of various labor skills and other resources computed from the linear programming model are taken to provide some indication about the desirable direction of change in the pattern of education and training facilities of different types through implicit calculations of the marginal social benefit from investment in education. For instance, the differences between the shadow prices of graduates of various types and their respective average earnings may provide some broad and notional estimate of the role of market incentives and prospective returns. Secondly, it is a mark of great flexibility that this type of model allows for the simultaneous computation of an optimal pattern of growth in the economy and an optimal pattern of enrollments and resource use in the educational system. The demands for skilled and educated labor are generated endogenously and in a sense recursively by the optimal pattern of economic and educational growth.

However, it is perhaps necessary to mention the need for cautious interpretation of this type of model. First of all, the shadow prices are strongly conditioned by the way the coefficients of the objective function and of the restraints are set up, e.g., the estimates of relative productivity coefficients of labor with various levels of education are very crucial in determining the shadow prices. To that extent the statistical sensitivity to errors in specification or estimation presents quite a complicated problem. Secondly, the linearity of the coefficient structure generally prevents any variation in the marginal rates of substitution between different education and skill levels and this means that the substitution rates between different component goals in the overall goal of the central objective function are fixed once for all for the not-too-short planning horizon. This could be relaxed by postulating nonlinear, maybe up to quadratic, relations with changes in relative marginal rates of substitution. This would also facilitate the analysis of sensitivity of the optimal solutions of the linear program. Thirdly, a very important difficulty with the programming formulation is that the optimal solutions are not available in an analytic form such as the regression of a set of dependent variables on the set of independent variables and hence the extrapolation of optimal solutions beyond the period considered or with slightly altered or added constraints is fraught with great problems. One way in which the problems could be tackled is to compute not only the optimal solution but also the second-best and third-best basic feasible solutions [22], which could be utilized when the coefficients in the objective function (for instance) reflecting relative marginal productivities are subject to revision and updating.

The second-best and third-best solutions may provide an indication of the range of variation of the optimal solution (i.e., the first-best solution) when the coefficients of the objective function are liable to small perturbations. For instance, whenever the Euclidean distance between the first-best and the second-best solutions is large, this indicates in a broad sense a high degree of sensitivity of the first-best optimal solution. Another interesting possibility is to investigate the size of region through which the optimal solution of the linear program would retain approximate optimality, the approximation referring to the point usually stressed in chance-constrained programming that violation of some constraints may be permitted to different degrees, provided the optimal solution can still be specified in the interior of the region so constructed.

In a somewhat specific and more or less analytic (or predictive) approach, the models in category D deal with a particular component of the overall educational system (implicitly, in a partial equilibrium setup) and analyze the impact of variation in some of the coefficients on the relevant endogenous variables of the system. An interesting problem at this level is the allocation of scientific effort between teaching and research in relation to the needs of prospective growth of an economy. This has been considered by Stoikov and others [15].

Denote by $S_t$ the total volume of scientific personnel in an economy engaged in teaching or research in period $t$, out of which $R_t$ denotes those who are engaged in research and $E_t$ represents the rest, those who are engaged in teaching. The growth of total scientific personnel $(S_t)$ and total number of teachers $(E_t)$ are assumed to be explained as follows:

$$S_{t+1} - S_t = gE_t - hS_t; \tag{7.17}$$

$$E_{t+1} - E_t = agE_t - hE_t; \tag{7.18}$$

$$S_t = R_t + E_t, \tag{7.19}$$

where $g$ is the number of students trained per scientist-year of teaching, $h$ is the rate of exit and dropout of scientists from the profession per year due to retirement and other causes, assumed to be the same for both teaching and research personnel, and $a$ is the fraction of graduating scientists entering teaching as a career. Define by $Q_t$ the quantum of research effort with a finite planning horizon $[0, T]$ measured by the sum total of research scientist manyears for the entire planning horizon, then the policy problem posed is: how should the newly trained scientists be allocated between teaching and research, i.e., what should be the most appropriate or optimal value of the ratio $a$?

From equations (7.17) through (7.19) one could solve for $R_t$ and $Q_T$ as

$$R_t = (1 - h)^t \left( R_0 - \frac{1 - a}{a} E_0 \right) + \frac{(1 - a) E_0}{a} (1 + ag - h)^t; \qquad (7.20)$$

$$Q_T = \sum_0^T R_t = \left( \frac{(1 - h)^{T+1} - 1}{h} \right) \left( \frac{(1 - a) E_0}{a} - R_0 \right)$$
$$+ \left( \frac{(1 - a) E_0}{a} \right) \frac{(1 + ag - h)^{T+1} - 1}{ag - h}, \qquad (7.21)$$

where the subscript zero indicates initial values. One way to analyze the problem is to vary the ratio $a$ along with plausible values of other coefficients for an economy, observe the effect on the quantum of research effort with alternative durations of the finite planning horizon, and then decide taxonomically on the most reasonably appropriate value of $a$ which very nearly maximizes in an approximate sense the variable $Q_T$. If the actual value of $a$ deviates far from the approximately optimal value so computed, then appropriate policy measures (e.g., appropriate emphasis on the incentives and prospects in teaching and research, etc.) need be conceived so as to minimize the gap between the two ratios.

Another approximate but analytic way of solving the problem is to consider a continuous (differential) equation form of the relations (7.17) through (7.19) in the model and express $Q_T$ approximately as

$$Q_T \simeq (R_0/h) \left( \exp(- hT) - 1 \right) - \frac{E_0(1 + a)}{a} \cdot (T + T^2 (ag - h)/2). \qquad (7.21)'$$

Equating the derivative of $Q_T$ with respect to $a$ to zero, we obtain the relation determining the optimal value $a^*$, i.e.,

$$a^{*^2} = 2/(gT) - h/g. \qquad (7.22)$$

Taking the positive value of the square root as economically meaningful we finally get

$$a^* = \left[ \frac{2}{gT} - \frac{h}{g} \right]^{\frac{1}{2}}, \qquad (7.23)$$

provided $hT \leqslant 2$, a condition required for economic feasibility of the solution. This approximate solution which is analytic can of course be improved through successive iterations on the approximate values of $Q_T$.

It may appear that this model is very specific and simplistic, but this need not be true. First of all, the competitive relation between teaching and research postulated by the basic equations of the model may be easily modified to allow for ranges of complementarity. Similarly, the exogenous role of needs of economic growth can be very easily incorporated by postulating the relative marginal contribution of research effort to the total real output of the national economy. Secondly, the activities of teaching and research could be further disaggregated into different levels and fields, so that $E_t$, $R_t$, and $S_t$ could be interpreted as vectors and likewise the coefficient $a$ could be interpreted as a suitably defined matrix, the elements of which could provide the decision variables to be optimally determined. Further, the costs of allocation, training and research along with the constraints of the non-education sector could be incorporated as secondary boundary conditions. Thirdly, this type of formulation is suitable for deriving linear decision rules with a quadratic preference function of the policy maker, provided the desired levels and values can be preassigned by the policy maker [2] and that the decision rules have a sequential character of self-correction in the face of uncertainty in data, represented by equational errors.

A recursive framework of supply and demand relations, analytically and estimation-wise more general than that of Stoikov and others, has been proposed by Fox [15]. In this setup, if the US National Register of Scientific and Technical Personnel data for different years are fully comparable, the changes in the number $(q_i)$ and average salary $(p_i)$ of scientists in speciality $i$ $(i = 1, 2, ..., m)$ ought to follow some kind of "cobweb" model, i.e.,

Demand function: $p_i(t) = a_i + b_i q_i(t) + c_i y(t) + u_i(t),$

Supply function: $q_i(t) = \alpha_i + \beta_i p_i(t - 1) + \gamma_i z(t) + v_i(t),$

$(i = 1, 2, ..., m),$

where the variable $y$ is a demand factor and the variable $z$ is a supply factor which in practice might include lagged salaries for several previous periods rather than one only and the variables $u_i(t)$, $v_i(t)$ are the equational error terms concerning which the usual assumptions about the statistical distribution are required for estimation purposes.

Some aspects of the flexibility of this type of model are worth emphasizing at this stage. First, the demand factor $y(t)$, the supply factor $z(t)$ and the definition of specialty could be given a more generalized interpretation, provided of course the conditions of econometric identification of the above model are not violated. For instance the demand factor $y(t)$ could be related to the trend of growth of prospective student population, to the relative attractiveness or otherwise of different specialties and so on. Similarly, the specialty category $i$ may refer to the different subcategories of a discipline, economics for example. The supply factor $z(t)$ may likewise be broadly interpreted to include national policies (e.g., specific budget provisions directed toward increasing the supply of scientists of specialty category $i$) and/or improved salary standards, etc. These generalizations could in principle be grafted through partial submodels allowing for interactions between subcategories of a given specialty category $i$, whenever it is feasible and operational to do so. Secondly, the aspects of stabilization and optimization [1] could be easily built into the above framework, by defining appropriate policies in terms of the policy variables $y$ and $z$. For instance, if $z(t)$ represents policies about improved relative salary standards, say, and the above cobweb-type model generates cobweb-type fluctuations, then in some cases an appropriate selection of values for the policy variable $z(t)$ may help to reduce those fluctuations. Again, if there is a demand-supply gap, an analysis of losses (in terms of potential losses of national income) can be made. By introducing a quadratic or other form of disutility function (as a function of the potential loss) it is sometimes possible to define an intertemporal path of values of the policy variable $z(t)$, or a combination of $y(t)$ and $z(t)$, which would be optimal in the sense of minimizing the cumulative sum of potential loss over time [1, 2].

### 7.1.2. Microanalysis and disaggregative models

Although the general techniques and methodology of the aggregative approach would retain much of their validity and usefulness in a microanalytic context, in which (for example) the optimization problem is discussed as a problem of resource allocation within a university or a specific department, the empirical framework of a microeconomic decision unit is likely to have several advantages. This is so for several reasons. First of all, since the aggregation difficulties are much less in this specific context, the coefficients of the model in terms of explicit or implicit prices and costs, the specific constraints of budget, manpower, faculty time available for research, etc., and most important, perhaps, the identification of sources of interaction between decision makers at different levels, are likely to be much more meaningful and representative in the specification of policies directed towards various goals. Secondly, the evolution of a university or a specific department provides some indication of the various facets of effects of alternative policies pursued by policy makers at different levels. Similarly, a cross-section or time series comparison of two universities or two departments is likely to suggest interesting insights about the quality of performance and/or excellence. However, there is one major bottleneck in the microanalytic approach: the generalization from the case history of one university or one department may be very misleading unless all the peculiarities of the specific case are explicitly recognized and taken into account.

Section 7.2 presents several illustrations of the microanalytic approach. The methods used include integer linear programming (of a special type); dynamic linear programming; and the Kornai-Liptak approach to two-level planning, a particular kind of decomposition or decentralization technique. Some summary remarks on microanalytic models of universities and their components are made at the end of section 7.3.

## 7.2. *Some applications of optimizing models to educational institutions*

The methods to be used in this section have been enumerated in the preceding paragraph. Four specific applications will be presented. In each case the mathematical structure of the model will be briefly stated. In addition, some highlights of the specific numerical inputs and results will be given as a basis for pointing out the potentialities and limitations of the approach.

### 7.2.1. *Integer linear programming: the faculty assignment model*

This model, from Fox, McCamley and Plessner [4], deals with the problem of allocating a given faculty among alternative teaching and research assignments. The model can be defined in terms of (1) a set of constraints which must be satisfied and (2) an objective function the value of which is to be maximized subject to the constraints.

We assume that commitments are expressed in terms of units such as "teaching a three-credit-hour course for one quarter", and that the amount of time of each faculty member which can be allocated to satisfy the commitments is measured in the same units. Thus, if the $i$th faculty member were responsible for teaching three three-credit-hour courses each quarter, or nine such courses for the academic year as a whole, $a_i = 9$. Similarly, if the $j$th commitment consists of offering two independent sections of a specified three-hour course in each of three quarters, $b_j = 6$. If the $i$th faculty member is assigned to teach all six of these offerings of the $j$th course, we have $x_{ij} = 6$, and the $i$th faculty member is still available to teach three other courses, presumably one in each quarter.

Suppose we have a department with $n$ faculty members and $m$ different sorts of commitments to fulfill. The constraints faced by this department can be written as:

$$\sum_{j=1}^{m} x_{ij} \leqslant a_i, \qquad i = 1, 2, ..., n \tag{7.24}$$

$$\sum_{i=1}^{n} x_{ij} = b_j, \qquad j = 1, 2, ..., m \tag{7.25}$$

$$x_{ij} \geqslant 0, \qquad i = 1, 2, ..., n; \qquad j = 1, 2, ..., m. \tag{7.26}$$

The type (7.24) inequalities insure that the total of the allocations of each faculty member's time does not exceed the amount available for such allocation. The type (7.25) equalities insure that all of the commitments are fulfilled. The type (7.26) inequalities preclude negative assignments (e.g. assigning some faculty member to teach a negative number of sections of some course).

The $x_{ij}$'s represent the amount of the $i$th faculty member's time allocated to the $j$th commitment. The $a_i$'s indicate the number of units of the $i$th faculty member's time which is available to the department. The $b_j$'s indicate the number of units of faculty time required by the $j$th commitment.

If $\sum_{i=1}^{n} a_i < \sum_{j=1}^{m} b_j$ no feasible solution exists, i.e., the department is either overcommitted or understaffed.

If $\sum_{i=1}^{n} a_i \geqslant \sum_{j=1}^{m} b_j$, feasible solutions exist. If $\sum_{i=1}^{n} a_i > \sum_{j=1}^{m} b_j$, the department is overstaffed or undercommitted. If $\sum_{i=1}^{n} a_i = \sum_{j=1}^{m} b_j$, there is a balance between staff and commitments. In that case the constraints have the same form as the constraints of the so-called "transportation model" and the model can be solved by any of the methods applicable for the solution of such models.[3]

We assume a linear objective function

$$\sum_{i=1}^{n} \sum_{j=1}^{m} c_{ij} x_{ij},$$

where $c_{ij}$ is a measure of the value per unit resulting when, for example,

---

[3] The "transportation model" specifies that there are $a_i$ units of a product at the $i$th shipping point ($i = 1, 2, ..., n$) and that $b_j$ units of the product are needed at the $j$th destination ($j = 1, 2, ..., m$); also $\sum_{i=1}^{n} a_i = \sum_{j=1}^{m} b_j$. Given the transportation cost, $c_{ij}$, from each of the $n$ shipping points to each of the $m$ destinations, the problem is to allocate the supply at each shipping point to a destination or destinations in such a way that (1) all destination requirements are satisfied and (2) the total transportation cost is minimized; that is, $\sum_{i=1}^{n} \sum_{j=1}^{m} c_{ij} x_{ij}$ is a minimum, where $x_{ij}$ is the number of units of the product transported from shipping point $i$ to destination $j$.

course $j$ is taught by faculty member $i$ and $x_{ij}$ is the number of units of his time assigned to course $j$.

For small problems such a model may be solved by hand. The solution procedure consists of two stages. During the first stage a feasible solution is obtained. During the second stage an optimal solution is obtained.

The first stage consists of a single step which is repeated until feasibility is obtained. Choose the largest of the $c_{ij}$'s for which both $b_j$ and $a_i$ are greater than zero. If this element is $c_{rs}$, set $x_{rs}$ equal to the smaller of the current values of $b_r$ and $a_s$. Update the values of $b_r$ and $a_s$ by subtracting $x_{rs}$ from both. This step is repeated until all $b_j$'s and $a_i$'s are equal to zero.

During the second stage the solution is improved until an optimum solution is obtained. The only way to improve the solution is to increase some allocation vector (one of the $x_{ij}$'s) from a zero level to a positive level. The first step involves determining which activity level to increase. Usually most of the activity levels will be zero and in addition there will often be several ways of increasing any given activity level. In such a case the easiest way to determine which activity level to increase is to first solve the dual of the model. The dual variables $u_i$ (the marginal value of a unit of input supplied by the $i$th staff member) and $v_j$ (the marginal value of a unit of input demanded by the $j$th task) must satisfy the relationship

$$c_{ij} = u_i - v_j,$$

if $x_{ij}$ is greater than zero. This leads to a system of $n+m-1$ (or fewer) equations which can easily be solved for the $u_i$'s and $v_j$'s. Those $x_{ij}$'s for which $c_{ij} - u_i + v_j$ is greater than zero are candidates for increases in activity levels. The $x_{ij}$ to increase first is the one for which $c_{ij} - u_i + v_j$ is the largest.

The next step involves determining how to increase the activity level. In order to increase the level of any activity (say $x_{rs}$) it is necessary to decrease the levels of at least two other activities and increase the level of at least one other activity. The method of changing the level of activity $x_{rs}$ should be chosen so that

$$\sum_{i=1}^{n} \sum_{j=1}^{m} \Delta x_{ij} c_{ij}$$

is maximized subject to

$$\sum_{i=1}^{n} \Delta x_{ij} = 0, \qquad j = 1, 2, ..., m,$$

$$\sum_{j=1}^{m} \Delta x_{ij} = 0, \qquad i = 1, 2, ..., n,$$

and

$$\Delta x_{rs} = 1, \, x_{ij} + \Delta x_{ij} \geqslant 0, \qquad i = 1, 2, ..., n,$$
$$j = 1, 2, ..., m.$$

Once the best way of changing $x_{rs}$ is determined, $x_{rs}$ is set equal to the largest value permitted by that method of changing the activity level.

The second stage steps are repeated until at some point

$$c_{ij} \leqslant u_i - v_j \quad \text{for} \quad i = 1, 2, ..., n,$$
$$j = 1, 2, ..., m.$$

At that point an optimum solution has been obtained.

Consider a department which has four faculty members each of whom teaches nine sections per year or contributes equivalent inputs to teaching and research assignments. It also offers six courses which during a given year it must offer at the rate of 9, 7, 6, 5, 4, and 3 sections per year. It also is conducting two small research projects which require respectively two units of faculty inputs and one unit of faculty input. It will be assumed that scheduling of sections among quarters and hours of the day is sufficiently flexible that the allocation for a whole year can be obtained without worrying about which quarter a particular section will be taught.

The information relevant to this problem is given in compact form in table 7.1. There are 32 possible activities. One unit of activity $x_{ij}$ assigns one unit of the time of faculty member $i$ to course $j$. This subtracts one unit from $a_i$ and adds one unit to $b_j$. The $a_i$'s are given positive signs; they are stocks or surpluses to be drawn down ultimately to zero. The $b_j$'s are given

TABLE 7.1

Faculty allocation problem with four faculty members, six courses, and two research projects.

| Faculty member | 1 | 2 | Courses 3 | 4 | 5 | 6 | Research 7 | 8 | Time units available $a_i$ |
|---|---|---|---|---|---|---|---|---|---|
| 1 | 10 | 7 | 5 | 9 | 15 | 4 | 6 | 3 | 9 |
| 2 | 6 | 8 | 4 | 3 | 7 | 5 | 12 | 2 | 9 |
| 3 | 7 | 7 | 6 | 11 | 10 | 9 | 5 | 1 | 9 |
| 4 | 5 | 6 | 2 | 5 | 3 | 8 | 7 | 6 | 9 |
| Time units required $b_j$ | 9 | 7 | 5 | 5 | 4 | 3 | 2 | 1 | 36 |

TABLE 7.2

Faculty allocation problem: optimal solution in matrix equation form.

| Faculty member ($F_i$) and courses and projects ($R_j$) | $x_{11}$ | $x_{15}$ | $x_{22}$ | $x_{27}$ | $x_{33}$ | $x_{34}$ | $x_{41}$ | $x_{43}$ | $x_{46}$ | $x_{48}$ | Units assigned | Availabilities and requirements |
|---|---|---|---|---|---|---|---|---|---|---|---|---|
| $F_1$ | 1 | 1 | 0 | 0 | 0 | 0 | 0 | 0 | 0 | 0 | 5 | 9 |
| $F_2$ | 0 | 0 | 1 | 1 | 0 | 0 | 0 | 0 | 0 | 0 | 4 | 9 |
| $F_3$ | 0 | 0 | 0 | 0 | 1 | 1 | 0 | 0 | 0 | 0 | 7 | 9 |
| $F_4$ | 0 | 0 | 0 | 0 | 0 | 0 | 1 | 1 | 1 | 1 | 2 | 9 |
| $R_1$ | −1 | 0 | 0 | 0 | 0 | 0 | −1 | 0 | 0 | 0 | 4 | −9 |
| $R_2$ | 0 | 0 | −1 | 0 | 0 | 0 | 0 | 0 | 0 | 0 | 5 | −7 |
| $R_3$ | 0 | 0 | 0 | 0 | −1 | 0 | 0 | −1 | 0 | 0 | 4 | −5 |
| $R_4$ | 0 | 0 | 0 | 0 | 0 | −1 | 0 | 0 | 0 | 0 | 1 | −5 |
| $R_5$ | 0 | −1 | 0 | 0 | 0 | 0 | 0 | 0 | 0 | 0 | 3 | −4 |
| $R_6$ | 0 | 0 | 0 | 0 | 0 | 0 | 0 | 0 | −1 | 0 | 1 | −3 |
| $R_7$ | 0 | 0 | 0 | −1 | 0 | 0 | 0 | 0 | 0 | 0 |  | −2 |
| $R_8$ | 0 | 0 | 0 | 0 | 0 | 0 | 0 | 0 | 0 | −1 |  | −1 |

(matrix) × (Units assigned) = (Availabilities and requirements)

TABLE 7.3

Dual of optimal solution in matrix equation form.

$$
\begin{bmatrix}
1 & 0 & 0 & 0 & -1 & 0 & 0 & 0 & 0 & 0 & 0 & 0 \\
1 & 0 & 0 & 0 & 0 & 0 & 0 & 0 & -1 & 0 & 0 & 0 \\
0 & 1 & 0 & 0 & 0 & -1 & 0 & 0 & 0 & 0 & -1 & 0 \\
0 & 1 & 0 & 0 & 0 & 0 & 0 & 0 & 0 & 0 & 0 & 0 \\
0 & 0 & 1 & 0 & 0 & 0 & -1 & 0 & 0 & 0 & 0 & 0 \\
0 & 0 & 1 & 0 & 0 & 0 & 0 & -1 & 0 & 0 & 0 & 0 \\
0 & 0 & 0 & 1 & -1 & 0 & 0 & 0 & 0 & 0 & 0 & 0 \\
0 & 0 & 0 & 1 & 0 & 0 & -1 & 0 & 0 & 0 & 0 & 0 \\
0 & 0 & 0 & 1 & 0 & 0 & 0 & 0 & 0 & -1 & 0 & 0 \\
0 & 0 & 0 & 1 & 0 & 0 & 0 & 0 & 0 & 0 & 0 & -1
\end{bmatrix}
\begin{bmatrix}
u_1 \\ u_2 \\ u_3 \\ u_4 \\ v_1 \\ v_2 \\ v_3 \\ v_4 \\ v_5 \\ v_6 \\ v_7 \\ v_8
\end{bmatrix}
=
\begin{bmatrix}
10 \\ 15 \\ 8 \\ 12 \\ 6 \\ 11 \\ 5 \\ 2 \\ 8 \\ 6
\end{bmatrix}
$$

negative signs; they are needs or deficits to be satisfied or made good until ultimately no deficits remain.

Tables 7.2 and 7.3 show the optimal solution and its dual in matrix equation form. The resulting faculty assignments are as follows:

| Faculty member | Assignments (units) | | | | | | | | |
| | Course | | | | | | Research | | |
| | 1 | 2 | 3 | 4 | 5 | 6 | 7 | 8 | $a_i$ |
| --- | --- | --- | --- | --- | --- | --- | --- | --- | --- |
| 1 | 5 | | | | 4 | | | | 9 |
| 2 | | 7 | | | | | 2 | | 9 |
| 3 | | | 4 | 5 | | | | | 9 |
| 4 | 4 | | 1 | | | 3 | | 1 | 9 |
| $b_j$ | 9 | 7 | 5 | 5 | 4 | 3 | 2 | 1 | 36 |

The value of the objective function, $W = \sum_{i=1}^{4} \sum_{j=1}^{8} c_{ij} x_{ij}$, is 321 in the optimal solution compared with 310 in the first feasible solution, which was obtained in the manner outlined on page 375.

*7.2.1.1. Some technical aspects of the objective function weights $(c_{ij}\text{s})$.* The $c_{ij}$'s in real situations would most likely be based on the judgment of the department chairman. Once specified, they guide the allocation process to an optimal solution. But the chairman's judgment in specifying the $c_{ij}$'s may be fallible. It is worth considering, then, how sensitive the optimal set of assignments may be to variations in the $c_{ij}$'s. We can state the following points:

(1) If all $m \cdot n$ of the $c_{ij}$'s are multiplied by the same constant, the optimal set of assignments will not be changed.

(2) If the same positive constant is added to all $m \cdot n$ of the $c_{ij}$'s the optimal set of assignments will not be changed.[4]

(3) If all $m \cdot n$ of the $c_{ij}$'s are multiplied by the same constant $\beta$ *and* are also all increased by the same constant $\alpha$, the optimal set of assignments will not be changed.

Thus, *any linear transformation* applied to all $m \cdot n$ of the $c_{ij}$'s will leave the optimal set of assignments unchanged, provided that no $c_{ij}$ is reduced below zero by the transformation.

The reason for this rather encouraging stability of the optimal assignment set in the face of linear transformations or "codings" of the $c_{ij}$'s may be clarified by an illustration:

| | Course 1 | Course 2 | Units available $(a_i)$ |
|---|---|---|---|
| Faculty member 1 | 10 | 7 | 3 |
| Faculty member 2 | 8 | 6 | 3 |
| Units required $(b_j)$ | 4 | 2 | 6 |

The optimal solution is $x_{11}=3$, $x_{12}=0$, $x_{21}=1$ and $x_{22}=2$; $W=3(10) +0(7)+1(8)+2(6)=50$.

What happens if we now transfer one unit of faculty member 1's time *from* course 1 *to* course 2? Clearly, we must transfer one unit of faculty member 2's time in the opposite direction, *from* course 2 *to* course 1. The "gain" in rearranging faculty member 1's time is $(-10+7)$; the gain in rearranging faculty member 2's time is $(-6+8)$. Thus, we lose 3 points on faculty member 1 and gain 2 points on faculty member 2; the net loss on the rearrangements is

$$(-c_{11}+c_{12})+(-c_{22}+c_{21})=(-10+7)+(-6+8)=(-3)+(2).$$

---

[4] Instead of adding a constant to each $c_{ij}$ we could subtract a constant *provided that no $c_{ij}$ is reduced below zero.*

The optimal solution is stable because any attempt to change it results in a loss-to-gain ratio of $-\frac{3}{2}$. If we add a constant, say 2, to each $c_{ij}$, we have $(-12+9)+(-8+10)=(-3)+(2)$; the numerator and denominator of the loss-to-gain ratio are unchanged, so the ratio itself is unchanged. If we multiply each $c_{ij}$ by a constant, say 0.5, we have $(-5+3.5)+(-3+4)=(-1.5)+(1)$; the loss-to-gain ratio is still $-1.5/1 = -\frac{3}{2}$, as before.

Thus, the stability of the optimal set of assignments depends on the stability of *relative differences* or loss-to-gain ratios associated with unit rearrangements; each rearrangement, as we have seen, involves four $c_{ij}$'s. Transformations of the type $c_{ij}^* = \alpha + \beta c_{ij}$, $i=1, 2, ..., n$, $j=1, 2, ..., m$, where $\alpha$ and $\beta$ are arbitrary positive constants, do not change the relative difference.

In the present example, the optimal assignment set would be stable under slightly less restrictive conditions. For example, we could multiply $c_{11}$ and $c_{12}$ by $\beta$ and $c_{21}$ and $c_{22}$ by any constant strictly less than $1.5\beta$ (we assume $\beta > 0$) without changing the optimal solution. But it is hard to generalize when we go beyond uniform linear codings. In any particular case a sensitivity analysis can, however, be made to determine the ranges of values over which stipulated $c_{ij}$'s may be varied without changing the optimal set of assignments.

*7.2.1.2. Some logical and practical aspects of the objective function weights* ($c_{ij}$'s). Despite the technical points we have just discussed, it seems desirable to specify the $c_{ij}$'s as approximations to magnitudes which, in principle, could be given economic values and/or other values in the larger society. The vocational value of a college education is one of the most tangible of these magnitudes, and a good deal has been written on this subject by Schultz [23], Becker [10] and others. When a university president allocates funds between the professional schools and the College of Liberal Arts, some implicit judgments may be inferred – for example, the last million dollars allocated to Liberal Arts *should* be as productive (in terms of the president's value system or objective function) as the last million dollars allocated to the professional schools in which career income is an important and fairly predictable output of the training received.

If we value faculty member 1's contribution in a section of course 5 at 15 points and in a section of course 1 at 10 points, we ought to mean that we think he accomplishes $\frac{15}{10}$ as much "good" in course 5 as in course 1. If faculty member 2's contribution in a section of course 5 is rated at 7 points, we ought to mean that we think he accomplishes $\frac{7}{15}$ as much "good" per section in that course as does faculty member 1. In a vocationally-oriented department, "good" may be roughly proportional to "increase in probable career income of students taking the course".

We might alternatively think of the $c_{ij}$'s as estimates of the national market values per course (i.e., the average salary cost per course) of professors who can teach course $j$ as well as faculty member $i$. Would it cost about $\$15\,000$ to hire another professor who could teach course 5 as well as faculty member 1? Would it cost about $\$10\,000$ to hire someone who could teach course 1 as well as faculty member 1? Competition for faculty members does express itself in terms of salaries, teaching loads, class sizes and other considerations, most of which have a direct bearing on salary cost per course or per student quarter, so there would be some realism in trying to relate the $c_{ij}$'s to salary costs of hiring comparable performance in the national market. In general, it seems that the salary costs per section in different courses should be roughly proportional to the amounts of "good" done to the students, so the two approaches could lead to approximately the same set of $c_{ij}$'s.

For the moment, let us assume that the $c_{ij}$'s in table 7.3 are estimates of the national average salary cost of obtaining the specified levels of performance in the stipulated courses. If $c_{15} = 15$, in other words, we assume faculty member 1 would justify a $\$15\,000$ salary *if* he were teaching nine sections of course 5. (We leave aside the question of need for variety in one's teaching program.)

Given the size of the particular department, however, there are only four sections of course 5 to be taught. The best use of faculty member 1's talents within this department is four units of course 5 and five units of course 1, and the average value of these services would be

$$\frac{4(15) + 5(10)}{9} = \frac{60 + 50}{9} = 12.222, \quad \text{or} \quad \$12\,222.$$

If we apply this interpretation of the $c_{ij}$'s to all four faculty members we may summarize the results as follows. (see top of page 382).

In arriving at these figures, we have multiplied each $c_{ij}$ by $\frac{1000}{9}$. If we reverse this procedure and multiply each of the column (3) and column (4) totals by $\frac{9}{1000}$ we have

$$35\,667 \left( \frac{9}{1000} \right) = 321$$

and

$$34\,444 \left( \frac{9}{1000} \right) = 310.$$

| Faculty member | (1) Value as specialist in his best course (9 sections of it) | (2) Value if assigned to the 9 sections in which he has highest value to this department | (3) Value in optimal solution for department as a whole | (4) Value if used as in the first feasible solution |
|---|---|---|---|---|
| 1 | $15000 | $12222 | $12222 | $12222 |
| 2 | 12000 | 8889 | 8889 | 8889 |
| 3 | 11000 | 10556 | 8778 | 9889 |
| 4 | 8000 | 6889 | 5778 | 3444 |
| Totals | $46000 | $38556 | $35667 | $34444 |

The second result (310) will be recognized as the value of the objective function associated with the first feasible solution, while 321 is the value of the objective function associated with the optimal solution.

A few more comments are in order:

(1) The optimal assignment set for each faculty member depends on the array of talents of all other faculty members in the department. Once faculty member 4 has been hired, the optimal use pattern for faculty member 3 is one valued at $8778.

(2) If faculty member 4 is on a one-year appointment while the other three members have tenure, in planning for the next following year it might be desirable to assign faculty member 3 to courses in which his total value is $9889 (as in the first feasible solution) and try to recruit a new faculty member 4 who would be strong in courses 1 and 3. (If faculty member 1 should leave, faculty member 3 could be assigned to courses in which his value is $10556.)

(3) Faculty member 2 is evidently stronger in research than in teaching and might reasonably move to another institution which provides more time and facilities for research.

(4) Faculty member 1 has unusual qualifications for course 5. These might extend to one or two closely related courses in the same field (perhaps at the first-year graduate level as well as at the advanced undergraduate level). A larger department with more enrollment in course 5 and closely related courses could afford to offer faculty member 1 about $15000.

(5) The faculty allocation model maximizes an objective function pertaining to the department as a whole in a single year. Longer-run goals for the department could also be expressed as values of the objective function. Is it realistic to plan for a department in which the average $c_{ij}$ is 15 for the optimal assignment pattern? If so, the faculty would be worth (and would probably require) an average salary level of about $15000, not counting the upward trend over time in the national salary structure for persons of given ability.

Faculty member 1 is evidently of the desired quality, if used as a specialist. However, the peak performances of faculty members 2, 3 and 4 in their best courses are currently valued at $12000, $11000 and $8000. Is this simply a matter of inexperience and other remediable factors? If not, the long-run goal for the department (average $c_{ij}$ to equal 15) may be incompatible with the retention of some or all of these faculty members. Or, the goal might be redefined to state that *new* faculty members should be of the desired quality or potential (expected $c_{ij}$'s of 15); an average performance level of less than 15 for new and existing faculty members combined would be accepted as a fact of life during a fairly long transition period.

### 7.2.2. Dynamic linear programming I: optimal admissions policy with a ten-year planning horizon

The following dynamic programming model is presented in Fox, McCamley and Plessner [4]:

$$\max \sum_t (c_{1t}x_{1t} + c_{2t}x_{2t}), \qquad\qquad t = 1, 2, ..., 10 \qquad (7.27)$$

subject to

$$x_{1,t-1} + x_{1t} \leqslant x_{3t} + x_{4t}, \qquad\qquad t = 1, 2, ..., 10, \qquad (7.28)$$

$$x_{1,t-3} + x_{1,t-2} + 0.6x_{3t} + x_{4t} + x_{5t} \leqslant 84, \qquad t = 1, 2, ..., 10, \qquad (7.29)$$

$$4x_{2,t-1} + 3x_{2t} - 3x_{5t} \leqslant 36, \qquad\qquad t = 1, 2, ..., 10, \qquad (7.30)$$

$$x_{1t} \leqslant 30, \qquad\qquad t = 1, 2, ..., 10, \qquad (7.31)$$

$$x_{2t} \leqslant 7, \qquad\qquad t = 1, 2, ..., 10, \qquad (7.32)$$

$$x_{1,t-3} \leqslant 21, \qquad\qquad t = 1 \qquad (7.33)$$

$$x_{1,t-2} \leqslant 22, \qquad\qquad t = 1, 2 \qquad (7.34)$$

$$x_{1,t-2} \leqslant 23, \qquad\qquad t = 1, 2, 3 \qquad (7.35)$$

$$x_{2,t-1} \leqslant 7, \qquad\qquad t = 1 \qquad (7.36)$$

$$x_{it} \geqslant 0, \qquad i = 1, 2, 3, 4 \text{ and } 5; \qquad t = 1, 2, ..., 10. \qquad (7.37)$$

TABLE 7.4

Dynamic programming model to optimize undergraduate and graduate admissions over a 10-year period.

| Item | | | | Year | | | | | | |
|---|---|---|---|---|---|---|---|---|---|---|
| | 1 | 2 | 3 | 4 | 5 | 6 | 7 | 8 | 9 | 10 |
| **Variables to be optimized (computed values rounded down if not integers):** | | | | | | | | | | |
| **Other variables:** | | | | | | | | | | |
| $x_{1t}$ | 30 | 24 | 23 | 23 | 24 | 25 | 26 | 24 | 25 | 26 |
| $x_{2t}$ | 7 | 7 | 5 | 6 | 3 | 7 | 7 | 6 | 6 | 7 |
| $x_{1t-3}$ | 21 | 22 | 23 | 30 | 24 | 23 | 23 | 24 | 25 | 26 |
| $x_{1t-2}$ | 22 | 23 | 30 | 24 | 23 | 23 | 24 | 25 | 26 | 24 |
| $x_{1t-1}$ | 23 | 30 | 24 | 23 | 23 | 24 | 25 | 26 | 24 | 25 |
| $x_{2t-1}$ | 6 | 7 | 7 | 5 | 6 | 3 | 7 | 7 | 6 | 6 |
| $x_{3t}$ | 50 | 50 | 48 | 47 | 12 | 50 | 50 | 50 | 49 | 50 |
| $x_{4t}$ | 3 | 5 | 0 | 0 | 36 | 0 | 2 | 0 | 0 | 1 |
| $x_{5t}$ | 4 | 4 | 2 | 1 | 1 | 0 | 4 | 4 | 3 | 3 |
| **Shadow prices corresponding to restrictions:** | | | | | | | | | | |
| (2) | 0 | 0.85 | 0.40 | 0.60 | 0.75 | 0.85 | 0.40 | 0.91 | 0.45 | 0.94 |
| (3) | 0 | 0.85 | 0.67 | 1.00 | 0.75 | 1.25 | 0.40 | 1.00 | 0.75 | 0.94 |
| (4) | 0 | 0.28 | 0.22 | 0.33 | 0.25 | 0.31 | 0.13 | 0.33 | 0.25 | 0.31 |
| **Objective function weights:** | | | | | | | | | | |
| $c_{1t}$ | 3.00 | 3.00 | 3.00 | 3.00 | 3.00 | 3.00 | 3.00 | (3.00)* | (3.00)* | (3.00)* |
| $c_{2t}$ | 2.00 | 2.00 | 2.00 | 2.00 | 2.00 | 2.00 | 2.00 | 2.00 | (2.00)* | (2.00)* |

Objective function value, $W = 644.19$*

* Freshmen admitted in years 1 through 7 receive B.S. degrees in years 4 through 10 and enter the objective function; freshmen admitted in years 8, 9 and 10 do not enter the objective function.
Graduate students admitted in years 1 through 9 receive M.S. degrees in years 2 through 10; those admitted in year 10 do not figure in the objective function value.

Constraint (7.28) insures that all freshmen and sophomore students are taught the required number of courses.

Constraint (7.29) insures that juniors and seniors receive the required amount of instruction.

Constraint (7.30) insures that graduate students receive the required amount of instruction.

Constraints (7.33) through (7.36) are initial conditions applying only to the first one to three years of the period.

The principal features and results of this model, optimized over a ten-year planning period, are summarized in table 7.4. The complete activity matrix (not shown) has a concentration of blocks of elements on its diagonal and additional elements below the diagonal. Each block involves the activity levels and restrictions specific to a given year; elements below a block indicate that some of the activity levels selected in a given year (such as the number of freshmen admitted) also commit resources in specified future years. This structure is characteristic of dynamic programming models.

The complete model involves 50 activities (5 activities in each of ten years) and 30 restrictions (3 restrictions in each of ten years). The activity levels in, say, year 3 depend partly on the numbers of freshmen admitted in years 0, 1 and 2 and the number of beginning graduate students admitted in year 2. The activities and restrictions *directly* relevant to year 3 are as follows:

| | | Relevant activities | | | | | | |
|---|---|---|---|---|---|---|---|---|
| | Years 0, 1 and 2: | | | | | Year 3 | | |
| | B.S.0 | B.S.1 | B.S.2 | M.S.2 | B.S.3 | M.S.3 | $I3$ | $T3$ | $TR3$ |
| $c_{it}$ | * | * | * | * | 3.00 | 2.00 | | | |
| $J3$ | | | 1.0 | | 1.0 | | $-1.0$ | $-1.0$ | $\leqslant 0$ |
| $U3$ | 1.0 | 1.0 | | | | | 0.6 | 1.0 | 1.0 | $\leqslant 84$ |
| $G3$ | | | | 4.0 | | 3.0 | | | $-3.0$ | $\leqslant 36$ |
| $X_{it}$ | 23 | 30 | 24 | 7 | 23 | 5 | 48 | 0 | 2 |

$W_3 = 23(3.00) + 5(2.00) = 69.00 + 10.00 = 79.00.$

* Not used in calculating $W_3$.

The objective of the department is to convert 48 sections' worth of faculty time each year (over the ten-year period) into as many "output points" as possible, given that each B.S. degree is valued at 3 points and each M.S. degree at 2 points. (As the M.S. candidates already have the B.S. degree, the 2 points represent an increment of value added over and above the B.S. degree.)

There is only one activity available for producing M.S. degrees but there are two alternative activities for producing B.S. degrees. The cost of a unit level of each activity in sections of faculty time is:

> M.S.:        1.17 sections of faculty time
> B.S. (I):    2.00 sections of faculty time
> B.S. (II):   1.60 sections of faculty time.

(The B.S. (II) activity also requires 0.40 sections of teaching assistant time, but we will disregard the cost of this input for our present purpose.)

The value of output per section of faculty time in each activity is:

$$\text{M.S.:} \qquad \frac{2.00 \text{ points}}{1.17 \text{ sections}} = 1.70 \text{ points per section}$$

$$\text{B.S. (I):} \qquad \frac{3.00 \text{ points}}{2.00 \text{ sections}} = 1.50 \text{ points per section}$$

$$\text{B.S. (II):} \qquad \frac{3.00 \text{ points}}{1.60 \text{ sections}} = 1.88 \text{ points per section}.$$

Within the terms of the problem, activity B.S. (II) produces the greatest value per section; activity M.S. is second and activity B.S. (I) is third.

Of the three restrictions in each year, $J$ insures that freshmen and sophomores get the required amount of instruction, $U$ that juniors and seniors get the required amount of instruction, and $G$ that graduate students get the required amount of instruction and thesis supervision. The unit of measure in restrictions $J$ and $U$ is one-half sections of faculty time; the unit for $G$ is one-sixth section of faculty time.

In table 7.4, the shadow prices corresponding to each restriction in a given year indicate the number of points by which the value of the objective function could be increased if one more unit of the restricting resource were available (one more half-section in $J$ and $U$, one more sixth-section in $G$). The difference in units is inconvenient, so we multiply the shadow prices of $J$ and $U$ by 2 and that of $G$ by 6 to obtain the increase in value of the objective function *per additional section of faculty time* in all three cases, with the following results:

| Year | Shadow prices per section of faculty time | | | Levels of selected activities | | |
|------|------|------|------|------|------|------|
| | $J$ | $U$ | $G$ | $x_3(=I)$ | $x_4(=T)$ | $x_5(=TR)$ |
| 1 | 0 | 0 | 0 | 50 | 3 | 4 |
| 2 | 1.70 | 1.70 | 1.70 | 50 | 5 | 4 |
| 3 | 0.80 | 1.33 | 1.33 | 48 | 0 | 2 |
| 4 | 1.20 | 2.00 | 2.00 | 47 | 0 | 1 |
| 5 | 1.50 | 1.50 | 1.50 | 12 | 36 | 1 |
| 6 | 1.70 | 2.50 | 1.86 | 50 | 0 | 0 |
| 7 | 0.80 | 0.80 | 0.80 | 50 | 2 | 4 |
| 8 | 1.82 | 2.00 | 2.00 | 50 | 0 | 4 |
| 9 | 0.90 | 1.50 | 1.50 | 49 | 0 | 3 |
| 10 | 1.88 | 1.88 | 1.88 | 50 | 1 | 3 |

The basic economic problem is to allocate 48 sections of faculty time among freshman-sophomore, junior-senior and graduate level teaching so as to maximize the value of total output. The shadow prices are marginal value products; in the continuous cases usually stressed in economic theory, the value of an additional section of faculty time should be the same in all three uses.

In years 1, 2, 5, 7 and 10 this three-way equality applies. In years 3, 4, 8 and 9 the shadow prices of $U$ and $G$ are equal but the shadow price of $J$ (marginal value product of faculty time in freshman and sophomore teaching) is lower. In years 3, 4, and 9, the shadow price of $J$ is 0.6 times as large as the shadow price of $U$.

Activity $x_5$ has the effect of equating the shadow prices of $U$ and $G$ whenever $x_5 > 0$, and $x_5$ is greater than zero in all years except year 6. Activity $x_4$ has the effect of equating the shadow prices of $J$ and $U$ when $x_4 > 0$, as it is in years 1, 2, 5, 7 and 10. When activity $x_4 = 0$, in most (but not all) cases the marginal value product of faculty time in teaching freshmen and sophomores is only 60 percent as large as that in teaching juniors and seniors under the assumptions of our problem.

Evidently the solutions of dynamic programming models can be given common sense interpretations. The technique of solution is essentially that used for ordinary linear programming models. The total numbers of activities and restrictions increase with the number of years in the planning period

TABLE 7.5

The simplified simplex tableau.

**Activities (columns) — Activity no. and Objective coefficient:**

| No. | Activity | Obj. coeff. |
|---|---|---|
| 1 | Undergraduates (B.S.) | $c_1$ |
| 2 | Master's students (M.S.) | $c_2$ |
| 3 | Ph.D. candidates UP | $c_3$ |
| 4 | Ph.D. candidates IP | $c_4$ |
| 5 | Ph.D. candidates RP | $c_5$ |
| 6 | Research by existing faculty | $c_6$ |
| 7 | Research by new faculty / Hiring new faculty | $c_7$ |
| 8 | Office space addition | $c_8$ |
| 9 | Transfer of existing faculty time to undergraduate teaching | $c_9$ |
| 10 | Transfer of existing faculty time to undergraduate teaching | 0 |
| 11 | Transfer of existing faculty time to graduate teaching | 0 |
| 12 | Transfer of new faculty time to undergraduate teaching | 0 |
| 13 | Transfer of new faculty time to graduate teaching | 0 |
| 14 | Transfer of new faculty time to undergraduate administration | 0 |
| 15 | Transfer of new faculty time to graduate administration | 0 |

**Tableau (restrictions × activities):**

| Restrictions | 1 | 2 | 3 | 4 | 5 | 6 | 7 | 8 | 9 | 10 | 11 | 12 | 13 | 14 | 15 | Right-hand side |
|---|---|---|---|---|---|---|---|---|---|---|---|---|---|---|---|---|
| 1 Manpower for undergraduate teaching | $a_{11}$ | | | $-a_{14}$ | | | | | | $-1$ | | $-a_{1,12}$ | | | | $b_1$ |
| 2 Manpower for graduate teaching | | $a_{22}$ | $a_{23}$ | $a_{24}$ | $a_{25}$ | | | | | | $-1$ | | $-a_{2,13}$ | | | $b_2$ |
| 3 "Pool" of existing manpower | | | | | | $-1676$ | | | | $1$ | $1$ | | | | | $b_3$ |
| 4 "Pool" of new manpower | | | | | | | $1$ | | | | | $1$ | $1$ | $1$ | $1$ | $0$ |
| 5 Manpower for undergraduate administration | $a_{51}$ | | | | | | | | | | | | | $-1$ | | $b_5$ |
| 6 Manpower for graduate administration | | $a_{62}$ | $a_{63}$ | $a_{64}$ | $a_{65}$ | | | | | | | | | | $-1$ | $b_6$ |
| 7 Office space | | | | $a_{74}$ | $a_{75}$ | $a_{76}$ | | $1$ | | | | | | | | $b_7$ |
| 8 Admission of undergraduates | $1$ | | | | | | | | | | | | | | | $b_8$ |
| 9 Admission of graduates | | $1$ | | $1$ | $1$ | | | | | | | | | | | $b_9$ |
| 10 Ratio of IP to undergraduates | $-1$ | | | $a_{10,4}$ | | | | | | | | | | | | $0$ |
| 11 Ratio of M.S. to graduates | | $-.75$ | $.25$ | $.25$ | $.25$ | | | | | | | | | | | $0$ |
| 12 Manpower of RP | | | | | $-a_{12,5}$ | | $a_{12,7}$ | $a_{12,8}$ | | | | | | | | $0$ |
| 13 Dissertation supervision | | $a_{13,2}$ | $a_{13,3}$ | $a_{13,4}$ | $a_{13,5}$ | | $-a_{13,7}$ | | | | | | | | | $0$ |
| 14 Existing manpower transferable to undergraduate teaching | | | | | | | | | $-1$ | | $1$ | | | | | $b_{14}$ |
| 15 New manpower transferable to administration | | | | | | $-a_{15,6}$ | | | | $1$ | | | | | | $b_{15}$ |
| 16 Research | | | | | | $-a_{16,6}$ | $1$ | | | | | | | | | $b_{16}$ |

and also with the real complexity of the department and/or the degree of detail with which it is represented. The Plessner-Fox-Sanyal [5] model has 15 activities and 16 restrictions in each year of a four-year planning period, or 60 activities and 64 restrictions for the period as a whole.

The McCamley model [8] of a large economics department has 82 activities and 57 constraints for a single year; a ten-year dynamic programming version at this level of detail would have 820 activities and 570 restrictions. A model of this size would not exceed the capacity of modern computers; however, it remains to be seen whether this level of detail is needed (or is in some sense useful) in a ten-year planning model.

### 7.2.3. *Dynamic linear programming II: a four-year planning model involving faculty allocation and recruitment*

The Plessner-Fox-Sanyal [5] model mentioned in 7.2.2. has some interesting features distinct from those of the Fox-McCamley-Plessner [4] example of dynamic programming. Table 7.5 presents a simplified version of the model used. The simplification is due to the fact that the actual model constituted a four-year plan, with some interdependency between the years.

In this model we conceive of a *policy function* which includes an "economic" part and a "noneconomic" part. The term "objective function" is here used to refer only to the economic part, namely the outputs of activities 1, 2, 3, 4 and 5 with their respective prices $c_1$, $c_2$, $c_3$, $c_4$ and $c_5$. As is seen from the table, three different activities relate to Ph.D. candidates: those who do not enjoy any income from university sources during their studies (UP); those who are half-time instructors (IP) and those who are half-time research assistants (RP). Since we treated each candidate for a degree as though he holds the immediately preceding degree, the assumed norms for the duration of studies were as follows: B.S. or IP, four years; M.S., two years; UP or RP, three years.[5] The output of research activities was defined in terms of the inputs, i.e., a unit of output is whatever emerges from one hour of faculty time devoted to research.

Next in order are the coefficients of the objective function. For $j = 1, 2, ..., 5$ these were computed as

$$c_j = R_j \frac{(1 + r)^{n_j - k_j} - 1}{r(1 + r)^{n_j - 1}} - F_j \frac{(1 + r)^{m_j - k_j} - 1}{r(1 + r)^{m_j - 1}} = S_{R_j} - S_{F_j},$$

---

[5] In the case of a B.S. candidate the "immediately preceding degree" is a high school diploma.

where

$R_j$ = starting annual salary;

$F_j$ = annual income foregone;

$r$ = interest rate (4.3 percent);

$k_j$ = years elapsed from the start of the program to the year of admission; [6]

$n_j$ = expected worklife $+ k_j$; and

$m_j = n_j +$ years of study.

For M.S. and Ph.D. candidates $F_j$ was taken to be the starting salary of the holder of the immediately preceding degree; for B.S. candidates, $F_j$ was assumed to be the salary that a high school graduate can earn in industry. The data for $R_j$ were taken from an American Economic Association study of the salaries of US economists in 1964 [24].

For $c_6$ we assumed the starting salary of a new faculty member, and computed his total discounted salary from the time he entered the system until the end of the program. We defined $c_7$ and $c_8$ as the total research expenditures, other than faculty and student salaries, per hour of faculty research. These were computed from departmental data.

Research outputs were not priced directly, so at the beginning of the analysis the *policy* function (as distinct from the objective function) was not completely specified. A prime object of the analysis was to estimate, and hence make explicit, the value assigned to research which was *implicit* in the chairman's allocation of faculty time between teaching and research.

Our treatment was based on partitioning the objective function into two parts, which we shall label for convenience "economic" and "noneconomic". The "economic" part is represented in our model by the programming objective function, which consists of the capitalization of expected lifetime income earned by students who graduate from the department in all its programs less departmental expenses on *new* faculty and other expenditures associated with the teaching program. This function provides us with the required link between the department and the market or national economy.

It is quite reasonable to assume that the objective function so constituted is included in the chairman's policy function. That is, if $x$ is an $(n-s)$ vector and $y$ an $s$ vector, and the programming objective function is given by $f(x)$, then the policy function may be stated as $g[f(x), y]$, where $y$ represents what we called the "noneconomic" part. The parameters of this latter part we were not prepared to estimate directly. Specifically, we refer to outputs associated with research activities.

---

[6] I.e., if the program covers 1969–72 and a student enters the system in 1971, then $k_j = 2$.

Formulating $f(x)$, however, enables us, through the imposition of constraints,[7] to evaluate *subjective* rates of substitution between variables in $x$ and variables in $y$, expressed in terms of their effect on national income.

To demonstrate the procedure, consider the problem of finding an $n$ vector $x^0 \geq 0$ such that

$$c'x^0 \geq c'x$$

for all $x$ satisfying

$$Ax \leq b,$$

where $c$ is an $n$ vector specifying net capitalized contributions of a unit level of $x$ to national income, $A$ is the $m \times n$ technology matrix and $b > 0$ the $m$ vector of available resources. Suppose now that $x_n$ is a "$y$-type" variable, which in our case implies $c_n = 0$. Assume also that $a^n \geq 0$, where $a^n$ denotes the $n$th column of $A$, and $c_j > 0$ for all $j \neq n$. Depending on the resource vector $b$, $x_n$ may or may not enter the optimal basis.

The iterative procedure starts when the chairman, the individual who "is in charge of the policy function", expresses his dissatisfaction with a program in which $x_r = 0$. We assume he is able to state that it would seem reasonable to him to try positive levels of $x_n$ in some interval, say $[\alpha, \beta]$. It is then possible to solve an array of problems of the form

$$\max c'x$$

subject to

$$Ax \leq b$$

$$x_n \geq \eta_k$$

$$x \geq 0,$$

where $\eta_k \in [\alpha, \beta]$ and $k$ takes a finite number of values, such that $\eta_k < \eta_{k+1}$.

Associated with the solution of the $k$th problem will be a vector of "shadow prices" $u^k$ of the elements in $b$ and $\eta_k$. As $\eta_k$ varies over its index set, so does $u^k$. Characteristically, it will be true that $u^{k+1} \geq u^k$ while $(c'x)^{k+1} < (c'x)^k$ for all $k$. That is to say, the contribution to national income is seemingly

---

[7] Some of these constraints are imposed by the university administration, others result from departmental faculty preferences. The noneconomic part, $y$, and the subjective rates of substitution between variables in $x$ and variables in $y$ may be regarded as special cases of Simon's concept of satisficing behavior [25]. Charnes and Cooper, in their papers on repricing theorems [26] and on deterministic equivalents for optimizing and satisficing under chance constraints [27] have presented methods for incorporating satisficing behavior in programming models.

decreasing, while the amount "forgone" is reflected by $u^k$. As $\eta_k$ varies, $u^k$ varies discontinuously. There will be a range (or ranges) of variation in $\eta_k$ for which $u_k$ remains constant. Since $x_n$ is a nonprofitable activity, increasing values of $x_n$ will not increase the value of the objective function and in general will decrease it as $x_n$ draws limiting resources away from the profitable activities included in the initial solution.

The usefulness of the information so provided hinges on the assumption, which to us seems realistic, that the policy maker will be able to identify a magnitude of $u^k$ beyond which he is not willing to go. In so doing, he will have placed an upper bound on his subjective evaluation of the contribution of $x_n$ to national income – assuming, of course, that he accepts contribution to national income as the sole criterion for both the economic and the non-economic parts of his policy function.

By executing the experiment we do not in any way progress towards direct measurement of as yet unestimable quantities. Rather, we contribute to systematizing a procedure which (in the absence of market prices for research outputs) is practiced anyway. For let $x_n$ represent research output, and it is clear that the determination of allocation to research is a function of what people believe to be its contribution to national income (and other aspects of well being).

The shadow price per hour of the time of existing faculty members available for teaching and administration emerges in the following way:

(a) The chairman diverts an hour of existing faculty time from teaching to research.

(b) As enrollment is expanding rapidly, some new faculty members must be hired in any case. The chairman has just reduced the teaching-time capacity of the existing faculty by one hour. We must replace it by an additional hour (experienced-teacher equivalent) of teaching time from a new faculty member.

(c) But some percentage, $\lambda$, of the new faculty member's time will be devoted to research. To obtain an hour of inexperienced teaching time, we must pay for $1/(1-\lambda)$ hours of total time.

(d) If a new faculty member takes $\frac{10}{7}$ as much time to handle a given course as does an existing faculty member, and if 30 percent of a new faculty member's time is allocated to research, we must hire $10/7(0.7) = 10/4.9 = 2.04$ hours of new faculty time to repair our teaching program. Hence, apart from minor repercussions, the cost of withdrawing an hour of existing faculty time from teaching is 2.04 times the starting salary (per hour) of a new faculty member.

The full reduction in the value of the objective function associated with an increase of one hour in research by existing faculty members includes both the cost of repairing the teaching program and the cost of providing the average amount of secretarial, clerical, computing and other resources which were associated with each hour of faculty research in 1965.

If the starting salary of a new faculty member is $7 an hour, the chairman's implicit appraisal of the value of an hour of faculty research time must be at least 2.04 times $7, or $14.28. If he adds $10 of supporting resources to the hour of research time, he implies that an hour of the activity is worth at least $14.28 plus $10.00, or $24.28 (assuming that the use of supporting resources reduces potential GNP in other sectors or establishments).

If the numbers of new faculty positions available during years 1, 2, 3 and 4 were closely rationed, the chairman might find that the opportunity cost of increased faculty research time included a reduction in graduate or undergraduate enrollments. If we used the AER salary figures, the reduction of undergraduate enrollment would reduce the objective function by about $50000 per student, or about $200 per hour of faculty time involved! Before doing that, the AER figures imply that the M.S. program should be eliminated; if a second step were needed, the Ph.D. program should be reduced relative to the original plan. The relative numbers of half-time instructors, research assistants, and graduate students not supported by the university within the Ph.D. program would be scrutinized.

### 7.2.4. *Decomposition or decentralization techniques: two-level planning for the allocation of a college's central resources among its constituent departments*

This illustration of two-level planning is based on Fox, McCamley and Plessner [4].

Under a two-level decision-making scheme each department may be faced with a problem of the form (for the $i$th department):

$$\max \sum_{j=1}^{m_i} c_{ij} x_{ij} \qquad (7.38)$$

subject to

$$\sum_{j=1}^{m_i} a_{ijk} x_{ij} \leqq b_{ik}, \qquad k = 1, 2, ..., s_i, \qquad (7.39)$$

$$\sum_{j=1}^{m_i} d_{ijh} x_{ij} \leqq u_{ih}, \qquad h = 1, 2, ..., t, \qquad (7.40)$$

$$x_{ij} \geqq 0, \qquad j = 1, 2, ..., m_i. \qquad (7.41)$$

The $c_{ij}$'s are objective function weights, the $x_{ij}$'s are the activity levels for activities of the $i$th department, the $a_{ijk}$'s and $d_{ijh}$'s are technical coefficients which indicate the amounts of resources $k$ and $h$ used when the $j$th activity (of the $i$th department) is operated at the unit level. Further, $t$ equals the number of different resources allocated by the college dean, $s_i$ equals the number of constraints faced by department $i$ with respect to resources which are specialized to it and are not usable by other departments, and $m_i$ equals the number of activities available to department $i$.

Constraints (7.39) are constraints on resources (or outputs) used (or produced) only by the $i$th department.

Constraints (7.40) are constraints on resources (or outputs) which could be used (or produced) by other departments and which are allocated by the college dean.

Constraints (7.41) reflect the fact that negative activity levels are not permitted.

The problem faced by the college dean has the form:

$$\max \sum_{i=1}^{n} \sum_{j=1}^{m_i} c_{ij} x_{ij} \tag{7.42}$$

subject to

$$\sum_{i=1}^{n} u_{ih} \le b_h, \qquad h = 1, 2, \ldots, t, \tag{7.43}$$

and subject to restrictions (7.39), (7.40) and (7.41) being satisfied for all departments.

Here, $n$ equals the number of departments in the college, $u_{ih}$ indicates the amount of the $h$th resource which is allocated to the $i$th department, and $b_h$ indicates the amount of the $h$th resource which the college dean has available for allocation.

The constraints (7.43) insure that the totals of the allocations made by the college dean do not exceed the total amounts available.

The decision process that could be used to obtain an optimum set of quotas consists of several phases each of which can be described by describing the $N$th phase. During the $N$th phase the college dean solves a problem of the form: [8]

$$Z^N = \min \left[ \sum_{h=1}^{t} b_h V_h + \sum_{i=1}^{n} w_i \right] \tag{7.44}$$

---

[8] The dual of this problem is ordinarliy easier to solve and can be used to obtain the solution to (7.44) through (7.46).

subject to

$$\sum_{h=1}^{t} u_{ih}^K V_h + w_i \geqq r_i^K, \qquad i = 1, 2, ..., n,$$

$$K = 0, 1, 2, ..., N - 1, \qquad (7.45)$$

$$V_h \geqq 0, \qquad h = 1, 2, ..., t. \qquad (7.46)$$

The solution values are designated as $V_h^N$, $h = 1, 2, ..., t$, and $w_i^N$, $i = 1, 2, ..., n$. The $V_h^N$'s are the college dean's current estimates of the shadow prices (marginal values) of the resources which he allocates. The $w_i^N$'s are his current estimates of those resources (and output requirements) which can only be used (or produced) by the individual departments.

He reports the $V_i^N$'s and $w_h^N$'s to the departments. They solve problems which (for the $i$th department) have the form:

$$Z_i^N = \max \left[ \sum_{j=1}^{m_i} c_{ij} x_{ij} - \sum_{h=1}^{t} u_{ih} V_h^N \right] - w_i^N \qquad (7.47)$$

subject to constraints (7.39), (7.40) and (7.41). If $Z_i^N$ is greater than zero the $x_{ij}^N$'s and $u_{ih}^N$'s are set equal to the solution values of the $x_{ij}$'s and $u_{ih}$'s. They also then compute $r_i^N$ by setting it equal to $\sum_{j=1}^{m_i} c_{ij} x_{ij}^N$ and report the values of the $u_{ih}^N$'s and of $r_i^N$ to the college dean. If $Z_i^N$ is equal to zero the $i$th department reports only this fact to the college dean.

In order to initiate this process it is necessary to know initially (at the beginning of phase 1) some feasible values for the $u_{ih}^0$'s and $r_i^0$s. Ordinarily this information would be known by the college dean or could be obtained by modifying plans (allocations) for previous periods. If these values cannot be supplied by the college dean the decision-making process can be modified for as many phases as are required to obtain a feasible solution. The details of this modification can be found in McCamley [8, pp. 106–107]. Essentially the modification amounts, for the college dean's part of the $N$th phase, to

$$\text{minimizing} \left[ \sum_{h=1}^{t} b_h V_h + \sum_{i=1}^{n} w_i \right]$$

subject to

$$\sum_{h=1}^{t} u_{ih}^K V_h + w_i \geqslant 0, \qquad \begin{array}{l} i = 1, 2, ..., n, \\ K = 1, 2, ..., N - 1, \end{array}$$

$$0 \leqslant V_h \leqslant 1, \qquad h = 1, 2, ..., t,$$

$$w_i \geqslant -1, \qquad i = 1, 2, ..., n.$$

The departments react as before except that $Z_i^N = \max \left[ -\sum_{h=1}^{t} u_{ih} \right] - w_i^N$ subject to constraints (7.39), (7.40) and (7.41).

The decision process continues until at the end of some phase, say the $M$th, $Z_i^M$ is equal to zero for all relevant $i$. The college dean would then solve a problem of the form:

$$Z^M = \max \left[ \sum_{i=1}^{n} \sum_{K=1}^{M-1} r_i^K \lambda_i^K \right] \tag{7.48}$$

subject to

$$\sum_{i=1}^{n} \sum_{K=1}^{M-1} u_{ih}^K \lambda_i^K \leqslant b_h, \qquad h = 1, 2, ..., t, \tag{7.49}$$

$$\sum_{K=1}^{M-1} \lambda_i^K = 1, \qquad i = 1, 2, ..., n, \tag{7.50}$$

$$\lambda_i^K \geqslant 0, \qquad i = 1, 2, ... n, \qquad K = 1, 2, ..., M-1. \tag{7.51}$$

(This, of course, is the dual of the $M$th phase version of the problem defined by (7.44) through (7.46) and therefore the solution would already be known to him.) Designate by $\hat{\lambda}_i^K$'s the values of the $\lambda_i^K$'s which solve (7.48) through (7.51). An optimum set of quotas could then be obtained by setting

$$u_{ih} = \sum_{K=1}^{M-1} u_{ih}^K \hat{\lambda}_i^K \qquad \begin{array}{l} \text{for} \quad i = 1, 2, ..., n \\ \text{and} \quad h = 1, 2, ..., t. \end{array}$$

The procedure described above must be modified if unbounded solutions ($Z_i^K \to \infty$) are obtained by any of the departments at any stage. This modification is described in Dantzig [28, pp. 453–454].

*7.2.4.1. An illustration.* The example presented in Fox, McCamley and Plessner [4] assumes that the dean of a college is granted a certain budget for the operation of his college; he wishes to allocate this budget among departments so as to maximize an objective function.

In addition to the budget, which obviously needs to be allocated, we assume that there are certain services whose use and production must be coordinated. Specifically, we assume that there is a need to insure that the amounts of instruction required by graduate students outside their own departments do not exceed the total amounts supplied by the various departments which perform this "service" teaching. We consider the dean as being concerned with the allocation of that graduate instruction which is produced by one department for use by other departments within his college.

One way for the college dean to decide on the appropriate allocation of the various resources would be for him to treat his college as one large decision-making unit. He could decide how much of each output to produce and what input combination to use in producing it. A byproduct of these decisions would be decisions about the amount of each resource to allocate to each department.

Fortunately, in some cases the dean may be able to allocate resources among departments, let the departments make most of the output and other activity level decisions, and still accomplish whatever output objectives he may have in mind. One of these cases occurs when all of the constraints are linear, the college objective function is linear, and when in addition, the departmental objective functions assign the same weights to the various outputs and inputs as are assigned by the college objective function. The results of Kornai and Liptak [20] assure us that in such a case there exists a system of quotas (for the resources allocated by the college dean) that, if implemented, will insure that the college dean's objective function will be maximized. The decomposition algorithm of Dantzig and Wolfe [21] provides a basis for the construction of a decentralized decision-making approach which can be used to discover an optimum set of quotas. Under this approach the college dean would, at each phase, ask each department how much of each resource it could "profitably" use if certain "prices" were assigned to each resource. The information which the departments give him would be used to aid in the derivation of a new set of "prices". The college dean would then ask each department to tell him how much of each resource it would use at these new prices. This process would continue until an optimum set of quotas is obtained.

Consider a college having three departments (departments A, B, and C). Suppose that the college has a teaching budget of $220000 per year, that 80 (graduate) students from other colleges take courses in department A, 115 take courses in department B, and 210 take courses in department C. Suppose further that graduate students in departments B and C take courses in department A and that graduate students in department A take courses in department B. To simplify matters it will be assumed that undergraduate enrollment, curriculum, and distribution of undergraduate students among majors is predetermined.

Some of the assumptions which will be made concerning the individual departments are outlined in table 7.6. The specific models used for the departments are presented in [4]. These models all allow alternative input combinations in the production of research publications and in the teaching of undergraduate students. They classify graduate students according to means of support. They also permit varying amounts of research, graduate teaching, and undergraduate teaching per faculty member.

TABLE 7.6

Two-level decision model: some characteristics of departments A, B, and C.

| Item | Department A | Department B | Department C |
|---|---|---|---|
| No. of faculty members* | 5.5 | 8.5 | 7.5 |
| Undergraduate teaching required (no. of student courses) | 1850 | 2750 | 2250 |
| Graduate service teaching required (no. of student courses) | determined by college dean | | 210 |
| Research budget ($'s) | 40000 | 20000 | 45000 |
| Faculty salaries ($'s) | 11000 | 10000 | 12000 |
| Undergraduate class sizes faculty instructors | 35 | 30 | 40 |
| both faculty and graduate student instructors | 30 | 25 | 35 |
| Graduate class sizes | 24 | 15 | 18 |
| Thesis "class sizes" | 6.5 | 7.0 | 7.5 |
| Teaching assistant salaries ($'s) | 2800 | 2600 | 2750 |
| Research assistant salaries ($'s) | 2750 | – | 2700 |
| Number of inputs supplied by teaching assistants (sections taught per year) | 5 | 5 | 6 |
| Number of years required to obtain M.S. degree | 2 | 2 | 2 |
| Number of courses taken to obtain M.S. degree | | | |
| in: department A | 10 | 3 | 4 |
| in: department B | 3 | 10 | 0 |
| in: department C | 0 | 0 | 9 |
| thesis credits | 3 | 3 | 3 |
| Objective function weights research publications | 2.50 | 2.00 | 3.00 |
| M.S. degrees | 1.50 | 1.75 | 2.00 |

* Each department is assumed to have an integral number of faculty members one of whom devotes half of his time to administrative functions.

The model required 7 phases to reach an optimal set of quotas. Some characteristics of the three departments are shown in table 7.6. The structure of the complete model is indicated in table 7.7, but the activities (columns) are shown only for department A.

Table 7.8 reveals some interesting features of the two-level planning model. The first three columns are shadow prices obtained in optimal solutions when

TABLE 7.7

A portion of complete model of departments A, B and C with department-level and college-level restrictions.

| Row number | A1 5.00 | A2 3.75 | A3 2.75 | A4 1.50 | A5 1.50 | A6 1.50 | A7 | A8 | A9 | A10 | A11 | A12 | A13 | Department restrictions b Vector | College restrictions |
|---|---|---|---|---|---|---|---|---|---|---|---|---|---|---|---|
| | | | | | | | | | | | (c_Aj's) | | | | |
| **College-level restrictions** | | | | | | | | | | | | | | | |
| A1(U1) | | | | 10 | 10 | 10 | | | | | | | | ≤ UA1 | = U1 |
| B1(U1) | | | | | | | | | | | | | | ≤ UB1 | |
| C1(U1) | | | | | | | | | | | | | | ≤ UC1 | |
| A2(U2) | | | | | | | | | −24 | | | | | ≤ UA2 | = U2 |
| B2(U2) | | | | | | | | | | | | | | ≤ UB2 | |
| A3(U3) | | | | 3 | 3 | 3 | | | | | 7400 | 7400 | | ≤ UA3 | |
| B3(U3) | | | | | | 5600 | | | | | | | | ≤ UB3 | = U3 ≤ $220,000 |
| C3(U3) | | | | | 5500 | | | | | | | | | ≤ UC3 | |
| **Department A restrictions** | | | | | | | | | | | | | | | |
| 4a | 3 | 1 | | 3 | −2 | 3 | | | | | | | | ≤ 0 | |
| 5a | 1 | 1 | 1 | | | | | | | | | | | ≤ 0 | |
| 6a | 3500 | 1500 | 750 | | | | | | | | | | | ≤ 40,000 | |
| 7a | | | | | | −10 | −35 | | | −6.5 | | | | ≤ − 1,850 | |
| 8a | | | | | | | 1 | −30 | | | | | | ≤ 0 | |
| 9a | | | | | | | | 0.5 | 1 | | −1/3 | −1/3 | −1 | ≤ 0 | |
| 10a | | | | | | | | | | | 3600 | 3600 | 11,000 | ≤ 0 | |
| 11a | | | | | | | | 0.5 | | | −6 | −4 | | ≤ 0 | |
| 12a | | | | | | | | | | 1 | −2 | −4 | | ≤ 5.5 | |
| 13a | | | | 1 | | | | | | | 1 | 1 | 1 | ≤ 2.0 | |
| **Department B restrictions** | | | | | | | | | | | | | | | |
| 4b | | | | | | Department B activities omitted to save space | | | | | | | | ≤ 0 | |
| 5b | | | | | | | | | | | | | | ≤ 20,000 | |
| 6b | | | | | | | | | | | | | | ≤ − 2,750 | |
| 7b | | | | | | | | | | | | | | ≤ 0 | |
| 8b | | | | | | | | | | | | | | ≤ 0 | |
| 9b | | | | | | | | | | | | | | ≤ 0 | |
| 10b | | | | | | | | | | | | | | ≤ 0 | |
| 11b | | | | | | | | | | | | | | ≤ 8.5 | |
| 12b | | | | | | | | | | | | | | ≤ 1.0 | |
| **Department C restrictions** | | | | | | | | | | | | | | | |
| 3c | | | | | | Department C activities omitted to save space | | | | | | | | ≤ 0 | |
| 4c | | | | | | | | | | | | | | ≤ 45,000 | |
| 5c | | | | | | | | | | | | | | ≤ − 2,250 | |
| 6c | | | | | | | | | | | | | | ≤ − 210 | |
| 7c | | | | | | | | | | | | | | ≤ 0 | |
| 8c | | | | | | | | | | | | | | ≤ 0 | |
| 9c | | | | | | | | | | | | | | ≤ 0 | |
| 10c | | | | | | | | | | | | | | ≤ 0 | |
| 11c | | | | | | | | | | | | | | ≤ 7.5 | |
| 12c | | | | | | | | | | | | | | ≤ 3.0 | |
| 13c | | | | | | | | | | | | | | | |

TABLE 7.8

Shadow prices in optimal solutions for (1) separate department models and (2) college model.

| Shadow price Variable identification (department and row)* | Shadow prices Solution values in department model Department | | | Solution values in college model Department | | |
|---|---|---|---|---|---|---|
| | A | B | C | A | B | C |
| A1, B1, C1 | 0.004 | 0.000 | 0.000 | 0.059 | 0.059 | 0.059 |
| A2, B2 | 0.475 | 0.107 | – | 0.084 | 0.084 | – |
| A3, B3, C2 | 0.000 | 1.792 | 2.089 | 1.446 | 1.446 | 1.446 |
| A4, C3 | 0.491 | – | 0.444 | 0.491 | – | 0.384 |
| A5, B4, C4 | 2.991 | 2.085 | 3.573 | 2.991 | 1.968 | 3.610 |
| A6, B5, C5 | 0.179 | 0.121 | 0.165 | 0.178 | 0.166 | 0.213 |
| Subtotal | 3.661 | 2.206 | 4.182 | 3.660 | 2.134 | 4.207 |
| A7, B6, C6 | 0.001 | 0.053 | 0.053 | 0.037 | 0.042 | 0.036 |
| C7** | – | – | 0.124** | – | – | 0.085** |
| A8, B7, C8 | 0.013 | 0.228 | 0.296 | 0.219 | 0.179 | 0.205 |
| A9, B8, C9 | 0.084 | 1.598 | 2.222 | 1.423 | 1.256 | 1.534 |
| A10, B9, C10 | 0.084 | 1.598 | 2.222 | 1.423 | 1.256 | 1.534 |
| A11, B10, C11 | 0.000 | 0.932 | 0.958 | 0.810 | 0.732 | 0.631 |
| A12, B11, C12 | 1.027 | 0.874 | 1.599 | 1.037 | 0.307 | 1.055 |
| A13, B12, C13 | 0.000 | 0.000 | 0.000 | 0.000 | 0.197 | 0.382 |

* Using the department A row numbers to identify rows in this table, it should be noted that rows 1, 2 and 3 involve teaching budget allocations and quotas on graduate service teaching determined by the dean; other involve restrictions specific to each department. Rows 4, 5 and 6 involve restrictions specific to research programs, row 12 involves restrictions on numbers of faculty members, and rows 7, 8, 9, 10, 11 and 13 impinge directly on teaching programs.
** Involves restriction on graduate service teaching for students in other colleges of the university.

each department is treated as a separate unit subject only to the restrictions specific to it; the remaining columns are shadow prices obtained in the optimal solution when the college-level and all departmental restrictions are satisfied simultaneously.

In the college-level solutions, college-level resources and quotas are administered by the dean in such a way as to equalize shadow prices among the three departments affected (see the first three rows of table 7.8). Note also that the shadow prices associated with similar restrictions in different departments (remaining ten rows of table 7.8) show only moderate differences among departments. These moderate differences arise from some or all of the specifications of the model as shown in table 7.6. The objective function weights for (1) publications and (2) M.S. degrees are different for each department. Class sizes, graduate assistant salaries and faculty salaries also vary among departments. The subtotals for rows 4, 5, and 6 are in the same rank order as the corresponding weights (2.50, 2.00 and 3.00) for research publications in the objective function. The figures in rows 9 and 10 are influenced by the different objective function weights for M.S. degrees (1.50, 1.75 and 2.00) and also by the graduate class sizes and thesis "class sizes", and perhaps by additional coefficients. The shadow prices in row 7 reflect in part differences in undergraduate class sizes and those in row 8 partly reflect differences in thesis "class sizes".

If the dean had \$325 000 with no earmarkings between teaching and research and if all resources and activities were infinitely divisible, he should be able to allocate his money in such a way that the shadow prices corresponding to an additional dollar spent should be identical for all categories of personnel (and for research current expense) in all three departments. If it cost \$3 000 to produce an M.S. degree in department A (1.50 objective function points), the dean should be willing to spend \$3 500 and \$4 000 respectively to produce an M.S. degree in departments B and C (1.75 and 2.00 objective function points respectively). This is not likely to happen precisely in a linear programming formulation. However, the dean approaches this result fairly closely in the present model, as he has three policy instruments which affect department A, three which affect department B and two which affect department C, and he uses them to maximize the college objective function.

The first three columns of table 7.8 are also of interest. Several of the shadow prices in department A are very low relative to their values in the college solution, suggesting that some resources are underemployed. In contrast, several shadow prices in departments B and C are high relative to their values in the college solution, suggesting that some resources are being used too intensively. The resources which are out of balance are associated with the teaching program; the earmarking of research funds separately for each department is also a feature of the college model, so the shadow prices in rows 4, 5 and 6 are almost the same in the department solutions as in the college solution. The dean tightens the teaching resource constraints in department A and loosens them in departments B and C to equalize shadow prices for the shared resources and achieve a better (if not always equal) relationship between the shadow prices *per dollar* associated with the corresponding specific resources in the different departments.

Restriction C7 specifies that 210 student quarters of service teaching shall be supplied to graduate students majoring in other colleges of the university. This restricts the numbers of student quarters available for M.S. candidates in departments A, B and C – students who directly enter the dean's objective function. Thus, the shadow price of 0.085 (0.084 except for rounding errors) attached to restriction C7 in the college solution is equal to the shadow prices attached to restrictions A2 and B2; if the number of student quarters supplied to other colleges were reduced from 210 to 209, the dean's objective function could be increased by 0.084 points.

Presumably the figure of 210 was determined by the president of the university, as it involves an allocation between colleges. This logically implies another two-level allocation model in which shadow prices for university-level resources are equalized between colleges in terms of the president's objective function. The dean's total teaching budget of $220000 (presumably allocated by the president) would have similar implications.

In connection with the faculty assignment model we pointed out that if the same linear transformation is applied to every $c_{ij}$ the optimal solution in terms of activity levels will be unchanged. In the present case, multiplication of all the objective function weights by the same constant would leave the optimal solution unchanged. If the weight for an M.S. in department A were translated into an estimate of that part of the increase in the present value of career income (from B.S. to M.S.) that was attributable to the university's inputs, the same conversion factor applied to all six objective function weights would convert them into market-like magnitudes. If the weights in table 7.6 were based simply on intuition, their translation into dollar magnitudes should at least stimulate further introspection as to their rationale. The implied assignment of dollar values to research publications in general and in different departments opens up a most interesting field for exploration.

In table 7.6 the objective function weights are constant. Many other formulations would be possible and rational. For example:

(1) Constant weights could be derived from appraisals of the national market for M.S. graduates and from judgments concerning the relative importance of additional contributions to the national and international scientific literature in different fields. Then, if departments A, B and C will at most contribute one percent or so of the total M.S. degrees and research publications in these national and international "markets", the relevant national and international "prices" will not be significantly affected by changes in the department A, B and C programs.

(2) The dean might have notions as to balance or equity between departments which would lead to a nonlinear (perhaps quadratic) objective function such that an increase in the flow of research publications from any department would reduce the corresponding weight, and conversely.

(3) An incentive weight might be assigned to publications from a particular department for a limited number of years to encourage a rapid buildup in its research program, after which the weight could be reduced to an equilibrium level relative to those for other departments.

(4) If it is desired to confine a particular department to undergraduate teaching, a zero weight could be assigned to publications by its faculty members; a "price" far below the national average will discourage local production.

## 7.3. *Aspects of growth planning for an educational institution*

In section 7.2.1, we noted that aggregative models of educational systems have adopted three interrelated approaches:

(1) The growth of the education sector has been related to the important structural variables characterizing overall national growth, such as population growth and demographic evolution, manpower and skill requirements, expenditure on research and training and investment-cum-growth requirements of the rest of the economy [29, 30].

(2) A system analysis approach has been developed at a more dynamic level [31, 32] for the input and output components of an educational system which is defined to be a system of connected processes including all forms of education, training and retraining. This approach like the first is designed to make predictions about the growth of different components of the educational system that is required in equilibrium, given the growth rates of exogenous factors such as the potential number of students, economic growth for the rest of the economy, changes in earnings-differentials for different skill groups, and the like. Simulation methods have frequently been adopted in this approach to analyze the effects of variations of the parameters on the set of feasible solutions.

(3) An optimization approach has been developed, mostly on the lines of control theory applications, which seeks to specify an optimal intertemporal growth path [33, 34] of strategic variables such as the number of scientists engaged in teaching when the objective function imputes either a measure of social benefits as a source of value of educational outputs or a measure of contribution to the sectoral and national levels of real output.

When we consider a single academic department (the analysis can sometimes be extended to a cluster of departments) and its problem of expansion over time, it appears that the policy makers responsible for it are also in need of a meaningful concept of optimal growth. It is possible to develop the above three approaches used in aggregative models of educational systems with appropriate modifications so that they are suitable for the context of a single academic department. If we consider that the goal of an academic department is to make the best possible use of its resources over time, the lines of modification should incorporate, for the sake of realism and practicality if you will, some of the following considerations, most of which are considered very important in the theories of growth applied at the sectoral or the firm level:

(a) The decomposition aspects of decision-making, which, in view of the existence of multiple decision makers in the framework of an academic department vis-à-vis the whole university, require an analysis of the whole process of imputing appropriate marginal productivity contributions at various levels of decentralization [20].

(b) Insofar as growth involves an intertemporal comparison of alternative feasible time paths measured by appropriate performance variables, the intertemporal allocation aspects (e.g., through variation of budgets for teaching and research over time, changing the allocation of faculty time among different activities, or planning for additional investment of resources in certain new lines of teaching or research) should have clear time orientation regarding short-term and long-term objectives. In the short-run analysis, which could be very detailed as in the activity analysis approach (and the prediction of exogenous variables may be fairly precise in this framework), it may be necessary to impose bounds on the system in terms of maximum permissible growth (determined by "capacity" of the system) and minimum growth (determined by the conditions of minimal rates of student inflow over time, etc.). In the long- and medium-term analysis, the expansion of capacity itself has to be analyzed and there is some need here to identify the concept of capacity with quantitative and operational precision as far as possible. Two important factors appear to be relevant in this context, as the various models of capacity expansion for the firm [35–37] serve to point out: (i) the element of economies or diseconomies of scale of expansion in capacity and its implications, and (ii) the set of other elements such as the exogenous rate of discounting over time, the cost of obtaining funds for expansion and the limited rate of growth of maximum total demand which provide definite limits to the possibility of unlimited expansion of the academic department as a firm.

(c) The optimality aspects in the concept of optimal growth, which generally presume the existence of a set of feasible solutions defined by the restrictions and the conditions of the mathematical model, require at least three types of analysis, e.g.:

(i) the objective function which is optimized in the model should be viewed not only as a scalar payoff function but also as a vector, the different components of which provide alternative subgoals not all of which could be brought to a common denominator. The latter view of the objective function, which leads to a vector optimization problem and which has close similarity with the decomposition aspects of decision-making referred to before, contributes ample flexibility to the otherwise rigid structure of a linear (or quadratic) programming problem based on a scalar payoff function;

(ii) even when a scalar objective function is considered for specifying an optimality ordering among the set of feasible solutions, satisficing behavior in terms of second-best, third-best and/or other consistent but suboptimal solutions [38, 39] should be incorporated in the objective function, so that the alternative possibilities of trade-off between subgoals are explicitly allowed for; and further

(iii) the problems of specification of the scalar objective function can be considerably facilitated by incorporating facets of the objective function which preassign a set of desired levels of targets or norms for some or all of the important variables in the model. The preassigned targets or norms should initially be viewed in terms of the outlook of the decision maker of the academic department, although these may have to be revised as the implicit costs of achieving these norms become known. If the objective function can be set up as a quadratic function in terms of deviations of the activity variables from their desired values and the model used is linear, this approach leads to linear optimal decision rules, which under certain conditions have desirable statistical properties [2].

(d) Last but not the least important is the analysis of probabilistic aspects of the growth problem, which may be generated from different sources such as the time rate of arrival of new students in specified fields, the estimate of imputed cost of faculty time committed in a particular course and even the forecast trend in the overall budget provision for a given academic department.

### 7.3.1. *Intertemporal growth path analysis for an academic department*

The need for intertemporal growth path analysis of an academic department can be justified on several economic grounds. First, the time profiles of growth indicators and their determinants indicate the trend framework within which short- and medium-term analyses are defined. In the trend framework the assumption of fixity of resources has to be relaxed, so also the rigidity of substitution. Second, it is known from experience that short-run policies which look only at short-run prospects and objectives may sometimes pre-empt long-run policies which would have attained the short-run objectives much better. This situation could easily occur for an academic department, if its expansion cost function as a function of total investment in both human (e.g., building good faculty) and physical capital had important economies (or diseconomies) of scale and the short-run policies did not incorporate these scale effects. With significant economies of scale, it is possible to make a strong economic case for building ahead of demand (and the reverse holds for diseconomies of scale) but such a case must depend on an intertemporal growth path analysis of some kind. Third, the problem of formulation of a framework of intertemporal growth is in a sense much more basic and funda-mental than the short-run analyses, since the bottlenecks and restrictions on long-run growth require more effective formulation of both long- and short-run policies.

Technically speaking the methods of intertemporal growth path analysis, whether for a single firm or the whole economy, have been much facilitated in recent years by the extension of classical techniques of variational calculus and the development of algorithms in dynamic programming and especially control theory. In particular the control theory approach [40, 41] and its various applications to economic problems of growth and investment have led to considerable developments in the formulation of Pontryagin's so-called maximum principle in both continuous and discrete versions, and what is most important is that computer routines are now available [42, 43] in standard form for applying several versions of Pontryagin's maximum principle, particularly for linear difference equation models with linear and quadratic objective functions with boundary conditions on both the control and the output variables.

It is our intention to formulate very briefly three types of models useful for intertemporal growth path analysis. In the first case it is assumed that outputs and inputs can be clearly distinguished in the performance of an academic department and that the stock of students in different categories provides a measure of the output vector at any given time, whereas faculty time, research grants, building and equipment, etc., are considered as inputs. In the second type of model, activities or processes are defined at any given time and the input requirements and output flows are determined by the particular time profile of activity vector chosen or solved for. In the third type of model, some general questions are raised concerning the implications of indivisibility and interaction between different activities or processes, since the technical solution of the problem is yet unknown.

Consider now the first type of model, where the department is motivated to produce degree outputs mainly, independent research and other faculty activities being considered as byproducts. Denote by $S(t) = S_i(t)$ the vector of students in different categories ($i$) at time ($t$) (i.e., undergraduate, graduate, postdoctoral levels). The growth of the student population is assumed dependent on the level already attained, the rate of new entry and the rate of research fellowship and other support available, i.e.,

$$S(t + 1) = H_1 S(t) + a(t) N(t) + H_2 O(t) + H_3 J(t). \quad (7.52a)$$

This is a linear difference equation approximation for the growth of student population, where $N(t)$ is the total number of new arrivals in time (year) $t$, $a(t) = (a_i(t))$ is the vector of proportions indicating students in category $i$, $O(t)$ is the vector of outside research funds available for student support, $J(t)$ is the vector of departmental funds for fellowship support, and $H_1$, $H_2$, $H_3$ are appropriate conforming matrices. Note that each of the matrices $H_1$, $H_2$ and $H_3$ could be viewed as a linear combination of other matrices more specific to the activities concerned. For instance, the matrix $H_1$ may be viewed as the sum of two (square) matrices, one reflecting the proportion of transition from category $j$ to $i$ in the next period and the other representing the combined effects of teaching assistantships and other partial supports. Now denote by $Y(t)$ a matrix at time $t$, whose rows refer to different economic inputs (e.g., number of faculty manyears in different fields, say vector $F(t)$, building space, research equipment and other support facilities (evaluated by their user cost, say vector $B(t)$) and whose columns refer to the different educational levels or processes (e.g., different years of undergraduate college level, M.S., Ph.D., postdoctoral and other research levels). If the categories of students are so defined as to be identical and coextensive with all the different educational levels here defined, then one could easily obtain a matrix $V(t)$ of input-output coefficients per unit level of students in different categories, i.e.,

$$V(t) = Y(t) \hat{S}^{-1}(t), \quad (7.52b)$$

where $\hat{S}(t)$ denotes a diagonal matrix whose diagonal elements are the corresponding elements of the column vector $S(t)$ and $\hat{S}^{-1}(t)$ denotes its inverse. Now denote the vector of row-sums of matrix $Y(t)$ by $y(t)$, then for any preassigned level of the output vector $S(t)$ one could compute the required supply vector of economic inputs as

$$y(t) = V(t) S(t).$$ (7.52c)

In particular, a typical element of the supply vector $y(t)$ would be represented by faculty members in one field teaching in different educational levels; in other words, the vectors $F(t)$ and $B(t)$ appropriately defined would comprise the subvectors of $y(t)$. Two comments may be made before the complete supply relation is specified. First, the input-output coefficient matrix $V(t)$ in (7.52) has to be built as an average estimate, so that it retains structural stability in the immediate future. Second, the supplies of some of the inputs such as teaching and research assistantships and especially the physical support facilities are in part influenced by outside research funds (vector $O(t)$) and the departmental funds (vector $J(t)$). Combining all these factors, the supply vector may finally be written as a linear approximation as follows:

$$\begin{bmatrix} F(t) \\ B(t) \end{bmatrix} = y(t) = VS(t) + H_4 \begin{bmatrix} O(t) \\ J(t) \end{bmatrix},$$ (7.52d)

where $H_4$ is an appropriate matrix and $V$ is a structural estimate of matrix $V(t)$.

Now the relations (7.52a) and (7.52d) constitute the fundamental relations of growth of an academic department. Use of these relations for policy purposes may be made in several ways.

First, a purely predictive approach may be adopted and the structural relations may be used to forecast the future course of growth of outputs and inputs under different assumptions regarding the parametric coefficients.

Second, a system analysis approach [31, 32] could be adopted and by simulation on the coefficients and the exogenous time paths of the independent variables such as $O(t)$ and $J(t)$ through various admissible domains, solutions in terms of output vectors could be generated like a navigation chart and the policy maker (or policy makers) could select a particular time path of solutions as the most appropriate by looking at the chart and applying his own ordering rules.

Third, a balanced growth approach may be adopted according to which the growth of demand in the future is forecast as of now; this determines a forecast of growth in the elements of the output vector $S(t)$ by using (7.52a) if necessary. Plugging this forecast value in equation (7.52d) and assuming exogenous trends in $O(t)$ and $J(t)$, one could compute the required vector of supply of inputs. Then by comparing the existing supply-of-input structure with the required one, we may find the deficiency or otherwise of the present supply and estimate its consequences (e.g., a deficient supply system may be reflected in a lowering of academic standards, a postponement of the present rate of improvement, and so on).

Fourth, it is also possible to support the case of unbalanced growth in a limited sense, since for particular inputs such as team research amongst faculty in some fields, important economies of scale in expansion may exist and in these cases building supply ahead of demand may be more economic than ostensibly balanced growth.

Last but not the least important application is to interpret some variables such as $O(t)$ and $J(t)$ as control variables and then introduce a separate performance functional (i.e., the objective function) in order to optimize it subject to reasonable restrictions on the control variables and also the output vector. If the performance functional is written as

$$W_N = \sum_{t=0}^{N} f\left(S(t) - S^*(t), O(t) - O^*(t), J(t) - J^*(t)\right), \qquad (7.52e)$$

where the asterisk indicates desired values, then the case where the function $f(\cdot)$ in (7.52e) is at most quadratic and the restrictions in the output and control space are linear and convex (e.g., with maximum and minimum bounds) has well-known algorithms for solution. The estimation of the parameters of the performance functional must start out with indirect cost estimates associated with the vectors $S(t)$ and $S^*(t)$ and also the opportunity cost of maintaining or not maintaining balanced growth. One should note however that several choices of the performance functional in (7.52e) are available *a priori*, e.g., minimal time control with stipulated initial and terminal conditions, minimizing the maximum deviations, minimizing a linear or quadratic combination of deviations and their time derivatives, and so on. It would be an interesting empirical application to try several plausible performance functionals and compare the implications of resulting optimal paths and their shadow prices [44].

Now consider a typical model in the second category, where it is assumed that there are $n$ activities at time $t$ denoted by the vector $x(t) = (x_1(t), ..., x_n(t))$, e.g., teaching at various levels, research and other activities, producing $s$ "goods", $m$ of which are output-like (e.g., students who receive degrees, value of research, etc.) and the remaining $(s-m)$ goods are used as intermediate inputs to the system (e.g., some M.S. students continue for Ph.D. work, some Ph.D.'s continue for postdoctoral work, etc.). Denote by the $f_{ij}(x(t))$ matrix the input of the $i$th good for $j$th activity at time $t$ $(i=1, ..., m)$ and by the $g_{ij}(x(t))$ matrix the output of the $i$th good from the $j$th process

$(i = m + 1, ..., s)$. Up to a linear approximation the costs and returns for using all activities are given by

$$\sum_{j=1}^{n} p_i f_{ij} x_j(t) \quad \text{and} \quad \sum_{j=1}^{n} \pi_i g_{ij} x_j(t), \tag{7.53a}$$

where $p_i$, $\pi_i$ are unit costs and prices and $f_{ij}$, $g_{ij}$ are constant matrices by approximation. Now consider an objective functional as in the Von Neumann model [45, 46] of optimal growth, which specifies the principle of maximizing a concave functional defined on the terminal stock of outputs only, i.e.,

$$\text{maximize } z_N = z(x(N)) = z\left( \sum_{j=1}^{n} \pi_i g_{ij}(x(N)) \right), \tag{7.53b}$$

where $t = 0, 1, ..., N$ and $x(t) \geqslant 0$ and $g_{ij}(x(N))$ are concave functions. One linear approximation of the performance functional would be, for example

$$\text{maximize } z_N = \sum_{j=1}^{n} c_j x_j(N), \tag{7.53c}$$

where $c_j$ is the appropriate net value coefficient for maintaining the $j$th activity in the terminal year. The restrictions of this type of optimizing growth model may now be specified by the following conditions:

$$\sum_{j=1}^{n} p_i f_{ij} x_j(t + 1) \leqslant \sum_{j=1}^{n} \pi_i g_{ij} x_j(t) + q_i(t), \tag{7.53d}$$

where $q_i(t)$ is the initial availability of resource $i$ at time $t$ from exogenous sources and $p_i$, $\pi_i$ are estimated constant coefficients. This restriction (7.53d) states that the total cost of resource $i$ in all activities at time $t + 1$ cannot exceed the total return from using that resource in the preceding period plus the return from exogenous availability. Further, in the initial period $(t = 0)$, the stocks of resources are given at positive levels $v_i(0) > 0$ say, so that

$$\sum_{j=1}^{n} f_{ij} x_j(1) \leqslant v_i(0). \tag{7.53e}$$

Now the problem is to solve for the time profile of vectors $(x(1), x(2), ..., x(N))$ which maximizes $z_N$, for example, defined in (7.53c) subject to the restrictions of production (7.53d), (7.53e) and the nonnegativity condition $x(t) \geqslant 0$, for $t = 1, 2, ..., N$.[9]

---

[9] It has to be emphasized that not all the requirements and conditions of the classical Von Neumann model are introduced here; this would not serve much purpose in our case, since policy applications are of major interest here.

Our interest here is not so much in seeking balanced growth solutions that are also efficient in the Von Neumann sense, but in adapting the Von Neumann sort of model to specify the characteristics of an intertemporal growth path for an academic department. However, as the various turnpike theorems [47, 48] have indicated, some of the characteristics of the Von Neumann model may even be present in policy applications at least in the long run when the time horizon $N$ becomes very large. For policy purposes the model could be looked at from the standpoint of control theory in the following manner. First, the activities in the activity vector must include some like the diversion of faculty time from one field to another which could be used potentially as control variables. Similarly, the objective function (7.53c) could also include desired levels of activities or outputs for other periods before the terminal year. Second, the exogenous availability $q_i(t)$ must be viewed as a potential control variable, since it could be influenced through budget allocation policies and the like.

Two concluding remarks may be made about this type of model. First, the basic difference of this type of model from the earlier type is that it is a model of resource utilization, when the same resource may have alternative values for different activities in different uses as inputs or outputs. Second, the data requirements of this model are significantly greater. Yet in principle this is also a computable model and the computational algorithms are known. Further, the way we have presented the problem has a basic similarity with the decentralized decision-making process of Arrow and Hurwicz [49], which shows that the model is capable in principle of analyzing the various stages of the decentralization process of decision making regarding the input and output basis of several activities.

Consider a third type of model structure, where difficulties in specifying the restrictions may be introduced through indivisibility and mutual interaction or interdependence between activities. The indivisibility of departmental management and the infrastructure of personalities interacting over time through various means do provide stumbling blocks to any measurement and hence a large region remains quite obscure and unexplored. Similarly the possible effects and implications of mutual interaction between activities and between inputs provide a field of analysis, which though very important remains practically unexplored by economists.

An example would perhaps illustrate the nature of problems unexplored. Consider the research sector alone and assume that there are $n$ faculty members denoted by $F_1, ..., F_n$. It is further assumed that faculty members can interact only bilaterally, i.e., the $i$th faculty member can interact only with one other faculty member. If the $i$th faculty member interacts with the $j$th member, then the additional research payoff is assumed to be measured by the difference in payoffs with $i$ and $j$ $(i \neq j)$ working as a team and working separately. Denote the additional payoff by $G_{ij}$. The problem is to develop a procedure for building a hierarchy of research teams such that the total payoff is maximized over the set of all feasible interactions. This framework could be extended to multilateral interactions, and the problem of optimal resource allocation under varying patterns of interaction is still unsolved. Yet it cannot be denied that once a growing institution reaches a standard where certain types of specialization have been built initially through team-work, the process of self-sustained growth carries on. Clustering of activities, of students and of faculty in appropriate fields may have quite significant economies of scale after the minimum threshold is crossed. Economic growth as a diffusion process is still an unexplored area, especially in its endogenous aspects. The stochastic process models with branching processes may have some applicability here.

## REFERENCES

[1] Fox, K. A., J. K. Sengupta and E. Thorbecke, *The theory of quantitative economic policy*. Amsterdam: North-Holland Publishing Company and Chicago: Rand McNally, 1966.

[2] Theil, H., *Optimal decision rules for government and industry*. Amsterdam: North-Holland Publishing Company and Chicago: Rand McNally, 1964.

[3] Fox, K. A. and J. K. Sengupta, "The specification of econometric models for planning educational systems: an appraisal of alternative approaches", *Kyklos*, Vol. 21, No. 4, 1968, 665–694.

[4] Fox, K. A., F. P. McCamley, and Y. Plessner, *Formulation of management science models for selected problems of college administration*. Final report (cyclostyled) submitted to U.S. Department of Health, Education and Welfare, November 10, 1967, Department of Economics, Iowa State University, Ames, Iowa, 117 pp.

[5] Plessner, Y., Fox, K. A. and B. C. Sanyal, "On the allocation of resources in a university department", to be published in *Metroeconomica*, 1968.

[6] Fox. K. A., J. K. Sengupta, D. K. Bose, T. K. Kumar and B. C. Sanyal, *Operations analysis of higher education* (book manuscript scheduled for completion by December 1969), Department of Economics, Iowa State University, Ames, Iowa.

[7] Sengupta, J. K. and K. A. Fox, "A computable approach to optimal growth for an academic department" (to be published in *Zeitschrift für die Gesamte Staatswissenschaft*).

[8] McCamley, F. P., *Activity analysis models of educational institutions*. Unpublished Ph.D. dissertation. Ames: Iowa State University Library, 1967. 235 pp.

[9] Tinbergen, J. and H. C. Bos, "A planning model for the educational requirements of economic development". In: *Econometric models of education: some applications*, Paris: OECD Publications, 1965.

[10] Sengupta, J. K. and G. Tintner, "On some economic models of development planning", *Economia Internazionale*, Vol. 16, 1963, 34–50.
Tinbergen, J., *The design of development*. Baltimore: Johns Hopkins Press, 1958.

O.E.C.D., *Policy conference on economic growth and investment in education* held in Washington, D.C., October 16–20, 1961, report, Paris, 1962.

Harbison, F. H. and C. A. Myers, *Education, manpower and economic growth*. New York: McGraw-Hill, 1964.

Becker, G. S., *Human capital*. New York: National Bureau of Economic Research; distributed by Columbia University Press, 1964.

Parnes, H. S., *Forecasting educational needs for economic and social development*. Paris: OECD, 1962.

Mushkin, S. J. (ed.), *Economics of higher education*. Washington, D.C.: Department of Health, Education and Welfare, Office of Education, 1962.

[11] Stone, R., "A model of the educational system", *Minerva*, Vol. 3, No. 2, 1965, 172–186.

[12] Smith, D. S. and P. Armitage, "The development of computable models of the British educational system and their possible uses". In: OECD conference proceedings on *mathematical models in educational planning*, Paris, 1967.

Tinbergen, J., *op. cit.*

[13] Adelman, I., "A linear programming model of educational planning: a case study of Argentina". In: I. Adelman and E. Thorbecke (eds.), *The theory and design of economic development*. Baltimore: Johns Hopkins University Press, 1966.

[14] Stone, R. and A. Brown, *A programme for growth: a computable model of economic growth*. London: Chapman and Hall, 1962.

Moser, C. A. and P. Redfern, *A computable model of the educational system in England and Wales*. Read at the 35th session of the International Statistical Institute in Belgrade in September 1965 and published in the Bulletin of the International Statistical Institute, 1967.

[15] Stoikov, V., "The allocation of scientific effort: some important aspects". *Quarterly Journal of Economics*, Vol. 78, 1964. 307–323.

Intrilligator, M. and B. Smith, "Some aspects of the allocation of scientific effort between teaching and research", Rand Memorandum RM-4339-PR, 1966.

Bowles, S., "A planning model for the efficient allocation of resources in education", unpublished paper presented at the annual meetings of the Allied Social Sciences Association, New York, New York, December 1965 (mimeo.). Cambridge, Mass.: Harvard University, Department of Economics. Unpublished Ph. D. thesis in Harvard University Library.

Bolt, R. H. and others, "Doctoral feedback into higher education", *Science*, Vol. 148, 1964, 918–928.

Fox, K. A., In unpublished letter to Study Director, National Register of Scientific and Technical Personnel, National Science Foundation, September 22, 1966, 5 pp.

Fox, K. A., "Economists' salary and income relationships", unpublished memorandum, Department of Economics, Iowa State University, May 25, 1966, 24 pp.

[16] Moser, C. A. and P. Layard, "Planning the scale of higher education in Britain: some statistical problems", *Journal of Royal Statistical Society*, Series A, Vol. 4, 1964.

Moser, C. A. and P. Redfern, "Education and manpower: some current research". In: *Models for decision*. London: English Universities Press, 1965.

[17] Solow, R., "Competitive valuation in a dynamic input-output system", *Econometrica*, Vol. 27, 1959, 30–53.

[18] Johansen, L., *A multisectoral study of economic growth*. Amsterdam: North-Holland Publishing Company, 1960.

[19] Lange, O., "Output-investment ratio and input-output analysis", *Econometrica*, Vol. 28, 1960, 310–324.

[20] Tintner, G. and J. K. Sengupta, *The econometrics of development and planning*, to be published by Cambridge University Press.

Kornai, J. and Th. Liptak, "Two-level planning", *Econometrica*, January, 1965.

[21] Dantzig, G. and P. Wolfe, "Decomposition principles for linear programs", *Operations Research*, Vol. 8, 1960.

McCamley, F. P., *Activity analysis models of educational institutions*. Unpublished Ph. D. dissertation in Iowa State University Library, Ames, Iowa, 1967, 235 pp.

[22] Sengupta, J. K., "The stability of truncated solutions of stochastic linear programming", *Econometrica*, Vol. 34, 1966, 87–103.

Sengupta, J. K. and T. K. Kumar, "An application of sensitivity analysis to a linear programming problem", *Unternehmensforschung*, Vol. 9, 1965.

[23] Schultz, T. W., *The economic value of education*. New York: Columbia University Press, 1963.

[24] Committee on the National Science Foundation Report on the Economics Profession, *The structure of economists' employment and salaries, 1964*, American Economic *Review*, Vol. LV: 4, Part 2, (Supplement), December 1965.

[25] Simon, H. A., *Models of man*, Ch. 14. New York: John Wiley and Sons, 1957.

[26] Charnes, A. and W. W. Cooper, "Systems evaluation and repricing theorems", *Management Science*, IX, No. 1, October 1962, 33–49.

[27] Charnes, A. and W. W. Cooper, "Deterministic equivalents for optimizing and satisficing under chance constraints", *Operations Research*, XI, 1963, 18.

[28] Dantzig, G. B., *Linear programming and extensions*. Princeton: Princeton University Press, 1963.

[29] O.E.C.D. Research Group, *Policy conference on economic growth and investment in education*: report. Conference held in Washington, D.C., October 16–20, 1961, Paris: O.E.C.D., 1962.

Moser, C. A. and P. Redfern, "Education and manpower: some current research". In: *Models for decision*. London: English Universities Press, 1965.

Correa, H. and J. Tinbergen, "Quantitative adaptation of education to accelerated growth", *Kyklos*, Vol. 15, 1962.

[30] Robinson, E. A. G. and J. E. Vaizey (eds.), *Economics of education*. Proceedings of an International Conference organized by the International Economic Association. London: MacMillan and New York: St. Martin's Press, 1966.

Harbison, F. H. and C. A. Myers, *Education, manpower and economic growth*. New York: McGraw-Hill, 1964.

[31] Koenig, H. E. and others, *A system approach to higher education*. Interim Report of the Division of Engineering Research, Rpt. No. 3, May 15, East Lansing, Mich.: Michigan State University, 1966.

Keeney, M. G., H. E. Koenig and R. Zemach, *A systems approach to higher education*. Final Report of the Division of Engineering Research, March 27, East Lansing, Mich.: Michigan State University, 1967.

[32] Stone, R., "A model of the educational system", *Minerva*, vol. 3, No. 2, 1965, 172–186. Also reprinted in R. Stone, *Mathematics in the social sciences and other essays* Cambridge, Mass.: M.I.T. Press, 1966.

[33] Intrilligator, M. and B. Smith, "Some aspects of the allocation of scientific effort between teaching and research", RAND Memorandum RM4339-PR, 1966.

[34] Alper, P., "Introduction of control concepts in educational planning models". Paper presented at OECD Conference on System Analysis Techniques in Educational Planning, Paris, March 1966.

Bowles, S., "A planning model for the efficient allocation of resources in education". Unpublished paper presented at the Annual Meetings of the Allied Social Sciences Association, New York, December 1965, (mimeo).

[35] Sengupta, J. K. and A. Sen, "Models of optimal capacity expansion for the firm: an appraisal" (to be published in *Metroeconomica*).

[36] Manne, A. S. (ed.), Investments for capacity expansion. Cambridge, Mass.: M.I.T. Press, 1967.

[37] Arrow, K. J., M. J. Beckmann and S. Karlin, (eds.), "The optimal expansion of capacity of a firm". In: *Studies in the mathematical theory of inventory and production*. Stanford: Stanford University Press, 1958.

[38] Sengupta, J. K., "Truncated decision rules and optimal economic growth with a fixed horizon", *International Economic Review*, Vol. 7, 1966, 42–64.

Sengupta, J. K., "On the sensitivity of optimal solutions under investment planning and programming", *Arthaniti*, Vol. 8, 1965, 1–23.

[39] Aris, R., Discrete dynamic programming. New York: Ginn and Co., 1963.

Sengupta, J. K., "On the stability of truncated solutions under stochastic linear programming", *Econometrica*, Vol. 34, 1966, 77–104.

[40] Pontryagin, L. S. and others, *The mathematical theory of optimal processes*. New York: Interscience, 1962.

[41] Fox, K. A., J. K. Sengupta and E. Thorbecke, *The theory of quantitative economic policy, op. cit.* [20].

Dobell, A. R. and Y. C. Ho, "Optimal investment policy: an example of a control problem in economic theory", *IEEE Transactions on Automatic Control*, Vol. AC-12, No. 1, February 1967.

[42] Mesarovic, M. D. (ed.), *View on general systems theory*. New York: Wiley, 1964.

Bellman, R. and R. Kalaba, *Dynamic programming and modern control theory*. New York: Academic Press, 1965.

Florentin, J. J., J. H. Westcott and J. D. Pearson, "Approximation methods in optimal and adaptive control". *Proceedings of IFAC Second Congress*, Basel, Switzerland, 1963.

[43] Tou, J. T., *Optimum design of digital control systems*. New York: Academic Press, 1963.

Merriam, C. W., III, "Computational considerations for a class of optimal control systems". *Proceedings of First International Congress of IFAC*, Vol. 2, edited by J. F. Coales. London: Butterworth and Co., 1961, 694–701.

[44] Schultz, W. C. and V. C. Rideout, "Control system performance measures: past, present and future", *IRE Transactions on Automatic Control*, Vol. AC-6, No. 1, 1961, 22–35.

[45] Morishima, M., *Equilibrium, stability and growth, op. cit.* [19].

McKenzie, L. W., "The Dorfman-Samuelson-Solow turnpike theorem", *International Economic Review*, Vol. 4, No. 1, 1963.

[46] Kemeny, J. G., O. Morgenstern and G. L. Thompson, "A generalization of the von Neumann model of an expanding economy", *Econometrica*, Vol. 24, 1956.

Malinvaud, E., "Capital accumulation and the efficient allocation of resources", *Econometrica*, Vol. 21, 1953, 233–268.

Nikaido, H., "Persistence of continual growth near the von Neumann ray: a strong version of the Radner turnpike theorem", *Econometrica*, Vol. 32, 1964, 151–162.

[47] McKenzie, L. W., "Turnpike theorems for a generalized Leontief model", *Econometrica*, Vol. 31, Nos. 1–2, January–April, 1963.

Radner, R., "Paths of economic growth that are optimal with regard only to final states: a turnpike theorem", *Review of Economic Studies*, Vol. 28, No. 2, February 1961, 98–104.

[48] McKenzie, L. W., "Maximal paths in the von Neumann model". In: E. Malinvaud and M. O. L. Bacharach (eds.), *Activity analysis in the theory of growth and planning*, proceedings of a Conference held by the International Economic Association. New York: St. Martin's Press, 1967.

Morishima, M., "Balanced growth and technical progress in a log-linear multisectoral economy". In: *The econometric approach to development planning*, proceedings of a Conference. Amsterdam: North-Holland.

[49] Arrow, K. J. and L. Hurwicz, "Decentralization and computation in resource allocation". In: R. W. Pfouts (ed.), *Essays in economics and econometrics*. Chapel Hill, N.C.: University of North Carolina Press, 1960.

# Chapter 8

# MODELS OF DECOMPOSITION OR DECENTRALIZATION IN FIRM BEHAVIOR AND ECONOMIC POLICY

The first section of this chapter deals with a number of situations in which decomposition techniques must be combined with others. The emphasis is upon operational methods independently of specific contexts.

The second section deals with two areas of application which are of great importance in all countries but are illustrated here with examples which are partly specialized to the United States. With proper allowance for different modes of transportation and different income levels, the discussion of competition and complementarity among retail firms can be extended to most other economies. The discussion of regionalization of national economic policies can be similarly extended.

In discussing both retail trade and the regionalization of national policies we have taken explicit account of the existence of hierarchies of central places, which manifest themselves as national (or multinational) systems of cities and also as different kinds or levels of shopping centers within individual cities. The relevance of central place theory to multilevel coordination through a system of markets or through successive layers of government should be intuitively clear.

## 8.1. Situations requiring the combination of decomposition algorithms with other techniques

The objective of this section is to describe several important situations in which decomposition techniques need to be combined with other techniques before the latter can be operationally useful in problems involving internal decentralization of large firms or organizations. Considering a typical decomposition technique as a two-level problem, i.e., one involving the sectoral level and the central level, we will discuss some basic aspects of three fundamental characteristics of the decomposition process. These are (a) the specification of the sectoral and central optimization models, (b) the rules for aggregating or combining the optimal solutions of sectoral models (with or without a modified objective function as in the Dantzig-Wolfe algorithm) to compute a revised set of (shadow) price signals through the central programming model, and (c) the methods of converging to the complete optimal solution, i.e., the solution which has associated with it a system of shadow prices that lead to an optimal allocation of resources between the center and the sectors.

From an economist's viewpoint, the first two of the characteristics mentioned above raise some fundamental questions about the role of price-guided allocation procedures in competitive market situations, not all of which have been solved or even explored. Arrow [1] has pointed out in his analysis of the theory of internal pricing in firms through decomposition techniques that there are two important types of exceptions to the theorem that the price system under competitive conditions leads to an optimal allocation of resources, e.g., (1) there may be various types of interdependence between different firms or between different processes in any given firm and (2) there may be increasing returns to scale for some firms (one implication of which may be that a firm would tend to grow in size indefinitely until it was coextensive with the whole industry, unless some appropriate limits to growth were introduced).

The interdependence between firms may be compared with the concept of interdependence between investment projects discussed in ch. 6 (section 4). In linear programming models of the type considered in the Dantzig-Wolfe algorithm of decomposition, the interdependence between sectors is in terms of the use of the central resources alone; otherwise the sector problems are separable and relatively independent. However, even in this case situations are possible in which the price guidance rule is not specific to some firms. For instance, Charnes, Clower and Kortanek [2] have considered the following problem

$$\max z = 3x_1 + 4x_2$$

subject to

$$x_j \geqslant 0, \quad j = 1, 2$$

$$x_1 \leqslant 1, \quad x_2 \leqslant 1, \quad \binom{2}{1} x_1 + \binom{2}{3} x_2 \leqslant \binom{3}{4}$$

for an economy consisting of two firms with each firm operating one activity $x_j$, which has optimal solution $\bar{x}_1 = 1$, $\bar{x}_2 = 1$ with the shadow price vector $(\frac{3}{2}, 0)$. The subproblems for the two firms in this case are firm 1:    $\max\left[3-\left(\frac{3}{2},0\right)\binom{2}{1}\right]x_1$    subject to    $x_1 \leqslant 1, x_1 \geqslant 0$,

i.e., $\max 0\cdot x_1$ subject to $x_1 \leqslant 1, x_1 \geqslant 0$;

firm 2:    $\max\left[4-\left(\frac{3}{2},0\right)\binom{2}{3}\right]x_2$    subject to    $x_2 \leqslant 1, x_2 \geqslant 0$,

i.e., $\max 1\cdot x_2$ subject to $x_2 \leqslant 1$.

Here firm 2 is led to correct action by this system of prices but firm 1 is indifferent and depends either on orders from firm 2 (or higher authority) or a market clearing condition. The fact that such orders (or higher authority) or the market clearing condition may not lead to unique closures (or solutions) in cases with more than two firms shows the need for introducing additional information or coordination.

Mathematically, the presence of decreasing marginal costs in the cost functions implies that the objective function of the original profit-maximization problem or the sectoral problem may not be concave (e.g., it may have domains of both concavity and convexity); in such cases the shadow-price guided allocation system requires more care in the specification and satisfaction of the sufficient conditions for a maximum of the overall objective function. Results developed in connection with quasi-concave programming in ch. 3 are especially relevant in this connection [3].

When the objective function of the original problem is a vector rather than a scalar function but the programming problem satisfies certain regularity conditions (e.g., Kuhn-Tucker constraint qualifications), then the gradient method applied to such a problem can still be given a decomposition-type interpretation. Consider for instance the following vector maximization problem: to find a vector $\bar{x}$ that maximizes the vector function $F(x)$ of vector $x$ subject to the constraints $g(x)\geqslant 0$, $x\geqslant 0$ where $x=(x_1,...,x_n)$, $g(x)=(g_i(x), i=1,...,m)$; (i.e., to find a vector $\bar{x}$ satisfying the constraints such that for no other feasible $x$ will it hold that $F(x)\geqslant F(\bar{x})$). The vector functions $F_i(x)$ in $F(x)=(F_i(x); i=1,...,m)$ are assumed differentiable and concave in $x$, the constraint functions $g_i(x)$ are assumed concave and differentiable, satisfying the so-called Kuhn-Tucker constraint qualifications (i.e., attention is restricted to those solutions $\bar{x}$ of the vector maximum problem which are *proper* in the sense that for any vector differential $dx$ it holds that $(\partial F(x)/\partial x)_{x=\bar{x}}\cdot dx\geqslant 0$, if the vector $\bar{x}$ belongs to the interior of the constraint set $g(x)\geqslant 0$).

Under the above conditions the following theorem has been proved by Kuhn and Tucker [4]:

*Theorem 1*

In order that the vector $\bar{x}$ be a (proper) optimal solution of the vector maximization problem: $\max F(x)$, $g(x) \geqslant 0$, $x \geqslant 0$, it is necessary that there exist a vector $\bar{v} > 0$ such that the associated vector $\bar{x}$ and some vector $\bar{u}$ of Lagrange multipliers satisfy conditions (i) and (ii) below for the Lagrangian function

$$\phi(x, u) = \bar{v}' F(x) + u' g(x) \qquad u, v: m.1 \qquad (8.1)$$

where

  (i) $\phi_{\bar{x}} \leqslant 0$, $\phi'_{\bar{x}} \bar{x} = 0$, $\bar{x} \geqslant 0$

  (ii) $\phi_{\bar{u}} \geqslant 0$, $\phi'_{\bar{x}} \bar{u} = 0$, $\bar{u} \geqslant 0$.

(Here the notation $\phi_{\bar{x}}$ is used for $(\partial \phi / \partial x)_{x = \bar{x}}$, similarly for $\phi_{\bar{u}}$.) The sufficient conditions are that the scalar function $\phi(x, u)$ satisfies conditions (i), (ii) above and also

  (iii) $\phi(x, \bar{u}) \leqslant \phi(\bar{x}, \bar{u}) + \phi'_{\bar{x}}(x - \bar{x})$

for all feasible $x$ (i.e., the function $\phi(x, \bar{u})$ is concave in $x$ around $\bar{x}$ for $u$ fixed at $\bar{u}$).

Note that since the vector objective function $F(x)$ can be interpreted as the specification of multiple goals of one or several policy makers, the above theorem is useful in characterizing a decentralization process with several policy makers. However, two basic problems may arise when the goals of the multiple policy-makers are not mutually compatible either due to their difference in weighting or to their specification of sectoral constraints which are not consistent with one another. Partial solutions to these problems may be suggested. First, the condition of mutual consistency may be incorporated by defining penalty costs associated with those goals or those constraints which tend to prevent feasibility. This method is usually followed in the control theory literature as a method of computation [5]. Second, the idea of a hierarchy of optimization criteria, each applicable at one level, may be introduced. For instance, consider the following control problem

$$\text{minimize } W = W_T(x, u) = \int_0^T f(x_t, u_t)\, dt \qquad (8.2a)$$

subject to

$$\dot{x} = Ax + Bu \qquad (8.2b)$$

$$u_t \in U, \quad x(0) = c_0, \qquad x(T) = c_T \qquad (c_0, c_T \text{ given constants}) \qquad (8.2c)$$

where $f(x_t, u_t)$ is a scalar function of vectors $x_t, u_t$ assumed convex and differentiable, $\dot{x} = dx/dt$, $u$ is the control vector and $x$ the state vector, $U$ is the set of constraints on $u_t$, assumed to be closed, bounded and convex. Now assume that the constraints (8.2c) and the linear dynamic model (8.2b) remain the same but we have three choices of the function $f(x_t, u_t)$ leading to three objective functions denoted by $W_I$, $W_{II}$, $W_{III}$ and assume that these can be arranged in a hierarchy as the primary, secondary and tertiary objectives. Let the optimal control solutions belonging to these three criteria and the relations (8.2b), (8.2c) be denoted by $(\bar{x}_I, \bar{u}_I)$, $(\bar{x}_{II}, \bar{u}_{II})$, $(\bar{x}_{III}, \bar{u}_{III})$. Two questions may now be posed:

(a) Does there exist any feasible solution $(x, u)$ belonging to the intersection of the three sets $(\bar{x}_I, \bar{u}_I)$, $(\bar{x}_{II}, \bar{u}_{II})$ and $(\bar{x}_{III}, \bar{u}_{III})$; i.e., for what types of hierarchy of objective function $W_I$, $W_{II}$, $W_{III}$ does such a solution exist?

(b) If there does not exist a feasible solution to (a) above, but we are prepared to sacrifice a small proportion of $\bar{W}_I$, the primary objective (i.e., $\bar{W}_I$ is allowed to be $(1+r)\bar{W}_I$, $r$ is a positive fraction preassigned) in order to obtain a feasible solution which also minimizes the secondary objective function $W_{II}$, then what is the smallest value of $r$ for which this can be done and what are its implications?

The second type of problem has been analyzed in the control theory literature from an operational viewpoint. Consider the following example due to Waltz [6] with one control variable $u$ and two optimization criteria:

$$\text{primary criterion:} \quad \text{minimize } T = W_I$$
$$\text{secondary criterion:} \quad \text{minimize control energy} =$$

$$\int_0^T u^2(t)\, dt = W_{II}$$

models and restrictions
$$\begin{cases} \dot{x}_1 = x_2; & x_1(0) = 0, \quad x_1(T) = 1; \quad |u| \leqslant 1 \\ \dot{x}_2 = ku; & k = \begin{cases} 4, & \text{if } t \leqslant 1 \\ 96, & \text{if } t > 1 \end{cases}; \quad x_2(0) = 0, \quad x_2(T) = 0. \end{cases}$$

Minimizing $T$ (i.e., the primary criterion) subject to the model and the restrictions gives the optimal solutions as

$$\bar{W}_I = T = 1.0, \ \bar{u}(t) = \begin{cases} 1, & \text{if } 0 \leqslant t < \tfrac{1}{2} \\ -1, & \text{if } \tfrac{1}{2} < t \leqslant 1 \end{cases}$$

hence
$$\int_0^1 \bar{u}^2(t)\, dt = 1.0.$$

Now the secondary criterion optimization problem is set up as follows:

$$\text{minimize } W_{\text{II}} = \int_0^T u^2(t)\,\mathrm{d}t$$

subject to $T \leqslant \frac{181}{180}$ and the model and restriction as before. Here the number $\frac{181}{180}$ which is very close to 1.0 is artificially imposed to guarantee that the resulting optimal control yields a time $T$ not exceeding the minimum value $1.0 = W_{\text{I}}$ by more than 0.555 percent. The optimal solution to this secondary problem is:

$$T = \tfrac{181}{180}; \qquad \bar{u}(t) = \begin{cases} 1, & \text{for } 0 \leqslant t \leqslant \frac{2}{15} \\[1mm] \dfrac{17 - 30t}{13}, & \text{for } \frac{2}{15} \leqslant t \leqslant 1 \\[1mm] -1, & \text{for } 1 \leqslant t \leqslant \frac{181}{180} \end{cases}$$

and

$$W_{\text{II}} = \tfrac{77}{180}.$$

Note that in this specific example, with an increase of only 0.555 percent in $T$ (i.e., $r = 0.00555$ in $(1+r)\,W_{\text{I}}$) we obtain a decrease of about 57.2 percent in the total control energy. This example could be generalized to include more optimization criteria arranged in a hierarchy. The example shows how the rates of tradeoff (or marginal rates of substitution) between the primary, secondary and tertiary objective functions may be analyzed and applied to practical cases. However more research work is needed to formulate the most appropriate and realistic hierarchy of objective functions for any given optimization problem.

One other source of infeasibility that may be mentioned in this connection is due to the presence of random components in the parameter of the original linear (or nonlinear) programming problem in which the Dantzig-Wolfe type of decomposition is envisaged. In this case the methods of probabilistic programming must first be appropriately incorporated to convert the stochastic problem into a deterministic form; then, at the second stage, the decomposition algorithms if applicable may be invoked. However, this process of conversion may lead to special difficulties due to nonlinearities and the fact that there may be several methods of conversion possible.

Now we consider the relationship between the methods of decomposition and aggregation. The standard decomposition methods (e.g., Dantzig-Wolfe type methods) invariably start from an overall model and specify a procedure for decomposing it into specific and smaller submodels linked in some fashion.

We may also pose the question the other way round, i.e., given a set of submodels, each of which may be a linear or quadratic programming problem, how may we construct an overall programming model which in some sense links (or aggregates) the submodels through a revised set of facets in the sectoral objective functions? In contrast to decomposition, this method, may be called the method of superposition or aggregation. (In principle, the methods of aggregation [7] discussed in economic theory should be viewed as a special case of the methods of superposition; however, the role of compatibility of optimizing objective functions is usually not made explicit in aggregation techniques for equational models.)

Note that two additional problems arise in the methods of superposition. First, the objective functions of different submodels may not be compatible with one another, unless the penalty cost functions or other means of achieving consistency are incorporated. Second, the overall objective function when constructed must in principle have not only the facets which are basically related to, if not identical with, the submodel objective functions but also a specific facet which reflects the net effect of interaction between the submodels, i.e., external economies or diseconomies so to say, external to each submodel but internal to the overall superposed problem.

In order to discuss the specific role of aggregation in the context of de-composition methods in general, consider a two-level problem of national planning with the center as the coordinator and the sectors as firms. There are $m$ firms, each using (either producing as outputs or utilizing as inputs) one or more of $n$ goods, where $g_{ik}$ denotes the net output of good $i$ ($i = 1, ..., n$) by firm $k$ ($k = 1, ..., m$); if $g_{ik} < 0$, then good $i$ is used as an "input" but if $g_{ik} > 0$, then good $i$ is an "output". Final consumption of good $i$ as an output is denoted by $y_i$ and the total excess demand by $d_i$ where $d_i = y_i - \sum_{k=1}^{m} g_{ik}$ (i.e., in vector notation $d = y - \sum_k g_k$, where $g_k$ denotes the vector ($g_{ik}$) and $d = (d_i)$, $y = (y_i)$ respectively). The constraints on each $y_i$, $g_k$, $d_i$ are denoted by the sets $Y$, $G_k$, $W$, respectively, where each of the sets $Y$, $G_k$, $W$ are assumed closed, bounded and convex, i.e.,

$$y_i \in Y, \quad g_k \in G_k, \quad d_i \leqslant w_i \quad \text{where} \quad w_i \in W; \quad (w_i = \text{availability limit}). \ (8.3a)$$

The center is assumed to have a concave (scalar) utility function $f(y)$ of vector $y$. The center does not know the technology set $G_k$ specific to each firm; firm $k$ does not know the technology sets of other firms, nor does it know the overall consumption set $Y$ and the demand set $W$. The center has information about the sets $Y$ and $W$.

Under the above conditions let us consider the two-way process of price guidance between the center and the firms. Denote a specific stage of the two-way process by the superscript $t$ and assume that each firm is a price taker in the sense that it cannot affect the price vector $p^{(t)} = (p_i^{(t)})$ by its own operation (i.e., this assumes perfect competition in the factor and the output markets). Now given the price vector $p^{(t)}$, the firm $k$ maximizes its own profit, i.e.,

$$p^{(t)'} g_k = \sum_{i=1}^{n} p_i^{(t)} g_{ik} \tag{8.3b}$$

subject to its own technology constraints $g_k \in G_k$ and this determines the optimal output vector $\bar{g}_k^{(t)}$ for the firm $k$ at time $t$. On the basis of $\bar{g}_k^{(t)}$ for each of the $m$ ($k = 1, ..., m$) firms, the center computes at stage $t$ the following demand:

$$d^{(t)} = y^{(t)} - \sum_k \bar{g}_k^{(t)}, \qquad y \in Y \tag{8.3c}$$

and the net excess demand

$$e^{(t)} = d^{(t)} - w = (d_i^{(t)}) - (w_i). \tag{8.3d}$$

If $e_i^{(t)} > 0$, excess demand is positive and if $e_i^{(t)} < 0$, then there is excess supply, i.e., a negative excess demand. The positive excess demand case is used in (8.3f).

Now the center could use this information on aggregate demand (or aggregate excess demand) to compute a revised set of prices $p^{t+1}$ at stage $t+1$. This could be done in several ways. The first way would be to solve the programming problem

$$\text{maximize} f\left(y^{(t)}\right) - p^{(t)'} y^{(t)}$$

under the conditions

$$d_i^{(t)} \leqslant w_i; \qquad w_i \in W; \qquad (i = 1, ..., n) \tag{8.3e}$$

and let the optimal dual vector corresponding to the constraints (this vector consists of the optimal values of the Lagrange multipliers) be denoted by $p^{(t+1)}$. The vector $p^{(t+1)}$ provides the prices at stage $t+1$ which each firm accepts as given (and maximizes its own profit). The successive stages of computation ·in the $t$-space could be interpreted as two-way exchanges between the center and the firms, till the optimal solution is reached. A second way would be to determine the price vector $p^{(t+1)}$ according to the following Arrow-Hurwicz rule which is essentially a rule of price adjustment under competitive market conditions, i.e.,

$$p_i^{(t+1)} = \max\left(0, p_i^{(t)} + h_i(d_i^{(t)} - w_i)\right); \qquad i = 1, ..., n \tag{8.3f}$$

where the function $h_i(d_i^{(t)} - w_i)$, which may be linearly approximated by $h_i \cdot (d_i^{(t)} - w_i)$ where $h_i$ is a small positive constant, expresses the effect of net excess demand on the prices in the next period (positive if excess demand is positive and negative if excess demand is negative).

Note that neither of the above rules consider the interfirm differences in efficiency of production, since the rule of aggregation used in (8.3c) assigns equal weights to all firms. Also, the fact that there is interdependence between the center's objective function (i.e., maximize either $f(y)$ or $f(y) - p'y$) and the firms' objective functions (i.e., maximize $p'g_k = \sum_i p_i g_{ik}$) is not explicitly recognized. In economic terms, however, the center's objective function could be interpreted as one of maximizing the total "consumers' surplus", whereas the aggregate of firms may be reasonably interpreted to be maximizing their total "producers' surplus". A plausible way to combine both these objectives would be to seek solutions (through provisional market prices $p^{(t+1)}$) which maximize the sum total of consumers' and producers' surpluses (i.e., which minimize the net total economic rent). We consider now the implications of incorporating the two characteristics, i.e., the interfirm differences and the maximization of the total consumers' and producers' surpluses, into the decomposition process.

Now consider good $i$ (as output) produced by different firms and define the unweighted means ($M_i$) and variances $\sigma_i^2$ at any stage of the computation $t$ by

$$M_i^{(t)} = \frac{1}{m} \sum_{k=1}^m \bar{g}_{ik}^{(t)}; \qquad \sigma_i^{2(t)} = \frac{1}{m} \sum_{k=1}^m (\bar{g}_{ik}^{(t)} - M_i^{(t)})^2. \qquad (8.4a)$$

Similarly the dispersion matrix composed of covariances for two outputs $i$ and $j$ may be computed as $V^{(t)} = (\sigma_{ij}^{(t)})$. Note also that if $\bar{g}_{ik}$ of the $k$th firm is given a nonnegative weight of $w_{ik}$, then the mean and variance of $g_i$ for the $i$th good produced by different firms can be similarly computed as weighted quantities, i.e.,

$$M_i^{(t)} = \sum_{k=1}^m w_{ik} \bar{g}_{ik}^{(t)} \Bigg/ \sum_{k=1}^n w_{ik}$$

$$\sigma_i^{2(t)} = \sum_{k=1}^m w_{ik} (\bar{g}_{ik}^{(t)})^2 \Bigg/ \sum_{k=1}^n w_{ik} - (M_i^{(t)})^2; \qquad i = 1, \dots, n.$$

With these concepts the rules for aggregating $\bar{g}_{ik}^{(t)}$ over $m$ firms may be improved. For instance, the simple unweighted aggregation rule assumed in (8.3c) could be replaced by a weighted aggregation rule, the weights being inversely proportional to the contribution of a given firm to the total variance $\sigma_i^2$ for output $i$ at time $t$. Also to each sector program (8.3b) we may adjoin in its objective function a facet to reflect the interfirm differences,[1] i.e.,

$$\text{maximize} \sum_{i=1}^{n} p_i^{(t)} g_{ik} - \sum_{i=1}^{n} r_i (g_{ik} - M_i^{(t)})^2$$

subject to

$$g_k \in G_k; \qquad r_i = \text{small positive constant}.$$

Note that the revised objective function now reflects the fact that firm $k$'s output of good $i$ must be close in some sense to the aggregate average $M_i$. Also in the Arrow-Hurwicz rule (8.3f) this could be incorporated through a revision of the pricing rule as follows:

$$p_i^{(t+1)} = \max \left[ 0, \, p_i^{(t)} + h_i \cdot (d_i^{(t)} - w_i) + s_i \sigma_i^{2^{(t)}} \right] \tag{8.4b}$$

where $s_i = $ a small positive constant.

(The term $s_i \sigma_i^2$ could be replaced by $(s_i^+ \sigma_i^{+2} + s_i^- \sigma_i^{-2})$ where $\sigma_i^{+2}, \sigma_i^{-2}$ are semi-variances based on positive and negative deviations respectively, $s_i^+ > 0$ and $s_i^- < 0$). Here the effects of variability between firms are additionally introduced over and above the net excess demand.

Now consider the second problem of maximizing the total of consumers' and producers' surpluses and incorporating this idea into the decomposition process. Consider now one "output" $i$ and denote by $g_i$ the sum total of this output produced by all the firms, i.e., $g_i = \sum_k g_{ik}$; this output is viewed as a supply function, i.e.,

$$S_i(p_i, \bar{p}_i) = g_i(p_i, \bar{p}_i) = g_i, \tag{8.5a}$$

where $\bar{p}_i$ is the minimum price necessary to induce the quantity of supply $g_i$ and any feasible $p_i$ in the market (or preassigned by the center) must be greater than or equal to $\bar{p}_i$. Also denote the consumption $y_i$ of output $i$ by the following demand function

$$D_i(p_i, p_i^0) = y_i,$$

where $p_i^0$ is the maximum price the consumers in general would be prepared to pay rather than forego the quantity of consumption $y_i$. Hence any feasible market price (or price preassigned by the center) $p_i$ must be less than or equal to $p_i^0$. Now given the preassigned quantities $\bar{p}_i, p_i^0$, the competitive market

---

[1] Incidentally the concept of an economic distance between firms (or sectors) based on these interfirm differences is closely related to the problem of statistical discriminant functions [8] and its applications in problems of classification of regions according to levels of development are now available [9].

solution specifies the static equilibrium condition which implies the minimization of total virtual rent $R_i$ received by demanders (buyers) and sellers
(suppliers):

$$R_i = \int\limits_{P_i}^{p_i{}^0} D_i(p_i, p_i^0) \, \mathrm{d}p_i + \int\limits_{\bar{p}_i}^{P_i} S_i(p_i, \bar{p}_i) \, \mathrm{d}p_i. \tag{8.5c}$$

Now assume that the firms are like "spatially separated" markets such that
demand for product $i$ has to be directed to any one of the $m$ markets (firms).
Denote by $D_{ik}(p_i^{(k)}, p_i^0)$ the demand allocated to market $k$ and by $S_{ik}(p_i^{(k)}, \bar{p}_i)$
the supply in market $k$ of commodity $i$, where $p_i^{(k)}$ is the price prevailing in
market (firm) $k$. Now the social rent $R_i$ becomes

$$R_i = \sum_{k=1}^{m} \left[ \int\limits_{P_i^{(k)}}^{p_i{}^0} D_{ik}(p_i^{(k)}, p_i^0) \, \mathrm{d}p_i + \int\limits_{p_i}^{P_i^{(k)}} S_{ik}(p_i^{(k)}, \bar{p}_i) \, \mathrm{d}p_i \right]. \tag{8.5d}$$

Now our objective is to minimize this rent $R_i$ subject to the constraints
which say that the prices prevailing in any pair of markets (i.e., any pair
of firms) cannot differ by an amount which exceeds the unit transportation
cost (i.e., the unit economic distance) between the two markets (i.e., firms).
These constraints are

$$P_i^{(k)} - P_i^{(j)} + T_i^{(kj)} \geqslant 0, \qquad k, j = 1, ..., m; \qquad k < j \tag{8.5e}$$

$$P_i^{(j)} - P_i^{(k)} + T_i^{(jk)} \geqslant 0, \qquad k, j = 1, ..., m; \qquad k < j \tag{8.5f}$$

where $P_i^{(k)}$ are market prices of good $i$ in the $k$th market (i.e., $k$th firm)
and $T_i^{(jk)}$ is the unit cost of transportation of good $i$ from market $j$ to market $k$.

Now for well-behaved demand and supply functions (with $\partial D_{ik}/\partial p_i^{(k)} < 0$
and $\partial S_{ik}/\partial p_i^{(k)} > 0$) the objective function $R_i$ in (8.5d) is concave in $P_i^{(k)}$ and
hence the problem of minimizing $R_i$ in (8.5d) subject to the constraints
(8.5e) and (8.5f) could in principle be solved, provided the usual regularity
conditions were satisfied. It is obvious that if both (8.5e) and (8.5f) hold
with strict inequality for all $k, j$ then the markets (or firms) are all independent and the optimal solution is given by equating $\partial R_i/\partial P_i^{(k)}$ to zero:

$$D_{ik}(P_i^{(k)}) = S_{ik}(P_i^{(k)}) \qquad k = 1, ..., m$$

with

$$\bar{p}_i \leqslant P_i^{(k)} \leqslant p_i^0.$$

This is the same type of solution which would be obtained from (8.5c) by equating $\partial R_i / \partial p_i$ to zero, i.e.,

$$D_i(P_i) = S_i(P_i); \qquad \bar{p}_i \leqslant P_i \leqslant p_i^0 .$$

In the simple case in which $R_i$ is given by (8.5c), the center could modify the process of computation of optimal shadow prices $p^{t+1}$ by substituting in place of (8.3c) the following programming problem

$$\text{minimize} \sum_{i=1}^{n} p_i^{(t)} R_i^{(t)}$$

under the conditions

$$d_i^{(t)} = y_i^{(t)} - g_i^{(t)} = D_i^{(t)} - S_i^{(t)} \leqslant w_i; \qquad w_i \in W$$
$$(i = 1, ..., n); \quad \text{and} \quad R_i^{(t)} = R_i \text{ of (8.5c) at time } t.$$

In the more general case of (8.5d), the possibility of transfer of demand (or supply) from one market (firm) to another would open up the possibility of central coordination in several ways. First, the economic distance between different firms may be explicitly recognized, before the decision to revise the prices $p_i^t$ in some optimizing fashion is taken. Second, the center could make available to each firm not only the revised set of prices for the next period $(t+1)$ but also the information about the average indicators $M_i^{(t)}$ and $\sigma^2{}_i^{(t)}$ defined in (8.4a) and how they are changing. This would help the convergence process.

However, one should note that the analogy of the spatial equilibrium models [10] does not carry over into the decomposition procedures in all respects and it is yet an unsolved problem how to incorporate features such as deviations from the competitive market standard and various other market imperfections (e.g., collusion, merger, etc.) into the framework of this discussion. Possible answers may be sought for perhaps in the various game theoretic models, e.g., nonzero sum and cooperative games [11].

### 8.2. Decomposition or decentralization techniques in analyzing (1) competition among retail firms and (2) regionalization of national economic policies

In section 7.2.4. we illustrated a two-level planning model in which the dean of a college allocates resources among its constituent departments. A similar model could be used to illustrate the allocation of resources by the president of a university among its respective colleges. The president, deans and department chairmen constitute a three-stage administrative hierarchy. If the same set of objective function weights (i.e., "prices" of specified outputs) is prescribed or validated by the president and accepted explicitly by all chairmen and deans, each chairman and dean has the task of maximizing gross revenue from whatever bundle of resources is made available to him. Maximizing gross revenue is equivalent to maximizing output in an index number sense, i.e., with each specific output weighted by its prescribed price. Coordination is achieved through direct, personalized communication between pairs of administrators.

We will be concerned in the present section with another kind of hierarchy which has emerged in most economies impersonally (i.e., without coordinated planning). This is the hierarchy of "central places" which figures so prominently in location theory but which is so frequently disregarded in other fields of economics in which the spatial distribution of activities is nonetheless important. An extensive bibliography on central place theory and empirical studies has been published by Berry and Pred [12].

The present book emphasizes techniques rather than phenomena. We will therefore state a number of propositions without proof, though there is evidence that they are approximately true for the United States economy as of the 1960's.

(1) The United States can be subdivided approximately into 350 or more *commuting fields*, each centered upon the largest city in that field. Fox [13–16] has used the term *functional economic areas* (FEAs) to describe such areas.

Berry [17], using all of the home-to-work commuting data in the 1960 Census, delineated 358 FEAs; these areas contained some 96 percent of the total United States population. Thus, the FEA serves as a frame of reference for 96 percent of all labor market activity in the United States (probably 97 percent by 1970) and for nearly 100 percent of retail trade and service activities which normally require direct contact with consumers, citizens, taxpayers, students, patients, etc. (Some 3 or 4 percent of the total population lives in gaps between commuting fields, often in mountainous, hilly or desert areas with low population densities and limited transportation facilities.)

(2) In nonmetropolitan areas, a typical FEA contains three levels of central places, including a *regional capital*, a few *small cities* and a large number of *towns*, to use the terminology of Berry and Harris [18]. The trade area of the regional capital tends to be coextensive with the home-to-work commuting field, covering several counties; the trade area of a small city (often a county seat) is usually equivalent to one or two counties; and the trade area of a town is usually considerably smaller than a county. Some

goods are found only in the regional capital; some are found there and also in the small cities; and some are found at all three levels (regional capital, small cities and towns).

(3) In metropolitan areas, the same three-stage hierarchy is found [19]. The *regional, district,* and *neighborhood shopping plazas* or centers have shopping facilities corresponding respectively to those of the regional capital, small cities and towns in a nonmetropolitan FEA. (Let us call these R, D and N level centers respectively, for "regional", "district" and "neighborhood".) The shopping facilities of the regional plazas are in most respects as complete as those of the central business district. In terms of *minutes,* including delays at traffic lights, parking lots and the like, the effective "distances" between shopping centers of any given level in the metropolis are not much less than those between shopping centers of the same hierarchical level in nonmetropolitan FEAs.

The nonmetropolitan FEA provides a particularly useful framework within which to analyze competition among retail stores. The partitioning of the United States into (say) 358 relatively self-contained commuting fields or labor market areas offers a useful framework within which to consider the regionalization of national economic policies. The nonmetropolitan FEA, in which the trade area of the regional capital roughly coincides with the commuting field, has been referred to by Fox [16] as a "mononuclear FEA". A large metropolis containing many regional shopping plazas is equivalent to a compound or multifaceted FEA in which the different R-level areas may be relatively independent for shopping purposes but interdependent as suppliers of labor for the central business district (facilitated by rapid transit systems and freeways).

### 8.2.1. *Firm behavior in an FEA framework: the Holdren model of monopolistic competition among multiproduct retail firms*

Holdren [20] has made a brilliant extension and application of monopolistic competition theory to multiproduct retail firms – specifically, food supermarkets. Holdren says in his preface that he went into a particular retail market asking the question, "What decision variables does the entrepreneur believe to be open to him?"... Once the decision variables were identified, a definitive model of retail firms was developed and the nature of the relationships between firms established. The departure from previous studies lies largely in the fact that a self-conscious attempt was made to construct a model specialized for the market in hand and which includes all the important decision variables objectively and subjectively open to the entrepreneur.[2] Fox [21] and Zusman [22] have commented upon Holdren's results and extended them in particular respects.

Holdren's formulation of the demand functions facing the operator of a food supermarket (one of several supermarkets in a city of 50000 or more people) is capable of generalization to shopping centers at N, D and R levels. It is worth noting that the product lines carried by food supermarkets in the United States can absorb approximately 30 percent of all personal consumption expenditures for goods and services other than house rents and public utilities (electricity, gas, water, telephone service) which are delivered to the home.

From a (monopolistically) competitive policy standpoint, Holdren partitions the products sold by a supermarket operator into (1) commodities with a significant effect in transferring customers' patronage from other supermarkets to his own (and vice versa), (2) commodities the retail prices of which are fixed (as by retail price maintenance laws), and (3) other commodities which (for reasons he presents) have little or no impact in transferring customers.[3]

The prices of $K$-class commodities (the ones with transfer effects) are the only useful instruments available to the supermarket operator for carrying out aggressive or defensive *price competition*. In addition, Holdren gives explicit and detailed consideration to the various *nonprice offer variations* that can also be used as instruments of monopolistic competition.

Holdren formulates the basic set of demand functions confronting a supermarket operator for the $n$ commodities he sells as:

$$q_1 = f_1(p_1, p_2, ..., p_n, a_1, a_2, ... a_m)$$
$$\vdots$$
$$q_n = f_n(p_1, p_2, ..., p_n, a_1, a_2, ... a_m),$$

(8.6a)

that is, the quantity the supermarket sells of each commodity will be (potentially) a function of the prices $p_i$, $i = 1, 2, ..., n$, of all commodities in the store, and of all the nonprice offer variations $a_j$, $j = 1, 2, ..., m$, of the store.

For a commodity with a significant transfer effect, the demand curve could be operationalized as follows:

$$q_K = \pi B_K dg_K \sum_{j=1}^{m} S_j(a_j - a_{0j}) \left[ B_K w_K \alpha_K (p_{0K} - p_K) \right.$$
$$\left. + \sum_{i=1}^{K-1} \alpha_i B_i g_i w_i (p_{0i} - p_i) + \sum_{j=1}^{m} V_j(a_j - a_{0j}) + \sum_{i=1}^{n} t_i g_i \right].$$

(8.6b)

---

[2] Holdren, *op. cit.*, p. vii.
[3] *Ibid.*, pp. 134–153.

The components of equation (8.6b), from left to right, have the following interpretation: $q_K$ is the sales level of commodity $K$, $B_K$ is the average number of units of the commodity purchased per unit of time per household, $d$ is the density of households per unit area, $g_K$ is the percentage of households that consumes the commodity, and $\pi$ equals 3.1416. The appearance of $\pi$ in this expression rightly suggests that the store's trade area is regarded as a circle (at least to a first approximation). However, the $r^2$ of the formula for the area of a circle appears in the rest of the expression (8.6b) in a highly disguised form.[4]

Without other qualifications, equation (8.6b) could be written very simply as

$$q_K = B_K d g_K r^2 \pi. \qquad (8.6c)$$

Equation (8.6c) is, however, nonlinear in the prices ($r$ is a linear function of $p$, so $q$ is a quadratic function of $p$) and in order to do away with this nonlinearity Holdren proposes the following linear substitution for $r^2$:

$$r^2 \approx V(a - a_0) + \alpha B(p_0 - p). \qquad (8.6d)$$

The terms in parentheses refer back to an expression

$$u = \phi[A, D, p], \qquad (8.6e)$$

in which $u$ is the utility of the store's offer as evaluated by a consumer living a specified distance $D$ from the store; $A$ and $p$ may be regarded as index numbers summarizing respectively all nonprice and price aspects of the store's offer. Holdren's substitution for $r^2$ makes the trading area of the store a linear function of the level of nonprice offer variation in the store $(a - a_0)$ and of variations of prices charged by the store $(p_0 - p)$. Both $V$ and $\alpha B$ in equation (8.6d) have positive signs. As Holdren observes, "so long as the range of offer variation is comparatively small (and it is), such a substitution does little violence to reality".[5]

In equation (8.6b) then, $r^2$ is expanded into a rather complicated expres-

---

[4] *Ibid.*, p. 123. In equation (8.6b), $p_{0K}$ and $p_{0i}$ are the prices associated with zero sales of commodity $K$, and $a_{0j}$ is the level of the $j$th type of nonprice offer variation associated with zero sales of commodity $K$. In effect, $p_{0K}$, $p_{0i}$, and $a_{0j}$ are the intercepts when $q_K$ equals zero of linearized functions describing the dependence of $q_K$ on $p_K$, $p_i$ and $a_j$ respectively.

[5] *Ibid.*, pp. 118–119. Holdren's original notation on pp. 118–119 has been slightly modified to conform with that in equation (8.6b). Equations (8.6c), (8.6d), and (8.6e) apply to a single commodity and a single type of nonprice offer variation. The subscripts of $p_K$, $p_i$, and $a_j$ in equation (8.6b) recognize the dependence of $q_K$ on prices of all commodities sold and all nonprice offer variations used by the store.

sion that states that the sales of the $K$th commodity are affected by its own price, the prices of the other $K-1$ commodities which have significant transfer effects, and the levels of the $m$ types of nonprice offer variation in the store. Further, $S_j$ reflects the fact that some of the nonprice offer variations adopted by supermarkets have the effect of reducing the frequency of trips by consumers to areas outside the supermarket's trading area and hence increasing the percentage of household purchases obtained by a given store within its trading area. The symbol $w_i$ reflects the level of information on the part of consumers – if $w_i=1$ consumers are perfectly informed. The last term on the right-hand side, $\sum_{i=1}^{n} t_i g_i$, is "an expression which is intended to cover the budget effect and the fact that, quite independently of price, a wider product line reduces the number of trips any consumer must make outside the store's trading area".[6]

Holdren then considers the nature of competition among several supermarkets, given their cost and production functions (which he describes in his third chapter) and their demand functions.

Although there are only nine or ten supermarkets in Center City (a real but anonymous Midwestern city of 50000 population), Holdren presents convincing arguments for his conclusion that "oligopoly agreement is virtually impossible and we are left with a market which is best described as monopolistically competitive but which is subject to many other imperfections which preclude a long-run adjustment to a zero profit equilibrium".[7]

In principle, Holdren's model could be extended in a number of respects, (see Fox [21]). First, competition among the nine or ten supermarkets could be expressed as a spatial equilibrium model. This model could be constructed at various levels of aggregation with respect to (1) the number of groups of (particularly) $K$-class commodities whose prices are specifically recognized as policy instruments and (2) the number of areas (and hence groups of households) into which the consuming population of the city is subdivided. The basic model could probably be supplemented by some stochastic elements which would allow for the fact that individual households may shop in more than one supermarket under any given constellation of price and nonprice offer variations on the parts of stores actually visited and of stores not visited in a given time period.[8]

---

[6] *Ibid.*, p. 124.
[7] *Ibid.*, pp. 180–182.
[8] Households would typically have some information about the stores not visited in a particular month on the basis of visits to these stores in earlier months, of comments by friends and neighbors, and of current and past advertisements by the stores.

Now suppose we think in terms of competition among *shopping centers*, each with its cluster of complementary stores, rather than among supermarkets only. We must remember that each individual store in a shopping center is presumably an optimizing unit and carries out its own particular competitive strategies with respect to firms offering the same product line at other shopping centers. From the standpoint of consumers visiting a shopping center, the partitioning of the center's total product line into the product lines of individual firms (drug stores, men's clothing stores, shoe stores, and the like) lends itself to a "utility tree" formulation of consumer demand.

We could conceive of the entire "offer" of a shopping center in terms of a consumer demand matrix containing every individual product offered by any store in the shopping center. If there were ten different stores in the shopping center, each offering a different nonoverlapping product line, the demand matrix for the shopping center as a whole would be very nearly block-diagonal. The proprietor of each store would carry out his own price and nonprice offer variation policies. However, the policies of one store would also influence the number of customers who visit the shopping center and *therefore* do some shopping at other stores in it. Operationally, this complementarity among stores in a shopping center could perhaps be handled on an aggregative level, as with a $10 \times 10$ matrix of coefficients indicating the percentage increase in total sales of store I resulting from an increase of 1 percent in the number of customers specifically attracted to store J by store J's price and nonprice offer variations.

If we think in terms of a group of shopping centers of roughly similar total sales volumes, it appears that an extension of Holdren's model to a collection of shopping centers would be fairly manageable. However, we would still have the problem of linking shopping centers of different hierarchical levels into a complete system.

Assume that the consumer goods and services offered in an R-level area consist of three categories that we shall label R, D and N respectively. The R-level goods are found only in the R-level shopping center; D-level goods are found in R-level and D-level shopping centers; and N-level goods are found at R, D and N-level shopping centers. These categories account for the great majority of consumer expenditures. The remainder (apart from tourist expenditures and other special purchases outside of the area) would consist of utilities delivered directly to the home, cash or imputed rentals of dwellings, and other services for which the consumer is not required to travel within the area.

Assume further that a household living closer to the R-level center than to any center of the D- or N-types can acquire its three categories of goods (the three that require personal travel and inspection) without incurring any transportation costs. The household may then be regarded as attempting to maximize an objective function,

$$W = f\left(q_r, q_d, q_n\right)$$

subject to the demand matrix

$$\begin{bmatrix} q_r \\ q_d \\ q_n \end{bmatrix} = \begin{bmatrix} b_{rr} & b_{rd} & b_{rn} \\ b_{dr} & b_{dd} & b_{dn} \\ b_{nr} & b_{nd} & b_{nn} \end{bmatrix} \begin{bmatrix} p_r \\ p_d \\ p_n \end{bmatrix} + \begin{bmatrix} e_r \\ e_d \\ e_n \end{bmatrix} y + \begin{bmatrix} a_r \\ a_d \\ a_n \end{bmatrix}$$

and the budget constraint

$$\sum_i q_i p_i = y, \qquad i = r, d, n.$$

(We may include the fourth category, rents and household utilities, in the maximization process formally or, for expository purposes, we can assume that the consumer has allocated a fixed total sum to be spent on the three categories of goods that normally require travel and inspection on his part.)

A household located closer to any other center than to R will incur transportation costs in acquiring one or more categories of commodities. Such a household must (at least initially) squeeze the cost of shopping travel out of its fixed income. We may think of the "brought home" price of any category of goods from any shopping center as equal to the retail store price at that center plus the (round-trip) transportation cost from the center home. In the absence of stochastic and/or irrational elements the household may be seen as trying to maximize its utility in terms of goods and services "brought home" subject to its overall budget constraint and the vector of travel costs (round-trip) between its home and each of the towns or shopping centers within a reasonable distance that offers one or more of the three categories of goods.

Assuming that each household's demand function for each category of goods is linear over the range of probable short-run experience, each household's objective function is quadratic and the household's problem is one of maximizing a quadratic objective function that requires it to specify the particular set of centers from which it should purchase its various categories of goods and services.

### 8.2.2. *Further comments on the Holdren model and its extensions*

Certain points should perhaps be emphasized.

First, Holdren's demand function should not be regarded as a consumer demand function. Suppose that our FEA is strictly self-contained, so that every household in the area spends its entire disposable income at stores located in the FEA; we assume that the money income of each household is fixed. Then the weighted average income elasticity of demand for all goods and services by each household is 1 and the corresponding weighted average of own-price and cross-price elasticities of demand is $-1$ (see Fox [23, pp. 517–520]). As these respective elasticities, 1 and $-1$, are identical for all households, we can aggregate over all households and still get an income elasticity of 1 and a price elasticity of $-1$ for total purchases of goods and services by all households.

This formulation implies that the total gross revenue of all consumer-oriented establishments in the area is fixed. Competition among all establishments becomes a zero sum game. Competition might conceivably increase the total amount spent at (say) clothing stores and reduce the total amount spent at food stores; however, cross-price elasticities between such dissimilar commodities as food and clothing are likely to be considerably smaller (in absolute value) than own-price elasticities; for food purchased at stores the latter figure is in the order of $-0.3$ to $-0.4$. Own-price elasticities for nonfoods average somewhat more (in absolute value) than $-1$, but probably not more than $-2$.

The main object of competition within an FEA is to transfer customers *to* one store *from* other stores selling the same generic products. If the stores are located in different shopping centers, it will take any given consumer more minutes to reach some centers than others. Thus the disutility of distance (measured in minutes) is an important factor which must be offset by price and nonprice offer variations. Holdren [20, p. 181] comments that: "In Center City in 1956, store A lowered its price level by 5 percent and doubled its sales level. Thus, A's own elasticity of demand was approximately 20. Store D adjusted to this change by reducing prices 3 percent, but still went down in volume from \$ 40000 per week to \$ 30000 per week." Holdren concludes that the remaining price differential of 2 percent is responsible for the 25 percent reduction in store D's sales, implying a cross-price elasticity of demand for store D's products of 12.5 with respect to changes in $p_D/p_A$.

This change in the price ratio (2 percent) would amount to \$ 0.40 on a grocery bill of \$ 20, a fairly typical weekly bill for a family of three persons in 1956. If the disutility of distance was equivalent for most consumers to $ 0.10 per mile each way, a consumer would have been justified in traveling up to a mile farther than usual (each way) for a trip involving purchases of $ 10 or more. A square mile of residential area even in small cities will often include more than a thousand households, respresenting total consumer expenditures of several million dollars.

This underscores the fact that central place theory, general location theory and spatial equilibrium models are extremely important in explaining firm behavior, and in choosing short-run and long-run policies for individual consumer-oriented firms, in an FEA framework.

Second, Holdren gives considerable attention to nonprice offer variations. In simplified terms, he states that

$$q = f(p, a),$$

where $q$ is a vector of quantities sold by a store, $p$ is a vector of prices, and $a$ is a vector of nonprice offer variations or amenities (such as good parking facilities, air conditioning, automatic doors, facilities for paying utility bills, a lunch counter, and other features not directly related to the store's product line). The equation implies that both price and nonprice offer variations can be evaluated in terms of their effects on quantities sold, e.g.,

$$\frac{\partial q}{\partial p_i} = \lambda_{ij}\left(\frac{\partial q}{\partial a_j}\right),$$

where $\lambda_{ij}$ is the effect on sales of a unit change in the $i$th price *relative to* that of a unit change in the $j$th amenity (which may in some cases be a zero-one variable). As the firm's gross revenue is

$$W = p'q$$

it also follows that

$$\frac{\partial W}{\partial p_i} = \lambda_{ij}\left(\frac{\partial W}{\partial a_j}\right)$$

so that the price and nonprice instruments can be compared in terms of their contributions to the firm's objective function.

If we specify that total consumer expenditures in an FEA are fixed, it appears that consumers collectively must pay for all amenities in all stores; if they pay more for air conditioning, they presumably have less to spend for commodities as such. (Over time, of course, real incomes have increased, so consumers have been able to buy more commodities and also pay for more amenities; however, this does not change the fact of competition between commodities and amenities for shares of the consumers' budget.)

Third, the set of independent firms in a shopping center (we assume a shopping center containing only one firm of each given type so that there is little overlapping of product lines) poses a problem of vector versus scalar optimization. Suppose that all these stores were merged into a single firm; then the objective would presumably be to maximize total net revenue for the shopping center-firm. An entire store could be operated at a loss if the resulting transfer effect (attracting customers away from other shopping centers to this one) increased net revenue for the other $m-1$ stores by a more-than-offsetting amount.

If the stores continued as private firms, it would (in principle) still be possible to maintain precisely the same array of price and nonprice offer variations as before, but to pool revenues and reallocate them among firms according to their contributions to the total net revenue of the center. Strictly independent operation would require each store to (try to) at least break even; yet it would be hard to ignore the fact that the ability of store 1 to break even would be strongly conditioned by the policies of the other $m-1$ stores (no doubt by some more than others).

In practice, there would be problems of communication and coordination, as one mind (or a committee) must now deal with (say) $n \cdot m$ products instead of $n$. We have here a version of the two-level planning problem. One possibility would be to treat a limited number of the most powerful price and nonprice instruments of each store as "central resources" to be used in a coordinated way to increase revenue for the shopping center as a whole. The remaining instruments could be left to the discretion of the proprietor of each store, who would be free to use them to maximize his own net income *subject to* the prescribed values of the centrally coordinated instruments.

Also, the strategies of competing firms in other shopping centers would have to be countered; this would involve primarily competition between stores with similar product lines. If firms in several shopping centers are directly or indirectly involved in such competition, causes may be difficult to trace. Holdren [20, p. 182], referring to food supermarkets, states that "the multidimensional character of response paths and the presence of consumer ignorance means that there is a long lag between the initiation of action (by one firm) and the time when the results of the action are felt by competitors. In the interim, many parameters have changed and the competitors are never sure just what caused their change in sales." If the firms in a given shopping center had a fairly sophisticated model of the system as a whole, of course, they might be able to unravel causes with considerably more precision than is implied in Holdren's statement, based on observations in the mid-1950's. However, sufficient uncertainty might remain to cast doubt on the optimality of any specific centrally coordinated response, so the initiative and responsibility for competition "in detail" might better be left with the individual proprietors.

Simon's [24] characterization of man as a creature of bounded rationality and limited computing capacity seems relevant here. The example in section 8.1.1. in which a small increase in allowable response time permitted a very large reduction in the required control energy is also suggestive. It might be possible in the case of the shopping center-firm to estimate the theoretical maximum revenue obtainable by optimizing at the level of $n \cdot m$ instruments and then (1) to estimate the reductions of revenue involved if only the most powerful 10, 20 or 40 instruments were used in the optimization or (2) to specify permissible reductions in revenue of (say) 1, 2 and 5 percent and estimate the minimum numbers of instruments required to achieve each of these "satisficing" levels.

An alternative approach so far as price instruments are concerned might be to specify the centrally controlled variables as *price index numbers* at different levels of aggregation such as (for a supermarket) all foods, or all meats, or (all cuts of) beef. The "all foods" level would imply a single instrument; the "all meats" level would permit four or five instruments (such as for meats; fresh fruits and vegetables; dairy products; groceries; etc.); while the "beef" level might permit twenty or more instruments. The centrally controlled set might include one or a few of the total instruments available at any given level of aggregation, and instruments might be selected from different levels of aggregation.

Aggregative controls, of course, lose various degrees of precision relative to detailed controls, as suggested by the following example:

$$\begin{bmatrix} q_1 \\ q_2 \end{bmatrix} = \begin{bmatrix} -5 & 0 \\ 0 & -10 \end{bmatrix} \begin{bmatrix} p_1 \\ p_2 \end{bmatrix},$$

and

$$q_T = (0.5q_1 + 0.5q_2), \qquad p_T = (0.5p_1 + 0.5p_2),$$

where $q_1$ and $q_2$ are quantity relatives, $p_1$ and $p_2$ are price relatives, the coefficients $-5$ and $-10$ represent the transfer effects of one percent changes in $p_1$ and $p_2$ respectively, and the coefficients 0.5 and 0.5 are weights (proportions of total dollar sales of $q_1$ and $q_2$ combined in some base period) in the index numbers $q_T$ and $p_T$. Then

$$\frac{\partial q_T}{\partial p_1} = (0.5)(-5) = -2.5$$

and

$$\frac{\partial q_T}{\partial p_2} = (0.5)(-10) = -5;$$

hence a one percent reduction in $p_2$ will have twice as much effect on $q_T$ as will a one percent reduction in $p_1$.

If we specify only that $p_T$ be reduced by one percent without stipulating anything about $p_1$ and/or $p_2$ separately, the transfer effect may range from 5 percent (if $p_1$ is used exclusively) to 10 percent (if $p_2$ is used exclusively). If both $p_1$ and $p_2$ are varied simultaneously without restrictions as to upper and lower bounds for either one, the range of transfer effects associated with $\Delta p_T = 1.00 - 0.99 = -0.01$ could include such values as 15 percent (for $p_1 = 1.02$ and $p_2 = 0.96$), no change (for $p_1 = 0.96$ and $p_2 = 1.02$), or even wider extremes. The proprietor's choice would depend on his own self-interest.

Suppose that the proprietor's wholesale costs are 0.80 per unit for each commodity and that other costs do not vary with sales volume. Then his net revenue is

$$N = (p_1 - 0.80)\, q_1 + (p_2 - 0.80)\, q_2.$$

The first term reaches a maximum for $p_1 = 1.00$ and the second term reaches a maximum for $p_2 = 0.93$. Thus, his own self-interest would be best served by choosing these two prices, yielding $p_T = 0.965$ and an increase of 25 percent in $q_T$.

If the proprietor were required to set $p_T \leqslant 0.95$ his net revenue would be forced below the unrestricted maximum by about 2 percent so (in our example) a conflict of interest in this amount would exist and would have to be offset (say) by a payment from the shopping center-firm. We may note in passing that if the proprietor were required to set $p_1 \leqslant 0.95$ *and* $p_2 \leqslant 0.95$ his net revenue would be forced down another one percent; this would be the cost to him of the additional restriction and would have to be offset to justify his cooperation.

The shopping center in general provides a good example of *external economies*. Store I's revenue is larger because the (noncompeting) store J is in the same center, and conversely. External economies will exist even if the two stores make no attempt to coordinate their policies. Additional gains through coordination (as in the shopping center-firm conceptualization) would also be external economies from the standpoint of each individual store, though the costs of coordination would have to be subtracted from the increase in total gross revenue for the shopping center as a whole.

The parking area of a shopping center provides an example of *indivisibility*. Also, consider the possibility of enclosing and air conditioning a central mall onto which all stores open. This nonprice offer variation, if successful, would benefit every store; it raises the problem of (1) estimating the benefits to each store and (2) allocating the costs among stores. The central parking lot involves the same principles and problems.

### 8.2.3. Decentralization or regionalization of national economic policies

We have stated earlier that in the United States 96 or 97 percent of all labor market activity and nearly 100 percent of retail trade and service activities requiring direct contact with the public (as customers, pupils, students, patients, clients, voters, taxpayers, church-goers and the like) occur within functional economic areas (FEAs) or urban-centered commuting fields. Broadly speaking, an FEA may be regarded as a "macro-household" which is essentially self-contained with respect to resident-oriented activities that account (as of 1968) for about 60 percent of total employment. The remaining employment (on the order of 40 percent) in each FEA is part of an inter-area trading system. The "export-oriented" activities include agriculture, most manufacturing, most mining and forestry, tourist attractions, state universities, state capitals, and many other private and public establishments which, though located in one FEA, are designed to serve residents of several or many FEAs.

Thus, we might view the United States economy in terms of an inter-sectoral flow matrix of the following structure:

$$
\begin{array}{c}
 & \text{Destinations} \\
\text{Sources} &
\begin{array}{c}
\begin{array}{cccc}
R_1 & R_2 & E_1 & E_2
\end{array} \\
\begin{array}{c}
R_1 \\ R_2 \\ \\ E_1 \\ E_2
\end{array}
\left[
\begin{array}{cc|cc}
X & 0 & 0 & 0 \\
0 & X & 0 & 0 \\
\hline
X & X & X & X \\
X & X & X & X
\end{array}
\right]
\end{array}
\end{array}
$$

where $R_i$ and $E_i$ are respectively the residentiary and the export sectors of the $i$th FEA. In ideal form, no residentiary establishment in the $i$th region would provide goods or services to any firm or consumer in $R_j$ ($j \neq i$) or to any firm in any $E_i$ or $E_j$. Deliveries from any export sector to any residentiary sector might be regarded as deliveries to final demand (in the "macro-household" sense) while deliveries from $E_i$ to $E_j$ would be regarded as inter-industry sales.

The special definition of final demand just mentioned would lead to the following input-output-type matrix:

| Export sector originating sales and deliveries | Sales to export sectors | Deliveries to "final demand" | Total gross sales of export sector |
|---|---|---|---|

$$
\begin{array}{c}
\\ E_1 \\ E_2 \\ \vdots \\ E_n
\end{array}
\begin{array}{cccc}
E_1 & E_2 & \cdots & E_n
\end{array}
\begin{bmatrix}
e_{11} & e_{12} & \cdots & e_{1n} \\
e_{21} & e_{22} & \cdots & e_{2n} \\
\vdots & \vdots & & \vdots \\
e_{n1} & e_{n2} & \cdots & e_{nn}
\end{bmatrix}
+
\begin{array}{cccc}
R_1 & R_2 & \cdots & R_n
\end{array}
\begin{bmatrix}
r_{11} & r_{12} & \cdots & r_{1n} \\
r_{21} & r_{22} & \cdots & r_{2n} \\
\vdots & \vdots & & \vdots \\
r_{n1} & r_{n2} & \cdots & r_{nn}
\end{bmatrix}
=
\begin{bmatrix}
X_{1e} \\ X_{2e} \\ \vdots \\ X_{ne}
\end{bmatrix}
$$

$$+$$

Primary inputs of export sector
$$
\begin{bmatrix}
w_{1e} & w_{2e} & \cdots & w_{ne} \\
k_{1e} & k_{2e} & \cdots & k_{ne}
\end{bmatrix}
$$

$$=$$

Total gross outlays of export sector
$$
\begin{bmatrix}
X_{1e} & X_{2e} & \cdots & X_{ne}
\end{bmatrix}
$$

or

$$E + R = X = E' + w' + k'$$

where the $w_{ie}$'s are total payments to labor (broadly defined) and the $k_{ie}$'s are total payments for other factors of production (net rent, interest, depreciation, etc.).

For some purposes this formulation may be awkward, but it expresses an important insight into the structure of the economy. Quite independently, Berry [25] has described the function of "the national system of cities" as follows:

1. We live in a specialized society in which there is progressively greater division of labor and scale of enterprise, accompanied by increasing degrees of specialization.
2. There is an increasing diversity of people as producers. But as consumers they are becoming more and more alike from one part of the country to another, consuming much

the same 'basket of goods' wherever they may live, as well as increasingly large baskets because of rising real incomes.

3. The physical problem in the economic system is therefore one of articulation – insuring that the specialized products of each segment of the country are shipped to final consumers, seeing that consumers in every part of the country receive the basket of goods and services they demand and are able to purchase, and bringing demands and supplies into equality over a period of time.

4. Articulation requires flows of messages, of goods and services, and of funds. The flows appear to be highly structured and channeled and major metropolitan centers serve as critical articulation points. These flows are as follows: products move from their specialized production areas to shipping points in the locally-dominant metropolitan centers; over the nation, products are transferred between metropolitan centers, with each metropolitan center shipping out the specialized products of its hinterland and collecting the entire range of specialized products from other metropolitan centers to satisfy the demands of the consumers residing in the area it dominates; distribution than takes place from the metropolis to its hinterland through wholesale and retail contacts. In the reverse direction move both requests for goods and services, and funds to pay for goods and services received, so that the flows are not unidirectional.

The great majority of central cities of functional economic areas (the regional capitals) are wholesale centers and hence "articulation points" in Berry's sense, as well as centers of commuting fields.

The matrix $E$ could be expanded to include any number $m$ of export-oriented production activities in each of the $n$ regions. Most extractive and manufacturing industries would be included in the $E$ matrix (along with strictly inter-FEA transportation); most personal, professional and public services and retailing, a great deal of wholesaling, and intra-FEA transportation would be included in the residentiary sector. (Matrix $R$ simply records deliveries from the export sectors to the residentiary sectors valued essentially at manufacturers' f.o.b. prices plus freight. To show the employment-generating activities within the residentiary sector we would need a different and more detailed model, as presented in Fox, Sengupta and Thorbecke [26, pp. 351–370].)

If disposable consumer income in the $j$th FEA is increased (for example, due to a reduction in tax rates on personal incomes) at least some of the $nr_{ij}$'s will increase. We assume here that the price vector $p_{ij}$ $(i = 1, 2, ..., n)$ does not change, so that the $r_{ij}$'s are essentially indexes of quantities demanded. The increased demands will ramify through the interregional trading system, so that employment and income payments in the $n$ export sectors (or $n \cdot m$ region-and-industry sectors) will increase to varying degrees. An increase in purchases from $E_j$ by the federal government or by other countries (not explicitly provided for in the model) would also increase employment and income in the $j$th FEA, with effects on the $r_{ij}$'s and the general economy as before.

In section 1.2.1 we outlined the theory of quantitative economic policy in terms of aggregative variables at the national level and considered a linear macroeconomic model with five equations. The target variables were employment ($N$) and the balance of payments ($B$); the instruments were government expenditures for current operations ($G_c$) and government expenditures ($G_i$) on new buildings, roads and other types of gross capital formation.

We could extend this model to indicate the relations between national and local (FEA-level) policy makers with respect to a particular FEA, say $FEA_1$, as follows:

FEA$_1$ output:
$$Y_1 = C_1 + I_{1p} + X_{1p} + G_{1c} + G_{1i}$$
$$+ (\lambda_{11} + \lambda_{21} + \lambda_{31}) G_f,$$

FEA$_1$ imports:
$$M_1 = a_{11}C_1 + a_{21}I_{1p} + a_{31}X_{1p} + a_{41}G_{1c} + a_{51}G_{1i}$$
$$+ (a_{21}\lambda_{11} + a_{31}\lambda_{21} + a_{51}\lambda_{31}) G_f,$$

FEA$_1$ consumption: $C_1 = b_1(1 - t_1) Y_1$,

FEA$_1$ employment: $N_1 = e_1 Y_1$,

FEA$_1$ balance of
payments:
$$B_1 = p_{x1}X_1 - p_{m1}M_1,$$
$$I_{1f} = \lambda_{11}G_f,$$
$$X_{1f} = \lambda_{21}G_f,$$
$$G_{1i(f)} = \lambda_{31}G_f,$$

Federal instruments: $\lambda_{11}, \lambda_{21}, \lambda_{31}, t_1, G_f$. (note that $\lambda_{11} + \lambda_{21} + \lambda_{31} = 1$),

Targets: $N_1^*, C_1^*$.

In these equations, $Y$ is income, $C$ consumption, $I_p$ private investment, $X_p$ private exports, $G_c$ expenditures by local government for current operations, $G_i$ expenditures of local government for investment purposes and $G_f$ expenditures by the federal government. The subscript 1 stands for region or $FEA_1$. The remaining variables are $M$ imports, $N$ employment, $B$ balance of payments, $p_x$ prices of exports, $p_m$ prices of imports, $I_f$ federal investment projects in the local FEA *or* investments induced by federal expenditures, $X_f$ exports purchased by the federal government and $G_{i(f)}$ local government investment activities *induced* by federal subsidies or other expenditures.

The endogenous variables of greatest concern to residents of the FEA are presumably $N_1$, $C_1$ and perhaps $Y_1$. The instruments available to the federal government in this model are the personal income tax ($t_1$), federal expenditures to encourage local private investment ($\lambda_{11}G_f$), federal expenditures for "exports" from the $FEA(\lambda_{21}G_f)$, and federal expenditures to encourage local government investment $(\lambda_{31}G_f)$. The $\lambda$'s are allocation coefficients which can presumably be set at different levels for different FEAs; so can the total federal expenditure in the area, $G_f$.

So far, the $FEA_1$ model ignores the inter-area trading system. We may illustrate the effects of inter-area trade by means of an even simpler macro-economic model. We assume to begin with a closed system consisting of two areas (FEAs). The models for each area separately are (see Fox [30]):

*Area* 1:

$$Y_1 = C_1 + I_1 + G_1 + E_1 - M_1$$
$$C_1 = c_1 Y_1$$
$$I_1 = i_1 Y_1$$
$$M_1 = m_1 Y_1$$

*Area* 2:

$$Y_2 = C_2 + I_2 + G_2 + E_2 - M_2$$
$$C_2 = c_2 Y_2$$
$$I_2 = i_2 Y_2$$
$$M_2 = m_2 Y_2 .$$

In area 1, we may (initially and naively) assume that $E_1$ (exports) is exogenous; $G_1$ (government expenditure) is our main policy instrument. Four variables, $Y_1$ (gross area product), $C_1$ (consumption), $I_1$ (domestic private investment), and $M_1$ (imports), are regarded as endogenous.

In our two-area model, of course, $E_1 = M_2$ and $E_2 = M_1$, so the export variables become *endogenous* to the closed system, which may be displayed as follows:

$$
\begin{bmatrix}
1 & -1 & -1 & & & & 1 & & -1 & & -1 & \\
-c_1 & 1 & 0 & & 0 & & & & & & & \\
-i_1 & 0 & 1 & & & & & & & & & \\
& & & 1 & -1 & -1 & 1 & & -1 & & & -1 \\
& 0 & & -c_2 & 1 & 0 & & & & & & \\
& & & -i_2 & 0 & 1 & & & & & & \\
-m_1 & & & & & & 1 & & & & & \\
& & & -m_2 & & & & 1 & & & & \\
& & & & & & -1 & 1 & & 0 & & \\
& & & & & & -1 & & 1 & & &
\end{bmatrix}
\begin{bmatrix}
Y_1 \\ C_1 \\ I_1 \\ Y_2 \\ C_2 \\ I_2 \\ M_1 \\ M_2 \\ E_1 \\ E_2 \\ G_1 \\ G_2
\end{bmatrix}
=
\begin{bmatrix}
0 \\ 0 \\ 0 \\ 0 \\ 0 \\ 0 \\ 0 \\ 0 \\ 0 \\ 0
\end{bmatrix}
$$

In this system there are now ten endogenous variables and only two exogenous or autonomous ones, $G_1$ and $G_2$. Because of feedbacks through area 2, the multiplier effect upon $Y_1$ of an increase in $G_1$ is larger than if imports $(M_1)$ were a genuine and complete leakage from the economy of area 1. For example, let $c_1 = c_2 = 0.5$, $i_1 = i_2 = 0.2$, and $m_1 = m_2 = 0.3$.

If $M_1$ were simply a leakage, the multiplier in area 1 would be

$$\frac{\partial Y_1}{\partial G_1} = \frac{1}{1 - 0.5 - 0.2 + 0.3} = \frac{1}{1 - 0.4} = \frac{1}{0.6} = 1.67.$$

However, in the two-area system the corresponding multiplier becomes

$$\frac{\partial Y_1}{\partial G_1} = \frac{(1 - 0.5 - 0.2 + 0.3)}{(1 - 0.5 - 0.2 + 0.3)^2 - (0.3)^2} = \frac{0.6}{0.36 - 0.09} = 2.22.$$

If the policy maker in each area understands the structure of the complete system he will presumably take account of the fact that his multiplier is 2.22 rather than 1.67 in deciding by how much government expenditures should be modified.

A four-area model (again treated as a closed system) opens up the possibility of multilateral trade. If we express the $G_i$ (government expenditures in area $i$) as functions of the $Y_i$, $i = 1, 2, 3, 4$, we obtain

$$G_1 = \phantom{-}k_1 Y_1 - m_{12} Y_2 - m_{13} Y_3 - m_{14} Y_4$$
$$G_2 = -m_{21} Y_1 + k_2 Y_2 - m_{23} Y_3 - m_{24} Y_4$$
$$G_3 = -m_{31} Y_1 - m_{32} Y_2 + k_3 Y_3 - m_{34} Y_4$$
$$G_4 = -m_{41} Y_1 - m_{42} Y_2 - m_{43} Y_3 + k_4 Y_4$$

where

$$k_i = 1 - c_i - i_i + \sum_{\substack{j=1 \\ (i \neq j)}}^{4} m_{ji}; \qquad i = 1, 2, 3, 4.$$

Or,

$$\begin{bmatrix} G_1^* \\ G_2^* \\ G_3^* \\ G_4^* \end{bmatrix} = \begin{bmatrix} k_1 & -m_{12} & -m_{13} & -m_{14} \\ -m_{21} & k_2 & -m_{23} & -m_{24} \\ -m_{31} & -m_{32} & k_3 & -m_{34} \\ -m_{41} & -m_{42} & -m_{43} & k_4 \end{bmatrix} \begin{bmatrix} Y_1^* \\ Y_2^* \\ Y_3^* \\ Y_4^* \end{bmatrix}$$

or

$$G^* = (k - M)Y^*$$

where the $Y_i^*$ are desired values of gross area product and the $G_i^*$ are the values of government expenditures needed to attain the $Y_i^*$. The model could be expanded to include any number of areas, $n$.

The model just outlined would also apply if the $Y_i^*$ $(i=1, 2, ..., n)$ were selected by a national policy maker and if the $G_i^*$ $(i=1, 2, ..., n)$ were also computed and implemented by him. As written, the model is just-identified, with $n$ targets and $n$ instruments.

In practice, the matrix $(k-M)$ might be rather stable for a year or two at a time, as most firms would try to maintain continuing relations with their existing customers wherever they are located. If the $Y_i^*$ were the explicit target variables of national policy, national GNP $(=\sum_{i=1}^{n} Y_i^*)$ and total federal expenditures $(=\sum_{i=1}^{n} G_i^*)$ would be calculated by simple addition. Employment, $N_i^*$, would be a more likely target of national policy than gross area product, $Y_i^*$, but if $Y_i^* = w_i N_i^*$ (where $w_i$ is average gross area product per worker in area $i$), we may simply rewrite the model as

$$G^* = (k - M) N^* w'.$$

As the functional economic area is a commuting field and a relatively self-contained labor market in the short-run, there is much to be said for maximizing employment FEA by FEA as a short-run policy goal (see Fox [27]). In a large metropolitan area regarded as a compound FEA, the employment targets should probably be stated for each R-level trade area within the metropolis. Interarea commuting would be fairly extensive. If the employment target $N_i^*$ applies to members of the labor force *residing* in area $i$ and the $G_i^*$ are calculated to increase the number of workers employed in *establishments* in area $i$, there is a potential difference between employment impacts by place of residence and those by place of work. If the initial interarea commuting pattern is known and can be assumed stable, we have

$$N^* = CN,$$

where a typical row is

$$N_1^* = c_{11}N_1 + c_{12}N_2 + \cdots + c_{1m}N_m$$

and there are $m$ R-level trade areas in the metropolis and environs. To find the set of $N_i$'s that will achieve the desired set of $N_i^*$, we multiply the first equation by $C^{-1}$, obtaining

$$N = C^{-1}N^*.$$

*8.2.3.1. Development planning models.* Suppose we now consider a model of the following type:

$$\max Y = v'x \qquad v, x : n.1$$

subject to

$$Ax \leqslant b \qquad A: m.n$$
$$x \geqslant 0 \qquad b: m.1$$

where $Y$ is gross area product, $v$ is a row vector of values added per unit of output in each of the $n$ industries in the area, $x$ is a vector of output levels in the $n$ industries, $b$ is a vector of restrictions on (1) numbers of workers of specified occupational categories available in the area and (2) capacities of specified industries, and $A$ is a matrix of input-output coefficients and drafts against the various capacity constraints. This is much like the model for Colombia presented by Adelman and Sparrow [28]. Value added might be further elaborated as

$$v_i = p_i - \sum_{j=1}^{n} a_{ji}p_j = p_i - \sum_{j=1}^{n} d_{ji}a_{ji}p_j - \sum_{j=1}^{n} (1 - d_{ji}) a_{ji}p_j$$

or

$$v_i = p_i - \sum_{j=1}^{n} d_j a_{ji}p_j - \sum_{j=1}^{n} m_{ji}a_{ji}p_j$$

where $i = 1, 2, ..., n$; $d_{ji}$ is the proportion of the $j$ input into the $i$th activity which is procured from firms in the same area, and $m_{ji} = 1 - d_{ji}$ is the proportion imported from other areas.

The structure of the model for each FEA separately could be refined in various ways; so could the treatment of interarea imports. For example, the trading pattern for outputs of each industry could be computed by solving a transportation model, given a matrix of transportation costs (for each kind of output) between all possible pairs of FEA central cities. Spatial equilibrium models might be appropriate for certain agricultural commodities, depending on the level of detail wanted [29, 30].

The model outlined appears to be a short-term production capacity model. In principle, it would yield a set of shadow prices for all restrictions in all areas, *given* no interarea mobility of labor, no increase in capacity, and no training of any kind to enable people to change occupations. High shadow prices for plant capacity in certain industries in certain FEAs would suggest likely opportunities for new investment; high shadow prices for certain occupations in certain areas would suggest (1) local retraining of some workers and (2) needs for recruiting workers from other areas.

We could place upper and lower bounds upon year-to-year changes in each plant capacity constraint and in the number of labor force members in each area having specified occupational skills. The model might then be applied recursively, using the shadow prices in one year to guide capacity expansion, interarea migration, training of new labor force entrants, and retraining of some existing members of the labor force. In principle, dynamic programming models could also be applied, though with 350 areas and 5- or 10-year planning horizons the computations might have to be done in segments and combined to yield an approximation (but only an approximation) to the optimal solution. The usefulness of high computational accuracy and great industry detail may, of course, be questionable given other major sources of uncertainty during a 5- or 10-year planning period.

One or more federal resources could be tentatively allocated according to specified shadow prices. Existing and alternative allocation formulas for various state and federal programs could in principle be tested by means of their effects on the values of FEA objective functions. Given problems of measurement and aggregation, the shadow prices would be indicative rather than precise guides to allocation; however, the approach should be helpful in demonstrating needless incongruities among programs and locating gaps which, if filled by appropriate new programs, would permit higher values of FEA objective functions to be achieved.

## REFERENCES

[1] Arrow, K. J., "Optimization, decentralization and internal pricing in business firms". In: *Contributions to scientific research in management*. Proceedings of the scientific program following the dedication of the Western Data Processing Center, Graduate School of Business Administration. Los Angeles: University of California, 1959.

[2] Charnes, A., R. W. Clower and K. O. Kortanek, "Effective control through coherent decentralization with pre-emptive goals", *Econometrica*, Vol. 35, No. 2, April 1967, 294–320.

[3] Hirshleifer, J., "On the economics of transfer pricing", *Journal of Business*, Vol. 29, 1956, 172–184.

Hurwicz, L., "Programming involving many variables and constraints". In: E. Malinvaud and M. O. L. Bacharach (eds.), *Activity analysis in the theory of growth and planning*. London: McMillan, 1967.

Malinvaud, E., "Decentralized procedures for planning". In: E. Malinvaud and M. O. L. Bacharach (eds.), *Activity analysis in the theory of growth and planning*, *op. cit.*

[4] Kuhn, H. W. and A. W. Tucker, "Nonlinear programming". In: J. Neyman (ed.), *Proceedings of Second Berkeley Symposium on Mathematical Statistics and Probability*. Berkeley: University of California Press, 1951, 481–492.

[5] Lasdon, L. S., A. D. Waren and R. K. Rice, "An interior penalty method for inequality constrained optimal control problems", *IEEE Transactions on Automatic Control*, August 1967, No. 4, 388.

[6] Waltz, F. M., "An engineering approach: hierarchical optimization criteria", *IEEE Transactions on Automatic Control*, Vol. AC-12, April 1967, 179–180.

[7] Theil, H., *Linear aggregation of economic relations*. Amsterdam: North-Holland Publishing Company, 1954.

[8] Porwit, K., *Central planning: evaluation of variants*, translated from Polish by J. Stadler. London: Pergamon Press, 1967.

Cornfield, J., "Discriminant functions", *Review of International Statistical Institute* Vol. 35, No. 2, 1967, 142–153.

[9] Ivanovic, B., "Classification of underdeveloped areas according to level of economic development". In: *Mathematical studies in economics and statistics in the USSR and Eastern Europe*, Vol. 1, No. 3, 1965, 83–116.

[10] Samuelson, P. A., "Spatial price equilibrium and linear programming", *American Economic Review*, Vol. 42, June 1952, 284–303.

[11] Shubik, M., *Strategy and market structure*. New York: John Wiley, 1959.

Marschak, T., "Centralization and decentralization in economic organizations", *Econometrica*, Vol. 27, 1959, 399–430.

Tinbergen, J., *Centralization and decentralization in economic policy*. Amsterdam: North-Holland Publishing Co., 1954.

[12] Berry, B. J. L. and A. Pred, *Central place studies: a bibliography of theory and applications*. Philadelphia: Regional Science Research Institute, G.P.O. Box 8776, 1961. See also *Supplement through 1964* to the above (same publisher) by H. G. Barnum, R. Kasperson and S. Kiuchi, 1965.

[13] Fox, K. A. and T. K. Kumar, "Functional economic areas: delineation and implications for economic analysis and policy", *Regional Science Association Papers*, Vol. XV, 1965, 57–85.

[14] Fox, K. A., "Functional economic areas and consolidated urban regions of the United States", *Social Science Research Council ITEMS*, Vol. 21, No. 4, December 1967, 45–49.

[15] Fox, K. A., "Metamorphosis in America: a new synthesis of rural and urban society". In: W. J. Gore and L. C. Hodapp (eds.), *Change in the small community: an interdisciplinary survey*. New York: Friendship Press, 1967, 62–104.

[16] Fox, K. A., "Strategies for area delineation in a national system of regional accounts". Paper prepared for a conference of the Committee on Regional Accounts, Los Angeles, California. January 24–26, 1968, 42 pp. cyclostyled, to be published.

[17] Berry, B. J . L. and others, *Metropolitan area definition: a re-evaluation of concept and statistical practice*, U.S. Department of Commerce, Bureau of the Census, Working Paper 28, June 1968, 45 pp.

[18] Berry, B. J. L. and C. D. Harris, "Central place". In: *International encyclopedia of the social sciences*. London: Macmillan Compnay and Free Press, 1968, Vol. 2, 365–370.

[19] Duncan, D. J., "Shopping centre (shopping plaza)". *Encyclopaedia Britannica*. Chicago: Encyclopaedia Britannica, Inc., Vol. 20, 1965, 575–576.

Berry, B. J. L., *Geography of market centers and retail distribution*. Englewood Cliffs, N.J.: Prentice-Hall, Inc., 1967.

[20] Holdren, B. R., *The structure of a retail market and the market behavior of retail units: a theory of the multi-product firm*. Englewood Cliffs, N.J.: Prentice-Hall, 1960.

[21] Fox, K. A., "Monopolistic competition in the food and agricultural sectors". In: R. E. Kuenne (ed.), *Monopolistic competition theory: studies in impact, essays in honor of Edward H. Chamberlin*, Ch. 16. New York: John Wiley, 1967, 329–356.

[22] Zusman, P., "The role of the retail trade in the competitive system". In: D. C. Hague (ed.), *Price formation in various economies*, Ch. 4. London: Macmillan and New York: St, Martin's Press, 1967, 50–67.

[23] Fox, K. A., *Intermediate economic statistics*. New York: John Wiley, 1968. See Ch. 14, "The measurement of economic aggregates", 495–536 and especially 517–520.

[24] Simon, H. A., *Models of man: social and rational*. New York: John Wiley and Sons, 1957.

[25] Berry, B. J. L., "Approaches to regional analysis: A synthesis", *Annals, Association of American Geographers*, Vol. 54, No. 1, March 1964, 2–11.

[26] Fox, K. A., J. K. Sengupta and E. Thorbecke, *The theory of quantitative economic policy: with applications to economic growth and stabilization*. Amsterdam: North-Holland Publishing Company and Chicago: Rand McNally, 1966, 351–370.

[27] Fox, K. A., "A program to promote maximum employment, human dignity and civic responsibility in the United States (author)", Department of Economics, Iowa State University, April 29, 1968, 33 pp., cyclostyled.

[28] Adelman, I. and F. T. Sparrow, "Experiments with linear and piece-wise linear dynamic programming models". In: I. Adelman and E. Thorbecke (eds.), *The theory and design of economic development*. Baltimore: Johns Hopkins Press, 1966, 291–317.

[29] Fox, K. A., "Spatial price equilibrium and process analysis in the food and agricultural sector". In: A. S. Manne and H. M. Markowitz (eds.), *Studies in process analysis: economy-wide production capabilities*, Cowles Foundation Monograph 18. New York: John Wiley, 1963, 215–233.

[30] Fox, K. A., "Toward a policy model of world economic development with special attention to the agricultural sector". In: E. Thorbecke (ed.), *The role of agriculture in economic development*, Universities-National Bureau of Economic Research, Columbia University Press; in press, expected publication date 1969.

# Chapter 9

# OPERATIONS RESEARCH AND COMPLEX SOCIAL SYSTEMS

In ch. 1 we reviewed three kinds of optimizing models that have been developed and used by economists. The *theory of the firm* employs a cardinal objective function and the weights applied to its various outputs are market prices. The *theory of consumption* employs an ordinal utility function; in equilibrium the marginal utilities of different commodities are proportional to their prices:

$$\frac{\partial U/\partial q_i}{\partial U/\partial q_j} = \frac{\lambda p_i}{\lambda p_j} = \frac{p_i}{p_j},$$

where $\lambda$, a Lagrangian multiplier, corresponds to the shadow price of the consumer's income constraint. If his income were increased by one dollar, the value of his utility function, $U$, would be increased by $\lambda$ units of his own internal and unspecified currency. The *theory of economic policy* as presented by Theil [1, 2] ascribes an ordinal utility function to a national policy maker. The ratio of the marginal "utilities" of any two instruments $x_j$ and $x_k$ can be expressed as

$$\frac{\partial W/\partial x_j}{\partial W/\partial x_k} = \frac{(\lambda_1 r_{1j} + \lambda_2 r_{2j} + \cdots + \lambda_n r_{nj})}{(\lambda_1 r_{1k} + \lambda_2 r_{2k} + \cdots + \lambda_n r_{nk})},$$

where the $r_{ij}$'s and $r_{ik}$'s reflect the real structure of the economy (net effects of a unit change in each instrument upon each target variable) and $\lambda_i$ is the increase in utility which would result if the $i$th restriction were relaxed by one unit. The ratio of $\partial W/\partial x_j$ to $\partial W/\partial x_k$ will not be affected if we multiply both numerator and denominator by the same scalar.

In the theory of the firm we assume that satisfactory cardinal measures exist for all quantities of outputs and inputs, all technical coefficients and all prices. Nearly all members of an industrial society have direct experience of prices, of budget constraints, and of some kinds of production processes in which inputs are transformed into outputs, so the assumption of measurability commends itself to "common sense" in such a society.

In a money economy, a multiproduct firm can convert a vector of outputs

$q_1$, $q_2$, ..., $q_m$ into a scalar money value of output $V = \sum_{i=1}^{m} p_i q_i$; a consumer can convert a scalar money value of income into a vector of quantities of goods and services. In terms of these scalars, we can make frequency distributions of family incomes and of the gross revenues of firms; we can also aggregate these scalars for an entire country to arrive at scalar components of the national income and product accounts. The most comprehensive measure of economic activity, the gross national product or GNP, is a scalar.

We could perhaps imagine an industrial society which abstained from the use of money. An elaborate system of multicommodity auction markets and brokerage firms might be envisaged to convert the gross output vector of each firm into a vector of goods used in production *plus* consumer goods supplied to employees and stockholders. Business records would be maintained in terms of physical quantities of each input and each differentiated output, and the "gross national product" would be a tremendously long $N$ times 1 vector of physical quantities.

If records of all barter transactions in the country were maintained throughout the year, some procedure might be found for computing an $N$ times $N$ matrix of average "barter terms of trade" between all possible pairs of commodities. A unit of commodity $i$ could have been exchanged on the average for specified numbers of units of each commodity $j$, where $j = 1, 2, 3, ..., i, ..., N$. If we asked how much a unit of commodity $i$ had been worth last year, there would be $N-1$ answers in terms of individual commodities and an infinite number of answers in terms of combinations of two or more commodities.

Operations research techniques have been highly successful in fields characterized by well-defined units of measurement. In such fields the numerical data are accepted (to use Ijiri's terminology [3]) as *surrogates* which represent real phenomena or *principals* with a satisfactory degree of accuracy. Thus, distances on a map are surrogates for distances on the earth's surface; the product of a north-south distance and an east-west distance on a map is a surrogate for the area of the corresponding portion of the earth's surface. For a small area the discrepancy between our surrogate (which implies a "flat" earth or Mercator's projection) and the corresponding portion of the earth's sphere may be of no consequence; for a large area our surrogate might have to be based on spherical rather than plane trigonometry. Optimizing techniques are useful to the extent that computations based upon numerical measurements (surrogates) accurately predict the consequences of manipulations of the corresponding physical or economic systems (principals).

In some areas in the social sciences, relations between surrogates and principals are as yet poorly defined. In the United States as of 1968 there is considerable interest in "social indicators"; the word "indicators" suggests that only a *vector* representation of the performance of a society is deemed possible in the forseeable future. The state of the art as of 1966 is suggested by Bauer [4] and the nature of the data available for different countries as of 1964 can be seen in Russett et al. [5].

The willingness to settle for vector representations of the performance of society as a whole contrasts sharply with the scalar representation of economic performance embodied in the national income and product accounts. At present, cost and benefit analyses, planning, programming and budgeting systems, and optimizing models of nonmarket institutions are all limited by the common problems of (1) measuring the quantities of inputs and outputs and (2) specifying generally acceptable "prices" or objective function weights. Once basic units of measurement were defined for the various noneconomic outputs of a social system, aggregation and scalarization of subsets of these outputs could proceed and provisional scalarizations combining economic and noneconomic outputs could be undertaken. Many of the optimizing models used in development planning for nations, regions, cities and functional economic areas could be applied to these more comprehensive measures of societal outputs, and the sensitivity of optimal plans to different weighting schemes for combining economic and other societal outputs could be explored.

The existence of a scalar measure called (say) "gross social product" (GSP) need not imply its selection as the sole component of an objective function for development planning models. But if we simply try to maximize GNP we may be assigning zero weight to some important human goals. And, some of the extreme polarizations that arise in connection with proposed institutional reforms might be avoided if the noneconomic considerations could be combined with the economic ones using some reasonable range of finite weights.

### 9.1. *Problems of measurement in complex social systems*

Churchman [6] asserts that "measurement is the most intricate and complex of all human decision processes". Crombie [7] discusses a period in the history of physics when scholars had very little interest in measurement. His discussion suggests analogies with the present situation in the social sciences.

Crombie distinguishes between quantified procedures and quantified concepts. A quantified procedure in science is "one that aims at measurement, that is, any procedure that assigns numbers in a scale. To be complete, such a procedure must comprise both mathematical techniques for operating the scale theoretically and measuring techniques for using it to explore the world. Technology need contain little more than procedures of these kinds.... But most sciences aim beyond these at providing explanations by means of a system of theory. So a quantified science, as distinct from quantified technology, comprises not only quantified procedures but also quantified explanatory concepts, each applicable to the other within a theoretical system. The development of a science then takes place through a dialogue between its theories and its procedures, the former offering an explanation of the expected world ... and the latter confronting these theoretical expectations with the test of quantified data".[1]

Crombie asserts that in medieval (thirteenth and fourteenth century) physics this dialogue between concepts and procedures was incomplete or absent and that "a far greater need was felt that concepts and theoretical and mathematical procedures should be quantified than that actual measurements should be made.... Departure from this purely theoretical emphasis occurred only when there was a strong external, practical demand for exact measurements. When this was present, theoretical concepts and procedures became quantified in such a way that measurement was applicable, accurate measurements were made and used to test and decide between different theories, and instruments were developed to get increasing precision".[2]

Today in the social sciences one can point to many evidences of convergence among quantitative geographers, regional scientists, urban and regional economists and planners, political scientists, organization theorists, sociologists and psychologists toward the idea of a comprehensive social science (see for example, [8, 9 and 10]). Recent phrases and titles such as "experimental cities", "model cities", "transactions analysis" (Berne [11, 12]), "behavior settings" (Barker [13, 14]), *Models of man* (Simon [8]), *An economic theory of democracy* (Downs [15]), *A systems analysis of political life* (Easton [16]), "Systems analysis: social systems" (Parsons [17]) and "General social, political and economic equilibrium for a system of regions" (Isard and Isard [18]) are suggestive of the models and concepts that are beginning to coalesce.

---

[1] Crombie, *op. cit.*, p. 188.
[2] Crombie, *op. cit.*, p. 206.

So far, no one has attempted an empirical model of a general social system on the level of specificity of (say) the Brookings quarterly econometric model of the United States. However, the complex problems of our largest cities are forcing policy makers to make decisions *as if* they knew the terms of trade between traffic congestion, air pollution, water pollution, schools, playgrounds, museums, rapid transit systems, and various patterns of urban renewal. The recent (1968) publication of the *International encyclopedia of the social sciences* [19], the first of its kind since the 1930's, should greatly facilitate communication among social scientists in connection with these and other multidisciplinary concerns.

### 9.1.1. *Social systems and generalized media of (social, economic and political) exchange*

Talcott Parsons [17] includes in his conceptualization of the "human action system" four generic types of subsystems: (1) the organism, (2) the social system, (3) the cultural system (including beliefs, ideas and symbols that give the action system its primary "sense of direction"), and (4) the personality. The social system and the personality are the levels with which we are here concerned. Parson states that:

"From the viewpoint of the psychology of the personality, the positive outputs from the social system are rewards ... Conversely, outputs from the personality to the social system ... from the viewpoint of the receiving social system, are *contributions* to its functioning, insofar as the two systems are integrated with each other."

Also,

"The unit of interpenetration between a personality and a social system is not the individual but a *role* or complex of *roles*. The *same* personality may participate in *several* social systems in different roles."

Parsons [17, pp. 470–471] also speaks of "generalized media of exchange", of which money is only one. In addition, he includes political power; prestige or influence, i.e., "the capacity to achieve 'consensus' with other members of an associated group through persuasion, without having to give fully adequate reasons" (acceptance of a physician's advice, for example); generalized commitments to the implementation of cultural values; affect, recognition and response; ideology; conscience; reputation; and faith (the last four in somewhat special connotations).

Economists focus their attention upon those contributions (or inputs) from personalities to the social system and those rewards (or outputs) from the social system to personalities which are commonly valued in money terms. Hours of labor are sold for money, and the money is spent for goods and services which are consumed outside of working hours.

However, much of the quality of life depends on interactions within families, schools and voluntary organizations and in various informal settings. It is intuitively plausible that a comprehensive measure of the outputs of a social system should include rewards received by each of its members throughout the 24 hours of the day or 8760 hours of the year.

Converse [20] points out that "time budget" research has a fairly long history, with large-scale studies dating back to the 1920's. He notes, however, that "a wide gulf still exists between the manifest activity as it is recorded and the latent functions of the activity for the individual which give it ultimate meaning or significance...." [3]

Barker [13] proposes what appears to be a very fruitful concept, that of "behavior settings":

"Behavior settings are units of the environment that have relevance for behavior ... A behavior setting coerces people and things to confirm to its temporal-spatial pattern." [4]

Barker identified about 220 *genotype* settings in a town of 830 people. Examples of his genotype settings include grocery stores, hardware stores, ice cream socials, kindergarten classes, business meetings, religion classes, hallways, bus stops, and many others. When individual grocery stores, churches and the like were recognized as separate or *specific* behavior settings, Barker found 884 "public" behavior settings in the town. He did not attempt to record or estimate behavior settings in private homes.

Each individual in a behavior setting has a role (student or teacher, grocer or customer, chairman or member, etc.). If two or more persons are involved in a behavior setting, "transactions" take place (in the terminology of Berne [11]) involving recognition and response. The utility of a behavior setting to an individual is a function of the setting as such, his own role in the setting, and his perception of his effectiveness in the role as evidenced by the behavior of other participants toward him.

We might postulate, then, that a "rational" personality will allocate his time among behavior-setting-and-role combinations in such a way as to maximize their (expected) total utility. If a role has a quality dimension, more preparation time may be required to perform it well than to perform it at the threshold of adequacy.

---

[3] Converse, *op. cit.*, p. 46.
[4] Barker, *op. cit.*, pp. 158–159.

Churchman [6, *op. cit.*, p. 58] is perhaps too modest in his characterization of value measurements:

"We can say in a very general way what a set of value measurements for a person is: it is a set of numbers that predict the probability that the person will make certain behavior choices in certain environments, given perfect awareness and knowledge on his part."

If we assume that a consumer can rate any two arrays of commodities as "A preferred to B", "B preferred to A", or "indifferent as between A and B", it may be equally reasonable to assume that a personality can make similar orderings of two arrays of behavior setting, role and quality-of-performance-in-role combinations. The personality must be able to perceive (through observation, trial participation, reading, film strips and other means) what it would feel like to "live" each of the arrays being compared.

It is not our purpose here to develop a comprehensive set of measurements for the outputs of a social system. We are, however, suggesting that such measurements would be useful in judging the performance of a complete social system and anticipating the consequences of modifying or reforming one or more of its subsystems in specified ways. It appears that useful concepts are at hand to initiate a dialogue leading to sequential improvements in measurements and theories.

## 9.2. Generalization of consumption theory to all outputs of a social system

In the case of economic transactions, we multiply observed market prices by quantities of the respective goods and services produced in a nation and compute gross national product (GNP). The ratios of market prices are (in principle) equal to the ratios of the marginal utilities of the corresponding commodities to each and every consumer. If the market prices for some base year are used as fixed weights, we can compute changes in "real" GNP over a period of years.

Would it mean anything to perform the same operation for all of Parson's media of exchange? Perhaps so, if we visualize the individual as trying to maximize his total utility by using his total capacities in the most effective way. If there are $s$ media of exchange, $n$ potential activities representing essentially all forms of human behavior, and $s$ restrictions limiting the amount of each medium that a given individual can use ("spend") as inputs into the social system, our model becomes:

$$\max U = f(q_1, q_2, ..., q_n)$$

subject to

$$\sum_{i=1}^{n} q_i p_i = Y = b_1 \qquad (Y = \text{money income})$$

$$\sum_{i=1}^{n} q_i t_i = H = b_2 \qquad (H = \text{time})$$

$$\sum_{i=1}^{n} q_i m_{3i} = M_3 = b_3$$

$$\sum_{i=1}^{n} q_i m_{4i} = M_4 = b_4$$

$$\vdots$$

$$\sum_{i=1}^{n} q_i m_{si} = M_s = b_s.$$

Then

$$\frac{\partial U}{\partial q_i} - \lambda_1 p_i - \lambda_2 t_i - \lambda_3 m_{3i} - \cdots - \lambda_s m_{si} = 0$$

for all

$$i = 1, 2, 3, \ldots, n,$$

and

$$\frac{\partial U/\partial q_i}{\partial U/\partial q_j} = \frac{\lambda_1 p_i + \lambda_2 t_i + \lambda_3 m_{3i} + \cdots + \lambda_s m_{si}}{\lambda_1 p_j + \lambda_2 t_j + \lambda_3 m_{3j} + \cdots + \lambda_s m_{sj}}.$$

Each activity $q_i$ uses up some time; many activities use up some money; some use personal influence; some use professional reputation; and so on. Each $q_i$ involves occupying a behavior setting and performing some role in it at a specified quality level. Each medium of exchange corresponds to a goal of activity for some if not all personalities. Some of Parsons' media seem to be *stocks* (for example, professional reputation) which yield a flow of inputs into the social system and bring in a flow of outputs or rewards from the social system. Intense application may increase professional reputation; diversion of effort to politics or gardening may cause it (or permit it) to decline. In measuring the utility enjoyed by a personality during a given year only the *flows* of rewards associated with possession of stock-like media would be included.

Some activities bring in only one or two of the $s$ kinds of rewards from the social system and use only one or a few kinds of the $s$ resources or "contributions", so there would be many zeros in the $n$ times $m$ "technology" matrix and hence in the expressions for the $\partial U/\partial q_i$, $i = 1, 2, \ldots, n$. If the individual is free to convert time into money income and into flows of each of the other $s-2$ resources, the initial $b_i$'s can be adjusted until the marginal utilities of time converted into all other limiting resources are equal.

If so, we have (from the exchange rate matrix on p. 461):

$$\lambda_2 = k_{21}\lambda_1$$
$$\lambda_3 = k_{32}\lambda_2 = k_{32}k_{21}\lambda_1$$
$$\lambda_4 = k_{42}\lambda_2 = k_{42}k_{21}\lambda_1$$
$$\vdots$$
$$\lambda_s = k_{s2}\lambda_2 = k_{s2}k_{21}\lambda_1 .$$

Hence, in this kind of equilibrium for the individual, we may write,

$$\frac{\partial U}{\partial q_i} - \lambda_1 (p_i + k_{21}t_i + k_{32}k_{21}m_{3i} + \cdots + k_{s2}k_{21}m_{si}) = 0$$

and

$$\frac{\partial U/\partial q_i}{\partial U/\partial q_j} = \frac{\lambda_1 (p_i + k_{21}t_i + k_{32}k_{21}m_{3i} + \cdots + k_{s2}k_{21}m_{si})}{\lambda_1 (p_j + k_{21}t_j + k_{32}k_{21}m_{3j} + \cdots + k_{s2}k_{21}m_{sj})} .$$

If we multiply $\partial U/\partial q_i$ by $q_i/\lambda_1$ and sum, the first term, $\sum_{i=1}^{n} q_i p_i = Y$, is a component of GNP; i.e., the total consumption expenditures of the individual. The remaining terms are also expressed in dollars.

Several additional points are worth noting. First, the $q_i$'s are separated from one another along the spatial-temporal boundaries that enclose particular behavior settings. We have commented that the activity matrix involving $n$ activities, $s$ contributions and $s$ rewards would contain many zeros. These imply that the behavior settings can be clustered or aggregated in various ways to identify interactions within one's family, within the organization of one's primary paid employment, within one's church, one's political party, one's national professional association and so on. "Home" as a location is important and is the locus of most but by no means all family interactions; "place of work" is the locus of most (but not all) interactions relevant to the flow of rewards associated with membership in the employing organization; and so on. Political power as a medium of exchange would be used mainly within specifically political behavior settings; in fact, various subsystems could be delimited largely on the basis of the dominant media of exchange used within them. The individual may use the same medium (for example, recognition and response) in many different environments; for describing and analyzing the community as a whole, the environments may be classed as church-related, or as parts of the political subsystem. etc., and an individual's resources may not be fully transferable from one subsystem to another.

Second, the effects of distances and of modes of transportation could also be incorporated into the model for a given individual. Consider the following matrix of exchange rates among marginal utilities of the $s$ resources:

$$
\begin{array}{c}
\begin{array}{cccccc}
\underline{\lambda_1} & \underline{\lambda_2} & \underline{\lambda_3} & \underline{\lambda_4} & \cdots & \underline{\lambda_s}
\end{array}\\
\begin{array}{c}
\lambda_1\\ \lambda_2\\ \lambda_3\\ \lambda_4\\ \vdots\\ \lambda_s
\end{array}
\begin{bmatrix}
1 & k_{12} & k_{13} & k_{14} & \cdots & k_{1s}\\
k_{21} & 1 & k_{23} & k_{24} & \cdots & k_{2s}\\
k_{31} & k_{32} & 1 & k_{34} & \cdots & k_{3s}\\
k_{41} & k_{42} & k_{43} & 1 & \cdots & k_{4s}\\
\vdots & \vdots & \vdots & \vdots & & \vdots\\
k_{s1} & k_{s2} & k_{s3} & k_{s4} & & 1
\end{bmatrix}
\end{array}
$$

The second row indicates the marginal rates at which time can be converted into the other $s-1$ media (note that $k_{ij}=1/k_{ji}$ for all $i,j$).

The activity matrix by definition includes activities which use up all of the individual's time. Most trips start from home or office, so the activity "going to a two-hour movie at the Downtown Theater" could be defined to include an hour of travel (roundtrip) between home and movie. However, "in the theater" is a different behavior setting than "in the car". On a formal level, we might specify an $n$ by $n$ matrix of distances between all possible pairs of the $n$ locationally fixed behavior settings. For any given mode of transport, the distance $d_{ij}$ requires time in all cases, money in some, and emotional energy, perhaps, if hazardous intersections or frustrating traffic congestion are involved. For a university professor, the time spent walking between office, classes and committee meetings may well exceed the time spent on roundtrips between home and office.

To reduce detail, however, we might partition the $n$ by $n$ matrix of distances and leave those "within work", "within home" and so on for separate consideration. The remaining $d_{ij}$'s would involve distances among home, office, stores (shopping centers), church and the like.

Without laboring the point further, we might simply note that a change in the marginal rate of transformation of distance into time enables the individual to "consume" more miles without disturbing his allocations of time within and among the locationally fixed behavior settings. Or, he can consume the same number of miles, in which case he has more time that can be converted into money and into the various other media. At the new point of equilibrium, all of the exchange rates $k_{ij}$ may be somewhat different than before; however, it seems likely that the major changes would occur in the second row (and second column) involving exchange rates between time and the other media. Some businessmen, school officials and others who perceive major economies of scale in the kinds of establishments in which they are interested begin to compete for a major share of the time released by faster transportation, drawing workers and customers to bigger establishments from longer distances. Similarly, if the time required to travel among the larger cities, involving the upper echelons of national and regional firms, organizations and systems, is sharply reduced, official travel time is saved; the saving can then be allocated among the existing locationally fixed behavior settings or, if some of the latter have potential economies of scale, the upper-echelon settings themselves may be clustered in a smaller number of (more widely separated) locations.

Ratios such as $(\partial U/\partial q_i)/(\partial U/\partial q_j)$ can in principle be treated as price ratios once the other $s-1$ marginal contributions are converted into money equivalents. Suppose we can cluster the activities in such a way as to minimize overlaps among (say) $s$ subsystems according to the dominant media of exchange used or, for that matter, in any other fashion. If the consumer is making an optimal allocation of his time, the equivalent money value of the utility produced by an additional hour of time should be the same for all of the aggregative activities.

To simplify, suppose all activities are combined into the two aggregates $Q_1$ and $Q_2$; the point $(q_1, q_2)$ is presumably located on the individual's production possibilities frontier. The ratio $(\partial Q_1/\partial T)/(\partial Q_2/\partial T)$ is the slope of the tangent to the frontier at the point $q_1, q_2$. If we did not know the individual's exchange rates among media but *did* know his capabilities for producing different combinations of $Q_1$ and $Q_2$ over some reasonable range, we would know the slope of the tangent to the production possibilities frontier at each point. At $(q_1, q_2)$, $\partial Q_1/\partial Q_2 = -r$; at point $(q'_1, q'_2)$, $\partial Q_1/\partial Q_2 = -r'$. If we associate "prices" with $Q_1$ and $Q_2$, we have $r = P_2/P_1$ and $r' = P'_2/P'_1$. Hence, if a rational individual made the shift from $(Q_1, Q_2)$ to $(Q'_1, Q'_2)$, it would imply that his conception of the relative marginal utilities of $Q_1$ and $Q_2$ had shifted from $r$ to $r'$.

If the outputs aggregated into $Q_1$ are mostly such as can be translated into market values with reasonable accuracy, we can make rough determinations of $P_1$ and $P'_1$ in dollar terms; the implicit estimates of $P_2$ and $P'_2$ could be computed as $P_2 = rP_1$ and $P'_2 = r'P'_1$, where $P_2$ and $P'_2$ are also expressed in dollar terms.

### 9.3. Further comments on optimizing models of nonmarket institutions

The argument just presented could evidently be adapted to a nonmarket institution such as a university. First, assume that a university president understands the internal "technology" of the university very well and can compute rather accurately what would happen to various measurable out-puts (such as numbers of B.S., M.S. and Ph.D. graduates in specific fields, numbers of research publications in specific fields, and so on) if a million dollars a year were withdrawn from one cluster of activities and added to another cluster. For simplicity, assume that all outputs are aggregated into two and that all limiting resources are converted into two, say (1) funds for current operations (mostly salaries for professors and supporting staff) and (2) physical plant (classrooms, office space, laboratories, library facilities and the like). Given these two constraints, he chooses to operate the two activities $Q_1$ and $Q_2$ at the levels $q_1$ and $q_2$.

We infer a utility function and an optimizing model:

$$\max W = f(Q_1, Q_2)$$

subject to the nonlinear production functions

$$Q_1 = f_1(F, B)$$
$$Q_2 = f_2(F, B),$$

the production transformation curve

$$g(Q_1, Q_2) = 0$$

and the constraints

$$F \leqslant F_0$$
$$B \leqslant B_0.$$

We assume that the president's utility function (like the consumer's) is simply ordinal but has the property of diminishing marginal rates of sub-stitution of $Q_i$ for $Q_j$ ($i, j = 1, 2, i \neq j$); also, that the production possibilities frontier has the property of diminishing marginal rates of transformation of $Q_i$ into $Q_j$.

If the point $(q_1, q_2)$ is optimal under the specified restrictions, it is a point of tangency between the president's utility function and the transformation function. Assume that the (continuous) transformation function is specified numerically over a reasonable range of values of $Q_1$ and $Q_2$; then the slope $-r$ of the tangent at $(q_1, q_2)$ is

$$-r = \frac{\partial Q_1}{\partial Q_2} = \frac{\{\partial g(Q_1, Q_2)\}/\partial Q_2}{\{\partial g(Q_1, Q_2)\}/\partial Q_1}.$$

If a vice-president agrees with the specification of the transformation function but believes that the (constrained) optimal point at which to operate would be $(q'_1, q'_2)$ at which the absolute value of the slope of the tangent is $|r'| > |r|$, we infer that he sets a higher value on $Q_2$ relative to $Q_1$ than does the president. If both utility functions are ordinal and no market-like prices are available for $Q_1$ and $Q_2$, there is no objective way to choose between the two views. Quantification of the ratios determined from the transformation function as (say) $r = 1.5$ and $r' = 2.0$ might provoke a clarifying exchange of "reasons why". If $Q_1$ and $Q_2$ are disaggregated into more sharply defined components, such as Ph.D. degrees in biological sciences versus Ph.D. degrees in social sciences, each party can specify his "barter terms of trade" at this more detailed level. Different assumptions about *facts* can be checked against factual data, and the areas of disagreement over as yet unmeasurable values can be more clearly delimited. The result might lead to some changes in both objective functions and the selection of a point $(q''_1, q''_2)$ as optimal.

If the detailed components of $Q_1$ can be assigned market-like prices, such as the net increases in expected career earnings associated with taking B.S. degrees rather than starting work with high school diplomas, we can compute a "market" price $P_1$ and infer an implicit price, $P_2 = rP_1$, for $Q_2$. The next challenge would be to analyze the suboutputs of $Q_2$ in more detail as inputs into various subsystems of the society; determine the media of exchange (in Parsons' sense) in which these inputs should be priced; and probe more deeply into the measurement of exchange rates between media which would be more or less appropriate for a society rather than simply for a particular individual (our earlier discussion was in terms of one individual's terms of trade among media).

The analogy of GNP calculations based on market prices seems to be the logical starting point. Many problems of measurement and aggregation are involved in computing gross national product. Yet the development of national income and product accounts in the 1930's and 1940's was prerequisite to the development and implementation of rational macroeconomic policies and the theory of quantitative economic policy in general. We should regard the "prices" of university outputs not as unmeasurable but simply as not yet measured.

We should note also that the discussion of external economies among firms in a shopping center is directly transferable to clusters of departments within a university. Suppose that $Q_1$ and $Q_2$ are aggregates of two kinds of outputs, say Ph.D. degrees $(Q_{1i})$ and B.S. degrees $(Q_{2i})$ in $m$ departments

$(i = 1, 2, ..., m)$. If each department operates independently, we have a set of $m$ production possibilities frontiers, one for each department. Suppose now that by pooling one or more of the limiting resources among all the departments, we are able to advance the production possibilities frontiers for all $m$ departments simultaneously. The economies which were external to the departments individually are now internal to the cluster as a whole.

If we assume that the $i$th department policy maker (chairman or faculty consensus) has an ordinal preference function such that an increase in either or both outputs $Q_{1i}$ and/or $Q_{2i}$ will be regarded as an improvement, the external economies can be allocated among departments in many different patterns all of which will leave some departments better off than before and none worse off than before. All of these solutions are Pareto-better than the situation prevailing before certain resources were pooled.

The president might allocate the benefits according to his own ordinal preference function. However, he may perceive features of "technology" which are not perceived by department chairmen generally but may be recognized by those most directly involved. For example, the president may have good reason to believe that department $i$ is operating in a range of increasing returns to scale and should therefore be given considerably more resources. A Schumpeterian innovation in one department may stimulate a wave of emulation in others. As in the market economy, new "profit" opportunities are continually appearing within (and between) universities – "profit" as perceived by particular decision makers at various levels in the universities. So long as several of the media of exchange are left unspecified (or at least not quantified) and exchange rates between media are undefined, comparisons between the expected "profits" from alternative innovations remain highly subjective.

It seems clear that careful measurement of the quantities of outputs (and inputs) of universities should be attempted, so that at least the quantity component of "gross university output" will be defined. Even if the prices were left relatively arbitrary, any specified set of (price) weights could be used to compute quantity index numbers for a given university over a period of years and to make rough but numerically reproducible comparisons between the quantities of output of different universities. The same (price) weights could be used in specifying *cardinal* objective functions for optimizing models of different universities; discussions of the implications of the results would lead to further clarification as to the rationales for (1) relative prices and (2) absolute prices ascribed to the various outputs.

On the operational level, perhaps, these endeavors are justified by the prospect of "increasing the efficiency of the university". On the scientific level, they would contribute to our understanding of the manner in which the market and nonmarket subsystems of the society are linked and how their functioning might be improved both "within and between" – initially and primarily by providing fuller and more accurate information about the system as a whole to decision makers active in the various subsystems.

The problems with which we are now faced within and between nations involve all subsystems of society and, in fact, all ecological systems. In dealing with many of these problems, disciplinary boundaries among engineering, economics and other social sciences must be freely crossed.

## REFERENCES

[1] Theil, H., *Economic forecasts and policy*. Amsterdam: North-Holland Publishing Co., 1958. Second revised edition, 1961, 424–444.

[2] Theil, H., *Optimal decision rules for government and industry*. Amsterdam: North-Holland Publishing Company and Chicago: Rand McNally, 1964.

[3] Ijiri, Y., *The foundations of accounting measurement*, Ch. 1. Englewood Cliffs, N.J.: Prentice-Hall, 1967, 3–31.

[4] Bauer, R. A. (ed.), *Social indicators*. Cambridge, Mass.: M.I.T. Press, 1966.

[5] Russett, B. M., H. R. Alker, Jr., K. W. Deutsch and H. D. Lasswell, *World handbook of social and political indicators*. New Haven: Yale University Press, 1964.

[6] Churchman, C. W., "Problems of value measurement for a theory of induction and decisions". In: J. Neyman (ed.), *Proceedings of the Third Berkeley Symposium on Mathematical Statistics and Probability*, Vol. V. Berkeley: University of California Press, 1956, 35–59.

[7] Crombie, A. C., "Quantification in medieval physics". In: S. L. Thrupp (ed.), *Change in medieval society*. New York: Appleton-Century-Crofts, 1964, 188–207.

[8] Simon, H. A., *Models of man: social and rational*. New York: John Wiley and Sons: 1957, esp. vii–x.

[9] Warntz, W., "Global science and the tyranny of space", *The Regional Science Association Papers*, Vol. XIX, 7–19.

[10] Iatridis, D., "Social scientists in physical development planning: A practitioner's viewpoint", *International Social Science Journal*, Vol. XVIII, No. 4, 1966, 473–493.

[11] Berne, E., *Games people play: the psychology of human relationships*. New York: Grove Press, Inc., 1964.

[12] Berne, E., *Transactional analysis in psychotherapy*. New York: Grove Press, Inc., 1961.

[13] Barker, R. G., L. S. Barker and D. D. M. Ragle, "The churches of Midwest, Kansas and Yoredale, Yorkshire: their contributions to the environments of the towns". In: W. J. Gore and L. C. Hodapp (eds.), *Change in the small community: an interdisciplinary survey*. New York: Friendship Press 1967, 155–189, specific quotation from 158–159.

[14] Barker, R. G., "On the nature of the environment", *Journal of Sociological Issues*, Vol. 19, No. 4, 1963, 17–38.

[15] Downs, A., *An economic theory of democracy*. New York: Harper, 1957.

[16] Easton, D., *A systems analysis of political life*. New York: John Wiley and Sons, 1965.

[17] Parsons, T., "Systems analysis: II. Social systems", *International encyclopedia of the social sciences*, Vol. 15. London: Macmillan and Free Press, 1968, 458–473.

[18] Isard, W. and P. Isard, "General social, political and economic equilibrium for a system of regions: part I", *Regional Science Association Papers*, Vol. XIV, 1965, 1–33. See also part II in Vol. XV, also published in 1965.

[19] *International encyclopedia of the social sciences*. London: Macmillan and Free Press, 1968, 17 volumes.

[20] Converse, P. E., "Time budgets", *International encyclopedia of the social sciences*. London: Macmillan and Free Press, 1968, Vol. 16, 42–47.

# SUBJECT INDEX

# AUTHOR INDEX